Part of the six-volume
Microsoft® SQL Server™ 2000 Reference Library

M000011509

The essential reference set for anyone who works with
Microsoft® SQL Server™ 2000

T-SQL Language Reference

David Iseminger
Series Editor

PUBLISHED BY
Microsoft Press
A Division of Microsoft Corporation
One Microsoft Way
Redmond, Washington 98052-6399

Copyright © 2001 by Microsoft Corporation; portions copyright © 2001 by David Iseminger

All rights reserved. No part of the contents of this book may be reproduced or transmitted in any form or by any means without the written permission of the publisher.

Library of Congress Cataloging-in-Publication Data
Iseminger, David, 1969-
    Microsoft SQL Server 2000 Reference Library / David Iseminger.
       p. cm.
    ISBN 0-7356-1280-3
    1. Client/server computing. 2. SQL server. I. Microsoft Corporation. II. Title
    QA76.9.C55 I84 2000
    005.75'85--dc21   00-046054

Printed and bound in the United States of America.

1 2 3 4 5 6 7 8 9   QWT   6 5 4 3 2 1

Distributed in Canada by Penguin Books Canada Limited.

A CIP catalogue record for this book is available from the British Library.

Microsoft Press books are available through booksellers and distributors worldwide. For further information about international editions, contact your local Microsoft Corporation office or contact Microsoft Press International directly at fax (425) 936-7329. Visit our Web site at *mspress.microsoft.com.* Send comments to *mspinput@microsoft.com.*

Active Directory, ActiveX, BizTalk, FoxPro, Georgia, Microsoft, Microsoft Press, MS-DOS, MSDN, PivotTable, Visual Basic, Visual C++, Visual C#, Visual FoxPro, Visual InterDev, Visual J++, Visual Studio, Win32, Windows, and Windows NT are either registered trademarks or trademarks of Microsoft Corporation in the United States and/or other countries. Other product and company names mentioned herein may be the trademarks of their respective owners.

Unless otherwise noted, the example companies, organizations, products, people, and events depicted herein are fictitious. No association with any real company, organization, product, person, or event is intended or should be inferred.

Acquisitions Editor: Juliana Aldous
Project Editor: Denise Bankaitis

Part No. 097-0003482

Acknowledgements

There are some people in the SQL Server group who deserve special recognition. I met with **Maura Dunn, Bryan Franz** and **Ann Beebe** long ago to discuss creating the *SQL Server 2000 Reference Library*, and their receptiveness and feedback on the library were both extensive and helpful. Throughout the process, they each were quick to provide help and direction. Thanks to each of them!

Orchestrating this library's march into publication was **Denise Bankaitis**, who again deserves thanks for keeping everything in order, on time, and moving forward.

Thanks also to the usual suspects involved in making this project become a reality, including **Mark Hoffman** for his concise descriptions that capture its merits, and **Rob Heiret** for a swift job of turning text and graphics into tables, pages and chapters.

Thanks also to **Margot Hutchison** for her role in the whole process.

Contents

Introduction

Imagine taking your Great Dane to the veterinarian on the back of your moped—that's how I felt while putting together the *SQL Server 2000 Reference Library*. All told, there was about three times as much SQL Server 2000 Books Online reference material as there was room in the *SQL Server 2000 Reference Library*, so I had to figure out the most widely used, appropriate, and pertinent parts of Books Online, and have included those parts in the library you now have in your possession.

Despite those woes, I believe you'll find the *SQL Server 2000 Reference Library* full of must-have information about SQL Server 2000. From architecture and XML, to Analysis Services (formerly OLAP) and T-SQL, this reference library contains the essential reference information you need to program, administer, deploy, or optimize your SQL Server 2000 solution… without monitor-induced eyestrain.

The SQL Server 2000 Reference Library is part of the Windows Programming Reference Series (WPRS), a series of libraries dedicated to providing printed development and IT material in a timely, intelligently organized, and well-conceived manner. You can find out more about WPRS and other available reference libraries (including the *COM+ Developer's Reference Library* and the *Active Directory Developer's Reference Library*) at www.iseminger.com—a website dedicated to providing additional information about the series, and other books also by yours truly.

How the SQL Server 2000 Reference Library is Structured

The *SQL Server 2000 Reference Library* consists of six volumes, each of which focuses on one or more specific areas of SQL Server 2000. These guides and programming reference volumes have been divided into the following:

Volume 1: SQL Server 2000 Architecture and XML/Internet Support

Volume 2: Database Creation, Warehousing, and Optimization

Volume 3: Analysis Services

Volume 4: Replication and English Query

Volume 5: T-SQL Language Reference

Volume 6: T-SQL Stored Procedures and Tables Reference

Dividing the *SQL Server 2000 Reference Library* into these categories enables you, the reader, to quickly identify the volume you need, based on your task, and facilitates your maintenance of focus for that task. This approach allows you to keep one reference book open and handy, or tucked under your arm while running between server racks.

In addition to the overall library structure, each volume in the *SQL Server 2000 Reference Library* is divided into parts that concentrate on a given subject. In order to provide a quick overview of a part's contents, each begins with a Part Introduction page that outlines what you'll find therein.

Finding Related Topics and Working With the Topic Index

Throughout this library, you're going to see references to related topics; some of them within the text of a given paragraph, and others placed in a special section called **Related Topics**. Since the entire body of SQL Server 2000 Books Online constitutes more topics than what you'll find in these volumes, you may occasionally come across a referenced topic that doesn't correspond to a section in this library. Don't worry; you can get to that information through the SQL Server 2000 Books Online. Most of the references *will* pertain to items in these volumes, but there might be some reference you're interested in that will lead you online.

To make locating topics as easy as possible, and to enable you to quickly identify which topics are found in this library (versus which are found only in Books Online), Volumes 1 through 4 include a special index called **Topics in the SQL Server 2000 Reference Library**. There's some good information about the topic index (as I'll refer to it from now on) that will help you understand how to get the most use out of it and out of the *SQL Server 2000 Reference Library*.

For starters, the topic index contains *topics only found in the SQL Server 2000 Reference Library*. So, say you're reading through a chapter in this library, and you come across text that refers you to another topic, such as the following:

Related Topics

Building and Processing Cubes, Updating Cubes and Dimensions

Or something like the following:

>...For more information about which editions support which features, see Features Supported by the Editions of SQL Server 2000.

You can then look through this alphabetical listing of topics included in this library for the referenced topic, and when you find it, you'll be directed to the Volume and Chapter where that topic can be found, as shown here:

If two topics with the same title exist (as shown here), each will be listed separately. As previously mentioned, most references refer to topics also found in this library, but for those that don't, you can go to Books Online to get more information.

There are important exceptions to topic references and the topic index: *T-SQL statements and other programming elements are **not** included in the topic index*. Each volume that contains programming elements (such as T-SQL stored procedures, or English Query statements) has its own index of programming elements. Rather than cluttering this index up with programming elements (or vice versa), I've provided separate indexes to help you find the information you need faster.

Since Volumes 5 and 6 are almost entirely dedicated to statement definitions, including the topic index in those volumes didn't seem like a good use of (precious) pages.

The Idea Behind SQL Server 2000 Reference Library

The *SQL Server 2000 Reference Library*, like all libraries in the Windows Programming Reference Series, is designed to deliver the most pertinent information in the most accessible way possible. The *SQL Server 2000 Reference Library* is also designed to integrate seamlessly with SQL Server 2000 Books Online (and with MSDN Online) by providing a look-and-feel that is consistent with the electronic means of disseminating SQL Server 2000 reference information. In other words, the way that a given function reference appears on the pages of this book has been designed specifically to emulate the way that Books Online presents its reference pages.

The reason for maintaining such integration is simple: make it easy for you—the administrator or developer of SQL Server 2000 solutions—to use the tools and get the ongoing information you need to do your job. By providing a "common interface" among reference resources, your familiarity with the *SQL Server 2000 Reference Library* reference material can be immediately applied to Books Online, and vice-versa. In a word, it means *consistency*.

You'll find this philosophy of consistency and simplicity applied throughout Windows Programming Reference Series publications. I've designed the series to go hand-in-hand with online resources. Such consistency lets you leverage your familiarity with electronic reference material, then apply that familiarity to enable you to get away from your computer if you'd like, take a book with you, and—in the absence of keyboards and e-mail and upright chairs—get your reading and research done. Of course, each of the *SQL Server 2000 Reference Library* volumes fits nicely right next to your mouse pad as well, even when opened to a particular reference page.

With any job, the simpler and more consistent your tools are, the more time you can spend doing work rather than figuring out how to use your tools. The structure and design of the *SQL Server 2000 Reference Library* provides you with a comprehensive, pre-sharpened toolset to quickly program, administer, or optimize SQL Server 2000 deployments.

T-SQL Language Reference Overview

Transact-SQL is central to the use of Microsoft SQL Server. All applications that communicate with SQL Server do so by sending Transact-SQL statements to the server, regardless of an application's user interface.

Transact-SQL is generated from many kinds of applications, including:

- General office productivity applications.
- Applications that use a graphical user interface (GUI) to allow users to select the tables and columns from which they want to see data.
- Applications that use general language sentences to determine what data a user wants to see.
- Line of business applications that store their data in SQL Server databases. These can include both applications from other vendors and applications written in-house.
- Transact-SQL scripts that are run using utilities such as **osql**.
- Applications created with development systems such as Microsoft Visual C++, Microsoft Visual Basic, or Microsoft Visual J++ that use database application programming interfaces (APIs) such as ADO, OLE DB, and ODBC.
- Web pages that extract data from SQL Server databases.
- Distributed database systems from which data from SQL Server is replicated to various databases or distributed queries are executed.
- Data warehouses in which data is extracted from online transaction processing (OLTP) systems and summarized for decision-support analysis.

Transact-SQL Syntax Conventions

The syntax diagrams in the Transact-SQL Reference use these conventions.

Convention	Used for
UPPERCASE	Transact-SQL keywords.
italic	User-supplied parameters of Transact-SQL syntax.
| (vertical bar)	Separating syntax items within brackets or braces. You can choose only one of the items.
[ ] (brackets)	Optional syntax items. Do not type the brackets.
{ } (braces)	Required syntax items. Do not type the braces.
[,...*n*]	Indicating that the preceding item can be repeated *n* number of times. The occurrences are separated by commas.
[...*n*]	Indicating that the preceding item can be repeated *n* number of times. The occurrences are separated by blanks.
bold	Database names, table names, column names, index names, stored procedures, utilities, data type names, and text that must be typed exactly as shown.
<label> ::=	The name for a block of syntax. This convention is used to group and label portions of lengthy syntax or a unit of syntax that can be used in more than one place within a statement. Each location in which the block of syntax can be used is indicated with the label enclosed in chevrons: <label>.

Unless specified otherwise, all Transact-SQL references to the name of a database object can be a four-part name in the form:

```
[
    server_name.[database_name].[owner_name].
    | database_name.[owner_name].
    | owner_name.
    ]
]
object_name
```

- *server_name* specifies a linked server name or remote server name.

- *database_name* specifies the name of a Microsoft SQL Server database when the object resides in a SQL Server database. It specifies an OLE DB catalog when the object is in a linked server.

- *owner_name* specifies the user that owns the object if the object is in a SQL Server database. It specifies an OLE DB schema name when the object is in a linked server.

- *object_name* refers to the name of the object.

When referencing a specific object, you do not always have to specify the server, database, and owner for SQL Server to identify the object. Intermediate nodes can be omitted; use periods to indicate these positions. The valid formats of object names are:

server.database.owner.object

server.database..object

server..owner.object

server...object

database.owner.object

database..object

owner.object

object

Code Example Conventions

Unless stated otherwise, the examples were tested using SQL Query Analyzer and its default settings for these options:

- QUOTED_IDENTIFIER
- ANSI_NULLS
- ANSI_WARNINGS
- ANSI_PADDING
- ANSI_NULL_DFLT_ON
- CONCAT_NULL_YIELDS_NULL

Most code examples in the Transact-SQL Reference have been tested on servers running a case-sensitive sort order. The test servers were usually running the ANSI/ISO 1252 code page.

Transact-SQL Data Type Categories

Data types with similar characteristics are classified into categories. Categories that contain two or three data types generally have a category name derived from the data types in that category. For example, the **money** and **smallmoney** category contains the **money** data type and the **smallmoney** data type. Data type names always appear in bold, even when used as part of a category name.

Transact-SQL Data Type Hierarchy

The following data type hierarchy shows the SQL Server data type categories, subcategories, and data types used in the SQL Server documentation. For example, the exact numeric category contains three subcategories: integers, **decimal**, and **money** and **smallmoney**.

The exact numeric category also contains all of the data types in these three subcategories: **bigint**, **int**, **smallint**, **tinyint**, **bit**, **decimal**, **money**, and **smallmoney**. Any reference to exact numeric in the Transact-SQL Reference refers to these eight data types.

In this hierarchy the category names built from two or more data types use the conjunction "and." The conjunction "or" may be used in the Transact-SQL Reference if it is more appropriate for the context in which the name is used.

The data types specified in this hierarchy also pertain to synonyms. For example, **int** refers to both **int** and its synonym **integer**. For more information, see Data Types.

```
numeric
        exact numeric
                integer
                        bigint
                        int
                        smallint
                        tinyint
                bit
                decimal and numeric
                        decimal
                        numeric
                money and smallmoney
                        money
                        smallmoney
        approximate numeric
                float
                real
        datetime and smalldatetime
                datetime
                smalldatetime
```

character and binary string
    character string
        char, **varchar**, and **text**
            char and **varchar**
                char
                varchar
            text
        Unicode character string
            nchar and **nvarchar**
                nchar
                nvarchar
            ntext
    binary strings
        binary and **varbinary**
            binary
            varbinary
        image

cursor

sql_variant

table

timestamp

uniqueidentifier

Additional data type categories used in the Transact-SQL Reference are described in these two hierarchies:

text, **ntext**, and **image**
    text and **ntext**
        text
        ntext
    image

short string
    short character
        char and **varchar**
            char
            varchar
        nchar and **nvarchar**
            nchar
            nvarchar
    binary and **varbinary**
        binary
        varbinary

CHAPTER 2

New and Enhanced Features in Transact-SQL

Transact-SQL in Microsoft SQL Server 2000 provides new and enhanced statements, stored procedures, functions, data types, DBCC statements, and information schema views.

Data Types

New data types
bigint
sql_variant
table

Database Console Commands (DBCC)

New commands

DBCC CHECKCONSTRAINTS
DBCC CLEANTABLE
DBCC CONCURRENCYVIOLATION

DBCC DROPCLEANBUFFERS
DBCC FREEPROCCACHE
DBCC INDEXDEFRAG

Enhanced commands

DBCC CHECKALLOC
DBCC CHECKDB
DBCC CHECKTABLE
DBCC CHECKFILEGROUP
DBCC SHOWCONTIG

Functions

New functions

BINARY_CHECKSUM

CHECKSUM

CHECKSUM_AGG

COLLATIONPROPERTY

COUNT_BIG

DATABASEPROPERTYEX

fn_helpcollations

fn_listextendedproperty

fn_servershareddrives

fn_trace_geteventinfo

fn_trace_getfilterinfo

fn_trace_getinfo

fn_trace_gettable

fn_virtualfilestats

GETUTCDATE

HAS_DBACCESS

IDENT_CURRENT

INDEXKEY_PROPERTY

OBJECTPROPERTY

OPENDATASOURCE

OPENXML

ROWCOUNT_BIG

SCOPE_IDENTITY

SERVERPROPERTY

SESSIONPROPERTY

SQL_VARIANT_PROPERTY

Information Schema Views

New information schema views

PARAMETERS

ROUTINES

ROUTINE_COLUMNS

Replication Stored Procedures

New replication stored procedures

sp_addmergealternatepublisher

sp_addscriptexec

sp_adjustpublisheridentityrange

sp_attachsubscription

sp_browsesnapshotfolder

sp_browsemergesnapshotfolder

sp_changesubscriptiondtsinfo

sp_copysnapshot

sp_disableagentoffload

sp_dropanonymouseagent

sp_dropmergealternatepublisher

sp_enableagentoffload

sp_getagentoffloadinfo

sp_getqueuedrows

sp_getsubscriptiondtspackagename

sp_helparticledts

sp_helpmergealternatepublisher

sp_helpreplicationoption

sp_ivindexhasnullcols

sp_marksubscriptionvalidation

sp_mergearticlecolumn

sp_repladdcolumn

sp_repldropcolumn

sp_restoredbreplication

sp_resyncmergesubscription

sp_vupgrade_replication

Reserved Keywords

COLLATE, FUNCTION, and OPENXML are reserved keywords in SQL Server 2000.

The following words have been **un**reserved.

AVG
CONFIRM
COUNT
FLOPPY
LEVEL
MIN
ONCE
PERM
PIPE
PRIVILEGES
SERIALIZABLE
TAPE
TEMPORARY
WORK

COMMITTED
CONTROLROW
ERROREXIT
ISOLATION
MAX
MIRROREXIT
ONLY
PERMANENT
PREPARE
REPEATABLE
SUM
TEMP
UNCOMMITTED

Statements

New statements

ALTER FUNCTION
CREATE FUNCTION
DROP FUNCTION

Enhanced statements

ALTER DATABASE
ALTER TABLE
BACKUP
COLUMNPROPERTY
CREATE INDEX
CREATE STATISTICS

CREATE TABLE
CREATE TRIGGER
INDEXPROPERTY
OBJECTPROPERTY
RESTORE

System Stored Procedures

New system stored procedures

sp_addextendedproperty
sp_add_log_shipping_database
sp_add_log_shipping_plan
sp_add_log_shipping_plan_database
sp_add_log_shipping_primary
sp_add_log_shipping_secondary
sp_add_maintenance_plan
sp_add_maintenance_plan_db
sp_add_maintenance_plan_job
sp_can_tlog_be_applied
sp_change_monitor_role
sp_change_primary_role
sp_change_secondary_role
sp_create_log_shipping_monitor_account
sp_define_log_shipping_monitor
sp_delete_log_shipping_database
sp_delete_log_shipping_plan
sp_delete_log_shipping_plan_database
sp_delete_log_shipping_primary
sp_delete_log_shipping_secondary
sp_delete_maintenance_plan
sp_delete_maintenance_plan_db

sp_delete_maintenance_plan_job
sp_dropextendedproperty
sp_get_log_shipping_monitor_info
sp_helpconstraint
sp_helpindex
sp_help_maintenance_plan
sp_invalidate_textptr
sp_remove_log_shipping_monitor
sp_resolve_logins
sp_settriggerorder
sp_trace_create
sp_trace_generateevent
sp_trace_setevent
sp_trace_setfilter
sp_trace_setstatus
sp_updateextendedproperty
sp_update_log_shipping_monitor_info
sp_update_log_shipping_plan
sp_update_log_shipping_plan_database
sp_xml_preparedocument
sp_xml_removedocument

Enhanced system stored procedures

sp_helptrigger
sp_tableoption
sp_serveroption
sp_who

System Tables

New system tables

logmarkhistory
log_shipping_databases
log_shipping_monitor
log_shipping_plan_databases
log_shipping_plan_history
log_shipping_plans
log_shipping_secondaries
Mssub_identity_range

MSsync_states
sysdbmaintplan_databases
sysdbmaintplan_history
sysdbmaintplan_jobs
sysdbmaintplans
sysmergeschemaarticles
sysopentapes

CHAPTER 3

T-SQL Data Types

This chapter explains important information about T-SQL data types. A detailed language definition for each T-SQL data type (such as its syntax, arguments, return types, examples, and the like) is provided in alphabetical order in Chapter 11, T-SQL Reference.

In Microsoft SQL Server, each column, local variable, expression, and parameter has a related data type, which is an attribute that specifies the type of data (integer, character, **money**, and so on) that the object can hold. SQL Server supplies a set of system data types that define all of the types of data that can be used with SQL Server. The set of system-supplied data types is shown below.

User-defined data types, which are aliases for system-supplied data types, can also be defined. For more information about user-defined data types, see sp_addtype and Creating User-defined Data Types.

When two expressions that have different data types, collations, precision, scale, or length are combined by an operator:

- The data type of the resulting value is determined by applying the rules of data type precedence to the data types of the input expressions. For more information, see Data Type Precedence.

- If the result data type is **char**, **varchar**, **text**, **nchar**, **nvarchar**, or **ntext**, the collation of the result value is determined by the rules of collation precedence. For more information, see Collation Precedence.

- The precision, scale, and length of the result depend on the precision, scale, and length of the input expressions. For more information, see Precision, Scale, and Length.

SQL Server provides data type synonyms for SQL-92 compatibility. For more information, see Data Type Synonyms.

Exact Numerics

Integers

bigint
> Integer (whole number) data from -2^{63} (-9223372036854775808) through $2^{63} - 1$ (9223372036854775807).

int
>   Integer (whole number) data from –2^31 (–2,147,483,648) through 2^31 – 1
>   (2,147,483,647).

smallint
>   Integer data from 2^15 (–32,768) through 2^15 – 1 (32,767).

tinyint
>   Integer data from 0 through 255.

bit

bit
>   Integer data with either a 1 or 0 value.

decimal and numeric

decimal
>   Fixed precision and scale numeric data from –10^38 +1 through 10^38 – 1.

numeric
>   Functionally equivalent to **decimal.**

money and smallmoney

money
>   Monetary data values from –2^63 (–922,337,203,685,477.5808) through
>   2^63 – 1 (+922,337,203,685,477.5807), with accuracy to a ten-thousandth of a
>   monetary unit.

smallmoney
>   Monetary data values from –214,748.3648 through +214,748.3647, with accuracy
>   to a ten-thousandth of a monetary unit.

Approximate Numerics

float
>   Floating precision number data from –1.79E + 308 through 1.79E + 308.

real
>   Floating precision number data from –3.40E + 38 through 3.40E + 38.

datetime and smalldatetime

datetime
>   Date and time data from January 1, 1753, through December 31, 9999, with an
>   accuracy of three-hundredths of a second, or 3.33 milliseconds.

smalldatetime
>   Date and time data from January 1, 1900, through June 6, 2079, with an accuracy
>   of one minute.

Character Strings

char
> Fixed-length non-Unicode character data with a maximum length of 8,000 characters.

varchar
> Variable-length non-Unicode data with a maximum of 8,000 characters.

text
> Variable-length non-Unicode data with a maximum length of
> $2^{31} - 1$ (2,147,483,647) characters.

Unicode Character Strings

nchar
> Fixed-length Unicode data with a maximum length of 4,000 characters.

nvarchar
> Variable-length Unicode data with a maximum length of 4,000 characters.
> **sysname** is a system-supplied user-defined data type that is functionally equivalent
> to **nvarchar(128)** and is used to reference database object names.

ntext
> Variable-length Unicode data with a maximum length of $2^{30} - 1$ (1,073,741,823)
> characters.

Binary Strings

binary
> Fixed-length binary data with a maximum length of 8,000 bytes.

varbinary
> Variable-length binary data with a maximum length of 8,000 bytes.

image
> Variable-length binary data with a maximum length of $2^{31} - 1$ (2,147,483,647)
> bytes.

Other Data Types

cursor
> A reference to a cursor.

sql_variant
> A data type that stores values of various SQL Server-supported data types, except
> **text**, **ntext**, **timestamp**, and **sql_variant**.

table
> A special data type used to store a result set for later processing.

timestamp
> A database-wide unique number that gets updated every time a row gets updated.

uniqueidentifier
> A globally unique identifier (GUID).

Related Topics

CREATE PROCEDURE, CREATE TABLE, DECLARE @local_variable,
EXECUTE, Expressions, Functions, LIKE, SET, sp_bindefault, sp_bindrule,
sp_droptype, sp_help, sp_rename, sp_unbindefault, sp_unbindrule,
Using Unicode Data

Data Type Precedence

When two expressions of different data types are combined by an operator, the data type precedence rules specify which data type is converted to the other. The data type with the lower precedence is converted to the data type with the higher precedence. If the conversion is not a supported implicit conversion, an error is returned. When both operand expressions have the same data type, the result of the operation has that data type.

This is the precedence order for the Microsoft SQL Server 2000 data types:

- **sql_variant** (highest)
- **datetime**
- **smalldatetime**
- **float**
- **real**
- **decimal**
- **money**
- **smallmoney**
- **bigint**
- **int**
- **smallint**
- **tinyint**
- **bit**
- **ntext**
- **text**

- **image**
- **timestamp**
- **uniqueidentifier**
- **nvarchar**
- **nchar**
- **varchar**
- **char**
- **varbinary**
- **binary** (lowest)

Collation Precedence

Collation precedence, also known as collation coercion rules, is the term given to the set of rules that determine:

- The collation of the final result of an expression that is evaluated to a character string.
- The collation used by collation-sensitive operators that use character string inputs but do not return a character string, such as LIKE and IN.

The collation precedence rules apply only to the character string data types, **char**, **varchar**, **text**, **nchar**, **nvarchar**, and **ntext**. Objects with other data types do not participate in collation evaluations.

The collation of all objects falls into one of four categories. The name of each category is called the collation label.

Collation label	Types of objects
Coercible-default	Any Transact-SQL character string variable, parameter, literal, or the output of a catalog built-in function, or a built-in function that does not take string inputs but produces a string output.
	If the object is declared in a user-defined function, stored procedure, or trigger, it is assigned the default collation of the database in which the function, stored procedure, or trigger is created. If the object is declared in a batch, it is assigned the default collation of the current database for the connection.

(continued)

(continued)

Collation label	Types of objects
Implicit X	A column reference. The collation of the expression (denoted by X) is taken from the collation defined for the column in the table or view. Even if the column was explicitly assigned a collation by a COLLATE clause in the CREATE TABLE or CREATE VIEW statement, the column reference is classified as implicit.
Explicit X	An expression that is explicitly cast to a specific collation (denoted by X) using a COLLATE clause in the expression.
No-collation	Indicates that the value of an expression is the result of an operation between two strings with conflicting collations of the implicit collation label. The expression result is defined as not having a collation.

The collation label of a simple expression that references only one character string object is the collation label of the referenced object.

The collation label of a complex expression that references two operand expressions with the same collation label is the collation label of the operand expressions.

The collation label of the final result of a complex expression that references two operand expressions with different collations is based on these rules:

- Explicit takes precedence over implicit. Implicit takes precedence over coercible-default. In other words,

  Explicit > Implicit > Coercible-Default

- Combining two explicit expressions that have been assigned different collations generates an error.

  Explicit X + Explicit Y = Error

- Combining two implicit expressions that have different collations yields a result of no-collation.

  Implicit X + Implicit Y = No-collation

- Combining an expression with no-collation with an expression of any label, except explicit collation (see following bullet), yields a result that has the no-collation label.

  No-collation + anything = No-collation

- Combining an expression with no-collation with an expression that has an explicit collation, yields an expression with an explicit label.

  No-collation + Explicit X = Explicit

These examples illustrate the rules.

```
USE tempdb
GO

CREATE TABLE TestTab (
    id int,
    GreekCol nvarchar(10) collate greek_ci_as,
    LatinCol nvarchar(10) collate latin1_general_cs_as
    )
INSERT TestTab VALUES (1, N'A', N'a')
GO
```

The predicate in the following query has collation conflict and generates an error:

```
SELECT *
FROM TestTab
WHERE GreekCol = LatinCol
```

This is the result set.

```
Msg 446, Level 16, State 9, Server CTSSERV, Line 1
Cannot resolve collation conflict for equal to operation.
```

The predicate in the following query is evaluated in collation greek_ci_as because the right expression has the explicit label, which takes precedence over the implicit label of the right expression:

```
SELECT *
FROM TestTab
WHERE GreekCol = LatinCol COLLATE greek_ci_as
```

This is the result set.

```
id          GreekCol              LatinCol
----------- --------------------- ---------------------
          1 a                     A

(1 row affected)
```

The case expressions in the following queries have no collation label so they cannot appear in the select list or be operated by collation-sensitive operators. However, the expressions can be operated on by collation-insensitive operators.

```
SELECT (CASE WHEN id > 10 THEN GreekCol ELSE LatinCol END)
FROM TestTab
```

Here is the result set.

```
Msg 451, Level 16, State 1, Line 1
Cannot resolve collation conflict for column 1 in SELECT statement.

SELECT PATINDEX((CASE WHEN id > 10 THEN GreekCol ELSE LatinCol END), 'a')
FROM TestTab
```

Here is the result set.

```
Msg 446, Level 16, State 9, Server LEIH2, Line 1
Cannot resolve collation conflict for patindex operation.

SELECT (CASE WHEN id > 10 THEN GreekCol ELSE LatinCol END) COLLATE Latin1_General_CI_AS
FROM TestTab
```

Here is the result set.

```
--------------------
a

(1 row affected)
```

This table summarizes the rules.

Operand coercion label	Explicit X	Implicit X	Coercible-default	No-collation
Explicit Y	Generates Error	Result is Explicit Y	Result is Explicit Y	Result is Explicit Y
Implicit Y	Result is Explicit X	Result is No-collation	Result is Implicit Y	Result is No-collation
Coercible-default	Result is Explicit X	Result is Implicit X	Result is Coercible-default	Result is No-collation
No-collation	Result is Explicit X	Result is No-collation	Result is No-collation	Result is No-collation

Operators and functions are either collation sensitive or insensitive:

- Collation sensitive means that specifying a no-collation operand is a compile-time error. The expression result cannot be no-collation.
- Collation insensitive means that the operands and result can be no-collation.

The comparison operators, and the MAX, MIN, BETWEEN, LIKE, and IN operators, are collation sensitive. The string used by the operators is assigned the collation label of the operand that has the higher precedence. The UNION operator is also collation sensitive, and all string operands and the final result is assigned the collation of the operand with the highest precedence. The collation precedence of the UNION operands and result are evaluated column by column.

The assignment operator is collation insensitive and the right expression is cast to the left collation.

The string concatenation operator is collation insensitive, the two string operands and the result are assigned the collation label of the operand with the highest collation precedence. The UNION ALL and CASE operators are collation insensitive, and all string operands and the final results are assigned the collation label of the operand with the highest precedence. The collation precedence of the UNION ALL operands and result are evaluated column by column.

THE CAST, CONVERT, and COLLATE functions are collation sensitive for **char**, **varchar**, and **text** data types. If the input and output of the CAST and CONVERT functions are character strings, the output string has the collation label of the input string. If the input is not a character string, the output string is coercible-default and assigned the collation of the current database for the connection, or the database containing the user-defined function, stored procedure, or trigger in which the CAST or CONVERT is referenced.

For the built-in functions that return a string but do not take a string input, the result string is coercible-default and is assigned either the collation of the current database, or the collation of the database containing the user-defined function, stored procedure, or trigger in which the function is referenced.

These functions are collation-sensitive and their output strings have the collation label of the input string:

- CHARINDEX
- DIFFERENCE
- ISNUMERIC
- LEFT
- LEN
- LOWER
- PATINDEX
- REPLACE
- REVERSE
- RIGHT

- SOUNDEX
- STUFF
- SUBSTRING
- UPPER

These additional rules also apply to collation precedence:

- You cannot have multiple COLLATE clauses on an expression that is already an explicit expression. For example, this WHERE clause is illegal because a COLLATE clause is specified for an expression that is already an explicit expression:

```
WHERE ColumnA = ( 'abc' COLLATE French_CI_AS) COLLATE French_CS_AS
```

- Code page conversions for **text** data types are not allowed. You cannot cast a text expression from one collation to another if they have the different code pages. The assignment operator cannot assign values if the collation of the right text operand has a different code page than the left text operand.

Determination of collation precedence takes place after data type conversion. The operand from which the resulting collation is taken can be different from the operand that supplies the data type of the final result. For example, consider this batch:

```
CREATE TABLE TestTab
    (PrimaryKey int PRIMARY KEY,
     CharCol char(10) COLLATE French_CI_AS
     )

SELECT *
FROM TestTab
WHERE CharCol LIKE N'abc'
```

The Unicode data type of the simple expression N'abc' has a higher data type precedence, so the resulting expression has the Unicode data type assigned to N'abc'. The expression **CharCol**, however, has a collation label of Implicit, while N'abc' has a lower coercion label of coercible-default, so the collation used is the **French_CI_AS** collation of **CharCol**.

Related Topics

COLLATE, Data Type Conversion

Precision, Scale, and Length

Precision is the number of digits in a number. Scale is the number of digits to the right of the decimal point in a number. For example, the number 123.45 has a precision of 5 and a scale of 2.

The default maximum precision of **numeric** and **decimal** data types is 38. In previous versions of SQL Server, the default maximum was 28.

Length for a numeric data type is the number of bytes used to store the number. Length for a character string or Unicode data type is the number of characters. The length for **binary**, **varbinary**, and **image** data types is the number of bytes. For example, an **int** data type can hold 10 digits, is stored in 4 bytes, and does not accept decimal points. The **int** data type has a precision of 10, a length of 4, and a scale of 0.

When two **char**, **varchar**, **binary**, or **varbinary** expressions are concatenated, the length of the resulting expression is the sum of the lengths of the two source expressions or 8,000 characters, whichever is less.

When two **nchar** or **nvarchar** expressions are concatenated, the length of the resulting expression is the sum of the lengths of the two source expressions, or 4,000 characters, whichever is less.

The precision and scale of the numeric data types besides **decimal** are fixed. If an arithmetic operator has two expressions of the same type, then the result has the same data type with the precision and scale defined for that type. If an operator has two expressions with different numeric data types, then the rules of data type precedence define the data type of the result. The result has the precision and scale defined for its data type.

This table defines how the precision and scale of the result are calculated when the result of an operation is of type **decimal**. The result is **decimal** when:

- Both expressions are **decimal**.
- One expression is **decimal** and the other is a data type with a lower precedence than **decimal**.

The operand expressions are denoted as expression e1, with precision p1 and scale s1, and expression e2, with precision p2 and scale s2. The precision and scale for any expression that is not **decimal** is the precision and scale defined for the data type of the expression.

Operation	Result precision	Result scale *
e1 + e2	max(s1, s2) + max(p1–s1, p2–s2) + 1	max(s1, s2)
e1 – e2	max(s1, s2) + max(p1–s1, p2–s2)	max(s1, s2)
e1 * e2	p1 + p2 + 1	s1 + s2
e1 / e2	p1 – s1 + s2 + max(6, s1 + p2 + 1)	max(6, s1 + p2 + 1)

* The result precision and scale have an absolute maximum of 38. When a result precision is greater than 38, the corresponding scale is reduced to prevent the integral part of a result from being truncated.

Data Type Synonyms

Data type synonyms are included for SQL-92 compatibility.

Synonym	Mapped to system data type
Binary varying	Varbinary
char varying	Varchar
character	Char
character	char(1)
character(n)	char(n)
character varying(n)	varchar(n)
Dec	decimal
Double precision	float
float[(n)] for $n = 1$–7	real
float[(n)] for $n = 8$–15	float
integer	int
national character(n)	nchar(n)
national char(n)	nchar(n)
national character varying(n)	nvarchar(n)
national char varying(n)	nvarchar(n)
national text	ntext
rowversion	timestamp

Data type synonyms can be used in place of the corresponding base data type name in data definition language (DDL) statements, such as CREATE TABLE, CREATE PROCEDURE, or DECLARE @variable. The synonyms have no visibility after the object is created, however. When the object is created, it is assigned the base data type associated with the synonym, and there is no record that the synonym was specified in the statement that created the object.

All objects derived from the original object, such as result set columns or expressions, are assigned the base data type. All subsequent meta data functions performed on the original object and any derived objects will report the base data type, not the synonym. This includes meta data operations, such as **sp_help** and other system stored procedures, the information schema views, or the various data access API meta data operations that report the data types of table or result set columns.

Data type synonyms also cannot be specified in the graphical administration utilities, such as SQL Server Enterprise Manager.

For example, you can create a table specifying **national character varying**:

```
CREATE TABLE ExampleTable (PriKey int PRIMARY KEY, VarCHarCol national character
varying(10))
```

VarCharCol is actually assigned an **nvarchar(10)** data type, and all subsequent meta data functions will report it as an **nvarchar(10)** column. The meta data functions will never report them as **national character varying(10)** column.

T-SQL Operators

This chapter explains important information about T-SQL operators. This chapter also includes detailed language definitions for each T-SQL operator.

T-SQL Operator Overview

An operator is a symbol specifying an action that is performed on one or more expressions. Microsoft SQL Server 2000 uses these operator categories:

- Arithmetic operators
- Assignment operator
- Bitwise operators
- Comparison operators
- Logical operators
- String concatenation operator
- Unary operators

Arithmetic Operators

Arithmetic operators perform mathematical operations on two expressions of any of the data types of the numeric data type category. For more information about data type categories, see Transact-SQL Syntax Conventions.

Operator	Meaning
+ (Add)	Addition.
- (Subtract)	Subtraction.
* (Multiply)	Multiplication.
/ (Divide)	Division.
% (Modulo)	Returns the integer remainder of a division. For example, 12 % 5 = 2 because the remainder of 12 divided by 5 is 2.

The plus (+) and minus (-) can also be used to perform arithmetic operations on **datetime** and **smalldatetime** values.

For more information about the precision and scale of the result of an arithmetic operation, see Precision, Scale, and Length.

Assignment Operator

Transact-SQL has one assignment operator, the equals sign (=). In this example, the **@MyCounter** variable is created. Then, the assignment operator sets **@MyCounter** to a value returned by an expression.

```
DECLARE @MyCounter INT
SET @MyCounter = 1
```

The assignment operator can also be used to establish the relationship between a column heading and the expression defining the values for the column. This example displays two column headings named **FirstColumnHeading** and **SecondColumnHeading**. The string xyz is displayed in the **FirstColumnHeading** column heading for all rows. Then, each product ID from the **Products** table is listed in the **SecondColumnHeading** column heading.

```
USE Northwind
GO
SELECT FirstColumnHeading = 'xyz',
       SecondColumnHeading = ProductID
FROM Products
GO
```

Bitwise Operators

Bitwise operators perform bit manipulations between two expressions of any of the data types of the integer data type category.

Operator	Meaning
& (Bitwise AND)	Bitwise AND (two operands).
| (Bitwise OR)	Bitwise OR (two operands).
^ (Bitwise Exclusive OR)	Bitwise exclusive OR (two operands).

The operands for bitwise operators can be any of the data types of the integer or binary string data type categories (except for the **image** data type), with the exception that both operands cannot be any of the data types of the binary string data type category. The table shows the supported operand data types.

Left operand	Right operand
binary	**int**, **smallint**, or **tinyint**
bit	**int**, **smallint**, **tinyint**, or **bit**
int	**int**, **smallint**, **tinyint**, **binary**, or **varbinary**
smallint	**int**, **smallint**, **tinyint**, **binary**, or **varbinary**
tinyint	**int**, **smallint**, **tinyint**, **binary**, or **varbinary**
varbinary	**int**, **smallint**, or **tinyint**

Comparison Operators

Comparison operators test whether or not two expressions are the same. Comparison operators can be used on all expressions except expressions of the **text**, **ntext**, or **image** data types.

Operator	Meaning
= (Equals)	Equal to
> (Greater Than)	Greater than
< (Less Than)	Less than
>= (Greater Than or Equal To)	Greater than or equal to
<= (Less Than or Equal To)	Less than or equal to
<> (Not Equal To)	Not equal to
!= (Not Equal To)	Not equal to (not SQL-92 standard)
!< (Not Less Than)	Not less than (not SQL-92 standard)
!> (Not Greater Than)	Not greater than (not SQL-92 standard)

The result of a comparison operator has the Boolean data type, which has three values: TRUE, FALSE, and UNKNOWN. Expressions that return a Boolean data type are known as Boolean expressions.

Unlike other SQL Server data types, a Boolean data type cannot be specified as the data type of a table column or variable, and cannot be returned in a result set.

When SET ANSI_NULLS is ON, an operator that has one or two NULL expressions returns UNKNOWN. When SET ANSI_NULLS is OFF, the same rules apply, except an equals operator returns TRUE if both expressions are NULL. For example, NULL = NULL returns TRUE if SET ANSI_NULLS is OFF.

Expressions with Boolean data types are used in the WHERE clause to filter the rows that qualify for the search conditions and in control-of-flow language statements such as IF and WHILE, for example:

```
USE Northwind
GO
DECLARE @MyProduct int
SET @MyProduct = 10
IF (@MyProduct <> 0)
   SELECT *
   FROM Products
   WHERE ProductID = @MyProduct
GO
```

Logical Operators

Logical operators test for the truth of some condition. Logical operators, like comparison operators, return a Boolean data type with a value of TRUE or FALSE.

Operator	Meaning
ALL	TRUE if all of a set of comparisons are TRUE.
AND	TRUE if both Boolean expressions are TRUE.
ANY	TRUE if any one of a set of comparisons are TRUE.
BETWEEN	TRUE if the operand is within a range.
EXISTS	TRUE if a subquery contains any rows.
IN	TRUE if the operand is equal to one of a list of expressions.

(continued)

(continued)

Operator	Meaning
LIKE	TRUE if the operand matches a pattern.
NOT	Reverses the value of any other Boolean operator.
OR	TRUE if either Boolean expression is TRUE.
SOME	TRUE if some of a set of comparisons are TRUE.

For more information about logical operators, see the specific logical operator topic.

String Concatenation Operator

The string concatenation operator allows string concatenation with the addition sign (+), which is also known as the string concatenation operator. All other string manipulation is handled through string functions such as SUBSTRING.

By default, an empty string is interpreted as an empty string in INSERT or assignment statements on data of the **varchar** data type. In concatenating data of the **varchar**, **char**, or **text** data types, the empty string is interpreted as an empty string. For example, 'abc' + '' + 'def' is stored as 'abcdef'. However, if the **sp_dbcmptlevel** compatibility level setting is 65, empty constants are treated as a single blank character and 'abc' + '' + 'def' is stored as 'abc def'. For more information about the interpretation of empty strings, see sp_dbcmptlevel.

When two character strings are concatenated, the collation of the result expression is set following the rules of collation precedence. For more information, see Collation Precedence.

Unary Operators

Unary operators perform an operation on only one expression of any of the data types of the numeric data type category.

Operator	Meaning
+ (Positive)	Numeric value is positive.
- (Negative)	Numeric value is negative.
~ (Bitwise NOT)	Returns the ones complement of the number.

The + (Positive) and - (Negative) operators can be used on any expression of any of the data types of the numeric data type category. The ~ (Bitwise NOT) operator can be used only on expressions of any of the data types of the integer data type category.

Operator Precedence

When a complex expression has multiple operators, operator precedence determines the sequence in which the operations are performed. The order of execution can significantly affect the resulting value.

Operators have these precedence levels. An operator on higher levels is evaluated before an operator on a lower level:

- \+ (Positive), - (Negative), ~ (Bitwise NOT)
- * (Multiply), / (Division), % (Modulo)
- \+ (Add), (+ Concatenate), - (Subtract)
- =, >, <, >=, <=, <>, !=, !>, !< (Comparison operators)
- ^ (Bitwise Exclusive OR), & (Bitwise AND), | (Bitwise OR)
- NOT
- AND
- ALL, ANY, BETWEEN, IN, LIKE, OR, SOME
- = (Assignment)

When two operators in an expression have the same operator precedence level, they are evaluated left to right based on their position in the expression. For example, in the expression used in the SET statement of this example, the subtraction operator is evaluated before the addition operator.

```
DECLARE @MyNumber int
SET @MyNumber = 4 - 2 + 27
-- Evaluates to 2 + 27 which yields an expression result of 29.
SELECT @MyNumber
```

Use parentheses to override the defined precedence of the operators in an expression. Everything within the parentheses is evaluated first to yield a single value before that value can be used by any operator outside of the parentheses.

For example, in the expression used in the SET statement of this example, the multiplication operator has a higher precedence than the addition operator, so it gets evaluated first; the expression result is 13.

```
DECLARE @MyNumber int
SET @MyNumber = 2 * 4 + 5
-- Evaluates to 8 + 5 which yields an expression result of 13.
SELECT @MyNumber
```

In the expression used in the SET statement of this example, the parentheses causes the addition to be performed first; the expression result is 18.

```
DECLARE @MyNumber int
SET @MyNumber = 2 * (4 + 5)
-- Evaluates to 2 * 9 which yields an expression result of 18.
SELECT @MyNumber
```

If an expression has nested parentheses, the most deeply nested expression is evaluated first. This example contains nested parentheses, with the expression 5 - 3 in the most deeply nested set of parentheses. This expression yields a value of 2. Then, the addition operator (+) adds this result to 4, which yields a value of 6. Finally, the 6 is multiplied by 2 to yield an expression result of 12.

```
DECLARE @MyNumber int
SET @MyNumber = 2 * (4 + (5 - 3) )
-- Evaluates to 2 * (4 + 2) which further evaluates to 2 * 6, and
-- yields an expression result of 12.
SELECT @MyNumber
```

T-SQL Operator Reference

This section provides complete reference for T-SQL operators.

+ (Add)

Adds two numbers. This addition arithmetic operator can also add a number, in days, to a date.

Syntax

```
expression + expression
```

Arguments

expression
Is any valid Microsoft SQL Server expression of any of the data types in the numeric category except the **bit** data type.

Result Types

Returns the data type of the argument with the higher precedence. For more information, see Data Type Precedence.

Examples

A. Use the addition operator to calculate the total units available for customers to order

This example adds the current number of products in stock and the number of units currently on order for all products in the **Products** table.

```
USE Northwind
GO
SELECT ProductName, UnitsInStock + UnitsOnOrder
FROM Products
ORDER BY ProductName ASC
GO
```

B. Use the addition operator to add days to date and time values

This example adds a number of days to a **datetime** date.

```
USE master
GO
SET NOCOUNT ON
DECLARE @startdate datetime, @adddays int
SET @startdate = '1/10/1900 12:00 AM'
SET @adddays = 5
SET NOCOUNT OFF
SELECT @startdate + 1.25 AS 'Start Date',
   @startdate + @adddays AS 'Add Date'
```

Here is the result set:

```
Start Date                  Add Date
-------------------------   ----------------------------
Jan 11 1900  6:00AM         Jan 15 1900 12:00AM

(1 row(s) affected)
```

C. Add character and integer data types

This example adds an **int** data type value and a character value by converting the character data type to **int**. If an invalid character exists in the **char** string, SQL Server returns an error.

```
DECLARE @addvalue int
SET @addvalue = 15
SELECT '125127' + @addvalue
```

Here is the result set:

```
-----------------------
125142

(1 row(s) affected)
```

Related Topics

CAST and CONVERT, Data Type Conversion, Data Types, Expressions, Functions, Operators, SELECT

+ (Positive)

A unary operator that returns the positive value of a numeric expression (a unary operator).

Syntax

```
+ numeric_expression
```

Arguments

numeric_expression
Is any valid Microsoft SQL Server expression of any of the data types in the numeric data type category except the **datetime** or **smalldatetime** data types.

Result Types

Returns the data type of *numeric_expression*, except that an unsigned **tinyint** expression is promoted to a **smallint** result.

Example

This example sets a variable to a positive value.

```
DECLARE @MyNumber decimal(10,2)
SET @MyNumber = +123.45
```

Related Topics

Data Types, Expressions, Operators

+ (String Concatenation)

An operator in a string expression that concatenates two or more character or binary strings, columns, or a combination of strings and column names into one expression (a string operator).

Syntax

```
expression + expression
```

Arguments

expression

Is any valid Microsoft SQL Server expression of any of the data types in the character and binary data type category, except the **image**, **ntext**, or **text** data types. Both expressions must be of the same data type, or one expression must be able to be implicitly converted to the data type of the other expression.

An explicit conversion to character data must be used when concatenating binary strings and any characters between the binary strings. The following example shows when CONVERT (or CAST) must be used with binary concatenation and when CONVERT (or CAST) does not need to be used.

```
DECLARE @mybin1 binary(5), @mybin2 binary(5)
SET @mybin1 = 0xFF
SET @mybin2 = 0xA5
-- No CONVERT or CAST function is necessary because this example
-- concatenates two binary strings.
SELECT @mybin1 + @mybin2
-- A CONVERT or CAST function is necessary because this example
-- concatenates two binary strings plus a space.
SELECT CONVERT(varchar(5), @mybin1) + ' '
   + CONVERT(varchar(5), @mybin2)
-- Here is the same conversion using CAST
SELECT CAST(@mybin1 AS varchar(5)) + ' '
   + CAST(@mybin2 AS varchar(5))
```

Result Types

Returns the data type of the argument with the highest precedence. For more information, see Data Type Precedence.

Remarks

When you concatenate null values, either the **concat null yields null** setting of **sp_dboption** or SET CONCAT_NULL_YIELDS_NULL determines the behavior when one *expression* is NULL. With either **concat null yields null** or SET CONCAT_NULL_YIELDS_NULL enabled ON, 'string' + NULL returns NULL. If either **concat null yields null** or SET CONCAT_NULL_YIELDS_NULL is disabled, the result is 'string'.

Examples

A. Use string concatenation

This example creates a single column (under the column heading Name) from multiple character columns, with the author's last name followed by a comma, a single space, and then the author's first name. The result set is in ascending, alphabetical order by the author's last name, and then by the author's first name.

```
USE pubs
SELECT (au_lname + ', ' + au_fname) AS Name
FROM authors
ORDER BY au_lname ASC, au_fname ASC
```

Here is the result set:

```
Name
----------------------------------------------------------------
Bennet, Abraham
Blotchet-Halls, Reginald
Carson, Cheryl
DeFrance, Michel
del Castillo, Innes
Dull, Ann
Green, Marjorie
Greene, Morningstar
Gringlesby, Burt
Hunter, Sheryl
Karsen, Livia
Locksley, Charlene
MacFeather, Stearns
McBadden, Heather
O'Leary, Michael
Panteley, Sylvia
Ringer, Albert
Ringer, Anne
Smith, Meander
Straight, Dean
Stringer, Dirk
White, Johnson
Yokomoto, Akiko

(23 row(s) affected)
```

B. Combine numeric and date data types

This example uses the CAST function to concatenate **numeric** and **date** data types.

```
USE pubs
SELECT 'The order date is ' + CAST(ord_date AS varchar(30))
FROM sales
WHERE ord_num = 'A2976'
ORDER BY ord_num
```

Here is the result set:

```
-------------------------------------------------
The order date is May 24 1993 12:00AM

(1 row(s) affected)
```

C. Use multiple string concatenation

This example concatenates multiple strings to form one long string. To display the last name and the first initial of each author living in the state of California, a comma is placed after the last name and a period after the first initial.

```
USE pubs
SELECT (au_lname + ',' + SPACE(1) + SUBSTRING(au_fname, 1, 1) + '.') AS Name
FROM authors
WHERE state = 'CA'
ORDER BY au_lname ASC, au_fname ASC
```

Here is the result set:

```
Name
-------------------------------------------------
Bennet, A.
Carson, C.
Dull, A.
Green, M.
Gringlesby, B.
Hunter, S.
Karsen, L.
Locksley, C.
MacFeather, S.
McBadden, H.
O'Leary, M.
Straight, D.
Stringer, D.
White, J.
Yokomoto, A.

(15 row(s) affected)
```

Related Topics

CAST and CONVERT, Data Type Conversion, Data Types, Expressions, Functions, Operators, SELECT, SET, Setting Database Options, sp_dboption

- (Negative)

Is a unary operator that returns the negative value of a numeric expression (a unary operator).

Syntax

```
- numeric_expression
```

Arguments

numeric_expression

Is any valid Microsoft SQL Server expression of any of the data types of the numeric data type category except the **datetime** or **smalldatetime** data types.

Result Types

Returns the data type of *numeric_expression*, except that an unsigned **tinyint** expression is promoted to a signed **smallint** result.

Examples

A. Set a variable to a negative value

This example sets a variable to a negative value.

```
DECLARE @MyNumber decimal(10,2)
@MyNumber = -123.45
```

B. Negate a value

This example negates a variable.

```
DECLARE @Num1 int
SET @Num1 = 5
SELECT -@Num1
```

Related Topics

Data Types, Expressions, Operators

- (Subtract)

Subtracts two numbers. This subtraction arithmetic operator can also subtract a number, in days, from a date.

Syntax

```
expression - expression
```

Arguments

expression

Is any valid Microsoft SQL Server expression of any of the data types of the numeric data type category except the **bit** data type.

Result Types

Returns the data type of the argument with the higher precedence. For more information, see Data Type Precedence.

Examples

A. Use subtraction in a SELECT statement

This example returns the amount of the year-to-date revenues retained by the company for each book title.

```
USE pubs
GO
SELECT title,
    (
        (price * ytd_sales) * CAST( ( (100 - royalty) / 100.0 )
            AS MONEY)
        ) AS IncomeAfterRoyalty
FROM titles
WHERE royalty <> 0
ORDER BY title_id ASC
GO
```

Parentheses can be used to change the order of execution. Calculations inside parentheses are evaluated first. If parentheses are nested, the most deeply nested calculation has precedence. For example, the result and meaning of the preceding query can be changed if you use parentheses to force the evaluation of subtraction before multiplication, which in this case would yield a meaningless number.

B. Use date subtraction

This example subtracts a number of days from a **datetime** date.

```
USE pubs
GO
DECLARE @altstartdate datetime
SET @altstartdate = '1/10/1900 3:00 AM'
SELECT @altstartdate - 1.5 AS 'Subtract Date'
```

Here is the result set:

```
Subtract Date
-------------------
Jan 8 1900  3:00PM

(1 row(s) affected)
```

Related Topics

Data Types, Expressions, Functions, Operators, SELECT

---

* (Multiply)

Multiplies two expressions (an arithmetic multiplication operator).

Syntax

```
expression * expression
```

Arguments

expression

Is any valid Microsoft SQL Server expression of any of the data types of the numeric data type category except the **datetime** or **smalldatetime** data types.

Result Types

Returns the data type of the argument with the higher precedence. For more information, see Data Type Precedence.

Example

This example retrieves the title identification number and the price of modern cookbooks, and uses the * arithmetic operator to multiply the price by 1.15.

```
USE pubs
SELECT title_id, price * 1.15 AS NewPrice
FROM titles
WHERE type = 'mod_cook'
ORDER BY title_id ASC
```

Related Topics

Data Types, Expressions, Functions, Operators, SELECT, WHERE

/ (Divide)

Divides one number by another (an arithmetic division operator).

Syntax

```
dividend / divisor
```

Arguments

dividend

Is the numeric expression to divide. *dividend* can be any valid Microsoft SQL Server expression of any of the data types of the numeric data type category except the **datetime** and **smalldatetime** data types.

divisor

Is the numeric expression to divide the dividend by. *divisor* can be any valid SQL Server expression of any of the data types of the numeric data type category except the **datetime** and **smalldatetime** data types.

Result Types

Returns the data type of the argument with the higher precedence. For more information about data type precedence, see Data Type Precedence.

If an integer *dividend* is divided by an integer *divisor*, the result is an integer that has any fractional part of the result truncated.

Remarks

The actual value returned by the / operator is the quotient of the first expression divided by the second expression.

Example

This example uses the division arithmetic operator to calculate the royalty amounts due for authors who have written business books.

```
USE pubs
GO
SELECT ((ytd_sales * price) * royalty)/100 AS 'Royalty Amount'
FROM titles
WHERE type = 'business'
ORDER BY title_id
```

Related Topics

Data Types, Expressions, Functions, Operators, SELECT, WHERE

% (Modulo)

Provides the remainder of one number divided by another.

Syntax

```
dividend % divisor
```

Arguments

dividend

Is the numeric expression to divide. *dividend* must be any valid Microsoft
SQL Server expression of the integer data type category. (A modulo is the integer
that remains after two integers are divided.)

divisor

Is the numeric expression to divide the dividend by. *divisor* must be any valid
SQL Server expression of any of the data types of the integer data type category.

Result Types

int

Remarks

The modulo arithmetic operator can be used in the select list of the SELECT statement
with any combination of column names, numeric constants, or any valid expression of
the integer data type category.

Example

This example returns the book title number and any modulo (remainder) of dividing
the price (converted to an integer value) of each book into the total yearly sales
(**ytd_sales * price**).

```
USE pubs
GO
SELECT title_id,
    CAST((ytd_sales * price) AS int) % CAST(price AS int) AS Modulo
FROM titles
WHERE price IS NOT NULL and type = 'trad_cook'
ORDER BY title_id
GO
```

Related Topics

Expressions, Functions, LIKE, Operators, SELECT

% (Wildcard—Character(s) to Match)

Matches any string of zero or more characters. This wildcard character can be used as either a prefix or a suffix.

Related Topics

LIKE

& (Bitwise AND)

Performs a bitwise logical AND operation between two integer values.

Syntax

```
expression & expression
```

Arguments

expression

Is any valid Microsoft SQL Server expression of any of the data types of the integer data type category. *expression* is an integer parameter that is treated and transformed into a binary number for the bitwise operation.

Result Types

Returns an **int** if the input values are **int**, a **smallint** if the input values are **smallint**, or a **tinyint** if the input values are **tinyint**.

Remarks

The bitwise & operator performs a bitwise logical AND between the two expressions, taking each corresponding bit for both expressions. The bits in the result are set to 1 if and only if both bits (for the current bit being resolved) in the input expressions have a value of 1; otherwise, the bit in the result is set to 0.

The & bitwise operator can be used only on expressions of the integer data type category.

If the left and right expressions have different integer data types (for example, the left *expression* is **smallint** and the right *expression* is **int**), the argument of the smaller data type is converted to the larger data type. In this example, the **smallint** *expression* is converted to an **int**.

Examples

This example creates a table with **int** data types to show the values, and puts the table into one row.

```
USE master
GO
IF EXISTS (SELECT * FROM INFORMATION_SCHEMA.TABLES
        WHERE TABLE_NAME = 'bitwise')
    DROP TABLE bitwise
GO
CREATE TABLE bitwise
(
 a_int_value int NOT NULL,
 b_int_value int NOT NULL
)
GO
INSERT bitwise VALUES (170, 75)
GO
```

This query performs the bitwise AND between the **a_int_value** and **b_int_value** columns.

```
USE MASTER
GO
SELECT a_int_value & b_int_value
FROM bitwise
GO
```

Here is the result set:

```
-----------
10

(1 row(s) affected)
```

The binary representation of 170 (**a_int_value** or A, below) is 0000 0000 1010 1010. The binary representation of 75 (**b_int_value** or B, below) is 0000 0000 0100 1011. Performing the bitwise AND operation on these two values produces the binary result 0000 0000 0000 1010, which is decimal 10.

```
(A & B)
        0000    0000 1010 1010
        0000 0000 0100 1011
        --------------------
        0000 0000 0000 1010
```

Related Topics

Expressions, Operators (Bitwise Operators)

| (Bitwise OR)

Performs a bitwise logical OR operation between two given integer values as translated to binary expressions within Transact-SQL statements.

Syntax

```
expression | expression
```

Arguments

expression

Is any valid Microsoft SQL Server expression of any of the data types of the integer data type category. *expression* is an integer that is treated and transformed into a binary number for the bitwise operation.

Result Types

Returns an **int** if the input values are **int**, a **smallint** if the input values are **smallint**, or a **tinyint** if the input values are **tinyint**.

Remarks

The bitwise | operator performs a bitwise logical OR between the two expressions, taking each corresponding bit for both expressions. The bits in the result are set to 1 if either or both bits (for the current bit being resolved) in the input expressions have a value of 1; if neither bit in the input expressions is 1, the bit in the result is set to 0.

The | bitwise operator requires two expressions, and it can be used on expressions of only the integer data type category.

If the left and right expressions have different integer data types (for example, the left *expression* is **smallint** and the right *expression* is **int**), the argument of the smaller data type is converted to the larger data type. In this example, the **smallint** *expression* is converted to an **int**.

Examples

This example creates a table with **int** data types to show the original values and puts the table into one row.

```
USE master
GO
IF EXISTS (SELECT * FROM INFORMATION_SCHEMA.TABLES
      WHERE TABLE_NAME = 'bitwise')
   DROP TABLE bitwise
GO
CREATE TABLE bitwise
(
 a_int_value int NOT NULL,
b_int_value int NOT NULL
)
GO
INSERT bitwise VALUES (170, 75)
GO
```

This query performs the bitwise OR on the **a_int_value** and **b_int_value** columns.

```
USE MASTER
GO
SELECT a_int_value | b_int_value
FROM bitwise
GO
```

Here is the result set:

```
-----------
235

(1 row(s) affected)
```

The binary representation of 170 (**a_int_value** or A, below) is 0000 0000 1010 1010.
The binary representation of 75 (**b_int_value** or B, below) is 0000 0000 0100 1011.
Performing the bitwise OR operation on these two values produces the binary result
0000 0000 1110 1011, which is decimal 235.

```
(A | B)
        0000 0000 1010 1010
        0000 0000 0100 1011
        -------------------
        0000 0000 1110 1011
```

Related Topics

Expressions, Operators (Bitwise Operators)

^ (Bitwise Exclusive OR)

Performs a bitwise exclusive OR operation between two given integer values as translated to binary expressions within Transact-SQL statements.

Syntax

```
expression ^ expression
```

Arguments

expression

Is any valid Microsoft SQL Server expression of any of the data types of the integer data type category, or of the **binary** or **varbinary** data type. *expression* is an integer that is treated and transformed into a binary number for the bitwise operation.

> **Note**   Only one *expression* can be of either **binary** or **varbinary** data type in a bitwise operation.

Result Types

Returns an **int** if the input values are **int**, a **smallint** if the input values are **smallint**, or a **tinyint** if the input values are **tinyint**.

Remarks

The bitwise ^ operator performs a bitwise logical ^ between the two expressions, taking each corresponding bit for both expressions. The bits in the result are set to 1 if either (but not both) bits (for the current bit being resolved) in the input expressions have a value of 1; if both bits are either a value of 0 or 1, the bit in the result is cleared to a value of 0.

The ^ bitwise operator can be used only on columns of the integer data type category.

If the left and right expressions have different integer data types (for example, the left *expression* is **smallint** and the right *expression* is **int**), then the argument of the smaller data type is converted to the larger data type. In this example, the **smallint** *expression* is converted to an **int**.

Examples

This example creates a table with **int** data types to show the original values, and puts the table into one row.

```
USE master
GO
IF EXISTS (SELECT * FROM INFORMATION_SCHEMA.TABLES
      WHERE TABLE_NAME = 'bitwise')
   DROP TABLE bitwise
GO
CREATE TABLE bitwise
(
 a_int_value int NOT NULL,
b_int_value int NOT NULL
)
GO
INSERT bitwise VALUES (170, 75)
GO
```

This query performs the bitwise exclusive OR on the **a_int_value** and **b_int_value** columns.

```
USE MASTER
GO
SELECT a_int_value ^ b_int_value
FROM bitwise
GO
```

Here is the result set:

```
-----------
225

(1 row(s) affected)
```

The binary representation of 170 (**a_int_value** or A, below) is 0000 0000 1010 1010. The binary representation of 75 (**b_int_value** or B, below) is 0000 0000 0100 1011. Performing the bitwise exclusive OR operation on these two values produces the binary result 0000 0000 1110 0001, which is decimal 225.

```
(A ^ B)
        0000 0000 1010 1010
        0000 0000 0100 1011
        -------------------
        0000 0000 1110 0001
```

Related Topics

Expressions, Operators (Bitwise Operators)

~ (Bitwise NOT)

Performs a bitwise logical NOT operation for one given integer value as translated to binary expressions within Transact-SQL statements.

Syntax

```
~ expression
```

Arguments

expression

Is any valid Microsoft SQL Server expression of any of the data types of the integer data type category, or of the **binary** or **varbinary** data type. *expression* is an integer that is treated and transformed into a binary number for the bitwise operation.

Result Types

Returns an **int** if the input values are **int**, a **smallint** if the input values are **smallint**, a **tinyint** if the input values are **tinyint**, or a **bit** if the input values are **bit**.

Remarks

The bitwise ~ operator performs a bitwise logical NOT for the *expression*, taking each corresponding bit. The bits in the result are set to 1 if one bit (for the current bit being resolved) in *expression* has a value of 0; otherwise, the bit in the result is cleared to a value of 1.

The ~ bitwise operator can be used only on columns of the integer data type category.

> **Important**   When performing any kind of bitwise operation, the storage length of the expression used in the bitwise operation is important. It is recommended that you use the same number of bytes when storing values. For example, storing the decimal value of 5 as a **tinyint**, **smallint**, or **int** produces a value stored with different numbers of bytes. **tinyint** stores data using 1 byte, **smallint** stores data using 2 bytes, and **int** stores data using 4 bytes. Therefore, performing a bitwise operation on an **int** decimal value can produce different results as compared to a direct binary or hexadecimal translation, especially when the ~ (bitwise NOT) operator is used. The bitwise NOT operation may occur on a variable of a shorter length that, when converted to a longer data type variable, may not have the bits in the upper 8 bits set to the expected value. It is recommended that you convert the smaller data type variable to the larger data type, and then perform the NOT operation on the result.

Examples

This example creates a table with **int** data types to show the values, and puts the table into one row.

```
USE master
GO
IF EXISTS (SELECT * FROM INFORMATION_SCHEMA.TABLES
     WHERE TABLE_NAME = 'bitwise')
  DROP TABLE bitwise
GO
CREATE TABLE bitwise
(
 a_int_value tinyint NOT NULL,
b_int_value tinyint NOT NULL
)
GO
INSERT bitwise VALUES (170, 75)
GO
```

This query performs the bitwise NOT on the **a_int_value** and **b_int_value** columns.

```
USE MASTER
GO
SELECT ~ a_int_value, ~ b_int_value
FROM bitwise
```

Here is the result set:

```
--- ---
85  180

(1 row(s) affected)
```

The binary representation of 170 (**a_int_value** or A, below) is 0000 0000 1010 1010. Performing the bitwise NOT operation on this value produces the binary result 0000 0000 0101 0101, which is decimal 85.

```
(~A)
        0000 0000 1010 1010
        ------------------
        0000 0000 0101 0101
```

Related Topics

Expressions, Operators (Bitwise Operators)

= (Equals)

Compares two expressions (a comparison operator). When you compare nonnull expressions, the result is TRUE if both operands are equal; otherwise, the result is FALSE. If either or both operands are NULL and SET ANSI_NULLS is set to ON, the result is NULL. If SET ANSI_NULLS is set to OFF, the result is FALSE if one of the operands is NULL, and TRUE if both operands are NULL.

Syntax

```
expression = expression
```

Arguments

expression

Is any valid Microsoft SQL Server expression. Both expressions must have implicitly convertible data types. The conversion depends on the rules of data type precedence. For more information, see Data Type Precedence.

Result Types

Boolean

Related Topics

Data Types, Expressions, Operators (Comparison Operators)

> (Greater Than)

Compares two expressions (a comparison operator). When you compare nonnull expressions, the result is TRUE if the left operand has a higher value than the right operand; otherwise, the result is FALSE. If either or both operands are NULL and SET ANSI_NULLS is set to ON, the result is NULL. If SET ANSI_NULLS is set to OFF, the result is FALSE if one of the operands is NULL, and TRUE if both operands are NULL.

Syntax

```
expression > expression
```

Arguments

expression

Is any valid Microsoft SQL Server expression. Both expressions must have implicitly convertible data types. The conversion depends on the rules of data type precedence. For more information, see Data Type Precedence.

Result Types

Boolean

Related Topics

Data Types, Expressions, Operators (Comparison Operators)

< (Less Than)

Compares two expressions (a comparison operator). When you compare nonnull expressions, the result is TRUE if the left operand has a lower value than the right operand; otherwise, the result is FALSE. If either or both operands are NULL and SET ANSI_NULLS is set to ON, the result is NULL. If SET ANSI_NULLS is set to OFF, the result is FALSE if one of the operands is NULL, and TRUE if both operands are NULL.

Syntax

```
expression < expression
```

Arguments

expression

Is any valid Microsoft SQL Server expression. Both expressions must have implicitly convertible data types. The conversion depends on the rules of data type precedence. For more information, see Data Type Precedence.

Result Types

Boolean

Related Topics

Data Types, Expressions, Operators (Comparison Operators)

>= (Greater Than or Equal To)

Compares two expressions (a comparison operator). When you compare nonnull expressions, the result is TRUE if the left operand has a higher or equal value than the right operand; otherwise, the result is FALSE. If either or both operands are NULL and SET ANSI_NULLS is set to ON, the result is NULL. If SET ANSI_NULLS is set to OFF, the result is FALSE if one of the operands is NULL, and TRUE if both operands are NULL.

Syntax

```
expression > = expression
```

Arguments

expression

Is any valid Microsoft SQL Server expression. Both expressions must have implicitly convertible data types. The conversion depends on the rules of data type precedence. For more information, see Data Type Precedence.

Result Types

Boolean

Related Topics

Data Types, Expressions, Operators (Comparison Operators)

<= (Less Than or Equal To)

Compares two expressions (a comparison operator). When you compare nonnull expressions, the result is TRUE if the left operand has a lower or equal value than the right operand; otherwise, the result is FALSE. If either or both operands are NULL and SET ANSI_NULLS is set to ON, the result is NULL. If SET ANSI_NULLS is set to OFF, the result is FALSE if one of the operands is NULL, and TRUE if both operands are NULL.

Syntax

```
expression = < expression
```

Arguments

expression

Is any valid Microsoft SQL Server expression. Both expressions must have implicitly convertible data types. The conversion depends on the rules of data type precedence. For more information, see Data Type Precedence.

Result Types

Boolean

Related Topics

Data Types, Expressions, Operators (Comparison Operators)

<> (Not Equal To)

Compares two expressions (a comparison operator). When you compare nonnull expressions, the result is TRUE if the left operand is not equal to the right operand; otherwise, the result is FALSE. If either or both operands are NULL and SET ANSI_NULLS is set to ON, the result is NULL. If SET ANSI_NULLS is set to OFF, the result is FALSE if one of the operands is NULL, and TRUE if both operands are NULL.

Syntax

```
expression < > expression
```

Arguments

expression

Is any valid Microsoft SQL Server expression. Both expressions must have implicitly convertible data types. The conversion depends on the rules of data type precedence. For more information, see Data Type Precedence.

Result Types

Boolean

Related Topics

Data Types, Expressions, Operators (Comparison Operators)

!< (Not Less Than)

Compares two expressions (a comparison operator). When you compare nonnull expressions, the result is TRUE if the left operand does not have a lower value than the right operand; otherwise, the result is FALSE. If either or both operands are NULL and SET ANSI_NULLS is set to ON, the result is NULL. If SET ANSI_NULLS is set to OFF, the result is FALSE if one of the operands is NULL, and TRUE if both operands are NULL.

Syntax

```
expression ! < expression
```

Arguments

expression

Is any valid Microsoft SQL Server expression. Both expressions must have implicitly convertible data types. The conversion depends on the rules of data type precedence. For more information, see Data Type Precedence.

Result Types

Boolean

Related Topics

Data Types, Expressions, Operators (Comparison Operators)

!= (Not Equal To)

Tests whether one expression is not equal to another expression (a comparison operator). Functions the same as the Not Equal To (<>) comparison operator.

Related Topics

Expressions, <> (Not Equal To), Operators (Comparison Operators)

!> (Not Greater Than)

Compares two expressions (a comparison operator). When you compare nonnull expressions, the result is TRUE if the left operand does not have a higher value than the right operand; otherwise, the result is FALSE. If either or both operands are NULL and SET ANSI_NULLS is set to ON, the result is NULL. If SET ANSI_NULLS is set to OFF, the result is FALSE if one of the operands is NULL, and TRUE if both operands are NULL.

Syntax

```
expression ! > expression
```

Arguments

expression

Is any valid Microsoft SQL Server expression. Both expressions must have implicitly convertible data types. The conversion depends on the rules of data type precedence. For more information, see Data Type Precedence.

Result Types

Boolean

Related Topics

Data Types, Expressions, Operators (Comparison Operators)

-- (Comment)

Indicates user-provided text. Comments can be inserted on a separate line, nested
(-- only) at the end of a Transact-SQL command line, or within a Transact-SQL
statement. The comment is not evaluated by the server. Two hyphens (--) is the
SQL-92 standard indicator for comments.

Syntax

```
-- text_of_comment
```

Arguments

text_of_comment
   Is the character string containing the text of the comment.

Remarks

Use -- for single-line or nested comments. Comments inserted with -- are delimited by
the newline character.

There is no maximum length for comments.

   Note Including a GO command within a comment generates an error message.

Examples

This example uses the -- commenting characters.

```
-- Choose the pubs database.
USE pubs
-- Choose all columns and all rows from the titles table.
SELECT *
FROM titles
ORDER BY title_id ASC -- We don't have to specify ASC because that
-- is the default.
```

Related Topics

/*...*/ (Comment), Control-of-Flow Language, Using Comments

/*...*/ (Comment)

Indicates user-provided text. The text between the /* and */ commenting characters is
not evaluated by the server.

Syntax

```
/ * text_of_comment * /
```

Arguments

text_of_comment
> Is the character string(s) containing the text of the comment.

Remarks

Comments can be inserted on a separate line or within a Transact-SQL statement.
Multiple-line comments must be indicated by /* and */. A stylistic convention often
used for multiple-line comments is to begin the first line with /*, subsequent lines with
**, and end with */.

There is no maximum length for comments.

> **Note**   Including a GO command within a comment generates an error message.

Examples

This example uses comments to document and test the behavior during different
phases of development for a trigger. In this example, parts of the trigger are
commented out to narrow down problems and test only one of the conditions.
Both styles of comments are used; SQL-92 style (--) comments are shown both alone
and nested.

> **Note**   The following CREATE TRIGGER statement fails because a trigger named
> **employee_insupd** already exists in the **pubs** database.

```
CREATE TRIGGER employee_insupd
/*
    Because CHECK constraints can only reference the column(s)
    on which the column- or table-level constraint has
    been defined, any cross-table constraints (in this case,
    business rules) need to be defined as triggers.
```

(continued)

(continued)

```
     Employee job_lvls (on which salaries are based) should be within
     the range defined for their job. To get the appropriate range,
     the jobs table needs to be referenced. This trigger will be
     invoked for INSERT and UPDATES only.
*/
ON employee
FOR INSERT, UPDATE
AS
/* Get the range of level for this job type from the jobs table. */
DECLARE @min_lvl tinyint,      -- Minimum level var. declaration
    @max_lvl tinyint,          -- Maximum level var. declaration
    @emp_lvl tinyint,          -- Employee level var. declaration
    @job_id smallint           -- Job ID var. declaration
SELECT @min_lvl = min_lvl,     -- Set the minimum level
    @max_lvl = max_lvl,        -- Set the maximum level
    @emp_lvl = i.job_lvl,      -- Set the proposed employee level
    @job_id = i.job_id         -- Set the Job ID for comparison
FROM employee e, jobs j, inserted i
WHERE e.emp_id = i.emp_id AND i.job_id = j.job_id
IF (@job_id = 1) and (@emp_lvl <> 10)
BEGIN
    RAISERROR ('Job id 1 expects the default level of 10.', 16, 1)
    ROLLBACK TRANSACTION
END
/* Only want to test first condition. Remaining ELSE is commented out.
-- Comments within this section are unaffected by this commenting style.
ELSE
IF NOT (@emp_lvl BETWEEN @min_lvl AND @max_lvl) -- Check valid range
BEGIN
    RAISERROR ('The level for job_id:%d should be between %d and %d.',
        16, 1, @job_id, @min_lvl, @max_lvl)
    ROLLBACK TRANSACTION
END
*/
GO
```

Related Topics

-- (Comment), Control-of-Flow Language, Using Comments

[ ] (Wildcard—Character(s) to Match)

Matches any single character within the specified range or set that is specified inside the square brackets.

Related Topics

LIKE

[^] (Wildcard—Character(s) Not to Match)

Matches any single character not within the specified range or set that is specified inside the square brackets.

Related Topics

LIKE

_ (Wildcard—Match One Character)

Matches any single character, and can be used as either a prefix or suffix.

Related Topics

LIKE

Reserved Keywords

Microsoft SQL Server 2000 uses reserved keywords for defining, manipulating, and accessing databases. Reserved keywords are part of the grammar of the Transact-SQL language used by SQL Server to parse and understand Transact-SQL statements and batches. Although it is syntactically possible to use SQL Server reserved keywords as identifiers and object names in Transact-SQL scripts, this can be done only using delimited identifiers.

The following table lists SQL Server reserved keywords.

ADD	CLUSTERED	DBCC
ALL	COALESCE	DEALLOCATE
ALTER	COLLATE	DECLARE
AND	COLUMN	DEFAULT
ANY	COMMIT	DELETE
AS	COMPUTE	DENY
ASC	CONSTRAINT	DESC
AUTHORIZATION	CONTAINS	DISK
BACKUP	CONTAINSTABLE	DISTINCT
BEGIN	CONTINUE	DISTRIBUTED
BETWEEN	CONVERT	DOUBLE
BREAK	CREATE	DROP
BROWSE	CROSS	DUMMY
BULK	CURRENT	DUMP
BY	CURRENT_DATE	ELSE
CASCADE	CURRENT_TIME	END
CASE	CURRENT_TIMESTAMP	ERRLVL
CHECK	CURRENT_USER	ESCAPE
CHECKPOINT	CURSOR	EXCEPT
CLOSE	DATABASE	EXEC

(continued)

(continued)

EXECUTE	KILL	PROCEDURE
EXISTS	LEFT	PUBLIC
EXIT	LIKE	RAISERROR
FETCH	LINENO	READ
FILE	LOAD	READTEXT
FILLFACTOR	NATIONAL	RECONFIGURE
FOR	NOCHECK	REFERENCES
FOREIGN	NONCLUSTERED	REPLICATION
FREETEXT	NOT	RESTORE
FREETEXTTABLE	NULL	RESTRICT
FROM	NULLIF	RETURN
FULL	OF	REVOKE
FUNCTION	OFF	RIGHT
GOTO	OFFSETS	ROLLBACK
GRANT	ON	ROWCOUNT
GROUP	OPEN	ROWGUIDCOL
HAVING	OPENDATASOURCE	RULE
HOLDLOCK	OPENQUERY	SAVE
IDENTITY	OPENROWSET	SCHEMA
IDENTITY_INSERT	OPENXML	SELECT
IDENTITYCOL	OPTION	SESSION_USER
IF	OR	SET
IN	ORDER	SETUSER
INDEX	OUTER	SHUTDOWN
INNER	OVER	SOME
INSERT	PERCENT	STATISTICS
INTERSECT	PLAN	SYSTEM_USER
INTO	PRECISION	TABLE
IS	PRIMARY	TEXTSIZE
JOIN	PRINT	THEN
KEY	PROC	TO

(continued)

(continued)

TOP	UNIQUE	VIEW
TRAN	UPDATE	WAITFOR
TRANSACTION	UPDATETEXT	WHEN
TRIGGER	USE	WHERE
TRUNCATE	USER	WHILE
TSEQUAL	VALUES	WITH
UNION	VARYING	WRITETEXT

In addition, the SQL-92 standard defines a list of reserved keywords. Avoid using SQL-92 reserved keywords for object names and identifiers. The ODBC reserved keyword list (shown below) is the same as the SQL-92 reserved keyword list.

> **Note** The SQL-92 reserved keywords list sometimes can be more restrictive than SQL Server and at other times less restrictive. For example, the SQL-92 reserved keywords list contains INT, which SQL Server does not need to distinguish as a reserved keyword.

Transact-SQL reserved keywords can be used as identifiers or names of databases or database objects, such as tables, columns, views, and so on. Use either quoted identifiers or delimited identifiers. The use of reserved keywords as the names of variables and stored procedure parameters is not restricted. For more information, see Using Identifiers.

ODBC Reserved Keywords

The following words are reserved for use in ODBC function calls. These words do not constrain the minimum SQL grammar; however, to ensure compatibility with drivers that support the core SQL grammar, applications should avoid using these keywords.

This is the current list of ODBC reserved keywords. For more information, see *Microsoft ODBC 3.0 Programmer's Reference, Volume 2, Appendix C.*

ABSOLUTE	AND	AUTHORIZATION
ACTION	ANY	AVG
ADA	ARE	BEGIN
ADD	AS	BETWEEN
ALL	ASC	BIT
ALLOCATE	ASSERTION	BIT_LENGTH
ALTER	AT	BOTH

(continued)

(continued)

BY	CURSOR	FETCH
CASCADE	DATE	FIRST
CASCADED	DAY	FLOAT
CASE	DEALLOCATE	FOR
CAST	DEC	FOREIGN
CATALOG	DECIMAL	FORTRAN
CHAR	DECLARE	FOUND
CHAR_LENGTH	DEFAULT	FROM
CHARACTER	DEFERRABLE	FULL
CHARACTER_LENGTH	DEFERRED	GET
CHECK	DELETE	GLOBAL
CLOSE	DESC	GO
COALESCE	DESCRIBE	GOTO
COLLATE	DESCRIPTOR	GRANT
COLLATION	DIAGNOSTICS	GROUP
COLUMN	DISCONNECT	HAVING
COMMIT	DISTINCT	HOUR
CONNECT	DOMAIN	IDENTITY
CONNECTION	DOUBLE	IMMEDIATE
CONSTRAINT	DROP	IN
CONSTRAINTS	ELSE	INCLUDE
CONTINUE	END	INDEX
CONVERT	END-EXEC	INDICATOR
CORRESPONDING	ESCAPE	INITIALLY
COUNT	EXCEPT	INNER
CREATE	EXCEPTION	INPUT
CROSS	EXEC	INSENSITIVE
CURRENT	EXECUTE	INSERT
CURRENT_DATE	EXISTS	INT
CURRENT_TIME	EXTERNAL	INTEGER
CURRENT_TIMESTAMP	EXTRACT	INTERSECT
CURRENT_USER	FALSE	INTERVAL

(continued)

(continued)

INTO	OCTET_LENGTH	ROLLBACK
IS	OF	ROWS
ISOLATION	ON	SCHEMA
JOIN	ONLY	SCROLL
KEY	OPEN	SECOND
LANGUAGE	OPTION	SECTION
LAST	OR	SELECT
LEADING	ORDER	SESSION
LEFT	OUTER	SESSION_USER
LEVEL	OUTPUT	SET
LIKE	OVERLAPS	SIZE
LOCAL	PAD	SMALLINT
LOWER	PARTIAL	SOME
MATCH	PASCAL	SPACE
MAX	POSITION	SQL
MIN	PRECISION	SQLCA
MINUTE	PREPARE	SQLCODE
MODULE	PRESERVE	SQLERROR
MONTH	PRIMARY	SQLSTATE
NAMES	PRIOR	SQLWARNING
NATIONAL	PRIVILEGES	SUBSTRING
NATURAL	PROCEDURE	SUM
NCHAR	PUBLIC	SYSTEM_USER
NEXT	READ	TABLE
NO	REAL	TEMPORARY
NONE	REFERENCES	THEN
NOT	RELATIVE	TIME
NULL	RESTRICT	TIMESTAMP
NULLIF	REVOKE	TIMEZONE_HOUR
NUMERIC	RIGHT	TIMEZONE_MINUTE

(continued)

(continued)

TO	UPDATE	VIEW
TRAILING	UPPER	WHEN
TRANSACTION	USAGE	WHENEVER
TRANSLATE	USER	WHERE
TRANSLATION	USING	WITH
TRIM	VALUE	WORK
TRUE	VALUES	WRITE
UNION	VARCHAR	YEAR
UNIQUE	VARYING	ZONE
UNKNOWN		

Future Keywords

The following keywords could be reserved in future releases of SQL Server as new features are implemented. Consider avoiding the use of these words as identifiers.

ABSOLUTE	BOTH	CORRESPONDING
ACTION	BREADTH	CUBE
ADMIN	CALL	CURRENT_PATH
AFTER	CASCADED	CURRENT_ROLE
AGGREGATE	CAST	CYCLE
ALIAS	CATALOG	DATA
ALLOCATE	CHAR	DATE
ARE	CHARACTER	DAY
ARRAY	CLASS	DEC
ASSERTION	CLOB	DECIMAL
AT	COLLATION	DEFERRABLE
BEFORE	COMPLETION	DEFERRED
BINARY	CONNECT	DEPTH
BIT	CONNECTION	DEREF
BLOB	CONSTRAINTS	DESCRIBE
BOOLEAN	CONSTRUCTOR	DESCRIPTOR

(continued)

(continued)

DESTROY	INOUT	NEXT
DESTRUCTOR	INPUT	NO
DETERMINISTIC	INT	NONE
DICTIONARY	INTEGER	NUMERIC
DIAGNOSTICS	INTERVAL	OBJECT
DISCONNECT	ISOLATION	OLD
DOMAIN	ITERATE	ONLY
DYNAMIC	LANGUAGE	OPERATION
EACH	LARGE	ORDINALITY
END-EXEC	LAST	OUT
EQUALS	LATERAL	OUTPUT
EVERY	LEADING	PAD
EXCEPTION	LESS	PARAMETER
EXTERNAL	LEVEL	PARAMETERS
FALSE	LIMIT	PARTIAL
FIRST	LOCAL	PATH
FLOAT	LOCALTIME	POSTFIX
FOUND	LOCALTIMESTAMP	PREFIX
FREE	LOCATOR	PREORDER
GENERAL	MAP	PREPARE
GET	MATCH	PRESERVE
GLOBAL	MINUTE	PRIOR
GO	MODIFIES	PRIVILEGES
GROUPING	MODIFY	READS
HOST	MODULE	REAL
HOUR	MONTH	RECURSIVE
IGNORE	NAMES	REF
IMMEDIATE	NATURAL	REFERENCING
INDICATOR	NCHAR	RELATIVE
INITIALIZE	NCLOB	RESULT
INITIALLY	NEW	RETURNS

(continued)

(continued)

ROLE	SPECIFICTYPE	TRANSLATION
ROLLUP	SQL	TREAT
ROUTINE	SQLEXCEPTION	TRUE
ROW	SQLSTATE	UNDER
ROWS	SQLWARNING	UNKNOWN
SAVEPOINT	START	UNNEST
SCROLL	STATE	USAGE
SCOPE	STATEMENT	USING
SEARCH	STATIC	VALUE
SECOND	STRUCTURE	VARCHAR
SECTION	TEMPORARY	VARIABLE
SEQUENCE	TERMINATE	WHENEVER
SESSION	THAN	WITHOUT
SETS	TIME	WORK
SIZE	TIMESTAMP	WRITE
SMALLINT	TIMEZONE_HOUR	YEAR
SPACE	TIMEZONE_MINUTE	ZONE
SPECIFIC	TRAILING	

T-SQL Globals

This chapter explains provides detailed language definitions for T-SQL globals.

@@CONNECTIONS

Returns the number of connections, or attempted connections, since
Microsoft SQL Server was last started.

Syntax

```
@@CONNECTIONS
```

Return Types

integer

Remarks

Connections are different from users. Applications, for example, can open multiple
connections to SQL Server without the user observing the connections.

To display a report containing several SQL Server statistics, including connection
attempts, run **sp_monitor**.

Examples

This example shows the number of login attempts as of the current date and time.

```
SELECT GETDATE() AS 'Today's Date and Time',
   @@CONNECTIONS AS 'Login Attempts'
```

Here is the result set:

```
Today's Date and Time          Login Attempts
---------------------------    ---------------
1998-04-09 14:28:46.940        18
```

Related Topics

Configuration Functions, sp_monitor

@@CPU_BUSY

Returns the time in milliseconds (based on the resolution of the system timer) that the CPU has spent working since Microsoft SQL Server was last started.

Syntax

```
@@CPU_BUSY
```

Return Types

integer

Remarks

To display a report containing several SQL Server statistics, including CPU activity, run **sp_monitor**.

Example

This example shows SQL Server CPU activity as of the current date and time.

```
SELECT @@CPU_BUSY AS 'CPU ms', GETDATE() AS 'As of'
```

Here is the result set:

```
CPU ms                 As of
----------------       ----------------------------
20                     1998-04-18  14:43:08.180
```

Related Topics

@@IDLE, @@IO_BUSY, sp_monitor, System Statistical Functions

@@CURSOR_ROWS

Returns the number of qualifying rows currently in the last cursor opened on the connection. To improve performance, Microsoft SQL Server can populate large keyset and static cursors asynchronously. @@CURSOR_ROWS can be called to determine that the number of the rows that qualify for a cursor are retrieved at the time @@CURSOR_ROWS is called.

Return value	Description
-m	The cursor is populated asynchronously. The value returned (*-m*) is the number of rows currently in the keyset.
-1	The cursor is dynamic. Because dynamic cursors reflect all changes, the number of rows that qualify for the cursor is constantly changing. It can never be definitely stated that all qualified rows have been retrieved.
0	No cursors have been opened, no rows qualified for the last opened cursor, or the last-opened cursor is closed or deallocated.
n	The cursor is fully populated. The value returned (*n*) is the total number of rows in the cursor.

Syntax

```
@@CURSOR_ROWS
```

Return Types

integer

Remarks

The number returned by @@CURSOR_ROWS is negative if the last cursor was opened asynchronously. Keyset-driver or static cursors are opened asynchronously if the value for **sp_configure cursor threshold** is greater than 0, and the number of rows in the cursor result set is greater than the cursor threshold.

Example

This example declares a cursor and uses SELECT to display the value of @@CURSOR_ROWS. The setting has a value of 0 before the cursor is opened, and a value of –1 to indicate that the cursor keyset is populated asynchronously.

```
SELECT @@CURSOR_ROWS
DECLARE authors_cursor CURSOR FOR
SELECT au_lname FROM authors
OPEN authors_cursor
FETCH NEXT FROM authors_cursor
SELECT @@CURSOR_ROWS
CLOSE authors_cursor
DEALLOCATE authors_cursor
```

(continued)

(continued)

```
----------
0

(1 row(s) affected)

au_lname
---------------------------------------
White

(1 row(s) affected)


----------
-1

(1 row(s) affected)
```

Related Topics

Asynchronous Population, Cursor Functions, OPEN

@@DATEFIRST

Returns the current value of the SET DATEFIRST parameter, which indicates the specified first day of each week: 1 for Monday, 2 for Wednesday, and so on through 7 for Sunday.

Syntax

```
@@DATEFIRST
```

Return Types

tinyint

Remarks

The U.S. English default is 7, Sunday.

Example

This example sets the first day of the week to 5 (Friday), and assumes the current day to be Saturday. The SELECT statement returns the DATEFIRST value and the number of the current day of the week.

```
SET DATEFIRST 5
SELECT @@DATEFIRST AS '1st Day', DATEPART(dw, GETDATE()) AS 'Today'
```

Here is the result set. Counting from Friday, today (Saturday) is day 2.

```
1st Day          Today
---------------  --------------
5                2
```

Related Topics

DATEPART, Configuration Functions, SET DATEFIRST

@@DBTS

Returns the value of the current **timestamp** data type for the current database.
This **timestamp** is guaranteed to be unique in the database.

Syntax

```
@@DBTS
```

Return Types

varbinary

Remarks

@@DBTS returns the current database's last-used timestamp value. A new timestamp
value is generated when a row with a **timestamp** column is inserted or updated.

Example

This example returns the current **timestamp** from the **pubs** database.

```
USE pubs
SELECT @@DBTS
```

Related Topics

Configuration Functions, Cursor Concurrency, Data Types

@@ERROR

Returns the error number for the last Transact-SQL statement executed.

Syntax

```
@@ERROR
```

Return Types

integer

Remarks

When Microsoft SQL Server completes the execution of a Transact-SQL statement, @@ERROR is set to 0 if the statement executed successfully. If an error occurs, an error message is returned. @@ERROR returns the number of the error message until another Transact-SQL statement is executed. You can view the text associated with an @@ERROR error number in the **sysmessages** system table.

Because @@ERROR is cleared and reset on each statement executed, check it immediately following the statement validated, or save it to a local variable that can be checked later.

Examples

A. Use @@ERROR to detect a specific error

This example uses @@ERROR to check for a check constraint violation (error #547) in an UPDATE statement.

```
USE pubs
GO
UPDATE authors SET au_id = '172 32 1176'
WHERE au_id = "172-32-1176"

IF @@ERROR = 547
   print "A check constraint violation occurred"
```

B. Use @@ERROR to conditionally exit a procedure

The IF...ELSE statements in this example test @@ERROR after an INSERT statement in a stored procedure. The value of the @@ERROR variable determines the return code sent to the calling program, indicating success or failure of the procedure.

```
USE pubs
GO

-- Create the procedure.
CREATE PROCEDURE add_author
@au_id varchar(11),@au_lname varchar(40),
@au_fname varchar(20),@phone char(12),
@address varchar(40) = NULL,@city varchar(20) = NULL,
@state char(2) = NULL,@zip char(5) = NULL,
@contract bit = NULL
AS
```

(continued)

(continued)

```
-- Execute the INSERT statement.
INSERT INTO authors
(au_id,  au_lname, au_fname, phone, address,
 city, state, zip, contract) values
(@au_id,@au_lname,@au_fname,@phone,@address,
 @city,@state,@zip,@contract)

-- Test the error value.
IF @@ERROR <> 0
BEGIN
    -- Return 99 to the calling program to indicate failure.
    PRINT "An error occurred loading the new author information"
    RETURN(99)
END
ELSE
BEGIN
    -- Return 0 to the calling program to indicate success.
    PRINT "The new author information has been loaded"
    RETURN(0)
END
GO
```

C. Use @@ERROR to check the success of several statements

This example depends on the successful operation of the INSERT and DELETE
statements. Local variables are set to the value of @@ERROR after both statements
and are used in a shared error-handling routine for the operation.

```
USE pubs
GO
DECLARE @del_error int, @ins_error int
-- Start a transaction.
BEGIN TRAN

-- Execute the DELETE statement.
DELETE authors
WHERE au_id = '409-56-7088'

-- Set a variable to the error value for
-- the DELETE statement.
SELECT @del_error = @@ERROR
```

(continued)

(continued)

```
-- Execute the INSERT statement.
INSERT authors
   VALUES('409-56-7008', 'Bennet', 'Abraham', '415 658-9932',
   '6223 Bateman St.', 'Berkeley', 'CA', '94705', 1)
-- Set a variable to the error value for
-- the INSERT statement.
SELECT @ins_error = @@ERROR

-- Test the error values.
IF @del_error = 0 AND @ins_error = 0
BEGIN
   -- Success. Commit the transaction.
   PRINT "The author information has been replaced"
   COMMIT TRAN
END
ELSE
BEGIN
   -- An error occurred. Indicate which operation(s) failed
   -- and roll back the transaction.
   IF @del_error <> 0
      PRINT "An error occurred during execution of the DELETE
      statement."

   IF @ins_error <> 0
      PRINT "An error occurred during execution of the INSERT
      statement."

   ROLLBACK TRAN
END
GO
```

D. Use @@ERROR with @@ROWCOUNT

This example uses @@ERROR with @@ROWCOUNT to validate the operation of
an UPDATE statement. The value of @@ERROR is checked for any indication of an
error, and @@ROWCOUNT is used to ensure that the update was successfully
applied to a row in the table.

```
USE pubs
GO
CREATE PROCEDURE change_publisher
@title_id tid,
@new_pub_id char(4)
AS
```

(continued)

(continued)

```
-- Declare variables used in error checking.
DECLARE @error_var int, @rowcount_var int

-- Execute the UPDATE statement.
UPDATE titles SET pub_id = @new_pub_id
WHERE title_id = @title_id

-- Save the @@ERROR and @@ROWCOUNT values in local
-- variables before they are cleared.
SELECT @error_var = @@ERROR, @rowcount_var = @@ROWCOUNT

-- Check for errors. If an invalid @new_pub_id was specified
-- the UPDATE statement returns a foreign-key violation error #547.
IF @error_var <> 0
BEGIN
   IF @error_var = 547
   BEGIN
      PRINT "ERROR: Invalid ID specified for new publisher"
      RETURN(1)
   END
   ELSE
   BEGIN
      PRINT "ERROR: Unhandled error occurred"
      RETURN(2)
   END
END

-- Check the rowcount. @rowcount_var is set to 0
-- if an invalid @title_id was specified.
IF @rowcount_var = 0
BEGIN
   PRINT "Warning: The title_id specified is not valid"
   RETURN(1)
END
ELSE
BEGIN
   PRINT "The book has been updated with the new publisher"
   RETURN(0)
END
GO
```

Related Topics

Error Handling, @@ROWCOUNT, SET @local_variable, sysmessages, System Functions

@@FETCH_STATUS

Returns the status of the last cursor FETCH statement issued against any cursor currently opened by the connection.

Return value	Description
0	FETCH statement was successful.
-1	FETCH statement failed or the row was beyond the result set.
-2	Row fetched is missing.

Syntax

```
@@FETCH_STATUS
```

Return Types

integer

Remarks

Because @@FETCH_STATUS is global to all cursors on a connection, use @@FETCH_STATUS carefully. After a FETCH statement is executed, the test for @@FETCH_STATUS must occur before any other FETCH statement is executed against another cursor. The value of @@FETCH_STATUS is undefined before any fetches have occurred on the connection.

For example, a user executes a FETCH statement from one cursor, and then calls a stored procedure that opens and processes the results from another cursor. When control is returned from the called stored procedure, @@FETCH_STATUS reflects the last FETCH executed in the stored procedure, not the FETCH statement executed before the stored procedure is called.

Examples

This example uses @@FETCH_STATUS to control cursor activities in a
WHILE loop.

```
DECLARE Employee_Cursor CURSOR FOR
SELECT LastName, FirstName FROM Northwind.dbo.Employees
OPEN Employee_Cursor
FETCH NEXT FROM Employee_Cursor
WHILE @@FETCH_STATUS = 0
BEGIN
   FETCH NEXT FROM Employee_Cursor
END
CLOSE Employee_Cursor
DEALLOCATE Employee_Cursor
```

Related Topics

Cursor Functions, FETCH

@@IDENTITY

Returns the last-inserted identity value.

Syntax

```
@@IDENTITY
```

Return Types

numeric

Remarks

After an INSERT, SELECT INTO, or bulk copy statement completes, @@IDENTITY
contains the last identity value generated by the statement. If the statement did not
affect any tables with identity columns, @@IDENTITY returns NULL. If multiple
rows are inserted, generating multiple identity values, @@IDENTITY returns the last
identity value generated. If the statement fires one or more triggers that perform inserts
that generate identity values, calling @@IDENTITY immediately after the statement
returns the last identity value generated by the triggers. The @@IDENTITY value
does not revert to a previous setting if the INSERT or SELECT INTO statement or
bulk copy fails, or if the transaction is rolled back.

@@IDENTITY, SCOPE_IDENTITY, and IDENT_CURRENT are similar functions in that they return the last value inserted into the IDENTITY column of a table.

@@IDENTITY and SCOPE_IDENTITY will return the last identity value generated in any table in the current session. However, SCOPE_IDENTITY returns the value only within the current scope; @@IDENTITY is not limited to a specific scope.

IDENT_CURRENT is not limited by scope and session; it is limited to a specified table. IDENT_CURRENT returns the identity value generated for a specific table in any session and any scope. For more information, see IDENT_CURRENT.

Example

This example inserts a row into a table with an identity column and uses @@IDENTITY to display the identity value used in the new row.

```
INSERT INTO jobs (job_desc,min_lvl,max_lvl)
VALUES ('Accountant',12,125)
SELECT @@IDENTITY AS 'Identity'
```

Related Topics

CREATE TABLE, IDENT_CURRENT, INSERT, SCOPE_IDENTITY, SELECT, System Functions

@@IDLE

Returns the time in milliseconds (based on the resolution of the system timer) that Microsoft SQL Server has been idle since last started.

Syntax

```
@@IDLE
```

Return Types

integer

Remarks

To display a report containing several SQL Server statistics, run **sp_monitor**.

Example

This example shows the number of milliseconds SQL Server was idle between the start time and the current time.

```
SELECT @@IDLE AS 'Idle ms', GETDATE() AS 'As of'
```

Here is the result set:

```
Idle Ms            As of
----------------   --------------------------
277593             1998-04-18  16:41:07.160
```

Related Topics

@@CPU_BUSY, sp_monitor, @@IO_BUSY, System Statistical Functions

---

@@IO_BUSY

Returns the time in milliseconds (based on the resolution of the system timer) that Microsoft SQL Server has spent performing input and output operations since it was last started.

Syntax

```
@@IO_BUSY
```

Return Types

integer

Remarks

To display a report containing several SQL Server statistics, run **sp_monitor**.

Example

This example shows the number of milliseconds SQL Server has spent performing input/output operations between start time and the current time.

```
SELECT @@IO_BUSY AS 'IO ms', GETDATE() AS 'As of'
```

Here is the result set:

```
IO ms              As of
----------------   --------------------------
31                 1998-04-18  16:49:49.650
```

Related Topics

@@CPU_BUSY, sp_monitor, System Statistical Functions

@@LANGID

Returns the local language identifier (ID) of the language currently in use.

Syntax

```
@@LANGID
```

Return Types

smallint

Remarks

To view information about language settings (including language ID numbers), run
sp_helplanguage with no parameter specified.

Example

This example sets the language for the current session to Italian, and then uses
@@LANGID to return the ID for Italian.

```
SET LANGUAGE 'Italian'
SELECT @@LANGID AS 'Language ID'
```

Here is the result set:

```
Language ID
--------------------
6
```

Related Topics

Configuration Functions, SET LANGUAGE, sp_helplanguage

@@LANGUAGE

Returns the name of the language currently in use.

Syntax

```
@@LANGUAGE
```

Return Types

nvarchar

Remarks

To view information about language settings (including valid official language names), run **sp_helplanguage** with no parameter specified.

Example

This example returns the language for the current session.

```
SELECT @@LANGUAGE AS 'Language Name'
```

Here is the result set:

```
Language Name
- - - - - - - - - - - - - - - - - - - - - - - - - - -
us_english
```

Related Topics

Configuration Functions, SET LANGUAGE, sp_helplanguage

@@LOCK_TIMEOUT

Returns the current lock time-out setting, in milliseconds, for the current session.

Syntax

```
@@LOCK_TIMEOUT
```

Return Types

integer

Remarks

SET LOCK_TIMEOUT allows an application to set the maximum time that a statement waits on a blocked resource. When a statement has waited longer than the LOCK_TIMEOUT setting, the blocked statement is automatically canceled, and an error message is returned to the application.

At the beginning of a connection, @@LOCK_TIMEOUT returns a value of –1.

Examples

This example shows the result set when a LOCK_TIMEOUT value is not set.

```
SELECT @@LOCK_TIMEOUT
```

Here is the result set:

```
----------------
-1
```

This example sets LOCK_TIMEOUT to 1800 milliseconds, and then calls
@@LOCK_TIMEOUT.

```
SET LOCK_TIMEOUT 1800
SELECT @@LOCK_TIMEOUT
```

Here is the result set:

```
-------------------------------
1800
```

Related Topics

Configuration Functions, Customizing the Lock Time-out, SET LOCK_TIMEOUT

@@MAX_CONNECTIONS

Returns the maximum number of simultaneous user connections allowed on a
Microsoft SQL Server. The number returned is not necessarily the number currently
configured.

Syntax

```
@@MAX_CONNECTIONS
```

Return Types

integer

Remarks

The actual number of user connections allowed also depends on the version of
SQL Server installed and the limitations of your application(s) and hardware.

To reconfigure SQL Server for fewer connections, use **sp_configure**.

Example

This example assumes that SQL Server has not been reconfigured for fewer user
connections.

```
SELECT @@MAX_CONNECTIONS
```

Here is the result set:

```
- - - - - - - - - - - - - - - -
32767
```

Related Topics

sp_configure, Configuration Functions, user connections Option

@@MAX_PRECISION

Returns the precision level used by **decimal** and **numeric** data types as currently set in the server.

Syntax

```
@@MAX_PRECISION
```

Return Types

tinyint

Remarks

By default, the maximum precision returns 38.

Example

```
SELECT @@MAX_PRECISION
```

Related Topics

Configuration Functions, decimal and numeric, "Precision, Scale, and Length"

@@NESTLEVEL

Returns the nesting level of the current stored procedure execution (initially 0).

Syntax

```
@@NESTLEVEL
```

Return Types

integer

Remarks

Each time a stored procedure calls another stored procedure, the nesting level is incremented. When the maximum of 32 is exceeded, the transaction is terminated.

Example

This example creates two procedures: one that calls the other, and one that displays the @@NESTLEVEL setting of each.

```
CREATE PROCEDURE innerproc as
select @@NESTLEVEL AS 'Inner Level'
GO

CREATE PROCEDURE outerproc as
select @@NESTLEVEL AS 'Outer Level'
EXEC innerproc
GO

EXECUTE outerproc
GO
```

Here is the result set:

```
Outer Level
----------------
1

Inner Level
----------------
2
```

Related Topics

Configuration Functions, Creating a Stored Procedure, @@TRANCOUNT

@@OPTIONS

Returns information about current SET options.

Syntax

```
@@OPTIONS
```

Return Types

integer

Remarks

SET options can be modified as a whole by using the **sp_configure user options** configuration option. Each user has an @@OPTIONS function that represents the configuration. When first logging on, all users are assigned a default configuration set by the system administrator.

You can change the language and query-processing options by using the SET statement.

Example

This example sets NOCOUNT ON and then tests the value of @@OPTIONS. The NOCOUNT ON option prevents the message about the number of rows affected from being sent back to the requesting client for every statement in a session. The value of @@OPTIONS is set to 512 (0x0200), which represents the NOCOUNT option. This example tests whether the NOCOUNT option is enabled on the client. For example, it can help track performance differences on a client.

```
SET NOCOUNT ON
IF @@OPTIONS & 512 > 0
   RAISERROR ('Current user has SET NOCOUNT turned on.',1,1)
```

Related Topics

Configuration Functions, sp_configure, user options Option

@@PACK_RECEIVED

Returns the number of input packets read from the network by Microsoft SQL Server since last started.

Syntax

```
@@PACK_RECEIVED
```

Return Types

integer

Remarks

To display a report containing several SQL Server statistics, including packets sent and received, run **sp_monitor**.

Example

```
SELECT @@PACK_RECEIVED
```

Related Topics

@@PACK_SENT, sp_monitor, System Statistical Functions

@@PACK_SENT

Returns the number of output packets written to the network by Microsoft SQL Server since last started.

Syntax

```
@@PACK_SENT
```

Return Types

integer

Remarks

To display a report containing several SQL Server statistics, including packets sent and received, run **sp_monitor**.

Example

```
SELECT @@PACK_SENT
```

Related Topics

@@PACK_RECEIVED, sp_monitor, System Statistical Functions

@@PACKET_ERRORS

Returns the number of network packet errors that have occurred on Microsoft SQL Server connections since SQL Server was last started.

Syntax

```
@@PACKET_ERRORS
```

Return Types

integer

Remarks

To display a report containing several SQL Server statistics, including packet errors, run **sp_monitor**.

Example

```
SELECT @@PACKET_ERRORS
```

Related Topics

@@PACK_RECEIVED, @@PACK_SENT, sp_monitor, System Statistical Functions

---

@@PROCID

Returns the stored procedure identifier (ID) of the current procedure.

Syntax

```
@@PROCID
```

Return Types

integer

Examples

This example creates a procedure that uses SELECT to display the @@PROCID
setting from inside the procedure.

```
CREATE PROCEDURE testprocedure AS
SELECT @@PROCID AS 'ProcID'
GO
EXEC testprocedure
GO
```

Related Topics

CREATE PROCEDURE, Metadata Functions

@@REMSERVER

Returns the name of the remote Microsoft SQL Server database server as it appears in
the login record.

Syntax

```
@@REMSERVER
```

Return Types

nvarchar(256)

Remarks
@@REMSERVER enables a stored procedure to check the name of the database server from which the procedure is run.

Example
This example creates a procedure, **check_server**, that returns the name of the remote server.

```
CREATE PROCEDURE check_server
AS
SELECT @@REMSERVER
```

The stored procedure is created on **SEATTLE1**, the local server. The user logs on to a remote server, **LONDON2**, and runs **check_server**.

```
exec SEATTLE1...check_server
```

Here is the result set:

```
----------------
LONDON2
```

Related Topics
Configuration Functions, Configuring Remote Servers

@@ROWCOUNT

Returns the number of rows affected by the last statement.

Syntax
```
@@ROWCOUNT
```

Return Types
integer

Remarks
This variable is set to 0 by any statement that does not return rows, such as an IF statement.

Example

This example executes UPDATE and uses @@ROWCOUNT to detect if any rows were changed.

```
UPDATE authors SET au_lname = 'Jones'
WHERE au_id = '999-888-7777'
IF @@ROWCOUNT = 0
    print 'Warning: No rows were updated'
```

Related Topics

@@ERROR, System Functions

@@SERVERNAME

Returns the name of the local server running Microsoft SQL Server.

Syntax

```
@@SERVERNAME
```

Return Types

nvarchar

Remarks

SQL Server Setup sets the server name to the computer name during installation. Change @@SERVERNAME by using **sp_addserver** and then restarting SQL Server. This method, however, is not usually required.

With multiple instances of SQL Server installed, @@SERVERNAME returns the following local server name information if the local server name has not been changed since setup.

Instance	Server information
Default instance	*'servername'*
Named instance	*'servername\instancename'*
Virtual server - default instance	*'virtualservername'*
Virtual server - named instance	*'virtualservername\instancename'*

Although the @@SERVERNAME function and the SERVERNAME property of SERVERPROPERTY function may return strings with similar formats, the information can be different. The SERVERNAME property automatically reports changes in the network name of the computer.

In contrast, @@SERVERNAME does not report such changes. @@SERVERNAME reports changes made to the local server name using the **sp_addserver** or **sp_dropserver** stored procedure.

Example

```
SELECT @@SERVERNAME
```

Related Topics

Configuration Functions, SERVERPROPERTY, sp_addserver

@@SERVICENAME

Returns the name of the registry key under which Microsoft SQL Server is running. @@SERVICENAME returns MSSQLServer if the current instance is the default instance; this function returns the instance name if the current instance is a named instance.

Syntax

```
@@SERVICENAME
```

Return Types

nvarchar

Remarks

SQL Server runs as a service named MSSQLServer on Microsoft Windows NT. It does not run as a service on Windows 95/98 because the operating system does not support services.

Example

```
SELECT @@SERVICENAME
```

Here is the result set:

```
---------------------------------
MSSQLServer
```

Related Topics

Configuration Functions, MSSQLServer Service

@ @SPID

Returns the server process identifier (ID) of the current user process.

Syntax

```
@@SPID
```

Return Types

smallint

Remarks

@ @SPID can be used to identify the current user process in the output of **sp_who**.

Example

This example returns the process ID, login name, and user name for the current user process.

```
SELECT @@SPID AS 'ID', SYSTEM_USER AS 'Login Name', USER AS 'User Name'
```

Here is the result set:

```
ID      Login Name      User Name
-----   -------------   -----------
11      sa              dbo
```

Related Topics

Configuration Functions, sp_lock, sp_who

@ @TEXTSIZE

Returns the current value of the TEXTSIZE option of the SET statement, which specifies the maximum length, in bytes, of **text** or **image** data that a SELECT statement returns.

Syntax

```
@@TEXTSIZE
```

Return Types

integer

Remarks

The default size is 4096 bytes.

Example

This example uses SELECT to display the @ @TEXTSIZE value before and after it is changed with the SET TEXTSIZE statement.

```
SELECT @@TEXTSIZE
SET TEXTSIZE 2048
SELECT @@TEXTSIZE
```

Here is the result set:

```
------------------------
64512

------------------------
2048
```

Related Topics

Configuration Functions, SET TEXTSIZE

@ @TIMETICKS

Returns the number of microseconds per tick.

Syntax

```
@@TIMETICKS
```

Return Types

integer

Remarks

The amount of time per tick is computer-dependent. Each tick on the operating system is 31.25 milliseconds, or one thirty-second of a second.

Example

```
SELECT @@TIMETICKS
```

Related Topics

System Statistical Functions

@@TOTAL_ERRORS

Returns the number of disk read/write errors encountered by Microsoft SQL Server since last started.

Syntax

```
@@TOTAL_ERRORS
```

Return Types

integer

Remarks

To display a report containing several SQL Server statistics, including total number of errors, run **sp_monitor**.

Example

This example shows the number of errors encountered by SQL Server as of the current date and time.

```
SELECT @@TOTAL_ERRORS AS 'Errors', GETDATE() AS 'As of'
```

Here is the result set:

```
Errors       As of
-------      -------------------------------
0            1998-04-21  22:07:30.013
```

Related Topics

sp_monitor, System Statistical Functions

@@TOTAL_READ

Returns the number of disk reads (not cache reads) by Microsoft SQL Server since last started.

Syntax

```
@@TOTAL_READ
```

Return Types

integer

Remarks

To display a report containing several SQL Server statistics, including read and write activity, run **sp_monitor**.

Example

This example shows the total number of disk read and writes as of the current date and time.

```
SELECT @@TOTAL_READ AS 'Reads', @@TOTAL_WRITE AS 'Writes', GETDATE() AS 'As of'
```

Here is the result set:

```
Reads        Writes        As of
---------    -----------   -------------------------------
978          124           1998-04-21 22:14:22.37
```

Related Topics

sp_monitor, System Statistical Functions, @@TOTAL_WRITE

@@TOTAL_WRITE

Returns the number of disk writes by Microsoft SQL Server since last started.

Syntax

```
@@TOTAL_WRITE
```

Return Types

integer

Remarks

To display a report containing several SQL Server statistics, including read and write activity, run **sp_monitor**.

Example

This example shows the total number of disk reads and writes as of the current date and time.

```
SELECT @@TOTAL_READ AS 'Reads', @@TOTAL_WRITE AS 'Writes', GETDATE() AS 'As of'
```

Here is the result set:

```
Reads        Writes        As of
---------    -----------   -------------------------------
978          124           1998-04-21 22:14:22.37
```

Related Topics

sp_monitor, System Statistical Functions, @@TOTAL_READ

@@TRANCOUNT

Returns the number of active transactions for the current connection.

Syntax

```
@@TRANCOUNT
```

Return Types

integer

Remarks

The BEGIN TRANSACTION statement increments @@TRANCOUNT by 1.
ROLLBACK TRANSACTION decrements @@TRANCOUNT to 0, except for
ROLLBACK TRANSACTION *savepoint_name*, which does not affect
@@TRANCOUNT. COMMIT TRANSACTION or COMMIT WORK decrement
@@TRANCOUNT by 1.

Example

This example uses @@TRANCOUNT to test for open transactions that should be
committed.

```
BEGIN TRANSACTION
UPDATE authors SET au_lname = upper(au_lname)
WHERE au_lname = 'White'
IF @@ROWCOUNT = 2
   COMMIT TRAN

IF @@TRANCOUNT > 0
BEGIN
   PRINT 'A transaction needs to be rolled back'
   ROLLBACK TRAN
END
```

Related Topics

BEGIN TRANSACTION, COMMIT TRANSACTION, ROLLBACK
TRANSACTION, System Functions

@ @VERSION

Returns the date, version, and processor type for the current installation of Microsoft SQL Server.

Syntax

```
@@VERSION
```

Return Types

nvarchar

Remarks

The information returned by @ @VERSION is similar to the product name, version, platform, and file data returned by the **xp_msver** stored procedure, which provides more detailed information.

Example

This example returns the date, version, and processor type for the current installation.

```
SELECT @@VERSION
```

Related Topics

Configuration Functions, xp_msver

CHAPTER 7

T-SQL Functions

This chapter explains important information about T-SQL functions. A detailed language definition for each T-SQL function (such as its syntax, arguments, return types, examples, and the like) is provided in alphabetical order in Chapter 9, T-SQL Reference.

The Transact-SQL programming language provides three types of functions:

- Rowset functions

  Can be used like table references in an SQL statement. For more information about a list of these functions, see Rowset Functions.

- Aggregate functions

  Operate on a collection of values but return a single, summarizing value. For more information about a list of these functions, see Aggregate Functions.

- Scalar functions

  Operate on a single value and then return a single value. Scalar functions can be used wherever an expression is valid. This table categorizes the scalar functions.

Function category	Explanation
Configuration Functions	Returns information about the current configuration.
Cursor Functions	Returns information about cursors.
Date and Time Functions	Performs an operation on a date and time input value and returns either a string, numeric, or date and time value.
Mathematical Functions	Performs a calculation based on input values provided as parameters to the function, and returns a numeric value.
Metadata Functions	Returns information about the database and database objects.

(continued)

(continued)

Function category	Explanation
Security Functions	Returns information about users and roles.
String Functions	Performs an operation on a string (**char** or **varchar**) input value and returns a string or numeric value.
System Functions	Performs operations and returns information about values, objects, and settings in Microsoft SQL Server.
System Statistical Functions	Returns statistical information about the system.
Text and Image Functions	Performs an operation on a text or image input values or column, and returns information about the value.

Function Determinism

SQL Server 2000 built-in functions are either deterministic or nondeterministic. Functions are deterministic when they always return the same result any time they are called with a specific set of input values. Functions are nondeterministic when they could return different results each time they are called, even with the same specific set of input values.

The determinism of functions dictate whether they can be used in indexed computed columns and indexed views. Index scans must always produce consistent results. Thus, only deterministic functions can be used to define computed columns and views that are to be indexed.

Configuration, cursor, meta data, security, and system statistical functions are nondeterministic. In addition, the following built-in functions are also always nondeterministic:

@@ERROR	FORMATMESSAGE	NEWID
@@IDENTITY	GETANSINULL	PERMISSIONS
@@ROWCOUNT	GETDATE	SESSION_USER
@@TRANCOUNT	HOST_ID	STATS_DATE
APP_NAME	HOST_NAME	SYSTEM_USER
CURRENT_TIMESTAMP	IDENT_INCR	TEXTPTR
CURRENT_USER	IDENT_SEED	TEXTVALID
DATENAME	IDENTITY	USER_NAME

Function Collation

Functions that take a character string input and return a character string output use the collation of the input string for the output.

Functions that take non-character inputs and return a character string use the default collation of the current database for the output.

Functions that take multiple character string inputs and return a character string use the rules of collation precedence to set the collation of the output string. For more information, see Collation Precedence.

CREATE FUNCTION, Deterministic and Nondeterministic Functions, User-defined Functions

Aggregate Functions

Aggregate functions perform a calculation on a set of values and return a single value. With the exception of COUNT, aggregate functions ignore null values. Aggregate functions are often used with the GROUP BY clause of the SELECT statement.

All aggregate functions are deterministic; they return the same value any time they are called with a given set of input values. For more information about function determinism, see Deterministic and Nondeterministic Functions.

Aggregate functions are allowed as expressions only in:

- The select list of a SELECT statement (either a subquery or an outer query).
- A COMPUTE or COMPUTE BY clause.
- A HAVING clause.

The Transact-SQL programming language provides these aggregate functions:

AVG	MAX
BINARY_CHECKSUM	MIN
CHECKSUM	SUM
CHECKSUM_AGG	STDEV
COUNT	STDEVP
COUNT_BIG	VAR
GROUPING	VARP

Configuration Functions

These scalar functions return information about current configuration option settings.

@@DATEFIRST
@@DBTS
@@LANGID
@@LANGUAGE
@@LOCK_TIMEOUT
@@MAX_CONNECTIONS
@@MAX_PRECISION
@@NESTLEVEL

@@OPTIONS
@@REMSERVER
@@SERVERNAME
@@SERVICENAME
@@SPID
@@TEXTSIZE
@@VERSION

All configuration functions are nondeterministic; they do not always return the same results every time they are called with a specific set of input values. For more information about function determinism, see Deterministic and Nondeterministic Functions.

Cursor Functions

These scalar functions return information about cursors:

@@CURSOR_ROWS
@@FETCH_STATUS
CURSOR_STATUS

All cursor functions are nondeterministic; they do not always return the same results every time they are called with a specific set of input values. For more information about function determinism, see Deterministic and Nondeterministic Functions.

Date and Time Functions

These scalar functions perform an operation on a date and time input value and return a string, numeric, or date and time value.

This table lists the date and time functions and their determinism property. For more information about function determinism, see Deterministic and Nondeterministic Functions.

Function	Determinism
DATEADD	Deterministic
DATEDIFF	Deterministic
DATENAME	Nondeterministic

(continued)

(continued)

Function	Determinism
DATEPART	Deterministic except when used as DATEPART (dw, date). dw, the weekday datepart, depends on the value set by SET DATEFIRST, which sets the first day of the week.
DAY	Deterministic
GETDATE	Nondeterministic
GETUTCDATE	Nondeterministic
MONTH	Deterministic
YEAR	Deterministic

Mathematical Functions

These scalar functions perform a calculation, usually based on input values provided as arguments, and return a numeric value.

ABS	DEGREES	RAND
ACOS	EXP	ROUND
ASIN	FLOOR	SIGN
ATAN	LOG	SIN
ATN2	LOG10	SQUARE
CEILING	PI	SQRT
COS	POWER	TAN
COT	RADIANS	

Note   Arithmetic functions, such as ABS, CEILING, DEGREES, FLOOR, POWER, RADIANS, and SIGN, return a value having the same data type as the input value. Trigonometric and other functions, including EXP, LOG, LOG10, SQUARE, and SQRT, cast their input values to **float** and return a **float** value.

All mathematical functions, except for RAND, are deterministic functions; they return the same results each time they are called with a specific set of input values. RAND is deterministic only when a seed parameter is specified. For more information about function determinism, see Deterministic and Nondeterministic Functions.

Meta Data Functions

These scalar functions return information about the database and database objects.

COL_LENGTH
COL_NAME
COLUMNPROPERTY
DATABASEPROPERTY
DATABASEPROPERTYEX
DB_ID
DB_NAME
FILE_ID
FILE_NAME
FILEGROUP_ID
FILEGROUP_NAME
FILEGROUPPROPERTY
FILEPROPERTY

fn_listextendedproperty
FULLTEXTCATALOGPROPERTY
FULLTEXTSERVICEPROPERTY
INDEX_COL
INDEXKEY_PROPERTY
INDEXPROPERTY
OBJECT_ID
OBJECT_NAME
OBJECTPROPERTY
@@PROCID
SQL_VARIANT_PROPERTY
TYPEPROPERTY

All meta data functions are nondeterministic. They do not always return the same results every time they are called with a specific set of input values. For more information about function determinism, see Deterministic and Nondeterministic Functions.

Rowset Functions

These rowset functions return an object that can be used in place of a table reference in a Transact-SQL statement.

CONTAINSTABLE
OPENDATASOURCE
OPENROWSET

FREETEXTTABLE
OPENQUERY
OPENXML

All rowset functions are nondeterministic; they do not return the same results every time they are called with a specific set of input values. For more information about function determinism, see Deterministic and Nondeterministic Functions.

Security Functions

These scalar functions return information about users and roles.

fn_trace_geteventinfo	IS_SRVROLEMEMBER
fn_trace_getfilterinfo	SUSER_SID
fn_trace_getinfo	SUSER_SNAME
fn_trace_gettable	USER_ID
HAS_DBACCESS	USER
IS_MEMBER	

All security functions are nondeterministic. They do not always return the same results every time they are called with a specific set of input values. For more information about function determinism, see Deterministic and Nondeterministic Functions.

String Functions

These scalar functions perform an operation on a string input value and return a string or numeric value.

ASCII	NCHAR	SOUNDEX
CHAR	PATINDEX	SPACE
CHARINDEX	REPLACE	STR
DIFFERENCE	QUOTENAME	STUFF
LEFT	REPLICATE	SUBSTRING
LEN	REVERSE	UNICODE
LOWER	RIGHT	UPPER
LTRIM	RTRIM	

All built-in string functions, except for CHARINDEX and PATINDEX, are deterministic. They return the same value any time they are called with a given set of input values. For more information about function determinism, see Deterministic and Nondeterministic Functions.

System Functions

These scalar functions perform operations on and return information about values, objects, and settings in Microsoft SQL Server.

This table lists the system functions and their determinism property. For more information about function determinism, see Deterministic and Nondeterministic Functions.

Function	Determinism
APP_NAME	Nondeterministic
CASE expression	Deterministic
CAST and CONVERT	Deterministic unless used with **datetime**, **smalldatetime**, or **sql_variant**.
COALESCE	Deterministic
COLLATIONPROPERTY	Nondeterministic
CURRENT_TIMESTAMP	Nondeterministic
CURRENT_USER	Nondeterministic
DATALENGTH	Deterministic
@@ERROR	Nondeterministic
fn_helpcollations	Deterministic
fn_servershareddrives	Nondeterministic
fn_virtualfilestats	Nondeterministic
FORMATMESSAGE	Nondeterministic
GETANSINULL	Nondeterministic
HOST_ID	Nondeterministic
HOST_NAME	Nondeterministic
IDENT_CURRENT	Nondeterministic
IDENT_INCR	Nondeterministic
IDENT_SEED	Nondeterministic

(continued)

(continued)

Function	Determinism
@@IDENTITY	Nondeterministic
IDENTITY (Function)	Nondeterministic
ISDATE	Deterministic only if used with the CONVERT function, the CONVERT style parameter is specified and the style parameter is not equal to 0, 100, 9, or 109. Styles 0 and 100 use the default format mon dd yyyy hh:miAM (or PM). Styles 9 and 109 use the default format plus milliseconds mon dd yyyy hh:mi:ss:mmmAM (or PM).
ISNULL	Deterministic
ISNUMERIC	Deterministic
NEWID	Nondeterministic
NULLIF	Deterministic
PARSENAME	Deterministic
PERMISSIONS	Nondeterministic
@@ROWCOUNT	Nondeterministic
ROWCOUNT_BIG	Nondeterministic
SCOPE_IDENTITY	Nondeterministic
SERVERPROPERTY	Nondeterministic
SESSIONPROPERTY	Nondeterministic
SESSION_USER	Nondeterministic
STATS_DATE	Nondeterministic
SYSTEM_USER	Nondeterministic
@@TRANCOUNT	Nondeterministic
USER_NAME	Nondeterministic

System Statistical Functions

These scalar functions return statistical information about the system.

@@CONNECTIONS	@@PACK_RECEIVED
@@CPU_BUSY	@@PACK_SENT
fn_virtualfilestats	@@TIMETICKS
@@IDLE	@@TOTAL_ERRORS
@@IO_BUSY	@@TOTAL_READ
@@PACKET_ERRORS	@@TOTAL_WRITE

All system statistical functions are nondeterministic; they do not always return the same results every time they are called with a specific set of input values. For more information about function determinism, see Deterministic and Nondeterministic Functions.

Text and Image Functions

These scalar functions perform an operation on a text or image input value or column and return information about the value.

PATINDEX

TEXTPTR

TEXTVALID

These text and image functions are nondeterministic functions and they may not return the same results each time they are called, even with the same set of input values. For more information about function determinism, see Deterministic and Nondeterministic Functions.

CHAPTER 8

T-SQL DBCC Statements

This chapter explains important information about T-SQL DBCC statements. This chapter also provides detailed language definitions for each T-SQL DBCC statement.

T-SQL DBCC Statements Overview

The Transact-SQL programming language provides DBCC statements that act as Database Console Commands for Microsoft SQL Server 2000. These statements check the physical and logical consistency of a database. Many DBCC statements can fix detected problems.

Database Console Command statements are grouped into these categories:

Statement category	Perform
Maintenance statements	Maintenance tasks on a database, index, or filegroup.
Miscellaneous statements	Miscellaneous tasks such as enabling row-level locking or removing a dynamic-link library (DLL) from memory.
Status statements	Status checks.
Validation statements	Validation operations on a database, table, index, catalog, filegroup, system tables, or allocation of database pages.

The DBCC statements of SQL Server 2000 take input parameters and return values. All DBCC statement parameters can accept both Unicode and DBCS literals.

Using DBCC Result Set Outputs

Many DBCC commands can produce output in tabular form (using the WITH TABLERESULTS option). This information can be loaded into a table for further use. An example script is shown below:

```
-- Create the table to accept the results
CREATE TABLE #tracestatus (
   TraceFlag INT,
   Status INT
   )

-- Execute the command, putting the results in the table
```

(continued)

(continued)

```
INSERT INTO #tracestatus
    EXEC ('DBCC TRACESTATUS (-1) WITH NO_INFOMSGS')

-- Display the results
SELECT *
FROM #tracestatus
GO
```

Maintenance Statements

DBCC DBREINDEX
DBCC DBREPAIR
DBCC INDEXDEFRAG
DBCC SHRINKDATABASE
DBCC SHRINKFILE
DBCC UPDATEUSAGE

Miscellaneous Statements

DBCC dllname (FREE)
DBCC HELP
DBCC PINTABLE
DBCC ROWLOCK
DBCC TRACEOFF
DBCC TRACEON
DBCC UNPINTABLE

Status Statements

DBCC INPUTBUFFER
DBCC OPENTRAN
DBCC OUTPUTBUFFER
DBCC PROCCACHE
DBCC SHOWCONTIG
DBCC SHOW_STATISTICS
DBCC SQLPERF
DBCC TRACESTATUS
DBCC USEROPTIONS

Validation Statements

DBCC CHECKALLOC
DBCC CHECKCATALOG
DBCC CHECKCONSTRAINTS
DBCC CHECKDB
DBCC CHECKFILEGROUP
DBCC CHECKIDENT
DBCC CHECKTABLE
DBCC NEWALLOC

T-SQL DBCC Statements Reference

DBCC CHECKALLOC

Checks the consistency of disk space allocation structures for a specified database.

Syntax

```
DBCC CHECKALLOC
    ( 'database_name'
        [ , NOINDEX
          |
          { REPAIR_ALLOW_DATA_LOSS
              | REPAIR_FAST
              | REPAIR_REBUILD
          } ]
    ) [ WITH { [ ALL_ERRORMSGS | NO_INFOMSGS ]
              [ , [ TABLOCK ] ]
              [ , [ ESTIMATEONLY ] ]
          }
      ]
```

Arguments

'*database_name*'

Is the database for which to check allocation and page usage. If not specified, the default is the current database. Database names must conform to the rules for identifiers. For more information, see Using Identifiers.

NOINDEX

Specifies that nonclustered indexes for nonsystem tables should not be checked.

> **Note**   NOINDEX is maintained for backward compatibility only. All indexes are checked when executing DBCC CHECKALLOC.

REPAIR_ALLOW_DATA_LOSS I REPAIR_FAST I REPAIR_REBUILD

Specifies that DBCC CHECKALLOC repair the found errors. The given *database_name* must be in single-user mode to use one of these repair options, and can be one of the following.

Value	Description
REPAIR_ALLOW_DATA_LOSS	Performs all repairs done by REPAIR_REBUILD and includes allocation and deallocation of rows and pages for correcting allocation errors, structural row or page errors, and deletion of corrupted text objects. These repairs can result in some data loss. The repair can be done under a user transaction to allow the user to roll back the changes made. If repairs are rolled back, the database will still contain errors and should be restored from a backup. If a repair for an error has been skipped due to the provided repair level, any repairs that depend on the repair are also skipped. After repairs are completed, back up the database.
REPAIR_FAST	Performs minor, nontime-consuming repair actions such as repairing extra keys in nonclustered indexes. These repairs can be done quickly and without risk of data loss.
REPAIR_REBUILD	Performs all repairs done by REPAIR_FAST and includes time-consuming repairs such as rebuilding indexes. These repairs can be done without risk of data loss.

WITH
> Specifies options on the number of error messages returned, locks obtained, or estimating **tempdb** requirements. If neither ALL_ERRORMSGS nor NO_INFOMSGS is specified, Microsoft SQL Server 2000 returns all error messages.

ALL_ERRORMSGS
> Displays all error messages. If not specified, SQL Server displays a maximum of 200 error messages per object.

NO_INFOMSGS
> Suppresses all informational messages and the report of space used.

TABLOCK
> Causes DBCC command to obtain shared table locks. Ignored for DBCC CHECKALLOC.

ESTIMATE ONLY
> Displays the estimated amount of **tempdb** space required to run DBCC CHECKALLOC with all of the other specified options.

Remarks

DBCC CHECKALLOC checks allocation and page usage in a database, including indexed views. The NOINDEX option, used only for backward compatibility, also applies to indexed views.

It is not necessary to execute DBCC CHECKALLOC if DBCC CHECKDB has already been executed. DBCC CHECKDB is a superset of DBCC CHECKALLOC and includes allocation checks in addition to checks of index structure and data integrity.

DBCC CHECKDB is the safest repair statement because it identifies and repairs the widest possible range of errors. If only allocation errors are reported for a database, execute DBCC CHECKALLOC with a repair option to correct them. However, to ensure that all errors (including allocation errors) are repaired properly, execute DBCC CHECKDB with a repair option. DBCC CHECKALLOC messages are sorted by object ID, except for those messages generated from **tempdb**. DBCC CHECKALLOC validates the allocation of all data pages in the database while DBCC CHECKDB validates the page information used in the storage of data in addition to validating the allocation information.

DBCC CHECKALLOC does not acquire table locks by default. Instead, it acquires schema locks that prevent meta data changes but allow changes to the data while the DBCC CHECKALLOC is in progress. The DBCC statement collects information, and then scans the log for any additional changes made, merging the two sets of information together to produce a consistent view of the data at the end of the scan.

Result Sets

This table describes the information DBCC CHECKALLOC returns.

Item	Description
FirstIAM	Internal use only.
Root	Internal use only.
Dpages	Data page count from sysindexes.
Pages used	Allocated pages.
Dedicated extents	Extents allocated to the object.
	If mixed allocation pages are used, there may be pages allocated with no extents.

The second part of a DBCC CHECKALLOC report is an allocation summary for each index in each file. This summary gives users an idea of the distribution of the data.

Item	Description
Reserved	Pages allocated to the index and the unused pages in allocated extents.
Used	Pages allocated and in use by the index.

Whether or not any options (except WITH NO_INFOMSGS) are specified, DBCC CHECKALLOC returns this result set (values may vary):

```
DBCC results for 'master'.
*********************************************************************
Table sysobjects                    Object ID 1.
Index ID 1          FirstIAM (1:11)    Root (1:12)      Dpages 22.
    Index ID 1. 24 pages used in 5 dedicated extents.
Index ID 2          FirstIAM (1:1368)   Root (1:1362)     Dpages 10.
    Index ID 2. 12 pages used in 2 dedicated extents.
Index ID 3          FirstIAM (1:1392)   Root (1:1408)     Dpages 4.
    Index ID 3. 6 pages used in 0 dedicated extents.
Total number of extents is 7.
*********************************************************************
'...'
*********************************************************************
Table spt_server_info               Object ID 1938105945.
Index ID 1          FirstIAM (1:520)   Root (1:508)     Dpages 1.
    Index ID 1. 3 pages used in 0 dedicated extents.
Total number of extents is 0.
*********************************************************************
Processed 52 entries in sysindexes for database ID 1.
File 1. Number of extents = 210, used pages = 1126, reserved pages = 1280.
          File 1 (number of mixed extents = 73, mixed pages = 184).
    Object ID 1, Index ID 0, data extents 5, pages 24, mixed extent pages 9.
'...'
    Object ID 1938105945, Index ID 0, data extents 0, pages 3, mixed extent pages 3.
Total number of extents = 210, used pages = 1126, reserved pages = 1280 in this database.
      (number of mixed extents = 73, mixed pages = 184) in this database.
CHECKALLOC found 0 allocation errors and 0 consistency errors in database 'master'.
DBCC execution completed. If DBCC printed error messages, contact your system
administrator.
```

DBCC CHECKALLOC returns this result set when the ESTIMATE ONLY option is specified.

```
Estimated TEMPDB space needed for CHECKALLOC (KB)
--------------------------------------------------
34

(1 row(s) affected)

DBCC execution completed. If DBCC printed error messages, contact your system
administrator.
```

Permissions

DBCC CHECKALLOC permissions default to members of the **sysadmin** fixed server role or the **db_owner** fixed database role, and are not transferable.

Examples

This example executes DBCC CHECKALLOC for the current database and for the **pubs** database.

```
-- Check the current database.
DBCC CHECKALLOC
GO
-- Check the pubs database.
DBCC CHECKALLOC ('pubs')
GO
```

Related Topics

DBCC, DBCC NEWALLOC, Space Allocation and Reuse, sp_dboption

DBCC CHECKCATALOG

Checks for consistency in and between system tables in the specified database.

Syntax

```
DBCC CHECKCATALOG
    ( 'database_name'
    ) [ WITH NO_INFOMSGS ]
```

Arguments

'database_name'
> Is the database for which to check system table consistency. If not specified, the default is the current database. Database names must conform to the rules for identifiers. For more information, see Using Identifiers.

WITH NO_INFOMSGS
> Suppresses all informational messages and the report of space used when there are less than 200 error messages. If not specified, DBCC CHECKCATALOG displays all error messages. DBCC CHECKCATALOG messages are sorted by object ID, except for those messages generated from **tempdb**.

Remarks

DBCC CHECKCATALOG checks that every data type in **syscolumns** has a matching entry in **systypes** and that every table and view in **sysobjects** has at least one column in **syscolumns**.

Result Sets

If no database is specified, DBCC CHECKCATALOG returns this result set (message):

```
DBCC results for 'current database'.
DBCC execution completed. If DBCC printed error messages, contact your system
administrator.
```

If **Northwind** is provided as a database name, DBCC CHECKCATALOG returns this result set (message):

```
DBCC results for 'Northwind'.
DBCC execution completed. If DBCC printed error messages, contact your system
administrator.
```

Permissions

DBCC CHECKCATALOG permissions default to members of the **sysadmin** fixed server role, the **db_owner** and **db_backupoperator** fixed database roles, and are not transferable.

Examples

This example checks the allocation and structural integrity of objects in both the current database and in the **pubs** database.

```
-- Check the current database.
DBCC CHECKCATALOG
GO
-- Check the pubs database.
DBCC CHECKCATALOG ('pubs')
GO
```

Related Topics

DBCC, System Tables

DBCC CHECKCONSTRAINTS

Checks the integrity of a specified constraint or all constraints on a specified table.

Syntax

```
DBCC CHECKCONSTRAINTS
    [( 'table_name' | 'constraint_name'
    )]
    [ WITH { ALL_ERRORMSGS | ALL_CONSTRAINTS } ]
```

Arguments

'table_name' | *'constraint_name'*

Is the table or constraint to be checked. If *table_name* is specified, all enabled constraints on that table are checked. If *constraint_name* is specified, only that constraint is checked. If neither a *table_name* nor a *constraint_name* is specified, all enabled constraints on all tables in the current database are checked.

A constraint name uniquely identifies the table to which it belongs. For more information, see Using Identifiers.

ALL_CONSTRAINTS

Checks all enabled and disabled constraints on the table, if the table name is specified or if all tables are checked. Otherwise, checks only the enabled constraint. ALL_CONSTRAINTS has no effect when a constraint name is specified.

ALL_ERRORMSGS

Returns all rows that violate constraints in the table checked. The default is the first 200 rows.

Remarks

DBCC CHECKCONSTRAINTS constructs and executes a query for all foreign key constraints and check constraints on a table.

For example, a foreign key query will be of the form:

```
SELECT columns
FROM table_being_checked LEFT JOIN referenced_table
  ON table_being_checked.fkey1 = referenced_table.pkey1
  AND table_being_checked.fkey2 = referenced_table.pkey2
WHERE table_being_checked.fkey1 IS NOT NULL
  AND referenced_table.pkey1 IS NULL
  AND table_being_checked.fkey2 IS NOT NULL
  AND referenced_table.pkey2 IS NULL
```

The query data is stored in a temp table. When all requested tables or constraints have been checked, the result set is returned.

DBCC CHECKCONSTRAINTS checks the integrity of foreign key and checked constraints, but does not check the integrity of a table's on-disk data structures. These data structure checks can be performed with DBCC CHECKDB and DBCC CHECKTABLE.

Result Sets

DBCC CHECKCONSTRAINTS return a rowset with the following columns.

Column name	Data type	Description
Table Name	varchar	Name of the table.
Constraint Name	varchar	Name of the constraint violated.
Where	varchar	Column value assignments that identify the row or rows violating the constraint.
		The value in this column may be used in a WHERE clause of a SELECT statement querying for rows violating the constraint.

For example, a DBCC CHECKCONSTRAINT on the **orders** table yields the following result.

```
Table Name   Constraint Name      Where
----------   ------------------   ------------------------
orders       PartNo_FKey          PartNo = '12'
```

The value PartNo = '12' in the Where column can be used in a SELECT statement that identifies the row violating the constraint **PartNo_FKEY**.

```
Select *
From orders
Where PartNo = '12'
```

The user then may decide to modify, delete or otherwise adjust the rows.

Permissions

DBCC CHECKCONSTRAINTS permissions default to members of the **sysadmin** fixed server role and the **db_owner** fixed database role, and are not transferable.

Examples

A. Check a table.

This example checks the constraint integrity of the **orders** table in the **pubs** database.

```
DBCC CHECKCONSTRAINTS ('authors')
GO
```

B. Check a specific constraint

This example checks the integrity of the **PartNo_FKey** constraint. The constraint name uniquely identifies the table it is declared upon.

```
DBCC CHECKCONSTRAINTS ('PartNo_Fkey')
GO
```

C. Check all enabled and disabled constraints on all tables

This example checks the integrity of all enabled and disabled constraints on all tables in the current database.

```
DBCC CHECKCONSTRAINTS WITH ALL_CONSTRAINTS
GO
```

DBCC CHECKDB

Checks the allocation and structural integrity of all the objects in the specified database.

Syntax

```
DBCC CHECKDB
    ( 'database_name'
        [ , NOINDEX
            | { REPAIR_ALLOW_DATA_LOSS
                | REPAIR_FAST
                | REPAIR_REBUILD
            } ]
    ) [ WITH { [ ALL_ERRORMSGS ]
               [ , [ NO_INFOMSGS ] ]
               [ , [ TABLOCK ] ]
               [ , [ ESTIMATEONLY ] ]
               [ , [ PHYSICAL_ONLY ] ]
             }
      ]
```

Arguments

'database_name'

Is the database for which to check all object allocation and structural integrity. If not specified, the default is the current database. Database names must conform to the rules for identifiers. For more information, see Using Identifiers.

NOINDEX

Specifies that nonclustered indexes for nonsystem tables should not be checked. NOINDEX decreases the overall execution time because it does not check nonclustered indexes for user-defined tables. NOINDEX has no effect on system tables, because DBCC CHECKDB always checks all system table indexes.

REPAIR_ALLOW_DATA_LOSS | REPAIR_FAST| REPAIR_REBUILD

Specifies that DBCC CHECKDB repair the found errors. The given *database_name* must be in single-user mode to use a repair option and can be one of the following.

Value	Description
REPAIR_ALLOW_DATA_LOSS	Performs all repairs done by REPAIR_REBUILD and includes allocation and deallocation of rows and pages for correcting allocation errors, structural row or page errors, and deletion of corrupted text objects. These repairs can result in some data loss. The repair may be done under a user transaction to allow the user to roll back the changes made. If repairs are rolled back, the database will still contain errors and should be restored from a backup. If a repair for an error has been skipped due to the provided repair level, any repairs that depend on the repair are also skipped. After repairs are completed, back up the database.
REPAIR_FAST	Performs minor, nontime-consuming repair actions such as repairing extra keys in nonclustered indexes. These repairs can be done quickly and without risk of data loss.
REPAIR_REBUILD	Performs all repairs done by REPAIR_FAST and includes time-consuming repairs such as rebuilding indexes. These repairs can be done without risk of data loss.

WITH

Specifies options on the number of error messages returned, locks obtained, or estimating **tempdb** requirements.

ALL_ERRORMSGS

Displays an unlimited number of errors per object. If ALL_ERRORMSGS is not specified, displays up to 200 error messages for each object. Error messages are sorted by object ID, except for those messages generated from **tempdb**.

NO_INFOMSGS

Suppresses all informational messages (Severity 10) and the report of space used.

TABLOCK

Causes DBCC CHECKDB to obtain shared table locks. TABLOCK will cause DBCC CHECKDB to run faster on a database under heavy load, but decreases the concurrency available on the database while DBCC CHECKDB is running.

ESTIMATE ONLY

>Displays the estimated amount of **tempdb** space needed to run DBCC CHECKDB with all of the other specified options. The check is not performed.

PHYSICAL_ONLY

>Limits the checking to the integrity of the physical structure of the page and record headers, and to the consistency between the pages' object ID and index ID and the allocation structures. Designed to provide a low overhead check of the physical consistency of the database, this check also detects torn pages and common hardware failures that can compromise a user's data. PHYSICAL_ONLY always implies NO_INFOMSGS and is not allowed with any of the repair options.

Remarks

DBCC CHECKDB performs a physical consistency check on indexed views. The NOINDEX option, used only for backward compatibility, also applies to any secondary indexes on indexed views.

DBCC CHECKDB is the safest repair statement because it identifies and repairs the widest possible errors. If only allocation errors are reported for a database, execute DBCC CHECKALLOC with a repair option to repair these errors. However, to ensure that all errors, including allocation errors, are properly repaired, execute DBCC CHECKDB with a repair option rather than DBCC CHECKALLOC with a repair option.

DBCC CHECKDB validates the integrity of everything in a database. There is no need to run DBCC CHECKALLOC or DBCC CHECKTABLE if DBCC CHECKDB either is currently or has been recently executed.

DBCC CHECKDB performs the same checking as if both a DBCC CHECKALLOC statement and a DBCC CHECKTABLE statement were executed for each table in the database.

DBCC CHECKDB does not acquire table locks by default. Instead, it acquires schema locks that prevent meta data changes but allow changes to the data. The schema locks acquired will prevent the user from getting an exclusive table lock required to build a clustered index, drop any index, or truncate the table.

The DBCC statement collects information, and then scans the log for any additional changes made, merging the two sets of information together to produce a consistent view of the data at the end of the scan.

When the TABLOCK option is specified, DBCC CHECKDB acquires shared table locks. This allows more detailed error messages for some classes of errors and minimizes the amount of **tempdb** space required by avoiding the use of transaction log data. The TABLOCK option will not block the truncation of the log and will allow the command to run faster.

DBCC CHECKDB checks the linkages and sizes of **text**, **ntext**, and **image** pages for each table, and the allocation of all the pages in the database.

For each table in the database, DBCC CHECKDB checks that:

- Index and data pages are correctly linked.
- Indexes are in their proper sort order.
- Pointers are consistent.
- The data on each page is reasonable.
- Page offsets are reasonable.

Errors indicate potential problems in the database and should be corrected immediately.

By default, DBCC CHECKDB performs parallel checking of objects. The degree of parallelism is determined automatically by the query processor. The maximum degree of parallelism is configured in the same manner as that of parallel queries. Use the sp_configure system stored procedure to restrict the maximum number of processors available for DBCC checking. For more information, see max degree of parallelism Option.

Parallel checking can be disabled by using trace flag 2528. For more information, see Trace Flags.

Result Sets

Whether or not any options (except for the NO_INFOMSGS or NOINDEX options) are specified, DBCC CHECKDB returns this result set for the current database, if no database is specified (values may vary):

```
DBCC results for 'master'.
DBCC results for 'sysobjects'.
There are 862 rows in 13 pages for object 'sysobjects'.
DBCC results for 'sysindexes'.
There are 80 rows in 3 pages for object 'sysindexes'.
'...'
DBCC results for 'spt_provider_types'.
There are 23 rows in 1 pages for object 'spt_provider_types'.
CHECKDB found 0 allocation errors and 0 consistency errors in database 'master'.
DBCC execution completed. If DBCC printed error messages, contact your system administrator.
```

IF the NO_INFOMSGS option is specified, DBCC CHECKDB returns this result set (message):

```
The command(s) completed successfully.
```

DBCC CHECKDB returns this result set when the ESTIMATEONLY option is specified.

```
Estimated TEMPDB space needed for CHECKALLOC (KB)
-------------------------------------------------
13

(1 row(s) affected)

Estimated TEMPDB space needed for CHECKTABLES (KB)
--------------------------------------------------
57

(1 row(s) affected)

DBCC execution completed. If DBCC printed error messages, contact your system
administrator.
```

Permissions

DBCC CHECKDB permissions default to members of the **sysadmin** fixed server role or the **db_owner** fixed database role, and are not transferable.

Examples

A. Check both the current and the pubs database

This example executes DBCC CHECKDB for the current database and for the **pubs** database.

```
-- Check the current database.
DBCC CHECKDB
GO
-- Check the pubs database without nonclustered indexes.
DBCC CHECKDB ('pubs', NOINDEX)
GO
```

B. Check the current database, suppressing informational messages

This example checks the current database and suppresses all informational messages.

```
DBCC CHECKDB WITH NO_INFOMSGS
GO
```

Related Topics

Features Supported by the Editions of SQL Server 2000, How to configure the number of processors available for parallel queries (Enterprise Manager), Physical Database Architecture, sp_helpdb, System Tables

DBCC CHECKFILEGROUP

Checks the allocation and structural integrity of all tables (in the current database) in the specified filegroup.

Syntax

```
DBCC CHECKFILEGROUP
    ( [ { 'filegroup' | filegroup_id } ]
      [ , NOINDEX ]
    ) [ WITH { [ ALL_ERRORMSGS | NO_INFOMSGS ]
               [ , [ TABLOCK ] ]
               [ , [ ESTIMATEONLY ] ]
             }
      ]
```

Arguments

'filegroup'

Is the name of the filegroup for which to check table allocation and structural integrity. If not specified, the default is the primary filegroup. Filegroup names must conform to the rules for identifiers. For more information, see Using Identifiers.

filegroup_id

Is the filegroup identification (ID) number for which to check table allocation and structural integrity. Obtain *filegroup_id* from either the FILEGROUP_ID function or the **sysfilegroups** system table in the database containing the filegroup.

NOINDEX

Specifies that nonclustered indexes for nonsystem tables should not be checked. This decreases execution time. NOINDEX has no effect on system tables. DBCC CHECKFILEGROUP always checks all system table indexes when run on the default filegroup.

WITH

Specifies options on the number of error messages returned, locks obtained, or estimating **tempdb** requirements. If neither ALL_ERRORMSGS nor NO_INFOMSGS is specified, Microsoft SQL Server returns all error messages.

ALL_ERRORMSGS

Displays all error messages. If not specified, SQL Server displays a maximum of 200 error messages per table. Error messages are sorted by object ID, except for those messages generated from **tempdb**.

NO_INFOMSGS
> Suppresses all informational messages and the report of space used.

TABLOCK
> Causes DBCC CHECKFILEGROUP to obtain shared table locks.

ESTIMATE ONLY
> Displays the estimated amount of **tempdb** space required to run DBCC CHECKFILEGROUP with all of the other specified options.

Remarks

DBCC CHECKFILEGROUP and DBCC CHECKDB are similar DBCC statements. The main difference lies in the check conducted by DBCC CHECKFILEGROUP: it is limited to the single specified filegroup and required tables.

Executing DBCC CHECKFILEGROUP statements on all filegroups in a database is the same as running a single DBCC CHECKDB statement. The only difference is that any table with indexes on different filegroups has the table and indexes checked multiple times (one time for each filegroup holding the table or any of its indexes).

DBCC CHECKFILEGROUP prevents modification of all tables and indexes in the filegroup (as well as tables in other filegroups whose indexes are in the filegroup currently checked) for the duration of the operation.

During DBCC CHECKFILEGROUP execution, table creation and deletion actions are not allowed.

DBCC CHECKFILEGROUP does not acquire table locks by default. Instead, it acquires schema locks that prevent meta data changes but allow changes to the data. The DBCC statement collects information, then scans the log for any additional changes made, merging the two sets of information together to produce a consistent view of the data at the end of the scan.

When the TABLOCK option is specified, DBCC CHECKFILEGROUP acquires shared table locks. This allows more detailed error messages for some classes of errors and minimizes the amount of **tempdb** space required by avoiding the use of transaction log data.

DBCC CHECKFILEGROUP checks the linkages and sizes of **text**, **ntext**, and **image** pages for each filegroup, and the allocation of all the pages in the filegroup.

DBCC CHECKFILEGROUP also performs a physical consistency check on indexed views. The NOINDEX option, used only for backward compatibility, also applies to indexed views.

For each table in the filegroup, DBCC CHECKFILEGROUP checks that:

- Index and data pages are correctly linked.
- Indexes are in their proper sort order.
- Pointers are consistent.
- The data on each page is reasonable.
- Page offsets are reasonable.

If a nonclustered index in the filegroup being explicitly checked is associated with a table in another filegroup, the table in the other filegroup (not originally explicitly checked) is also checked because verifying the index also requires verification of the base table structure. If a table in the filegroup being checked has a nonclustered index in another filegroup, however, the index is not checked because:

- The base table structure is not dependent on the structure of a nonclustered index.
- The DBCC CHECKFILEGROUP statement is focused on validating only objects in the filegroup. Nonclustered indexes do not have to be scanned to validate the base table.
- Only checking the index when the filegroup holding it is specifically checked reduces duplicate processing when DBCC CHECKFILEGROUP is run on multiple filegroups in a database.

It is not possible to have a clustered index and a table on different filegroups, so these considerations only apply to nonclustered indexes.

The references to *filegroup* and *filegroup_id* are only relevant in the current database. Be sure to switch context to the proper database before executing DBCC CHECKFILEGROUP. For more information about changing the current database, see USE.

By default, DBCC CHECKFILEGROUP performs parallel checking of objects. The degree of parallelism is determined automatically by the query processor. The maximum degree of parallelism is configured in the same manner as that of parallel queries. Use the sp_configure system stored procedure to restrict the maximum number of processors available for DBCC checking. For more information, see max degree of parallelism Option.

Parallel checking can be disabled by using trace flag 2528. For more information, see Trace Flags.

Result Sets

Whether or not any options (except NOINDEX) are specified, DBCC CHECKFILEGROUP returns this result set for the current database, if no database is specified (values may vary):

```
DBCC results for 'master'.
DBCC results for 'sysobjects'.
There are 862 rows in 13 pages for object 'sysobjects'.
DBCC results for 'sysindexes'.
There are 80 rows in 3 pages for object 'sysindexes'.
'...'
DBCC results for 'spt_provider_types'.
There are 23 rows in 1 pages for object 'spt_provider_types'.
CHECKFILEGROUP found 0 allocation errors and 0 consistency errors in database 'master'.
DBCC execution completed. If DBCC printed error messages, contact your system
administrator.
```

DBCC CHECKFILEGROUP returns this result set if the NO_INFOMSGS option is specified:

```
DBCC execution completed. If DBCC printed error messages, contact your system
administrator.
```

DBCC CHECKFILEGROUP returns this result set when the ESTIMATEONLY option is specified.

```
Estimated TEMPDB space needed for CHECKALLOC (KB)
-------------------------------------------------
15

(1 row(s) affected)

Estimated TEMPDB space needed for CHECKTABLES (KB)
-------------------------------------------------
207

(1 row(s) affected)

DBCC execution completed. If DBCC printed error messages, contact your system
administrator.
```

Permissions

DBCC CHECKFILEGROUP permissions default to members of the **sysadmin** fixed server role or the **db_owner** fixed database role, and are not transferable.

Examples

A. Check the PRIMARY filegroup in the pubs database

This example checks the **pubs** database primary filegroup.

```
USE pubs
GO
DBCC CHECKFILEGROUP
GO
```

B. Check the pubs PRIMARY filegroup without nonclustered indexes

This example checks the **pubs** database primary filegroup (excluding nonclustered indexes) by specifying the identification number of the primary filegroup, and by specifying the NOINDEX option.

```
USE pubs
GO
DBCC CHECKFILEGROUP (1, NOINDEX)
GO
```

Related Topics

Features Supported by the Editions of SQL Server 2000, FILEGROUP_ID, How to configure the number of processors available for parallel queries (Enterprise Manager), Physical Database Architecture, sp_helpfile, sp_helpfilegroup, sysfilegroups

DBCC CHECKIDENT

Checks the current identity value for the specified table and, if needed, corrects the identity value.

Syntax

```
DBCC CHECKIDENT
  ( 'table_name'
    [ , { NORESEED
          | { RESEED [ , new_reseed_value ] } }
      }
    ]
  )
```

Arguments

'table_name'
> Is the name of the table for which to check the current identity value. Table names must conform to the rules for identifiers. For more information, see Using Identifiers. The table specified must contain an identity column.

NORESEED
> Specifies that the current identity value should not be corrected.

RESEED
> Specifies that the current identity value should be corrected.

new_reseed_value
> Is the value to use in reseeding the identity column.

Remarks

If necessary, DBCC CHECKIDENT corrects the current identity value for a column. The current identity value is not corrected, however, if the identity column was created with the NOT FOR REPLICATION clause (in either the CREATE TABLE or ALTER TABLE statement).

Invalid identity information can cause error message 2627 when a primary key or unique key constraint exists on the identity column.

The specific corrections made to the current identity value depend on the parameter specifications.

DBCC CHECKIDENT statement	Identity correction(s) made
DBCC CHECKIDENT ('*table_name*', NORESEED)	The current identity value is not reset. DBCC CHECKIDENT returns a report indicating the current identity value and what it should be.
DBCC CHECKIDENT ('*table_name*') or DBCC CHECKIDENT ('*table_name*', RESEED)	If the current identity value for a table is lower than the maximum identity value stored in the column, it is reset using the maximum value in the identity column.
DBCC CHECKIDENT ('*table_name*', RESEED, *new_reseed_value*)	The current identity value is set to the *new_reseed_value*. If no rows have been inserted to the table since it was created, the first row inserted after executing DBCC CHECKIDENT will use *new_reseed_value* as the identity. Otherwise, the next row inserted will use *new_reseed_value* + 1. If the value of *new_reseed_value* is less than the maximum value in the identity column, error message 2627 will be generated on subsequent references to the table.

The current identity value can be larger than the maximum value in the table. DBCC CHECKIDENT does not reset the current identity value automatically in this case. To reset the current identity value when it is larger than the maximum value in the column, use either of two methods:

- Execute DBCC CHECKIDENT (*'table_name'*, NORESEED) to determine the current maximum value in the column, and then specify that as the *new_reseed_value* in a DBCC CHECKIDENT (*'table_name'*, RESEED, *new_reseed_value*) statement.
- Execute DBCC CHECKIDENT (*'table_name'*, RESEED, *new_reseed_value*) with *new_reseed_value* set to a very low value, and then run DBCC CHECKIDENT (*'table_name'*, RESEED).

Result Sets

Whether or not any of the options are specified (for a table containing an identity column; this example uses the **jobs** table of the **pubs** database), DBCC CHECKIDENT returns this result set (values may vary):

```
Checking identity information: current identity value '14', current column value '14'.
DBCC execution completed. If DBCC printed error messages, contact your system
administrator.
```

Permissions

DBCC CHECKIDENT permissions default to the table owner, members of the **sysadmin** fixed server role, and the **db_owner** and **db_ddladmin** fixed database role, and are not transferable.

Examples

A. Reset the current identity value, if needed

This example resets the current identity value, if needed, of the **jobs** table.

```
USE pubs
GO
DBCC CHECKIDENT (jobs)
GO
```

B. Report the current identity value

This example reports the current identity value in the **jobs** table, and does not correct the identity value, if incorrect.

```
USE pubs
GO
DBCC CHECKIDENT (jobs, NORESEED)
GO
```

C. Force the current identity value to 30

This example forces the current identity value in the **jobs** table to a value of 30.

```
USE pubs
GO
DBCC CHECKIDENT (jobs, RESEED, 30)
GO
```

Related Topics

ALTER TABLE, CREATE TABLE, DBCC, IDENTITY (Property), USE

DBCC CHECKTABLE

Checks the integrity of the data, index, **text**, **ntext**, and **image** pages for the specified table or indexed view.

Syntax

```
DBCC CHECKTABLE
    ( 'table_name' | 'view_name'
      [ , NOINDEX
          | index_id
          | { REPAIR_ALLOW_DATA_LOSS
            | REPAIR_FAST
            | REPAIR_REBUILD }
      ]
    ) [ WITH { [ ALL_ERRORMSGS | NO_INFOMSGS ]
               [ , [ TABLOCK ] ]
               [ , [ ESTIMATEONLY ] ]
               [ , [ PHYSICAL_ONLY ] ]
             }
      ]
```

Arguments

'*table_name*' | '*view_name*'

Is the table or indexed view for which to check data page integrity. Table or view names must conform to the rules for identifiers. For more information, see Using Identifiers.

NOINDEX

Specifies that nonclustered indexes for nonsystem tables should not be checked.

REPAIR_ALLOW_DATA_LOSS I REPAIR_FAST I REPAIR_REBUILD
Specifies that DBCC CHECKTABLE repair the found errors. The database must
be in single-user mode to use a repair option and can be one of the following.

Value	Description
REPAIR_ALLOW_DATA_LOSS	Performs all repairs done by REPAIR_REBUILD and includes allocation and deallocation of rows and pages for correcting allocation errors, structural row or page errors, and deletion of corrupted text objects. These repairs can result in some data loss. The repair may be done under a user transaction to allow the user to roll back the changes made. If repairs are rolled back, the database will still contain errors and should be restored from a backup. If a repair for an error has been skipped due to the provided repair level, any repairs that depend on the repair are also skipped. After repairs are completed, back up the database.
REPAIR_FAST	Performs minor, nontime-consuming repair actions such as repairing extra keys in nonclustered indexes. These repairs can be done quickly and without risk of data loss.
REPAIR_REBUILD	Performs all repairs done by REPAIR_FAST and includes time-consuming repairs such as rebuilding indexes. These repairs can be done without risk of data loss.

index_id
Is the index identification (ID) number for which to check data page integrity. If an
index_id is specified, DBCC CHECKTABLE checks only that index.

WITH
Specifies options on the number of error messages returned, locks obtained, or
estimating **tempdb** requirements. If neither ALL_ERRORMSGS nor
NO_INFOMSGS is specified, Microsoft SQL Server returns all error messages.

ALL_ERRORMSGS
Displays all error messages. If not specified, SQL Server displays a maximum of
200 error messages per table. Error messages are sorted by object ID.

NO_INFOMSGS
Suppresses all informational messages and the report of space used.

TABLOCK
Causes DBCC CHECKTABLE to obtain a shared table lock.

ESTIMATE ONLY
Displays the estimated amount of **tempdb** space needed to run
DBCC CHECKTABLE with all of the other specified options.

PHYSICAL_ONLY

Limits the checking to the integrity of the physical structure of the page and record headers, and to the consistency between the pages' object ID and index ID and the allocation structures. Designed to provide a low overhead check of the physical consistency of the database, this check also detects torn pages and common hardware failures that can compromise a user's data. PHYSICAL_ONLY always implies NO_INFOMSGS and is not allowed with any of the repair options.

Remarks

DBCC CHECKTABLE performs a physical consistency check on tables and indexed views. The NOINDEX option, used only for backward compatibility, also applies to indexed views.

For the specified table, DBCC CHECKTABLE checks that:

- Index and data pages are correctly linked.
- Indexes are in their proper sort order.
- Pointers are consistent.
- The data on each page is reasonable.
- Page offsets are reasonable.

DBCC CHECKTABLE checks the linkages and sizes of **text**, **ntext**, and **image** pages for the specified table. However, DBCC CHECKTABLE does not verify the consistency of all the allocation structures in the database. Use DBCC CHECKALLOC to do this verification.

DBCC CHECKTABLE does not acquire a table lock by default. Instead, it acquires a schema lock that prevents meta data changes but allows changes to the data. The DBCC statement collects information, then scans the log for any additional changes made, merging the two sets of information together to produce a consistent view of the data at the end of the scan.

When the TABLOCK option is specified, DBCC CHECKTABLE acquires a shared table lock. This allows more detailed error messages for some classes of errors and minimizes the amount of **tempdb** space required by avoiding the use of transaction log data.

To perform DBCC CHECKTABLE on every table in the database, use DBCC CHECKDB.

By default, DBCC CHECKTABLE performs parallel checking of objects. The degree of parallelism is determined automatically by the query processor. The maximum degree of parallelism is configured in the same manner as that of parallel queries. Use the sp_configure system stored procedure to restrict the maximum number of processors available for DBCC checking. For more information, see max degree of parallelism Option.

Parallel checking can be disabled by using trace flag 2528. For more information, see Trace Flags.

Result Sets

DBCC CHECKTABLE returns this result set (same result set is returned if you specify only the table name or if you provide any of the options); this example specifies the **authors** table in the **pubs** database (values may vary):

```
DBCC results for 'authors'.
There are 23 rows in 1 pages for object 'authors'.
DBCC execution completed. If DBCC printed error messages, contact your system
administrator.
```

DBCC CHECKTABLE returns this result set when the ESTIMATEONLY option is specified.

```
Estimated TEMPDB space needed for CHECKTABLES (KB)
--------------------------------------------------
2

(1 row(s) affected)

DBCC execution completed. If DBCC printed error messages, contact your system
administrator.
```

Permissions

DBCC CHECKTABLE permissions default to members of the **sysadmin** fixed server role or the **db_owner** fixed database role, or the table owner, and are not transferable.

Examples

A. Check a specific table

This example checks the data page integrity of the **authors** table.

```
DBCC CHECKTABLE ('authors')
GO
```

B. Check the table without checking nonclustered indexes

This example checks the data page integrity of the **authors** table without checking nonclustered indexes.

```
DBCC CHECKTABLE ('authors') WITH PHYSICAL_ONLY
GO
```

C. Check a specific index

This example checks a specific index, obtained by accessing **sysindexes**.

```
USE pubs
DECLARE @indid int
SELECT @indid = indid
FROM sysindexes
WHERE id = OBJECT_ID('authors') AND name = 'aunmind'
DBCC CHECKTABLE ('authors', @indid)
GO
```

Related Topics

DBCC, Features Supported by the Editions of SQL Server 2000, How to configure the number of processors available for parallel queries (Enterprise Manager), Table and Index Architecture

DBCC CLEANTABLE

Reclaims space for dropped variable length columns and text columns.

Syntax

```
DBCC CLEANTABLE
    ( { 'database_name' | database_id }
      , { 'table_name' | table_id | 'view_name' | view_id }
      [ , batch_size ]
    )
```

Arguments

'database_name' | *database_id*
    Is the database in which the table to be cleaned belongs.

'table_name' | *table_id* | *'view_name'* | *view_id*
    Is the table or view to be cleaned.

batch_size
    Is the number of rows processed per transaction. If not specified, the statement processes the entire table in one transaction.

Remarks

DBCC CLEANTABLE reclaims space after a variable length column or a **text** column is dropped using the ALTER TABLE DROP COLUMN statement. It does not reclaim space after a fixed length column is dropped.

DBCC CLEANTABLE runs as one or more transactions. If a batch size is not specified, the statement processes the entire row in one transaction. For some large tables, the length of the single transaction and the log space required may be too much. If a batch size is specified, the statement runs in a series of transactions, each including the specified number of rows. DBCC CLEANTABLE cannot be run as a transaction inside another transaction.

This operation is fully logged.

DBCC CLEANTABLE is not supported for use on system tables or temporary tables.

Result Sets

```
DBCC execution completed. If DBCC printed error messages, contact your system
administrator.
```

Permissions

DBCC CLEANTABLE permissions default to members of the **sysadmin** fixed server role, the **db_owner** and **db_ddladmin** fixed database roles, and the table owner.

DBCC CONCURRENCYVIOLATION

Displays statistics on how many times more than five batches were executed concurrently on SQL Server 2000 Desktop Engine or SQL Server 2000 Personal Edition. Also Controls whether these statistics are also recorded in the SQL Server error log.

Syntax

```
DBCC CONCURRENCYVIOLATION [ ( DISPLAY | RESET | STARTLOG | STOPLOG ) ]
```

Arguments

DISPLAY

Displays the current values of the concurrency violation counters. The counters record how many times more than 5 batches were executed concurrently since logging was started or the counters were last reset. DISPLAY is the default if no option is specified.

RESET

Sets all the concurrency violation counters to zero.

STARTLOG

Enables logging the concurrency violation counters in the SQL Server event log once a minute whenever there are more than 5 concurrent batches.

STOPLOG

Stops the periodic logging of the concurrency violation counters in the SQL Server event log.

Remarks

DBCC CONCURRENCYVIOLATION can be executed on any Edition of SQL Server 2000, but is only effective on the SQL Server 2000 editions that have a concurrent workload governor: SQL Server 2000 Desktop Engine and SQL Server 2000 Personal Edition. On all other editions, it has no effect other than returning the message:

```
DBCC execution completed. If DBCC printed error messages, contact your system
administrator.
```

SQL Server 2000 Desktop Edition and SQL Server 2000 Personal Edition have a concurrent workload governor that limits performance when more than 5 batches are executed concurrently. As the number of batches executing concurrently increases, the governor lowers the performance of the system by increasing amounts. Counts of the number of times more than 5 batches are executed concurrently are maintained in internal counters. You can display the contents of these counters using the DBCC CONCURRENCYVIOLATION statement with either the DISPLAY parameter or no parameter. You should consider upgrading to another edition of SQL Server 2000 if performance on a well-tuned system is slow, and DBCC CONCURRENCYVIOLATIONS shows that the database engine has often had significantly more than 5 batches executing concurrently.

You can enable periodic logging of the concurrency violation counters in the SQL Server event log using the DBCC CONCURRENCYVIOLATION(STARTLOG) statement. When logging is enabled, the concurrency violation counters are logged in the event log once a minute if there are more than 5 concurrent batches being executed. The counters are not written to the error log whenever there are 4 or less concurrent batches.

The primary output of the DBCC CONCURRENCYVIOLATION statement is in these lines:

```
Concurrency violations since 2000-02-02 11:03:17.20
 1    2    3    4    5    6    7    8    9   10-100   >100
 5    3    1    0    0    0    0    0    0     0        0
```

- The first line indicates how long the counters have been accumulating statistics.

- The second line is built of headings that indicate which counter is being reported in that field of the message. Each heading indicates how far over the 5-batch limit each violation was. The 1 represents the count of the number of times 6 batches (5 batch limit + 1 violation) were executing concurrently, the 2 represents the count of the number of times 7 batches (5 + 2) were executing concurrently, and so on. The heading 10-100 represents the count of the number of times the system was between 10 and 100 batches over the limit, and the heading >100 indicates the number of times the system was more than 100 batches over the limit.

- The third line reports how many times the indicated number of batches were executing concurrently. In the example line above, there were 5 times when the system was 1 batch over the limit, 3 times it was 2 batches over the limit, and 1 time it was 3 batches over the limit.

When periodic logging is enabled, a message in this format is placed in the SQL Server error log once a minute whenever more than 5 batches are executing concurrently:

```
2000-02-02 11:03:17.20 spid 12  This SQL Server has been opimized for 5 concurrent
queries. This limit has been exceeded by 2 queries and performance may be adversely
affected.
```

Result Sets

If periodic logging of the concurrency violation counters is enabled, DBCC CONCURRENCYVIOLATION returns this result set (message):

```
Concurrency violations since 2000-02-02 11:03:17.20
 1   2   3   4   5   6   7   8   9   10-100   >100
 5   3   1   0   0   0   0   0   0     0        0
Concurrency violations will be written to the SQL Server error log.
DBCC execution completed. If DBCC printed error messages, contact your system
administrator.
```

If periodic logging of the concurrency violation counters is not enabled, DBCC CONCURRENCYVIOLATION returns this result set (message):

```
Concurrency violations since 2000-02-02 11:03:17.20
 1   2   3   4   5   6   7   8   9   10-100   >100
 5   3   1   0   0   0   0   0   0     0        0
Concurrency violations will not be written to the SQL Server error log.
DBCC execution completed. If DBCC printed error messages, contact your system
administrator.
```

Permissions

DBCC CONCURRENCYVIOLATION permissions default to members of the **sysadmin** fixed server role and are not transferable.

Examples

This example displays the current counter values, and then resets the counters.

```
-- Display the current counter values.
DBCC CONCURRENCYVIOLATION
GO
-- Reset the counter values to 0.
DBCC CONCURRENCYVIOLATION(RESET)
GO
```

Related Topics

DBCC, SQL Server 2000 Databases on the Desktop

DBCC DBREPAIR

Drops a damaged database.

> **Important** DBCC DBREPAIR is included in Microsoft SQL Server 2000 for backward compatibility only. It is recommended that DROP DATABASE be used to drop damaged databases. In a future version of SQL Server, DBCC DBREPAIR may not be supported.

Related Topics

DBCC, DROP DATABASE

DBCC DBREINDEX

Rebuilds one or more indexes for a table in the specified database.

Syntax

```
DBCC DBREINDEX
    ( [ 'database.owner.table_name'
        [ , index_name
            [ , fillfactor ]
        ]
    ]
    ) [ WITH NO_INFOMSGS ]
```

Arguments

'*database.owner.table_name*'

Is the name of the table for which to rebuild the specified index(es). Database, owner, and table names must conform to the rules for identifiers. For more information, see Using Identifiers. The entire *database.owner.table_name* must be enclosed in single quotation marks (') if either the *database* or *owner* parts are supplied. The single quotation marks are not necessary if only *table_name* is specified.

index_name

Is the name of the index to rebuild. Index names must conform to the rules for identifiers. If *index_name* is not specified or is specified as ' ', all indexes for the table are rebuilt.

fillfactor

Is the percentage of space on each index page to be used for storing data when the index is created. *fillfactor* replaces the original fillfactor as the new default for the index and for any other nonclustered indexes rebuilt because a clustered index is rebuilt. When *fillfactor* is 0, DBCC DBREINDEX uses the original *fillfactor* specified when the index was created.

WITH NO_INFOMSGS

Suppresses all informational messages (with severity levels from 0 through 10).

Remarks

DBCC DBREINDEX rebuilds an index for a table or all indexes defined for a table. By allowing an index to be rebuilt dynamically, indexes enforcing either PRIMARY KEY or UNIQUE constraints can be rebuilt without having to drop and re-create those constraints. This means an index can be rebuilt without knowing the table's structure or constraints, which could occur after a bulk copy of data into the table.

If either *index_name* or *fillfactor* is specified, all preceding parameters must also be specified.

DBCC DBREINDEX can rebuild all of the indexes for a table in one statement, which is easier than coding multiple DROP INDEX and CREATE INDEX statements. Because the work is done by one statement, DBCC DBREINDEX is automatically atomic, while individual DROP INDEX and CREATE INDEX statements would have to be put in a transaction to be atomic. Also, DBCC DBREINDEX can take advantage of more optimizations with DBCC DBREINDEX than it can with individual DROP INDEX and CREATE INDEX statements.

DBCC DBREINDEX is not supported for use on system tables.

Result Sets

Whether or not any of the options (except NO_INFOMSGS) are specified (the table name must be specified), DBCC DBREINDEX returns this result set; this example uses the **authors** table of the **pubs** database (values will vary):

```
Index (ID = 1) is being rebuilt.
Index (ID = 2) is being rebuilt.
DBCC execution completed. If DBCC printed error messages, contact your system
administrator.
```

DBCC DBREINDEX returns this result set (message) if the NO_INFOMSGS option is specified:

```
DBCC execution completed. If DBCC printed error messages, contact your system
administrator.
```

Permissions

DBCC DBREINDEX permissions default to members of the **sysadmin** fixed server role, the **db_owner** and **db_ddladmin** fixed database roles, and the table owner, and are not transferable.

Examples

A. Rebuild an index

This example rebuilds the **au_nmind** clustered index with a fillfactor of 80 on the **authors** table in the **pubs** database.

```
DBCC DBREINDEX ('pubs.dbo.authors', UPKCL_auidind, 80)
```

B. Rebuild all indexes

This example rebuilds all indexes on the **authors** table using a fillfactor value of 70.

```
DBCC DBREINDEX (authors, '', 70)
```

Related Topics

ALTER TABLE, CREATE TABLE, DBCC, Table and Index Architecture

DBCC dllname (FREE)

Unloads the specified extended stored procedure dynamic-link library (DLL) from memory.

Syntax

```
DBCC dllname ( FREE )
```

Arguments

dllname

Is the name of the DLL to release from memory.

Remarks

When an extended stored procedure is executed, the DLL remains loaded by Microsoft SQL Server until the server is shut down. This statement allows a DLL to be unloaded from memory without shutting down SQL Server. Execute **sp_helpextendedproc** to display the DLL files currently loaded by SQL Server.

Result Sets

DBCC dllname (FREE) returns this result set (message) when a valid DLL is specified:

```
DBCC execution completed. If DBCC printed error messages, contact your system administrator.
```

Permissions

DBCC *dllname* (FREE) permissions default to members of the **sysadmin** fixed server role or the **db_owner** fixed database role, and are not transferable.

Examples

This example assumes an extended procedure **xp_sample** is implemented as Xp_sample.dll and has been executed. It uses the DBCC *dllname* (FREE) statement to unload the Xp_sample.dll file associated with the **xp_sample** extended procedure.

```
DBCC xp_sample (FREE)
```

Related Topics

DBCC, Execution Characteristics of Extended Stored Procedures, sp_addextendedproc, sp_dropextendedproc, sp_helpextendedproc, Unloading an Extended Stored Procedure DLL

DBCC DROPCLEANBUFFERS

Removes all clean buffers from the buffer pool.

Syntax

```
DBCC DROPCLEANBUFFERS
```

Remarks

Use DBCC DROPCLEANBUFFERS to test queries with a cold buffer cache without shutting down and restarting the server.

Result Sets

```
DBCC execution completed. If DBCC printed error messages, contact your system administrator.
```

Permissions

DBCC DROPCLEANBUFFERS permissions default to members of the **sysadmin** fixed server role only, and are not transferable.

DBCC FREEPROCCACHE

Removes all elements from the procedure cache.

Syntax

```
DBCC FREEPROCCACHE
```

Remarks

Use DBCC FREEPROCCACHE to clear the procedure cache. Freeing the procedure cache would cause, for example, an ad-hoc SQL statement to be recompiled rather than reused from the cache.

Result Sets

```
DBCC execution completed. If DBCC printed error messages, contact your system administrator.
```

Permissions

DBCC FREEPROCACHE permissions default to members of the **sysadmin** and **serveradmin** fixed server role only, and are not transferable.

DBCC HELP

Returns syntax information for the specified DBCC statement.

Syntax

```
DBCC HELP ( 'dbcc_statement' | @dbcc_statement_var | '?' )
```

Arguments

dbcc_statement | *@dbcc_statement_var*

Is the name of the DBCC statement for which to receive syntax information. Provide only the portion of the DBCC statement following the DBCC part of the statement. For example, CHECKDB rather than DBCC CHECKDB.

?

Specifies that Microsoft SQL Server return all DBCC statements (minus the "DBCC" portion of the statement) for which help information can be obtained.

Result Sets

DBCC HELP returns a result set displaying the syntax for the specified DBCC statement. Syntax varies between the DBCC statements.

Permissions

DBCC HELP permissions default to members of the **sysadmin** fixed server role only, and are not transferable.

Examples

A. Use DBCC HELP with a variable

This example returns syntax information for DBCC CHECKDB.

```
DECLARE @dbcc_stmt sysname
SET @dbcc_stmt = 'CHECKDB'
DBCC HELP (@dbcc_stmt)
GO
```

B. Use DBCC HELP with the ? option

This example returns all DBCC statements for which help is available.

```
DBCC HELP ('?')
GO
```

Related Topics

DBCC

DBCC INDEXDEFRAG

Defragments clustered and secondary indexes of the specified table or view.

Syntax

```
DBCC INDEXDEFRAG
  ( { database_name | database_id | 0 }
    , { table_name | table_id | 'view_name' | view_id }
    , { index_name | index_id }
  ) [ WITH NO_INFOMSGS ]
```

Arguments

database_name | database_id | 0

Is the database for which to defragment an index. Database names must conform to the rules for identifiers. For more information, see Using Identifiers. If 0 is specified, then the current database is used.

table_name | table_id | 'view_name' | view_id

Is the table or view for which to defragment an index. Table and view names must conform to the rules for identifiers.

index_name | index_id

Is the index to defragment. Index names must conform to the rules for identifiers.

WITH NO_INFOMSGS

Suppresses all informational messages (with severity levels from 0 through 10).

Remarks

DBCC INDEXDEFRAG can defragment clustered and nonclustered indexes on tables and views. DBCC INDEXDEFRAG defragments the leaf level of an index so that the physical order of the pages matches the left-to-right logical order of the leaf nodes, thus improving index-scanning performance.

DBCC INDEXDEFRAG also compacts the pages of an index, taking into account the FILLFACTOR specified when the index was created. Any empty pages created as a result of this compaction will be removed. For more information about FILLFACTOR, see CREATE INDEX.

If an index spans more than one file, DBCC INDEXDEFRAG defragments one file at a time. Pages do not migrate between files.

Every five minutes, DBCC INDEXDEFRAG will report to the user an estimated percentage completed. DBCC INDEXDEFRAG can be terminated at any point in the process, and any completed work is retained.

Unlike DBCC DBREINDEX (or the index building operation in general), DBCC INDEXDEFRAG is an online operation. It does not hold locks long term and thus will not block running queries or updates. A relatively unfragmented index can be defragmented faster than a new index can be built because the time to defragment is related to the amount of fragmentation. A very fragmented index might take considerably longer to defragment than to rebuild. In addition, the defragmentation is always fully logged, regardless of the database recovery model setting (see ALTER DATABASE). The defragmentation of a very fragmented index can generate more log than even a fully logged index creation. The defragmentation, however, is performed as a series of short transactions and thus does not require a large log if log backups are taken frequently or if the recovery model setting is SIMPLE.

Also, DBCC INDEXDEFRAG will not help if two indexes are interleaved on the disk because INDEXDEFRAG shuffles the pages in place. To improve the clustering of pages, rebuild the index.

DBCC INDEXDEFRAG is not supported for use on system tables.

Result Sets

DBCC INDEXDEFRAG returns this result set unless WITH NO_INFOMSGS is specified (values may vary):

```
Pages Scanned Pages Moved Pages Removed
------------- ----------- -------------
359           346         8

(1 row(s) affected)

DBCC execution completed. If DBCC printed error messages, contact your system
administrator.
```

Permissions

DBCC INDEXDEFRAG permissions default to members of the **sysadmin** fixed server role, the **db_owner** and **db_ddladmin** fixed database role, and the table owner, and are not transferable.

Examples

```
DBCC INDEXDEFRAG (Northwind, Orders, CustomersOrders)
GO
```

DBCC INPUTBUFFER

Displays the last statement sent from a client to Microsoft SQL Server.

Syntax

```
DBCC INPUTBUFFER (spid)
```

Arguments

spid

Is the system process ID (SPID) for the user connection as displayed in the output of the **sp_who** system stored procedure.

Result Sets

DBCC INPUTBUFFER returns a rowset with the following columns.

Column name	Data type	Description
EventType	**nvarchar(30)**	Event type, for example: RPC, Language, or No Event.
Parameters	**Int**	0 = text 1- *n* = parameters
EventInfo	**nvarchar(255)**	For an **EventType** of RPC, **EventInfo** contains only the procedure name. For an **EventType** of Language or No Event, only the first 255 characters of the event are displayed.

For example, DBCC INPUTBUFFER returns the following result set when the last event in the buffer is DBCC INPUTBUFFER(11).

```
EventType        Parameters  EventInfo
--------------   ----------  ---------------------
Language Event   0           DBCC INPUTBUFFER (11)

(1 row(s) affected)

DBCC execution completed. If DBCC printed error messages, contact your system
administrator.
```

Note There are very brief transitional periods between events when no event can be displayed on Windows NT. On Windows 98, an event is displayed only when active.

Permissions

DBCC INPUTBUFFER permissions default to members of the **sysadmin** fixed server role only, who can see any SPID. Other users can see any SPID they own. Permissions are not transferable.

Examples

This example assumes a valid SPID of 10.

```
DBCC INPUTBUFFER (10)
```

Related Topics

DBCC, sp_who, Trace Flags

DBCC NEWALLOC

Checks the allocation of data and index pages for each table within the extent structures of the database.

> **Important**   DBCC NEWALLOC is identical to DBCC CHECKALLOC and is included in Microsoft SQL Server 2000 for backward compatibility only. It is recommended that DBCC CHECKALLOC be used to check the allocation and use of all pages in the specified database. In a future version of Microsoft SQL Server, DBCC NEWALLOC may not be supported.

Related Topics

DBCC, DBCC CHECKDB, DBCC CHECKALLOC, sqlmaint Utility

DBCC OPENTRAN

Displays information about the oldest active transaction and the oldest distributed and nondistributed replicated transactions, if any, within the specified database. Results are displayed only if there is an active transaction or if the database contains replication information. An informational message is displayed if there are no active transactions.

Syntax

```
DBCC OPENTRAN
    ( { 'database_name' | database_id} )
        [ WITH TABLERESULTS
            [ , NO_INFOMSGS ]
        ]
```

Arguments

'database_name'

Is the name of the database for which to display the oldest transaction information. Database names must conform to the rules for identifiers. For more information, see Using Identifiers.

database_id

Is the database identification (ID) number for which to display the oldest transaction information. Obtain the database ID using the DB_ID function.

WITH TABLERESULTS

Specifies results in a tabular format that can be loaded into a table. Use this option to create a table of results that can be inserted into a table for comparisons. When this option is not specified, results are formatted for readability.

NO_INFOMSGS

Suppresses all informational messages.

Remarks

If neither *database_name* nor *database_id* is specified, the default is the current database.

Use DBCC OPENTRAN to determine whether an open transaction exists within the log. When using the BACKUP LOG statement, only the inactive portion of the log can be truncated; an open transaction can cause the log to not truncate completely. In earlier versions of Microsoft SQL Server, either all users had to log off or the server had to be shut down and restarted to clear uncommitted transactions from the log. With DBCC OPENTRAN, an open transaction can be identified (by obtaining the system process ID from the **sp_who** output) and terminated, if necessary.

Result Sets

DBCC OPENTRAN returns this result set when there are no open transactions:

```
No active open transactions.
DBCC execution completed. If DBCC printed error messages, contact your system
administrator.
```

Permissions

DBCC OPENTRAN permissions default to members of the **sysadmin** fixed server role or the **db_owner** fixed database role, and are not transferable.

Examples

This example obtains transaction information for the current database and for the **pubs** database.

```
-- Display transaction information only for the current database.
DBCC OPENTRAN
GO
-- Display transaction information for the pubs database.
DBCC OPENTRAN('pubs')
GO
```

Related Topics

BEGIN TRANSACTION, COMMIT TRANSACTION, DBCC, DB_ID, ROLLBACK TRANSACTION

DBCC OUTPUTBUFFER

Returns the current output buffer in hexadecimal and ASCII format for the specified system process ID (SPID).

Syntax

```
DBCC OUTPUTBUFFER ( spid )
```

Arguments

spid

Is the system process ID for the user connection as displayed in the output of the **sp_who** system stored procedure.

Remarks

When you use DBCC OUTPUTBUFFER, DBCC OUTPUTBUFFER displays the results sent to the specified client (*spid*). For processes that do not contain output streams, an error message is returned.

To show the statement executed that returned the results displayed by DBCC OUTPUTBUFFER, execute DBCC INPUTBUFFER.

Result Sets

DBCC OUTPUTBUFFER returns this result set (values may vary):

```
Output Buffer
----------------------------------------------------------------------
01fb8028:   04 00 01 5f 00 00 00 00 e3 1b 00 01 06 6d 00 61   ..._.........m.a
01fb8038:   00 73 00 74 00 65 00 72 00 06 6d 00 61 00 73 00   .s.t.e.r..m.a.s.
'…'
```

(continued)

(continued)

```
01fb8218:   04 17 00 00 00 00 00 d1 04 18 00 00 00 00 00 d1   ...............
01fb8228:    .

(33 row(s) affected)

DBCC execution completed. If DBCC printed error messages, contact your system
administrator.
```

Permissions

DBCC OUTPUTBUFFER permissions default only to members of the **sysadmin** fixed
server role, who can see any SPID. Permissions are not transferable.

Examples

This example returns current output buffer information for an assumed SPID of 13.

```
DBCC OUTPUTBUFFER (13)
```

Related Topics

DBCC, sp_who, Trace Flags

DBCC PINTABLE

Marks a table to be pinned, which means Microsoft SQL Server does not flush the
pages for the table from memory.

Syntax

```
DBCC PINTABLE ( database_id , table_id )
```

Arguments

database_id
> Is the database identification (ID) number of the table to be pinned. To determine
> the database ID, use the DB_ID function.

table_id
> Is the object identification number of the table to be pinned. To determine the table
> ID, use the OBJECT_ID function.

Remarks

DBCC PINTABLE does not cause the table to be read into memory. As the pages from the table are read into the buffer cache by normal Transact-SQL statements, they are marked as pinned pages. SQL Server does not flush pinned pages when it needs space to read in a new page. SQL Server still logs updates to the page and, if necessary, writes the updated page back to disk. SQL Server does, however, keep a copy of the page available in the buffer cache until the table is unpinned with the DBCC UNPINTABLE statement.

DBCC PINTABLE is best used to keep small, frequently referenced tables in memory. The pages for the small table are read into memory one time, then all future references to their data do not require a disk read.

> **CAUTION**   Although DBCC PINTABLE can provide performance improvements, it must be used with care. If a large table is pinned, it can start using a large portion of the buffer cache and not leave enough cache to service the other tables in the system adequately. If a table larger than the buffer cache is pinned, it can fill the entire buffer cache. A member of the **sysadmin** fixed server role must shut down SQL Server, restart SQL Server, and then unpin the table. Pinning too many tables can cause the same problems as pinning a table larger than the buffer cache.

Result Sets

Here is the result set:

```
Warning: Pinning tables should be carefully considered. If a pinned table is larger, or
grows larger, than the available data cache, the server may need to be restarted and the
table unpinned.
DBCC execution completed. If DBCC printed error messages, contact your system
administrator.
```

Permissions

DBCC PINTABLE permissions default to members of the **sysadmin** fixed server role and are not transferable.

Examples

This example pins the **authors** table in the **pubs** database.

```
DECLARE @db_id int, @tbl_id int
USE pubs
SET @db_id = DB_ID('pubs')
SET @tbl_id = OBJECT_ID('pubs..authors')
DBCC PINTABLE (@db_id, @tbl_id)
```

Related Topics

DBCC, Memory Architecture, DBCC UNPINTABLE, sp_tableoption

DBCC PROCCACHE

Displays information in a table format about the procedure cache.

Syntax

```
DBCC PROCCACHE
```

Remarks

SQL Server Performance Monitor uses DBCC PROCCACHE to obtain information about the procedure cache.

Result Sets

This table describes the columns of the result set.

Column name	Description
num proc buffs	Number of possible stored procedures that could be in the procedure cache.
num proc buffs used	Number of cache slots holding stored procedures.
num proc buffs active	Number of cache slots holding stored procedures that are currently executing.
proc cache size	Total size of the procedure cache.
proc cache used	Amount of the procedure cache holding stored procedures.
proc cache active	Amount of the procedure cache holding stored procedures that are currently executing.

Permissions

DBCC PROCCACHE permissions default to members of the **sysadmin** fixed server role or the **db_owner** fixed database role, and are not transferable.

Related Topics

DBCC, Memory Architecture

DBCC ROWLOCK

Used for Microsoft SQL Server version 6.5, enabling Insert Row Locking (IRL) operations on tables.

> **Important**   Row-level locking is enabled by default in SQL Server. The locking strategy of SQL Server is row locking with possible promotion to page or table locking. DBCC ROWLOCK does not alter the locking behavior of SQL Server (it has no effect) and is included in Microsoft SQL Server 2000 for backward compatibility of existing scripts and procedures only. In a future version of SQL Server, DBCC ROWLOCK may not be supported.

Related Topics

DBCC

DBCC SHOWCONTIG

Displays fragmentation information for the data and indexes of the specified table.

Syntax

```
DBCC SHOWCONTIG
    [ ( { table_name | table_id | view_name | view_id }
        [ , index_name | index_id ]
      )
    ]
    [ WITH { ALL_INDEXES
             | FAST [ , ALL_INDEXES ]
             | TABLERESULTS [ , { ALL_INDEXES } ]
             [ , { FAST | ALL_LEVELS } ]
           }
    ]
```

Arguments

table_name | *table_id* | *view_name* | *view_id*
   Is the table or view for which to check fragmentation information. If not specified, all tables and indexed views in the current database are checked. To obtain the table or view ID, use the OBJECT_ID function.

index_name | *index_id*
   Is the index for which to check fragmentation information. If not specified, the statement processes the base index for the specified table or view. To obtain the index ID, use **sysindexes**.

WITH
>Specifies options for the type of information returned by the DBCC statement.

FAST
>Specifies whether to perform a fast scan of the index and output minimal information. A fast scan does not read the leaf or data level pages of the index.

TABLERESULTS
>Displays results as a rowset, with additional information.

ALL_INDEXES
>Displays results for all the indexes for the specified tables and views, even if a particular index is specified.

ALL_LEVELS
>Can only be used with the TABLERESULTS option. Cannot be used with the FAST option. Specifies whether to produce output for each level of each index processed. If not specified, only the index leaf level or table data level will be processed.

Remarks

The DBCC SHOWCONTIG statement traverses the page chain at the leaf level of the specified index when *index_id* is specified. If only *table_id* is specified, or if *index_id* is 0, the data pages of the specified table are scanned.

DBCC SHOWCONTIG determines whether the table is heavily fragmented. Table fragmentation occurs through the process of data modifications (INSERT, UPDATE, and DELETE statements) made against the table. Because these modifications are not usually distributed equally among the rows of the table, the fullness of each page can vary over time. For queries that scan part or all of a table, such table fragmentation can cause additional page reads, which hinders parallel scanning of data.

When an index is heavily fragmented, there are two choices for reducing fragmentation:

- Drop and re-create a clustered index.

 Re-creating a clustered index reorganizes the data, and results in full data pages. The level of fullness can be configured using the FILLFACTOR option. The drawbacks of this method are that the index is offline during the drop/re-create cycle and that the operation is atomic. If the index creation is interrupted, the index is not re-created.

- Use DBCC INDEXDEFRAG to reorder the leaf level pages of the index in a logical order.

 The DBCC INDEXDEFRAG command is an online operation, so the index is available while the command is running. The operation is also interruptible without loss of completed work. The drawback of this method is that it does not do as good a job of reorganizing the data as a clustered index drop/re-create operation.

The **Avg. Bytes free per page** and **Avg. Page density (full)** statistic in the result set give an indication of the fullness of index pages. The **Avg. Bytes free per page** figure should be low and the **Avg. Page density (full)** figure should be high. Dropping and recreating a clustered index, with the FILLFACTOR option specified, can improve these statistics. Also, the DBCC INDEXDEFRAG command will compact an index, taking into account its FILLFACTOR, which will improve these statistics.

The fragmentation level of an index can be determined in two ways:

- Comparing the values of **Extent Switches** and **Extents Scanned**.

  Note: This method of determining fragmentation does not work if the index spans multiple files. The value of **Extent Switches** should be as close as possible to that of **Extents Scanned**. This ratio is calculated as the **Scan Density** value, which should be as high as possible. This can be improved by either method of reducing fragmentation discussed earlier.

- Understanding **Logical Scan Fragmentation** and **Extent Scan Fragmentation** values.

  Logical Scan Fragmentation and, to a lesser extent, **Extent Scan Fragmentation** values give the best indication of a table's fragmentation level. Both these values should be as close to zero as possible (although a value from 0% through 10% may be acceptable). It should be noted that the **Extent Scan Fragmentation** value will be high if the index spans multiple files. Both methods of reducing fragmentation can be used to reduce these values.

Result Sets

This table describes the information in the result set.

Statistic	Description
Pages Scanned	Number of pages in the table or index.
Extents Scanned	Number of extents in the table or index.
Extent Switches	Number of times the DBCC statement moved from one extent to another while it traversed the pages of the table or index.
Avg. Pages per Extent	Number of pages per extent in the page chain.
Scan Density [Best Count: Actual Count]	Best count is the ideal number of extent changes if everything is contiguously linked. Actual count is the actual number of extent changes. The number in scan density is 100 if everything is contiguous; if it is less than 100, some fragmentation exists. Scan density is a percentage.

(continued)

(continued)

Statistic	Description
Logical Scan Fragmentation	Percentage of out-of-order pages returned from scanning the leaf pages of an index. This number is not relevant to heaps and text indexes. An out of order page is one for which the next page indicated in an IAM is a different page than the page pointed to by the next page pointer in the leaf page.
Extent Scan Fragmentation	Percentage of out-of-order extents in scanning the leaf pages of an index. This number is not relevant to heaps. An out-of-order extent is one for which the extent containing the current page for an index is not physically the next extent after the extent containing the previous page for an index.
Avg. Bytes free per page	Average number of free bytes on the pages scanned. The higher the number, the less full the pages are. Lower numbers are better. This number is also affected by row size; a large row size can result in a higher number.
Avg. Page density (full)	Average page density (as a percentage). This value takes into account row size, so it is a more accurate indication of how full your pages are. The higher the percentage, the better.

When a table ID and the FAST option are specified, DBCC SHOWCONTIG returns a result set with only the following columns:

- Pages Scanned
- Extent Switches
- Scan Density [Best Count:Actual Count]
- Logical Scan Fragmentation

When TABLERESULTS is specified, DBCC SHOWCONTIG returns these eight columns, described in the first table, and the following additional columns.

- ExtentSwitches
- AverageFreeBytes
- AveragePageDensity
- ScanDensity
- BestCount
- ActualCount
- LogicalFragmentation
- ExtentFragmentation

Statistic	Description
ObjectName	Name of the table or view processed.
ObjectId	ID of the object name.
IndexName	Name of the index processed. IndexName is NULL for a heap.
IndexId	ID of the index. IndexId is 0 for a heap.
Level	Level of the index. Level 0 is the leaf (or data) level of the index. The level number increases moving up the tree toward the index root. Level is 0 for a heap.
Pages	Number of pages comprising that level of the index or entire heap.
Rows	Number of data or index records at that level of the index. For a heap, this is the number of data records in the entire heap.
MinimumRecordSize	Minimum record size in that level of the index or entire heap.
MaximumRecordSize	Maximum record size in that level of the index or entire heap.
AverageRecordSize	Average record size in that level of the index or entire heap.
ForwardedRecords	Number of forwarded records in that level of the index or entire heap.
Extents	Number of extents in that level of the index or entire heap.

DBCC SHOWCONTIG returns the following columns when TABLERESULTS and FAST are specified.

- ObjectName
- ObjectId
- IndexName
- IndexId
- Pages
- ExtentSwitchs
- ScanDensity
- BestCount
- ActualCount
- LogicalFragmentation

Permissions

DBCC SHOWCONTIG permissions default to members of the **sysadmin** fixed server role, the **db_owner** and **db_ddladmin** fixed database roles, and the table owner, and are not transferable.

Examples

A. Display fragmentation information for a table

This example displays fragmentation information for the table with the specified table name.

```
USE Northwind
GO
DBCC SHOWCONTIG (Employees)
GO
```

B. Use OBJECT_ID to obtain the table ID and sysindexes to obtain the index ID

This example uses OBJECT_ID and **sysindexes** to obtain the table ID and index ID for the **aunmind** index of the **authors** table.

```
USE pubs
GO
DECLARE @id int, @indid int
SET @id = OBJECT_ID('authors')
SELECT @indid = indid
FROM sysindexes
WHERE id = @id
    AND name = 'aunmind'
DBCC SHOWCONTIG (@id, @indid)
GO
```

C. Display an abbreviated result set for a table

This example returns an abbreviated result set for the **authors** table in the **pubs** database.

```
USE pubs
DBCC SHOWCONTIG ('authors', 1) WITH FAST
```

D. Display the full result set for every index on every table in a database

This example returns a full table result set for every index on every table in the **pubs** database.

```
USE pubs
DBCC SHOWCONTIG WITH TABLERESULTS, ALL_INDEXES
```

E. Use DBCC SHOWCONTIG and DBCC INDEXDEFRAG to defragment the indexes in a database

This example shows a simple way to defragment all indexes in a database that is fragmented above a declared threshold.

```
/*Perform a 'USE <database name>' to select the database in which to run the script.*/
-- Declare variables
SET NOCOUNT ON
DECLARE @tablename VARCHAR (128)
DECLARE @execstr   VARCHAR (255)
DECLARE @objectid  INT
DECLARE @indexid   INT
DECLARE @frag      DECIMAL
DECLARE @maxfrag   DECIMAL

-- Decide on the maximum fragmentation to allow
SELECT @maxfrag = 30.0

-- Declare cursor
DECLARE tables CURSOR FOR
   SELECT TABLE_NAME
   FROM INFORMATION_SCHEMA.TABLES
   WHERE TABLE_TYPE = 'BASE TABLE'

-- Create the table
CREATE TABLE #fraglist (
   ObjectName CHAR (255),
   ObjectId INT,
   IndexName CHAR (255),
   IndexId INT,
   Lvl INT,
   CountPages INT,
   CountRows INT,
   MinRecSize INT,
   MaxRecSize INT,
   AvgRecSize INT,
   ForRecCount INT,
   Extents INT,
   ExtentSwitches INT,
   AvgFreeBytes INT,
   AvgPageDensity INT,
   ScanDensity DECIMAL,
   BestCount INT,
```

(continued)

(continued)

```
    ActualCount INT,
    LogicalFrag DECIMAL,
    ExtentFrag DECIMAL)

-- Open the cursor
OPEN tables

-- Loop through all the tables in the database
FETCH NEXT
    FROM tables
    INTO @tablename

WHILE @@FETCH_STATUS = 0
BEGIN
-- Do the showcontig of all indexes of the table
    INSERT INTO #fraglist
    EXEC ('DBCC SHOWCONTIG (''' + @tablename + ''')
        WITH FAST, TABLERESULTS, ALL_INDEXES, NO_INFOMSGS')
    FETCH NEXT
        FROM tables
        INTO @tablename
END

-- Close and deallocate the cursor
CLOSE tables
DEALLOCATE tables

-- Declare cursor for list of indexes to be defragged
DECLARE indexes CURSOR FOR
    SELECT ObjectName, ObjectId, IndexId, LogicalFrag
    FROM #fraglist
    WHERE LogicalFrag >= @maxfrag
        AND INDEXPROPERTY (ObjectId, IndexName, 'IndexDepth') > 0

-- Open the cursor
OPEN indexes

-- loop through the indexes
FETCH NEXT
    FROM indexes
    INTO @tablename, @objectid, @indexid, @frag
```

(continued)

(continued)

```
WHILE @@FETCH_STATUS = 0
BEGIN
   PRINT 'Executing DBCC INDEXDEFRAG (0, ' + RTRIM(@tablename) + ',
      ' + RTRIM(@indexid) + ') - fragmentation currently '
      + RTRIM(CONVERT(varchar(15),@frag)) + '%'
   SELECT @execstr = 'DBCC INDEXDEFRAG (0, ' + RTRIM(@objectid) + ',
      ' + RTRIM(@indexid) + ')'
   EXEC (@execstr)

   FETCH NEXT
      FROM indexes
      INTO @tablename, @objectid, @indexid, @frag
END

-- Close and deallocate the cursor
CLOSE indexes
DEALLOCATE indexes

-- Delete the temporary table
DROP TABLE #fraglist
GO
```

Related Topics

CREATE INDEX, DBCC, DBCC DBREINDEX, DBCC INDEXDEFRAG, DROP INDEX, OBJECT_ID, Space Allocation and Reuse, sysindexes, Table and Index Architecture

DBCC SHOW_STATISTICS

Displays the current distribution statistics for the specified target on the specified table.

Syntax

```
DBCC SHOW_STATISTICS ( table , target )
```

Arguments

table

Is the name of the table for which to display statistics information. Table names must conform to the rules for identifiers. For more information, see Using Identifiers.

target

Is the name of the object (index name or collection) for which to display statistics information. Target names must conform to the rules for identifiers. If *target* is both an index name and a statistics collection name, both index and column statistics are returned. If no index or statistics collection is found with the specified name, an error is returned.

Remarks

The results returned indicate the selectivity of an index (the lower the density returned, the higher the selectivity) and provide the basis for determining whether or not an index is useful to the query optimizer. The results returned are based on distribution steps of the index.

To see the last date the statistics were updated, use STATS_DATE.

Result Sets

This table describes the columns in the result set.

Column name	Description
Updated	Date and time the statistics were last updated.
Rows	Number of rows in the table.
Rows Sampled	Number of rows sampled for statistics information.
Steps	Number of distribution steps.
Density	Selectivity of the first index column prefix (non-frequent).
Average key length	Average length of the first index column prefix.
All density	Selectivity of a set of index column prefixes (frequent).
Average length	Average length of a set of index column prefixes.
Columns	Names of index column prefixes for which **All density** and **Average length** are displayed.
RANGE_HI_KEY	Upper bound value of a histogram step.

(continued)

(continued)

Column name	Description
RANGE_ROWS	Number of rows from the sample that fall within a histogram step, excluding the upper bound.
EQ_ROWS	Number of rows from the sample that are equal in value to the upper bound of the histogram step.
DISTINCT_RANGE_ROWS	Number of distinct values within a histogram step, excluding the upper bound.
AVG_RANGE_ROWS	Average number of duplicate values within a histogram step, excluding the upper bound (RANGE_ROWS / DISTINCT_RANGE_ROWS for DISTINCT_RANGE_ROWS > 0).

Permissions

DBCC SHOW_STATISTICS permissions default to members of the **sysadmin** fixed server role, the **db_owner** and **db_ddladmin** fixed database role, and the table owner, and are not transferable.

Examples

This example displays statistics information for the **UPKCL_auidind** index of the **authors** table.

```
USE pubs
DBCC SHOW_STATISTICS (authors, UPKCL_auidind)
GO
```

Here is the result set:

```
Statistics for INDEX 'UPKCL_auidind'.
Updated                Rows    Rows Sampled    Steps    Density
-------------------    ------  --------------  -------  --------------
Mar  1 2000  4:58AM    23      23              23       4.3478262E-2

Average key length
------------------
11.0

(1 row(s) affected)
```

(continued)

(continued)

```
All density            Average Length          Columns
---------------------  ----------------------  ----------------
4.3478262E-2           11.0                    au_id

(1 row(s) affected)

RANGE_HI_KEY RANGE_ROWS EQ_ROWS DISTINCT_RANGE_ROWS AVG_RANGE_ROWS
------------ ---------- ------- ------------------- --------------
172-32-1176  0.0        1.0     0                   0.0
213-46-8915  0.0        1.0     0                   0.0
238-95-7766  0.0        1.0     0                   0.0
267-41-2394  0.0        1.0     0                   0.0
274-80-9391  0.0        1.0     0                   0.0
341-22-1782  0.0        1.0     0                   0.0
409-56-7008  0.0        1.0     0                   0.0
427-17-2319  0.0        1.0     0                   0.0
472-27-2349  0.0        1.0     0                   0.0
486-29-1786  0.0        1.0     0                   0.0
527-72-3246  0.0        1.0     0                   0.0
648-92-1872  0.0        1.0     0                   0.0
672-71-3249  0.0        1.0     0                   0.0
712-45-1867  0.0        1.0     0                   0.0
722-51-5454  0.0        1.0     0                   0.0
724-08-9931  0.0        1.0     0                   0.0
724-80-9391  0.0        1.0     0                   0.0
756-30-7391  0.0        1.0     0                   0.0
807-91-6654  0.0        1.0     0                   0.0
846-92-7186  0.0        1.0     0                   0.0
893-72-1158  0.0        1.0     0                   0.0
899-46-2035  0.0        1.0     0                   0.0
998-72-3567  0.0        1.0     0                   0.0

(23 row(s) affected)
```

Related Topics

CREATE INDEX, CREATE STATISTICS, DBCC, Distribution Statistics, DROP
STATISTICS, sp_autostats, sp_createstats, sp_dboption, STATS_DATE, UPDATE
STATISTICS, USE

DBCC SHRINKDATABASE

Shrinks the size of the data files in the specified database.

Syntax

```
DBCC SHRINKDATABASE
    ( database_name [ , target_percent ]
      [ , { NOTRUNCATE | TRUNCATEONLY } ]
    )
```

Arguments

database_name

Is the name of the database to be shrunk. Database names must conform to the rules for identifiers. For more information, see Using Identifiers.

target_percent

Is the desired percentage of free space left in the database file after the database has been shrunk.

NOTRUNCATE

Causes the freed file space to be retained in the database files. If not specified, the freed file space is released to the operating system.

TRUNCATEONLY

Causes any unused space in the data files to be released to the operating system and shrinks the file to the last allocated extent, reducing the file size without moving any data. No attempt is made to relocate rows to unallocated pages. *target_percent* is ignored when TRUNCATEONLY is used.

Remarks

Microsoft SQL Server can shrink:

- All data and log files for a specific database. Execute DBCC SHRINKDATABASE.

- One data or log file at a time for a specific database. Execute DBCC SHRINKFILE.

DBCC SHRINKDATABASE shrinks data files on a per-file basis. However, DBCC SHRINKDATABASE shrinks log files as if all the log files existed in one contiguous log pool.

Assume a database named **mydb** with two data files and two log files. Both data and log files are 10 MB in size. The first data file contains 6 MB of data.

For each file, SQL Server calculates a target size, which is the size to which the file is to be shrunk. When DBCC SHRINKDATABASE is specified with *target_percent*, SQL Server calculates target size to be the *target_percent* amount of space free in the file after shrinking. For example, if you specify a *target_percent* of 25 for shrinking **mydb**. SQL Server calculates the target size for this file to be 8 MB (6 MB of data plus 2 MB of free space). Therefore, SQL Server moves any data from the last 2 MB of the data file to any free space in the first 8 MB of the data file and then shrinks the file.

Assume the first data file of **mydb** contains 7 MB of data. Specifying *target_percent* of 30 allows this data file to be shrunk to the desired free percentage of 30. However, specifying a *target_percent* of 40 does not shrink the data file because SQL Server will not shrink a file to a size smaller than the data currently occupies. You can also think of this issue another way: 40 percent desired free space + 70 percent full data file (7 MB out of 10 MB) is greater than 100 percent. Because the desired percentage free plus the current percentage that the data file occupies is over 100 percent (by 10 percent), any *target_size* greater than 30 will not shrink the data file.

For log files, SQL Server uses *target_percent* to calculate the target size for the entire log; therefore, *target_percent* is the amount of free space in the log after the shrink operation. Target size for the entire log is then translated to target size for each log file. DBCC SHRINKDATABASE attempts to shrink each physical log file to its target size immediately. If no part of the logical log resides in the virtual logs beyond the log file's target size, the file is successfully truncated and DBCC SHRINKDATABASE completes with no messages. However, if part of the logical log resides in the virtual logs beyond the target size, SQL Server frees as much space as possible and then issues an informational message. The message tells you what actions you need to perform to move the logical log out of the virtual logs at the end of the file. After you perform the actions, you can then reissue the DBCC SHRINKDATABASE command to free the remaining space. For more information about shrinking transaction logs, see Shrinking the Transaction Log.

Because a log file can only be shrunk to a virtual log file boundary, it may not be possible to shrink a log file to a size smaller than the size of a virtual log file, even if it is not being used. For example, a database with a log file of 1 GB can have the log file shrunk to only 128 MB. For more information about truncation, see Truncating the Transaction Log. For more information about determining virtual log file sizes, see Virtual Log Files.

The target size for data and log files as calculated by DBCC SHRINKDATABASE can never be smaller than the minimum size of a file. The minimum size of a file is the size specified when the file was originally created, or the last explicit size set with a file size changing operation such as ALTER DATABASE with the MODIFY FILE option or DBCC SHRINKFILE. For example, if all the data and log files of **mydb** were specified to be 10 MB at the time CREATE DATABASE was executed, the minimum size of each file is 10 MB. DBCC SHRINKDATABASE cannot shrink any of the files smaller than 10 MB. If one of the files is explicitly grown to a size of 20 MB by using ALTER DATABASE with the MODIFY FILE option, the new minimum size of the file is 20 MB. To shrink a file to a size smaller than its minimum size, use DBCC SHRINKFILE and specify the new size. Executing DBCC SHRINKFILE changes the minimum file size to the new size specified.

When using data files, DBCC SHRINKDATABASE has the NOTRUNCATE and TRUNCATEONLY options. Both options are ignored if specified for log files. DBCC SHRINKDATABASE with neither option is equivalent to a DBCC SHRINKDATABASE with the NOTRUNCATE option followed by a DBCC SHRINKDATABASE with the TRUNCATEONLY option.

The NOTRUNCATE option, with or without specifying *target_percent*, performs the actual data movement operations of DBCC SHRINKDATABASE including the movement of allocated pages from the end of a file to unallocated pages in the front of the file. However, the free space at the end of the file is not returned to the operating system and the physical size of the file does not change. Therefore, data files appear not to shrink when the NOTRUNCATE option is specified. For example, assume you are using the **mydb** database again. **mydb** has two data files and two log files. The second data file and second log file are both 10 MB in size. When DBCC SHRINKDATABASE **mydb** NOTRUNCATE is executed, Microsoft SQL Server moves the data from the later pages to the front pages of the data file. However, the file still remains 10 MB in size.

The TRUNCATEONLY option reclaims all free space at the end of the file to the operating system. However, TRUNCATEONLY does not perform any page movement inside the file or files. The specified file is shrunk only to the last allocated extent. *target_percent* is ignored if specified with the TRUNCATEONLY option.

The database cannot be made smaller than the size of the **model** database.

The database being shrunk does not have to be in single user mode; other users can be working in the database when it is shrunk. This includes system databases.

Result Sets

This table describes the columns in the result set.

Column name	Description
DbId	Database identification number of the file SQL Server attempted to shrink.
FileId	The file identification number of the file SQL Server attempted to shrink.
CurrentSize	The number of 8-KB pages the file currently occupies.
MinimumSize	The number of 8-KB pages the file could occupy, at minimum. This corresponds to the minimum size or originally created size of a file.
UsedPages	The number of 8-KB pages currently used by the file.
EstimatedPages	The number of 8-KB pages that SQL Server estimates the file could be shrunk down to.

Note   SQL Server does not display rows for those files not shrunk.

Permissions

DBCC SHRINKDATABASE permissions default to members of the **sysadmin** fixed server role or the **db_owner** fixed database role, and are not transferable.

Examples

This example decreases the size of the files in the **UserDB** user database to allow 10 percent free space in the files of **UserDB**.

```
DBCC SHRINKDATABASE (UserDB, 10)
GO
```

Related Topics

ALTER DATABASE, DBCC, Physical Database Files and Filegroups

DBCC SHRINKFILE

Shrinks the size of the specified data file or log file for the related database.

Syntax

```
DBCC SHRINKFILE
    ( { file_name | file_id }
      { [ , target_size ]
          | [ , { EMPTYFILE | NOTRUNCATE | TRUNCATEONLY } ]
      }
    )
```

Arguments

file_name
> Is the logical name of the file shrunk. File names must conform to the rules for identifiers. For more information, see Using Identifiers.

file_id
> Is the identification (ID) number of the file to be shrunk. To obtain a file ID, use the FILE_ID function or search **sysfiles** in the current database.

target_size
> Is the desired size for the file in megabytes, expressed as an integer. If not specified, DBCC SHRINKFILE reduces the size to the default file size.
>
> If *target_size* is specified, DBCC SHRINKFILE attempts to shrink the file to the specified size. Used pages in the part of the file to be freed are relocated to available free space in the part of the file retained. For example, if there is a 10-MB data file, a DBCC SHRINKFILE with a *target_size* of 8 causes all used pages in the last 2 MB of the file to be reallocated into any available free slots in the first 8 MB of the file. DBCC SHRINKFILE does not shrink a file past the size needed to store the data in the file. For example, if 7 MB of a 10-MB data file is used, a DBCC SHRINKFILE statement with a *target_size* of 6 shrinks the file to only 7 MB, not 6 MB.

EMPTYFILE

Migrates all data from the specified file to other files in the same filegroup. Microsoft SQL Server no longer allows data to be placed on the file used with the EMPTYFILE option. This option allows the file to be dropped using the ALTER DATABASE statement.

NOTRUNCATE

Causes the freed file space to be retained in the files.

When NOTRUNCATE is specified along with *target_size*, the space freed is not released to the operating system. The only effect of the DBCC SHRINKFILE is to relocate used pages from above the *target_size* line to the front of the file. When NOTRUNCATE is not specified, all freed file space is returned to the operating system.

TRUNCATEONLY

Causes any unused space in the files to be released to the operating system and shrinks the file to the last allocated extent, reducing the file size without moving any data. No attempt is made to relocate rows to unallocated pages. *target_size* is ignored when TRUNCATEONLY is used.

Remarks

DBCC SHRINKFILE applies to the files in the current database. Switch context to the database to issue a DBCC SHRINKFILE statement referencing a file in that particular database. For more information about changing the current database, see USE.

The database cannot be made smaller than the size of the **model** database.

Use DBCC SHRINKFILE to reduce the size of a file to smaller than its originally created size. The minimum file size for the file is then reset to the newly specified size.

To remove any data that may be in a file, execute DBCC SHRINKFILE(*'file_name'*, EMPTYFILE) before executing ALTER DATABASE.

The database being shrunk does not have to be in single-user mode; other users can be working in the database when the file is shrunk. You do not have to run SQL Server in single-user mode to shrink the system databases.

For log files, SQL Server uses *target_size* to calculate the target size for the entire log; therefore, *target_size* is the amount of free space in the log after the shrink operation. Target size for the entire log is then translated to target size for each log file. DBCC SHRINKFILE attempts to shrink each physical log file to its target size immediately. If no part of the logical log resides in the virtual logs beyond the log file's target size, the file is successfully truncated and DBCC SHRINKFILE completes with no messages. However, if part of the logical log resides in the virtual logs beyond the target size, SQL Server frees as much space as possible and then issues an informational message. The message tells you what actions you need to perform to move the logical log out of the virtual logs at the end of the file. After you perform the actions, you can then reissue the DBCC SHRINKFILE command to free the remaining space. For more information about shrinking transaction logs, see Shrinking the Transaction Log.

Because a log file can only be shrunk to a virtual log file boundary, it may not be possible to shrink a log file to a size smaller than the size of a virtual log file, even if it is not being used. For example, a database with a log file of 1 GB can have the log file shrunk to only 128 MB. For more information about truncation, see Truncating the Transaction Log. For more information about determining virtual log file sizes, see Virtual Log Files.

Result Sets

This table describes the columns in the result set.

Column name	Description
DbId	Database identification number of the file SQL Server attempted to shrink.
FileId	The file identification number of the file SQL Server attempted to shrink.
CurrentSize	The number of 8-KB pages the file currently occupies.
MinimumSize	The number of 8-KB pages the file could occupy, at minimum. This corresponds to the minimum size or originally created size of a file.
UsedPages	The number of 8-KB pages currently used by the file.
EstimatedPages	The number of 8-KB pages that SQL Server estimates the file could be shrunk down to.

Permissions

DBCC SHRINKFILE permissions default to members of the **sysadmin** fixed server role or the **db_owner** fixed database role, and are not transferable.

Examples

This example shrinks the size of a file named DataFil1 in the **UserDB** user database to 7 MB.

```
USE UserDB
GO
DBCC SHRINKFILE (DataFil1, 7)
GO
```

Related Topics
ALTER DATABASE, DBCC, FILE_ID, Physical Database Files and Filegroups, sysfiles

---

DBCC SQLPERF

Provides statistics about the use of transaction-log space in all databases.

Syntax

```
DBCC SQLPERF ( LOGSPACE )
```

Remarks

The transaction log accumulates information about changes to data in each database. The information returned by DBCC SQLPERF(LOGSPACE) can be used to monitor the amount of space used and indicates when to back up or truncate the transaction log.

Result Sets

This table describes the columns in the result set.

Column name	Definition
Database Name	Name of the database for the log statistics displayed.
Log Size (MB)	The actual amount of space available for the log. This amount is smaller than the amount originally allocated for log space because Microsoft SQL Server reserves a small amount of disk space for internal header information.
Log Space Used (%)	Percentage of the log file currently occupied with transaction log information.
Status	Status of the log file (always contains 0).

Permissions

DBCC SQLPERF permissions default to any user.

Examples

This example displays LOGSPACE information for all databases currently installed.

```
DBCC SQLPERF(LOGSPACE)
GO
```

Here is the result set:

```
Database Name Log Size (MB) Log Space Used (%) Status
------------- ------------- ------------------ -----------
pubs               1.99219             4.26471           0
msdb               3.99219            17.0132            0
tempdb             1.99219             1.64216           0
model              1.0               12.7953            0
master             3.99219            14.3469            0
```

Related Topics

DBCC, sp_spaceused

DBCC TRACEOFF

Disables the specified trace flag(s).

Syntax

```
DBCC TRACEOFF ( trace# [ ,...n ] )
```

Arguments

trace#

    Is the number of the trace flag to disable.

n

    Is a placeholder indicating that multiple trace flags can be specified.

Remarks

Trace flags are used to customize certain characteristics controlling how Microsoft SQL Server operates.

To find out information about the status of trace flags, use DBCC TRACESTATUS. To enable certain trace flags, use DBCC TRACEON.

Result Sets

DBCC TRACEOFF returns this result set (message):

```
DBCC execution completed. If DBCC printed error messages, contact your system
administrator.
```

Permissions

DBCC TRACEOFF permissions default to members of the **sysadmin** fixed server role only, and are not transferable.

Examples

This example disables the effects of trace flag 3205.

```
DBCC TRACEOFF (3205)
GO
```

Related Topics

DBCC, DBCC TRACEON, DBCC TRACESTATUS, Trace Flags

DBCC TRACEON

Turns on (enables) the specified trace flag.

Syntax

```
DBCC TRACEON ( trace# [ ,...n ] )
```

Arguments

trace#

Is the number of the trace flag to turn on.

n

Is a placeholder indicating that multiple trace flags can be specified.

Remarks

Trace flags are used to customize certain characteristics controlling how
Microsoft SQL Server operates. Trace flags remain enabled in the server until disabled
by executing a DBCC TRACEOFF statement. New connections into the server do not
see any trace flags until a DBCC TRACEON statement is issued. Then, the connection
will see all trace flags currently enabled in the server, even those enabled by another
connection.

For more information about the status of trace flags, see DBCC TRACESTATUS.

Result Sets

DBCC TRACEON returns this result set (message):

```
DBCC execution completed. If DBCC printed error messages, contact your system
administrator.
```

Permissions

DBCC TRACEON permissions default to members of the **sysadmin** fixed server role
only, and are not transferable.

Examples

This example disables hardware compression for tape drivers.

```
DBCC TRACEON (3205)
GO
```

Related Topics

DBCC, DBCC TRACEOFF, DBCC TRACESTATUS, Trace Flags

DBCC TRACESTATUS

Displays the status of trace flags.

Syntax

```
DBCC TRACESTATUS ( trace# [ ,...n ] )
```

Arguments

trace#

Is the number of the trace flag whose status will be displayed.

n

Is a placeholder that indicates multiple trace flags can be specified.

Result Sets

DBCC TRACESTATUS returns a column for the trace flag number and a column for the status, indicating whether the trace flag is ON (1) or OFF (0). To get status information for all trace flags currently turned on, specify -1 for *trace#*.

Remarks

To enable certain trace flags, use DBCC TRACEON. To disable trace flags, use DBCC TRACEOFF.

Permissions

DBCC TRACESTATUS permissions default to any user.

Examples

A. Display the status of all trace flags currently enabled

This example displays the status of all currently enabled trace flags by specifying a value of –1.

```
DBCC TRACESTATUS(-1)
GO
```

B. Display the status of multiple trace flags

This example displays the status of trace flags 2528 and 3205.

```
DBCC TRACESTATUS (2528, 3205)
GO
```

Related Topics

DBCC, DBCC TRACEOFF, DBCC TRACEON, Trace Flags

DBCC UNPINTABLE

Marks a table as unpinned. After a table is marked as unpinned, the table pages in the buffer cache can be flushed.

Syntax

```
DBCC UNPINTABLE ( database_id , table_id )
```

Arguments

database_id
> Is the database identification (ID) number of the database containing the table to be pinned. To obtain the database ID, use DB_ID.

table_id
> Is the object ID of the table to be pinned. To determine the object ID, use OBJECT_ID.

Remarks

DBCC UNPINTABLE does not cause the table to be immediately flushed from the data cache. It specifies that all of the pages for the table in the buffer cache can be flushed if space is needed to read in a new page from disk.

Result Sets

DBCC UNPINTABLE returns this result set (message):

```
DBCC execution completed. If DBCC printed error messages, contact your system
administrator.
```

Permissions

DBCC UNPINTABLE permissions default to members of the **sysadmin** fixed server role and are not transferable.

Examples

This example unpins the **authors** table in the **pubs** database.

```
DECLARE @db_id int, @tbl_id int
USE pubs
SET @db_id = DB_ID('pubs')
SET @tbl_id = OBJECT_ID('pubs..authors')
DBCC UNPINTABLE (@db_id, @tbl_id)
```

Related Topics

DB_ID, DBCC, DBCC PINTABLE, Memory Architecture, OBJECT_ID, sp_tableoption

---

DBCC UPDATEUSAGE

Reports and corrects inaccuracies in the **sysindexes** table, which may result in incorrect space usage reports by the **sp_spaceused** system stored procedure.

Syntax

```
DBCC UPDATEUSAGE
    ( { 'database_name' | 0 }
      [ , { 'table_name' | 'view_name' }
      [ , { index_id | 'index_name' } ] ]
    )
    [ WITH[ COUNT_ROWS ] [ , NO_INFOMSGS ]
      ]
```

Arguments

'database_name' | 0

Is the name of the database for which to report and correct space usage statistics. Database names must conform to the rules for identifiers. For more information, see Using Identifiers. If 0 is specified, then the current database is used.

'table_name' | *'view_name'*

Is the name of the table or indexed view for which to report and correct space usage statistics. Table and view names must conform to the rules for identifiers.

index_id | *'index_name'*

Is the identification (ID) number or index name of the index to use. If not specified, the statement processes all indexes for the specified table or view.

COUNT_ROWS

Specifies that the **rows** column of **sysindexes** is updated with the current count of the number of rows in the table or view. This applies only to **sysindexes** rows that have an **indid** of 0 or 1. This option can affect performance on large tables and indexed views.

NO_INFOMSGS

Suppresses all informational messages.

Remarks

DBCC UPDATEUSAGE corrects the **rows**, **used**, **reserved**, and **dpages** columns of the **sysindexes** table for tables and clustered indexes. Size information is not maintained for nonclustered indexes.

If there are no inaccuracies in **sysindexes**, DBCC UPDATEUSAGE returns no data. If inaccuracies are found and corrected and the WITH NO_INFOMSGS option is not used, UPDATEUSAGE returns the rows and columns being updated in **sysindexes**.

Use UPDATEUSAGE to synchronize space-usage counters. DBCC UPDATEUSAGE can take some time to run on large tables or databases, so it should typically be used only when you suspect incorrect values returned by **sp_spaceused**. **sp_spaceused** accepts an optional parameter to run DBCC UPDATEUSAGE before returning space information for the table or index.

Result Sets

DBCC UPDATEUSAGE returns this result set for the **Northwind** database (values may vary):

```
DBCC UPDATEUSAGE: sysindexes row updated for table 'Orders' (index ID 4):
        USED pages: Changed from (2) to (4) pages.
        RSVD pages: Changed from (2) to (4) pages.
DBCC UPDATEUSAGE: sysindexes row updated for table 'Orders' (index ID 5):
        USED pages: Changed from (2) to (4) pages.
        RSVD pages: Changed from (2) to (4) pages.
'...'
DBCC execution completed. If DBCC printed error messages, contact your system
administrator.
```

Permissions

DBCC UPDATEUSAGE permissions default to members of the **sysadmin** fixed
server role or the **db_owner** fixed database role, and are not transferable.

Examples

A. Update sysindexes by specifying 0 for the current database

This example specifies 0 for the database name and Microsoft SQL Server reports
information for the current database.

```
DBCC UPDATEUSAGE (0)
GO
```

B. Update sysindexes for pubs, suppressing informational messages

This example specifies **pubs** as the database name, and suppresses all informational
messages.

```
DBCC UPDATEUSAGE ('pubs') WITH NO_INFOMSGS
GO
```

C. Update sysindexes for the authors table

This example reports information about the **authors** table.

```
DBCC UPDATEUSAGE ('pubs','authors')
GO
```

D. Update sysindexes for a specified index

This example uses the index name, **UPKCL_auidind**.

```
DBCC UPDATEUSAGE ('pubs', 'authors', 'UPKCL_auidind')
```

Related Topics

DBCC, sp_spaceused, sysindexes, Table and Index Architecture,
UPDATE STATISTICS

DBCC USEROPTIONS

Returns the SET options active (set) for the current connection.

Syntax

```
DBCC USEROPTIONS
```

Result Sets

DBCC USEROPTIONS returns this result set (values and entries may vary):

```
Set Option                     Value
---------------------------    ---------------------------------------------
textsize                       64512
language                       us_english
dateformat                     mdy
datefirst                      7
ansi_null_dflt_on              SET
ansi_warnings                  SET
ansi_padding                   SET
ansi_nulls                     SET
concat_null_yields_null        SET

(9 row(s) affected)

DBCC execution completed. If DBCC printed error messages, contact your system
administrator.
```

DBCC USEROPTIONS returns a column for the name of the SET option and a
column for the setting of the option.

Permissions

DBCC USEROPTIONS permissions default to any user.

Examples

This example returns the active SET options for the current connection.

```
DBCC USEROPTIONS
```

Related Topics

DBCC, Customizing Transaction Isolation Level, SET, SET TRANSACTION
ISOLATION LEVEL

CHAPTER 9

T-SQL Reference

This chapter provides detailed language definitions for T-SQL language programming elements, including data types and functions. Language definitions for certain T-SQL language elements are found in different chapters in this volume, per the following:

- Operators—discussed and defined in Chapter 4, T-SQL Operators
- Globals—discussed and defined in Chapter 6, T-SQL Globals
- DBCC Statements—discussed and defined in Chapter 8, T-SQL DBCC Statements
- Reserved Keywords—discussed and defined in Chapter 5, T-SQL Reserved Keywords

Complete treatment of the following T-SQL language elements are found in Volume 6, T-SQL Stored Procedures and Tables Reference:

- T-SQL Information Schema Views—discussed and defined in Volume 6, Chapter 3
- T-SQL Stored Procedures—discussed and defined in Volume 6, Chapter 4
- T-SQL Tables—discussed and defined in Volume 6, Chapter 6

That still leaves a lot of T-SQL programming elements to discuss in this chapter—over 750 pages worth of programming elements, to be more precise.

ABS

Returns the absolute, positive value of the given numeric expression.

Syntax

```
ABS ( numeric_expression )
```

Arguments

numeric_expression
> Is an expression of the exact numeric or approximate numeric data type category, except for the **bit** data type.

Return Types

Returns the same type as *numeric_expression*.

Examples

This example shows the effect of the ABS function on three different numbers.

```
SELECT ABS(-1.0), ABS(0.0), ABS(1.0)
```

Here is the result set:

```
---- ---- ----
1.0  .0   1.0
```

The ABS function can produce an overflow error, for example:

```
SELECT ABS(convert(int, -2147483648))
```

Here is the error message:

```
Server: Msg 8115, Level 16, State 2
Arithmetic overflow error converting expression to type int.
```

Related Topics

CAST and CONVERT, Data Types, Mathematical Functions

ACOS

Returns the angle, in radians, whose cosine is the given **float** expression; also called arccosine.

Syntax

```
ACOS ( float_expression )
```

Arguments

float_expression

Is an expression of the type **float** or **real**, with a value from −1 through 1. Values outside this range return NULL and report a domain error.

Return Types

float

Examples

This example returns the ACOS of the given angle.

```
SET NOCOUNT OFF
DECLARE @angle float
SET @angle = -1
SELECT 'The ACOS of the angle is: ' + CONVERT(varchar, ACOS(@angle))
```

Here is the result set:

```
----------------------------------
The ACOS of the angle is: 3.14159

(1 row(s) affected)
```

This example sets **@angle** to a value outside the valid range.

```
SET NOCOUNT OFF
DECLARE @angle float
SET @angle = 1.01
SELECT 'The ACOS of the angle is: ' + CONVERT(varchar, ACOS(@angle))
```

Here is the result set:

```
------------------------------------------------------------
NULL

(1 row(s) affected)

A domain error occurred.
```

Related Topics

Mathematical Functions

ALL

Compares a scalar value with a single-column set of values.

Syntax

```
scalar_expression { = | <> | != | > | >= | !> | < | <= | !< } ALL ( subquery )
```

Arguments

scalar_expression

Is any valid Microsoft SQL Server expression.

{ = | <> | != | > | >= | !> | < | <= | !< }

Is a comparison operator.

subquery

> Is a subquery that returns a result set of one column. The data type of the returned column must be the same data type as the data type of *scalar_expression*.

> Is a restricted SELECT statement (the ORDER BY clause, the COMPUTE clause, and the INTO keyword are not allowed).

Return Types

Boolean

Result Value

Returns TRUE when the comparison specified is TRUE for all pairs (*scalar_expression*, *x*) where *x* is a value in the single-column set; otherwise returns FALSE.

Related Topics

CASE, Expressions, Functions, LIKE, Operators (Logical Operators), SELECT (Subqueries), WHERE

ALTER DATABASE

Adds or removes files and filegroups from a database. Can also be used to modify the attributes of files and filegroups, such as changing the name or size of a file. ALTER DATABASE provides the ability to change the database name, filegroup names, and the logical names of data files and log files.

ALTER DATABASE supports the setting of database options. In previous versions of Microsoft SQL Server, these options could be set with the **sp_dboption** stored procedure. SQL Server continues to support **sp_dboption** in this release but may not do so in the future. Use the **DATABASEPROPERTYEX** function to retrieve current settings for database options.

Syntax

```
ALTER DATABASE database
{ ADD FILE < filespec > [ ,...n ] [ TO FILEGROUP filegroup_name ]
| ADD LOG FILE < filespec > [ ,...n ]
| REMOVE FILE logical_file_name
| ADD FILEGROUP filegroup_name
| REMOVE FILEGROUP filegroup_name
| MODIFY FILE < filespec >
| MODIFY NAME = new_dbname
```

(continued)

(continued)

```
| MODIFY FILEGROUP filegroup_name {filegroup_property | NAME = new_filegroup_name }
/ SET < optionspec > [ ,…n ] [ WITH < termination > ]
| COLLATE < collation_name >
}
< filespec > ::= . ( NAME = logical_file_name
   [ , NEWNAME = new_logical_name ]
   [ , FILENAME = 'os_file_name' ]
   [ , SIZE = size ]
   [ , MAXSIZE = { max_size | UNLIMITED } ]
   [ , FILEGROWTH = growth_increment ] )

< optionspec > ::= . < state_option >
   | < cursor_option >
   | < auto_option >
   | < sql_option >
   | < recovery_option >

   < state_option > ::=
       { SINGLE_USER | RESTRICTED_USER | MULTI_USER }
       | { OFFLINE | ONLINE }
       | { READ_ONLY | READ_WRITE }

   < termination > ::=
       ROLLBACK AFTER integer [ SECONDS ]
       | ROLLBACK IMMEDIATE
       | NO_WAIT
   < cursor_option > ::=
       CURSOR_CLOSE_ON_COMMIT { ON | OFF }
       | CURSOR_DEFAULT { LOCAL | GLOBAL }

   < auto_option > ::=
       AUTO_CLOSE { ON | OFF }
       | AUTO_CREATE_STATISTICS { ON | OFF }
       | AUTO_SHRINK { ON | OFF }
       | AUTO_UPDATE_STATISTICS { ON | OFF }

   < sql_option > ::=
       ANSI_NULL_DEFAULT { ON | OFF }
       | ANSI_NULLS { ON | OFF }
       | ANSI_PADDING { ON | OFF }
       | ANSI_WARNINGS { ON | OFF }
       | ARITHABORT { ON | OFF }
```

(continued)

(continued)

```
      | CONCAT_NULL_YIELDS_NULL { ON | OFF }
      | NUMERIC_ROUNDABORT { ON | OFF }
      | QUOTED_IDENTIFIER { ON | OFF }
      | RECURSIVE_TRIGGERS { ON | OFF }


  < recovery_option > ::=
      RECOVERY { FULL | BULK_LOGGED | SIMPLE }
      | TORN_PAGE_DETECTION { ON | OFF }
```

Arguments

database

Is the name of the database changed.

ADD FILE

Specifies that a file is added.

TO FILEGROUP

Specifies the filegroup to which to add the specified file.

filegroup_name

Is the name of the filegroup to add the specified file to.

ADD LOG FILE

Specifies that a log file be added to the specified database.

REMOVE FILE

Removes the file description from the database system tables and deletes the physical file. The file cannot be removed unless empty.

ADD FILEGROUP

Specifies that a filegroup is to be added.

filegroup_name

Is the name of the filegroup to add or drop.

REMOVE FILEGROUP

Removes the filegroup from the database and deletes all the files in the filegroup. The filegroup cannot be removed unless empty.

MODIFY FILE

Specifies the given file that should be modified, including the FILENAME, SIZE, FILEGROWTH, and MAXSIZE options. Only one of these properties can be changed at a time. NAME must be specified in the <filespec> to identify the file to be modified. If SIZE is specified, the new size must be larger than the current file size. FILENAME can be specified only for files in the **tempdb** database, and the new name does not take effect until Microsoft SQL Server is restarted.

To modify the logical name of a data file or log file, specify in NAME the logical file name to be renamed, and specify for NEWNAME the new logical name for the file.

Thus:

MODIFY FILE (NAME = *logical_file_name*, NEWNAME = *new_logical_name*…).

For optimum performance during multiple modify-file operations, several ALTER DATABASE *database* MODIFY FILE statements can be run concurrently.

MODIFY NAME = *new_dbname*
Renames the database.

MODIFY FILEGROUP *filegroup_name* { *filegroup_property* | NAME = *new_filegroup_name* }
Specifies the filegroup to be modified and the change needed.

If *filegroup_name* and NAME = *new_filegroup_name* are specified, changes the filegroup name to the *new_filegroup_name*.

If *filegroup_name* and *filegroup_property* are specified, indicates the given filegroup property be applied to the filegroup. The values for *filegroup_property* are:

READONLY
Specifies the filegroup is read-only. Updates to objects in it are not allowed. The primary filegroup cannot be made read-only. Only users with exclusive database access can mark a filegroup read-only.

READWRITE
Reverses the READONLY property. Updates are enabled for the objects in the filegroup. Only users who have exclusive access to the database can mark a filegroup read/write.

DEFAULT
Specifies the filegroup as the default database filegroup. Only one database filegroup can be default. CREATE DATABASE sets the primary filegroup as the initial default filegroup. New tables and indexes are created in the default filegroup—if no filegroup is specified in the CREATE TABLE, ALTER TABLE, or CREATE INDEX statements.

WITH <termination>
Specifies when to roll back incomplete transactions when the database is transitioned from one state to another. Only one termination clause can be specified and it follows the SET clauses.

ROLLBACK AFTER *integer* [SECONDS] | ROLLBACK IMMEDIATE
Specifies whether to roll back after the specified number of seconds or immediately. If the termination clause is omitted, transactions are allowed to commit or roll back on their own.

NO_WAIT
Specifies that if the requested database state or option change cannot complete immediately without waiting for transactions to commit or roll back on their own, the request will fail.

COLLATE < *collation_name* >
Specifies the collation for the database. Collation name can be either a Windows collation name or a SQL collation name. If not specified, the database is assigned the default collation of the SQL Server instance.

For more information about the Windows and SQL collation names, see COLLATE.

<filespec>
Controls the file properties.

NAME
Specifies a logical name for the file.

logical_file_name
Is the name used in Microsoft SQL Server when referencing the file. The name must be unique within the database and conform to the rules for identifiers. The name can be a character or Unicode constant, a regular identifier, or a delimited identifier. For more information, see Using Identifiers.

FILENAME
Specifies an operating system file name. When used with MODIFY FILE, FILENAME can be specified only for files in the **tempdb** database. The new **tempdb** file name takes effect only after SQL Server is stopped and restarted.

'*os_file_name*'
Is the path and file name used by the operating system for the file. The file must reside in the server in which SQL Server is installed. Data and log files should not be placed on compressed file systems.

If the file is on a raw partition, *os_file_name* must specify only the drive letter of an existing raw partition. Only one file can be placed on each raw partition. Files on raw partitions do not autogrow; therefore, the MAXSIZE and FILEGROWTH parameters are not needed when *os_file_name* specifies a raw partition.

SIZE
Specifies the file size.

size
Is the size of the file. The KB, MB, GB, and TB suffixes can be used to specify kilobytes, megabytes, gigabytes, or terabytes. The default is MB. Specify a whole number; do not include a decimal. The minimum value for *size* is 512 KB, and the default if *size* is not specified is 1 MB. When specified with ADD FILE, *size* is the initial size for the file. When specified with MODIFY FILE, *size* is the new size for the file, and must be larger than the current file size.

MAXSIZE
Specifies the maximum file size.

max_size
> Is the maximum file size. The KB, MB, GB, and TB suffixes can be used to specify kilobytes, megabytes, gigabytes, or terabytes. The default is MB. Specify a whole number; do not include a decimal. If *max_size* is not specified, the file size will increase until the disk is full. The Microsoft Windows NT application log warns an administrator when a disk is about to become full.

UNLIMITED
> Specifies that the file increases in size until the disk is full.

FILEGROWTH
> Specifies file increase increment.

growth_increment
> Is the amount of space added to the file each time new space is needed. A value of 0 indicates no increase. The value can be specified in MB, KB, or %. Specify a whole number; do not include a decimal. When % is specified, the increment size is the specified percentage of the file size at the time the increment occurs. If a number is specified without an MB, KB, or % suffix, the default is MB. The default value if FILEGROWTH is not specified is 10%, and the minimum value is 64 KB. The size specified is rounded to the nearest 64 KB.

<state_option>
> Controls user access to the database, whether the database is online, and whether writes are allowed.

SINGLE_USER | RESTRICTED_USER | MULTI_USER
> Controls which users may access the database. When SINGLE_USER is specified, only one user at a time can access the database. When RESTRICTED_USER is specified, only members of the **db_owner**, **dbcreator**, or **sysadmin** roles can use the database. MULTI_USER returns the database to its normal operating state.

OFFLINE | ONLINE
> Controls whether the database is offline or online.

READ_ONLY | READ_WRITE
> Specifies whether the database is in read-only mode. In read-only mode, users can read data from the database, not modify it. The database cannot be in use when READ_ONLY is specified. The **master** database is the exception, and only the system administrator can use **master** while READ_ONLY is set. READ_WRITE returns the database to read/write operations.

<cursor_option>
> Controls cursor options.

CURSOR_CLOSE_ON_COMMIT ON | OFF

If ON is specified, any cursors open when a transaction is committed or rolled back are closed. If OFF is specified, such cursors remain open when a transaction is committed; rolling back a transaction closes any cursors except those defined as INSENSITIVE or STATIC.

CURSOR_DEFAULTLOCAL | GLOBAL

Controls whether cursor scope defaults to LOCAL or GLOBAL.

<auto_option>

Controls automatic options.

AUTO_CLOSE ON | OFF

If ON is specified, the database is shut down cleanly and its resources are freed after the last user exits. If OFF is specified, the database remains open after the last user exits.

AUTO_CREATE_STATISTICS ON | OFF

If ON is specified, any missing statistics needed by a query for optimization are automatically built during optimization.

AUTO_SHRINK ON | OFF

If ON is specified, the database files are candidates for automatic periodic shrinking.

AUTO_UPDATE_STATISTICS ON | OFF

If ON is specified, any out-of-date statistics required by a query for optimization are automatically built during optimization. If OFF is specified, statistics must be updated manually.

<sql_option>

Controls the ANSI compliance options.

ANSI_NULL_DEFAULT ON | OFF

If ON is specified, CREATE TABLE follows SQL-92 rules to determine whether a column allows null values.

ANSI_NULLS ON | OFF

If ON is specified, all comparisons to a null value evaluate to UNKNOWN. If OFF is specified, comparisons of non-UNICODE values to a null value evaluate to TRUE if both values are NULL.

ANSI_PADDING ON | OFF

If ON is specified, strings are padded to the same length before comparison or insert. If OFF is specified, strings are not padded.

ANSI_WARNINGS ON | OFF

If ON is specified, errors or warnings are issued when conditions such as divide-by-zero occur.

ARITHABORT ON | OFF

If ON is specified, a query is terminated when an overflow or divide-by-zero error occurs during query execution.

CONCAT_NULL_YIELDS_NULL ON | OFF

If ON is specified, the result of a concatenation operation is NULL when either operand is NULL. If OFF is specified, the null value is treated as an empty character string. The default is OFF.

QUOTED_IDENTIFIER ON | OFF

If ON is specified, double quotation marks can be used to enclose delimited identifiers.

NUMERIC_ROUNDABORT ON | OFF

If ON is specified, an error is generated when loss of precision occurs in an expression.

RECURSIVE_TRIGGERS ON | OFF

If ON is specified, recursive firing of triggers is allowed.
RECURSIVE_TRIGGERS OFF, the default, prevents direct recursion only. To disable indirect recursion as well, set the **nested triggers** server option to 0 using **sp_configure**.

<recovery_options>

Controls database recovery options.

RECOVERY FULL | BULK_LOGGED | SIMPLE

If FULL is specified, complete protection against media failure is provided. If a data file is damaged, media recovery can restore all committed transactions.

If BULK_LOGGED is specified, protection against media failure is combined with the best performance and least amount of log memory usage for certain large scale or bulk operations. These operations include SELECT INTO, bulk load operations (**bcp** and BULK INSERT), CREATE INDEX, and text and image operations (WRITETEXT and UPDATETEXT).

Under the bulk-logged recovery model, logging for the entire class is minimal and cannot be controlled on an operation-by-operation basis.

If SIMPLE is specified, a simple backup strategy that uses minimal log space is provided. Log space can be automatically reused when no longer needed for server failure recovery.

> **Important** The simple recovery model is easier to manage than the other two models but at the expense of higher data loss exposure if a data file is damaged. All changes since the most recent database or differential database backup are lost and must be re-entered manually.

The default recovery model is determined by the recovery model of the **model** database. To change the default for new databases, use ALTER DATABASE to set the recovery option of the **model** database.

TORN_PAGE_DETECTION ON | OFF

If ON is specified, incomplete pages can be detected. The default is ON.

Remarks

To remove a database, use DROP DATABASE. To rename a database, use
sp_renamedb. For more information about decreasing the size of a database, see
DBCC SHRINKDATABASE.

Before you apply a different or new collation to a database, ensure the following
conditions are in place:

1. You are the only one currently using the database.

2. No schema bound object is dependent on the collation of the database.

   If the following objects, which are dependent on the database collation, exist in the
   database, the ALTER DATABASE database COLLATE statement will fail. SQL Server
   will return an error message for each object blocking the ALTER action:

   - User-defined functions and views created with SCHEMABINDING.

   - Computed columns.

   - CHECK constraints.

   - Table-valued functions that return tables with character columns with collations
     inherited from the default database collation.

3. Altering the database collation does not create duplicates among any system names
   for the database objects.

   These namespaces may cause the failure of a database collation alteration if
   duplicate names result from the changed collation:

   - Object names (such as procedure, table, trigger, or view).

   - Schema names (such as group, role, or user).

   - Scalar-type names (such as system and user-defined types).

   - Full-text catalog names.

   - Column or parameter names within an object.

   - Index names within a table.

   Duplicate names resulting from the new collation will cause the alter action to fail
   and SQL Server will return an error message specifying the namespace where the
   duplicate was found.

You cannot add or remove a file while a BACKUP statement is executing.

To specify a fraction of a megabyte in the size parameters, convert the value to
kilobytes by multiplying the number by 1024. For example, specify 1536 KB instead
of 1.5MB (1.5 x 1024 = 1536).

Permissions

ALTER DATABASE permissions default to members of the **sysadmin** and **dbcreator** fixed server roles, and to members of the **db_owner** fixed database roles. These permissions are not transferable.

Examples

A. Add a file to a database

This example creates a database and alters it to add a new 5-MB data file.

```
USE master
GO
CREATE DATABASE Test1 ON
(
 NAME = Test1dat1,
 FILENAME = 'c:\Program Files\Microsoft SQL Server\MSSQL\Data\t1dat1.ndf',
 SIZE = 5MB,
 MAXSIZE = 100MB,
 FILEGROWTH = 5MB
)
GO
ALTER DATABASE Test1
ADD FILE
(
 NAME = Test1dat2,
 FILENAME = 'c:\Program Files\Microsoft SQL Server\MSSQL\Data\t1dat2.ndf',
 SIZE = 5MB,
 MAXSIZE = 100MB,
 FILEGROWTH = 5MB
)
GO
```

B. Add a filegroup with two files to a database

This example creates a filegroup in the **Test 1** database created in Example A and adds two 5-MB files to the filegroup. It then makes **Test1FG1** the default filegroup.

```
USE master
GO
ALTER DATABASE Test1
ADD FILEGROUP Test1FG1
GO

ALTER DATABASE Test1
ADD FILE
```

(continued)

(continued)

```
( NAME = test1dat3,
  FILENAME = 'c:\Program Files\Microsoft SQL Server\MSSQL\Data\t1dat3.ndf',
  SIZE = 5MB,
  MAXSIZE = 100MB,
  FILEGROWTH = 5MB),
( NAME = test1dat4,
  FILENAME = 'c:\Program Files\Microsoft SQL Server\MSSQL\Data\t1dat4.ndf',
  SIZE = 5MB,
  MAXSIZE = 100MB,
  FILEGROWTH = 5MB)
TO FILEGROUP Test1FG1

ALTER DATABASE Test1
MODIFY FILEGROUP Test1FG1 DEFAULT
GO
```

C. Add two log files to a database

This example adds two 5-MB log files to a database.

```
USE master
GO
ALTER DATABASE Test1
ADD LOG FILE
( NAME = test1log2,
  FILENAME = 'c:\Program Files\Microsoft SQL Server\MSSQL\Data\test2log.ldf',
  SIZE = 5MB,
  MAXSIZE = 100MB,
  FILEGROWTH = 5MB),
( NAME = test1log3,
  FILENAME = 'c:\Program Files\Microsoft SQL Server\MSSQL\Data\test3log.ldf',
  SIZE = 5MB,
  MAXSIZE = 100MB,
  FILEGROWTH = 5MB)
GO
```

D. Remove a file from a database

This example removes one of the files added to the **Test1** database in Example B.

```
USE master
GO
ALTER DATABASE Test1
REMOVE FILE test1dat4
GO
```

E. Modify a file

This example increases the size of one of the files added to the **Test1** database in Example B.

```
USE master
GO
ALTER DATABASE Test1
MODIFY FILE
   (NAME = test1dat3,
   SIZE = 20MB)
GO
```

F. Make the primary filegroup the default

This example makes the primary filegroup the default filegroup if another filegroup was made the default earlier.

```
USE master
GO
ALTER DATABASE MyDatabase
MODIFY FILEGROUP [PRIMARY] DEFAULT
GO
```

Related Topics

CREATE DATABASE, DROP DATABASE, sp_helpdb, sp_helpfile, sp_helpfilegroup, sp_renamedb, sp_spaceused, Using Recovery Models

ALTER FUNCTION

Alters an existing user-defined function, previously created by executing the CREATE FUNCTION statement, without changing permissions and without affecting any dependent functions, stored procedures, or triggers.

For more information about the parameters used in the ALTER FUNCTION statement, see CREATE FUNCTION.

Syntax

Scalar Functions

```
ALTER FUNCTION [ owner_name. ] function_name
   ( [ { @parameter_name scalar_parameter_data_type [ = default ] } [ ,...n ] ] )
RETURNS scalar_return_data_type
[ WITH < function_option> [,...n] ]
[ AS ]
```

(continued)

(continued)

```
BEGIN
    function_body
    RETURN scalar_expression
END
```

Inline Table-valued Functions

```
ALTER FUNCTION [ owner_name. ] function_name
    ( [ { @parameter_name scalar_parameter_data_type [ = default ] } [ ,...n ] ] )
RETURNS TABLE
[ WITH < function_option > [ ,...n ] ]
[ AS ]
RETURN [ ( ] select-stmt [ ) ]
```

Multi-statement Table-valued Functions

```
ALTER FUNCTION [ owner_name. ] function_name
    ( [ { @parameter_name scalar_parameter_data_type [ = default ] } [ ,...n ] ] )
RETURNS @return_variable TABLE < table_type_definition >
[ WITH < function_option > [ ,...n ] ]
[ AS ]
BEGIN
    function_body
    RETURN
END

< function_option > ::=
    { ENCRYPTION | SCHEMABINDING }
< table_type_definition > :: =
    ( { column_definition | table_constraint } [ ,...n ] )
```

Arguments

owner_name

Is the name of the user ID that owns the user-defined function to be changed. *owner_name* must be an existing user ID.

function_name

Is the user-defined function to be changed. Function names must conform to the rules for identifiers and must be unique within the database and to its owner.

@parameter_name

Is a parameter in the user-defined function. One or more parameters can be declared. A function can have a maximum of 1,024 parameters. The value of each declared parameter must be supplied by the user when the function is executed (unless a default for the parameter is defined). When a parameter of the function has a default value, the keyword "default" must be specified when calling the function in order to get the default value. This behavior is different from parameters with default values in stored procedures in which omitting the parameter also implies the default value.

Specify a parameter name using an at sign (@) as the first character. The parameter name must conform to the rules for identifiers. Parameters are local to the function; the same parameter names can be used in other functions. Parameters can take the place only of constants; they cannot be used in place of table names, column names, or the names of other database objects.

scalar_parameter_data_type

Is the parameter data type. All scalar data types, including **bigint** and **sql_variant**, can be used as a parameter for user-defined functions. The **timestamp** data type is not supported. Nonscalar types such as **cursor** and **table** cannot be specified.

scalar_return_data_type

Is the return value of a scalar user-defined function. *scalar_return_data_type* can be any of the scalar data types supported by SQL Server, except **text**, **ntext**, **image**, and **timestamp**.

scalar_expression

Specifies that the scalar function returns a scalar value.

TABLE

Specifies that the return value of the table-valued function is a table.

In inline table-valued functions, the TABLE return value is defined through a single SELECT statement. Inline functions do not have associated return variables.

In multi-statement table-valued functions, *@return_variable* is a TABLE variable, used to store and accumulate the rows that should be returned as the value of the function.

function_body

Specifies that a series of Transact-SQL statements, which together do not produce a side effect, define the value of the function. *function_body* is used only in scalar functions and multi-statement table-valued functions.

In scalar functions, *function_body* is a series of Transact-SQL statements that together evaluate to a scalar value.

In multi-statement table-valued functions, *function_body* is a series of Transact-SQL statements that populate a table return variable.

select-stmt

Is the single SELECT statement that defines the return value of an inline table-valued function.

ENCRYPTION

Indicates that SQL Server encrypts the system table columns containing the text of the CREATE FUNCTION statement. Using ENCRYPTION prevents the function from being published as part of SQL Server replication.

SCHEMABINDING

Specifies that the function is bound to the database objects that it references. This condition will prevent changes to the function if other schema bound objects are referencing it.

The binding of the function to the objects it references is removed only when one of two actions take place:

- The function is dropped.

- The function is altered (using the ALTER statement) with the SCHEMABINDING option not specified.

For a list of conditions that must be met before a function can be schema bound, see CREATE FUNCTION.

Remarks

ALTER FUNCTION cannot be used to change a scalar-valued function to a table-valued function, or vice versa. Also, ALTER FUNCTION cannot be used to change an inline function to a multistatement function, or vice versa.

Permissions

ALTER FUNCTION permissions default to members of the **sysadmin** fixed server role, and the **db_owner** and **db_ddladmin** fixed database roles, and the owner of the function, and are not transferable.

Owners of functions have EXECUTE permission on their functions. However, other users may be granted such permissions as well.

Related Topics

CREATE FUNCTION, DROP FUNCTION

ALTER PROCEDURE

Alters a previously created procedure, created by executing the CREATE PROCEDURE statement, without changing permissions and without affecting any dependent stored procedures or triggers. For more information about the parameters used in the ALTER PROCEDURE statement, see CREATE PROCEDURE.

Syntax

```
ALTER PROC [ EDURE ] procedure_name [ ; number ]
   [ { @parameter data_type }
      [ VARYING ] [ = default ] [ OUTPUT ]
   ] [ ,...n ]
[ WITH
   { RECOMPILE | ENCRYPTION
      | RECOMPILE , ENCRYPTION
   }
]
[ FOR REPLICATION ]
AS
   sql_statement [ ...n ]
```

Arguments

procedure_name
> Is the name of the procedure to change. Procedure names must conform to the rules for identifiers.

;number
> Is an existing optional integer used to group procedures of the same name so that they can be dropped together with a single DROP PROCEDURE statement.

@parameter
> Is a parameter in the procedure.

data_type
> Is the data type of the parameter.

VARYING
> Specifies the result set supported as an output parameter (constructed dynamically by the stored procedure and whose contents can vary). Applies only to cursor parameters.

default

Is a default value for the parameter.

OUTPUT

Indicates that the parameter is a return parameter.

n

Is a placeholder indicating up to 2,100 parameters can be specified.

{RECOMPILE | ENCRYPTION | RECOMPILE, ENCRYPTION}

RECOMPILE indicates that Microsoft SQL Server does not cache a plan for this procedure and the procedure is recompiled at run time.

ENCRYPTION indicates that SQL Server encrypts the **syscomments** table entry that contains the text of the ALTER PROCEDURE statement. Using ENCRYPTION prevents the procedure from being published as part of SQL Server replication.

> **Note** During an upgrade, SQL Server uses the encrypted comments stored in **syscomments** to re-create encrypted procedures.

FOR REPLICATION

Specifies that stored procedures created for replication cannot be executed on the Subscriber. A stored procedure created with the FOR REPLICATION option is used as a stored procedure filter and only executed during replication. This option cannot be used with the WITH RECOMPILE option.

AS

Are the actions the procedure is to take.

sql_statement

Is any number and type of Transact-SQL statements to be included in the procedure. Some limitations do apply. For more information, see *sql_statement* Limitations in CREATE PROCEDURE.

n

Is a placeholder indicating that multiple Transact-SQL statements can be included in the procedure. For more information, see CREATE PROCEDURE.

Remarks

For more information about ALTER PROCEDURE, see Remarks in CREATE PROCEDURE.

> **Note** If a previous procedure definition was created using WITH ENCRYPTION or WITH RECOMPILE, these options are only enabled if they are included in ALTER PROCEDURE.

Permissions

ALTER PROCEDURE permissions default to members of the **sysadmin** fixed server role, and the **db_owner** and **db_ddladmin** fixed database roles, and the owner of the procedure, and are not transferable.

Permissions and the startup property remain unchanged for a procedure modified with ALTER PROCEDURE.

Examples

This example creates a procedure called **Oakland_authors** that, by default, contains all authors from the city of Oakland, California. Permissions are granted. Then, when the procedure must be changed to retrieve all authors from California, ALTER PROCEDURE is used to redefine the stored procedure.

```
USE pubs
GO
IF EXISTS(SELECT name FROM sysobjects WHERE name = 'Oakland_authors' AND type = 'P')
    DROP PROCEDURE Oakland_authors
GO
-- Create a procedure from the authors table that contains author
-- information for those authors who live in Oakland, California.
USE pubs
GO
CREATE PROCEDURE Oakland_authors
AS
SELECT au_fname, au_lname, address, city, zip
FROM pubs..authors
WHERE city = 'Oakland'
and state = 'CA'
ORDER BY au_lname, au_fname
GO
-- Here is the statement to actually see the text of the procedure.
SELECT o.id, c.text
FROM sysobjects o INNER JOIN syscomments c ON o.id = c.id
WHERE o.type = 'P' and o.name = 'Oakland_authors'
-- Here, EXECUTE permissions are granted on the procedure to public.
GRANT EXECUTE ON Oakland_authors TO public
GO
-- The procedure must be changed to include all
-- authors from California, regardless of what city they live in.
-- If ALTER PROCEDURE is not used but the procedure is dropped
-- and then re-created, the above GRANT statement and any
-- other statements dealing with permissions that pertain to this
-- procedure must be re-entered.
```

(continued)

(continued)

```
ALTER PROCEDURE Oakland_authors
WITH ENCRYPTION
AS
SELECT au_fname, au_lname, address, city, zip
FROM pubs..authors
WHERE state = 'CA'
ORDER BY au_lname, au_fname
GO
-- Here is the statement to actually see the text of the procedure.
SELECT o.id, c.text
FROM sysobjects o INNER JOIN syscomments c ON o.id = c.id
WHERE o.type = 'P' and o.name = 'Oakland_authors'
GO
```

Related Topics

Data Types, DROP PROCEDURE, EXECUTE, Programming Stored Procedures,
System Tables, Using Identifiers

ALTER TABLE

Modifies a table definition by altering, adding, or dropping columns and constraints, or
by disabling or enabling constraints and triggers.

Syntax

```
ALTER TABLE table
{ [ ALTER COLUMN column_name
    { new_data_type [ ( precision [ , scale ] ) ]
      [ COLLATE < collation_name > ]
      [ NULL | NOT NULL ]
      | {ADD | DROP } ROWGUIDCOL }
    ]
  | ADD
      { [ < column_definition > ]
      |   column_name AS computed_column_expression
      } [ ,...n ]
  | [ WITH CHECK | WITH NOCHECK ] ADD
      { < table_constraint > } [ ,...n ]
  | DROP
      { [ CONSTRAINT ] constraint_name
        | COLUMN column } [ ,...n ]
```

(continued)

(continued)

```
    | { CHECK | NOCHECK } CONSTRAINT
        { ALL | constraint_name [ ,...n ] }
    | { ENABLE | DISABLE } TRIGGER
        { ALL | trigger_name [ ,...n ] }
}
< column_definition > ::=
    { column_name data_type }
    [ [ DEFAULT constant_expression ] [ WITH VALUES ]
    | [ IDENTITY [ (seed , increment ) [ NOT FOR REPLICATION ] ] ]
        ]
    [ ROWGUIDCOL ]
    [ COLLATE < collation_name > ]
    [ < column_constraint > ] [ ...n ]
< column_constraint > ::=
    [ CONSTRAINT constraint_name ]
    { [ NULL | NOT NULL ]
        | [ { PRIMARY KEY | UNIQUE }
            [ CLUSTERED | NONCLUSTERED ]
            [ WITH FILLFACTOR = fillfactor ]
            [ ON { filegroup | DEFAULT } ]
            ]
        | [ [ FOREIGN KEY ]
            REFERENCES ref_table [ ( ref_column ) ]
            [ ON DELETE { CASCADE | NO ACTION } ]
            [ ON UPDATE { CASCADE | NO ACTION } ]
            [ NOT FOR REPLICATION ]
            ]
        | CHECK [ NOT FOR REPLICATION ]
            ( logical_expression )
    }
< table_constraint > ::=
    [ CONSTRAINT constraint_name ]
    { [ { PRIMARY KEY | UNIQUE }
        [ CLUSTERED | NONCLUSTERED ]
        { ( column [ ,...n ] ) }
        [ WITH FILLFACTOR = fillfactor ]
        [ ON {filegroup | DEFAULT } ]
        ]
        | FOREIGN KEY
            [ ( column [ ,...n ] ) ]
            REFERENCES ref_table [ ( ref_column [ ,...n ] ) ]
            [ ON DELETE { CASCADE | NO ACTION } ]
```

(continued)

(continued)

```
        [ ON UPDATE { CASCADE | NO ACTION } ]
        [ NOT FOR REPLICATION ]
    | DEFAULT constant_expression
        [ FOR column ] [ WITH VALUES ]
    | CHECK [ NOT FOR REPLICATION ]
        ( search_conditions )
}
```

Arguments

table

Is the name of the table to be altered. If the table is not in the current database or owned by the current user, the database and owner can be explicitly specified.

ALTER COLUMN

Specifies that the given column is to be changed or altered. ALTER COLUMN is not allowed if the compatibility level is 65 or earlier. For more information, see sp_dbcmptlevel.

The altered column cannot be:

- A column with a **text**, **image**, **ntext**, or **timestamp** data type.

- The ROWGUIDCOL for the table.

- A computed column or used in a computed column.

- A replicated column.

- Used in an index, unless the column is a **varchar**, **nvarchar**, or **varbinary** data type, the data type is not changed, and the new size is equal to or larger than the old size.

- Used in statistics generated by the CREATE STATISTICS statement. First remove the statistics using the DROP STATISTICS statement. Statistics automatically generated by the query optimizer are automatically dropped by ALTER COLUMN.

- Used in a PRIMARY KEY or [FOREIGN KEY] REFERENCES constraint.

- Used in a CHECK or UNIQUE constraint, except that altering the length of a variable-length column used in a CHECK or UNIQUE constraint is allowed.

- Associated with a default, except that changing the length, precision, or scale of a column is allowed if the data type is not changed.

Some data type changes may result in a change in the data. For example, changing an **nchar** or **nvarchar** column to **char** or **varchar** can result in the conversion of extended characters. For more information, see CAST and CONVERT. Reducing the precision and scale of a column may result in data truncation.

column_name

Is the name of the column to be altered, added, or dropped. For new columns, *column_name* can be omitted for columns created with a **timestamp** data type. The name **timestamp** is used if no *column_name* is specified for a **timestamp** data type column.

new_data_type

Is the new data type for the altered column. Criteria for the *new_data_type* of an altered column are:

- The previous data type must be implicitly convertible to the new data type.

- *new_data_type* cannot be **timestamp**.

- ANSI null defaults are always on for ALTER COLUMN; if not specified, the column is nullable.

- ANSI padding is always on for ALTER COLUMN.

- If the altered column is an identity column, *new_data_type* must be a data type that supports the identity property.

- The current setting for SET ARITHABORT is ignored. ALTER TABLE operates as if the ARITHABORT option is ON.

precision

Is the precision for the specified data type. For more information about valid precision values, see Precision, Scale, and Length.

scale

Is the scale for the specified data type. For more information about valid scale values, see Precision, Scale, and Length.

COLLATE < *collation_name* >

Specifies the new collation for the altered column. Collation name can be either a Windows collation name or a SQL collation name. For a list and more information, see Windows Collation Name and SQL Collation Name.

The COLLATE clause can be used to alter the collations only of columns of the **char**, **varchar**, **text**, **nchar**, **nvarchar**, and **ntext** data types. If not specified, the column is assigned the default collation of the database.

ALTER COLUMN cannot have a collation change if any of the following conditions apply:

- If a check constraint, foreign key constraint, or computed columns reference the column changed.

- If any index, statistics, or full-text index are created on the column. Statistics created automatically on the column changed will be dropped if the column collation is altered.

- If a SCHEMABOUND view or function references the column.

For more information about the COLLATE clause, see COLLATE.

NULL | NOT NULL

Specifies whether the column can accept null values. Columns that do not allow null values can be added with ALTER TABLE only if they have a default specified. A new column added to a table must either allow null values, or the column must be specified with a default value.

If the new column allows null values and no default is specified, the new column contains a null value for each row in the table. If the new column allows null values and a default definition is added with the new column, the WITH VALUES option can be used to store the default value in the new column for each existing row in the table.

If the new column does not allow null values, a DEFAULT definition must be added with the new column, and the new column automatically loads with the default value in the new columns in each existing row.

NULL can be specified in ALTER COLUMN to make a NOT NULL column allow null values, except for columns in PRIMARY KEY constraints. NOT NULL can be specified in ALTER COLUMN only if the column contains no null values. The null values must be updated to some value before the ALTER COLUMN NOT NULL is allowed, such as:

```
UPDATE MyTable SET NullCol = N'some_value' WHERE NullCol IS NULL

ALTER TABLE MyTable ALTER COLUMN NullCol NVARCHAR(20) NOT NULL
```

If NULL or NOT NULL is specified with ALTER COLUMN, *new_data_type* [(*precision* [, *scale*])] must also be specified. If the data type, precision, and scale are not changed, specify the current column values.

[{ADD | DROP} ROWGUIDCOL]

Specifies the ROWGUIDCOL property is added to or dropped from the specified column. ROWGUIDCOL is a keyword indicating that the column is a row global unique identifier column. Only one **uniqueidentifier** column per table can be designated as the ROWGUIDCOL column. The ROWGUIDCOL property can be assigned only to a **uniqueidentifier** column.

The ROWGUIDCOL property does not enforce uniqueness of the values stored in the column. It also does not automatically generate values for new rows inserted into the table. To generate unique values for each column, either use the NEWID function on INSERT statements or specify the NEWID function as the default for the column.

ADD

Specifies that one or more column definitions, computed column definitions, or table constraints are added.

computed_column_expression

Is an expression that defines the value of a computed column. A computed column is a virtual column not physically stored in the table but computed from an expression using other columns in the same table. For example, a computed column could have the definition: **cost AS price * qty**. The expression can be a noncomputed column name, constant, function, variable, and any combination of these connected by one or more operators. The expression cannot be a subquery.

Computed columns can be used in select lists, WHERE clauses, ORDER BY clauses, or any other locations where regular expressions can be used, with these exceptions:

- A computed column cannot be used as a DEFAULT or FOREIGN KEY constraint definition or with a NOT NULL constraint definition. However, a computed column can be used as a key column in an index or as part of any PRIMARY KEY or UNIQUE constraint, if the computed column value is defined by a deterministic expression and the data type of the result is allowed in index columns.

  For example, if the table has integer columns **a** and **b**, the computed column **a+b** may be indexed but computed column **a+DATEPART(dd, GETDATE())** cannot be indexed because the value may change in subsequent invocations.

- A computed column cannot be the target of an INSERT or UPDATE statement.

  Note Because each row in a table may have different values for columns involved in a computed column, the computed column may not have the same result for each row.

n

Is a placeholder indicating that the preceding item can be repeated *n* number of times.

WITH CHECK | WITH NOCHECK

Specifies whether the data in the table is or is not validated against a newly added or re-enabled FOREIGN KEY or CHECK constraint. If not specified, WITH CHECK is assumed for new constraints, and WITH NOCHECK is assumed for re-enabled constraints.

The WITH CHECK and WITH NOCHECK clauses cannot be used for PRIMARY KEY and UNIQUE constraints.

If you do not want to verify new CHECK or FOREIGN KEY constraints against existing data, use WITH NOCHECK. This is not recommended except in rare cases. The new constraint will be evaluated in all future updates. Any constraint violations suppressed by WITH NOCHECK when the constraint is added may cause future updates to fail if they update rows with data that does not comply with the constraint.

Constraints defined WITH NOCHECK are not considered by the query optimizer. These constraints are ignored until all such constraints are re-enabled using ALTER TABLE *table* CHECK CONSTRAINT ALL.

DROP { [CONSTRAINT] *constraint_name* | COLUMN *column_name* }
Specifies that *constraint_name* or *column_name* is removed from the table. DROP COLUMN is not allowed if the compatibility level is 65 or earlier. Multiple columns and constraints can be listed. A column cannot be dropped if it is:

- A replicated column.

- Used in an index.

- Used in a CHECK, FOREIGN KEY, UNIQUE, or PRIMARY KEY constraint.

- Associated with a default defined with the DEFAULT keyword, or bound to a default object.

- Bound to a rule.

{ CHECK | NOCHECK} CONSTRAINT
Specifies that *constraint_name* is enabled or disabled. When disabled, future inserts or updates to the column are not validated against the constraint conditions. This option can only be used with FOREIGN KEY and CHECK constraints.

ALL
Specifies that all constraints are disabled with the NOCHECK option, or enabled with the CHECK option.

{ENABLE | DISABLE} TRIGGER
Specifies that *trigger_name* is enabled or disabled. When a trigger is disabled it is still defined for the table; however, when INSERT, UPDATE, or DELETE statements are executed against the table, the actions in the trigger are not performed until the trigger is re-enabled.

ALL
Specifies that all triggers in the table are enabled or disabled.

trigger_name
Specifies the name of the trigger to disable or enable.

column_name data_type
Is the data type for the new column. *data_type* can be any Microsoft SQL Server or user-defined data type.

DEFAULT
Is a keyword that specifies the default value for the column. DEFAULT definitions can be used to provide values for a new column in the existing rows of data. DEFAULT definitions cannot be added to columns that have a **timestamp** data type, an IDENTITY property, an existing DEFAULT definition, or a bound default. If the column has an existing default, the default must be dropped before the new default can be added. To maintain compatibility with earlier versions of SQL Server, it is possible to assign a constraint name to a DEFAULT.

IDENTITY

Specifies that the new column is an identity column. When a new row is added to the table, SQL Server provides a unique, incremental value for the column. Identity columns are commonly used in conjunction with PRIMARY KEY constraints to serve as the unique row identifier for the table. The IDENTITY property can be assigned to a **tinyint**, **smallint**, **int**, **bigint**, **decimal(p,0)**, or **numeric(p,0)** column. Only one identity column can be created per table. The DEFAULT keyword and bound defaults cannot be used with an identity column. Either both the seed and increment must be specified, or neither. If neither are specified, the default is (1,1).

Seed

Is the value used for the first row loaded into the table.

Increment

Is the incremental value added to the identity value of the previous row loaded.

NOT FOR REPLICATION

Specifies that the IDENTITY property should not be enforced when a replication login, such as **sqlrepl**, inserts data into the table. NOT FOR REPLICATION can also be specified on constraints. The constraint is not checked when a replication login inserts data into the table.

CONSTRAINT

Specifies the beginning of a PRIMARY KEY, UNIQUE, FOREIGN KEY, or CHECK constraint, or a DEFAULT definition.

constraint_name

Is the new constraint. Constraint names must follow the rules for identifiers, except that the name cannot begin with a number sign (#). If *constraint_name* is not supplied, a system-generated name is assigned to the constraint.

PRIMARY KEY

Is a constraint that enforces entity integrity for a given column or columns through a unique index. Only one PRIMARY KEY constraint can be created for each table.

UNIQUE

Is a constraint that provides entity integrity for a given column or columns through a unique index.

CLUSTERED | NONCLUSTERED

Specifies that a clustered or nonclustered index is created for the PRIMARY KEY or UNIQUE constraint. PRIMARY KEY constraints default to CLUSTERED; UNIQUE constraints default to NONCLUSTERED.

If a clustered constraint or index already exists on a table, CLUSTERED cannot be specified in ALTER TABLE. If a clustered constraint or index already exists on a table, PRIMARY KEY constraints default to NONCLUSTERED.

WITH FILLFACTOR = *fillfactor*

Specifies how full SQL Server should make each index page used to store the index data. User-specified *fillfactor* values can be from 1 through 100. If a value is not specified, the default is 0. A lower *fillfactor* value creates an index with more space available for new index entries without having to allocate new space. For more information, see CREATE INDEX.

ON { *filegroup* **| DEFAULT}**

Specifies the storage location of the index created for the constraint. If *filegroup* is specified, the index is created in the named filegroup. If DEFAULT is specified, the index is created in the default filegroup. If ON is not specified, the index is created in the filegroup that contains the table. If ON is specified when adding a clustered index for a PRIMARY KEY or UNIQUE constraint, the entire table is moved to the specified filegroup when the clustered index is created.

DEFAULT, in this context, is not a keyword. DEFAULT is an identifier for the default filegroup and must be delimited, as in ON "DEFAULT" or ON [DEFAULT].

FOREIGN KEY...REFERENCES

Is a constraint that provides referential integrity for the data in the column. FOREIGN KEY constraints require that each value in the column exists in the specified column in the referenced table.

ref_table

Is the table referenced by the FOREIGN KEY constraint.

ref_column

Is a column or list of columns in parentheses referenced by the new FOREIGN KEY constraint.

ON DELETE {CASCADE | NO ACTION}

Specifies what action occurs to a row in the table altered, if that row has a referential relationship and the referenced row is deleted from the parent table. The default is NO ACTION.

If CASCADE is specified, a row is deleted from the referencing table if that row is deleted from the parent table. If NO ACTION is specified, SQL Server raises an error and the delete action on the row in the parent table is rolled back.

The CASCADE action ON DELETE cannot be defined if an INSTEAD OF trigger ON DELETE already exists on the table in question.

For example, in the **Northwind** database, the **Orders** table has a referential relationship with the **Customers** table. The **Orders.CustomerID** foreign key references the **Customers.CustomerID** primary key.

If a DELETE statement is executed on a row in the **Customers** table, and an ON DELETE CASCADE action is specified for **Orders.CustomerID**, SQL Server checks for one or more dependent rows in the **Orders** table. If any exist, the dependent row in the **Orders** table will be deleted, as well as the row referenced in the **Customers** table.

On the other hand, if NO ACTION is specified, SQL Server raises an error and rolls back the delete action on the **Customers** row if there is at least one row in the **Orders** table that references it.

ON UPDATE {CASCADE | NO ACTION}

Specifies what action occurs to a row in the table altered, if that row has a referential relationship and the referenced row is updated in the parent table. The default is NO ACTION.

If CASCADE is specified, the row is updated in the referencing table if that row is updated in the parent table. If NO ACTION is specified, SQL Server raises an error and the update action on the row in the parent table is rolled back.

The CASCADE action ON UPDATE cannot be defined if an INSTEAD OF trigger ON UPDATE already exists on the table in question.

For example, in the **Northwind** database, the **Orders** table has a referential relationship with the **Customers** table. The **Orders.CustomerID** foreign key references the **Customers.CustomerID** primary key.

If an UPDATE statement is executed on a row in the **Customers** table, and an ON UPDATE CASCADE action is specified for **Orders.CustomerID**, SQL Server checks for one or more dependent rows in the **Orders** table. If any exist, the dependent row in the **Orders** table will be updated, as well as the row referenced in the **Customers** table.

On the other hand, if NO ACTION is specified, SQL Server raises an error and rolls back the update action on the **Customers** row if there is at least one row in the **Orders** table that references it.

[ASC | DESC]

Specifies the order in which the column or columns participating in table constraints are sorted. The default is ASC.

WITH VALUES

Specifies that the value given in DEFAULT *constant_expression* is stored in a new column added to existing rows. WITH VALUES can be specified only when DEFAULT is specified in an ADD column clause. If the added column allows null values and WITH VALUES is specified, the default value is stored in the new column added to existing rows. If WITH VALUES is not specified for columns that allow nulls, the value NULL is stored in the new column in existing rows. If the new column does not allow nulls, the default value is stored in new rows regardless of whether WITH VALUES is specified.

column[,...n]

Is a column or list of columns in parentheses used in a new constraint.

constant_expression

Is a literal value, a NULL, or a system function used as the default column value.

FOR *column*

Specifies the column associated with a table-level DEFAULT definition.

CHECK

Is a constraint that enforces domain integrity by limiting the possible values that can be entered into a column or columns.

logical_expression

Is a logical expression used in a CHECK constraint and returns TRUE or FALSE. *Logical_expression* used with CHECK constraints cannot reference another table but can reference other columns in the same table for the same row.

Remarks

To add new rows of data, use the INSERT statement. To remove rows of data, use the DELETE or TRUNCATE TABLE statements. To change the values in existing rows, use UPDATE.

The changes specified in ALTER TABLE are implemented immediately. If the changes require modifications of the rows in the table, ALTER TABLE updates the rows. ALTER TABLE acquires a schema modify lock on the table to ensure no other connections reference even the meta data for the table during the change. The modifications made to the table are logged and fully recoverable. Changes that affect all the rows in very large tables, such as dropping a column or adding a NOT NULL column with a default, can take a long time to complete and generate many log records. These ALTER TABLE statements should be executed with the same care as any INSERT, UPDATE, or DELETE statement that affects a large number of rows.

If there are any execution plans in the procedure cache referencing the table, ALTER TABLE marks them to be recompiled on their next execution.

If the ALTER TABLE statement specifies changes on column values referenced by other tables, either of two events occurs depending on the action specified by ON UPDATE or ON DELETE in the referencing tables.

- If no value or NO ACTION (the default) is specified in the referencing tables, an ALTER TABLE statement against the parent table that causes a change to the column value referenced by the other tables will be rolled back and SQL Server raises an error.

- If CASCADE is specified in the referencing tables, changes caused by an ALTER TABLE statement against the parent table are applied to the parent table and its dependents.

ALTER TABLE statements that add a **sql_variant** column can generate the following warning:

```
The total row size (xx) for table 'yy' exceeds the maximum number of bytes per row (8060).
Rows that exceed the maximum number of bytes will not be added.
```

This warning occurs because **sql_variant** can have a maximum length of 8016 bytes. When a **sql_variant** column contains values close to the maximum length, it can overshoot the row's maximum size limit.

The restrictions that apply to ALTER TABLE statements on tables with schema bound views are the same as the restrictions currently applied when altering tables with a simple index. Adding a column is allowed. However, removing or changing a column that participates in any schema bound view is not allowed. If the ALTER TABLE statement requires altering a column used in a schema bound view, the alter action fails and SQL Server raises an error message. For more information about SCHEMABINDING and indexed views, see CREATE VIEW.

Adding or removing triggers on base tables is not affected by creating a schema bound view referencing the tables.

Indexes created as part of a constraint are dropped when the constraint is dropped. Indexes that were created with CREATE INDEX must be dropped with the DROP INDEX statement. The DBCC DBREINDEX statement can be used to rebuild an index part of a constraint definition; the constraint does not need to be dropped and added again with ALTER TABLE.

All indexes and constraints based on a column must be removed before the column can be removed.

When constraints are added, all existing data is verified for constraint violations. If any violations occur, the ALTER TABLE statement fails and an error is returned.

When a new PRIMARY KEY or UNIQUE constraint is added to an existing column, the data in the column(s) must be unique. If duplicate values are found, the ALTER TABLE statement fails. The WITH NOCHECK option has no effect when adding PRIMARY KEY or UNIQUE constraints.

Each PRIMARY KEY and UNIQUE constraint generates an index. The number of UNIQUE and PRIMARY KEY constraints cannot cause the number of indexes on the table to exceed 249 nonclustered indexes and 1 clustered index.

If a column is added having a **uniqueidentifier** data type, it can be defined with a default that uses the NEWID() function to supply the unique identifier values in the new column for each existing row in the table.

SQL Server does not enforce an order in which DEFAULT, IDENTITY, ROWGUIDCOL, or column constraints are specified in a column definition.

The ALTER COLUMN clause of ALTER TABLE does not bind or unbind any rules on a column. Rules must be bound or unbound separately using **sp_bindrule** or **sp_unbindrule**.

Rules can be bound to a user-defined data type. CREATE TABLE then automatically binds the rule to any column defined having the user-defined data type. ALTER COLUMN does not unbind the rule when changing the column data type. The rule from the original user-defined data type remains bound to the column. After ALTER COLUMN has changed the data type of the column, any subsequent **sp_unbindrule** execution that unbinds the rule from the user-defined data type does not unbind it from the column for which data type was changed. If ALTER COLUMN changes the data type of a column to a user-defined data type bound to a rule, the rule bound to the new data type is not bound to the column.

Permissions

ALTER TABLE permissions default to the table owner, members of the **sysadmin** fixed server role, and the **db_owner** and **db_ddladmin** fixed database roles, and are not transferable.

Examples

A. Alter a table to add a new column

This example adds a column that allows null values and has no values provided through a DEFAULT definition. Each row will have a NULL in the new column.

```
CREATE TABLE doc_exa ( column_a INT)
GO
ALTER TABLE doc_exa ADD column_b VARCHAR(20) NULL
GO
EXEC sp_help doc_exa
GO
DROP TABLE doc_exa
GO
```

B. Alter a table to drop a column

This example modifies a table to remove a column.

```
CREATE TABLE doc_exb ( column_a INT, column_b VARCHAR(20) NULL)
GO
ALTER TABLE doc_exb DROP COLUMN column_b
GO
EXEC sp_help doc_exb
GO
DROP TABLE doc_exb
GO
```

C. Alter a table to add a column with a constraint

This example adds a new column with a UNIQUE constraint.

```
CREATE TABLE doc_exc ( column_a INT)
GO
ALTER TABLE doc_exc ADD column_b VARCHAR(20) NULL
    CONSTRAINT exb_unique UNIQUE
GO
EXEC sp_help doc_exc
GO
DROP TABLE doc_exc
GO
```

D. Alter a table to add an unverified constraint

This example adds a constraint to an existing column in the table. The column has a value that violates the constraint; therefore, WITH NOCHECK is used to prevent the constraint from being validated against existing rows, and to allow the constraint to be added.

```
CREATE TABLE doc_exd ( column_a INT)
GO
INSERT INTO doc_exd VALUES (-1)
GO
ALTER TABLE doc_exd WITH NOCHECK
ADD CONSTRAINT exd_check CHECK (column_a > 1)
GO
EXEC sp_help doc_exd
GO
DROP TABLE doc_exd
GO
```

E. Alter a table to add several columns with constraints

This example adds several columns with constraints defined with the new column. The first new column has an IDENTITY property; each row in the table has new incremental values in the identity column.

```
CREATE TABLE doc_exe ( column_a INT CONSTRAINT column_a_un UNIQUE)
GO
ALTER TABLE doc_exe ADD

/* Add a PRIMARY KEY identity column. */
column_b INT IDENTITY
CONSTRAINT column_b_pk PRIMARY KEY,
```

(continued)

217

(continued)

```
/* Add a column referencing another column in the same table. */
column_c INT NULL
CONSTRAINT column_c_fk
REFERENCES doc_exe(column_a),

/* Add a column with a constraint to enforce that    */
/* nonnull data is in a valid phone number format.   */
column_d VARCHAR(16) NULL
CONSTRAINT column_d_chk
CHECK
(column_d IS NULL OR
column_d LIKE "[0-9][0-9][0-9]-[0-9][0-9][0-9][0-9]" OR
column_d LIKE
"([0-9][0-9][0-9]) [0-9][0-9][0-9]-[0-9][0-9][0-9][0-9]"),

/* Add a nonnull column with a default. */
column_e DECIMAL(3,3)
CONSTRAINT column_e_default
DEFAULT .081
GO
EXEC sp_help doc_exe
GO
DROP TABLE doc_exe
GO
```

F. Add a nullable column with default values

This example adds a nullable column with a DEFAULT definition, and uses WITH VALUES to provide values for each existing row in the table. If WITH VALUES is not used, each row has the value NULL in the new column.

```
ALTER TABLE MyTable
ADD AddDate smalldatetime NULL
CONSTRAINT AddDateDflt
DEFAULT getdate() WITH VALUES
```

G. Disable and reenable a constraint

This example disables a constraint that limits the salaries accepted in the data. WITH NOCHECK CONSTRAINT is used with ALTER TABLE to disable the constraint and allow an insert that would normally violate the constraint. WITH CHECK CONSTRAINT re-enables the constraint.

```
CREATE TABLE cnst_example
(id INT NOT NULL,
 name VARCHAR(10) NOT NULL,
 salary MONEY NOT NULL
    CONSTRAINT salary_cap CHECK (salary < 100000)
)

-- Valid inserts
INSERT INTO cnst_example VALUES (1,"Joe Brown",65000)
INSERT INTO cnst_example VALUES (2,"Mary Smith",75000)

-- This insert violates the constraint.
INSERT INTO cnst_example VALUES (3,"Pat Jones",105000)

-- Disable the constraint and try again.
ALTER TABLE cnst_example NOCHECK CONSTRAINT salary_cap
INSERT INTO cnst_example VALUES (3,"Pat Jones",105000)

-- Reenable the constraint and try another insert, will fail.
ALTER TABLE cnst_example CHECK CONSTRAINT salary_cap
INSERT INTO cnst_example VALUES (4,"Eric James",110000)
```

H. Disable and reenable a trigger

This example uses the DISABLE TRIGGER option of ALTER TABLE to disable the
trigger and allow an insert that would normally violate the trigger. It then uses
ENABLE TRIGGER to re-enable the trigger.

```
CREATE TABLE trig_example
(id INT,
name VARCHAR(10),
salary MONEY)
go
-- Create the trigger.
CREATE TRIGGER trig1 ON trig_example FOR INSERT
as
IF (SELECT COUNT(*) FROM INSERTED
WHERE salary > 100000) > 0
BEGIN
print "TRIG1 Error: you attempted to insert a salary > $100,000"
ROLLBACK TRANSACTION
END
GO
-- Attempt an insert that violates the trigger.
INSERT INTO trig_example VALUES (1,"Pat Smith",100001)
```

(continued)

(continued)

```
GO
-- Disable the trigger.
ALTER TABLE trig_example DISABLE TRIGGER trig1
GO
-- Attempt an insert that would normally violate the trigger
INSERT INTO trig_example VALUES (2,"Chuck Jones",100001)
GO
-- Re-enable the trigger.
ALTER TABLE trig_example ENABLE TRIGGER trig1
GO
-- Attempt an insert that violates the trigger.
INSERT INTO trig_example VALUES (3,"Mary Booth",100001)
GO
```

Related Topics

DROP TABLE, sp_help

ALTER TRIGGER

Alters the definition of a trigger created previously by the CREATE TRIGGER
statement. For more information about the parameters used in the ALTER TRIGGER
statement, see CREATE TRIGGER.

Syntax

```
ALTER TRIGGER trigger_name
ON ( table | view )
[ WITH ENCRYPTION ]
{
   { ( FOR | AFTER | INSTEAD OF ) { [ DELETE ] [ , ] [ INSERT ] [ , ] [ UPDATE ] }
     [ NOT FOR REPLICATION ]
     AS
     sql_statement [ ...n ]
   }
   |
   { ( FOR | AFTER | INSTEAD OF ) { [ INSERT ] [ , ] [ UPDATE ] }
     [ NOT FOR REPLICATION ]
     AS
     { IF UPDATE ( column )
     [ { AND | OR } UPDATE ( column ) ]
     [ ...n ]
```

(continued)

(continued)

```
    | IF ( COLUMNS_UPDATED ( ) { bitwise_operator } updated_bitmask )
    { comparison_operator } column_bitmask [ ...n ]
    }
    sql_statement [ ...n ]
  }
}
```

Arguments

trigger_name
> Is the existing trigger to alter.

table | view
> Is the table or view on which the trigger is executed.

WITH ENCRYPTION
> Encrypts the **syscomments** entries that contain the text of the ALTER TRIGGER
> statement. Using WITH ENCRYPTION prevents the trigger from being published
> as part of SQL Server replication.
>
> > **Note** If a previous trigger definition was created using WITH ENCRYPTION
> > or RECOMPILE, these options are only enabled if they are included in ALTER
> > TRIGGER.

AFTER
> Specifies that the trigger is fired only after the triggering SQL statement is
> executed successfully. All referential cascade actions and constraint checks also
> must have been successful before this trigger executes.
>
> AFTER is the default, if only the FOR keyword is specified.
>
> AFTER triggers may be defined only on tables.

INSTEAD OF
> Specifies that the trigger is executed instead of the triggering SQL statement, thus
> overriding the actions of the triggering statements.
>
> At most, one INSTEAD OF trigger per INSERT, UPDATE, or DELETE statement
> can be defined on a table or view. However, it is possible to define views on views
> where each view has its own INSTEAD OF trigger.
>
> INSTEAD OF triggers are not allowed on views created with WITH CHECK
> OPTION. SQL Server will raise an error if an INSTEAD OF trigger is added to a
> view for which WITH CHECK OPTION was specified. The user must remove that
> option using ALTER VIEW before defining the INSTEAD OF trigger.

{ [DELETE] [,] [INSERT] [,] [UPDATE] } | { [INSERT] [,] [UPDATE]}

> Are keywords that specify which data modification statements, when attempted against this table or view, activate the trigger. At least one option must be specified. Any combination of these in any order is allowed in the trigger definition. If more than one option is specified, separate the options with commas.
>
> For INSTEAD OF triggers, the DELETE option is not allowed on tables that have a referential relationship specifying a cascade action ON DELETE. Similarly, the UPDATE option is not allowed on tables that have a referential relationship specifying a cascade action ON UPDATE. For more information, see ALTER TABLE.

NOT FOR REPLICATION

> Indicates that the trigger should not be executed when a replication login such as **sqlrepl** modifies the table involved in the trigger.

AS

> Are the actions the trigger is to take.

sql_statement

> Is the trigger condition(s) and action(s).

n

> Is a placeholder indicating that multiple Transact-SQL statements can be included in the trigger.

IF UPDATE (*column*)

> Tests for an INSERT or UPDATE action to a specified column and is not used with DELETE operations.
>
> UPDATE(*column*) can be used anywhere inside the body of the trigger.

{AND | OR}

> Specifies another column to test for either an INSERT or UPDATE action.

column

> Is the name of the column to test for either an INSERT or UPDATE action.

IF (COLUMNS_UPDATED())

> Tests to see, in an INSERT or UPDATE trigger only, whether the mentioned column or columns were inserted or updated. COLUMNS_UPDATED returns a **varbinary** bit pattern that indicates which columns of the table were inserted or updated.
>
> COLUMNS_UPDATED can be used anywhere inside the body of the trigger.

bitwise_operator

> Is the bitwise operator to use in the comparison.

updated_bitmask

> Is the integer bitmask of those columns actually updated or inserted. For example, table **t1** contains columns **C1**, **C2**, **C3**, **C4**, and **C5**. To check whether columns **C2**, **C3**, and **C4** are all updated (with table **t1** having an UPDATE trigger), specify a value of **14**. To check whether only **C2** is updated, specify a value of **2**.

comparison_operator
> Is the comparison operator. Use the equal sign (=) to check whether all columns specified in *updated_bitmask* are actually updated. Use the greater than symbol (>) to check whether any or not all columns specified in the *updated_bitmask* are updated.

column_bitmask
> Is the integer *bitmask* of the columns to check.

Remarks

For more information about ALTER TRIGGER, see Remarks in CREATE TRIGGER.

> **Note** Because Microsoft does not support the addition of user-defined triggers on system tables, it is recommended that no user-defined triggers be created on system tables.

ALTER TRIGGER supports manually updateable views through INSTEAD OF triggers on tables and views. Microsoft SQL Server applies ALTER TRIGGER the same way for all types of triggers (AFTER, INSTEAD-OF).

The first and last AFTER triggers to be executed on a table may be specified by using **sp_settriggerorder**. Only one first and one last AFTER trigger may be specified on a table; if there are other AFTER triggers on the same table, they will be executed in an undefined sequence.

If an ALTER TRIGGER statement changes a first or last trigger, the first or last attribute set on the modified trigger is dropped, and the order value must be reset with **sp_settriggerorder**.

An AFTER trigger is executed only after the triggering SQL statement, including all referential cascade actions and constraint checks associated with the object updated or deleted, is executed successfully. The AFTER trigger operation checks for the effects of the triggering statement as well as all referential cascade UPDATE and DELETE actions caused by the triggering statement.

When a DELETE action to a child or referencing table is the result of a CASCADE on a DELETE from the parent table, and an INSTEAD OF trigger on DELETE is defined on that child table, the trigger is ignored and the DELETE action is executed.

Permissions

ALTER TRIGGER permissions default to members of the **db_owner** and **db_ddladmin** fixed database roles, and to the table owner. These permissions are not transferable.

Examples

This example creates a trigger that prints a user-defined message to the client when a user tries to add or change data in the **roysched** table. Then, the trigger is altered using ALTER TRIGGER to apply the trigger only on INSERT activities. This trigger is helpful because it reminds the user who updates or inserts rows into this table to also notify the book authors and publishers.

```
USE pubs
GO
CREATE TRIGGER royalty_reminder
ON roysched
WITH ENCRYPTION
FOR INSERT, UPDATE
AS RAISERROR (50009, 16, 10)

-- Now, alter the trigger.
USE pubs
GO
ALTER TRIGGER royalty_reminder
ON roysched
FOR INSERT
AS RAISERROR (50009, 16, 10)
```

Message 50009 is a user-defined message in **sysmessages**. For more information about creating user-defined messages, see **sp_addmessage**.

Related Topics

DROP TRIGGER, Programming Stored Procedures, sp_addmessage, Transactions, Using Identifiers

ALTER VIEW

Alters a previously created view (created by executing CREATE VIEW), including indexed views, without affecting dependent stored procedures or triggers and without changing permissions. For more information about the parameters used in the ALTER VIEW statement, see CREATE VIEW.

Syntax

```
ALTER VIEW [ < database_name > . ] [ < owner > . ] view_name [ ( column [ ,...n ] ) ]
[ WITH < view_attribute > [ ,...n ] ]
AS
    select_statement
```

(continued)

(continued)

```
[ WITH CHECK OPTION ]

< view_attribute > ::=
    { ENCRYPTION | SCHEMABINDING | VIEW_METADATA }
```

Arguments

view_name
> Is the view to change.

column
> Is the name of one or more columns, separated by commas, to be part of the given view.

> **Important** Column permissions are maintained only when columns have the same name before and after ALTER VIEW is performed.

> **Note** In the columns for the view, the permissions for a column name apply across a CREATE VIEW or ALTER VIEW statement, regardless of the source of the underlying data. For example, if permissions are granted on the **title_id** column in a CREATE VIEW statement, an ALTER VIEW statement can rename the **title_id** column (for example, to **qty**) and still have the permissions associated with the view using **title_id**.

n
> Is a placeholder indicating the *column* can be repeated *n* number of times.

WITH ENCRYPTION
> Encrypts the **syscomments** entries that contain the text of the ALTER VIEW statement. Using WITH ENCRYPTION prevents the view from being published as part of SQL Server replication.

SCHEMABINDING
> Binds the view to the schema. When SCHEMABINDING is specified, the *select_statement* must include the two-part name (owner.object) of tables, views, or user-defined functions referenced.

> Views or tables participating in a view created with the schema binding clause cannot be dropped unless that view is dropped or changed so it no longer has schema binding. Otherwise, SQL Server raises an error. In addition, ALTER TABLE statements on tables that participate in views having schema binding will fail if these statements affect the view definition.

VIEW_METADATA

Specifies that SQL Server will return to the DBLIB, ODBC, and OLE DB APIs the meta data information about the view, instead of the base table or tables, when browse-mode meta data is being requested for a query that references the view. Browse-mode meta data is additional meta data returned by SQL Server to the client-side DB-LIB, ODBC, and OLE DB APIs, which allow the client-side APIs to implement updateable client-side cursors. Browse-mode meta data includes information about the base table that the columns in the result set belong to.

For views created with VIEW_METADATA option, the browse-mode meta data returns the view name as opposed to the base table names when describing columns from the view in the result set.

When a view is created WITH VIEW_METADATA, all its columns (except for **timestamp**) are updateable if the view has INSERT or UPDATE INSTEAD OF triggers. See Updateable Views in CREATE VIEW.

AS

Are the actions the view is to take.

select_statement

Is the SELECT statement that defines the view.

WITH CHECK OPTION

Forces all data modification statements executed against the view to adhere to the criteria set within the *select_statement* defining the view.

Remarks

For more information about ALTER VIEW, see Remarks in CREATE VIEW.

Note If the previous view definition was created using WITH ENCRYPTION or CHECK OPTION, these options are enabled only if included in ALTER VIEW.

If a view currently in use is modified by using ALTER VIEW, Microsoft SQL Server takes an exclusive schema lock on the view. When the lock is granted, and there are no active users of the view, SQL Server deletes all copies of the view from the procedure cache. Existing plans referencing the view remain in the cache but are recompiled when invoked.

ALTER VIEW can be applied to indexed views. However, ALTER VIEW unconditionally drops all indexes on the view.

Permissions

ALTER VIEW permissions default to members of the **db_owner** and **db_ddladmin** fixed database roles, and to the view owner. These permissions are not transferable.

To alter a view, the user must have ALTER VIEW permission along with SELECT permission on the tables, views, and table-valued functions being referenced in the view, and EXECUTE permission on the scalar-valued functions being invoked in the view.

In addition, to alter a view WITH SCHEMABINDING, the user must have REFERENCES permissions on each table, view, and user-defined function that is referenced.

Examples

A. Alter a view

This example creates a view that contains all authors called **All_authors**. Permissions are granted to the view, but requirements are changed to select authors from Utah. Then, ALTER VIEW is used to replace the view.

```
-- Create a view from the authors table that contains all authors.
CREATE VIEW All_authors (au_fname, au_lname, address, city, zip)
AS
SELECT au_fname, au_lname, address, city, zip
FROM pubs..authors
GO
-- Grant SELECT permissions on the view to public.
GRANT SELECT ON All_authors TO public
GO
-- The view needs to be changed to include all authors
-- from Utah.
-- If ALTER VIEW is not used but instead the view is dropped and
-- re-created, the above GRANT statement and any other statements
-- dealing with permissions that pertain to this view
-- must be re-entered.
ALTER VIEW All_authors (au_fname, au_lname, address, city, zip)
AS
SELECT au_fname, au_lname, address, city, zip
FROM pubs..authors
WHERE state = 'UT'
GO
```

B. Use @@ROWCOUNT function in a view

This example uses the @@ROWCOUNT function as part of the view definition.

```
USE pubs
GO
CREATE VIEW yourview
AS
    SELECT title_id, title, mycount = @@ROWCOUNT, ytd_sales
    FROM titles
GO
SELECT *
```

(continued)

(continued)

```
FROM yourview
GO
-- Here, the view is altered.
USE pubs
GO
ALTER VIEW yourview
AS
    SELECT title, mycount = @@ ROWCOUNT, ytd_sales
    FROM titles
    WHERE type = 'mod_cook'
GO
SELECT *
FROM yourview
GO
```

Related Topics

CREATE TABLE, CREATE VIEW, DROP VIEW, Programming Stored Procedures, SELECT, Using Identifiers

---

AND

Combines two Boolean expressions and returns TRUE when both expressions are TRUE. When more than one logical operator is used in a statement, AND operators are evaluated first. You can change the order of evaluation by using parentheses.

Syntax

```
boolean_expression AND boolean_expression
```

Arguments

boolean_expression

Is any valid Microsoft SQL Server expression that returns a Boolean value: TRUE, FALSE, or UNKNOWN.

Result Types

Boolean

Result Value

Returns TRUE when both expressions are TRUE.

Remarks

This chart outlines the outcomes when you compare TRUE and FALSE values using the AND operator.

	TRUE	FALSE	UNKNOWN
TRUE	TRUE	FALSE	UNKNOWN
FALSE	FALSE	FALSE	FALSE
UNKNOWN	UNKNOWN	FALSE	UNKNOWN

Related Topics

Expressions, Functions, Operators (Logical Operators), SELECT, WHERE

ANY

Compares a scalar value with a single-column set of values. For more information, see SOME | ANY.

APP_NAME

Returns the application name for the current session if set by the application.

Syntax

```
APP_NAME ( )
```

Return Types

nvarchar(128)

Examples

This example checks whether the client application that initiated this process is a SQL Query Analyzer session.

```
DECLARE @CurrentApp varchar(35)
SET @CurrentApp = APP_NAME()
IF @CurrentApp <> 'MS SQL Query Analyzer'
PRINT 'This process was not started by a SQL Query Analyzer query session.'
```

Related Topics

System Functions

ASCII

Returns the ASCII code value of the leftmost character of a character expression.

Syntax

```
ASCII ( character_expression )
```

Arguments

character_expression
    Is an expression of the type **char** or **varchar**.

Return Types

int

Examples

This example, which assumes an ASCII character set, returns the ASCII value and **char** character for each character in the string "Du monde entier."

```
SET TEXTSIZE 0
SET NOCOUNT ON
-- Create the variables for the current character string position
-- and for the character string.
DECLARE @position int, @string char(15)
-- Initialize the variables.
SET @position = 1
SET @string = 'Du monde entier'
WHILE @position <= DATALENGTH(@string)
   BEGIN
   SELECT ASCII(SUBSTRING(@string, @position, 1)),
      CHAR(ASCII(SUBSTRING(@string, @position, 1)))
   SET @position = @position + 1
   END
SET NOCOUNT OFF
GO
```

Here is the result set:

```
----------- -
68          D


----------- -
117         u
```

(continued)

(continued)

```
----------- -
32

----------- -
109        m

----------- -
111        o

----------- -
110        n

----------- -
100        d

----------- -
101        e

----------- -
32

----------- -
101        e

----------- -
110        n

----------- -
116        t

----------- -
105        i

----------- -
101        e

----------- -
114        r
```

Related Topics

String Functions

ASIN

Returns the angle, in radians, whose sine is the given **float** expression (also called arcsine).

Syntax

```
ASIN ( float_expression )
```

Arguments

float_expression

Is an expression of the type **float**, with a value from −1 through 1. Values outside this range return NULL and report a domain error.

Return Types

float

Examples

This example takes a **float** expression and returns the ASIN of the given angle.

```
-- First value will be -1.01, which fails.
DECLARE @angle float
SET @angle = -1.01
SELECT 'The ASIN of the angle is: ' + CONVERT(varchar, ASIN(@angle))
GO

-- Next value is -1.00.
DECLARE @angle float
SET @angle = -1.00
SELECT 'The ASIN of the angle is: ' + CONVERT(varchar, ASIN(@angle))
GO

-- Next value is 0.1472738.
DECLARE @angle float
SET @angle = 0.1472738
SELECT 'The ASIN of the angle is: ' + CONVERT(varchar, ASIN(@angle))
GO
```

Here is the result set:

```
------------------------
The ASIN of the angle is:

(1 row(s) affected)
```

(continued)

(continued)

```
Domain error occurred.


----------------------------------
The ASIN of the angle is: -1.5708

(1 row(s) affected)


----------------------------------
The ASIN of the angle is: 0.147811

(1 row(s) affected)
```

Related Topics

CEILING, Mathematical Functions, SET ARITHIGNORE, SET ARITHABORT

ATAN

Returns the angle in radians whose tangent is the given **float** expression (also called arctangent).

Syntax

```
ATAN ( float_expression )
```

Arguments

float_expression
  Is an expression of the type **float**.

Return Types

float

Examples

This example takes a **float** expression and returns the ATAN of the given angle.

```
SELECT 'The ATAN of -45.01 is: ' + CONVERT(varchar, ATAN(-45.01))
SELECT 'The ATAN of -181.01 is: ' + CONVERT(varchar, ATAN(-181.01))
SELECT 'The ATAN of 0 is: ' + CONVERT(varchar, ATAN(0))
SELECT 'The ATAN of 0.1472738 is: ' + CONVERT(varchar, ATAN(0.1472738))
SELECT 'The ATAN of 197.1099392 is: ' + CONVERT(varchar, ATAN(197.1099392))
GO
```

Here is the result set:

```
------------------------------------
The ATAN of -45.01 is: -1.54858

(1 row(s) affected)


------------------------------------
The ATAN of -181.01 is: -1.56527

(1 row(s) affected)


------------------------------------
The ATAN of 0 is: 0

(1 row(s) affected)


------------------------------------
The ATAN of 0.1472738 is: 0.146223

(1 row(s) affected)



------------------------------------
The ATAN of 197.1099392 is: 1.56572

(1 row(s) affected)
```

Related Topics

CEILING, Mathematical Functions

ATN2

Returns the angle, in radians, whose tangent is between the two given **float** expressions (also called arctangent).

Syntax

```
ATN2 ( float_expression , float_expression )
```

Arguments

float_expression

Is an expression of the **float** data type.

Return Types

float

Examples

This example calculates the ATN2 for the given angles.

```
DECLARE @angle1 float
DECLARE @angle2 float
SET @angle1 = 35.175643
SET @angle2 = 129.44
SELECT 'The ATN2 of the angle is: ' + CONVERT(varchar,ATN2(@angle1,@angle2 ))
GO
```

Here is the result set:

```
The ATN2 of the angle is: 0.265345

(1 row(s) affected)
```

Related Topics

CAST and CONVERT, float and real, Mathematical Functions

AVG

Returns the average of the values in a group. Null values are ignored.

Syntax

```
AVG ( [ ALL | DISTINCT ] expression )
```

Arguments

ALL
    Applies the aggregate function to all values. ALL is the default.

DISTINCT
    Specifies that AVG be performed only on each unique instance of a value,
    regardless of how many times the value occurs.

expression
    Is an expression of the exact numeric or approximate numeric data type category,
    except for the **bit** data type. Aggregate functions and subqueries are not permitted.

Return Types

The return type is determined by the type of the evaluated result of *expression*.

Expression result	Return type
integer category	**int**
decimal category (p, s)	**decimal(38, s)** divided by **decimal(10, 0)**
money and **smallmoney** category	**money**
float and **real** category	**float**

> **Important**   Distinct aggregates, for example, AVG(DISTINCT *column_name*), COUNT(DISTINCT *column_name*), MAX(DISTINCT *column_name*), MIN(DISTINCT *column_name*), and SUM(DISTINCT *column_name*), are not supported when using CUBE or ROLLUP. If used, Microsoft SQL Server returns an error message and cancels the query.

Examples

A. Use SUM and AVG functions for calculations

This example calculates the average advance and the sum of year-to-date sales for all business books. Each of these aggregate functions produces a single summary value for all of the retrieved rows.

```
USE pubs

SELECT AVG(advance), SUM(ytd_sales)
FROM titles
WHERE type = 'business'
```

Here is the result set:

```
-------------------------- -----------
6,281.25                   30788

(1 row(s) affected)
```

B. Use SUM and AVG functions with a GROUP BY clause

When used with a GROUP BY clause, each aggregate function produces a single value for each group, rather than for the whole table. This example produces summary values for each type of book that include the average advance for each type of book and the sum of year-to-date sales for each type of book.

```
USE pubs

SELECT type, AVG(advance), SUM(ytd_sales)
FROM titles
GROUP BY type
ORDER BY type
```

Here is the result set:

```
type
------------ --------------------------- -----------
business     6,281.25                    30788
mod_cook     7,500.00                    24278
popular_comp 7,500.00                    12875
psychology   4,255.00                    9939
trad_cook    6,333.33                    19566
UNDECIDED    NULL                        NULL

(6 row(s) affected)
```

C. Use AVG with DISTINCT

This statement returns the average price of business books.

```
USE pubs

SELECT AVG(DISTINCT price)
FROM titles
WHERE type = 'business'
```

Here is the result set:

```
--------------------------
11.64

(1 row(s) affected)
```

D. Use AVG without DISTINCT

Without DISTINCT, the AVG function finds the average price of all business titles in the **titles** table.

```
USE pubs

SELECT AVG(price)
FROM titles
WHERE type = 'business'
```

Here is the result set:

```
- - - - - - - - - - - - - - - - - - - - - - - - - - -
13.73

(1 row(s) affected)
```

Related Topics

Aggregate Functions

BACKUP

Backs up an entire database, transaction log, or one or more files or filegroups.
For more information about database backup and restore operations, see Backing Up
and Restoring Databases.

Syntax

Backing up an entire database:

```
BACKUP DATABASE { database_name | @database_name_var }
TO < backup_device > [ ,...n ]
[ WITH
  [ BLOCKSIZE = { blocksize | @blocksize_variable } ]
  [ [ , ] DESCRIPTION = { 'text' | @text_variable } ]
  [ [ , ] DIFFERENTIAL ]
  [ [ , ] EXPIREDATE = { date | @date_var }
    | RETAINDAYS = { days | @days_var } ]
  [ [ , ] PASSWORD = { password | @password_variable } ]
  [ [ , ] FORMAT | NOFORMAT ]
  [ [ , ] { INIT | NOINIT } ]
  [ [ , ] MEDIADESCRIPTION = { 'text' | @text_variable } ]
  [ [ , ] MEDIANAME = { media_name | @media_name_variable } ]
  [ [ , ] MEDIAPASSWORD = { mediapassword | @mediapassword_variable } ]
  [ [ , ] NAME = { backup_set_name | @backup_set_name_var } ]
  [ [ , ] { NOSKIP | SKIP } ]
  [ [ , ] { NOREWIND | REWIND } ]
  [ [ , ] { NOUNLOAD | UNLOAD } ]
  [ [ , ] RESTART ]
  [ [ , ] STATS [ = percentage ] ]
]
```

Backing up specific files or filegroups:

```
BACKUP DATABASE { database_name | @database_name_var }
   < file_or_filegroup > [ ,...n ]
TO < backup_device > [ ,...n ]
[ WITH
   [ BLOCKSIZE = { blocksize | @blocksize_variable } ]
   [ [ , ] DESCRIPTION = { 'text' | @text_variable } ]
   [ [ , ] DIFFERENTIAL ]
   [ [ , ] EXPIREDATE = { date | @date_var }
     | RETAINDAYS = { days | @days_var } ]
   [ [ , ] PASSWORD = { password | @password_variable } ]
   [ [ , ] FORMAT | NOFORMAT ]
   [ [ , ] { INIT | NOINIT } ]
   [ [ , ] MEDIADESCRIPTION = { 'text' | @text_variable } ]
   [ [ , ] MEDIANAME = { media_name | @media_name_variable } ]
   [ [ , ] MEDIAPASSWORD = { mediapassword | @mediapassword_variable } ]
   [ [ , ] NAME = { backup_set_name | @backup_set_name_var } ]
   [ [ , ] { NOSKIP | SKIP } ]
   [ [ , ] { NOREWIND | REWIND } ]
   [ [ , ] { NOUNLOAD | UNLOAD } ]
   [ [ , ] RESTART ]
   [ [ , ] STATS [ = percentage ] ]
]
```

Backing up a transaction log:

```
BACKUP LOG { database_name | @database_name_var }
{
   TO < backup_device > [ ,...n ]
   [ WITH
       [ BLOCKSIZE = { blocksize | @blocksize_variable } ]
       [ [ , ] DESCRIPTION = { 'text' | @text_variable } ]
       [ [ ,] EXPIREDATE = { date | @date_var }
         | RETAINDAYS = { days | @days_var } ]
       [ [ , ] PASSWORD = { password | @password_variable } ]
       [ [ , ] FORMAT | NOFORMAT ]
       [ [ , ] { INIT | NOINIT } ]
       [ [ , ] MEDIADESCRIPTION = { 'text' | @text_variable } ]
       [ [ , ] MEDIANAME = { media_name | @media_name_variable } ]
       [ [ , ] MEDIAPASSWORD = { mediapassword | @mediapassword_variable } ]
       [ [ , ] NAME = { backup_set_name | @backup_set_name_var } ]
       [ [ , ] NO_TRUNCATE ]
       [ [ , ] { NORECOVERY | STANDBY = undo_file_name } ]
       [ [ , ] { NOREWIND | REWIND } ]
```

(continued)

(continued)

```
      [ [ , ] { NOSKIP | SKIP } ]
      [ [ , ] { NOUNLOAD | UNLOAD } ]
      [ [ , ] RESTART ]
      [ [ , ] STATS [ = percentage ] ]
   ]
}
< backup_device > ::=
   {
      { logical_backup_device_name | @logical_backup_device_name_var }
      |
      { DISK | TAPE } =
         { 'physical_backup_device_name' | @physical_backup_device_name_var }
   }
< file_or_filegroup > ::=
   {
      FILE = { logical_file_name | @logical_file_name_var }
      |
      FILEGROUP = { logical_filegroup_name | @logical_filegroup_name_var }
   }
```

Truncating the transaction log:

```
BACKUP LOG { database_name | @database_name_var }
{
   [ WITH
      { NO_LOG | TRUNCATE_ONLY } ]
}
```

Arguments

DATABASE

Specifies a complete database backup. If a list of files and filegroups is specified, only those files and filegroups are backed up.

> **Note** During a full database or differential backup, Microsoft SQL Server backs up enough of the transaction log to produce a consistent database for when the database is restored. Only a full database backup can be performed on the **master** database.

{ *database_name* | @*database_name_var* }

Is the database from which the transaction log, partial database, or complete database is backed up. If supplied as a variable (@*database_name_var*), this name can be specified either as a string constant (@*database_name_var* = database name) or as a variable of character string data type, except for the **ntext** or **text** data types.

< backup_device >

Specifies the logical or physical backup device to use for the backup operation. Can be one or more of the following:

{ *logical_backup_device_name* } | { *@logical_backup_device_name_var* }

Is the logical name, which must follow the rules for identifiers, of the backup device(s) (created by **sp_addumpdevice**) to which the database is backed up. If supplied as a variable (*@logical_backup_device_name_var*), the backup device name can be specified either as a string constant (*@logical_backup_device_name_var* = logical backup device name) or as a variable of character string data type, except for the **ntext** or **text** data types.

{ DISK | TAPE } =
'*physical_backup_device_name*' | *@physical_backup_device_name_var*

Allows backups to be created on the specified disk or tape device. The physical device specified need not exist prior to executing the BACKUP statement. If the physical device exists and the INIT option is not specified in the BACKUP statement, the backup is appended to the device.

When specifying TO DISK or TO TAPE, enter the complete path and file name. For example, DISK = 'C:\Program Files\Microsoft SQL Server\MSSQL\BACKUP\Mybackup.dat' or TAPE = '\\.\TAPE0'.

> **Note** If a relative path name is entered for a backup to disk, the backup file is placed in the default backup directory. This directory is set during installation and stored in the BackupDirectory registry key under KEY_LOCAL_MACHINE\Software\Microsoft\MSSQLServer\-MSSQLServer.

If using a network server with a Uniform Naming Convention (UNC) name or using a redirected drive letter, specify a device type of disk.

When specifying multiple files, logical file names (or variables) and physical file names (or variables) can be mixed. However, all devices must be of the same type (disk, tape, or pipe).

Backup to tape is not supported on Windows 98.

n

Is a placeholder that indicates multiple backup devices may be specified. The maximum number of backup devices is 64.

BLOCKSIZE = { *blocksize* | *@blocksize_variable* }

Specifies the physical block size, in bytes. On Windows NT systems, the default is the default block size of the device. Generally, this parameter is not required as SQL Server will choose a blocksize that is appropriate to the device. On Windows 2000-based computers, the default is 65,536 (64 KB, which is the maximum size SQL Server supports).

For DISK, BACKUP automatically determines the appropriate block size for disk devices.

Note   To transfer the resulting backup set to a CD-ROM and then restore from that CD-ROM, set BLOCKSIZE to 2048.

The default BLOCKSIZE for tape is 65,536 (64 KB). Explicitly stating a block size overrides SQL Server's selection of a block size.

DESCRIPTION = { *'text'* | *@text_variable* }
Specifies the free-form text describing the backup set. The string can have a maximum of 255 characters.

DIFFERENTIAL
Specifies the database or file backup should consist only of the portions of the database or file changed since the last full backup. A differential backup usually takes up less space than a full backup. Use this option so that all individual log backups since the last full backup do not need to be applied. For more information, see Differential Database Backups and File Differential Backups.

Note   During a full database or differential backup, SQL Server backs up enough of the transaction log to produce a consistent database when the database is restored.

EXPIREDATE = { *date* | *@date_var* }
Specifies the date when the backup set expires and can be overwritten. If supplied as a variable (*@date_var*), this date is specified as either a string constant (*@date_var* = date), as a variable of character string data type (except for the **ntext** or **text** data types), a **smalldatetime**, or **datetime** variable, and must follow the configured system **datetime** format.

RETAINDAYS = { *days* | *@days_var* }
Specifies the number of days that must elapse before this backup media set can be overwritten. If supplied as a variable (*@days_var*), it must be specified as an integer.

Important   If EXPIREDATE or RETAINDAYS is not specified, expiration is determined by the **media retention** configuration setting of **sp_configure**. These options only prevent SQL Server from overwriting a file. Tapes can be erased using other methods, and disk files can be deleted through the operating system. For more information about expiration verification, see SKIP and FORMAT in this topic.

PASSWORD = { *password* | *@password_variable* }
Sets the password for the backup set. PASSWORD is a character string. If a password is defined for the backup set, the password must be supplied to perform any restore operation from the backup set.

Important   A backup set password protects the contents of the backup set from unauthorized access through SQL Server 2000 tools, but does not protect the backup set from being overwritten.

For more information about using passwords, see the Permissions section.

FORMAT

Specifies that the media header should be written on all volumes used for this backup operation. Any existing media header is overwritten. The FORMAT option invalidates the entire media contents, ignoring any existing content.

Important Use FORMAT carefully. Formatting one backup device or medium renders the entire media set unusable. For example, if a single tape belonging to an existing striped media set is initialized, the entire media set is rendered useless.

By specifying FORMAT, the backup operation implies SKIP and INIT; these do not need to be explicitly stated.

NOFORMAT

Specifies the media header should not be written on all volumes used for this backup operation and does not rewrite the backup device unless INIT is specified.

INIT

Specifies that all backup sets should be overwritten, but preserves the media header. If INIT is specified, any existing backup set data on that device is overwritten.

The backup media is not overwritten if any one of the following conditions is met:

- All backup sets on the media have not yet expired. For more information, see the EXPIREDATE and RETAINDAYS options.

- The backup set name given in the BACKUP statement, if provided, does not match the name on the backup media. For more information, see the NAME clause.

Use the SKIP option to override these checks. For more information about interactions when using SKIP, NOSKIP, INIT, and NOINIT, see the Remarks section.

Note If the backup media is password protected, SQL Server does not write to the media unless the media password is supplied. This check is not overridden by the SKIP option. Password-protected media may be overwritten only by reformatting it. For more information, see the FORMAT option.

NOINIT

Indicates that the backup set is appended to the specified disk or tape device, preserving existing backup sets. NOINIT is the default.

The FILE option of the RESTORE command is used to select the appropriate backup set at restore time. For more information, see RESTORE.

If a media password is defined for the media set, the password must be supplied.

MEDIADESCRIPTION = { *text* | *@text_variable* }

Specifies the free-form text description, maximum of 255 characters, of the media set.

MEDIANAME = { *media_name* | *@media_name_variable* **}**

Specifies the media name, a maximum of 128 characters, for the entire backup media set. If MEDIANAME is specified, it must match the previously specified media name already existing on the backup volume(s). If not specified or if the SKIP option is specified, there is no verification check of the media name.

MEDIAPASSWORD = { *mediapassword* | *@mediapassword_variable* **}**

Sets the password for the media set. MEDIAPASSWORD is a character string.

If a password is defined for the media set, the password must be supplied to create a backup set on that media set. In addition, that media password also must be supplied to perform any restore operation from the media set. Password-protected media may be overwritten only by reformatting it. For more information, see the FORMAT option.

For more information about using passwords, see the Permissions section.

NAME = { *backup_set_name* | *@backup_set_var* **}**

Specifies the name of the backup set. Names can have a maximum of 128 characters. If NAME is not specified, it is blank.

NORECOVERY

Used only with BACKUP LOG. Backs up the tail of the log and leaves the database in the Restoring state. NORECOVERY is useful when failing over to a secondary database or when saving the tail of the log prior to a RESTORE operation.

**STANDBY = ** *undo_file_name*

Used only with BACKUP LOG. Backs up the tail of the log and leaves the database in read-only and standby mode. The undo file name specifies storage to hold rollback changes which must be undone if RESTORE LOG operations are to be subsequently applied.

If the specified undo file name does not exist, SQL Server creates it. If the file does exist, SQL Server overwrites it. For more information, see Using Standby Servers.

NOREWIND

Specifies that SQL Server will keep the tape open after the backup operation. NOREWIND implies NOUNLOAD. SQL Server will retain ownership of the tape drive until a BACKUP or RESTORE command is used WITH REWIND.

If a tape is inadvertently left open, the fastest way to release the tape is by using the following RESTORE command:

```
RESTORE LABELONLY FROM TAPE = <name> WITH REWIND
```

A list of currently open tapes can be found by querying the **sysopentapes** table in the **master** database.

REWIND

Specifies that SQL Server will release and rewind the tape. If neither NOREWIND nor REWIND is specified, REWIND is the default.

NOSKIP

Instructs the BACKUP statement to check the expiration date of all backup sets on the media before allowing them to be overwritten.

SKIP

Disables the backup set expiration and name checking usually performed by the BACKUP statement to prevent overwrites of backup sets. For more information, see the Remarks section.

NOUNLOAD

Specifies the tape is not unloaded automatically from the tape drive after a backup. NOUNLOAD remains set until UNLOAD is specified. This option is used only for tape devices.

UNLOAD

Specifies that the tape is automatically rewound and unloaded when the backup is finished. UNLOAD is set by default when a new user session is started. It remains set until that user specifies NOUNLOAD. This option is used only for tape devices.

RESTART

Specifies that SQL Server restarts an interrupted backup operation. The RESTART option saves time because it restarts the backup operation at the point it was interrupted. To RESTART a specific backup operation, repeat the entire BACKUP statement and add the RESTART option. Using the RESTART option is not required but can save time.

> **Important** This option can only be used for backups directed to tape media and for backups that span multiple tape volumes. A restart operation never occurs on the first volume of the backup.

STATS [= *percentage*]

Displays a message each time another *percentage* completes, and is used to gauge progress. If *percentage* is omitted, SQL Server displays a message after each 10 percent is completed.

< file_or_filegroup >

Specifies the logical names of the files or filegroups to include in the database backup. Multiple files or filegroups may be specified.

FILE = { *logical_file_name* | *@logical_file_name_var* }

Names one or more files to include in the database backup.

FILEGROUP = { *logical_filegroup_name* | *@logical_filegroup_name_var* }

Names one or more filegroups to include in the database backup.

> **Note** Back up a file when the database size and performance requirements make a full database backup impractical. To back up the transaction log separately, use BACKUP LOG.

Important To recover a database using file and filegroup backups, a separate backup of the transaction log must be provided by using BACKUP LOG. For more information about file backups, see Backing up Using File Backups.

File and filegroup backups are not allowed if the recovery model is simple.

n

Is a placeholder indicating that multiple files and filegroups may be specified. There is no maximum number of files or filegroups.

LOG

Specifies a backup of the transaction log only. The log is backed up from the last successfully executed LOG backup to the current end of the log. Once the log is backed up, the space may be truncated when no longer required by replication or active transactions.

Note If backing up the log does not appear to truncate most of the log, an old open transaction may exist in the log. Log space can be monitored with DBCC SQLPERF (LOGSPACE). For more information, see Transaction Log Backups.

NO_LOG | TRUNCATE_ONLY

Removes the inactive part of the log without making a backup copy of it and truncates the log. This option frees space. Specifying a backup device is unnecessary because the log backup is not saved. NO_LOG and TRUNCATE_ONLY are synonyms.

After backing up the log using either NO_LOG or TRUNCATE_ONLY, the changes recorded in the log are not recoverable. For recovery purposes, immediately execute BACKUP DATABASE.

NO_TRUNCATE

Allows backing up the log in situations where the database is damaged.

Remarks

Database or log backups can be appended to any disk or tape device, allowing a database, and its transaction logs, to be kept within one physical location.

SQL Server uses an online backup process to allow a database backup while the database is still in use. The following list includes operations that cannot run during a database or transaction log backup:

- File management operations such as the ALTER DATABASE statement with either the ADD FILE or REMOVE FILE options; INSERT, UPDATE, or DELETE statements are allowed during a backup operation.
- Shrink database or shrink file. This includes autoshrink operations.

If a backup is started when one of these operations is in progress, the backup ends. If a backup is running and one of these operations is attempted, the operation fails.

Cross-platform backup operations, even between different processor types, can be performed as long as the collation of the database is supported by the operating system. For more information, see SQL Server Collation Fundamentals.

Backup File Format

SQL Server backups can coexist on tape media with Windows NT backups because the SQL Server 2000 backup format conforms to Microsoft Tape Format (MTF); the same format used by Windows NT tape backups. To ensure interoperability, the tape should be formatted by NTBackup.

Backup Types

Backup types supported by SQL Server include:

- Full database backup, which backs up the entire database including the transaction log.
- Differential database backup performed between full database backups.
- Transaction log backup.

  A sequence of log backups provides for a continuous chain of transaction information to support recovery forward from database, differential, or file backups.

- File(s) and Filegroup(s) backup.

  Use BACKUP to back up database files and filegroups instead of the full database when time constraints make a full database backup impractical. To back up a file instead of the full database, put procedures in place to ensure that all files in the database are backed up regularly. Also, separate transaction log backups must be performed. After restoring a file backup, apply the transaction log to roll the file contents forward to make it consistent with the rest of the database.

Backup devices used in a stripe set must always be used in a stripe set (unless reinitialized at some point with FORMAT) with the same number of devices. After a backup device is defined as part of a stripe set, it cannot be used for a single device backup unless FORMAT is specified. Similarly, a backup device that contains nonstriped backups cannot be used in a stripe set unless FORMAT is specified. Use FORMAT to split a striped backup set.

If neither MEDIANAME nor MEDIADESCRIPTION is specified when a media header is written, the media header field corresponding to the blank item is empty.

BACKUP LOG cannot be used if the recovery model is SIMPLE. Use BACKUP DATABASE instead.

Interaction of SKIP, NOSKIP, INIT, and NOINIT

This table shows how the { INIT I NOINIT } and { NOSKIP I SKIP } clauses interact.

Note In all these interactions, if the tape media is empty or the disk backup file does not exist, write a media header and proceed. If the media is not empty and does not contain a valid media header, give feedback that this is not valid MTF media and abort the backup.

	INIT	NOINIT
SKIP	If the volume contains a valid[1] media header, verify the media password and overwrite any backup sets on the media, preserving only the media header. If the volume does not contain a valid media header, generate one with the given MEDIANAME, MEDIAPASSWORD, and MEDIADESCRIPTION, if any.	If the volume contains a valid media header, verify the media password and append the backup set, preserving all existing backup sets. If the volume does not contain a valid media header, an error occurs.
NOSKIP	If the volume contains a valid media header, perform the following checks: • Verify the media password.[2] • If MEDIANAME was specified, verify that the given media name matches the media header's media name. • Verify that there are no unexpired backup set(s) already on the media. If there are, abort the backup. If these checks pass, overwrite any backup sets on the media, preserving only the media header. If the volume does not contain a valid media header, generate one with the given MEDIANAME, MEDIAPASSWORD, and MEDIADESCRIPTION, if any.	If the volume contains a valid media header, verify the media password* and verify that the media name matches the given MEDIANAME, if any. If it matches, append the backup set, preserving all existing backup sets. If the volume does not contain a valid media header, an error occurs.

1 Validity includes the MTF version number and other header information. If the version specified is unsupported or an unexpected value, an error occurs.

2 The user must belong to the appropriate fixed database or server roles and provide the correct media password to perform a backup operation.

Note To maintain backward compatibility, the DUMP keyword can be used in place of the BACKUP keyword in the BACKUP statement syntax. In addition, the TRANSACTION keyword can be used in place of the LOG keyword.

Backup History Tables

SQL Server includes these backup history tables that track backup activity:

- backupfile
- backupmediafamily
- backupmediaset
- backupset

When a RESTORE is performed, the backup history tables are modified.

Compatibility Considerations

CAUTION   Backups created with Microsoft SQL Server 2000 cannot be restored in earlier versions of SQL Server.

Permissions

BACKUP DATABASE and BACKUP LOG permissions default to members of the **sysadmin** fixed server role and the **db_owner** and **db_backupoperator** fixed database roles.

In addition, the user may specify passwords for a media set, a backup set, or both. When a password is defined on a media set, it is not enough that a user is a member of appropriate fixed server and database roles to perform a backup. The user also must supply the media password to perform these operations. Similarly, restore is not allowed unless the correct media password and backup set password are specified in the restore command.

Defining passwords for backup sets and media sets is an optional feature in the BACKUP statement. The passwords will prevent unauthorized restore operations and unauthorized appends of backup sets to media using SQL Server 2000 tools, but passwords do not prevent overwrite of media with the FORMAT option.

Thus, although the use of passwords can help protect the contents of media from unauthorized access using SQL Server tools, passwords do not protect contents from being destroyed. Passwords do not fully prevent unauthorized access to the contents of the media because the data in the backup sets is not encrypted and could theoretically be examined by programs specifically created for this purpose. For situations where security is crucial, it is important to prevent access to the media by unauthorized individuals.

It is an error to specify a password for objects that were not created with associated passwords.

BACKUP creates the backup set with the backup set password supplied through the PASSWORD option. In addition, BACKUP will normally verify the media password given by the MEDIAPASSWORD option prior to writing to the media. The only time that BACKUP will not verify the media password is when it formats the media, which overwrites the media header. BACKUP formats the media only:

- If the FORMAT option is specified.
- If the media header is invalid and INIT is specified.
- If the operation is writing a continuation volume.

If BACKUP writes the media header, BACKUP will assign the media set password to the value specified in the MEDIAPASSWORD option.

For more information about the impact of passwords on SKIP, NOSKIP, INIT, and NOINIT options, see the Remarks section.

Ownership and permission problems on the backup device's physical file can interfere with a backup operation. SQL Server must be able to read and write to the device; the account under which the SQL Server service runs must have write permissions. However, **sp_addumpdevice**, which adds an entry for a device in the system tables, does not check file access permissions. Such problems on the backup device's physical file may not appear until the physical resource is accessed when the backup or restore is attempted.

Examples

A. Back up the entire MyNwind database

Note   The **MyNwind** database is shown for illustration only.

This example creates a logical backup device in which a full backup of the **MyNwind** database is placed.

```
-- Create a logical backup device for the full MyNwind backup.
USE master
EXEC sp_addumpdevice 'disk', 'MyNwind_1',
   DISK ='c:\Program Files\Microsoft SQL Server\MSSQL\BACKUP\MyNwind_1.dat'

-- Back up the full MyNwind database.
BACKUP DATABASE MyNwind TO MyNwind_1
```

B. Back up the database and log

This example creates both a full database and log backup. The database is backed up to a logical backup device called **MyNwind_2**, and then the log is backed up to a logical backup device called **MyNwindLog1**.

Note   Creating a logical backup device needs to be done only once.

```
-- Create the backup device for the full MyNwind backup.
USE master
EXEC sp_addumpdevice 'disk', 'MyNwind_2',
   'c:\Program Files\Microsoft SQL Server\MSSQL\BACKUP\MyNwind_2.dat'

--Create the log backup device.
USE master
EXEC sp_addumpdevice 'disk', 'MyNwindLog1',
   'c:\Program Files\Microsoft SQL Server\MSSQL\BACKUP\MyNwindLog1.dat'

-- Back up the full MyNwind database.
BACKUP DATABASE MyNwind TO MyNwind_2

-- Update activity has occurred since the full database backup.

-- Back up the log of the MyNwind database.
BACKUP LOG MyNwind
   TO MyNwindLog1
```

Related Topics

Backup Formats, DBCC SQLPERF, RESTORE, RESTORE FILELISTONLY,
RESTORE HEADERONLY, RESTORE LABELONLY, RESTORE VERIFYONLY,
sp_addumpdevice, sp_configure, sp_dboption, sp_helpfile, sp_helpfilegroup, Using
Identifiers, Using Media Sets and Families

BEGIN...END

Encloses a series of Transact-SQL statements so that a group of Transact-SQL
statements can be executed. BEGIN and END are control-of-flow language keywords.

Syntax

```
BEGIN
   {
      sql_statement
      | statement_block
   }
END
```

Arguments

{ *sql_statement* | *statement_block* }
    Is any valid Transact-SQL statement or statement grouping as defined with a
    statement block.

Remarks

BEGIN...END blocks can be nested.

Although all Transact-SQL statements are valid within a BEGIN...END block, certain Transact-SQL statements should not be grouped together within the same batch (statement block). For more information, see Batches and the individual statements used.

Examples

In this example, BEGIN and END define a series of Transact-SQL statements that execute together. If the BEGIN...END block were not included, the IF condition would cause only the ROLLBACK TRANSACTION to execute, and the print message would not be returned.

```
USE pubs
GO
CREATE TRIGGER deltitle
ON titles
FOR delete
AS
IF (SELECT COUNT(*) FROM deleted, sales
      WHERE sales.title_id = deleted.title_id) > 0
   BEGIN
      ROLLBACK TRANSACTION
      PRINT 'You can't delete a title with sales.'
END
```

Related Topics

ALTER TRIGGER, Control-of-Flow Language, CREATE TRIGGER, END (BEGIN...END)

BEGIN DISTRIBUTED TRANSACTION

Specifies the start of a Transact-SQL distributed transaction managed by Microsoft Distributed Transaction Coordinator (MS DTC).

Syntax

```
BEGIN DISTRIBUTED TRAN [ SACTION ]
  [ transaction_name | @tran_name_variable ]
```

Arguments

transaction_name
>Is a user-defined transaction name used to track the distributed transaction within MS DTC utilities. *transaction_name* must conform to the rules for identifiers but only the first 32 characters are used.

@tran_name_variable
>Is the name of a user-defined variable containing a transaction name used to track the distributed transaction within MS DTC utilities. The variable must be declared with a **char**, **varchar**, **nchar**, or **nvarchar** data type.

Remarks

The server executing the BEGIN DISTRIBUTED TRANSACTION statement is the transaction originator and controls the completion of the transaction. When a subsequent COMMIT TRANSACTION or ROLLBACK TRANSACTION statement is issued for the connection, the controlling server requests that MS DTC manage the completion of the distributed transaction across the servers involved.

There are two ways remote SQL servers are enlisted in a distributed transaction:

- A connection already enlisted in the distributed transaction performs a remote stored procedure call referencing a remote server.

- A connection already enlisted in the distributed transaction executes a distributed query referencing a remote server.

For example, if BEGIN DISTRIBUTED TRANSACTION is issued on **ServerA**, the connection calls a stored procedure on **ServerB** and another stored procedure on **ServerC**, and the stored procedure on **ServerC** executes a distributed query against **ServerD**, then all four SQL servers are involved in the distributed transaction. **ServerA** is the originating, controlling server for the transaction.

The connections involved in Transact-SQL distributed transactions do not get a transaction object they can pass to another connection for it to explicitly enlist in the distributed transaction. The only way for a remote server to enlist in the transaction is to be the target of a remote stored procedure call or a distributed query.

The **sp_configure remote proc trans** option controls whether calls to remote stored procedures in a local transaction automatically cause the local transaction to be promoted to a distributed transaction managed by MS DTC. The connection-level SET option REMOTE_PROC_TRANSACTIONS can be used to override the server default established by **sp_configure remote proc trans**. With this option set on, a remote stored procedure call causes a local transaction to be promoted to a distributed transaction. The connection that creates the MS DTC transaction becomes the originator for the transaction. COMMIT TRANSACTION initiates an MS DTC coordinated commit. If the **sp_configure remote proc trans** option is set on, remote stored procedure calls in local transactions are automatically protected as part of distributed transactions without having to rewrite applications to specifically issue BEGIN DISTRIBUTED TRANSACTION instead of BEGIN TRANSACTION.

When a distributed query is executed in a local transaction, the transaction is automatically promoted to a distributed transaction if the target OLE DB data source supports **ITransactionLocal**. If the target OLE DB data source does not support **ITransactionLocal**, only read-only operations are allowed in the distributed query.

For more information about the distributed transaction environment and process, see the Microsoft Distributed Transaction Coordinator documentation.

Permissions

BEGIN DISTRIBUTED TRANSACTION permissions default to any valid user.

Examples

This example updates the author's last name on the local and remote databases. The local and remote databases will both either commit or roll back the transaction.

Note   Unless MS DTC is currently installed on the computer running Microsoft SQL Server, this example produces an error message. For more information about installing MS DTC, see the Microsoft Distributed Transaction Coordinator documentation.

```
USE pubs
GO
BEGIN DISTRIBUTED TRANSACTION
UPDATE authors
    SET au_lname = 'McDonald' WHERE au_id = '409-56-7008'
EXECUTE remote.pubs.dbo.changeauth_lname '409-56-7008','McDonald'
COMMIT TRAN
GO
```

Related Topics

BEGIN TRANSACTION, COMMIT TRANSACTION, COMMIT WORK, Distributed Transactions, ROLLBACK TRANSACTION, ROLLBACK WORK, SAVE TRANSACTION

BEGIN TRANSACTION

Marks the starting point of an explicit, local transaction. BEGIN TRANSACTION increments @@TRANCOUNT by 1.

Syntax

```
BEGIN TRAN [ SACTION ] [ transaction_name | @tran_name_variable
   [ WITH MARK [ 'description' ] ] ]
```

Arguments

transaction_name

Is the name assigned to the transaction. *transaction_name* must conform to the rules for identifiers but identifiers longer than 32 characters are not allowed. Use transaction names only on the outermost pair of nested BEGIN...COMMIT or BEGIN...ROLLBACK statements.

@tran_name_variable

Is the name of a user-defined variable containing a valid transaction name. The variable must be declared with a **char**, **varchar**, **nchar**, or **nvarchar** data type.

WITH MARK ['*description*']

Specifies the transaction is marked in the log. *description* is a string that describes the mark.

If WITH MARK is used, a transaction name must be specified. WITH MARK allows for restoring a transaction log to a named mark.

Remarks

BEGIN TRANSACTION represents a point at which the data referenced by a connection is logically and physically consistent. If errors are encountered, all data modifications made after the BEGIN TRANSACTION can be rolled back to return the data to this known state of consistency. Each transaction lasts until either it completes without errors and COMMIT TRANSACTION is issued to make the modifications a permanent part of the database, or errors are encountered and all modifications are erased with a ROLLBACK TRANSACTION statement.

BEGIN TRANSACTION starts a local transaction for the connection issuing the statement. Depending on the current transaction isolation level settings, many resources acquired to support the Transact-SQL statements issued by the connection are locked by the transaction until it is completed with either a COMMIT TRANSACTION or ROLLBACK TRANSACTION statement. Transactions left outstanding for long periods of time can prevent other users from accessing these locked resources.

Although BEGIN TRANSACTION starts a local transaction, it is not recorded in the transaction log until the application subsequently performs an action that must be recorded in the log, such as executing an INSERT, UPDATE, or DELETE statement. An application can perform actions such as acquiring locks to protect the transaction isolation level of SELECT statements, but nothing is recorded in the log until the application performs a modification action.

Naming multiple transactions in a series of nested transactions with a transaction name has little effect on the transaction. Only the first (outermost) transaction name is registered with the system. A rollback to any other name (other than a valid savepoint name) generates an error. None of the statements executed before the rollback are in fact rolled back at the time this error occurs. The statements are rolled back only when the outer transaction is rolled back.

BEGIN TRANSACTION starts a local transaction. The local transaction is escalated to a distributed transaction if the following actions are performed before it is committed or rolled back:

- An INSERT, DELETE, or UPDATE statement is executed that references a remote table on a linked server. The INSERT, UPDATE, or DELETE statement fails if the OLE DB provider used to access the linked server does not support the **ITransactionJoin** interface.

- A call is made to a remote stored procedure when the REMOTE_PROC_TRANSACTIONS option is set to ON.

The local copy of SQL Server becomes the transaction controller and uses MS DTC to manage the distributed transaction.

Marked Transactions

The WITH MARK option causes the transaction name to be placed in the transaction log. When restoring a database to an earlier state, the marked transaction can be used in place of a date and time. For more information, see Restoring a Database to a Prior State, Recovering to a Named Transaction, and RESTORE.

Additionally, transaction log marks are necessary if you need to recover a set of related databases to a logically consistent state. Marks can be placed in the transaction logs of the related databases by a distributed transaction. Recovering the set of related databases to these marks results in a set of databases that are transactionally consistent. Placement of marks in related databases requires special procedures. For more information, see Backup and Recovery of Related Databases.

The mark is placed in the transaction log only if the database is updated by the marked transaction. Transactions that do not modify data are not marked.

BEGIN TRAN *new_name* WITH MARK can be nested within an already existing transaction that is not marked. Upon doing so, *new_name* becomes the mark name for the transaction, despite the name that the transaction may already have been given. In the following example, M2 is the name of the mark.

```
BEGIN TRAN T1
UPDATE table1 ...
BEGIN TRAN M2 WITH MARK
UPDATE table2 ...
SELECT * from table1
COMMIT TRAN M2
UPDATE table3 ...
COMMIT TRAN T1
```

Attempting to mark a transaction that is already marked results in a warning (not error) message:

```
BEGIN TRAN T1 WITH MARK
UPDATE table1 ...
BEGIN TRAN M2 WITH MARK

Server: Msg 3920, Level 16, State 1, Line 3
WITH MARK option only applies to the first BEGIN TRAN WITH MARK.
The option is ignored.
```

Permissions

BEGIN TRANSACTION permissions default to any valid user.

Examples

A. Naming a transaction

This example demonstrates how to name a transaction. Upon committing the named transaction, royalties paid for all popular computer books are increased by 10 percent.

```
DECLARE @TranName VARCHAR(20)
SELECT @TranName = 'MyTransaction'

BEGIN TRANSACTION @TranName
GO
USE pubs
GO
UPDATE roysched
SET royalty = royalty * 1.10
WHERE title_id LIKE 'Pc%'
GO

COMMIT TRANSACTION MyTransaction
GO
```

B. Marking a transaction

This example demonstrates how to mark a transaction. The transaction named "RoyaltyUpdate" is marked.

```
BEGIN TRANSACTION RoyaltyUpdate
   WITH MARK 'Update royalty values'
GO
USE pubs
GO
UPDATE roysched
```

(continued)

257

(continued)

```
    SET royalty = royalty * 1.10
    WHERE title_id LIKE 'Pc%'
GO
COMMIT TRANSACTION RoyaltyUpdate
GO
```

Related Topics

BEGIN DISTRIBUTED TRANSACTION, COMMIT TRANSACTION, COMMIT
WORK, RESTORE, Recovering to a Named Transaction, ROLLBACK
TRANSACTION, ROLLBACK WORK, SAVE TRANSACTION, Transactions

BETWEEN

Specifies a range to test.

Syntax

```
test_expression [ NOT ] BETWEEN begin_expression AND end_expression
```

Arguments

test_expression

Is the expression to test for in the range defined by *begin_expression* and
end_expression. *test_expression* must be the same data type as both
begin_expression and *end_expression*.

NOT

Specifies that the result of the predicate be negated.

begin_expression

Is any valid Microsoft SQL Server expression. *begin_expression* must be the same
data type as both *test_expression* and *end_expression*.

end_expression

Is any valid SQL Server expression. *end_expression* must be the same data type as
both *test_expression* and *begin_expression*.

AND

Acts as a placeholder indicating that *test_expression* should be within the range
indicated by *begin_expression* and *end_expression*.

Result Types

Boolean

Result Value

BETWEEN returns TRUE if the value of *test_expression* is greater than or equal to the value of *begin_expression* and less than or equal to the value of *end_expression*.

NOT BETWEEN returns TRUE if the value of *test_expression* is less than the value of *begin_expression* or greater than the value of *end_expression*.

Remarks

To specify an exclusive range, use the greater than (>) and less than operators (<). If any input to the BETWEEN or NOT BETWEEN predicate is NULL, the result is UNKNOWN.

Examples

A. Use BETWEEN

This example returns title identifiers for books with year-to-date unit sales from 4,095 through 12,000.

```
USE pubs
GO
SELECT title_id, ytd_sales
FROM titles
WHERE ytd_sales BETWEEN 4095 AND 12000
GO
```

Here is the result set:

```
title_id ytd_sales
-------- -----------
BU1032   4095
BU7832   4095
PC1035   8780
PC8888   4095
TC7777   4095

(5 row(s) affected)
```

B. Use > and < instead of BETWEEN

This example, which uses greater than (>) and less than (<) operators, returns different results because these operators are not inclusive.

```
USE pubs
GO
SELECT title_id, ytd_sales
FROM titles
WHERE ytd_sales > 4095 AND ytd_sales < 12000
GO
```

Here is the result set:

```
title_id ytd_sales
-------- -----------
PC1035   8780

(1 row(s) affected)
```

C. Use NOT BETWEEN

This example finds all rows outside a specified range (from 4,095 through 12,000).

```
USE pubs
GO
SELECT title_id, ytd_sales
FROM titles
WHERE ytd_sales NOT BETWEEN 4095 AND 12000
GO
```

Here is the result set:

```
title_id ytd_sales
-------- -----------
BU1111   3876
BU2075   18722
MC2222   2032
MC3021   22246
PS1372   375
PS2091   2045
PS2106   111
PS3333   4072
PS7777   3336
TC3218   375
TC4203   15096

(11 row(s) affected)
```

Related Topics

> (Greater Than), < (Less Than), Expressions, Functions, Operators (Logical Operators), SELECT (Subqueries), WHERE

binary and varbinary

Binary data types of either fixed-length (**binary**) or variable-length (**varbinary**).

binary [(*n*)]

Fixed-length binary data of *n* bytes. *n* must be a value from 1 through 8,000. Storage size is *n*+4 bytes.

varbinary [(*n*)]

Variable-length binary data of *n* bytes. *n* must be a value from 1 through 8,000. Storage size is the actual length of the data entered + 4 bytes, not *n* bytes. The data entered can be 0 bytes in length. The SQL-92 synonym for **varbinary** is **binary varying**.

Remarks

When *n* is not specified in a data definition, or variable declaration statement, the default length is 1. When *n* is not specified with the CAST function, the default length is 30.

Use **binary** when column data entries are consistent in size.

Use **varbinary** when column data entries are inconsistent in size.

Related Topics

ALTER TABLE, CAST and CONVERT, CREATE TABLE, Data Type Conversion, Data Types, DECLARE @local_variable, DELETE, INSERT, SET @local_variable, UPDATE

BINARY_CHECKSUM

Returns the binary checksum value computed over a row of a table or over a list of expressions. BINARY_CHECKSUM can be used to detect changes to a row of a table.

Syntax

```
BINARY_CHECKSUM ( * | expression [ ,...n ] )
```

Arguments

*

Specifies that the computation is over all the columns of the table. BINARY_CHECKSUM ignores columns of noncomparable data types in its computation. Noncomparable data types are **text**, **ntext**, **image**, and **cursor**, as well as **sql_variant** with any of the above types as its base type.

expression

> Is an expression of any type. BINARY_CHECKSUM ignores expressions of noncomparable data types in its computation.

Remarks

BINARY_CHECKSUM(*), computed on any row of a table, returns the same value as long the row is not subsequently modified. BINARY_CHECKSUM(*) will return a different value for most, but not all, changes to the row, and can be used to detect most row modifications.

BINARY_CHECKSUM can be applied over a list of expressions, and returns the same value for a given list. BINARY_CHECKSUM applied over any two lists of expressions returns the same value if the corresponding elements of the two lists have the same type and byte representation. For this definition, NULL values of a given type are considered to have the same byte representation.

BINARY_CHECKSUM and CHECKSUM are similar functions: they can be used to compute a checksum value on a list of expressions, and the order of expressions affects the resultant value. The order of columns used in the case of BINARY_CHECKSUM(*) is the order of columns specified in the table or view definition, including computed columns.

CHECKSUM and BINARY_CHECKSUM return different values for the string data types, where locale can cause strings with different representation to compare equal. The string data types are **char**, **varchar**, **nchar**, **nvarchar**, or **sql_variant** (if the base type of **sql_variant** is a string data type). For example, the BINARY_CHECKSUM values for the strings "McCavity" and "Mccavity" are different. In contrast, in a case-insensitive server, CHECKSUM returns the same checksum values for those strings. CHECKSUM values should not be compared against BINARY_CHECKSUM values.

Examples

A. Use BINARY_CHECKSUM to detect changes in the rows of a table

This example uses BINARY_CHECKSUM to detect changes in a row of the **Products** table in the **Northwind** database.

```
/*Get the checksum value before the values in the specific rows (#13-15) are changed.*/
USE Northwind
GO
CREATE TABLE TableBC (ProductID int, bchecksum int)
INSERT INTO TableBC
        SELECT ProductID, BINARY_CHECKSUM(*)
        FROM      Products
```

(continued)

(continued)

```
/*TableBC contains a column of 77 checksum values corresponding to each row in the
Products table.*/

--A large company bought products 13-15.
--The new company modified the products names and unit prices.
--Change the values of ProductsName and UnitPrice for rows 13, 14, and 15 of the Products
table.*/
UPDATE Products
SET ProductName='Oishi Konbu', UnitPrice=5
WHERE ProductName='Konbu'

UPDATE Products
SET ProductName='Oishi Tofu', UnitPrice=20
WHERE ProductName='Tofu'

UPDATE Products
SET ProductName='Oishi Genen Shouyu', UnitPrice=12
WHERE ProductName='Genen Shouyu'

--Determine the rows that have changed.
SELECT ProductID
FROM     TableBC
WHERE EXISTS (
     SELECT ProductID
     FROM      Products
     WHERE     Products.ProductID = TableBC.ProductID
     AND BINARY_CHECKSUM(*) <> TableBC.bchecksum)
```

Here is the result set:

```
ProductID
13
14
15
```

Related Topics

CHECKSUM, CHECKSUM_AGG

bit

Integer data type 1, 0, or NULL.

Remarks

Columns of type **bit** cannot have indexes on them.

Microsoft SQL Server optimizes the storage used for **bit** columns. If there are 8 or fewer **bit** columns in a table, the columns are stored as 1 byte. If there are from 9 through 16 **bit** columns, they are stored as 2 bytes, and so on.

Related Topics

ALTER TABLE, CAST and CONVERT, CREATE TABLE, Data Type Conversion, Data Types, DECLARE @local_variable, DELETE, INSERT, SET @local_variable, syscolumns, UPDATE

BREAK

Exits the innermost WHILE loop. Any statements following the END keyword are ignored. BREAK is often, but not always, activated by an IF test.

Related Topics

Control-of-Flow Language, WHILE

BULK INSERT

Copies a data file into a database table or view in a user-specified format.

Syntax

```
BULK INSERT [ [ 'database_name'.] [ 'owner' ].] { 'table_name' FROM 'data_file' }
   [ WITH
      (
         [ BATCHSIZE [ = batch_size ] ]
         [ [ , ] CHECK_CONSTRAINTS ]
         [ [ , ] CODEPAGE [ = 'ACP' | 'OEM' | 'RAW' | 'code_page' ] ]
         [ [ , ] DATAFILETYPE [ =
            { 'char' | 'native'| 'widechar' | 'widenative' } ] ]
         [ [ , ] FIELDTERMINATOR [ = 'field_terminator' ] ]
         [ [ , ] FIRSTROW [ = first_row ] ]
         [ [ , ] FIRE_TRIGGERS ]
```

(continued)

(continued)

```
        [ [ , ] FORMATFILE = 'format_file_path' ]
        [ [ , ] KEEPIDENTITY ]
        [ [ , ] KEEPNULLS ]
        [ [ , ] KILOBYTES_PER_BATCH [ = kilobytes_per_batch ] ]
        [ [ , ] LASTROW [ = last_row ] ]
        [ [ , ] MAXERRORS [ = max_errors ] ]
        [ [ , ] ORDER ( { column [ ASC | DESC ] } [ ,...n ] ) ]
        [ [ , ] ROWS_PER_BATCH [ = rows_per_batch ] ]
        [ [ , ] ROWTERMINATOR [ = 'row_terminator' ] ]
        [ [ , ] TABLOCK ]
    )
]
```

Arguments

'database_name'

Is the database name in which the specified table or view resides. If not specified, this is the current database.

'owner'

Is the name of the table or view owner. *owner* is optional if the user performing the bulk copy operation owns the specified table or view. If *owner* is not specified and the user performing the bulk copy operation does not own the specified table or view, Microsoft SQL Server returns an error message, and the bulk copy operation is canceled.

'table_name'

Is the name of the table or view to bulk copy data into. Only views in which all columns refer to the same base table can be used. For more information about the restrictions for copying data into views, see INSERT.

'data_file'

Is the full path of the data file that contains data to copy into the specified table or view. BULK INSERT can copy data from a disk (including network, floppy disk, hard disk, and so on).

data_file must specify a valid path from the server on which SQL Server is running. If *data_file* is a remote file, specify the Universal Naming Convention (UNC) name.

BATCHSIZE [= *batch_size*]

Specifies the number of rows in a batch. Each batch is copied to the server as one transaction. SQL Server commits or rolls back, in the case of failure, the transaction for every batch. By default, all data in the specified data file is one batch.

CHECK_CONSTRAINTS
Specifies that any constraints on *table_name* are checked during the bulk copy operation. By default, constraints are ignored.

CODEPAGE [= 'ACP' | 'OEM' | 'RAW' | '*code_page*']
Specifies the code page of the data in the data file. CODEPAGE is relevant only if the data contains **char**, **varchar**, or **text** columns with character values greater than 127 or less than 32.

CODEPAGE value	Description
ACP	Columns of **char**, **varchar**, or **text** data type are converted from the ANSI/Microsoft Windows code page (ISO 1252) to the SQL Server code page.
OEM (default)	Columns of **char**, **varchar**, or **text** data type are converted from the system OEM code page to the SQL Server code page.
RAW	No conversion from one code page to another occurs; this is the fastest option.
code_page	Specific code page number, for example, 850.

DATAFILETYPE [= { 'char' | 'native' | 'widechar' | 'widenative' }]
Specifies that BULK INSERT performs the copy operation using the specified default.

DATAFILETYPE value	Description
char (default)	Performs the bulk copy operation from a data file containing character data.
native	Performs the bulk copy operation using the **native** (database) data types. The data file to load is created by bulk copying data from SQL Server using the **bcp** utility.
widechar	Performs the bulk copy operation from a data file containing Unicode characters.
widenative	Performs the same bulk copy operation as **native**, except **char**, **varchar**, and **text** columns are stored as Unicode in the data file. The data file to be loaded was created by bulk copying data from SQL Server using the **bcp** utility. This option offers a higher performance alternative to the **widechar** option, and is intended for transferring data from one computer running SQL Server to another by using a data file. Use this option when transferring data that contains ANSI extended characters in order to take advantage of **native** mode performance.

FIELDTERMINATOR [= *'field_terminator'*]
Specifies the field terminator to be used for **char** and **widechar** data files.
The default is \t (tab character).

FIRSTROW [= *first_row*]
Specifies the number of the first row to copy. The default is 1, indicating the first row in the specified data file.

FIRE_TRIGGERS
Specifies that any insert triggers defined on the destination table will execute during the bulk copy operation. If FIRE_TRIGGERS is not specified, no insert triggers will execute.

FORMATFILE [= *'format_file_path'*]
Specifies the full path of a format file. A format file describes the data file that contains stored responses created using the **bcp** utility on the same table or view. The format file should be used in cases in which:

- The data file contains greater or fewer columns than the table or view.

- The columns are in a different order.

- The column delimiters vary.

- There are other changes in the data format. Format files are usually created by using the **bcp** utility and modified with a text editor as needed. For more information, see bcp Utility.

KEEPIDENTITY
Specifies that the values for an identity column are present in the file imported. If KEEPIDENTITY is not given, the identity values for this column in the data file imported are ignored, and SQL Server automatically assigns unique values based on the seed and increment values specified during table creation. If the data file does not contain values for the identity column in the table or view, use a format file to specify that the identity column in the table or view should be skipped when importing data; SQL Server automatically assigns unique values for the column. For more information, see DBCC CHECKIDENT.

KEEPNULLS
Specifies that empty columns should retain a null value during the bulk copy operation, rather than have any default values for the columns inserted.

KILOBYTES_PER_BATCH [= *kilobytes_per_batch*]
Specifies the approximate number of kilobytes (KB) of data per batch (as *kilobytes_per_batch*). By default, KILOBYTES_PER_BATCH is unknown.

LASTROW [= *last_row*]
Specifies the number of the last row to copy. The default is 0, indicating the last row in the specified data file.

MAXERRORS [= *max_errors*]

Specifies the maximum number of errors that can occur before the bulk copy operation is canceled. Each row that cannot be imported by the bulk copy operation is ignored and counted as one error. If *max_errors* is not specified, the default is 10.

ORDER ({ *column* [ASC | DESC] } [,...*n*])

Specifies how the data in the data file is sorted. Bulk copy operation performance is improved if the data loaded is sorted according to the clustered index on the table. If the data file is sorted in a different order, or there is no clustered index on the table, the ORDER clause is ignored. The column names supplied must be valid columns in the destination table. By default, the bulk insert operation assumes the data file is unordered.

n

Is a placeholder indicating that multiple columns can be specified.

ROWS_PER_BATCH [= *rows_per_batch*]

Specifies the number of rows of data per batch (as *rows_per_batch*). Used when BATCHSIZE is not specified, resulting in the entire data file sent to the server as a single transaction. The server optimizes the bulk load according to *rows_per_batch*. By default, ROWS_PER_BATCH is unknown.

ROWTERMINATOR [= '*row_terminator*']

Specifies the row terminator to be used for **char** and **widechar** data files. The default is \n (newline character).

TABLOCK

Specifies that a table-level lock is acquired for the duration of the bulk copy operation. A table can be loaded concurrently by multiple clients if the table has no indexes and TABLOCK is specified. By default, locking behavior is determined by the table option **table lock on bulk load**. Holding a lock only for the duration of the bulk copy operation reduces lock contention on the table, significantly improving performance.

Remarks

The BULK INSERT statement can be executed within a user-defined transaction. Rolling back a user-defined transaction that uses a BULK INSERT statement and BATCHSIZE clause to load data into a table or view using multiple batches rolls back all batches sent to SQL Server.

Permissions

Only members of the **sysadmin** and **bulkadmin** fixed server roles can execute BULK INSERT.

Examples

This example imports order detail information from the specified data file using a pipe (|) as the field terminator and \n as the row terminator.

```
BULK INSERT Northwind.dbo.[Order Details]
   FROM 'f:\orders\lineitem.tbl'
   WITH
      (
         FIELDTERMINATOR = '|',
         ROWTERMINATOR = '|\n'
      )
```

This example specifies the FIRE_TRIGGERS argument.

```
BULK INSERT Northwind.dbo.[Order Details]
   FROM 'f:\orders\lineitem.tbl'
   WITH
      (
         FIELDTERMINATOR = '|',
         ROWTERMINATOR = ':\n',
         FIRE_TRIGGERS
      )
```

Related Topics

bcp Utility, Collations, Copying Data Between Different Collations, Copying Data Using bcp or BULK INSERT, Parallel Data Loads, sp_tableoption, Using Format Files

CASE

Evaluates a list of conditions and returns one of multiple possible result expressions.

CASE has two formats:

- The simple CASE function compares an expression to a set of simple expressions to determine the result.
- The searched CASE function evaluates a set of Boolean expressions to determine the result.

Both formats support an optional ELSE argument.

Syntax

Simple CASE function:

```
CASE input_expression
    WHEN when_expression THEN result_expression
        [ ...n ]
    [
        ELSE else_result_expression
    ]
END
```

Searched CASE function:

```
CASE
    WHEN Boolean_expression THEN result_expression
        [ ...n ]
    [
        ELSE else_result_expression
    ]
END
```

Arguments

input_expression

Is the expression evaluated when using the simple CASE format. *input_expression* is any valid Microsoft SQL Server expression.

WHEN *when_expression*

Is a simple expression to which *input_expression* is compared when using the simple CASE format. *when_expression* is any valid SQL Server expression. The data types of *input_expression* and each *when_expression* must be the same or must be an implicit conversion.

n

Is a placeholder indicating that multiple WHEN *when_expression* THEN *result_expression* clauses, or multiple WHEN *Boolean_expression* THEN *result_expression* clauses can be used.

THEN *result_expression*

Is the expression returned when *input_expression* equals *when_expression* evaluates to TRUE, or *Boolean_expression* evaluates to TRUE. *result expression* is any valid SQL Server expression.

ELSE *else_result_expression*

Is the expression returned if no comparison operation evaluates to TRUE. If this argument is omitted and no comparison operation evaluates to TRUE, CASE returns NULL. *else_result_expression* is any valid SQL Server expression. The data types of *else_result_expression* and any *result_expression* must be the same or must be an implicit conversion.

WHEN *Boolean_expression*
> Is the Boolean expression evaluated when using the searched CASE format. *Boolean_expression* is any valid Boolean expression.

Result Types

Returns the highest precedence type from the set of types in *result_expressions* and the optional *else_result_expression*. For more information, see Data Type Precedence.

Result Values

Simple CASE function:

- Evaluates *input_expression*, and then, in the order specified, evaluates *input_expression* = *when_expression* for each WHEN clause.

- Returns the *result_expression* of the first (*input_expression* = *when_expression*) that evaluates to TRUE.

- If no *input_expression* = *when_expression* evaluates to TRUE, SQL Server returns the *else_result_expression* if an ELSE clause is specified, or a NULL value if no ELSE clause is specified.

Searched CASE function:

- Evaluates, in the order specified, *Boolean_expression* for each WHEN clause.

- Returns *result_expression* of the first *Boolean_expression* that evaluates to TRUE.

- If no *Boolean_expression* evaluates to TRUE, SQL Server returns the *else_result_expression* if an ELSE clause is specified, or a NULL value if no ELSE clause is specified.

Examples

A. Use a SELECT statement with a simple CASE function

Within a SELECT statement, a simple CASE function allows only an equality check; no other comparisons are made. This example uses the CASE function to alter the display of book categories to make them more understandable.

```
USE pubs
GO
SELECT Category =
     CASE type
          WHEN 'popular_comp' THEN 'Popular Computing'
          WHEN 'mod_cook' THEN 'Modern Cooking'
          WHEN 'business' THEN 'Business'
          WHEN 'psychology' THEN 'Psychology'
          WHEN 'trad_cook' THEN 'Traditional Cooking'
```

(continued)

(continued)

```
        ELSE 'Not yet categorized'
    END,
  CAST(title AS varchar(25)) AS 'Shortened Title',
  price AS Price
FROM titles
WHERE price IS NOT NULL
ORDER BY type, price
COMPUTE AVG(price) BY type
GO
```

Here is the result set:

```
Category            Shortened Title          Price
------------------- ------------------------ --------------------------
Business            You Can Combat Computer S 2.99
Business            Cooking with Computers: S 11.95
Business            The Busy Executive's Data 19.99
Business            Straight Talk About Compu 19.99

                                             avg
                                             ==========================
                                             13.73


Category            Shortened Title          Price
------------------- ------------------------ --------------------------
Modern Cooking      The Gourmet Microwave    2.99
Modern Cooking      Silicon Valley Gastronomi 19.99

                                             avg
                                             ==========================
                                             11.49


Category            Shortened Title          Price
------------------- ------------------------ --------------------------
Popular Computing   Secrets of Silicon Valley 20.00
Popular Computing   But Is It User Friendly?  22.95

                                             avg
                                             ==========================
                                             21.48
```

(continued)

(continued)

```
Category             Shortened Title             Price
-------------------  --------------------------  -------------------------

Psychology           Life Without Fear           7.00
Psychology           Emotional Security: A New   7.99
Psychology           Is Anger the Enemy?         10.95
Psychology           Prolonged Data Deprivatio   19.99
Psychology           Computer Phobic AND Non-P   21.59

                                                 avg
                                                 =========================
                                                 13.50


Category             Shortened Title             Price
-------------------  --------------------------  -------------------------

Traditional Cooking  Fifty Years in Buckingham   11.95
Traditional Cooking  Sushi, Anyone?              14.99
Traditional Cooking  Onions, Leeks, and Garlic   20.95

                                                 avg
                                                 =========================
                                                 15.96

(21 row(s) affected)
```

B. Use a SELECT statement with simple and searched CASE function

Within a SELECT statement, the searched CASE function allows values to be replaced in the result set based on comparison values. This example displays the price (a **money** column) as a text comment based on the price range for a book.

```
USE pubs
GO
SELECT    'Price Category' =
      CASE
          WHEN price IS NULL THEN 'Not yet priced'
          WHEN price < 10 THEN 'Very Reasonable Title'
          WHEN price >= 10 and price < 20 THEN 'Coffee Table Title'
          ELSE 'Expensive book!'
      END,
    CAST(title AS varchar(20)) AS 'Shortened Title'
FROM titles
ORDER BY price
GO
```

Here is the result set:

```
Price Category          Shortened Title
--------------------    --------------------
Not yet priced          Net Etiquette
Not yet priced          The Psychology of Co
Very Reasonable Title   The Gourmet Microwav
Very Reasonable Title   You Can Combat Compu
Very Reasonable Title   Life Without Fear
Very Reasonable Title   Emotional Security:
Coffee Table Title      Is Anger the Enemy?
Coffee Table Title      Cooking with Compute
Coffee Table Title      Fifty Years in Bucki
Coffee Table Title      Sushi, Anyone?
Coffee Table Title      Prolonged Data Depri
Coffee Table Title      Silicon Valley Gastr
Coffee Table Title      Straight Talk About
Coffee Table Title      The Busy Executive's
Expensive book!         Secrets of Silicon V
Expensive book!         Onions, Leeks, and G
Expensive book!         Computer Phobic And
Expensive book!         But Is It User Frien

(18 row(s) affected)
```

C. Use CASE with SUBSTRING and SELECT

This example uses CASE and THEN to produce a list of authors, the book identification numbers, and the book types each author has written.

```
USE pubs
SELECT SUBSTRING((RTRIM(a.au_fname) + ' '+
  RTRIM(a.au_lname) + ' '), 1, 25) AS Name, a.au_id, ta.title_id,
  Type =
  CASE
    WHEN SUBSTRING(ta.title_id, 1, 2) = 'BU' THEN 'Business'
    WHEN SUBSTRING(ta.title_id, 1, 2) = 'MC' THEN 'Modern Cooking'
    WHEN SUBSTRING(ta.title_id, 1, 2) = 'PC' THEN 'Popular Computing'
    WHEN SUBSTRING(ta.title_id, 1, 2) = 'PS' THEN 'Psychology'
    WHEN SUBSTRING(ta.title_id, 1, 2) = 'TC' THEN 'Traditional Cooking'
  END
FROM titleauthor ta JOIN authors a ON ta.au_id = a.au_id
```

Here is the result set:

```
Name                       au_id         title_id Type
-------------------------- ------------- -------- --------------------
Johnson White              172-32-1176   PS3333   Psychology
Marjorie Green             213-46-8915   BU1032   Business
Marjorie Green             213-46-8915   BU2075   Business
Cheryl Carson              238-95-7766   PC1035   Popular Computing
Michael O'Leary            267-41-2394   BU1111   Business
Michael O'Leary            267-41-2394   TC7777   Traditional Cooking
Dean Straight              274-80-9391   BU7832   Business
Abraham Bennet             409-56-7008   BU1032   Business
Ann Dull                   427-17-2319   PC8888   Popular Computing
Burt Gringlesby            472-27-2349   TC7777   Traditional Cooking
Charlene Locksley          486-29-1786   PC9999   Popular Computing
Charlene Locksley          486-29-1786   PS7777   Psychology
Reginald Blotchet-Halls    648-92-1872   TC4203   Traditional Cooking
Akiko Yokomoto             672-71-3249   TC7777   Traditional Cooking
Innes del Castillo         712-45-1867   MC2222   Modern Cooking
Michel DeFrance            722-51-5454   MC3021   Modern Cooking
Stearns MacFeather         724-80-9391   BU1111   Business
Stearns MacFeather         724-80-9391   PS1372   Psychology
Livia Karsen               756-30-7391   PS1372   Psychology
Sylvia Panteley            807-91-6654   TC3218   Traditional Cooking
Sheryl Hunter              846-92-7186   PC8888   Popular Computing
Anne Ringer                899-46-2035   MC3021   Modern Cooking
Anne Ringer                899-46-2035   PS2091   Psychology
Albert Ringer              998-72-3567   PS2091   Psychology
Albert Ringer              998-72-3567   PS2106   Psychology

(25 row(s) affected)
```

Related Topics

Data Type Conversion, Data Types, Expressions, SELECT, System Functions,
UPDATE, WHERE

CAST and CONVERT

Explicitly converts an expression of one data type to another. CAST and CONVERT provide similar functionality.

Syntax
Using CAST:

```
CAST ( expression AS data_type )
```

Using CONVERT:

```
CONVERT ( data_type [ ( length ) ] , expression [ , style ] )
```

Arguments

expression

Is any valid Microsoft SQL Server expression. For more information, see Expressions.

data_type

Is the target system-supplied data type, including **bigint** and **sql_variant**. User-defined data types cannot be used. For more information about available data types, see Data Types.

length

Is an optional parameter of **nchar**, **nvarchar**, **char**, **varchar**, **binary**, or **varbinary** data types.

style

Is the style of date format used to convert **datetime** or **smalldatetime** data to character data (**nchar**, **nvarchar**, **char**, **varchar**, **nchar**, or **nvarchar** data types), or the string format when converting **float**, **real**, **money**, or **smallmoney** data to character data (**nchar**, **nvarchar**, **char**, **varchar**, **nchar**, or **nvarchar** data types).

SQL Server supports the date format in Arabic style, using Kuwaiti algorithm.

In the table, the two columns on the left represent the *style* values for **datetime** or **smalldatetime** conversion to character data. Add 100 to a *style* value to get a four-place year that includes the century (yyyy).

Without century (yy)	With century (yyyy)	Standard	Input/Output**
-	0 or 100 (*)	Default	mon dd yyyy hh:miAM (or PM)
1	101	USA	mm/dd/yy
2	102	ANSI	yy.mm.dd

(continued)

(continued)

Without century (yy)	With century (yyyy)	Standard	Input/Output**
3	103	British/French	dd/mm/yy
4	104	German	dd.mm.yy
5	105	Italian	dd-mm-yy
6	106	-	dd mon yy
7	107	-	Mon dd, yy
8	108	-	hh:mm:ss
-	9 or 109 (*)	Default + milliseconds	mon dd yyyy hh:mi:ss:mmmAM (or PM)
10	110	USA	mm-dd-yy
11	111	JAPAN	yy/mm/dd
12	112	ISO	yymmdd
-	13 or 113 (*)	Europe default + milliseconds	dd mon yyyy hh:mm:ss:mmm(24h)
14	114	-	hh:mi:ss:mmm(24h)
-	20 or 120 (*)	ODBC canonical	yyyy-mm-dd hh:mi:ss(24h)
-	21 or 121 (*)	ODBC canonical (with milliseconds)	yyyy-mm-dd hh:mi:ss.mmm(24h)
-	126(***)	ISO8601	yyyy-mm-dd Thh:mm:ss:mmm (no spaces)
-	130*	Kuwaiti	dd mon yyyy hh:mi:ss:mmmAM
-	131*	Kuwaiti	dd/mm/yy hh:mi:ss:mmmAM

* The default values (*style* 0 or 100, 9 or 109, 13 or 113, 20 or 120, and 21 or 121) always return the century (yyyy).

** Input when converting to **datetime**; output when converting to character data.

*** Designed for XML use. For conversion from **datetime** or **smalldatetime** to **character** data, the output format is as described in the table. For conversion from **float**, **money**, or **smallmoney** to **character** data, the output is equivalent to *style* 2. For conversion from **real** to **character** data, the output is equivalent to *style* 1.

Important By default, SQL Server interprets two-digit years based on a cutoff year of 2049. That is, the two-digit year 49 is interpreted as 2049 and the two-digit year 50 is interpreted as 1950. Many client applications, such as those based on OLE Automation objects, use a cutoff year of 2030. SQL Server provides a configuration option (**two digit year cutoff**) that changes the cutoff year used by SQL Server and allows the consistent treatment of dates. The safest course, however, is to specify four-digit years.

When you convert to character data from **smalldatetime**, the styles that include seconds or milliseconds show zeros in these positions. You can truncate unwanted date parts when converting from **datetime** or **smalldatetime** values by using an appropriate **char** or **varchar** data type length.

This table shows the *style* values for **float** or **real** conversion to character data.

Value	Output
0 (default)	Six digits maximum. Use in scientific notation, when appropriate.
1	Always eight digits. Always use in scientific notation.
2	Always 16 digits. Always use in scientific notation.

In the following table, the column on the left represents the *style* value for **money** or **smallmoney** conversion to character data.

Value	Output
0 (default)	No commas every three digits to the left of the decimal point, and two digits to the right of the decimal point; for example, 4235.98.
1	Commas every three digits to the left of the decimal point, and two digits to the right of the decimal point; for example, 3,510.92.
2	No commas every three digits to the left of the decimal point, and four digits to the right of the decimal point; for example, 4235.9819.

Return Types

Returns the same value as *data type* 0.

Remarks

Implicit conversions are those conversions that occur without specifying either the CAST or CONVERT function. Explicit conversions are those conversions that require the CAST (CONVERT) function to be specified. This chart shows all explicit and implicit data type conversions allowed for SQL Server system-supplied data types, including **bigint** and **sql_variant**.

Data type conversion chart. Legend: ● Explicit conversion, ◐ Implicit conversion, ○ Conversion is not allowed, * Requires explicit CAST to prevent the loss of precision or scale that might occur in an implicit conversion. (Shaded/blank diagonal cells represent conversion of a type to itself.)

From \ To:	binary	varbinary	char	varchar	nchar	nvarchar	datetime	smalldatetime	decimal	numeric	float	real	bigint	int(INT4)	smalllint(INT2)	tinyint(INT1)	money	smallmoney	bit	timestamp	uniqueidentifier	image	ntext	text	sql_variant
binary		◐	◐	◐	◐	◐	◐	◐	◐	◐	◐	◐	◐	◐	◐	◐	◐	◐	◐	◐	◐	○	○	○	◐
varbinary	◐		◐	◐	◐	◐	◐	◐	◐	◐	◐	◐	◐	◐	◐	◐	◐	◐	◐	◐	◐	○	○	○	◐
char	●	●		◐	◐	◐	◐	◐	◐	◐	◐	◐	◐	◐	◐	◐	●	●	◐	●	◐	○	◐	◐	◐
varchar	●	●	◐		◐	◐	◐	◐	◐	◐	◐	◐	◐	◐	◐	◐	●	●	◐	●	◐	○	◐	◐	◐
nchar	●	●	◐	◐		◐	◐	◐	◐	◐	◐	◐	◐	◐	◐	◐	●	●	◐	●	◐	○	◐	○	◐
nvarchar	●	●	◐	◐	◐		◐	◐	◐	◐	◐	◐	◐	◐	◐	◐	●	●	◐	●	◐	○	○	○	◐
datetime	●	●	◐	◐	◐	◐		◐	●	●	●	●	●	●	●	●	●	●	●	●	○	○	○	○	◐
smalldatetime	●	●	◐	◐	◐	◐	◐		●	●	●	●	●	●	●	●	●	●	●	●	○	○	○	○	◐
decimal	◐	◐	◐	◐	◐	◐	○	○	*	*	◐	◐	◐	◐	◐	◐	◐	◐	◐	◐	○	○	○	○	◐
numeric	◐	◐	◐	◐	◐	◐	○	○	*	*	◐	◐	◐	◐	◐	◐	◐	◐	◐	◐	○	○	○	○	◐
float	◐	◐	◐	◐	◐	◐	◐	◐	◐	◐		◐	◐	◐	◐	◐	◐	◐	◐	◐	○	○	○	○	◐
real	◐	◐	◐	◐	◐	◐	◐	◐	◐	◐	◐		◐	◐	◐	◐	◐	◐	◐	◐	○	○	○	○	◐
bigint	◐	◐	◐	◐	◐	◐	◐	◐	◐	◐	◐	◐		◐	◐	◐	◐	◐	◐	◐	○	○	○	○	◐
int(INT4)	◐	◐	◐	◐	◐	◐	◐	◐	◐	◐	◐	◐	◐		◐	◐	◐	◐	◐	◐	○	○	○	○	◐
smalllint(INT2)	◐	◐	◐	◐	◐	◐	◐	◐	◐	◐	◐	◐	◐	◐		◐	◐	◐	◐	◐	○	○	○	○	◐
tinyint(INT1)	◐	◐	◐	◐	◐	◐	◐	◐	◐	◐	◐	◐	◐	◐	◐		◐	◐	◐	◐	○	○	○	○	◐
money	◐	◐	●	●	●	●	◐	◐	◐	◐	◐	◐	◐	◐	◐	◐		◐	◐	◐	○	○	○	○	◐
smallmoney	◐	◐	●	●	●	●	◐	◐	◐	◐	◐	◐	◐	◐	◐	◐	◐		◐	◐	○	○	○	○	◐
bit	◐	◐	◐	◐	◐	◐	○	○	◐	◐	◐	◐	◐	◐	◐	◐	◐	◐		◐	○	○	○	○	◐
timestamp	◐	◐	◐	◐	○	◐	◐	◐	◐	◐	○	◐	◐	◐	◐	◐	◐	◐	◐		○	○	○	○	◐
uniqueidentifier	◐	◐	◐	◐	◐	◐	○	○	○	○	○	○	○	○	○	○	○	○	○	○		○	○	○	◐
image	◐	◐	○	○	○	○	○	○	○	○	○	○	○	○	○	○	○	○	○	○	○		○	○	○
ntext	○	○	●	●	◐	◐	○	○	○	○	○	○	○	○	○	○	○	○	○	○	○	○		○	○
text	○	○	◐	◐	●	●	○	○	○	○	○	○	○	○	○	○	○	○	○	○	○	○	○		○
sql_variant	●	●	●	●	●	●	●	●	●	●	●	●	●	●	●	●	●	●	●	○	●	○	○	○	

● Explicit conversion
◐ Implicit conversion
○ Conversion is not allowed
* Requires explicit CAST to prevent the loss of precision or scale that might occur in an implicit conversion

Note Because Unicode data always uses an even number of bytes, use caution when converting **binary** or **varbinary** to or from Unicode supported data types. For example, this conversion does not return a hexadecimal value of 41, but of 4100: `SELECT CAST(CAST(0x41 AS nvarchar) AS varbinary)`

Automatic data type conversion is not supported for the **text** and **image** data types. You can explicitly convert **text** data to character data, and **image** data to **binary** or **varbinary**, but the maximum length is 8000. If you attempt an incorrect conversion (for example, if you convert a character expression that includes letters to an **int**), SQL Server generates an error message.

When the output of CAST or CONVERT is a character string, and the input is a character string, the output has the same collation and collation label as the input. If the input is not a character string, the output has the default collation of the database, and a collation label of coercible-default. For more information, see Collation Precedence.

To assign a different collation to the output, apply the COLLATE clause to the result expression of the CAST or CONVERT function. For example:

```
SELECT CAST('abc' AS varchar(5)) COLLATE French_CS_AS
```

There is no implicit conversion on assignment from the **sql_variant** data type but there is implicit conversion to **sql_variant**.

When converting character or binary expressions (**char**, **nchar**, **nvarchar**, **varchar**, **binary**, or **varbinary**) to an expression of a different data type, data can be truncated, only partially displayed, or an error is returned because the result is too short to display. Conversions to **char**, **varchar**, **nchar**, **nvarchar**, **binary**, and **varbinary** are truncated, except for the conversions shown in this table.

From data type	To data type	Result
int, **smallint**, or **tinyint**	**char**	*
	varchar	*
	nchar	E
	nvarchar	E
money, **smallmoney**, **numeric**, **decimal**, **float**, or **real**	**char**	E
	varchar	E
	nchar	E
	nvarchar	E

* Result length too short to display.
E Error returned because result length is too short to display.

Microsoft SQL Server guarantees that only roundtrip conversions, conversions that convert a data type from its original data type and back again, will yield the same values from release to release. This example shows such a roundtrip conversion:

```
DECLARE @myval decimal (5, 2)
SET @myval = 193.57
SELECT CAST(CAST(@myval AS varbinary(20)) AS decimal(10,5))
-- Or, using CONVERT
SELECT CONVERT(decimal(10,5), CONVERT(varbinary(20), @myval))
```

Do not attempt to construct, for example, **binary** values and convert them to a data type of the numeric data type category. SQL Server does not guarantee that the result of a **decimal** or **numeric** data type conversion to **binary** will be the same between releases of SQL Server.

This example shows a resulting expression too small to display.

```
USE pubs
SELECT SUBSTRING(title, 1, 25) AS Title, CAST(ytd_sales AS char(2))
FROM titles
WHERE type = 'trad_cook'
```

Here is the result set:

```
Title
------------------------- --
Onions, Leeks, and Garlic *
Fifty Years in Buckingham *
Sushi, Anyone?            *

(3 row(s) affected)
```

When data types are converted with a different number of decimal places, the value is truncated to the most precise digit. For example, the result of SELECT CAST(10.6496 AS **int**) is 10.

When data types in which the target data type has fewer decimal points than the source data type are converted, the value is rounded. For example, the result of CAST(10.3496847 AS **money**) is $10.3497.

SQL Server returns an error message when non-numeric **char**, **nchar**, **varchar**, or **nvarchar** data is converted to **int**, **float**, **numeric**, or **decimal**. SQL Server also returns an error when an empty string (" ") is converted to **numeric** or **decimal**.

Using Binary String Data

When **binary** or **varbinary** data is converted to character data and an odd number of values is specified following the x, SQL Server adds a 0 (zero) after the x to make an even number of values.

Binary data consists of the characters from 0 through 9 and from A through F (or from a through f), in groups of two characters each. Binary strings must be preceded by 0x. For example, to input FF, type 0xFF. The maximum value is a binary value of 8000 bytes, each of which is FF. The **binary** data types are not for hexadecimal data but rather for bit patterns. Conversions and calculations of hexadecimal numbers stored as binary data can be unreliable.

When specifying the length of a **binary** data type, every two characters count as one. A length of 10 signifies that 10 two-character groupings will be entered.

Empty binary strings, represented by 0x, can be stored as binary data.

Examples

A. Use both CAST and CONVERT

Each example retrieves the titles for those books that have a 3 in the first digit of year-to-date sales, and converts their **ytd_sales** to **char(20)**.

```
-- Use CAST.
USE pubs
GO
SELECT SUBSTRING(title, 1, 30) AS Title, ytd_sales
FROM titles
WHERE CAST(ytd_sales AS char(20)) LIKE '3%'
GO


-- Use CONVERT.
USE pubs
GO
SELECT SUBSTRING(title, 1, 30) AS Title, ytd_sales
FROM titles
WHERE CONVERT(char(20), ytd_sales) LIKE '3%'
GO
```

Here is the result set (for either query):

```
Title                           ytd_sales
------------------------------- -----------
Cooking with Computers: Surrep 3876
Computer Phobic AND Non-Phobic 375
Emotional Security: A New Algo 3336
Onions, Leeks, and Garlic: Coo 375

(4 row(s) affected)
```

B. Use CAST with arithmetic operators

This example calculates a single column computation (**Copies**) by dividing the total year-to-date sales (**ytd_sales**) by the individual book price (**price**). This result is converted to an **int** data type after being rounded to the nearest whole number.

```
USE pubs
GO
SELECT CAST(ROUND(ytd_sales/price, 0) AS int) AS 'Copies'
FROM titles
GO
```

Here is the result set:

```
Copies
------
205
324
6262
205
102
7440
NULL
383
205
NULL
17
187
16
204
418
18
1263
273

(18 row(s) affected)
```

C. Use CAST to concatenate

This example concatenates noncharacter, nonbinary expressions using the CAST data type conversion function.

```
USE pubs
GO
SELECT 'The price is ' + CAST(price AS varchar(12))
FROM titles
WHERE price > 10.00
GO
```

Here is the result set:

```
------------------
The price is 19.99
The price is 11.95
The price is 19.99
The price is 19.99
The price is 22.95
The price is 20.00
The price is 21.59
```

(continued)

(continued)

```
The price is 10.95
The price is 19.99
The price is 20.95
The price is 11.95
The price is 14.99

(12 row(s) affected)
```

D. Use CAST for more readable text

This example uses CAST in the select list to convert the **title** column to a **char(50)** column so the results are more readable.

```
USE pubs
GO
SELECT CAST(title AS char(50)), ytd_sales
FROM titles
WHERE type = 'trad_cook'
GO
```

Here is the result set:

```
                                                   ytd_sales
--------------------------------------------------  ---------
Onions, Leeks, and Garlic: Cooking Secrets of the   375
Fifty Years in Buckingham Palace Kitchens           15096
Sushi, Anyone?                                      4095

(3 row(s) affected)
```

E. Use CAST with LIKE clause

This example converts an **int** column (the **ytd_sales** column) to a **char(20)** column so that it can be used with the LIKE clause.

```
USE pubs
GO
SELECT title, ytd_sales
FROM titles
WHERE CAST(ytd_sales AS char(20)) LIKE '15%'
   AND type = 'trad_cook'
GO
```

Here is the result set:

```
title                                                           ytd_sales
--------------------------------------------------------------- -----------
Fifty Years in Buckingham Palace Kitchens                       15096

(1 row(s) affected)
```

Related Topics

Data Type Conversion, SELECT, System Functions

CEILING

Returns the smallest integer greater than, or equal to, the given numeric expression.

Syntax

```
CEILING ( numeric_expression )
```

Arguments

numeric_expression

Is an expression of the exact numeric or approximate numeric data type category, except for the **bit** data type.

Return Types

Returns the same type as *numeric_expression*.

Examples

This example shows positive numeric, negative, and zero values with the CEILING function.

```
SELECT CEILING($123.45), CEILING($-123.45), CEILING($0.0)
GO
```

Here is the result set:

```
---------- ---------- --------------------------
124.00     -123.00     0.00

(1 row(s) affected)
```

Related Topics

System Functions

char and varchar

Fixed-length (**char**) or variable-length (**varchar**) character data types.

char[(*n*)]

Fixed-length non-Unicode character data with length of *n* bytes. *n* must be a value from 1 through 8,000. Storage size is *n* bytes. The SQL-92 synonym for **char** is **character**.

varchar[(*n*)]

Variable-length non-Unicode character data with length of *n* bytes. *n* must be a value from 1 through 8,000. Storage size is the actual length in bytes of the data entered, not *n* bytes. The data entered can be 0 characters in length. The SQL-92 synonyms for **varchar** are **char varying** or **character varying**.

Remarks

When *n* is not specified in a data definition or variable declaration statement, the default length is 1. When *n* is not specified with the CAST function, the default length is 30.

Objects using **char** or **varchar** are assigned the default collation of the database, unless a specific collation is assigned using the COLLATE clause. The collation controls the code page used to store the character data.

Sites supporting multiple languages should consider using the Unicode **nchar** or **nvarchar** data types to minimize character conversion issues. If you use **char** or **varchar**:

- Use **char** when the data values in a column are expected to be consistently close to the same size.

- Use **varchar** when the data values in a column are expected to vary considerably in size.

If SET ANSI_PADDING is OFF when CREATE TABLE or ALTER TABLE is executed, a **char** column defined as NULL is handled as **varchar**.

When the collation code page uses double-byte characters, the storage size is still *n* bytes. Depending on the character string, the storage size of *n* bytes may be less than *n* characters.

Related Topics

CAST and CONVERT, COLLATE, Collations, Data Type Conversion, Data Types, sp_dbcmptlevel, Specifying Collations, Using char and varchar Data, Using Unicode Data

CHAR

A string function that converts an **int** ASCII code to a character.

Syntax

```
CHAR ( integer_expression )
```

Arguments

integer_expression
   Is an integer from 0 through 255. NULL is returned if the integer expression is not in this range.

Return Types

char(1)

Remarks

CHAR can be used to insert control characters into character strings. The table shows some commonly used control characters.

Control character	Value
Tab	CHAR(9)
Line feed	CHAR(10)
Carriage return	CHAR(13)

Examples

A. Use ASCII and CHAR to print ASCII values from a string

This example prints the ASCII value and character for each character in the string New Moon.

```
SET TEXTSIZE 0
-- Create variables for the character string and for the current
-- position in the string.
DECLARE @position int, @string char(8)
-- Initialize the current position and the string variables.
SET @position = 1
SET @string = 'New Moon'
WHILE @position <= DATALENGTH(@string)
```

(continued)

(continued)

```
    BEGIN
    SELECT ASCII(SUBSTRING(@string, @position, 1)),
        CHAR(ASCII(SUBSTRING(@string, @position, 1)))
    SET @position = @position + 1
    END
GO
```

Here is the result set:

```
----------- -
78          N


----------- -
101         e


----------- -
119         w


----------- -
32


----------- -
77          M


----------- -
111         o


----------- -
111         o


----------- -
110         n


----------- -
```

B. Use CHAR to insert a control character

This example uses CHAR(13) to print name, address, and city information on separate lines, when the results are returned in text.

```
USE Northwind
SELECT FirstName + ' ' + LastName, + CHAR(13) + Address,
    + CHAR(13) + City, + Region
FROM Employees
WHERE EmployeeID = 1
```

Here is the result set:

```
Nancy Davolio
507 - 20th Ave. E.
Apt. 2A
Seattle          WA
```

Note In this record, the data in the **Address** column also contains a control character.

Related Topics

+ (String Concatenation), String Functions

CHARINDEX

Returns the starting position of the specified expression in a character string.

Syntax

```
CHARINDEX ( expression1 , expression2 [ , start_location ] )
```

Arguments

expression1

Is an expression containing the sequence of characters to be found. *expression1* is an expression of the short character data type category.

expression2

Is an expression, usually a column searched for the specified sequence. *expression2* is of the character string data type category.

start_location

Is the character position to start searching for *expression1* in *expression2*. If *start_location* is not given, is a negative number, or is zero, the search starts at the beginning of *expression2*.

Return Types

int

Remarks

If either *expression1* or *expression2* is of a Unicode data type (**nvarchar** or **nchar**) and the other is not, the other is converted to a Unicode data type.

If either *expression1* or *expression2* is NULL, CHARINDEX returns NULL when the database compatibility level is 70 or later. If the database compatibility level is 65 or earlier, CHARINDEX returns NULL only when both *expression1* and *expression2* are NULL.

If *expression1* is not found within *expression2*, CHARINDEX returns 0.

Examples

The first code example returns the position at which the sequence "wonderful" begins in the **notes** column of the **titles** table. The second example uses the optional *start_location* parameter to begin looking for wonderful in the fifth character of the **notes** column. The third example shows the result set when *expression1* is not found within *expression2*.

```
USE pubs
GO
SELECT CHARINDEX('wonderful', notes)
FROM titles
WHERE title_id = 'TC3218'
GO


-- Use the optional start_location parameter to start searching
-- for wonderful starting with the fifth character in the notes
-- column.
USE pubs
GO
SELECT CHARINDEX('wonderful', notes, 5)
FROM titles
WHERE title_id = 'TC3218'
GO
```

Here is the result set for the first and second queries:

```
-----------
46

(1 row(s) affected)

USE pubs
GO
SELECT CHARINDEX('wondrous', notes)
FROM titles
WHERE title_id='TC3218'
GO
```

Here is the result set.

```
- - - - - - - - - - -
0

(1 row(s) affected)
```

Related Topics

+ (String Concatenation), String Functions

CHECKPOINT

Forces all dirty pages for the current database to be written to disk. Dirty pages are data or log pages modified after entered into the buffer cache, but the modifications have not yet been written to disk. For more information about log truncation, see Truncating the Transaction Log.

Syntax

```
CHECKPOINT
```

Remarks

The CHECKPOINT statement saves time in a subsequent recovery by creating a point at which all modifications to data and log pages are guaranteed to have been written to disk.

Checkpoints also occur:

- When a database option is changed with ALTER DATABASE. A checkpoint is executed in the database in which the option is changed.
- When a server is stopped, a checkpoint is executed in each database on the server. These methods of stopping Microsoft SQL Server 2000 checkpoint each database:
  - Using SQL Server Service Manager.
  - Using SQL Server Enterprise Manager.
  - Using the SHUTDOWN statement.
  - Using the Windows NT command **net stop mssqlserver** on the command prompt.
  - Using the **services** icon in the Windows NT control panel, selecting the **mssqlserver** service, and clicking the stop button.

The SHUTDOWN WITH NOWAIT statement shuts down SQL Server without executing a checkpoint in each database. This may cause the subsequent restart to take a longer time than usual to recover the databases on the server.

SQL Server 2000 also automatically checkpoints any database where the lesser of these conditions occur:

- The active portion of the log exceeds the size that the server could recover in the amount of time specified in the **recovery interval** server configuration option.
- If the database is in log truncate mode and the log becomes 70 percent full.

A database is in log truncate mode when both these conditions are TRUE:

- The database is using the simple recovery model.
- One of these events has occurred after the last BACKUP DATABASE statement referencing the database was executed:
  - A BACKUP LOG statement referencing the database is executed with either the NO_LOG or TRUNCATE_ONLY clauses.
  - A nonlogged operation is performed in the database, such as a nonlogged bulk copy operation or a nonlogged WRITETEXT statement is executed.
  - An ALTER DATABASE statement that adds or deletes a file in the database is executed.

Permissions

CHECKPOINT permissions default to members of the **sysadmin** fixed server role and the **db_owner** and **db_backupoperator** fixed database roles, and are not transferable.

Related Topics

ALTER DATABASE, Checkpoints and the Active Portion of the Log, recovery interval Option, Setting Database Options, SHUTDOWN

CHECKSUM

Returns the checksum value computed over a row of a table, or over a list of expressions. CHECKSUM is intended for use in building hash indices.

Syntax

```
CHECKSUM ( * | expression [ ,...n ] )
```

Arguments

*

Specifies that computation is over all the columns of the table. CHECKSUM returns an error if any column is of noncomparable data type. Noncomparable data types are **text**, **ntext**, **image**, and **cursor**, as well as **sql_variant** with any of the above types as its base type.

expression

Is an expression of any type except a noncomparable data type.

Return Types

int

Remarks

CHECKSUM computes a hash value, called the checksum, over its list of arguments. The hash value is intended for use in building hash indices. If the arguments to CHECKSUM are columns, and an index is built over the computed CHECKSUM value, the result is a hash index, which can be used for equality searches over the columns.

CHECKSUM satisfies the properties of a hash function: CHECKSUM applied over any two lists of expressions returns the same value if the corresponding elements of the two lists have the same type and are equal when compared using the equals (=) operator. For the purpose of this definition, NULL values of a given type are considered to compare as equal. If one of the values in the expression list changes, the checksum of the list also usually changes. However, there is a small chance that the checksum will not change.

BINARY_CHECKSUM and CHECKSUM are similar functions: they can be used to compute a checksum value on a list of expressions, and the order of expressions affects the resultant value. The order of columns used in the case of CHECKSUM(*) is the order of columns specified in the table or view definition, including computed columns.

CHECKSUM and BINARY_CHECKSUM return different values for the string data types, where locale can cause strings with different representation to compare equal. The string data types are **char**, **varchar**, **nchar**, **nvarchar**, or **sql_variant** (if its base type is a string data type). For example, the BINARY_CHECKSUM values for the strings "McCavity" and "Mccavity" are different. In contrast, in a case-insensitive server, CHECKSUM returns the same checksum values for those strings. CHECKSUM values should not be compared against BINARY_CHECKSUM values.

Examples

Using CHECKSUM to build hash indices

The CHECKSUM function may be used to build hash indices. The hash index is built by adding a computed checksum column to the table being indexed, then building an index on the checksum column.

```
-- Create a checksum index.
SET ARITHABORT ON
USE Northwind
GO
ALTER TABLE Products
ADD cs_Pname AS checksum(ProductName)
CREATE INDEX Pname_index ON Products (cs_Pname)
```

The checksum index can be used as a hash index, particularly to improve indexing speed when the column to be indexed is a long character column. The checksum index can be used for equality searches.

```
/*Use the index in a SELECT query. Add a second search
condition to catch stray cases where checksums match,
but the values are not identical.*/
SELECT *
FROM Products
WHERE checksum(N'Vegie-spread') = cs_Pname
AND ProductName = N'Vegie-spread'
```

Creating the index on the computed column materializes the checksum column, and any changes to the **ProductName** value will be propagated to the checksum column. Alternatively, an index could be built directly on the column indexed. However, if the key values are long, a regular index is not likely to perform as well as a checksum index.

Related Topics

BINARY_CHECKSUM, CHECKSUM_AGG

CHECKSUM_AGG

Returns the checksum of the values in a group. Null values are ignored.

Syntax

```
CHECKSUM_AGG ( [ ALL | DISTINCT ] expression )
```

Arguments

ALL
   Applies the aggregate function to all values. ALL is the default.

DISTINCT
   Specifies that CHECKSUM_AGG return the checksum of unique values.

expression
   Is a constant, column, or function, and any combination of arithmetic, bitwise, and string operators. *expression* is an expression of the **int** data type. Aggregate functions and subqueries are not allowed.

Return Types

Returns the checksum of all *expression* values as **int**.

Remarks

CHECKSUM_AGG can be used along with BINARY_CHECKSUM to detect changes in a table.

The order of the rows in the table does not affect the result of CHECKSUM_AGG. In addition, CHECKSUM_AGG functions may be used with the DISTINCT keyword and the GROUP BY clause.

If one of the values in the expression list changes, the checksum of the list also usually changes. However, there is a small chance that the checksum will not change.

CHECKSUM_AGG has similar functionality with other aggregate functions. For more information, see Aggregate Functions.

Examples

A. Use CHECKSUM_AGG with BINARY_CHECKSUM to detect changes in a table

This example uses CHECKSUM_AGG with the BINARY_CHECKSUM function to detect changes in the **Products** table.

```
USE Northwind
GO
SELECT CHECKSUM_AGG(BINARY_CHECKSUM(*))
FROM   Products
```

B. Use CHECKSUM_AGG with BINARY_CHECKSUM to detect changes in a column of a table

This example detects changes in **UnitsInStock** column of the **Products** table in the **Northwind** database.

```
--Get the checksum value before the column value is changed.
USE Northwind
GO
SELECT CHECKSUM_AGG(CAST(UnitsInStock AS int))
FROM   Products
```

Here is the result set:

```
57
```

```
--Change the value of a row in the column
UPDATE Products --
SET UnitsInStock=135
WHERE UnitsInStock=125
```

(continued)

(continued)

```
--Get the checksum of the modified column.
SELECT CHECKSUM_AGG(CAST(UnitsInStock AS int))
FROM   Products
```

Here is the result set:

```
195
```

Related Topics

BINARY_CHECKSUM, CHECKSUM

CLOSE

Closes an open cursor by releasing the current result set and freeing any cursor locks held on the rows on which the cursor is positioned. CLOSE leaves the data structures accessible for reopening, but fetches and positioned updates are not allowed until the cursor is reopened. CLOSE must be issued on an open cursor; it is not allowed on cursors that have only been declared or are already closed.

Syntax

```
CLOSE { { [ GLOBAL ] cursor_name } | cursor_variable_name }
```

Arguments

GLOBAL

Specifies that *cursor_name* refers to a global cursor.

cursor_name

Is the name of an open cursor. If both a global and a local cursor exist with *cursor_name* as their name, *cursor_name* refers to the global cursor when GLOBAL is specified; otherwise, *cursor_name* refers to the local cursor.

cursor_variable_name

Is the name of a cursor variable associated with an open cursor.

Examples

This example shows the correct placement of the CLOSE statement in a cursor-based process.

```
USE pubs
GO
```

(continued)

(continued)

```
DECLARE authorcursor CURSOR FOR
SELECT au_fname, au_lname
FROM authors
ORDER BY au_fname, au_lname

OPEN authorcursor
FETCH NEXT FROM authorcursor
WHILE @@FETCH_STATUS = 0
BEGIN
    FETCH NEXT FROM authorcursor
END

CLOSE authorcursor
DEALLOCATE authorcursor
GO
```

Related Topics

Cursors, DEALLOCATE, FETCH, OPEN

COALESCE

Returns the first nonnull expression among its arguments.

Syntax

```
COALESCE ( expression [ ,...n ] )
```

Arguments

expression

Is an expression of any type.

n

Is a placeholder indicating that multiple expressions can be specified. All expressions must be of the same type or must be implicitly convertible to the same type.

Return Types

Returns the same value as *expression*.

Remarks

If all arguments are NULL, COALESCE returns NULL.

COALESCE(*expression1*,...*n*) is equivalent to this CASE function:

```
CASE
    WHEN (expression1 IS NOT NULL) THEN expression1
    ...
    WHEN (expressionN IS NOT NULL) THEN expressionN
    ELSE NULL
```

Examples

In this example, the **wages** table is shown to include three columns with information about an employee's yearly wage: **hourly_wage**, **salary**, and **commission**. However, an employee receives only one type of pay. To determine the total amount paid to all employees, use the COALESCE function to receive only the nonnull value found in **hourly_wage**, **salary**, and **commission**.

```
SET NOCOUNT ON
GO
USE master
IF EXISTS (SELECT TABLE_NAME FROM INFORMATION_SCHEMA.TABLES
      WHERE TABLE_NAME = 'wages')
   DROP TABLE wages
GO
CREATE TABLE wages
(
   emp_id    tinyint   identity,
   hourly_wage decimal   NULL,
   salary    decimal   NULL,
   commission   decimal   NULL,
   num_sales tinyint   NULL
)
GO
INSERT wages VALUES(10.00, NULL, NULL, NULL)
INSERT wages VALUES(20.00, NULL, NULL, NULL)
INSERT wages VALUES(30.00, NULL, NULL, NULL)
INSERT wages VALUES(40.00, NULL, NULL, NULL)
INSERT wages VALUES(NULL, 10000.00, NULL, NULL)
INSERT wages VALUES(NULL, 20000.00, NULL, NULL)
INSERT wages VALUES(NULL, 30000.00, NULL, NULL)
INSERT wages VALUES(NULL, 40000.00, NULL, NULL)
INSERT wages VALUES(NULL, NULL, 15000, 3)
INSERT wages VALUES(NULL, NULL, 25000, 2)
```

(continued)

(continued)

```
INSERT wages VALUES(NULL, NULL, 20000, 6)
INSERT wages VALUES(NULL, NULL, 14000, 4)
GO
SET NOCOUNT OFF
GO
SELECT CAST(COALESCE(hourly_wage * 40 * 52,
    salary,
    commission * num_sales) AS money) AS 'Total Salary'
FROM wages
GO
```

Here is the result set:

```
Total Salary
------------
20800.0000
41600.0000
62400.0000
83200.0000
10000.0000
20000.0000
30000.0000
40000.0000
45000.0000
50000.0000
120000.0000
56000.0000

(12 row(s) affected)
```

Related Topics

CASE, System Functions

COLLATE

A clause that can be applied to a database definition or a column definition to define
the collation, or to a character string expression to apply a collation cast.

Syntax

```
COLLATE < collation_name >
< collation_name > :: =
    { Windows_collation_name } | { SQL_collation_name }
```

Arguments

collation_name

> Is the name of the collation to be applied to the expression, column definition, or database definition. collation_name can be only a specified *Windows_collation_name* or a *SQL_collation_name*.

> *Windows_collation_name*
>> Is the collation name for Windows collation. See Windows Collation Names.

> *SQL_collation_name*
>> Is the collation name for a SQL collation. See SQL Collation Names.

Remarks

The COLLATE clause can be specified at several levels, including the following:

1. Creating or altering a database.

   You can use the COLLATE clause of the CREATE DATABASE or ALTER DATABASE statement to specify the default collation of the database. You can also specify a collation when you create a database using SQL Server Enterprise Manager. If you do not specify a collation, the database is assigned the default collation of the SQL Server instance.

2. Creating or altering a table column.

   You can specify collations for each character string column using the COLLATE clause of the CREATE TABLE or ALTER TABLE statement. You can also specify a collation when you create a table using SQL Server Enterprise Manager. If you do not specify a collation, the column is assigned the default collation of the database.

   You can also use the database_default option in the COLLATE clause to specify that a column in a temporary table use the collation default of the current user database for the connection instead of **tempdb**.

3. Casting the collation of an expression.

   You can use the COLLATE clause to cast a character expression to a certain collation. Character literals and variables are assigned the default collation of the current database. Column references are assigned the definition collation of the column. For the collation of an expression, see Collation Precedence.

The collation of an identifier depends on the level at which it is defined. Identifiers of instance-level objects, such as logins and database names, are assigned the default collation of the instance. Identifiers of objects within a database, such as tables, views, and column names, are assigned the default collation of the database. For example, two tables with names differing only in case may be created in a database with case-sensitive collation, but may not be created in a database with case-insensitive collation.

Variables, GOTO labels, temporary stored procedures, and temporary tables can be created when the connection context is associated with one database, and then referenced when the context has been switched to another database. The identifiers for variables, GOTO labels, temporary stored procedures, and temporary tables are in the default collation of the instance.

The COLLATE clause can be applied only for the **char**, **varchar**, **text**, **nchar**, **nvarchar**, and **ntext** data types.

Collations are generally identified by a collation name. The exception is in Setup where you do not specify a collation name for Windows collations, but instead specify the collation designator, and then select check boxes to specify binary sorting or dictionary sorting that is either sensitive or insensitive to either case or accents.

You can execute the system function **fn_helpcollations** to retrieve a list of all the valid collation names for Windows collations and SQL collations:

```
SELECT *
FROM ::fn_helpcollations()
```

SQL Server can support only code pages that are supported by the underlying operating system. When you perform an action that depends on collations, the SQL Server collation used by the referenced object must use a code page supported by the operating system running on the computer. These actions can include:

- Specifying a default collation for a database when you create or alter the database.

- Specifying a collation for a column when creating or altering a table.

- When restoring or attaching a database, the default collation of the database and the collation of any **char**, **varchar**, and **text** columns or parameters in the database must be supported by the operating system.

  Code page translations are supported for **char** and **varchar** data types, but not for **text** data type. Data loss during code page translations is not reported.

If the collation specified or the collation used by the referenced object, uses a code page not supported by Windows, SQL Server issues error. For more information, see the Collations section in the SQL Server Architecture chapter of the SQL Server Books Online.

Related Topics

ALTER TABLE, Collation Options for International Support, Collation Precedence, Collations, Constants, CREATE DATABASE, CREATE TABLE, DECLARE @local_variable, table, Using Unicode Data

Windows Collation Name

Specifies the Windows collation name in the COLLATE clause. The Windows collations name is composed of the collation designator and the comparison styles.

Syntax

```
< Windows_collation_name > :: =
  CollationDesignator_<ComparisonStyle>
  < ComparisonStyle > :: =
    CaseSensitivity_AccentSensitivity
    [_KanatypeSensitive [_WidthSensitive ] ]
    | _BIN
```

Arguments

CollationDesignator

Specifies the base collation rules used by the Windows collation. The base collation rules cover:

- The alphabet or language whose sorting rules are applied when dictionary sorting is specified

- The code page used to store non-Unicode character data.

Examples are Latin1_General or French, both of which use code page 1252, or Turkish, which uses code page 1254.

CaseSensitivity

CI specifies case-insensitive, **CS** specifies case-sensitive.

AccentSensitivity

AI specifies accent-insensitive, **AS** specifies accent-sensitive.

KanatypeSensitive

Omitted specifies case-insensitive, **KS** specifies kanatype-sensitive.

WidthSensitivity

Omitted specifies case-insensitive, **WS** specifies case-sensitive.

BIN

Specifies the binary sort order is to be used.

Remarks

The collation designators for Microsoft SQL Server 2000 Windows collations are:

SQL Server 2000 Collation Designator	Code Page for non-Unicode data	Supported Windows Locales
Albanian	1250	Albanian
Arabic	1256	Arabic (Algeria), Arabic (Bahrain), Arabic (Egypt), Arabic (Iraq), Arabic (Jordan), Arabic (Kuwait), Arabic (Lebanon), Arabic (Libya), Arabic (Morocco), Arabic (Oman), Arabic (Qatar), Arabic (Saudi Arabia), Arabic (Syria), Arabic (Tunisia), Arabic (United Arab Emirates), Arabic (Yemen), Farsi, Urdu
Chinese_PRC	936	Chinese (Hong Kong S.A.R.), Chinese (People's Republic of China), Chinese (Singapore)
Chinese_PRC_Stroke	936	Stroke sort with Chinese (PRC)
Chinese_Taiwan_Bopomofo	950	Bopomofo with Chinese (Taiwan)
Chinese_Taiwan_Stroke	950	Chinese (Taiwan)
Croatian	1250	Croatia
Cyrillic_General	1251	Bulgarian, Byelorussian, Russian, Serbian
Czech	1250	Czech
Danish_Norwegian	1252	Danish, Norwegian (Bokmål), Norwegian (Nyorsk)
Estonian	1257	Estonian
Finnish_Swedish	1252	Finnish, Swedish
French	1252	French (Belgium), French (Canada), French (Luxembourg), French (Standard), French (Switzerland)
Georgian_Modern_Sort	1252	Modern Sort with Georgian
German_PhoneBook	1252	PhoneBook sort with German
Greek	1253	Greek

(continued)

(continued)

SQL Server 2000 Collation Designator	Code Page for non-Unicode data	Supported Windows Locales
Hebrew	1255	Hebrew
Hindi	For Unicode data types only	Hindi
Hungarian	1250	Hungarian
Hungarian_Technical	1250	
Icelandic	1252	Icelandic
Japanese	932	Japanese
Japanese_Unicode	932	
Korean_Wansung	949	Korean
Korean_Wansung_Unicode	949	
Latin1_General	1252	Afrikaans, Basque, Catalan, Dutch (Belgium), Dutch (Standard), English (Australia), English (Britain), English (Canada), English (Caribbean) English (Ireland), English (Jamaican), English (New Zealand), English (South Africa), English (United States), Faeroese, German (Austria), German (Liechtenstein), German (Luxembourg), German (Standard), German (Switzerland), Indonesian, Italian, Italian (Switzerland), Portuguese (Brazil), Portuguese (Standard)
Latvian	1257	Latvian
Lithuanian	1257	Lithuanian
Lithuanian_Classic	1257	
Macedonian	1251	Macedonian
Mexican_Trad_Spanish	1252	Spanish (Mexican), Spanish (Traditional Sort)

(continued)

(continued)

SQL Server 2000 Collation Designator	Code Page for non-Unicode data	Supported Windows Locales
Modern_Spanish	1252	Spanish (Argentina), Spanish (Bolivia), Spanish (Chile), Spanish (Colombia), Spanish (Costa Rica), Spanish (Dominican Republic), Spanish (Ecuador), Spanish (Guatemala), Spanish (Modern Sort), Spanish (Panama), Spanish (Paraguay), Spanish (Peru), Spanish (Uruguay), Spanish (Venezuela)
Polish	1250	Polish
Romanian	1250	Romanian
Slovak	1250	Slovak
Slovenian	1250	Slovenian
Thai	874	Thai
Turkish	1254	Turkish
Ukrainian	1251	Ukrainian
Vietnamese	1258	Vietnamese

Examples

These are some examples of Windows collation names:

- **Latin1_General_CI_AS**

  Collation uses the Latin1 General dictionary sorting rules, code page 1252. Is case-insensitive and accent-sensitive.

- **Estonian_CS_AS**

  Collation uses the Estonian dictionary sorting rules, code page 1257. Is case-sensitive and accent-sensitive.

- **Latin1_General_BIN**

  Collation uses code page 1252 and binary sorting rules. The Latin1 General dictionary sorting rules are ignored.

Related Topics

ALTER TABLE, Collation Settings in Setup, Constants, CREATE DATABASE, CREATE TABLE, DECLARE @local_variable, table, Windows Collation Names Table

SQL Collation Name

A single string that specifies the collation name for a SQL collation.

Syntax

```
< SQL_collation_name > :: =
    SQL_SortRules[_Pref]_CPCodepage_<ComparisonStyle>


<ComparisonStyle> ::=
    _CaseSensitivity_AccentSensitivity | _BIN
```

Arguments

SortRules

A string identifying the alphabet or language whose sorting rules are applied when dictionary sorting is specified. Examples are Latin1_General or Polish.

Pref

Specifies uppercase preference.

Codepage

Specifies a one to four digit number identifying the code page used by the collation. CP1 specifies code page 1252, for all other code pages the complete code page number is specified. For example, CP1251 specifies code page 1251 and CP850 specifies code page 850.

CaseSensitivity

CI specifies case-insensitive, **CS** specifies case-sensitive.

AccentSensitivity

AI specifies accent-insensitive, **AS** specifies accent-sensitive.

BIN

Specifies the binary sort order is to be used.

Remarks

This table lists the SQL collation names.

Sort order ID	SQL collation name
30	SQL_Latin1_General_Cp437_BIN
31	SQL_Latin1_General_Cp437_CS_AS
32	SQL_Latin1_General_Cp437_CI_AS
33	SQL_Latin1_General_Pref_CP437_CI_AS

(continued)

(continued)

Sort order ID	SQL collation name
34	SQL_Latin1_General_Cp437_CI_AI
40	SQL_Latin1_General_Cp850_BIN
41	SQL_Latin1_General_Cp850_CS_AS
42	SQL_Latin1_General_Cp850_CI_AS
43	SQL_Latin1_General_Pref_CP850_CI_AS
44	SQL_Latin1_General_Cp850_CI_AI
49	SQL_1Xcompat_CP850_CI_AS
50	Latin1_General_BIN
51	SQL_Latin1_General_Cp1_CS_AS
52	SQL_Latin1_General_Cp1_CI_AS
53	SQL_Latin1_General_Pref_CP1_CI_AS
54	SQL_Latin1_General_Cp1_CI_AI
55	SQL_AltDiction_Cp850_CS_AS
56	SQL_AltDiction_Pref_CP850_CI_AS
57	SQL_AltDiction_Cp850_CI_AI
58	SQL_Scandinavian_Pref_Cp850_CI_AS
59	SQL_Scandinavian_Cp850_CS_AS
60	SQL_Scandinavian_Cp850_CI_AS
61	SQL_AltDiction_Cp850_CI_AS
71	Latin1_General_CS_AS
72	Latin1_General_CI_AS
73	Danish_Norwegian_CS_AS
74	Finnish_Swedish_CS_AS
75	Icelandic_CS_AS

(continued)

(continued)

Sort order ID	SQL collation name
80	Hungarian_BIN (or Albanian_BIN, Czech_BIN, and so on)[1]
81	SQL_Latin1_General_Cp1250_CS_AS
82	SQL_Latin1_General_Cp1250_CI_AS
83	SQL_Czech_Cp1250_CS_AS
84	SQL_Czech_Cp1250_CI_AS
85	SQL_Hungarian_Cp1250_CS_AS
86	SQL_Hungarian_Cp1250_CI_AS
87	SQL_Polish_Cp1250_CS_AS
88	SQL_Polish_Cp1250_CI_AS
89	SQL_Romanian_Cp1250_CS_AS
90	SQL_Romanian_Cp1250_CI_AS
91	SQL_Croatian_Cp1250_CS_AS
92	SQL_Croatian_Cp1250_CI_AS
93	SQL_Slovak_Cp1250_CS_AS
94	SQL_Slovak_Cp1250_CI_AS
95	SQL_Slovenian_Cp1250_CS_AS
96	SQL_Slovenian_Cp1250_CI_AS
104	Cyrillic_General_BIN (or Ukrainian_BIN, Macedonian_BIN)
105	SQL_Latin1_General_Cp1251_CS_AS
106	SQL_Latin1_General_Cp1251_CI_AS
107	SQL_Ukrainian_Cp1251_CS_AS
108	SQL_Ukrainian_Cp1251_CI_AS
112	Greek_BIN

(continued)

(continued)

Sort order ID	SQL collation name
113	SQL_Latin1_General_Cp1253_CS_AS
114	SQL_Latin1_General_Cp1253_CI_AS
120	SQL_MixDiction_Cp1253_CS_AS
121	SQL_AltDiction_Cp1253_CS_AS
124	SQL_Latin1_General_Cp1253_CI_AI
128	Turkish_BIN
129	SQL_Latin1_General_Cp1254_CS_AS
130	SQL_Latin1_General_Cp1254_CI_AS
136	Hebrew_BIN
137	SQL_Latin1_General_Cp1255_CS_AS
138	SQL_Latin1_General_Cp1255_CI_AS
144	Arabic_BIN
145	SQL_Latin1_General_Cp1256_CS_AS
146	SQL_Latin1_General_Cp1256_CI_AS
153	SQL_Latin1_General_Cp1257_CS_AS
154	SQL_Latin1_General_Cp1257_CI_AS
155	SQL_Estonian_Cp1257_CS_AS
156	SQL_Estonian_Cp1257_CI_AS
157	SQL_Latvian_Cp1257_CS_AS
158	SQL_Latvian_Cp1257_CI_AS
159	SQL_Lithuanian_Cp1257_CS_AS
160	SQL_Lithuanian_Cp1257_CI_AS
183	SQL_Danish_Pref_Cp1_CI_AS

(continued)

(continued)

Sort order ID	SQL collation name
184	SQL_SwedishPhone_Pref_Cp1_CI_AS
185	SQL_SwedishStd_Pref_Cp1_CI_AS
186	SQL_Icelandic_Pref_Cp1_CI_AS
192	Japanese_BIN
193	Japanese_CI_AS
194	Korean_Wansung_BIN
195	Korean_Wansung_CI_AS
196	Chinese_Taiwan_Stroke_BIN
197	Chinese_Taiwan_Stroke_CI_AS
198	Chinese_PRC_BIN
199	Chinese_PRC_CI_AS
200	Japanese_CS_AS
201	Korean_Wansung_CS_AS
202	Chinese_Taiwan_Stroke_CS_AS
203	Chinese_PRC_CS_AS
204	Thai_BIN
205	Thai_CI_AS
206	Thai_CS_AS
210	SQL_EBCDIC037_CP1_CS_AS
211	SQL_EBCDIC273_CP1_CS_AS
212	SQL_EBCDIC277_CP1_CS_AS
213	SQL_EBCDIC278_CP1_CS_AS

(continued)

(continued)

Sort order ID	SQL collation name
214	SQL_EBCDIC280_CP1_CS_AS
215	SQL_EBCDIC284_CP1_CS_AS
216	SQL_EBCDIC285_CP1_CS_AS
217	SQL_EBCDIC297_CP1_CS_AS

1 For Sort Order ID 80, use any of the Window collations with the code page of 1250, and binary order. For example: Albanian_BIN, Croatian_BIN, Czech_BIN, Romanian_BIN, Slovak_BIN, Slovenian_BIN.

Related Topics

ALTER TABLE, Collation Settings in Setup, Constants, CREATE DATABASE, CREATE TABLE, DECLARE @local_variable, table, SQL Collation Names Table (Compatibility collations)

COLLATIONPROPERTY

Returns the property of a given collation.

Syntax

```
COLLATIONPROPERTY( collation_name, property )
```

Arguments

collation_name

Is the name of the collation. *collation_name* is **nvarchar(128)**, and has no default.

property

Is the property of the collation. *property* is **varchar(128)**, and can be any of these values:

Property name	Description
CodePage	The nonUnicode code page of the collation.
LCID	The Windows LCID of the collation. Returns NULL for SQL collations.
ComparisonStyle	The Windows comparison style of the collation. Returns NULL for binary or SQL collations.

Return Types

sql_variant

Examples

```
SELECT COLLATIONPROPERTY('Traditional_Spanish_CS_AS_KS_WS', 'CodePage')
```

Result Set

```
1252
```

Related Topics

fn_helpcollations

COL_LENGTH

Returns the defined length (in bytes) of a column.

Syntax

```
COL_LENGTH ( 'table' , 'column' )
```

Arguments

'table'

Is the name of the table for which to determine column length information. *table* is an expression of type **nvarchar**.

'column'

Is the name of the column for which to determine length. *column* is an expression of type **nvarchar**.

Return Types

int

Examples

This example shows the return values for a column of type **varchar(40)** and a column of type **nvarchar(40)**.

```
USE pubs
GO
CREATE TABLE t1
    (c1 varchar(40),
     c2 nvarchar(40)
)
```

(continued)

(continued)

```
GO
SELECT COL_LENGTH('t1','c1')AS 'VarChar',
       COL_LENGTH('t1','c2')AS 'NVarChar'
GO
DROP TABLE t1
```

Here is the result set.

```
VarChar     NVarChar
40          80
```

Related Topics

Expressions, Metadata Functions

COL_NAME

Returns the name of a database column given the corresponding table identification number and column identification number.

Syntax

```
COL_NAME ( table_id , column_id )
```

Arguments

table_id
> Is the identification number of the table containing the database column. *table_id* is of type **int**.

column_id
> Is the identification number of the column. *column_id* parameter is of type **int**.

Return Types

sysname

Remarks

The *table_id* and *column_id* parameters together produce a column name string.

For more information about obtaining table and column identification numbers, see OBJECT_ID.

Examples

This example returns the name of the first column in the **Employees** table of the **Northwind** database.

```
USE Northwind
SET NOCOUNT OFF
SELECT COL_NAME(OBJECT_ID('Employees'), 1)
```

Here is the result set:

```
EmployeeID

(1 row(s) affected)
```

Related Topics

Expressions, Metadata Functions, sysobjects

COLUMNPROPERTY

Returns information about a column or procedure parameter.

Syntax

```
COLUMNPROPERTY ( id , column , property )
```

Arguments

id

Is an expression containing the identifier (ID) of the table or procedure.

column

Is an expression containing the name of the column or parameter.

property

Is an expression containing the information to be returned for *id,* and can be any of these values.

Value	Description	Value returned
AllowsNull	Allows null values.	1 = TRUE 0 = FALSE NULL = Invalid input
IsComputed	The column is a computed column.	1 = TRUE 0 = FALSE NULL = Invalid input

(continued)

(continued)

Value	Description	Value returned
IsCursorType	The procedure parameter is of type CURSOR.	1 = TRUE 0 = FALSE NULL = Invalid input
IsDeterministic	The column is deterministic. This property applies only to computed columns and view columns.	1 = TRUE 0 = FALSE NULL = Invalid input. Not a computed column or view column.
IsFulltextIndexed	The column has been registered for full-text indexing.	1 = TRUE 0 = FALSE NULL = Invalid input
IsIdentity	The column uses the IDENTITY property.	1 = TRUE 0 = FALSE NULL = Invalid input
IsIdNotForRepl	The column checks for the IDENTITY_INSERT setting. If IDENTITY NOT FOR REPLICATION is specified, the IDENTITY_INSERT setting is not checked.	1 = TRUE 0 = FALSE NULL = Invalid input
IsIndexable	The column can be indexed.	1 = TRUE 0 = FALSE NULL = Invalid input
IsOutParam	The procedure parameter is an output parameter.	1 = TRUE 0 = FALSE NULL = Invalid input
IsPrecise	The column is precise. This property applies only to deterministic columns.	1 = TRUE 0 = FALSE NULL = Invalid input. Not a deterministic column
IsRowGuidCol	The column has the **uniqueidentifier** data type and is defined with the ROWGUIDCOL property.	1 = TRUE 0 = FALSE NULL = Invalid input

(continued)

315

(continued)

Value	Description	Value returned
Precision	Precision for the data type of the column or parameter.	The precision of the specified column data type
		NULL = Invalid input
Scale	Scale for the data type of the column or parameter.	The scale
		NULL = Invalid input
UsesAnsiTrim	ANSI padding setting was ON when the table was initially created.	1= TRUE
		0= FALSE
		NULL = Invalid input

Return Types

int

Remarks

When checking a column's deterministic property, test first whether the column is a computed column. **IsDeterministic** returns NULL for noncomputed columns.

Computed columns can be specified as index columns.

Examples

This example returns the length of the **au_lname** column.

```
SELECT COLUMNPROPERTY( OBJECT_ID('authors'),'au_lname','PRECISION')
```

Related Topics

Metadata Functions, OBJECTPROPERTY, TYPEPROPERTY

COMMIT TRANSACTION

Marks the end of a successful implicit or user-defined transaction.
If @@TRANCOUNT is 1, COMMIT TRANSACTION makes all data modifications performed since the start of the transaction a permanent part of the database, frees the resources held by the connection, and decrements @@TRANCOUNT to 0.
If @@TRANCOUNT is greater than 1, COMMIT TRANSACTION decrements @@TRANCOUNT only by 1.

Syntax

```
COMMIT [ TRAN [ SACTION ] [ transaction_name | @tran_name_variable ] ]
```

Arguments

transaction_name

Is ignored by Microsoft SQL Server. *transaction_name* specifies a transaction name assigned by a previous BEGIN TRANSACTION. *transaction_name* must conform to the rules for identifiers, but only the first 32 characters of the transaction name are used. *transaction_name* can be used as a readability aid by indicating to programmers which nested BEGIN TRANSACTION the COMMIT TRANSACTION is associated with.

@tran_name_variable

Is the name of a user-defined variable containing a valid transaction name. The variable must be declared with a **char**, **varchar**, **nchar**, or **nvarchar** data type.

Remarks

It is the responsibility of the Transact-SQL programmer to issue COMMIT TRANSACTION only at a point when all data referenced by the transaction is logically correct.

If the transaction committed was a Transact-SQL distributed transaction, COMMIT TRANSACTION triggers MS DTC to use a two-phase commit protocol to commit all the servers involved in the transaction. If a local transaction spans two or more databases on the same server, SQL Server uses an internal two-phase commit to commit all the databases involved in the transaction.

When used in nested transactions, commits of the inner transactions do not free resources or make their modifications permanent. The data modifications are made permanent and resources freed only when the outer transaction is committed. Each COMMIT TRANSACTION issued when @@TRANCOUNT is greater than 1 simply decrements @@TRANCOUNT by 1. When @@TRANCOUNT is finally decremented to 0, the entire outer transaction is committed. Because *transaction_name* is ignored by SQL Server, issuing a COMMIT TRANSACTION referencing the name of an outer transaction when there are outstanding inner transactions only decrements @@TRANCOUNT by 1.

Issuing a COMMIT TRANSACTION when @@TRANCOUNT is 0 results in an error that there is no corresponding BEGIN TRANSACTION.

You cannot roll back a transaction after a COMMIT TRANSACTION statement is issued because the data modifications have been made a permanent part of the database.

Examples

A. Commit a transaction

This example increases the advance to be paid to an author when year-to-date sales of a title are greater than $8,000.

```
BEGIN TRANSACTION
USE pubs
GO
UPDATE titles
SET advance = advance * 1.25
WHERE ytd_sales > 8000
GO
COMMIT
GO
```

B. Commit a nested transaction

This example creates a table, generates three levels of nested transactions, and then commits the nested transaction. Although each COMMIT TRANSACTION statement has a *transaction_name* parameter, there is no relationship between the COMMIT TRANSACTION and BEGIN TRANSACTION statements. The *transaction_name* parameters are simply readability aids to help the programmer ensure the proper number of commits are coded to decrement @@TRANCOUNT to 0, and thereby commit the outer transaction.

```
CREATE TABLE TestTran (Cola INT PRIMARY KEY, Colb CHAR(3))
GO
BEGIN TRANSACTION OuterTran -- @@TRANCOUNT set to 1.
GO
INSERT INTO TestTran VALUES (1, 'aaa')
GO
BEGIN TRANSACTION Inner1 -- @@TRANCOUNT set to 2.
GO
INSERT INTO TestTran VALUES (2, 'bbb')
GO
BEGIN TRANSACTION Inner2 -- @@TRANCOUNT set to 3.
GO
INSERT INTO TestTran VALUES (3, 'ccc')
GO
COMMIT TRANSACTION Inner2 -- Decrements @@TRANCOUNT to 2.
-- Nothing committed.
GO
COMMIT TRANSACTION Inner1 -- Decrements @@TRANCOUNT to 1.
-- Nothing committed.
GO
```

(continued)

(continued)

```
COMMIT TRANSACTION OuterTran -- Decrements @@TRANCOUNT to 0.
-- Commits outer transaction OuterTran.
GO
```

Related Topics

BEGIN DISTRIBUTED TRANSACTION, BEGIN TRANSACTION, COMMIT
WORK, ROLLBACK TRANSACTION, ROLLBACK WORK, SAVE
TRANSACTION, @@TRANCOUNT, Transactions

COMMIT WORK

Marks the end of a transaction.

Syntax

```
COMMIT [ WORK ]
```

Remarks

This statement functions identically to COMMIT TRANSACTION, except COMMIT
TRANSACTION accepts a user-defined transaction name. This COMMIT syntax,
with or without specifying the optional keyword WORK, is compatible with SQL-92.

Related Topics

BEGIN DISTRIBUTED TRANSACTION, BEGIN TRANSACTION, COMMIT
TRANSACTION, ROLLBACK TRANSACTION, ROLLBACK WORK, SAVE
TRANSACTION, @@TRANCOUNT

Constants

A constant, also known as a literal or a scalar value, is a symbol that represents a
specific data value. The format of a constant depends on the data type of the value it
represents.

Character string constants

> Character string constants are enclosed in single quotation marks and include
> alphanumeric characters (a–z, A–Z, and 0–9) and special characters, such as
> exclamation point (!), at sign (@), and number sign (#). Character string constants
> are assigned the default collation of the current database, unless the COLLATE
> clause is used to specify a collation. Character strings typed by users are evaluated
> through the code page of the computer and are translated to the database default
> code page if necessary. For more information, see Collations.

If the QUOTED_IDENTIFIER option has been set OFF for a connection, character strings can also be enclosed in double quotation marks, but the Microsoft OLE DB Provider for Microsoft SQL Server and ODBC driver automatically use SET QUOTED_IDENTIFIER ON. The use of single quotation marks is recommended.

If a character string enclosed in single quotation marks contains an embedded quotation mark, represent the embedded single quotation mark with two single quotation marks. This is not necessary in strings embedded in double quotation marks.

Examples of character strings are:

```
'Cincinnati'
'O''Brien'
'Process X is 50% complete.'
'The level for job_id: %d should be between %d and %d.'
"O'Brien"
```

Empty strings are represented as two single quotation marks with nothing in between. In 6.x compatibility mode, an empty string is treated as a single space.

Character string constants support enhanced collations.

Unicode strings

Unicode strings have a format similar to character strings but are preceded by an N identifier (N stands for National Language in the SQL-92 standard). The N prefix must be uppercase. For example, 'Michél' is a character constant while N'Michél' is a Unicode constant. Unicode constants are interpreted as Unicode data, and are not evaluated using a code page. Unicode constants do have a collation, which primarily controls comparisons and case sensitivity. Unicode constants are assigned the default collation of the current database, unless the COLLATE clause is used to specify a collation. Unicode data is stored using two bytes per character, as opposed to one byte per character for character data. For more information, see Using Unicode Data.

Unicode string constants support enhanced collations.

Binary constants

Binary constants have the suffix 0x and are a string of hexadecimal numbers. They are not enclosed in quotation marks. Examples of binary strings are:

```
0xAE
0x12Ef
0x69048AEFDD010E
0x  (empty binary string)
```

bit constants

bit constants are represented by the numbers zero or one, and are not enclosed in quotation marks. If a number larger than one is used, it is converted to one.

datetime constants

datetime constants are represented using character date values in specific formats, enclosed in single quotation marks. For more information about the formats for **datetime** constants, see Using Date and Time Data. Examples of date constants are:

```
'April 15, 1998'
'15 April, 1998'
'980415'
'04/15/98'
```

Examples of time constants are:

```
'14:30:24'
'04:24 PM'
```

integer constants

integer constants are represented by a string of numbers not enclosed in quotation marks and do not contain decimal points. **integer** constants must be whole numbers; they cannot contain decimals. Examples of **integer** constants are:

```
1894
2
```

decimal constants

decimal constants are represented by a string of numbers that are not enclosed in quotation marks and contain a decimal point. Examples of **decimal** constants are:

```
1894.1204
2.0
```

float and **real** constants

float and **real** constants are represented using scientific notation. Examples of **float** or **real** values are:

```
101.5E5
0.5E-2
```

money constants

money constants are represented as string of numbers with an optional decimal point and an optional currency symbol as a prefix. They are not enclosed in quotation marks. Examples of **money** constants are:

```
$12
$542023.14
```

uniqueidentifier constants

uniqueidentifier constants are a string representing a globally unique identifier (GUID) value. They can be specified in either a character or binary string format. Both of these examples specify the same GUID:

```
'6F9619FF-8B86-D011-B42D-00C04FC964FF'
0xff19966f868b11d0b42d00c04fc964ff
```

Specifying Negative and Positive Numbers

To indicate whether a number is positive or negative, apply the + or - unary operators to a numeric constant. This creates a numeric expression that represents the signed numeric value. Numeric constants default to positive if the + or - unary operators are not applied.

- Signed **integer** expressions:

```
+145345234
-2147483648
```

- Signed **decimal** expressions:

```
+145345234.2234
-2147483648.10
```

- Signed **float** expressions:

```
+123E-3
-12E5
```

- Signed **money** expressions:

```
-$45.56
+$423456.99
```

Enhanced Collations

SQL Server 2000 supports character and Unicode string constants that support enhanced collations.

To utilize enhanced collation, use the COLLATE clause.

Related Topics

Collations, Data Types, Expressions, Operators, Using Constants

---

CONTAINS

Is a predicate used to search columns containing character-based data types for precise or fuzzy (less precise) matches to single words and phrases, the proximity of words within a certain distance of one another, or weighted matches. CONTAINS can search for:

- A word or phrase.
- The prefix of a word or phrase.
- A word near another word.
- A word inflectionally generated from another (for example, the word drive is the inflectional stem of drives, drove, driving, and driven).
- A word that has a higher designated weighting than another word.

Syntax

```
CONTAINS
    ( { column | * } , '< contains_search_condition >'
    )
< contains_search_condition > ::=
      { < simple_term >
      | < prefix_term >
      | < generation_term >
      | < proximity_term >
      | < weighted_term >
      }
      | { ( < contains_search_condition > )
      { AND | AND NOT | OR } < contains_search_condition > [ ...n ]
      }
< simple_term > ::=
    word | " phrase "
< prefix term > ::=
    { "word * " | "phrase * " }
< generation_term > ::=
    FORMSOF ( INFLECTIONAL , < simple_term > [ ,...n ] )
< proximity_term > ::=
    { < simple_term > | < prefix_term > }
    { { NEAR | ~ } { < simple_term > | < prefix_term > } } [ ...n ]
< weighted_term > ::=
    ISABOUT
      ( { {
              < simple_term >
            | < prefix_term >
            | < generation_term >
            | < proximity_term >
            }
        [ WEIGHT ( weight_value ) ]
        } [ ,...n ]
      )
```

Arguments

column

Is the name of a specific column that has been registered for full-text searching. Columns of the character string data types are valid full-text searching columns.

*

Specifies that all columns in the table registered for full-text searching should be used to search for the given contains search condition(s). If more than one table is in the FROM clause, * must be qualified by the table name.

<contains_search_condition>

Specifies some text to search for in *column*. Variables cannot be used for the search condition.

word

Is a string of characters without spaces or punctuation.

phrase

Is one or more words with spaces between each word.

> **Note** Some languages, such as those in Asia, can have phrases that consist of one or more words without spaces between them.

<simple_term>

Specifies a match for an exact word (one or more characters without spaces or punctuation in single-byte languages) or a phrase (one or more consecutive words separated by spaces and optional punctuation in single-byte languages). Examples of valid simple terms are "blue berry", blueberry, and "Microsoft SQL Server". Phrases should be enclosed in double quotation marks (""). Words in a phrase must appear in the same order as specified in <contains_search_condition> as they appear in the database column. The search for characters in the word or phrase is case insensitive. Noise words (such as a, and, or the) in full-text indexed columns are not stored in the full-text index. If a noise word is used in a single word search, SQL Server returns an error message indicating that only noise words are present in the query. SQL Server includes a standard list of noise words in the directory \Mssql\Ftdata\Sqlserver\Config.

Punctuation is ignored. Therefore, CONTAINS(testing, "computer failure") matches a row with the value, "Where is my computer? Failure to find it would be expensive."

<prefix_term>

Specifies a match of words or phrases beginning with the specified text. Enclose a prefix term in double quotation marks ("") and add an asterisk (*) before the ending quotation mark, so that all text starting with the simple term specified before the asterisk is matched. The clause should be specified this way: CONTAINS (column, '"text*"') The asterisk matches zero, one, or more characters (of the root word or words in the word or phrase). If the text and asterisk are not delimited by double quotation marks, as in CONTAINS (column, 'text*'), full-text search considers the asterisk as a character and will search for exact matches to text*.

When <prefix_term> is a phrase, each word contained in the phrase is considered to be a separate prefix. Therefore, a query specifying a prefix term of "local wine *" matches any rows with the text of "local winery", "locally wined and dined", and so on.

<generation_term>

Specifies a match of words when the included simple terms include variants of the original word for which to search.

INFLECTIONAL

Specifies that the plural and singular, as well as the gender and neutral forms of nouns, verbs, and adjectives should be matched. The various tenses of verbs should be matched too.

A given <simple_term> within a <generation_term> will not match both nouns and verbs.

<proximity_term>

Specifies a match of words or phrases that must be close to one another. <proximity_term> operates similarly to the AND operator: both require that more than one word or phrase exist in the column being searched. As the words in <proximity_term> appear closer together, the better the match.

NEAR | ~

Indicates that the word or phrase on the left side of the NEAR or ~ operator should be approximately close to the word or phrase on the right side of the NEAR or ~ operator. Multiple proximity terms can be chained, for example:

```
a NEAR b NEAR c
```

This means that word or phrase a should be near word or phrase b, which should be near word or phrase c.

Microsoft SQL Server ranks the distance between the left and right word or phrase. A low rank value (for example, 0) indicates a large distance between the two. If the specified words or phrases are far apart from each other, the query is considered to be satisfied; however, the query has a very low (0) rank value. However, if <contains_search_condition> consists of only one or more NEAR proximity terms, SQL Server does not return rows with a rank value of 0. For more information about ranking, see CONTAINSTABLE.

<weighted_term>

Specifies that the matching rows (returned by the query) match a list of words and phrases, each optionally given a weighting value.

ISABOUT

Specifies the <weighted_term> keyword.

WEIGHT (weight_value)

Specifies a weight value which is a number from 0.0 through 1.0. Each component in <weighted_term> may include a *weight_value*. *weight_value* is a way to change how various portions of a query affect the rank value assigned to each row matching the query. Weighting forces a different measurement of the ranking of a value because all the components of <weighted_term> are used together to determine the match. A row is returned if there is a match on any one of the ISABOUT parameters, whether or not a weight value is assigned. To determine the rank values for each returned row that indicates the degree of matching between the returned rows, see CONTAINSTABLE.

AND | AND NOT | OR

Specifies a logical operation between two contains search conditions. When <contains_search_condition> contains parenthesized groups, these parenthesized groups are evaluated first. After evaluating parenthesized groups, these rules apply when using these logical operators with contains search conditions:

- NOT is applied before AND.

- NOT can only occur after AND, as in AND NOT. The OR NOT operator is not allowed. NOT cannot be specified before the first term (for example, CONTAINS (**mycolumn**, 'NOT "phrase_to_search_for" ').

- AND is applied before OR.

- Boolean operators of the same type (AND, OR) are associative and can therefore be applied in any order.

n

Is a placeholder indicating that multiple contains search conditions and terms within them can be specified.

Remarks

CONTAINS is not recognized as a keyword if the compatibility level is less than 70. For more information, see sp_dbcmptlevel.

Examples

A. Use CONTAINS with <simple_term>

This example finds all products with a price of $15.00 that contain the word "bottles."

```
USE Northwind
GO
SELECT ProductName
FROM Products
WHERE UnitPrice = 15.00
   AND CONTAINS(QuantityPerUnit, 'bottles')
GO
```

B. Use CONTAINS and phrase in <simple_term>

This example returns all products that contain either the phrase "sasquatch ale" or "steeleye stout."

```
USE Northwind
GO
SELECT ProductName
FROM Products
WHERE CONTAINS(ProductName, ' "sasquatch ale" OR "steeleye stout" ')
GO
```

C. Use CONTAINS with <prefix_term>

This example returns all product names with at least one word starting with the prefix choc in the **ProductName** column.

```
USE Northwind
GO
SELECT ProductName
FROM Products
WHERE CONTAINS(ProductName, ' "choc*" ')
GO
```

D. Use CONTAINS and OR with <prefix_term>

This example returns all category descriptions containing the strings "sea" or "bread."

```
USE Northwind
SELECT CategoryName
FROM Categories
WHERE CONTAINS(Description, '"sea*" OR "bread*"')
GO
```

E. Use CONTAINS with <proximity_term>

This example returns all product names that have the word "Boysenberry" near the word "spread."

```
USE Northwind
GO
SELECT ProductName
FROM Products
WHERE CONTAINS(ProductName, 'spread NEAR Boysenberry')
GO
```

F. Use CONTAINS with <generation_term>

This example searches for all products with words of the form dry: dried, drying, and so on.

```
USE Northwind
GO
SELECT ProductName
FROM Products
WHERE CONTAINS(ProductName, ' FORMSOF (INFLECTIONAL, dry) ')
GO
```

G. Use CONTAINS with <weighted_term>

This example searches for all product names containing the words spread, sauces, or relishes, and different weightings are given to each word.

```
USE Northwind
GO
SELECT CategoryName, Description
FROM Categories
WHERE CONTAINS(Description, 'ISABOUT (spread weight (.8),
   sauces weight (.4), relishes weight (.2) )' )
GO
```

H. Use CONTAINS with variables

This example uses a variable instead of a specific search term.

```
USE pubs
GO
DECLARE @SearchWord varchar(30)
SET @SearchWord ='Moon'
SELECT pr_info FROM pub_info WHERE CONTAINS(pr_info, @SearchWord)
```

Related Topics

FREETEXT, FREETEXTTABLE, Using the CONTAINS Predicate, WHERE

CONTAINSTABLE

Returns a table of zero, one, or more rows for those columns containing character-based data types for precise or fuzzy (less precise) matches to single words and phrases, the proximity of words within a certain distance of one another, or weighted matches. CONTAINSTABLE can be referenced in the FROM clause of a SELECT statement as if it were a regular table name.

Queries using CONTAINSTABLE specify contains-type full-text queries that return a relevance ranking value (RANK) for each row. The CONTAINSTABLE function uses the same search conditions as the CONTAINS predicate.

Syntax

```
CONTAINSTABLE ( table , { column | * } , ' < contains_search_condition > '
   [ , top_n_by_rank ] )
< contains_search_condition > ::=
     { < simple_term >
     | < prefix_term >
     | < generation_term >
```

(continued)

(continued)

```
        | < proximity_term >
        |   < weighted_term >
        }
        | { ( < contains_search_condition > )
        { AND | AND NOT | OR } < contains_search_condition > [ ...n ]
        }
< simple_term > ::=
    word | " phrase "
< prefix term > ::=
    { "word * " | "phrase * " }
< generation_term > ::=
    FORMSOF ( INFLECTIONAL , < simple_term > [ ,...n ] )
< proximity_term > ::=
    { < simple_term > | < prefix_term > }
    { { NEAR | ~ } { < simple_term > | < prefix_term > } } [ ...n ]
< weighted_term > ::=
    ISABOUT
        ( { {
                < simple_term >
                | < prefix_term >
                | < generation_term >
                | < proximity_term >
                }
            [ WEIGHT ( weight_value ) ]
            } [ ,...n ]
        )
```

Arguments

table

Is the name of the table that has been marked for full-text querying. *table* can be a one-, two-, or three-part database object name. For more information, see Transact-SQL Syntax Conventions. *table* cannot specify a server name and cannot be used in queries against linked servers.

column

Is the name of the column to search, which resides in *table*. Columns of the character string data types are valid full-text searching columns.

*

Specifies that all columns in the table that have been registered for full-text searching should be used to search for the given contains search condition(s).

top_n_by_rank

Specifies that only the *n* highest ranked matches, in descending order, are returned. Applies only when an integer value, *n*, is specified.

<contains_search_condition>

Specifies some text to search for in *column*. Variables cannot be used for the search condition. For more information, see CONTAINS.

Remarks

The table returned has a column named **KEY** that contains full-text key values. Each full-text indexed table has a column whose values are guaranteed to be unique, and the values returned in the **KEY** column are the full-text key values of the rows that match the selection criteria specified in the contains search condition. The **TableFulltextKeyColumn** property, obtained from the OBJECTPROPERTY function, provides the identity for this unique key column. To obtain the rows you want from the original table, specify a join with the CONTAINSTABLE rows. The typical form of the FROM clause for a SELECT statement using CONTAINSTABLE is:

```
SELECT select_list
FROM table AS FT_TBL INNER JOIN
    CONTAINSTABLE(table, column, contains_search_condition) AS KEY_TBL
    ON FT_TBL.unique_key_column = KEY_TBL.[KEY]
```

The table produced by CONTAINSTABLE includes a column named **RANK**. The **RANK** column is a value (from 0 through 1000) for each row indicating how well a row matched the selection criteria. This rank value is typically used in one of these ways in the SELECT statement:

- In the ORDER BY clause to return the highest-ranking rows as the first rows in the table.

- In the select list to see the rank value assigned to each row.

- In the WHERE clause to filter out rows with low rank values.

CONTAINSTABLE is not recognized as a keyword if the compatibility level is less than 70. For more information, see sp_dbcmptlevel.

Permissions

Execute permissions are available only by users with the appropriate SELECT privileges on the table or the referenced table's columns.

Examples

A. Return rank values using CONTAINSTABLE

This example searches for all product names containing the words breads, fish, or beers, and different weightings are given to each word. For each returned row matching this search criteria, the relative closeness (ranking value) of the match is shown. In addition, the highest ranking rows are returned first.

```
USE Northwind
GO
SELECT FT_TBL.CategoryName, FT_TBL.Description, KEY_TBL.RANK
FROM Categories AS FT_TBL INNER JOIN
   CONTAINSTABLE(Categories, Description,
   'ISABOUT (breads weight (.8),
   fish weight (.4), beers weight (.2) )' ) AS KEY_TBL
   ON FT_TBL.CategoryID = KEY_TBL.[KEY]
ORDER BY KEY_TBL.RANK DESC
GO
```

B. Return rank values greater than specified value using CONTAINSTABLE

This example returns the description and category name of all food categories for which the **Description** column contains the words "sweet and savory" near either the word "sauces" or the word "candies." All rows with a category name "Seafood" are disregarded. Only rows with a rank value of 2 or higher are returned.

```
USE Northwind
GO
SELECT FT_TBL.Description,
   FT_TBL.CategoryName,
   KEY_TBL.RANK
FROM Categories AS FT_TBL INNER JOIN
   CONTAINSTABLE (Categories, Description,
      '("sweet and savory" NEAR sauces) OR
      ("sweet and savory" NEAR candies)'
   ) AS KEY_TBL
   ON FT_TBL.CategoryID = KEY_TBL.[KEY]
WHERE KEY_TBL.RANK > 2
   AND FT_TBL.CategoryName <> 'Seafood'
ORDER BY KEY_TBL.RANK DESC
```

C. Return top 10 ranked results using CONTAINSTABLE and Top_n_by_rank

This example returns the description and category name of the top 10 food categories where the **Description** column contains the words "sweet and savory" near either the word "sauces" or the word "candies."

```
SELECT FT_TBL.Description,
   FT_TBL.CategoryName,
   KEY_TBL.RANK
FROM Categories AS FT_TBL INNER JOIN
   CONTAINSTABLE (Categories, Description,
      '("sweet and savory" NEAR sauces) OR
      ("sweet and savory" NEAR candies)'
      , 10
   ) AS KEY_TBL
   ON FT_TBL.CategoryID = KEY_TBL.[KEY]
```

Related Topics

CONTAINS, Full-text Querying SQL Server Data, Rowset Functions, SELECT, WHERE

CONTINUE

Restarts a WHILE loop. Any statements after the CONTINUE keyword are ignored. CONTINUE is often, but not always, activated by an IF test. For more information, see WHILE and Control-of-Flow Language.

Control-of-Flow Language

The table shows the Transact-SQL control-of-flow keywords.

Keyword	Description
BEGIN...END	Defines a statement block.
BREAK	Exits the innermost WHILE loop.
CONTINUE	Restarts a WHILE loop.
GOTO *label*	Continues processing at the statement following the *label* as defined by *label*.

(continued)

(continued)

Keyword	Description
IF...ELSE	Defines conditional, and optionally, alternate execution when a condition is FALSE.
RETURN	Exits unconditionally.
WAITFOR	Sets a delay for statement execution.
WHILE	Repeats statements while a specific condition is TRUE.

Other Transact-SQL statements that can be used with control-of-flow language statements are:

CASE

/*...*/ (Comment)

-- (Comment)

DECLARE @local_variable

EXECUTE

PRINT

RAISERROR

COS

A mathematic function that returns the trigonometric cosine of the given angle (in radians) in the given expression.

Syntax

```
COS ( float_expression )
```

Arguments

float_expression
   Is an *expression* of type **float**.

Return Types

float

Examples

This example returns the COS of the given angle.

```
DECLARE @angle float
SET @angle = 14.78
SELECT 'The COS of the angle is: ' + CONVERT(varchar,COS(@angle))
GO
```

Here is the result set:

```
The COS of the angle is: -0.599465

(1 row(s) affected)
```

Related Topics

Mathematical Functions

COT

A mathematic function that returns the trigonometric cotangent of the specified angle (in radians) in the given **float** expression.

Syntax

```
COT ( float_expression )
```

Arguments

float_expression
   Is an *expression* of type **float**.

Return Types

float

Examples

This example returns the COT for the given angle.

```
DECLARE @angle float
SET @angle = 124.1332
SELECT 'The COT of the angle is: ' + CONVERT(varchar,COT(@angle))
GO
```

Here is the result set:

```
The COT of the angle is: -0.040312

(1 row(s) affected)
```

Related Topics

Mathematical Functions

COUNT

Returns the number of items in a group.

Syntax

```
COUNT ( { [ ALL | DISTINCT ] expression ] | * } )
```

Arguments

ALL
> Applies the aggregate function to all values. ALL is the default.

DISTINCT
> Specifies that COUNT returns the number of unique nonnull values.

expression
> Is an expression of any type except **uniqueidentifier**, **text**, **image**, or **ntext**. Aggregate functions and subqueries are not permitted.

*
> Specifies that all rows should be counted to return the total number of rows in a table. COUNT(*) takes no parameters and cannot be used with DISTINCT. COUNT(*) does not require an *expression* parameter because, by definition, it does not use information about any particular column. COUNT(*) returns the number of rows in a specified table without eliminating duplicates. It counts each row separately, including rows that contain null values.

> **Important** Distinct aggregates, for example AVG(DISTINCT *column_name*), COUNT(DISTINCT *column_name*), MAX(DISTINCT *column_name*), MIN(DISTINCT *column_name*), and SUM(DISTINCT *column_name*), are not supported when using CUBE or ROLLUP. If used, Microsoft SQL Server returns an error message and cancels the query.

Return Types

int

Remarks

COUNT(*) returns the number of items in a group, including NULL values and duplicates.

COUNT(ALL *expression*) evaluates *expression* for each row in a group and returns the number of nonnull values.

COUNT(DISTINCT *expression*) evaluates *expression* for each row in a group and returns the number of unique, nonnull values.

Examples

A. Use COUNT and DISTINCT

This example finds the number of different cities in which authors live.

```
USE pubs
GO
SELECT COUNT(DISTINCT city)
FROM authors
GO
```

Here is the result set:

```
-----------
16

(1 row(s) affected)
```

B. Use COUNT(*)

This example finds the total number of books and titles.

```
USE pubs
GO
SELECT COUNT(*)
FROM titles
GO
```

Here is the result set:

```
-----------
18

(1 row(s) affected)
```

C. Use COUNT(*) with other aggregates

The example shows that COUNT(*) can be combined with other aggregate functions in the select list.

```
USE pubs
GO
SELECT COUNT(*), AVG(price)
FROM titles
WHERE advance > $1000
GO
```

Here is the result set:

```
----------- --------------------------
15          14.42

(1 row(s) affected)
```

Related Topics

Aggregate Functions

COUNT_BIG

Returns the number of items in a group. COUNT_BIG works like the COUNT function. The only difference between them is their return values: COUNT_BIG always returns a **bigint** data type value. COUNT always returns an **int** data type value.

Syntax

```
COUNT_BIG ( { [ ALL | DISTINCT ] expression } | * )
```

Arguments

ALL
  Applies the aggregate function to all values. ALL is the default.

DISTINCT
  Specifies that COUNT_BIG returns the number of unique nonnull values.

expression
  Is an expression of any type except **uniqueidentifier**, **text**, **image**, or **ntext**. Aggregate functions and subqueries are not permitted.

*
  Specifies that all rows should be counted to return the total number of rows in a table. COUNT_BIG(*) takes no parameters and cannot be used with DISTINCT. COUNT_BIG(*) does not require an *expression* parameter because, by definition, it does not use information about any particular column. COUNT_BIG(*) returns the number of rows in a specified table without eliminating duplicates. It counts each row separately, including rows that contain null values.

Return Types

bigint

Remarks

COUNT_BIG(*) returns the number of items in a group, including NULL values and duplicates.

COUNT_BIG(ALL *expression*) evaluates *expression* for each row in a group and returns the number of nonnull values.

COUNT_BIG(DISTINCT *expression*) evaluates *expression* for each row in a group and returns the number of unique, nonnull values.

Related Topics

int, bigint, smallint, and tinyint

CURRENT_TIMESTAMP

Returns the current date and time. This function is equivalent to GETDATE().

Syntax

```
CURRENT_TIMESTAMP
```

Return Types

datetime

Examples

A. Use CURRENT_TIMESTAMP to return the current date and time

This example returns the value of CURRENT_TIMESTAMP and a text description.

```
SELECT 'The current time is: '+ CONVERT(char(30), CURRENT_TIMESTAMP)
```

Here is the result set:

```
--------------------------------------------------
The current time is: Feb 24 1998  3:45PM

(1 row(s) affected)
```

B. Use CURRENT_TIMESTAMP as a DEFAULT constraint

This example creates a table that uses CURRENT_TIMESTAMP as a DEFAULT
constraint for the **sales_date** column of a sales row.

```
USE pubs
GO
CREATE TABLE sales2
(
 sales_id int IDENTITY(10000, 1) NOT NULL,
 cust_id  int NOT NULL,
 sales_date datetime NOT NULL DEFAULT CURRENT_TIMESTAMP,
 sales_amt money NOT NULL,
 delivery_date datetime NOT NULL DEFAULT DATEADD(dd, 10, GETDATE())
)
GO
INSERT sales2 (cust_id, sales_amt)
   VALUES (20000, 550)
```

This query selects all information from the **sales2** table.

```
USE pubs
GO
SELECT *
FROM sales2
GO
```

Here is the result set:

```
sales_id    cust_id    sales_date            sales_amt delivery_date
----------- ---------- --------------------- --------- --------------------

10000       20000      Mar 4 1998 10:06AM    550.00    Mar 14 1998 10:06AM

(1 row(s) affected)
```

Related Topics

ALTER TABLE, CREATE TABLE, System Functions

CURRENT_USER

Returns the current user. This function is equivalent to USER_NAME().

Syntax

```
CURRENT_USER
```

Return Types

sysname

Examples

A. Use CURRENT_USER to return the current username

This example declares a variable as **char**, assigns the current value of
CURRENT_USER to it, and then returns the variable with a text description.

```
SELECT 'The current user is: '+ convert(char(30), CURRENT_USER)
```

Here is the result set:

```
----------------------------------------------------
The current user is: dbo

(1 row(s) affected)
```

B. Use CURRENT_USER as a DEFAULT constraint

This example creates a table that uses CURRENT_USER as a DEFAULT constraint
for the **order_person** column on a sales row.

```
USE pubs
IF EXISTS (SELECT TABLE_NAME FROM INFORMATION_SCHEMA.TABLES
      WHERE TABLE_NAME = 'orders2')
   DROP TABLE orders2
GO
SET NOCOUNT ON
CREATE TABLE orders2
(
 order_id int IDENTITY(1000, 1) NOT NULL,
 cust_id  int NOT NULL,
 order_date datetime NOT NULL DEFAULT GETDATE(),
 order_amt money NOT NULL,
 order_person char(30) NOT NULL DEFAULT CURRENT_USER
)
```

(continued)

(continued)

```
GO
INSERT orders2 (cust_id, order_amt)
VALUES (5105, 577.95)
GO
SET NOCOUNT OFF
```

This query selects all information from the **orders2** table.

```
SELECT *
FROM orders2
```

Here is the result set:

```
order_id     cust_id      order_date              order_amt      order_person
-----------  -----------  --------------------    -------------  ---------------
1000         5105         Mar 4 1998 10:13AM      577.95               dbo

(1 row(s) affected)
```

Related Topics

ALTER TABLE, CREATE TABLE, System Functions

cursor

A data type for variables or stored procedure OUTPUT parameters that contain a reference to a cursor. Any variables created with the **cursor** data type are nullable.

The operations that can reference variables and parameters having a **cursor** data type are:

- The DECLARE *@local_variable* and SET *@local_variable* statements.
- The OPEN, FETCH, CLOSE, and DEALLOCATE cursor statements.
- Stored procedure output parameters.
- The CURSOR_STATUS function.
- The **sp_cursor_list**, **sp_describe_cursor**, **sp_describe_cursor_tables**, and **sp_describe_cursor_columns** system stored procedures.

  Important The **cursor** data type cannot be used for a column in a CREATE TABLE statement.

Related Topics

CAST and CONVERT, CURSOR_STATUS, Data Type Conversion, Data Types, DECLARE CURSOR, DECLARE @local_variable, SET @local_variable

CURSOR_STATUS

A scalar function that allows the caller of a stored procedure to determine whether or not the procedure has returned a cursor and result set for a given parameter.

Syntax

```
CURSOR_STATUS
    (
        { 'local' , 'cursor_name' }
        | { 'global' , 'cursor_name' }
        | { 'variable' , 'cursor_variable' }
    )
```

Arguments

'local'

Specifies a constant that indicates the source of the cursor is a local cursor name.

'cursor_name'

Is the name of the cursor. A cursor name must conform to the rules for identifiers.

'global'

Specifies a constant that indicates the source of the cursor is a global cursor name.

'variable'

Specifies a constant that indicates the source of the cursor is a local variable.

'cursor_variable'

Is the name of the cursor variable. A cursor variable must be defined using the **cursor** data type.

Return Types

smallint

Return value	Cursor name	Cursor variable
1	The result set of the cursor has at least one row and: • For insensitive and keyset cursors, the result set has at least one row. • For dynamic cursors, the result set can have zero, one, or more rows.	The cursor allocated to this variable is open and: • For insensitive and keyset cursors, the result set has at least one row. • For dynamic cursors, the result set can have zero, one, or more rows.
0	The result set of the cursor is empty.*	The cursor allocated to this variable is open, but the result set is definitely empty.*

(continued)

(continued)

Return value	Cursor name	Cursor variable
−1	The cursor is closed.	The cursor allocated to this variable is closed.
−2	Not applicable.	Can be: • No cursor was assigned to this OUTPUT variable by the previously called procedure. • A cursor was assigned to this OUTPUT variable by the previously called procedure, but it was in a closed state upon completion of the procedure. Therefore, the cursor is deallocated and not returned to the calling procedure. • There is no cursor assigned to a declared cursor variable.
−3	A cursor with the specified name does not exist.	A cursor variable with the specified name does not exist, or if one exists it has not yet had a cursor allocated to it.

* Dynamic cursors never return this result.

Examples

This example creates a procedure named **lake_list** and uses the output from executing **lake_list** as a check for CURSOR_STATUS.

Note   This example depends on a procedure named **check_authority**, which has not been created.

```
USE pubs
IF EXISTS (SELECT name FROM sysobjects
      WHERE name = 'lake_list' AND type = 'P')
   DROP PROCEDURE lake_list
GO
CREATE PROCEDURE lake_list
   ( @region varchar(30),
     @size integer,
     @lake_list_cursor CURSOR VARYING OUTPUT )
```

(continued)

(continued)

```
AS
BEGIN
   DECLARE @ok SMALLINT
   EXECUTE check_authority @region, username, @ok OUTPUT
   IF @ok = 1
      BEGIN
      SET @lake_list_cursor =CURSOR LOCAL SCROLL FOR
         SELECT name, lat, long, size, boat_launch, cost
         FROM lake_inventory
         WHERE locale = @region AND area >= @size
         ORDER BY name
      OPEN @lake_list_cursor
      END
END
DECLARE @my_lakes_cursor CURSOR
DECLARE @my_region char(30)
SET @my_region = 'Northern Ontario'
EXECUTE lake_list @my_region, 500, @my_lakes_cursor OUTPUT
IF Cursor_Status('variable', '@my_lakes_cursor') <= 0
   BEGIN
   /* Some code to tell the user that there is no list of
   lakes for him/her */
   END
ELSE
   BEGIN
      FETCH @my_lakes_cursor INTO -- Destination here
      -- Continue with other code here.
END
```

Related Topics

Cursor Functions, Data Types, Using Identifiers

Cursors

Microsoft SQL Server statements produce a complete result set, but there are times when the results are best processed one row at a time. Opening a cursor on a result set allows processing the result set one row at a time. SQL Server version 7.0 also introduces assigning a cursor to a variable or parameter with a **cursor** data type.

Cursor operations are supported on these statements:

CLOSE	DELETE
CREATE PROCEDURE	FETCH
DEALLOCATE	OPEN
DECLARE CURSOR	UPDATE
DECLARE @local_variable	SET

These system functions and system stored procedures also support cursors:

@@CURSOR_ROWS	sp_describe_cursor
CURSOR_STATUS	sp_describe_cursor_columns
@@FETCH_STATUS	sp_describe_cursor_tables
sp_cursor_list	

Related Topics

Cursors

CREATE DATABASE

Creates a new database and the files used to store the database, or attaches a database from the files of a previously created database.

Note For more information about backward compatibility with DISK INIT, see Devices (Level 3) in Microsoft SQL Server Backward Compatibility Details.

Syntax

```
CREATE DATABASE database_name
[ ON
   [ < filespec > [ ,...n ] ]
   [ , < filegroup > [ ,...n ] ]
]
[ LOG ON { < filespec > [ ,...n ] } ]
[ COLLATE collation_name ]
[ FOR LOAD | FOR ATTACH ]

< filespec > ::=
[ PRIMARY ]
( [ NAME = logical_file_name , ]
   FILENAME = 'os_file_name'
   [ , SIZE = size ]
```

(continued)

(continued)

```
    [ , MAXSIZE = { max_size | UNLIMITED } ]
    [ , FILEGROWTH = growth_increment ] ) [ ,...n ]
< filegroup > ::=
FILEGROUP filegroup_name < filespec > [ ,...n ]
```

Arguments

database_name

> Is the name of the new database. Database names must be unique within a server and conform to the rules for identifiers. *database_name* can be a maximum of 128 characters, unless no logical name is specified for the log. If no logical log file name is specified, Microsoft SQL Server generates a logical name by appending a suffix to *database_name*. This limits *database_name* to 123 characters so that the generated logical log file name is less than 128 characters.

ON

> Specifies that the disk files used to store the data portions of the database (data files) are defined explicitly. The keyword is followed by a comma-separated list of <filespec> items defining the data files for the primary filegroup. The list of files in the primary filegroup can be followed by an optional, comma-separated list of <filegroup> items defining user filegroups and their files.

n

> Is a placeholder indicating that multiple files can be specified for the new database.

LOG ON

> Specifies that the disk files used to store the database log (log files) are explicitly defined. The keyword is followed by a comma-separated list of <filespec> items defining the log files. If LOG ON is not specified, a single log file is automatically created with a system-generated name and a size that is 25 percent of the sum of the sizes of all the data files for the database.

FOR LOAD

> This clause is supported for compatibility with earlier versions of Microsoft SQL Server. The database is created with the **dbo use only** database option turned on, and the status is set to loading. This is not required in SQL Server version 7.0 because the RESTORE statement can recreate a database as part of the restore operation.

FOR ATTACH

> Specifies that a database is attached from an existing set of operating system files. There must be a <filespec> entry specifying the first primary file. The only other <filespec> entries needed are those for any files that have a different path from when the database was first created or last attached. A <filespec> entry must be specified for these files. The database attached must have been created using the same code page and sort order as SQL Server. Use the **sp_attach_db** system stored procedure instead of using CREATE DATABASE FOR ATTACH directly. Use CREATE DATABASE FOR ATTACH only when you must specify more than 16 <filespec> items.

If you attach a database to a server other than the server from which the database was detached, and the detached database was enabled for replication, you should run **sp_removedbreplication** to remove replication from the database.

collation_name

Specifies the default collation for the database. Collation name can be either a Windows collation name or a SQL collation name. If not specified, the database is assigned the default collation of the SQL Server instance.

For more information about the Windows and SQL collation names, see COLLATE.

PRIMARY

Specifies that the associated <filespec> list defines the primary file. The primary filegroup contains all of the database system tables. It also contains all objects not assigned to user filegroups. The first <filespec> entry in the primary filegroup becomes the primary file, which is the file containing the logical start of the database and its system tables. A database can have only one primary file. If PRIMARY is not specified, the first file listed in the CREATE DATABASE statement becomes the primary file.

NAME

Specifies the logical name for the file defined by the <filespec>. The NAME parameter is not required when FOR ATTACH is specified.

logical_file_name

Is the name used to reference the file in any Transact-SQL statements executed after the database is created. *logical_file_name* must be unique in the database and conform to the rules for identifiers. The name can be a character or Unicode constant, or a regular or delimited identifier.

FILENAME

Specifies the operating-system file name for the file defined by the <filespec>.

'*os_file_name*'

Is the path and file name used by the operating system when it creates the physical file defined by the <filespec>. The path in *os_file_name* must specify a directory on an instance of SQL Server. *os_file_name* cannot specify a directory in a compressed file system.

If the file is created on a raw partition, *os_file_name* must specify only the drive letter of an existing raw partition. Only one file can be created on each raw partition. Files on raw partitions do not autogrow; therefore, the MAXSIZE and FILEGROWTH parameters are not needed when *os_file_name* specifies a raw partition.

SIZE

Specifies the size of the file defined in the <filespec>. When a SIZE parameter is not supplied in the <filespec> for a primary file, SQL Server uses the size of the primary file in the **model** database. When a SIZE parameter is not specified in the <filespec> for a secondary or log file, SQL Server makes the file 1 MB.

size

Is the initial size of the file defined in the <filespec>. The kilobyte (KB), megabyte (MB), gigabyte (GB), or terabyte (TB) suffixes can be used. The default is MB. Specify a whole number; do not include a decimal. The minimum value for *size* is 512 KB. If *size* is not specified, the default is 1 MB. The size specified for the primary file must be at least as large as the primary file of the **model** database.

MAXSIZE

Specifies the maximum size to which the file defined in the <filespec> can grow.

max_size

Is the maximum size to which the file defined in the <filespec> can grow. The kilobyte (KB), megabyte (MB), gigabyte (GB), or terabyte (TB) suffixes can be used. The default is MB. Specify a whole number; do not include a decimal. If *max_size* is not specified, the file grows until the disk is full.

> **Note**   The Microsoft Windows NT S/B system log warns the SQL Server system administrator if a disk is almost full.

UNLIMITED

Specifies that the file defined in the <filespec> grows until the disk is full.

FILEGROWTH

Specifies the growth increment of the file defined in the <filespec>.
The FILEGROWTH setting for a file cannot exceed the MAXSIZE setting.

growth_increment

Is the amount of space added to the file each time new space is needed. Specify a whole number; do not include a decimal. A value of 0 indicates no growth. The value can be specified in MB, KB, GB, TB, or percent (%). If a number is specified without an MB, KB, or % suffix, the default is MB. When % is specified, the growth increment size is the specified percentage of the size of the file at the time the increment occurs. If FILEGROWTH is not specified, the default value is 10 percent and the minimum value is 64 KB. The size specified is rounded to the nearest 64 KB.

Remarks

You can use one CREATE DATABASE statement to create a database and the files that store the database. SQL Server implements the CREATE DATABASE statement in two steps:

1. SQL Server uses a copy of the **model** database to initialize the database and its meta data.

2. SQL Server then fills the rest of the database with empty pages, except for pages that have internal data recording how the space is used in the database.

Any user-defined objects in the **model** database are therefore copied to all newly created databases. You can add to the **model** database any objects, such as tables, views, stored procedures, data types, and so on, to be included in all databases.

Each new database inherits the database option settings from the **model** database (unless FOR ATTACH is specified). For example, the database option **select into/bulkcopy** is set to OFF in **model** and any new databases you create. If you use ALTER DATABASE to change the options for the **model** database, these option settings are in effect for new databases you create. If FOR ATTACH is specified on the CREATE DATABASE statement, the new database inherits the database option settings of the original database.

A maximum of 32,767 databases can be specified on a server.

There are three types of files used to store a database:

- The primary file contains the startup information for the database. The primary file is also used to store data. Every database has one primary file.

- Secondary files hold all of the data that does not fit in the primary data file. Databases need not have any secondary data files if the primary file is large enough to hold all of the data in the database. Other databases may be large enough to need multiple secondary data files, or they may use secondary files on separate disk drives to spread the data across multiple disks.

- Transaction log files hold the log information used to recover the database. There must be at least one transaction log file for each database, although there may be more than one. The minimum size for a transaction log file is 512 KB.

Every database has at least two files, a primary file and a transaction log file.

Although '*os_file_name*' can be any valid operating system file name, the name more clearly reflects the purpose of the file if you use the following recommended extensions.

File type	File name extension
Primary data file	.mdf
Secondary data file	.ndf
Transaction log file	.ldf

Note   The **master** database should be backed up when a user database is created.

Fractions cannot be specified in the SIZE, MAXSIZE, and FILEGROWTH parameters. To specify a fraction of a megabyte in SIZE parameters, convert to kilobytes by multiplying the number by 1,024. For example, specify 1,536 KB instead of 1.5 MB (1.5 multiplied by 1,024 equals 1,536).

When a simple CREATE DATABASE *database_name* statement is specified with no additional parameters, the database is made the same size as the **model** database.

All databases have at least a primary filegroup. All system tables are allocated in the primary filegroup. A database can also have user-defined filegroups. If an object is created with an ON *filegroup* clause specifying a user-defined filegroup, then all the pages for the object are allocated from the specified filegroup. The pages for all user objects created without an ON *filegroup* clause, or with an ON DEFAULT clause, are allocated from the default filegroup. When a database is first created the primary filegroup is the default filegroup. You can specify a user-defined filegroup as the default filegroup using ALTER DATABASE:

```
ALTER DATABASE database_name MODIFY FILEGROUP filegroup_name DEFAULT
```

Each database has an owner who has the ability to perform special activities in the database. The owner is the user who creates the database. The database owner can be changed with **sp_changedbowner**.

To display a report on a database, or on all the databases for an instance of SQL Server, execute **sp_helpdb**. For a report on the space used in a database, use **sp_spaceused**. For a report on the filegroups in a database use **sp_helpfilegroup**, and use **sp_helpfile** for a report of the files in a database.

Earlier versions of SQL Server used DISK INIT statements to create the files for a database before the CREATE DATABASE statement was executed. For backward compatibility with earlier versions of SQL Server, the CREATE DATABASE statement can also create a new database on files or devices created with the DISK INIT statement. For more information, see SQL Server Backward Compatibility Details.

Permissions

CREATE DATABASE permission defaults to members of the **sysadmin** and **dbcreator** fixed server roles. Members of the **sysadmin** and **securityadmin** fixed server roles can grant CREATE DATABASE permissions to other logins. Members of the **sysadmin** and **dbcreator** fixed server role can add other logins to the **dbcreator** role. The CREATE DATABASE permission must be explicitly granted; it is not granted by the GRANT ALL statement.

CREATE DATABASE permission is usually limited to a few logins to maintain control over disk usage on an instance of SQL Server.

Examples

A. Create a database that specifies the data and transaction log files

This example creates a database called **Sales**. Because the keyword PRIMARY is not used, the first file (**Sales_dat**) becomes the primary file. Because neither MB or KB is specified in the SIZE parameter for the **Sales_dat** file, it defaults to MB and is allocated in megabytes. The **Sales_log** file is allocated in megabytes because the MB suffix is explicitly stated in the SIZE parameter.

```
USE master
GO
CREATE DATABASE Sales
ON
( NAME = Sales_dat,
   FILENAME = 'c:\program files\microsoft sql server\mssql\data\saledat.mdf',
   SIZE = 10,
   MAXSIZE = 50,
   FILEGROWTH = 5 )
LOG ON
( NAME = 'Sales_log',
   FILENAME = 'c:\program files\microsoft sql server\mssql\data\salelog.ldf',
   SIZE = 5MB,
   MAXSIZE = 25MB,
   FILEGROWTH = 5MB )
GO
```

B. Create a database specifying multiple data and transaction log files

This example creates a database called **Archive** with three 100-MB data files and two 100-MB transaction log files. The primary file is the first file in the list and is explicitly specified with the PRIMARY keyword. The transaction log files are specified following the LOG ON keywords. Note the extensions used for the files in the FILENAME option: .mdf is used for primary data files, .ndf is used for the secondary data files, and .ldf is used for transaction log files.

```
USE master
GO
CREATE DATABASE Archive
ON
PRIMARY ( NAME = Arch1,
      FILENAME = 'c:\program files\microsoft sql server\mssql\data\archdat1.mdf',
      SIZE = 100MB,
      MAXSIZE = 200,
      FILEGROWTH = 20),
```

(continued)

(continued)

```
( NAME = Arch2,
   FILENAME = 'c:\program files\microsoft sql server\mssql\data\archdat2.ndf',
   SIZE = 100MB,
   MAXSIZE = 200,
   FILEGROWTH = 20),
( NAME = Arch3,
   FILENAME = 'c:\program files\microsoft sql server\mssql\data\archdat3.ndf',
   SIZE = 100MB,
   MAXSIZE = 200,
   FILEGROWTH = 20)
LOG ON
( NAME = Archlog1,
   FILENAME = 'c:\program files\microsoft sql server\mssql\data\archlog1.ldf',
   SIZE = 100MB,
   MAXSIZE = 200,
   FILEGROWTH = 20),
( NAME = Archlog2,
   FILENAME = 'c:\program files\microsoft sql server\mssql\data\archlog2.ldf',
   SIZE = 100MB,
   MAXSIZE = 200,
   FILEGROWTH = 20)
GO
```

C. Create a simple database

This example creates a database called **Products** and specifies a single file. The file specified becomes the primary file, and a 1-MB transaction log file is automatically created. Because neither MB or KB is specified in the **SIZE** parameter for the primary file, the primary file is allocated in megabytes. Because there is no <filespec> for the transaction log file, the transaction log file has no MAXSIZE and can grow to fill all available disk space.

```
USE master
GO
CREATE DATABASE Products
ON
( NAME = prods_dat,
   FILENAME = 'c:\program files\microsoft sql server\mssql\data\prods.mdf',
   SIZE = 4,
   MAXSIZE = 10,
   FILEGROWTH = 1 )
GO
```

D. Create a database without specifying files

This example creates a database named **mytest** and creates a corresponding primary and transaction log file. Because the statement has no <filespec> items, the primary database file is the size of the **model** database primary file. The transaction log is the size of the model database transaction log file. Because MAXSIZE is not specified, the files can grow to fill all available disk space.

```
CREATE DATABASE mytest
```

E. Create a database without specifying SIZE

This example creates a database named **products2**. The file **prods2_dat** becomes the primary file with a size equal to the size of the primary file in the **model** database. The transaction log file is created automatically and is 25 percent of the size of the primary file, or 512 KB, whichever is larger. Because MAXSIZE is not specified, the files can grow to fill all available disk space.

```
USE master
GO
CREATE DATABASE Products2
ON
( NAME = prods2_dat,
   FILENAME = 'c:\program files\microsoft sql server\mssql\data\prods2.mdf' )
GO
```

F. Create a database with filegroups

This example creates a database named **sales** with three filegroups:

- The primary filegroup with the files **Spri1_dat** and **Spri2_dat**. The FILEGROWTH increments for these files is specified as 15 percent.

- A filegroup named **SalesGroup1** with the files **SGrp1Fi1** and **SGrp1Fi2**.

- A filegroup named **SalesGroup2** with the files **SGrp2Fi1** and **SGrp2Fi2**.

```
CREATE DATABASE Sales
ON PRIMARY
( NAME = SPri1_dat,
   FILENAME = 'c:\program files\microsoft sql server\mssql\data\SPri1dat.mdf',
   SIZE = 10,
   MAXSIZE = 50,
   FILEGROWTH = 15% ),
( NAME = SPri2_dat,
   FILENAME = 'c:\program files\microsoft sql server\mssql\data\SPri2dt.ndf',
   SIZE = 10,
   MAXSIZE = 50,
   FILEGROWTH = 15% ),
```

(continued)

(continued)

```
FILEGROUP SalesGroup1
( NAME = SGrp1Fi1_dat,
    FILENAME = 'c:\program files\microsoft sql server\mssql\data\SG1Fi1dt.ndf',
    SIZE = 10,
    MAXSIZE = 50,
    FILEGROWTH = 5 ),
( NAME = SGrp1Fi2_dat,
    FILENAME = 'c:\program files\microsoft sql server\mssql\data\SG1Fi2dt.ndf',
    SIZE = 10,
    MAXSIZE = 50,
    FILEGROWTH = 5 ),
FILEGROUP SalesGroup2
( NAME = SGrp2Fi1_dat,
    FILENAME = 'c:\program files\microsoft sql server\mssql\data\SG2Fi1dt.ndf',
    SIZE = 10,
    MAXSIZE = 50,
    FILEGROWTH = 5 ),
( NAME = SGrp2Fi2_dat,
    FILENAME = 'c:\program files\microsoft sql server\mssql\data\SG2Fi2dt.ndf',
    SIZE = 10,
    MAXSIZE = 50,
    FILEGROWTH = 5 )
LOG ON
( NAME = 'Sales_log',
    FILENAME = 'c:\program files\microsoft sql server\mssql\data\salelog.ldf',
    SIZE = 5MB,
    MAXSIZE = 25MB,
    FILEGROWTH = 5MB )
GO
```

G. Attach a database

Example B creates a database named **Archive** with the following physical files:

```
c:\program files\microsoft sql server\mssql\data\archdat1.mdf
c:\program files\microsoft sql server\mssql\data\archdat2.ndf
c:\program files\microsoft sql server\mssql\data\archdat3.ndf
c:\program files\microsoft sql server\mssql\data\archlog1.ldf
c:\program files\microsoft sql server\mssql\data\archlog2.ldf
```

The database can be detached using the **sp_detach_db** stored procedure, and then reattached using CREATE DATABASE with the FOR ATTACH clause:

```
sp_detach_db Archive
GO
CREATE DATABASE Archive
ON PRIMARY (FILENAME = 'c:\program files\microsoft sql server\mssql\data\archdat1.mdf')
FOR ATTACH
GO
```

H. Use raw partitions

This example creates a database called **Employees** using raw partitions. The raw partitions must exist when the statement is executed, and only one file can go on each raw partition.

```
USE master
GO
CREATE DATABASE Employees
ON
( NAME = Empl_dat,
    FILENAME = 'f:',
    SIZE = 10,
    MAXSIZE = 50,
    FILEGROWTH = 5 )
LOG ON
( NAME = 'Sales_log',
    FILENAME = 'g:',
    SIZE = 5MB,
    MAXSIZE = 25MB,
    FILEGROWTH = 5MB )
GO
```

I. Use mounted drives

This example creates a database called **Employees** using mounted drives pointing to raw partitions. This feature is available only in Microsoft Windows 2000 Server. The mounted drives and raw partitions must exist when the statement is executed, and only one file can go on each raw partition. When creating a database file on a mounted drive, a trailing backslash (\) must end the drive path.

```
USE master
GO
CREATE DATABASE Employees
ON
( NAME = Empl_dat,
    FILENAME = 'd:\sample data dir\',
    SIZE = 10,
```

(continued)

(continued)

```
   MAXSIZE = 50,
   FILEGROWTH = 5 )
LOG ON
( NAME = 'Sales_log',
   FILENAME = 'd:\sample log dir\',
   SIZE = 5MB,
   MAXSIZE = 25MB,
   FILEGROWTH = 5MB )
GO
```

Related Topics

ALTER DATABASE, DROP DATABASE, sp_attach_db, sp_changedbowner, sp_detach_db, sp_helpdb, sp_helpfile, sp_helpfilegroup, sp_removedbreplication, sp_renamedb, sp_spaceused, Using Raw Partitions

CREATE DEFAULT

Creates an object called a *default*. When bound to a column or a user-defined data type, a default specifies a value to be inserted into the column to which the object is bound (or into all columns, in the case of a user-defined data type) when no value is explicitly supplied during an insert. Defaults, a backward compatibility feature, perform some of the same functions as default definitions created using the DEFAULT keyword of ALTER or CREATE TABLE statements. Default definitions are the preferred, standard way to restrict column data because the definition is stored with the table and automatically dropped when the table is dropped. A default is beneficial, however, when the default is used multiple times for multiple columns.

Syntax

```
CREATE DEFAULT default
   AS constant_expression
```

Arguments

default

Is the name of the default. Default names must conform to the rules for identifiers. Specifying the default owner name is optional.

constant_expression

Is an expression that contains only constant values (it cannot include the names of any columns or other database objects). Any constant, built-in function, or mathematical expression can be used. Enclose character and date constants in single quotation marks ('); monetary, integer, and floating-point constants do not require quotation marks. Binary data must be preceded by 0x, and monetary data must be preceded by a dollar sign ($). The default value must be compatible with the column data type.

Remarks

A default name can be created only in the current database. Within a database, default names must be unique by owner. When a default is created, use **sp_bindefault** to bind it to a column or to a user-defined data type.

If the default is not compatible with the column to which it is bound, Microsoft SQL Server generates an error message when trying to insert the default value. For example, N/A cannot be used as a default for a **numeric** column.

If the default value is too long for the column to which it is bound, the value is truncated.

CREATE DEFAULT statements cannot be combined with other Transact-SQL statements in a single batch.

A default must be dropped before creating a new one of the same name, and the default must be unbound by executing **sp_unbindefault** before it is dropped.

If a column has both a default and a rule associated with it, the default value must not violate the rule. A default that conflicts with a rule is never inserted, and SQL Server generates an error message each time it attempts to insert the default.

When bound to a column, a default value is inserted when:

- A value is not explicitly inserted.
- Either the DEFAULT VALUES or DEFAULT keywords are used with INSERT to insert default values.

If NOT NULL is specified when creating a column and a default is not created for it, an error message is generated when a user fails to make an entry in that column. This table illustrates the relationship between the existence of a default and the definition of a column as NULL or NOT NULL. The entries in the table show the result.

Column definition	No entry, no default	No entry, default	Enter NULL, no default	Enter NULL, default
NULL	NULL	default	NULL	NULL
NOT NULL	Error	default	error	error

> **Note**   Whether SQL Server interprets an empty string as a single space or as a true empty string is controlled by the **sp_dbcmptlevel** setting. If the compatibility level is less than or equal to 65, SQL Server interprets empty strings as single spaces. If the compatibility level is equal to 70, SQL Server interprets empty strings as empty strings. For more information, see sp_dbcmptlevel.

To rename a default, use **sp_rename**. For a report on a default, use **sp_help**.

Permissions

CREATE DEFAULT permissions default to members of the **sysadmin** fixed server role and the **db_ddladmin** and **db_owner** fixed database roles. Members of the **sysadmin**, **db_owner** and **db_securityadmin** roles can transfer permissions to other users.

Examples

A. Create a simple character default

This example creates a character default called unknown.

```
USE pubs
GO
CREATE DEFAULT phonedflt AS 'unknown'
```

B. Bind a default

This example binds the default created in example A. The default takes effect only if there is no entry in the **phone** column of the **authors** table. Note that no entry is not the same as an explicit null value.

Because a default named **phonedflt** does not exist, the following Transact-SQL statement fails. This example is for illustration only.

```
USE pubs
GO
sp_bindefault phonedflt, 'authors.phone'
```

Related Topics

ALTER TABLE, Batches, CREATE RULE, CREATE TABLE, DROP DEFAULT, DROP RULE, Expressions, INSERT, sp_bindefault, sp_help, sp_helptext, sp_rename, sp_unbindefault, Using Identifiers

CREATE FUNCTION

Creates a user-defined function, which is a saved Transact-SQL routine that returns a value. User-defined functions cannot be used to perform a set of actions that modify the global database state. User-defined functions, like system functions, can be invoked from a query. They also can be executed through an EXECUTE statement like stored procedures.

User-defined functions are modified using ALTER FUNCTION, and dropped using DROP FUNCTION.

Syntax

Scalar Functions

```
CREATE  FUNCTION [ owner_name. ] function_name
    ( [ { @parameter_name [AS] scalar_parameter_data_type [ = default ] } [ ,…n ] ] )
RETURNS scalar_return_data_type
[ WITH < function_option> [ [,] …n] ]
[ AS ]
BEGIN
    function_body
    RETURN scalar_expression
END
```

Inline Table-valued Functions

```
CREATE FUNCTION [ owner_name. ] function_name
    ( [ { @parameter_name [AS] scalar_parameter_data_type [ = default ] } [ ,…n ] ] )
RETURNS TABLE
[ WITH < function_option > [ [,] ...n ] ]
[ AS ]
RETURN [ ( ] select-stmt [ ) ]
```

Multi-statement Table-valued Functions

```
CREATE FUNCTION [ owner_name. ] function_name
    ( [ { @parameter_name [AS] scalar_parameter_data_type [ = default ] } [ ,…n ] ] )
RETURNS @return_variable TABLE < table_type_definition >
[ WITH < function_option > [ [,] ...n ] ]
[ AS ]
BEGIN
    function_body
    RETURN
END

< function_option > ::=
    { ENCRYPTION | SCHEMABINDING }
< table_type_definition > :: =
    ( { column_definition | table_constraint } [ ,...n ] )
```

Arguments

owner_name

Is the name of the user ID that owns the user-defined function. *owner_name* must be an existing user ID.

function_name

Is the name of the user-defined function. Function names must conform to the rules for identifiers and must be unique within the database and to its owner.

@*parameter_name*
> Is a parameter in the user-defined function. One or more parameters can be declared in a CREATE FUNCTION statement. A function can have a maximum of 1,024 parameters. The value of each declared parameter must be supplied by the user when the function is executed, unless a default for the parameter is defined. When a parameter of the function has a default value, the keyword "default" must be specified when calling the function in order to get the default value. This behavior is different from parameters with default values in stored procedures in which omitting the parameter also implies the default value.
>
> Specify a parameter name using an at sign (@) as the first character. The parameter name must conform to the rules for identifiers. Parameters are local to the function; the same parameter names can be used in other functions. Parameters can take the place only of constants; they cannot be used in place of table names, column names, or the names of other database objects.

scalar_parameter_data_type
> Is the parameter data type. All scalar data types, including **bigint** and **sql_variant**, can be used as a parameter for user-defined functions. The **timestamp** data type and user-defined data types not supported. Nonscalar types such as cursor and table cannot be specified.

scalar_return_data_type
> Is the return value of a scalar user-defined function. *scalar_return_data_type* can be any of the scalar data types supported by SQL Server, except **text**, **ntext**, **image**, and **timestamp**.

scalar_expression
> Specifies the scalar value that the scalar function returns.

TABLE
> Specifies that the return value of the table-valued function is a table.
>
> In inline table-valued functions, the TABLE return value is defined through a single SELECT statement. Inline functions do not have associated return variables.
>
> In multi-statement table-valued functions, @*return_variable* is a TABLE variable, used to store and accumulate the rows that should be returned as the value of the function.

function_body
> Specifies that a series of Transact-SQL statements, which together do not produce a side effect, define the value of the function. function_body is used only in scalar functions and multi-statement table-valued functions.
>
> In scalar functions, *function_body* is a series of Transact-SQL statements that together evaluate to a scalar value.
>
> In multi-statement table-valued functions, *function_body* is a series of Transact-SQL statements that populate a table return variable.

select-stmt
>Is the single SELECT statement that defines the return value of an inline table valued function.

ENCRYPTION
>Indicates that SQL Server encrypts the system table columns containing the text of the CREATE FUNCTION statement. Using ENCRYPTION prevents the function from being published as part of SQL Server replication.

SCHEMABINDING
>Specifies that the function is bound to the database objects that it references. If a function is created with the SCHEMABINDING option, then the database objects that the function references cannot be altered (using the ALTER statement) or dropped (using a DROP statement).

>The binding of the function to the objects it references is removed only when one of two actions take place:

>- The function is dropped.
>- The function is altered (using the ALTER statement) with the SCHEMABINDING option not specified.

>A function can be schema-bound only if the following conditions are true:

>- The user-defined functions and views referenced by the function are also schema-bound.
>- The objects referenced by the function are not referenced using a two-part name.
>- The function and the objects it references belong to the same database.
>- The user who executed the CREATE FUNCTION statement has REFERENCES permission on all the database objects that the function references.

>The CREATE FUNCTION statement with the SCHEMABINDING option specified will fail if the above conditions are not true.

Remarks

User-defined functions are either scalar-valued or table-valued. Functions are scalar-valued if the RETURNS clause specified one of the scalar data types. Scalar-valued functions can be defined using multiple Transact-SQL statements.

Functions are table-valued if the RETURNS clause specified TABLE. Depending on how the body of the function is defined, table-valued functions can be classified as inline or multi-statement functions.

If the RETURNS clause specifies TABLE with no accompanying column list, the function is an inline function. Inline functions are table-valued functions defined with a single SELECT statement making up the body of the function. The columns, including the data types, of the table returned by the function are derived from the SELECT list of the SELECT statement defining the function.

If the RETURNS clause specifies a TABLE type with columns and their data types, the function is a multi-statement table-valued function.

The following statements are allowed in the body of a multi-statement function. Statements not in this list are not allowed in the body of a function:

- Assignment statements.
- Control-of-Flow statements.
- DECLARE statements defining data variables and cursors that are local to the function.
- SELECT statements containing select lists with expressions that assign values to variables that are local to the function.
- Cursor operations referencing local cursors that are declared, opened, closed, and deallocated in the function. Only FETCH statements that assign values to local variables using the INTO clause are allowed; FETCH statements that return data to the client are not allowed.
- INSERT, UPDATE, and DELETE statements modifying **table** variables local to the function.
- EXECUTE statements calling an extended stored procedures.

Function Determinism and Side Effects

Functions are either deterministic or nondeterministic. They are deterministic when they always return the same result any time they are called with a specific set of input values. They are nondeterministic when they could return different result values each time they are called with the same specific set of input values.

Nondeterministic functions can cause side effects. Side effects are changes to some global state of the database, such as an update to a database table, or to some external resource, such as a file or the network (for example, modify a file or send an e-mail message).

Built-in nondeterministic functions are not allowed in the body of user-defined functions; they are as follows:

@@CONNECTIONS
@@CPU_BUSY
@@IDLE
@@IO_BUSY
@@MAX_CONNECTIONS
@@PACK_RECEIVED
@@PACK_SENT
@@PACKET_ERRORS
@@TIMETICKS

@@TOTAL_ERRORS
@@TOTAL_READ
@@TOTAL_WRITE
GETDATE
GETUTCDATE
NEWID
RAND
TEXTPTR

Although nondeterministic functions are not allowed in the body of user-defined functions, these user-defined functions still can cause side effects if they call extended stored procedures.

Functions that call extended stored procedures are considered nondeterministic because extended stored procedures can cause side effects on the database. When user defined functions call extended stored procedures that can have side effects on the database, do not rely on a consistent result set or execution of the function.

Calling extended stored procedures from functions

The extended stored procedure, when called from inside a function, cannot return result sets to the client. Any ODS APIs that return result sets to the client will return FAIL. The extended stored procedure could connect back to Microsoft SQL Server; however, it should not attempt to join the same transaction as the function that invoked the extended stored procedure.

Similar to invocations from a batch or stored procedure, the extended stored procedure will be executed in the context of the Windows security account under which SQL Server is running. The owner of the stored procedure should consider this when giving EXECUTE privileges on it to users.

Function Invocation

Scalar-valued functions may be invoked where scalar expressions are used, including computed columns and CHECK constraint definitions. When invoking scalar-valued functions, at minimum use the two-part name of the function.

```
[database_name.]owner_name.function_name ([argument_expr][,…])
```

If a user-defined function is used to define a computed column, the function's deterministic quality also defines whether an index may be created on that computed column. An index can be created on a computed column that uses a function only if the function is deterministic. A function is deterministic if it always returns the same value, given the same input.

Table-valued functions can be invoked using a single part name.

```
[database_name.][owner_name.]function_name ([argument_expr][,…])
```

System table functions that are included in Microsoft SQL Server 2000 need to be invoked using a '::' prefix before the function name.

```
SELECT *
FROM ::fn_helpcollations()
```

Transact-SQL errors that cause a statement to be stopped and then continued with the next statement in a stored procedure are treated differently inside a function. In functions, such errors will cause the function execution to be stopped. This in turn will cause the statement that invoked the function to be stopped.

Permissions

Users should have the CREATE FUNCTION permission to execute the CREATE FUNCTION statement.

CREATE FUNCTION permissions default to members of the **sysadmin** fixed server role, and the **db_owner** and **db_ddladmin** fixed database roles. Members of **sysadmin** and **db_owner** can grant CREATE FUNCTION permissions to other logins by using the GRANT statement.

Owners of functions have EXECUTE permission on their functions. Other users do not have EXECUTE permissions unless EXECUTE permissions on the specific function are granted to them.

In order to create or alter tables with references to user-defined functions in the CONSTRAINT, DEFAULT clauses, or computed column definition, the user must also have REFERENCES permission to the functions.

Examples

A. Scalar-valued user-defined function that calculates the ISO week

In this example, a user-defined function, ISOweek, takes a date argument and calculates the ISO week number. For this function to calculate properly, SET DATEFIRST 1 must be invoked before the function is called.

```
CREATE FUNCTION ISOweek  (@DATE datetime)
RETURNS int
AS
BEGIN
   DECLARE @ISOweek int
   SET @ISOweek= DATEPART(wk,@DATE)+1
       -DATEPART(wk,CAST(DATEPART(yy,@DATE) as CHAR(4))+'0104')
--Special cases: Jan 1-3 may belong to the previous year
   IF (@ISOweek=0)
       SET @ISOweek=dbo.ISOweek(CAST(DATEPART(yy,@DATE)-1
           AS CHAR(4))+'12'+ CAST(24+DATEPART(DAY,@DATE) AS CHAR(2)))+1
--Special case: Dec 29-31 may belong to the next year
   IF ((DATEPART(mm,@DATE)=12) AND
       ((DATEPART(dd,@DATE)-DATEPART(dw,@DATE))>= 28))
       SET @ISOweek=1
   RETURN(@ISOweek)
END
```

Here is the function call. Notice that DATEFIRST is set to 1.

```
SET DATEFIRST 1
SELECT master.dbo.ISOweek('12/26/1999') AS 'ISO Week'
```

Here is the result set.

```
ISO Week
----------------
52
```

B. Inline table-valued function

This example returns an inline table-valued function.

```
USE pubs
GO
CREATE FUNCTION SalesByStore (@storeid varchar(30))
RETURNS TABLE
AS
RETURN (SELECT title, qty
      FROM sales s, titles t
      WHERE s.stor_id = @storeid and
      t.title_id = s.title_id)
```

C. Multi-statement table-valued function

Given a table that represents a hierarchical relationship:

```
CREATE TABLE employees (empid nchar(5) PRIMARY KEY,
    empname nvarchar(50),
    mgrid nchar(5) REFERENCES employees(empid),
    title nvarchar(30)
    )
```

The table-valued function fn_FindReports(InEmpID), which—given an Employee ID—returns a table corresponding to all the employees that report to the given employee directly or indirectly. This logic is not expressible in a single query and is a good candidate for implementing as a user-defined function.

```
CREATE FUNCTION fn_FindReports (@InEmpId nchar(5))
RETURNS @retFindReports TABLE (empid nchar(5) primary key,
    empname nvarchar(50) NOT NULL,
    mgrid nchar(5),
    title nvarchar(30))
/*Returns a result set that lists all the employees who report to given
employee directly or indirectly.*/
AS
BEGIN
    DECLARE @RowsAdded int
    -- table variable to hold accumulated results
    DECLARE @reports TABLE (empid nchar(5) primary key,
        empname nvarchar(50) NOT NULL,
        mgrid nchar(5),
        title nvarchar(30),
        processed tinyint default 0)
-- initialize @Reports with direct reports of the given employee
    INSERT @reports
    SELECT empid, empname, mgrid, title, 0
    FROM employees
    WHERE empid = @InEmpId
    SET @RowsAdded = @@rowcount
    -- While new employees were added in the previous iteration
    WHILE @RowsAdded > 0
    BEGIN
        /*Mark all employee records whose direct reports are going to be
        found in this iteration with processed=1.*/
        UPDATE @reports
        SET processed = 1
        WHERE processed = 0
```

(continued)

(continued)

```
    -- Insert employees who report to employees marked 1.
    INSERT @reports
    SELECT e.empid, e.empname, e.mgrid, e.title, 0
    FROM employees e, @reports r
    WHERE e.mgrid=r.empid and e.mgrid <> e.empid and r.processed = 1
    SET @RowsAdded = @@rowcount
    /*Mark all employee records whose direct reports have been found
 in this iteration.*/
    UPDATE @reports
    SET processed = 2
    WHERE processed = 1
  END

    -- copy to the result of the function the required columns
    INSERT @retFindReports
    SELECT empid, empname, mgrid, title
    FROM @reports
    RETURN
END
GO


-- Example invocation
SELECT *
FROM fn_FindReports('11234')
GO
```

Related Topics

ALTER FUNCTION, DROP FUNCTION, Invoking User-defined Functions,
User-defined Functions

CREATE INDEX

Creates an index on a given table or view.

Only the table or view owner can create indexes on that table. The owner of a table or
view can create an index at any time, whether or not there is data in the table. Indexes
can be created on tables or views in another database by specifying a qualified
database name.

Syntax

```
CREATE [ UNIQUE ] [ CLUSTERED | NONCLUSTERED ] INDEX index_name
    ON { table | view } ( column [ ASC | DESC ] [ ,...n ] )
[ WITH < index_option > [ ,...n] ]
[ ON filegroup ]
< index_option > :: =
    { PAD_INDEX |
        FILLFACTOR = fillfactor |
        IGNORE_DUP_KEY |
        DROP_EXISTING |
    STATISTICS_NORECOMPUTE |
    SORT_IN_TEMPDB
}
```

Arguments

UNIQUE

Creates a unique index (one in which no two rows are permitted to have the same index value) on a table or view. A clustered index on a view must be UNIQUE.

Microsoft SQL Server checks for duplicate values when the index is created (if data already exists) and checks each time data is added with an INSERT or UPDATE statement. If duplicate key values exist, the CREATE INDEX statement is canceled and an error message giving the first duplicate is returned. Multiple NULL values are considered duplicates when UNIQUE index is created.

When a unique index exists, UPDATE or INSERT statements that would generate duplicate key values are rolled back, and SQL Server displays an error message. This is true even if the UPDATE or INSERT statement changes many rows but causes only one duplicate. If an attempt is made to enter data for which there is a unique index and the IGNORE_DUP_KEY clause is specified, only the rows violating the UNIQUE index fail. When processing an UPDATE statement, IGNORE_DUP_KEY has no effect.

SQL Server does not allow the creation of a unique index on columns that already include duplicate values, whether or not IGNORE_DUP_KEY is set. If attempted, SQL Server displays an error message; duplicates must be eliminated before a unique index can be created on the column(s).

CLUSTERED

Creates an object where the physical order of rows is the same as the indexed order of the rows, and the bottom (leaf) level of the clustered index contains the actual data rows. A table or view is allowed one clustered index at a time.

A view with a clustered index is called an indexed view. A unique clustered index must be created on a view before any other indexes can be defined on the same view.

Create the clustered index before creating any nonclustered indexes. Existing nonclustered indexes on tables are rebuilt when a clustered index is created.

If CLUSTERED is not specified, a nonclustered index is created.

Note Because the leaf level of a clustered index and its data pages are the same by definition, creating a clustered index and using the ON *filegroup* clause effectively moves a table from the file on which the table was created to the new filegroup. Before creating tables or indexes on specific filegroups, verify which filegroups are available and that they have enough empty space for the index. It is important that the filegroup have at least 1.2 times the space required for the entire table.

NONCLUSTERED

Creates an object that specifies the logical ordering of a table. With a nonclustered index, the physical order of the rows is independent of their indexed order. The leaf level of a nonclustered index contains index rows. Each index row contains the nonclustered key value and one or more row locators that point to the row that contains the value. If the table does not have a clustered index, the row locator is the row's disk address. If the table does have a clustered index, the row locator is the clustered index key for the row.

Each table can have as many as 249 nonclustered indexes (regardless of how they are created: implicitly with PRIMARY KEY and UNIQUE constraints, or explicitly with CREATE INDEX). Each index can provide access to the data in a different sort order.

For indexed views, nonclustered indexes can be created only on a view with a clustered index already defined. Thus, the row locator of a nonclustered index on an indexed view is always the clustered key of the row.

index_name

Is the name of the index. Index names must be unique within a table or view but do not need to be unique within a database. Index names must follow the rules of identifiers.

table

Is the table that contains the column or columns to be indexed. Specifying the database and table owner names is optional.

view

Is the name of the view to be indexed. The view must be defined with SCHEMABINDING in order to create an index on it. The view definition also must be deterministic. A view is deterministic if all expressions in the select list, and the WHERE and GROUP BY clauses are deterministic. Also, all key columns must be precise. Only nonkey columns of the view may contain float expressions (expressions that use **float** data type), and **float** expressions cannot be used anywhere else in the view definition.

To find a column in the view that is deterministic, use the COLUMNPROPERTY function (**IsDeterministic** property). The **IsPrecise** property of the function can be used to determine that the key columns are precise.

A unique clustered index must be created on a view before any nonclustered index is created.

Indexed views may be used by the query optimizer in SQL Server Enterprise or Developer edition to speed up the query execution. The view does not need to be referenced in the query for the optimizer to consider that view for a substitution.

When creating indexed views or manipulating rows in tables participating in an indexed view, seven SET options must be assigned specific values. The SET options ARITHABORT, CONCAT_NULL_YIELDS_NULL, QUOTED_IDENTIFIER, ANSI_NULLS, ANSI_PADDING, and ANSI_WARNING must be ON. The SET option NUMERIC_ROUNDABORT must be OFF.

If any of these settings is different, data modification statements (INSERT, UPDATE, DELETE) on any table referenced by an indexed view fail and SQL Server raises an error listing all SET options that violate setting requirements. In addition, for a SELECT statement that involves an indexed view, if the values of any of the SET options are not the required values, SQL Server processes the SELECT without considering the indexed view substitution. This ensures correctness of query result in cases where it can be affected by the above SET options.

If the application uses a DB-Library connection, all seven SET options on the server must be assigned the required values. (By default, OLE DB and ODBC connections have set all of the required SET options correctly, except for ARITHABORT.)

Some operations, like BCP, replication, or distributed queries may fail to execute their updates against tables participating in indexed views if not all of the listed SET options have the required value. In the majority of cases, this issue can be prevented by setting ARITHABORT to ON (through **user options** in the server configuration option).

It is strongly recommended that the ARITHABORT user option be set server-wide to ON as soon as the first indexed view or index on a computed column is created in any database on the server.

See the Remarks section for more information on considerations and restrictions on indexed views.

column

Is the column or columns to which the index applies. Specify two or more column names to create a composite index on the combined values in the specified columns. List the columns to be included in the composite index (in sort-priority order) inside the parentheses after *table*.

Note   Columns consisting of the **ntext**, **text**, or **image** data types cannot be specified as columns for an index. In addition, a view cannot include any **text**, **ntext**, or **image** columns, even if they are not referenced in the CREATE INDEX statement.

Composite indexes are used when two or more columns are best searched as a unit or if many queries reference only the columns specified in the index. As many as 16 columns can be combined into a single composite index. All the columns in a composite index must be in the same table. The maximum allowable size of the combined index values is 900 bytes. That is, the sum of the lengths of the fixed-size columns that make up the composite index cannot exceed 900 bytes. For more information about variable type columns in composite indexes, see the Remarks section.

[ASC | DESC]

Determines the ascending or descending sort direction for the particular index column. The default is ASC.

n

Is a placeholder indicating that multiple *column*s can be specified for any particular index.

PAD_INDEX

Specifies the space to leave open on each page (node) in the intermediate levels of the index. The PAD_INDEX option is useful only when FILLFACTOR is specified, because PAD_INDEX uses the percentage specified by FILLFACTOR. By default, SQL Server ensures that each index page has enough empty space to accommodate at least one row of the maximum size the index can have, given the set of keys on the intermediate pages. If the percentage specified for FILLFACTOR is not large enough to accommodate one row, SQL Server internally overrides the percentage to allow the minimum.

Note   The number of rows on an intermediate index page is never less than two, regardless of how low the value of FILLFACTOR.

FILLFACTOR = *fillfactor*

Specifies a percentage that indicates how full SQL Server should make the leaf level of each index page during index creation. When an index page fills up, SQL Server must take time to split the index page to make room for new rows, which is quite expensive. For update-intensive tables, a properly chosen FILLFACTOR value yields better update performance than an improper FILLFACTOR value. The value of the original FILLFACTOR is stored with the index in **sysindexes**.

When FILLFACTOR is specified, SQL Server rounds up the number of rows to be placed on each page. For example, issuing CREATE CLUSTERED INDEX ... FILLFACTOR = 33 creates a clustered index with a FILLFACTOR of 33 percent. Assume that SQL Server calculates that 5.2 rows is 33 percent of the space on a page. SQL Server rounds so that six rows are placed on each page.

Note An explicit FILLFACTOR setting applies only when the index is first created. SQL Server does not dynamically keep the specified percentage of empty space in the pages.

User-specified FILLFACTOR values can be from 1 through 100. If no value is specified, the default is 0. When FILLFACTOR is set to 0, only the leaf pages are filled. You can change the default FILLFACTOR setting by executing **sp_configure**.

Use a FILLFACTOR of 100 only if no INSERT or UPDATE statements will occur, such as with a read-only table. If FILLFACTOR is 100, SQL Server creates indexes with leaf pages 100 percent full. An INSERT or UPDATE made after the creation of an index with a 100 percent FILLFACTOR causes page splits for each INSERT and possibly each UPDATE.

Smaller FILLFACTOR values, except 0, cause SQL Server to create new indexes with leaf pages that are not completely full. For example, a FILLFACTOR of 10 can be a reasonable choice when creating an index on a table known to contain a small portion of the data that it will eventually hold. Smaller FILLFACTOR values also cause each index to take more storage space.

The following table illustrates how the pages of an index are filled up if FILLFACTOR is specified.

FILLFACTOR	Intermediate page	Leaf page
0 percent	One free entry	100 percent full
1–99 percent	One free entry	<= FILLFACTOR percent full
100 percent	One free entry	100 percent full

One free entry is the space on the page that can accommodate another index entry.

Important Creating a clustered index with a FILLFACTOR affects the amount of storage space the data occupies because SQL Server redistributes the data when it creates the clustered index.

IGNORE_DUP_KEY

Controls what happens when an attempt is made to insert a duplicate key value into a column that is part of a unique clustered index. If IGNORE_DUP_KEY was specified for the index and an INSERT statement that creates a duplicate key is executed, SQL Server issues a warning and ignores the duplicate row.

If IGNORE_DUP_KEY was not specified for the index, SQL Server issues an error message and rolls back the entire INSERT statement.

The table shows when IGNORE_DUP_KEY can be used.

Index type	Options
Clustered	Not allowed
Unique clustered	IGNORE_DUP_KEY allowed
Nonclustered	Not allowed
Unique nonclustered	IGNORE_DUP_KEY allowed

DROP_EXISTING

Specifies that the named, preexisting clustered or nonclustered index should be dropped and rebuilt. The index name specified must be the same as a currently existing index. Because nonclustered indexes contain the clustering keys, the nonclustered indexes must be rebuilt when a clustered index is dropped. If a clustered index is recreated, the nonclustered indexes must be rebuilt to take the new set of keys into account.

The DROP_EXISTING clause enhances performance when re-creating a clustered index (with either the same or a different set of keys) on a table that also has nonclustered indexes. The DROP_EXISTING clause replaces the execution of a DROP INDEX statement on the old clustered index followed by the execution of a CREATE INDEX statement for the new clustered index. The nonclustered indexes are rebuilt once, and only if the keys are different.

If the keys do not change (the same index name and columns as the original index are provided), the DROP_EXISTING clause does not sort the data again. This can be useful if the index must be compacted.

A clustered index cannot be converted to a nonclustered index using the DROP_EXISTING clause; however, a unique clustered index can be changed to a non-unique index, and vice versa.

> **Note**   When executing a CREATE INDEX statement with the DROP_EXISTING clause, SQL Server assumes that the index is consistent, that is, there is no corruption in the index. The rows in the specified index should be sorted by the specified key referenced in the CREATE INDEX statement.

STATISTICS_NORECOMPUTE

Specifies that out-of-date index statistics are not automatically recomputed. To restore automatic statistics updating, execute UPDATE STATISTICS without the NORECOMPUTE clause.

> **Important**   Disabling automatic recomputation of distribution statistics may prevent the SQL Server query optimizer from picking optimal execution plans for queries involving the table.

SORT_IN_TEMPDB
Specifies that the intermediate sort results used to build the index will be stored in the **tempdb** database. This option may reduce the time needed to create an index if **tempdb** is on a different set of disks than the user database, but it increases the amount of disk space used during the index build.

For more information, see tempdb and Index Creation.

ON *filegroup*
Creates the specified index on the given *filegroup*. The filegroup must have already been created by executing either CREATE DATABASE or ALTER DATABASE.

Remarks

Space is allocated to tables and indexes in increments of one extent (eight 8-kilobyte pages) at a time. Each time an extent is filled, another is allocated. Indexes on very small or empty tables will use single page allocations until eight pages have been added to the index and then will switch to extent allocations. For a report on the amount of space allocated and used by an index, use **sp_spaceused**.

Creating a clustered index requires space available in your database equal to approximately 1.2 times the size of the data. This is space in addition to the space used by the existing table; the data is duplicated in order to create the clustered index, and the old, nonindexed data is deleted when the index is complete. When using the DROP_EXISTING clause, the space needed for the clustered index is the amount of space equal to the space requirements of the existing index. The amount of additional space required also may be affected by the FILLFACTOR specified.

When creating an index in SQL Server 2000, you can use the SORT_IN_TEMPDB option to direct the database engine to store the intermediate index sort results in **tempdb**. This option may reduce the time needed to create an index if **tempdb** is on a different set of disks than the user database, but it increases the amount of disk space used to create an index. In addition to the space required in the user database to create the index, **tempdb** must have about the same amount of additional space to hold the intermediate sort results. For more information, see tempdb and Index Creation.

The CREATE INDEX statement is optimized like any other query. The SQL Server query processor may choose to scan another index instead of performing a table scan to save on I/O operations. The sort may be eliminated in some situations.

On multiprocessor computers on SQL Server Enterprise and Developer Editions, CREATE INDEX automatically uses more processors to perform the scan and sort, in the same way as other queries do. The number of processors employed to execute a single CREATE INDEX statement is determined by the configuration option **max degree of parallelism** as well as the current workload. If SQL Server detects that the system is busy, the degree of parallelism of the CREATE INDEX operation is automatically reduced before statement execution begins.

Entire filegroups affected by a CREATE INDEX statement since the last filegroup backup must be backed up as a unit. For more information about file and filegroup backups, see BACKUP.

Backup and CREATE INDEX operations do not block each other. If a backup is in progress, index is created in a fully logged mode, which may require extra log space.

To display a report on an object's indexes, execute **sp_helpindex**.

Indexes can be created on a temporary table. When the table is dropped or the session ends, all indexes and triggers are dropped.

Variable type columns in indexes

The maximum size allowed for an index key is 900 bytes, but SQL Server 2000 allows indexes to be created on columns that may have large variable type columns with a maximum size greater than 900 bytes.

During index creation, SQL Server checks the following conditions:

- The sum of all fixed data columns that participate in the index definition must be less or equal to 900 bytes. When the index to be created is composed of fixed data columns only, the total size of the fixed data columns must be less or equal to 900 bytes. Otherwise, the index will not be created and SQL Server will return an error.

- If the index definition is composed of fixed- and variable-type columns, and the fixed-data columns meet the previous condition (less or equal to 900 bytes), SQL Server still checks the total size of the variable type columns. If the maximum size of the variable-type columns plus the size of the fixed-data columns is greater than 900 bytes, SQL Server creates the index, but returns a warning to the user. The warning alerts the user that if subsequent insert or update actions on the variable-type columns result in a total size greater than 900 bytes, the action will fail and the user will get a run-time error. Likewise, if the index definition is composed of variable-type columns only, and the maximum total size of these columns is greater than 900 bytes, SQL Server will create the index, but return a warning.

For more information, see Maximum Size of Index Keys.

Considerations when indexing computed columns and views

In SQL Server 2000, indexes also can be created on computed columns and views. Creating a unique clustered index on a view improves query performance because the view is stored in the database in the same way a table with a clustered index is stored.

The UNIQUE or PRIMARY KEY may contain a computed column as long as it satisfies all conditions for indexing. Specifically, the computed column must be deterministic, precise, and must not contain **text**, **ntext**, or **image** columns. For more information about determinism, see Deterministic and Nondeterministic Functions.

Creation of an index on a computed column or view may cause the failure of an INSERT or UPDATE operation that previously worked. Such a failure may take place when the computed column results in arithmetic error. For example, although computed column **c** in the following table will result in an arithmetic error, the INSERT statement will work:

```
CREATE TABLE t1 (a int, b int, c AS a/b)
GO
INSERT INTO t1 VALUES ('1', '0')
GO
```

If, instead, after creating the table, you create an index on computed column **c**, the same INSERT statement now will fail.

```
CREATE TABLE t1 (a int, b int, c AS a/b)
GO
CREATE UNIQUE CLUSTERED INDEX Idx1 ON t1.c
GO
INSERT INTO t1 VALUES ('1', '0')
GO
```

The result of a query using an index on a view defined with numeric or **float** expressions may be different from a similar query that does not use the index on the view. This difference may be the result of rounding errors during INSERT, DELETE, or UPDATE actions on underlying tables.

To prevent SQL Server from using indexed views, include the OPTION (EXPAND VIEWS) hint on the query. Also, setting any of the listed options incorrectly will prevent the optimizer from using the indexes on the views. For more information about the OPTION (EXPAND VIEWS) hint, see SELECT.

Restrictions on indexed views

The SELECT statement defining an indexed view must not have the TOP, DISTINCT, COMPUTE, HAVING, and UNION keywords. It cannot have a subquery.

The SELECT list may not include asterisks (*), '*table*.*' wildcard lists, DISTINCT, COUNT(*), COUNT(*<expression>*), computed columns from the base tables, and scalar aggregates.

Nonaggregate SELECT lists cannot have expressions. Aggregate SELECT list (queries that contain GROUP BY) may include SUM and COUNT_BIG(<expression>); it must contain COUNT_BIG(*). Other aggregate functions (MIN, MAX, STDEV,…) are not allowed.

Complex aggregation using AVG cannot participate in the SELECT list of the indexed view. However, if a query uses such aggregation, the optimizer is capable of using this indexed view to substitute AVG with a combination of simple aggregates SUM and COUNT_BIG.

A column resulting from an expression that either evaluates to a **float** data type or uses **float** expressions for its evaluation cannot be a key of an index in an indexed view or on a computed column in a table. Such columns are called nonprecise. Use the COLUMNPROPERTY function to determine if a particular computed column or a column in a view is precise.

Indexed views are subject to these additional restrictions:

- The creator of the index must own the tables. All tables, the view, and the index, must be created in the same database.
- The SELECT statement defining the indexed view may not contain views, rowset functions, inline functions, or derived tables. The same physical table may occur only once in the statement.
- In any joined tables, no OUTER JOIN operations are allowed.
- No subqueries or CONTAINS or FREETEXT predicates are allowed in the search condition.
- If the view definition contains a GROUP BY clause, all grouping columns as well as the COUNT_BIG(*) expression must appear in the view's SELECT list. Also, these columns must be the only columns in the CREATE UNIQUE CLUSTERED INDEX clause.

The body of the definition of a view that can be indexed must be deterministic and precise, similar to the requirements on indexes on computed columns. See Creating Indexes on Computed Columns.

Permissions

CREATE INDEX permissions default to the **sysadmin** fixed server role and the **db_ddladmin** and **db_owner** fixed database roles and the table owner, and are not transferable.

Examples

A. Use a simple index

This example creates an index on the **au_id** column of the **authors** table.

```
SET NOCOUNT OFF
USE pubs
IF EXISTS (SELECT name FROM sysindexes
      WHERE name = 'au_id_ind')
   DROP INDEX authors.au_id_ind
GO
USE pubs
CREATE INDEX au_id_ind
   ON authors (au_id)
GO
```

B. Use a unique clustered index

This example creates an index on the **employeeID** column of the **emp_pay** table that enforces uniqueness. This index physically orders the data on disk because the CLUSTERED clause is specified.

```
SET NOCOUNT ON
USE pubs
IF EXISTS (SELECT * FROM INFORMATION_SCHEMA.TABLES
      WHERE TABLE_NAME = 'emp_pay')
   DROP TABLE emp_pay
GO
USE pubs
IF EXISTS (SELECT name FROM sysindexes
      WHERE name = 'employeeID_ind')
   DROP INDEX emp_pay.employeeID_ind
GO
USE pubs
GO
CREATE TABLE emp_pay
(
 employeeID int NOT NULL,
 base_pay money NOT NULL,
 commission decimal(2, 2) NOT NULL
)
INSERT emp_pay
   VALUES (1, 500, .10)
INSERT emp_pay
   VALUES (2, 1000, .05)
INSERT emp_pay
```

(continued)

(continued)

```
   VALUES (3, 800, .07)
INSERT emp_pay
   VALUES (5, 1500, .03)
INSERT emp_pay
   VALUES (9, 750, .06)
GO
SET NOCOUNT OFF
CREATE UNIQUE CLUSTERED INDEX employeeID_ind
   ON emp_pay (employeeID)
GO
```

C. Use a simple composite index

This example creates an index on the **orderID** and **employeeID** columns of the **order_emp** table.

```
SET NOCOUNT ON
USE pubs
IF EXISTS (SELECT * FROM INFORMATION_SCHEMA.TABLES
      WHERE TABLE_NAME = 'order_emp')
   DROP TABLE order_emp
GO
USE pubs
IF EXISTS (SELECT name FROM sysindexes
      WHERE name = 'emp_order_ind')
   DROP INDEX order_emp.emp_order_ind
GO
USE pubs
GO
CREATE TABLE order_emp
(
 orderID int IDENTITY(1000, 1),
 employeeID int NOT NULL,
 orderdate datetime NOT NULL DEFAULT GETDATE(),
 orderamount money NOT NULL
)

INSERT order_emp (employeeID, orderdate, orderamount)
   VALUES (5, '4/12/98', 315.19)
INSERT order_emp (employeeID, orderdate, orderamount)
   VALUES (5, '5/30/98', 1929.04)
INSERT order_emp (employeeID, orderdate, orderamount)
   VALUES (1, '1/03/98', 2039.82)
```

(continued)

(continued)

```
INSERT order_emp (employeeID, orderdate, orderamount)
   VALUES (1, '1/22/98', 445.29)
INSERT order_emp (employeeID, orderdate, orderamount)
   VALUES (4, '4/05/98', 689.39)
INSERT order_emp (employeeID, orderdate, orderamount)
   VALUES (7, '3/21/98', 1598.23)
INSERT order_emp (employeeID, orderdate, orderamount)
   VALUES (7, '3/21/98', 445.77)
INSERT order_emp (employeeID, orderdate, orderamount)
   VALUES (7, '3/22/98', 2178.98)
GO
SET NOCOUNT OFF
CREATE INDEX emp_order_ind
   ON order_emp (orderID, employeeID)
```

D. Use the FILLFACTOR option

This example uses the FILLFACTOR clause set to 100. A FILLFACTOR of 100 fills every page completely and is useful only when you know that index values in the table will never change.

```
SET NOCOUNT OFF
USE pubs
IF EXISTS (SELECT name FROM sysindexes
      WHERE name = 'zip_ind')
   DROP INDEX authors.zip_ind
GO
USE pubs
GO
CREATE NONCLUSTERED INDEX zip_ind
   ON authors (zip)
   WITH FILLFACTOR = 100
```

E. Use the IGNORE_DUP_KEY

This example creates a unique clustered index on the **emp_pay** table. If a duplicate key is entered, the INSERT or UPDATE statement is ignored.

```
SET NOCOUNT ON
USE pubs
IF EXISTS (SELECT * FROM INFORMATION_SCHEMA.TABLES
      WHERE TABLE_NAME = 'emp_pay')
   DROP TABLE emp_pay
GO
```

(continued)

(continued)

```
USE pubs
IF EXISTS (SELECT name FROM sysindexes
      WHERE name = 'employeeID_ind')
   DROP INDEX emp_pay.employeeID_ind
GO
USE pubs
GO
CREATE TABLE emp_pay
(
 employeeID int NOT NULL,
 base_pay money NOT NULL,
 commission decimal(2, 2) NOT NULL
)
INSERT emp_pay
   VALUES (1, 500, .10)
INSERT emp_pay
   VALUES (2, 1000, .05)
INSERT emp_pay
   VALUES (3, 800, .07)
INSERT emp_pay
   VALUES (5, 1500, .03)
INSERT emp_pay
   VALUES (9, 750, .06)
GO
SET NOCOUNT OFF
GO
CREATE UNIQUE CLUSTERED INDEX employeeID_ind
   ON emp_pay(employeeID)
   WITH IGNORE_DUP_KEY
```

F. Create an index with PAD_INDEX

This example creates an index on the author's identification number in the **authors** table. Without the PAD_INDEX clause, SQL Server creates leaf pages that are 10 percent full, but the pages above the leaf level are filled almost completely. With PAD_INDEX, the intermediate pages are also 10 percent full.

Note   At least two entries appear on the index pages of unique clustered indexes when PAD_INDEX is not specified.

```
SET NOCOUNT OFF
USE pubs
IF EXISTS (SELECT name FROM sysindexes
      WHERE name = 'au_id_ind')
```

(continued)

(continued)

```
    DROP INDEX authors.au_id_ind
GO
USE pubs
CREATE INDEX au_id_ind
   ON authors (au_id)
   WITH PAD_INDEX, FILLFACTOR = 10
```

G. Create an index on a view

This example will create a view and an index on that view. Then, two queries are included using the indexed view.

```
USE Northwind
GO


--Set the options to support indexed views.
SET NUMERIC_ROUNDABORT OFF
GO
SET
ANSI_PADDING,ANSI_WARNINGS,CONCAT_NULL_YIELDS_NULL,ARITHABORT,QUOTED_IDENTIFIER,ANSI_NULLS
ON
GO


--Create view.
CREATE VIEW V1
WITH   SCHEMABINDING
AS
   SELECT SUM(UnitPrice*Quantity*(1.00-Discount)) AS Revenue, OrderDate, ProductID,
COUNT_BIG(*) AS COUNT
   FROM   dbo.[Order Details] od, dbo.Orders o
   WHERE od.OrderID=o.OrderID
   GROUP BY OrderDate, ProductID
GO


--Create index on the view.
CREATE UNIQUE CLUSTERED INDEX IV1 ON V1 (OrderDate, ProductID)
GO


--This query will use the above indexed view.
SELECT SUM(UnitPrice*Quantity*(1.00-Discount)) AS Rev, OrderDate, ProductID
FROM   dbo.[Order Details] od, dbo.Orders o
WHERE od.OrderID=o.OrderID AND ProductID in (2, 4, 25, 13, 7, 89, 22, 34)
   AND OrderDate >= '05/01/1998'
GROUP BY OrderDate, ProductID
```

(continued)

(continued)

```
ORDER BY Rev DESC

--This query will use the above indexed view.
SELECT  OrderDate, SUM(UnitPrice*Quantity*(1.00-Discount)) AS Rev
FROM   dbo.[Order Details] od, dbo.Orders o
WHERE od.OrderID=o.OrderID AND DATEPART(mm,OrderDate)= 3
   AND DATEPART(yy,OrderDate) = 1998
GROUP BY OrderDate
ORDER BY OrderDate ASC
```

Related Topics

ALTER DATABASE, CREATE DATABASE, CREATE STATISTICS, CREATE TABLE, Data Types, DBCC SHOW_STATISTICS, Designing an Index, DROP INDEX, DROP STATISTICS, Indexes, INSERT, RECONFIGURE, SET, sp_autostats, sp_createstats, sp_dbcmptlevel, sp_dboption, sp_helpindex, sp_spaceused, sysindexes, Transactions, UPDATE, UPDATE STATISTICS, Using Identifiers

CREATE PROCEDURE

Creates a stored procedure, which is a saved collection of Transact-SQL statements that can take and return user-supplied parameters.

Procedures can be created for permanent use or for temporary use within a session (local temporary procedure) or for temporary use within all sessions (global temporary procedure).

Stored procedures can also be created to run automatically when Microsoft SQL Server starts.

Syntax

```
CREATE PROC [ EDURE ] procedure_name [ ; number ]
   [ { @parameter data_type }
      [ VARYING ] [ = default ] [ OUTPUT ]
   ] [ ,...n ]

[ WITH
   { RECOMPILE | ENCRYPTION | RECOMPILE , ENCRYPTION } ]

[ FOR REPLICATION ]

AS sql_statement [ ...n ]
```

Arguments

procedure_name

> Is the name of the new stored procedure. Procedure names must conform to the rules for identifiers and must be unique within the database and its owner. For more information, see Using Identifiers.
>
> Local or global temporary procedures can be created by preceding the *procedure_name* with a single number sign (#*procedure_name*) for local temporary procedures and a double number sign (##*procedure_name*) for global temporary procedures. The complete name, including # or ##, cannot exceed 128 characters. Specifying the procedure owner name is optional.

;number

> Is an optional integer used to group procedures of the same name so they can be dropped together with a single DROP PROCEDURE statement. For example, the procedures used with an application called orders may be named **orderproc**;1, **orderproc**;2, and so on. The statement DROP PROCEDURE **orderproc** drops the entire group. If the name contains delimited identifiers, the number should not be included as part of the identifier; use the appropriate delimiter around *procedure_name* only.

@parameter

> Is a parameter in the procedure. One or more parameters can be declared in a CREATE PROCEDURE statement. The value of each declared parameter must be supplied by the user when the procedure is executed (unless a default for the parameter is defined). A stored procedure can have a maximum of 2,100 parameters.
>
> Specify a parameter name using an at sign (@) as the first character. The parameter name must conform to the rules for identifiers. Parameters are local to the procedure; the same parameter names can be used in other procedures. By default, parameters can take the place only of constants; they cannot be used in place of table names, column names, or the names of other database objects. For more information, see EXECUTE.

data_type

> Is the parameter data type. All data types, including **text, ntext** and **image**, can be used as a parameter for a stored procedure. However, the **cursor** data type can be used only on OUTPUT parameters. When you specify a data type of **cursor**, the VARYING and OUTPUT keywords must also be specified. For more information about SQL Server-supplied data types and their syntax, see Data Types.
>
> > **Note** There is no limit on the maximum number of output parameters that can be of **cursor** data type.

VARYING

Specifies the result set supported as an output parameter (constructed dynamically by the stored procedure and whose contents can vary). Applies only to cursor parameters.

default

Is a default value for the parameter. If a default is defined, the procedure can be executed without specifying a value for that parameter. The default must be a constant or it can be NULL. It can include wildcard characters (%, _, [], and [^]) if the procedure uses the parameter with the LIKE keyword.

OUTPUT

Indicates that the parameter is a return parameter. The value of this option can be returned to EXEC[UTE]. Use OUTPUT parameters to return information to the calling procedure. **Text**, **ntext**, and **image** parameters can be used as OUTPUT parameters. An output parameter using the OUTPUT keyword can be a cursor placeholder.

n

Is a placeholder indicating that a maximum of 2,100 parameters can be specified.

{RECOMPILE | ENCRYPTION | RECOMPILE, ENCRYPTION}

RECOMPILE indicates that SQL Server does not cache a plan for this procedure and the procedure is recompiled at run time. Use the RECOMPILE option when using atypical or temporary values without overriding the execution plan cached in memory.

ENCRYPTION indicates that SQL Server encrypts the **syscomments** table entry containing the text of the CREATE PROCEDURE statement. Using ENCRYPTION prevents the procedure from being published as part of SQL Server replication.

> **Note** During an upgrade, SQL Server uses the encrypted comments stored in **syscomments** to re-create encrypted procedures.

FOR REPLICATION

Specifies that stored procedures created for replication cannot be executed on the Subscriber. A stored procedure created with the FOR REPLICATION option is used as a stored procedure filter and only executed during replication. This option cannot be used with the **WITH RECOMPILE** option.

AS

Specifies the actions the procedure is to take.

sql_statement

Is any number and type of Transact-SQL statements to be included in the procedure. Some limitations apply.

n

Is a placeholder that indicates multiple Transact-SQL statements may be included in this procedure.

Remarks

The maximum size of a stored procedure is 128 MB.

A user-defined stored procedure can be created only in the current database (except for temporary procedures, which are always created in **tempdb**). The CREATE PROCEDURE statement cannot be combined with other Transact-SQL statements in a single batch.

Parameters are nullable by default. If a NULL parameter value is passed and that parameter is used in a CREATE or ALTER TABLE statement in which the column referenced does not allow NULLs, SQL Server generates an error. To prevent passing a NULL parameter value to a column that does not allow NULLs, add programming logic to the procedure or use a default value (with the DEFAULT keyword of CREATE or ALTER TABLE) for the column.

It is recommended that you explicitly specify NULL or NOT NULL for each column in any CREATE TABLE or ALTER TABLE statement in a stored procedure, such as when creating a temporary table. The ANSI_DFLT_ON and ANSI_DFLT_OFF options control the way SQL Server assigns the NULL or NOT NULL attributes to columns if not specified in a CREATE TABLE or ALTER TABLE statement. If a connection executes a stored procedure with different settings for these options than the connection that created the procedure, the columns of the table created for the second connection can have different nullability and exhibit different behaviors. If NULL or NOT NULL is explicitly stated for each column, the temporary tables are created with the same nullability for all connections that execute the stored procedure.

SQL Server saves the settings of both SET QUOTED_IDENTIFIER and SET ANSI_NULLS when a stored procedure is created or altered. These original settings are used when the stored procedure is executed. Therefore, any client session settings for SET QUOTED_IDENTIFIER and SET ANSI_NULLS are ignored during stored procedure execution. SET QUOTED_IDENTIFIER and SET ANSI_NULLS statements that occur within the stored procedure do not affect the functionality of the stored procedure.

Other SET options, such as SET ARITHABORT, SET ANSI_WARNINGS, or SET ANSI_PADDINGS are not saved when a stored procedure is created or altered. If the logic of the stored procedure is dependent on a particular setting, include a SET statement at the start of the procedure to ensure the proper setting. When a SET statement is executed from a stored procedure, the setting remains in effect only until the stored procedure completes. The setting is then restored to the value it had when the stored procedure was called. This allows individual clients to set the options wanted without affecting the logic of the stored procedure.

Note Whether SQL Server interprets an empty string as either a single space or as a true empty string is controlled by the compatibility level setting. If the compatibility level is less than or equal to 65, SQL Server interprets empty strings as single spaces. If the compatibility level is equal to 70, SQL Server interprets empty strings as empty strings. For more information, see sp_dbcmptlevel.

Getting Information About Stored Procedures

To display the text used to create the procedure, execute **sp_helptext** in the database in which the procedure exists with the procedure name as the parameter.

Note Stored procedures created with the ENCRYPTION option cannot be viewed with **sp_helptext**.

For a report on the objects referenced by a procedure, use **sp_depends**.

To rename a procedure, use **sp_rename**.

Referencing Objects

SQL Server allows the creation of stored procedures that reference objects that do not yet exist. At creation time, only syntax checking is done. The stored procedure is compiled to generate an execution plan when executed, if a valid plan does not already exist in the cache. Only during compilation are all objects referenced in the stored procedure resolved. Thus, a syntactically correct stored procedure that references objects which do not exist can be created successfully, but will fail at run time because referenced objects do not exist. For more information, see Deferred Name Resolution and Compilation.

Deferred Name Resolution and Compatibility Level

SQL Server allows Transact-SQL stored procedures to refer to tables that do not exist at creation time. This ability is called deferred name resolution. If, however, the Transact-SQL stored procedure refers to a table defined within the stored procedure, a warning is issued at creation time if the compatibility level setting (set by executing **sp_dbcmptlevel**) is 65. An error message is returned at run time if the table referenced does not exist. For more information, see sp_dbcmptlevel and Deferred Name Resolution and Compilation.

Executing Stored Procedures

When a CREATE PROCEDURE statement is executed successfully, the procedure name is stored in the **sysobjects** system table and the text of the CREATE PROCEDURE statement is stored in **syscomments**. When executed for the first time, the procedure is compiled to determine an optimal access plan to retrieve the data.

Parameters Using the cursor Data Type

Stored procedures can use the **cursor** data type only for OUTPUT parameters. If the **cursor** data type is specified for a parameter, both the VARYING and OUTPUT parameters are required. If the VARYING keyword is specified for a parameter, the data type must be **cursor** and the OUTPUT keyword must be specified.

Note   The **cursor** data type cannot be bound to application variables through the database APIs such as OLE DB, ODBC, ADO, and DB-Library. Because OUTPUT parameters must be bound before an application can execute a stored procedure, stored procedures with **cursor** OUTPUT parameters cannot be called from the database APIs. These procedures can be called from Transact-SQL batches, stored procedures, or triggers only when the **cursor** OUTPUT variable is assigned to a Transact-SQL local **cursor** variable.

Cursor Output Parameters

The following rules pertain to **cursor** output parameters when the procedure is executed:

- For a forward-only cursor, the rows returned in the cursor's result set are only those rows at and beyond the position of the cursor at the conclusion of the stored procedure executed, for example:

  - A nonscrollable cursor is opened in a procedure on a result set named RS of 100 rows.

  - The procedure fetches the first 5 rows of result set RS.

  - The procedure returns to its caller.

  - The result set RS returned to the caller consists of rows from 6 through 100 of RS, and the cursor in the caller is positioned before the first row of RS.

- For a forward-only cursor, if the cursor is positioned before the first row upon completion of the stored procedure, the entire result set is returned to the calling batch, stored procedure, or trigger. When returned, the cursor position is set before the first row.

- For a forward-only cursor, if the cursor is positioned beyond the end of the last row upon completion of the stored procedure, an empty result set is returned to the calling batch, stored procedure, or trigger.

  Note   An empty result set is not the same as a null value.

- For a scrollable cursor, all the rows in the result set are returned to the calling batch, stored procedure, or trigger at the conclusion of the execution of the stored procedure. When returned, the cursor position is left at the position of the last fetch executed in the procedure.

- For any type of cursor, if the cursor is closed, then a null value is passed back to the calling batch, stored procedure, or trigger. This will also be the case if a cursor is assigned to a parameter, but that cursor is never opened.

    Note The closed state matters only at return time. For example, it is valid to close a cursor part way through the procedure, to open it again later in the procedure, and return that cursor's result set to the calling batch, stored procedure, or trigger.

Temporary Stored Procedures

SQL Server supports two types of temporary procedures: local and global. A local temporary procedure is visible only to the connection that created it. A global temporary procedure is available to all connections. Local temporary procedures are automatically dropped at the end of the current session. Global temporary procedures are dropped at the end of the last session using the procedure. Usually, this is when the session that created the procedure ends.

Temporary procedures named with # and ## can be created by any user. When the procedure is created, the owner of the local procedure is the only one who can use it. Permission to execute a local temporary procedure cannot be granted for other users. If a global temporary procedure is created, all users can access it; permissions cannot be revoked explicitly. Explicitly creating a temporary procedure in **tempdb** (naming without a number sign) can be performed only by those with explicit CREATE PROCEDURE permission in the **tempdb** database. Permission can be granted and revoked from these procedures.

    Note Heavy use of temporary stored procedures can create contention on the system tables in **tempdb** and adversely affect performance. It is recommended that **sp_executesql** be used instead. **sp_executesql** does not store data in the system tables and therefore avoids the problem.

Automatically Executing Stored Procedures

One or more stored procedures can execute automatically when SQL Server starts. The stored procedures must be created by the system administrator and executed under the **sysadmin** fixed server role as a background process. The procedure(s) cannot have any input parameters.

There is no limit to the number of startup procedures you can have, but be aware that each consumes one connection while executing. If you must execute multiple procedures at startup but do not need to execute them in parallel, make one procedure the startup procedure and have that procedure call the other procedures. This uses only one connection.

Execution of the stored procedures starts when the last database is recovered at startup. To skip launching these stored procedures, specify trace flag 4022 as a startup parameter. If you start SQL Server with minimal configuration (using the **-f** flag), the startup stored procedures are not executed. For more information, see Trace Flags.

To create a startup stored procedure, you must be logged in as a member of the **sysadmin** fixed server role and create the stored procedure in the **master** database.

Use **sp_procoption** to:

- Designate an existing stored procedure as a startup procedure.
- Stop a procedure from executing at SQL Server startup.
- View a list of all procedures that execute at SQL Server startup.

Stored Procedure Nesting

Stored procedures can be nested; that is one stored procedure calling another. The nesting level is incremented when the called procedure starts execution, and decremented when the called procedure finishes execution. Exceeding the maximum levels of nesting causes the whole calling procedure chain to fail. The current nesting level is returned by the @@NESTLEVEL function.

To estimate the size of a compiled stored procedure, use these Performance Monitor Counters.

Performance Monitor object name	Performance Monitor Counter name
SQLServer: Buffer Manager	Cache Size (pages)
SQLServer: Cache Manager	Cache Hit Ratio
	Cache Pages
	Cache Object Counts*

* These counters are available for various categories of cache objects including adhoc sql, prepared sql, procedures, triggers, and so on.

For more information, see SQL Server: Buffer Manager Object and SQL Server: Cache Manager Object.

sql_statement Limitations

Any SET statement can be specified inside a stored procedure except SET SHOWPLAN_TEXT and SET SHOWPLAN_ALL, which must be the only statements in the batch. The SET option chosen remains in effect during the execution of the stored procedure and then reverts to its former setting.

Inside a stored procedure, object names used with certain statements must be qualified with the name of the object owner if other users are to use the stored procedure. The statements are:

- ALTER TABLE
- CREATE INDEX
- CREATE TABLE
- All DBCC statements
- DROP TABLE
- DROP INDEX
- TRUNCATE TABLE
- UPDATE STATISTICS

Permissions

CREATE PROCEDURE permissions default to members of the **sysadmin** fixed server role, and the **db_owner** and **db_ddladmin** fixed database roles. Members of the **sysadmin** fixed server role and the **db_owner** fixed database role can transfer CREATE PROCEDURE permissions to other users. Permission to execute a stored procedure is given to the procedure owner, who can then set execution permission for other database users.

Examples

A. Use a simple procedure with a complex SELECT

This stored procedure returns all authors (first and last names supplied), their titles, and their publishers from a four-table join. This stored procedure does not use any parameters.

```
USE pubs
IF EXISTS (SELECT name FROM sysobjects
        WHERE name = 'au_info_all' AND type = 'P')
   DROP PROCEDURE au_info_all
GO
CREATE PROCEDURE au_info_all
AS
SELECT au_lname, au_fname, title, pub_name
   FROM authors a INNER JOIN titleauthor ta
      ON a.au_id = ta.au_id INNER JOIN titles t
      ON t.title_id = ta.title_id INNER JOIN publishers p
      ON t.pub_id = p.pub_id
GO
```

The **au_info_all** stored procedure can be executed in these ways:

```
EXECUTE au_info_all
-- Or
EXEC au_info_all
```

Or, if this procedure is the first statement within the batch:

```
au_info_all
```

B. Use a simple procedure with parameters

This stored procedure returns only the specified authors (first and last names supplied), their titles, and their publishers from a four-table join. This stored procedure accepts exact matches for the parameters passed.

```
USE pubs
IF EXISTS (SELECT name FROM sysobjects
        WHERE name = 'au_info' AND type = 'P')
   DROP PROCEDURE au_info
GO
USE pubs
GO
CREATE PROCEDURE au_info
   @lastname varchar(40),
   @firstname varchar(20)
AS
SELECT au_lname, au_fname, title, pub_name
   FROM authors a INNER JOIN titleauthor ta
      ON a.au_id = ta.au_id INNER JOIN titles t
      ON t.title_id = ta.title_id INNER JOIN publishers p
      ON t.pub_id = p.pub_id
   WHERE  au_fname = @firstname
      AND au_lname = @lastname
GO
```

The **au_info** stored procedure can be executed in these ways:

```
EXECUTE au_info 'Dull', 'Ann'
-- Or
EXECUTE au_info @lastname = 'Dull', @firstname = 'Ann'
-- Or
EXECUTE au_info @firstname = 'Ann', @lastname = 'Dull'
-- Or
EXEC au_info 'Dull', 'Ann'
-- Or
EXEC au_info @lastname = 'Dull', @firstname = 'Ann'
-- Or
EXEC au_info @firstname = 'Ann', @lastname = 'Dull'
```

Or, if this procedure is the first statement within the batch:

```
au_info 'Dull', 'Ann'
-- Or
au_info @lastname = 'Dull', @firstname = 'Ann'
-- Or
au_info @firstname = 'Ann', @lastname = 'Dull'
```

C. Use a simple procedure with wildcard parameters

This stored procedure returns only the specified authors (first and last names supplied), their titles, and their publishers from a four-table join. This stored procedure pattern matches the parameters passed or, if not supplied, uses the preset defaults.

```
USE pubs
IF EXISTS (SELECT name FROM sysobjects
      WHERE name = 'au_info2' AND type = 'P')
   DROP PROCEDURE au_info2
GO
USE pubs
GO
CREATE PROCEDURE au_info2
   @lastname varchar(30) = 'D%',
   @firstname varchar(18) = '%'
AS
SELECT au_lname, au_fname, title, pub_name
FROM authors a INNER JOIN titleauthor ta
   ON a.au_id = ta.au_id INNER JOIN titles t
   ON t.title_id = ta.title_id INNER JOIN publishers p
   ON t.pub_id = p.pub_id
WHERE au_fname LIKE @firstname
   AND au_lname LIKE @lastname
GO
```

The **au_info2** stored procedure can be executed in many combinations. Only a few combinations are shown here:

```
EXECUTE au_info2
-- Or
EXECUTE au_info2 'Wh%'
-- Or
EXECUTE au_info2 @firstname = 'A%'
-- Or
EXECUTE au_info2 '[CK]ars[OE]n'
-- Or
EXECUTE au_info2 'Hunter', 'Sheryl'
-- Or
EXECUTE au_info2 'H%', 'S%'
```

D. Use OUTPUT parameters

OUTPUT parameters allow an external procedure, a batch, or more than one Transact-SQL statements to access a value set during the procedure execution. In this example, a stored procedure (**titles_sum**) is created and allows one optional input parameter and one output parameter.

First, create the procedure:

```
USE pubs
GO
IF EXISTS(SELECT name FROM sysobjects
    WHERE name = 'titles_sum' AND type = 'P')
   DROP PROCEDURE titles_sum
GO
USE pubs
GO
CREATE PROCEDURE titles_sum @@TITLE varchar(40) = '%', @@SUM money OUTPUT
AS
SELECT 'Title Name' = title
FROM titles
WHERE title LIKE @@TITLE
SELECT @@SUM = SUM(price)
FROM titles
WHERE title LIKE @@TITLE
GO
```

Next, use the OUTPUT parameter with control-of-flow language.

> **Note** The OUTPUT variable must be defined during the table creation as well as during use of the variable.

The parameter name and variable name do not have to match; however, the data type and parameter positioning must match (unless @@SUM = *variable* is used).

```
DECLARE @@TOTALCOST money
EXECUTE titles_sum 'The%', @@TOTALCOST OUTPUT
IF @@TOTALCOST < 200
BEGIN
   PRINT ' '
   PRINT 'All of these titles can be purchased for less than $200.'
END
ELSE
   SELECT 'The total cost of these titles is $'
       + RTRIM(CAST(@@TOTALCOST AS varchar(20)))
```

Here is the result set:

```
Title Name
-----------------------------------------------------------------------
The Busy Executive's Database Guide
The Gourmet Microwave
The Psychology of Computer Cooking

(3 row(s) affected)

Warning, null value eliminated from aggregate.

All of these titles can be purchased for less than $200.
```

E. Use an OUTPUT cursor parameter

OUTPUT cursor parameters are used to pass a cursor that is local to a stored procedure back to the calling batch, stored procedure, or trigger.

First, create the procedure that declares and then opens a cursor on the titles table:

```
USE pubs
IF EXISTS (SELECT name FROM sysobjects
      WHERE name = 'titles_cursor' and type = 'P')
DROP PROCEDURE titles_cursor
GO
CREATE PROCEDURE titles_cursor @titles_cursor CURSOR VARYING OUTPUT
AS
SET @titles_cursor = CURSOR
FORWARD_ONLY STATIC FOR
SELECT *
FROM titles

OPEN @titles_cursor
GO
```

Next, execute a batch that declares a local cursor variable, executes the procedure to assign the cursor to the local variable, and then fetches the rows from the cursor.

```
USE pubs
GO
DECLARE @MyCursor CURSOR
EXEC titles_cursor @titles_cursor = @MyCursor OUTPUT
WHILE (@@FETCH_STATUS = 0)
BEGIN
   FETCH NEXT FROM @MyCursor
END
```

(continued)

(continued)

```
CLOSE @MyCursor
DEALLOCATE @MyCursor
GO
```

F. Use the WITH RECOMPILE option

The WITH RECOMPILE clause is helpful when the parameters supplied to the procedure will not be typical, and when a new execution plan should not be cached or stored in memory.

```
USE pubs
IF EXISTS (SELECT name FROM sysobjects
     WHERE name = 'titles_by_author' AND type = 'P')
   DROP PROCEDURE titles_by_author
GO
CREATE PROCEDURE titles_by_author @@LNAME_PATTERN varchar(30) = '%'
WITH RECOMPILE
AS
SELECT RTRIM(au_fname) + ' ' + RTRIM(au_lname) AS 'Authors full name',
   title AS Title
FROM authors a INNER JOIN titleauthor ta
   ON a.au_id = ta.au_id INNER JOIN titles t
   ON ta.title_id = t.title_id
WHERE au_lname LIKE @@LNAME_PATTERN
GO
```

G. Use the WITH ENCRYPTION option

The WITH ENCRYPTION clause hides the text of a stored procedure from users. This example creates an encrypted procedure, uses the **sp_helptext** system stored procedure to get information on that encrypted procedure, and then attempts to get information on that procedure directly from the **syscomments** table.

```
IF EXISTS (SELECT name FROM sysobjects
     WHERE name = 'encrypt_this' AND type = 'P')
   DROP PROCEDURE encrypt_this
GO
USE pubs
GO
CREATE PROCEDURE encrypt_this
WITH ENCRYPTION
AS
SELECT *
FROM authors
GO

EXEC sp_helptext encrypt_this
```

Here is the result set:

```
The object's comments have been encrypted.
```

Next, select the identification number and text of the encrypted stored procedure contents.

```
SELECT c.id, c.text
FROM syscomments c INNER JOIN sysobjects o
   ON c.id = o.id
WHERE o.name = 'encrypt_this'
```

Here is the result set:

> **Note** The **text** column output is shown on a separate line. When executed, this information appears on the same line as the **id** column information.

```
id          text
---------- -------------------------------------------------------------
1413580074
?????????????????????????????????e??????????????????????????????????????????????????????????????????????????????
????????????????????

(1 row(s) affected)
```

H. Create a user-defined system stored procedure

This example creates a procedure to display all the tables and their corresponding indexes with a table name beginning with the string **emp**. If not specified, this procedure returns all tables (and indexes) with a table name beginning with **sys**.

```
IF EXISTS (SELECT name FROM sysobjects
      WHERE name = 'sp_showindexes' AND type = 'P')
   DROP PROCEDURE sp_showindexes
GO
USE master
GO
CREATE PROCEDURE sp_showindexes
   @@TABLE varchar(30) = 'sys%'
AS
SELECT o.name AS TABLE_NAME,
   i.name AS INDEX_NAME,
   indid AS INDEX_ID
FROM sysindexes i INNER JOIN sysobjects o
   ON o.id = i.id
WHERE o.name LIKE @@TABLE
GO
USE pubs
EXEC sp_showindexes 'emp%'
GO
```

Here is the result set:

```
TABLE_NAME        INDEX_NAME        INDEX_ID
---------------   ---------------   ---------------
employee          employee_ind      1
employee          PK_emp_id         2

(2 row(s) affected)
```

I. Use deferred name resolution

This example shows four procedures and the various ways that deferred name resolution can be used. Each stored procedure is created, although the table or column referenced does not exist at compile time.

```
IF EXISTS (SELECT name FROM sysobjects
      WHERE name = 'proc1' AND type = 'P')
   DROP PROCEDURE proc1
GO
-- Creating a procedure on a nonexistent table.
USE pubs
GO
CREATE PROCEDURE proc1
AS
   SELECT *
   FROM does_not_exist
GO
-- Here is the statement to actually see the text of the procedure.
SELECT o.id, c.text
FROM sysobjects o INNER JOIN syscomments c
   ON o.id = c.id
WHERE o.type = 'P' AND o.name = 'proc1'
GO
USE master
GO
IF EXISTS (SELECT name FROM sysobjects
      WHERE name = 'proc2' AND type = 'P')
   DROP PROCEDURE proc2
GO
-- Creating a procedure that attempts to retrieve information from a
-- nonexistent column in an existing table.
USE pubs
GO
CREATE PROCEDURE proc2
AS
```

(continued)

(continued)

```
    DECLARE @middle_init char(1)
    SET @middle_init = NULL
    SELECT au_id, middle_initial = @middle_init
    FROM authors
GO
-- Here is the statement to actually see the text of the procedure.
SELECT o.id, c.text
FROM sysobjects o INNER JOIN syscomments c
    ON o.id = c.id
WHERE o.type = 'P' and o.name = 'proc2'
```

Related Topics

ALTER PROCEDURE, Batches, Control-of-Flow Language, Cursors, DBCC, DECLARE @local_variable, DROP PROCEDURE, Functions, GRANT, Programming Stored Procedures, SELECT, sp_addextendedproc, sp_depends, sp_helptext, sp_procoption, sp_recompile, sp_rename, System Tables, Using Comments, Using Variables and Parameters

CREATE RULE

Creates an object called a *rule*. When bound to a column or a user-defined data type, a rule specifies the acceptable values that can be inserted into that column. Rules, a backward compatibility feature, perform some of the same functions as check constraints. CHECK constraints, created using the CHECK keyword of ALTER or CREATE TABLE, are the preferred, standard way to restrict the values in a column (multiple constraints can be defined on one or multiple columns). A column or user-defined data type can have only one rule bound to it. However, a column can have both a rule and one or more check constraints associated with it. When this is true, all restrictions are evaluated.

Syntax

```
CREATE RULE rule
    AS condition_expression
```

Arguments

rule

Is the name of the new rule. Rule names must conform to the rules for identifiers. Specifying the rule owner name is optional.

condition_expression

Is the condition(s) defining the rule. A rule can be any expression valid in a WHERE clause and can include such elements as arithmetic operators, relational operators, and predicates (for example, IN, LIKE, BETWEEN). A rule cannot reference columns or other database objects. Built-in functions that do not reference database objects can be included.

condition_expression includes one variable. The at sign (@) precedes each local variable. The expression refers to the value entered with the UPDATE or INSERT statement. Any name or symbol can be used to represent the value when creating the rule, but the first character must be the at sign (@).

Remarks

The CREATE RULE statement cannot be combined with other Transact-SQL statements in a single batch. Rules do not apply to data already existing in the database at the time the rules are created, and rules cannot be bound to system data types. A rule can be created only in the current database. After creating a rule, execute **sp_bindrule** to bind the rule to a column or to a user-defined data type.

The rule must be compatible with the column data type. A rule cannot be bound to a **text**, **image**, or **timestamp** column. Be sure to enclose character and date constants with single quotation marks (') and to precede binary constants with 0x. For example, "@value LIKE A%" cannot be used as a rule for a numeric column. If the rule is not compatible with the column to which it is bound, Microsoft SQL Server returns an error message when inserting a value, but not when the rule is bound.

A rule bound to a user-defined data type is activated only when you attempt to insert a value into, or to update, a database column of the user-defined data type. Because rules do not test variables, do not assign a value to a user-defined data type variable that would be rejected by a rule bound to a column of the same data type.

To get a report on a rule, use **sp_help**. To display the text of a rule, execute **sp_helptext** with the rule name as the parameter. To rename a rule, use **sp_rename**.

A rule must be dropped (using DROP RULE) before a new one with the same name is created, and the rule must be unbound (using **sp_unbindrule**) before it is dropped. Use **sp_unbindrule** to unbind a rule from a column.

You can bind a new rule to a column or data type without unbinding the previous one; the new rule overrides the previous one. Rules bound to columns always take precedence over rules bound to user-defined data types. Binding a rule to a column replaces a rule already bound to the user-defined data type of that column. But binding a rule to a data type does not replace a rule bound to a column of that user-defined data type. The table shows the precedence in effect when binding rules to columns and to user-defined data types where rules already exist.

| | Old rule bound to | |
New rule bound to	user-defined data type	Column
User-defined data type	Old rule replaced	No change
Column	Old rule replaced	Old rule replaced

If a column has both a default and a rule associated with it, the default must fall within the domain defined by the rule. A default that conflicts with a rule is never inserted. SQL Server generates an error message each time it attempts to insert such a default.

> **Note** Whether SQL Server interprets an empty string as a single space or as a true empty string is controlled by the setting of **sp_dbcmptlevel**. If the compatibility level is less than or equal to 65, SQL Server interprets empty strings as single spaces. If the compatibility level is equal to 70, SQL Server interprets empty strings as empty strings. For more information, see sp_dbcmptlevel.

Permissions

CREATE RULE permissions default to the members of the **sysadmin** fixed server role and the **db_ddladmin** and **db_owner** fixed database roles. Members of the **sysadmin**, **db_owner** and **db_securityadmin** roles can transfer permissions to other users.

Examples

A. Rule with a range

This example creates a rule that restricts the range of integers inserted into the column(s) to which this rule is bound.

```
CREATE RULE range_rule
AS
@range >= $1000 AND @range < $20000
```

B. Rule with a list

This example creates a rule that restricts the actual values entered into the column or columns (to which this rule is bound) to only those listed in the rule.

```
CREATE RULE list_rule
AS
@list IN ('1389', '0736', '0877')
```

C. Rule with a pattern

This example creates a rule to follow a pattern of any two characters followed by a hyphen, any number of characters (or no characters), and ending with an integer from 0 through 9.

```
CREATE RULE pattern_rule
AS
@value LIKE '_ _-%[0-9]'
```

Related Topics

ALTER TABLE, Batches, CREATE DEFAULT, CREATE TABLE, DROP DEFAULT, DROP RULE, Expressions, sp_bindrule, sp_help, sp_helptext, sp_rename, sp_unbindrule, Using Identifiers, WHERE

CREATE SCHEMA

Creates a schema that can be thought of as a conceptual object containing definitions of tables, views, and permissions.

Syntax

```
CREATE SCHEMA AUTHORIZATION owner
    [ < schema_element > [ ...n ] ]
< schema_element > ::=
    { table_definition | view_definition | grant_statement }
```

Arguments

AUTHORIZATION *owner*
> Specifies the ID of the schema object owner. This identifier must be a valid security account in the database.

table_definition
> Specifies a CREATE TABLE statement that creates a table within the schema.

view_definition
> Specifies a CREATE VIEW statement that creates a view within the schema.

grant_statement
> Specifies a GRANT statement that grants permissions for a user or a group of users.

Remarks

CREATE SCHEMA provides a way to create tables and views and to grant permissions for objects with a single statement. If errors occur when creating any objects or granting any permissions specified in a CREATE SCHEMA statement, none of the objects are created.

The created objects do not have to appear in logical order, except for views that reference other views. For example, a GRANT statement can grant permission for an object before the object itself is created, or a CREATE VIEW statement can appear before the CREATE TABLE statements creating the tables referenced by the view. Also, CREATE TABLE statements can declare foreign keys to tables specified later. The exception is that if the select from one view references another view, the referenced view must be specified before the view that references it.

Permissions

CREATE SCHEMA permissions default to all users, but they must have permissions to create the objects that participate in the schema.

Examples

A. Grant access to objects before object creation

This example shows permissions granted before the objects are created.

```
CREATE SCHEMA AUTHORIZATION ross
GRANT SELECT on v1 TO public
CREATE VIEW v1(c1) AS SELECT c1 from t1
CREATE TABLE t1(c1 int)
```

B. Create mutually dependent FOREIGN KEY constraints

This example creates mutually dependent FOREIGN KEY constraints. Other methods would take several steps to accomplish what is enabled by this CREATE SCHEMA example.

```
CREATE SCHEMA AUTHORIZATION ross
CREATE TABLE t1 (c1 INT PRIMARY KEY, c2 INT REFERENCES t2(c1))
CREATE TABLE t2 (c1 INT PRIMARY KEY, c2 INT REFERENCES t1(c1))
```

CREATE STATISTICS

Creates a histogram and associated density groups (collections) over the supplied column or set of columns.

Syntax

```
CREATE STATISTICS statistics_name
ON { table | view } ( column [ ,...n ] )
   [ WITH
      [ [ FULLSCAN
         | SAMPLE number { PERCENT | ROWS } ] [ , ] ]
      [ NORECOMPUTE ]
   ]
```

Arguments

statistics_name

Is the name of the statistics group to create. Statistics names must conform to the rules for identifiers.

table

Is the name of the table on which to create the named statistics. Table names must conform to the rules for identifiers. *table* is the table with which the *column* is associated. Specifying the table owner name is optional. Statistics can be created on tables in another database by specifying a qualified database name.

view

Is the name of the view on which to create the named statistics. A view must have a clustered index before statistics can be created on it. View names must conform to the rules for identifiers. *view* is the view with which the *column* is associated. Specifying the view owner name is optional. Statistics can be created on views in another database by specifying a qualified database name.

column

Is the column or set of columns on which to create statistics. Computed columns and columns of the **ntext**, **text**, or **image** data types cannot be specified as statistics columns.

n

Is a placeholder indicating that multiple columns can be specified.

FULLSCAN

Specifies that all rows in *table* should be read to gather the statistics. Specifying FULLSCAN provides the same behavior as SAMPLE 100 PERCENT. This option cannot be used with the SAMPLE option.

SAMPLE *number* { PERCENT | ROWS }

Specifies that a percentage, or a specified number of rows, of the data should be read using random sampling to gather the statistics. *number* can be only an integer: if PERCENT, *number* should be from 0 through 100; if ROWS, *number* can be from 0 to the *n* total rows.

This option cannot be used with the FULLSCAN option. If no SAMPLE or FULLSCAN option is given, an automatic sample is computed by Microsoft SQL Server.

NORECOMPUTE

Specifies that automatic recomputation of the statistics should be disabled. If this option is specified, SQL Server continues to use previously created (old) statistics even as the data changes. The statistics are not automatically updated and maintained by SQL Server, which may produce suboptimal plans.

> **! WARNING** It is recommended that this option be used rarely and only by a trained system administrator.

Remarks

Only the table owner can create statistics on that table. The owner of a table can create a statistics group (collection) at any time, whether or not there is data in the table.

CREATE STATISTICS can be executed on views with clustered index, or indexed views. Statistics on indexed views are used by the optimizer only if the view is directly referenced in the query and the NOEXPAND hint is specified for the view. Otherwise, the statistics are derived from the underlying tables before the indexed view is substituted into the query plan. Such substitution is supported only on Microsoft SQL Server 2000 Enterprise and Developer Editions.

Permissions

CREATE STATISTICS permissions default to members of the **sysadmin** fixed server role and the **db_ddladmin** and **db_owner** fixed database roles and the table owner, and are not transferable.

Examples

A. Use CREATE STATISTICS with SAMPLE *number* PERCENT

This example creates the **names** statistics group (collection), which calculates random sampling statistics on five percent of the **CompanyName** and **ContactName** columns of the **Customers** table.

```
CREATE STATISTICS names
    ON Customers (CompanyName, ContactName)
    WITH SAMPLE 5 PERCENT
GO
```

B. Use CREATE STATISTICS with FULLSCAN and NORECOMPUTE

This example creates the **names** statistics group (collection), which calculates statistics for all rows in the **CompanyName** and **ContactName** columns of the **Customers** table and disables automatic recomputation of statistics.

```
CREATE STATISTICS names
    ON Northwind..Customers (CompanyName, ContactName)
    WITH FULLSCAN, NORECOMPUTE
GO
```

Related Topics

CREATE INDEX, DBCC SHOW_STATISTICS, DROP STATISTICS, sp_autostats, sp_createstats, sp_dboption, UPDATE STATISTICS

CREATE TABLE

Creates a new table.

Syntax

```
CREATE TABLE
    [ database_name.[ owner ] . | owner. ] table_name
    ( { < column_definition >
      | column_name AS computed_column_expression
      | < table_constraint > ::= [ CONSTRAINT constraint_name ] }
        | [ { PRIMARY KEY | UNIQUE } [ ,...n ]
    )

[ ON { filegroup | DEFAULT } ]
[ TEXTIMAGE_ON { filegroup | DEFAULT } ]

< column_definition > ::= { column_name data_type }
    [ COLLATE < collation_name > ]
    [ [ DEFAULT constant_expression ]
      | [ IDENTITY [ ( seed , increment ) [ NOT FOR REPLICATION ] ] ]
    ]
    [ ROWGUIDCOL]
    [ < column_constraint > ] [ ...n ]

< column_constraint > ::= [ CONSTRAINT constraint_name ]
    { [ NULL | NOT NULL ]
      | [ { PRIMARY KEY | UNIQUE }
          [ CLUSTERED | NONCLUSTERED ]
          [ WITH FILLFACTOR = fillfactor ]
          [ON {filegroup | DEFAULT} ] ]
      ]
      | [ [ FOREIGN KEY ]
          REFERENCES ref_table [ ( ref_column ) ]
          [ ON DELETE { CASCADE | NO ACTION } ]
          [ ON UPDATE { CASCADE | NO ACTION } ]
          [ NOT FOR REPLICATION ]
      ]
      | CHECK [ NOT FOR REPLICATION ]
      ( logical_expression )
    }
< table_constraint > ::= [ CONSTRAINT constraint_name ]
    { [ { PRIMARY KEY | UNIQUE }
        [ CLUSTERED | NONCLUSTERED ]
```

(continued)

(continued)

```
        { ( column [ ASC | DESC ] [ ,...n ] ) }
        [ WITH FILLFACTOR = fillfactor ]
        [ ON { filegroup | DEFAULT } ]
    ]
    | FOREIGN KEY
        [ ( column [ ,...n ] ) ]
        REFERENCES ref_table [ ( ref_column [ ,...n ] ) ]
        [ ON DELETE { CASCADE | NO ACTION } ]
        [ ON UPDATE { CASCADE | NO ACTION } ]
        [ NOT FOR REPLICATION ]
    | CHECK [ NOT FOR REPLICATION ]
        ( search_conditions )
    }
```

Arguments

database_name

Is the name of the database in which the table is created. *database_name* must specify the name of an existing database. *database_name* defaults to the current database if not specified. The login for the current connection must be associated with an existing user ID in the database specified by *database_name*, and that user ID must have create table permissions.

owner

Is the name of the user ID that owns the new table. *owner* must be an existing user ID in the database specified by *database_name*. *owner* defaults to the user ID associated with the login for the current connection in the database specified in *database_name*. If the CREATE TABLE statement is executed by a member of the **sysadmin** fixed server role, or a member of the **db_dbowner** or **db_ddladmin** fixed database roles in the database specified by *database_name*, *owner* can specify a user ID other than the one associated with the login of the current connection. If the CREATE TABLE statement is executed by a login associated with a user ID that has only create table permissions, *owner* must specify the user ID associated with the current login. Members of the **sysadmin** fixed server role, or logins aliased to the **dbo** user are associated with the user ID **dbo**; therefore, tables created by these users default to having **dbo** as the owner. Tables created by any logins not in either of these two roles have *owner* default to the user ID associated with the login.

table_name

Is the name of the new table. Table names must conform to the rules for identifiers. The combination of *owner.table_name* must be unique within the database. *table_name* can contain a maximum of 128 characters, except for local temporary table names (names prefixed with a single number sign (#)) that cannot exceed 116 characters.

column_name

Is the name of a column in the table. Column names must conform to the rules for identifiers and must be unique in the table. *column_name* can be omitted for columns created with a **timestamp** data type. The name of a **timestamp** column defaults to **timestamp** if *column_name* is not specified.

computed_column_expression

Is an expression defining the value of a computed column. A computed column is a virtual column not physically stored in the table. It is computed from an expression using other columns in the same table. For example, a computed column can have the definition: **cost** AS **price * qty**. The expression can be a noncomputed column name, constant, function, variable, and any combination of these connected by one or more operators. The expression cannot be a subquery.

Computed columns can be used in select lists, WHERE clauses, ORDER BY clauses, or any other locations in which regular expressions can be used, with the following exceptions:

- A computed column cannot be used as a DEFAULT or FOREIGN KEY constraint definition or with a NOT NULL constraint definition. However, a computed column can be used as a key column in an index or as part of any PRIMARY KEY or UNIQUE constraint, if the computed column value is defined by a deterministic expression and the data type of the result is allowed in index columns.

  For example, if the table has integer columns **a** and **b**, the computed column **a+b** may be indexed, but computed column **a+DATEPART(dd, GETDATE())** cannot be indexed because the value may change in subsequent invocations.

- A computed column cannot be the target of an INSERT or UPDATE statement.

  Note Each row in a table can have different values for columns involved in a computed column, therefore the computed column may not have the same value for each row.

The nullability of computed columns is determined automatically by SQL Server based on the expressions used. The result of most expressions is considered nullable even if only non-nullable columns are present because possible underflows or overflows will produce NULL results as well. Use the COLUMNPROPERTY function (AllowsNull property) to investigate the nullability of any computed column in a table. An expression *expr* that is nullable can be turned into a non-nullable one by specifying ISNULL(*check_expression*, constant) where the constant is a non-NULL value substituted for any NULL result.

ON {*filegroup* | DEFAULT}

Specifies the filegroup on which the table is stored. If *filegroup* is specified, the table is stored in the named filegroup. The filegroup must exist within the database. If DEFAULT is specified, or if ON is not specified at all, the table is stored on the default filegroup.

ON {*filegroup* | DEFAULT} can also be specified in a PRIMARY KEY or UNIQUE constraint. These constraints create indexes. If *filegroup* is specified, the index is stored in the named filegroup. If DEFAULT is specified, the index is stored in the default filegroup. If no filegroup is specified in a constraint, the index is stored on the same filegroup as the table. If the PRIMARY KEY or UNIQUE constraint creates a clustered index, the data pages for the table are stored in the same filegroup as the index.

> **Note** DEFAULT, in the context of ON {filegroup | DEFAULT} and TEXTIMAGE_ON {filegroup | DEFAULT}, is not a keyword. DEFAULT is an identifier for the default filegroup and must be delimited, as in ON "DEFAULT" or ON [DEFAULT] and TEXTIMAGE_ON "DEFAULT" or TEXTIMAGE_ON [DEFAULT].

TEXTIMAGE_ON

Are keywords indicating that the **text**, **ntext**, and **image** columns are stored on the specified filegroup. TEXTIMAGE ON is not allowed if there are no **text**, **ntext**, or **image** columns in the table. If TEXTIMAGE_ON is not specified, the **text**, **ntext**, and **image** columns are stored in the same filegroup as the table.

data_type

Specifies the column data type. System or user-defined data types are acceptable. User-defined data types are created with **sp_addtype** before they can be used in a table definition.

The NULL/NOT NULL assignment for a user-defined data type can be overridden during the CREATE TABLE statement. However, the length specification cannot be changed; you cannot specify a length for a user-defined data type in a CREATE TABLE statement.

DEFAULT

Specifies the value provided for the column when a value is not explicitly supplied during an insert. DEFAULT definitions can be applied to any columns except those defined as **timestamp**, or those with the IDENTITY property. DEFAULT definitions are removed when the table is dropped. Only a constant value, such as a character string; a system function, such as SYSTEM_USER(); or NULL can be used as a default. To maintain compatibility with earlier versions of SQL Server, a constraint name can be assigned to a DEFAULT.

constant_expression

Is a constant, NULL, or a system function used as the default value for the column.

IDENTITY

Indicates that the new column is an identity column. When a new row is added to the table, Microsoft SQL Server provides a unique, incremental value for the column. Identity columns are commonly used in conjunction with PRIMARY KEY constraints to serve as the unique row identifier for the table. The IDENTITY property can be assigned to **tinyint**, **smallint**, **int**, **bigint**, **decimal(p,0)**, or **numeric(p,0)** columns. Only one identity column can be created per table. Bound defaults and DEFAULT constraints cannot be used with an identity column. You must specify both the seed and increment or neither. If neither is specified, the default is (1,1).

seed

Is the value used for the very first row loaded into the table.

increment

Is the incremental value added to the identity value of the previous row loaded.

NOT FOR REPLICATION

Indicates that the IDENTITY property should not be enforced when a replication login such as **sqlrepl** inserts data into the table. Replicated rows must retain the key values assigned in the publishing database; the NOT FOR REPLICATION clause ensures that rows inserted by a replication process are not assigned new identity values. Rows inserted by other logins continue to have new identity values created in the usual way. It is recommended that a CHECK constraint with NOT FOR REPLICATION also be defined to ensure that the identity values assigned are within the range wanted for the current database.

ROWGUIDCOL

Indicates that the new column is a row global unique identifier column. Only one **uniqueidentifier** column per table can be designated as the ROWGUIDCOL column. The ROWGUIDCOL property can be assigned only to a **uniqueidentifier** column. The ROWGUIDCOL keyword is not valid if the database compatibility level is 65 or lower. For more information, see sp_dbcmptlevel.

The ROWGUIDCOL property does not enforce uniqueness of the values stored in the column. It also does not automatically generate values for new rows inserted into the table. To generate unique values for each column, either use the NEWID function on INSERT statements or use the NEWID function as the default for the column.

collation_name

Specifies the collation for the column. Collation name can be either a Windows collation name or a SQL collation name. The *collation_name* is applicable only for columns of the **char**, **varchar**, **text**, **nchar**, **nvarchar**, and **ntext** data types. If not specified, the column is assigned either the collation of the user-defined data type, if the column is of a user-defined data type, or the default collation of the database.

For more information about the Windows and SQL collation names, see COLLATE.

CONSTRAINT

Is an optional keyword indicating the beginning of a PRIMARY KEY, NOT NULL, UNIQUE, FOREIGN KEY, or CHECK constraint definition. Constraints are special properties that enforce data integrity and they may create indexes for the table and its columns.

constraint_name

Is the name of a constraint. Constraint names must be unique within a database.

NULL | NOT NULL

Are keywords that determine if null values are allowed in the column. NULL is not strictly a constraint but can be specified in the same manner as NOT NULL.

PRIMARY KEY

Is a constraint that enforces entity integrity for a given column or columns through a unique index. Only one PRIMARY KEY constraint can be created per table.

UNIQUE

Is a constraint that provides entity integrity for a given column or columns through a unique index. A table can have multiple UNIQUE constraints.

CLUSTERED | NONCLUSTERED

Are keywords to indicate that a clustered or a nonclustered index is created for the PRIMARY KEY or UNIQUE constraint. PRIMARY KEY constraints default to CLUSTERED and UNIQUE constraints default to NONCLUSTERED.

You can specify CLUSTERED for only one constraint in a CREATE TABLE statement. If you specify CLUSTERED for a UNIQUE constraint and also specify a PRIMARY KEY constraint, the PRIMARY KEY defaults to NONCLUSTERED.

[WITH FILLFACTOR = fillfactor]

Specifies how full SQL Server should make each index page used to store the index data. User-specified fillfactor values can be from 1 through 100, with a default of 0. A lower fill factor creates the index with more space available for new index entries without having to allocate new space.

FOREIGN KEY...REFERENCES

Is a constraint that provides referential integrity for the data in the column or columns. FOREIGN KEY constraints require that each value in the column exists in the corresponding referenced column(s) in the referenced table. FOREIGN KEY constraints can reference only columns that are PRIMARY KEY or UNIQUE constraints in the referenced table or columns referenced in a UNIQUE INDEX on the referenced table.

ref_table

Is the name of the table referenced by the FOREIGN KEY constraint.

(ref_column[,...n])

Is a column, or list of columns, from the table referenced by the FOREIGN KEY constraint.

ON DELETE {CASCADE | NO ACTION}

Specifies what action takes place to a row in the table created, if that row has a referential relationship and the referenced row is deleted from the parent table. The default is NO ACTION.

If CASCADE is specified, a row is deleted from the referencing table if that row is deleted from the parent table. If NO ACTION is specified, SQL Server raises an error and the delete action on the row in the parent table is rolled back.

For example, in the **Northwind** database, the **Orders** table has a referential relationship with the **Customers** table. The **Orders.CustomerID** foreign key references the **Customers.CustomerID** primary key.

If a DELETE statement is executed on a row in the **Customers** table, and an ON DELETE CASCADE action is specified for **Orders.CustomerID**, SQL Server checks for one or more dependent rows in the **Orders** table. If any, the dependent rows in the **Orders** table are deleted, as well as the row referenced in the **Customers** table.

On the other hand, if NO ACTION is specified, SQL Server raises an error and rolls back the delete action on the **Customers** row if there is at least one row in the **Orders** table that references it.

ON UPDATE {CASCADE | NO ACTION}

Specifies what action takes place to a row in the table created, if that row has a referential relationship and the referenced row is updated in the parent table. The default is NO ACTION.

If CASCADE is specified, the row is updated in the referencing table if that row is updated in the parent table. If NO ACTION is specified, SQL Server raises an error and the update action on the row in the parent table is rolled back.

For example, in the **Northwind** database, the **Orders** table has a referential relationship with the **Customers** table: **Orders.CustomerID** foreign key references the **Customers.CustomerID** primary key.

If an UPDATE statement is executed on a row in the **Customers** table, and an ON UPDATE CASCADE action is specified for **Orders.CustomerID**, SQL Server checks for one or more dependent rows in the **Orders** table. If any exist, the dependent rows in the **Orders** table are updated, as well as the row referenced in the **Customers**.

Alternately, if NO ACTION is specified, SQL Server raises an error and rolls back the update action on the **Customers** row if there is at least one row in the **Orders** table that references it.

CHECK

Is a constraint that enforces domain integrity by limiting the possible values that can be entered into a column or columns.

NOT FOR REPLICATION

Keywords used to prevent the CHECK constraint from being enforced during the distribution process used by replication. When tables are subscribers to a replication publication, do not update the subscription table directly, instead update the publishing table, and let replication distribute the data back to the subscribing table. A CHECK constraint can be defined on the subscription table to prevent users from modifying it. Unless the NOT FOR REPLICATION clause is added, however, the CHECK constraint also prevents the replication process from distributing modifications from the publishing table to the subscribing table. The NOT FOR REPLICATION clause means the constraint is enforced on user modifications but not on the replication process.

The NOT FOR REPLICATION CHECK constraint is applied to both the before and after image of an updated record to prevent records from being added to or deleted from the replicated range. All deletes and inserts are checked; if they fall within the replicated range, they are rejected.

When this constraint is used with an identity column, SQL Server allows the table not to have its identity column values reseeded when a replication user updates the identity column.

logical_expression

Is a logical expression that returns TRUE or FALSE.

column

Is a column or list of columns, in parentheses, used in table constraints to indicate the columns used in the constraint definition.

[ASC | DESC]

Specifies the order in which the column or columns participating in table constraints are sorted. The default is ASC.

n

Is a placeholder indicating that the preceding item can be repeated *n* number of times.

Remarks

SQL Server can have as many as two billion tables per database and 1,024 columns per table. The number of rows and total size of the table are limited only by the available storage. The maximum number of bytes per row is 8,060. If you create tables with **varchar**, **nvarchar**, or **varbinary** columns in which the total defined width exceeds 8,060 bytes, the table is created, but a warning message appears. Trying to insert more than 8,060 bytes into such a row or to update a row so that its total row size exceeds 8,060 produces an error message and the statement fails.

CREATE TABLE statements that include a **sql_variant** column can generate the following warning:

```
The total row size (xx) for table 'yy' exceeds the maximum number of bytes per row (8060).
Rows that exceed the maximum number of bytes will not be added.
```

This warning occurs because **sql_variant** can have a maximum length of 8016 bytes. When a **sql_variant** column contains values close to the maximum length, it can overshoot the row's maximum size limit.

Each table can contain a maximum of 249 nonclustered indexes and 1 clustered index. These include the indexes generated to support any PRIMARY KEY and UNIQUE constraints defined for the table.

SQL Server does not enforce an order in which DEFAULT, IDENTITY, ROWGUIDCOL, or column constraints are specified in a column definition.

Temporary Tables

You can create local and global temporary tables. Local temporary tables are visible only in the current session; global temporary tables are visible to all sessions.

Prefix local temporary table names with single number sign (*#table_name*), and prefix global temporary table names with a double number sign (*##table_name*).

SQL statements reference the temporary table using the value specified for *table_name* in the CREATE TABLE statement:

```
CREATE TABLE #MyTempTable (cola INT PRIMARY KEY)
INSERT INTO #MyTempTable VALUES (1)
```

If a local temporary table is created in a stored procedure or application that can be executed at the same time by several users, SQL Server has to be able to distinguish the tables created by the different users. SQL Server does this by internally appending a numeric suffix to each local temporary table name. The full name of a temporary table as stored in the **sysobjects** table in **tempdb** consists of table name specified in the CREATE TABLE statement and the system-generated numeric suffix. To allow for the suffix, *table_name* specified for a local temporary name cannot exceed 116 characters.

Temporary tables are automatically dropped when they go out of scope, unless explicitly dropped using DROP TABLE:

- A local temporary table created in a stored procedure is dropped automatically when the stored procedure completes. The table can be referenced by any nested stored procedures executed by the stored procedure that created the table. The table cannot be referenced by the process which called the stored procedure that created the table.

- All other local temporary tables are dropped automatically at the end of the current session.

- Global temporary tables are automatically dropped when the session that created the table ends and all other tasks have stopped referencing them. The association between a task and a table is maintained only for the life of a single Transact-SQL statement. This means that a global temporary table is dropped at the completion of the last Transact-SQL statement that was actively referencing the table when the creating session ended.

A local temporary table created within a stored procedure or trigger is distinct from a temporary table with the same name created before the stored procedure or trigger is called. If a query references a temporary table, and two temporary tables with the same name exist at that time, it is not defined which table the query is resolved against. Nested stored procedures can also create temporary tables with the same name as a temporary table created by the stored procedure that called it. All references to the table name in the nested stored procedure are resolved to the table created in the nested procedure, for example:

```
CREATE PROCEDURE Test2
AS
CREATE TABLE #t(x INT PRIMARY KEY)
INSERT INTO #t VALUES (2)
SELECT Test2Col = x FROM #t
GO
CREATE PROCEDURE Test1
AS
CREATE TABLE #t(x INT PRIMARY KEY)
INSERT INTO #t VALUES (1)
SELECT Test1Col = x FROM #t
EXEC Test2
GO
CREATE TABLE #t(x INT PRIMARY KEY)
INSERT INTO #t VALUES (99)
GO
EXEC Test1
GO
```

Here is the result set:

```
(1 row(s) affected)

Test1Col
-----------
1
```

(continued)

415

(continued)

```
(1 row(s) affected)

Test2Col
----------
2
```

When you create local or global temporary tables, the CREATE TABLE syntax supports constraint definitions with the exception of FOREIGN KEY constraints. If a FOREIGN KEY constraint is specified in a temporary table, the statement returns a warning message indicating that the constraint was skipped, and the table is still created without the FOREIGN KEY constraints. Temporary tables cannot be referenced in FOREIGN KEY constraints.

Consider using table variables instead of temporary tables. Temporary tables are useful in cases when indexes need to be created explicitly on them, or when the table values need to be visible across multiple stored procedures or functions. In general, table variables contribute to more efficient query processing. For more information, see table.

PRIMARY KEY Constraints

- A table can contain only one PRIMARY KEY constraint.

- The index generated by a PRIMARY KEY constraint cannot cause the number of indexes on the table to exceed 249 nonclustered indexes and 1 clustered index.

- If CLUSTERED or NONCLUSTERED is not specified for a PRIMARY KEY constraint, CLUSTERED is used if there are no clustered indexes specified for UNIQUE constraints.

- All columns defined within a PRIMARY KEY constraint must be defined as NOT NULL. If nullability is not specified, all columns participating in a PRIMARY KEY constraint have their nullability set to NOT NULL.

UNIQUE Constraints

- If CLUSTERED or NONCLUSTERED is not specified for a UNIQUE constraint, NONCLUSTERED is used by default.

- Each UNIQUE constraint generates an index. The number of UNIQUE constraints cannot cause the number of indexes on the table to exceed 249 nonclustered indexes and 1 clustered index.

FOREIGN KEY Constraints

- When a value other than NULL is entered into the column of a FOREIGN KEY constraint, the value must exist in the referenced column; otherwise, a foreign key violation error message is returned.

- FOREIGN KEY constraints are applied to the preceding column unless source columns are specified.

- FOREIGN KEY constraints can reference only tables within the same database on the same server. Cross-database referential integrity must be implemented through triggers. For more information, see CREATE TRIGGER.

- FOREIGN KEY constraints can reference another column in the same table (a self reference).

- The REFERENCES clause of a column-level FOREIGN KEY constraint can list only one reference column, which must have the same data type as the column on which the constraint is defined.

- The REFERENCES clause of a table-level FOREIGN KEY constraint must have the same number of reference columns as the number of columns in the constraint column list. The data type of each reference column must also be the same as the corresponding column in the column list.

- CASCADE may not be specified if a column of type **timestamp** is part of either the foreign key or the referenced key.

- It is possible to combine CASCADE and NO ACTION on tables that have referential relationships with each other. If SQL Server encounters NO ACTION, it terminates and rolls back related CASCADE actions. When a DELETE statement causes a combination of CASCADE and NO ACTION actions, all the CASCADE actions are applied before SQL Server checks for any NO ACTION.

- A table can contain a maximum of 253 FOREIGN KEY constraints.

- FOREIGN KEY constraints are not enforced on temporary tables.

- A table can reference a maximum of 253 different tables in its FOREIGN KEY constraints.

- FOREIGN KEY constraints can reference only columns in PRIMARY KEY or UNIQUE constraints in the referenced table or in a UNIQUE INDEX on the referenced table.

DEFAULT Definitions

- A column can have only one DEFAULT definition.

- A DEFAULT definition can contain constant values, functions, SQL-92 niladic functions, or NULL. The table shows the niladic functions and the values they return for the default during an INSERT statement.

SQL-92 niladic function	Value returned
CURRENT_TIMESTAMP	Current date and time.
CURRENT_USER	Name of user performing insert.
SESSION_USER	Name of user performing insert.
SYSTEM_USER	Name of user performing insert.
USER	Name of user performing insert.

- *constant_expression* in a DEFAULT definition cannot refer to another column in the table, or to other tables, views, or stored procedures.

- DEFAULT definitions cannot be created on columns with a **timestamp** data type or columns with an IDENTITY property.

- DEFAULT definitions cannot be created for columns with user-defined data types if the user-defined data type is bound to a default object.

CHECK Constraints

- A column can have any number of CHECK constraints, and the condition can include multiple logical expressions combined with AND and OR. Multiple CHECK constraints for a column are validated in the order created.

- The search condition must evaluate to a Boolean expression and cannot reference another table.

- A column-level CHECK constraint can reference only the constrained column, and a table-level CHECK constraint can reference only columns in the same table.

  CHECK CONSTRAINTS and rules serve the same function of validating the data during INSERT and DELETE statements.

- When a rule and one or more CHECK constraints exist for a column or columns, all restrictions are evaluated.

Additional Constraint Information

- An index created for a constraint cannot be dropped with the DROP INDEX statement; the constraint must be dropped with the ALTER TABLE statement. An index created for and used by a constraint can be rebuilt with the DBCC DBREINDEX statement.

- Constraint names must follow the rules for identifiers, except that the name cannot begin with a number sign (#). If *constraint_name* is not supplied, a system-generated name is assigned to the constraint. The constraint name appears in any error message about constraint violations.

- When a constraint is violated in an INSERT, UPDATE, or DELETE statement, the statement is terminated. However, the transaction (if the statement is part of an explicit transaction) continues to be processed. You can use the ROLLBACK TRANSACTION statement with the transaction definition by checking the @@ERROR system function.

If a table has FOREIGN KEY or CHECK CONSTRAINTS and triggers, the constraint conditions are evaluated before the trigger is executed.

For a report on a table and its columns, use **sp_help** or **sp_helpconstraint**. To rename a table, use **sp_rename**. For a report on the views and stored procedures that depend on a table, use **sp_depends**.

Space is generally allocated to tables and indexes in increments of one extent at a time. When the table or index is created, it is allocated pages from mixed extents until it has enough pages to fill a uniform extent. After it has enough pages to fill a uniform extent, another extent is allocated each time the currently allocated extents become full. For a report about the amount of space allocated and used by a table, execute **sp_spaceused**.

Nullability Rules Within a Table Definition

The nullability of a column determines whether or not that column can allow a null value (NULL) as the data in that column. NULL is not zero or blank: it means no entry was made or an explicit NULL was supplied, and it usually implies that the value is either unknown or not applicable.

When you create or alter a table with the CREATE TABLE or ALTER TABLE statements, database and session settings influence and possibly override the nullability of the data type used in a column definition. It is recommended that you always explicitly define a column as NULL or NOT NULL for noncomputed columns or, if you use a user-defined data type, that you allow the column to use the default nullability of the data type.

When not explicitly specified, column nullability follows these rules:

- If the column is defined with a user-defined data type:
  - SQL Server uses the nullability specified when the data type was created. Use **sp_help** to get the default nullability of the data type.

- If the column is defined with a system-supplied data type:
  - If the system-supplied data type has only one option, it takes precedence. **timestamp** data types must be NOT NULL.
  - If the setting of **sp_dbcmptlevel** is 65 or lower, **bit** data types default to NOT NULL if the column does not have an explicit NULL or NOT NULL. For more information, see sp_dbcmptlevel.
  - If any session settings are ON (turned on with the SET statement), then:

    If ANSI_NULL_DFLT_ON is ON, NULL is assigned.

    If ANSI_NULL_DFLT_OFF is ON, NOT NULL is assigned.
  - If any database settings are configured (changed with **sp_dboption**), then:

    If **ANSI null default** is **true**, NULL is assigned.

    If **ANSI null default** is **false**, NOT NULL is assigned.
- When neither of the ANSI_NULL_DFLT options is set for the session and the database is set to the default (**ANSI null default** is **false**), then the SQL Server default of NOT NULL is assigned.
- If the column is a computed column, its nullability is always determined automatically by SQL Server. Use the COLUMNPROPERTY function (**AllowsNull** property) to find out the nullability of such a column.

  Note   The SQL Server ODBC driver and Microsoft OLE DB Provider for SQL Server both default to having ANSI_NULL_DFLT_ON set to ON. ODBC and OLE DB users can configure this in ODBC data sources, or with connection attributes or properties set by the application.

Permissions

CREATE TABLE permission defaults to the members of the **db_owner** and **db_ddladmin** fixed database roles. Members of the **db_owner** fixed database role and members of the **sysadmin** fixed server role can transfer CREATE TABLE permission to other users.

Examples

A. Use PRIMARY KEY constraints

This example shows the column definition for a PRIMARY KEY constraint with a clustered index on the **job_id** column of the **jobs** table (allowing the system to supply the constraint name) in the **pubs** sample database.

```
job_id smallint
     PRIMARY KEY CLUSTERED
```

This example shows how a name can be supplied for the PRIMARY KEY constraint. This constraint is used on the **emp_id** column of the **employee** table. This column is based on a user-defined data type.

```
emp_id empid
      CONSTRAINT PK_emp_id PRIMARY KEY NONCLUSTERED
```

B. Use FOREIGN KEY constraints

A FOREIGN KEY constraint is used to reference another table. Foreign keys can be single-column keys or multicolumn keys. This example shows a single-column FOREIGN KEY constraint on the **employee** table that references the **jobs** table. Only the REFERENCES clause is required for a single-column FOREIGN KEY constraint.

```
job_id smallint    NOT NULL
      DEFAULT 1
      REFERENCES jobs(job_id)
```

You can also explicitly use the FOREIGN KEY clause and restate the column attribute. Note that the column name does not have to be the same in both tables.

```
FOREIGN KEY (job_id) REFERENCES jobs(job_id)
```

Multicolumn key constraints are created as table constraints. In the **pubs** database, the **sales** table includes a multicolumn PRIMARY KEY. This example shows how to reference this key from another table; an explicit constraint name is optional.

```
CONSTRAINT FK_sales_backorder FOREIGN KEY (stor_id, ord_num, title_id)
   REFERENCES sales (stor_id, ord_num, title_id)
```

C. Use UNIQUE constraints

UNIQUE constraints are used to enforce uniqueness on nonprimary key columns. A PRIMARY KEY constraint column includes a restriction for uniqueness automatically; however, a UNIQUE constraint can allow null values. This example shows a column called **pseudonym** on the **authors** table. It enforces a restriction that authors' pen names must be unique.

```
pseudonym varchar(30) NULL
UNIQUE NONCLUSTERED
```

This example shows a UNIQUE constraint created on the **stor_name** and **city** columns of the **stores** table, where the **stor_id** is actually the PRIMARY KEY; no two stores in the same city should be the same.

```
CONSTRAINT U_store UNIQUE NONCLUSTERED (stor_name, city)
```

D. Use DEFAULT definitions

Defaults supply a value (with the INSERT and UPDATE statements) when no value is supplied. In the **pubs** database, many DEFAULT definitions are used to ensure that valid data or placeholders are entered.

On the **jobs** table, a character string default supplies a description (column **job_desc**) when the actual description is not entered explicitly.

```
DEFAULT 'New Position - title not formalized yet'
```

In the **employee** table, the employees can be employed by an imprint company or by the parent company. When an explicit company is not supplied, the parent company is entered (note that, as shown here, comments can be nested within the table definition).

```
DEFAULT ('9952')
/* By default the Parent Company Publisher is the company
to whom each employee reports. */
```

In addition to constants, DEFAULT definitions can include functions. Use this example to get the current date for an entry:

```
DEFAULT (getdate())
```

Niladic-functions can also improve data integrity. To keep track of the user who inserted a row, use the niladic-function for USER (do not surround the niladic functions with parentheses):

```
DEFAULT USER
```

E. Use CHECK constraints

This example shows restrictions made to the values entered into the **min_lvl** and **max_lvl** columns of the **jobs** table. Both of these constraints are unnamed:

```
CHECK (min_lvl >= 10)
```

and

```
CHECK (max_lvl <= 250)
```

This example shows a named constraint with a pattern restriction on the character data entered into the **emp_id** column of the **employee** table.

```
CONSTRAINT CK_emp_id CHECK (emp_id LIKE
   '[A-Z][A-Z][A-Z][1-9][0-9][0-9][0-9][0-9][FM]' OR
   emp_id LIKE '[A-Z]-[A-Z][1-9][0-9][0-9][0-9][0-9][FM]')
```

This example specifies that the **pub_id** must be within a specific list or follow a given pattern. This constraint is for the **pub_id** of the **publishers** table.

```
CHECK (pub_id IN ('1389', '0736', '0877', '1622', '1756')
   OR pub_id LIKE '99[0-9][0-9]')
```

F. Complete table definitions

This example shows complete table definitions with all constraint definitions for three
tables (**jobs**, **employee**, and **publishers**) created in the **pubs** database.

```
/* *********************** jobs table *********************** */
CREATE TABLE jobs
(
   job_id  smallint
      IDENTITY(1,1)
      PRIMARY KEY CLUSTERED,
   job_desc         varchar(50)      NOT NULL
      DEFAULT 'New Position - title not formalized yet',
   min_lvl tinyint NOT NULL
      CHECK (min_lvl >= 10),
   max_lvl tinyint NOT NULL
      CHECK (max_lvl <= 250)
)

/* *********************** employee table *********************** */
CREATE TABLE employee
(
   emp_id  empid
      CONSTRAINT PK_emp_id PRIMARY KEY NONCLUSTERED
      CONSTRAINT CK_emp_id CHECK (emp_id LIKE
         '[A-Z][A-Z][A-Z][1-9][0-9][0-9][0-9][0-9][FM]' or
         emp_id LIKE '[A-Z]-[A-Z][1-9][0-9][0-9][0-9][0-9][FM]'),
      /* Each employee ID consists of three characters that
      represent the employee's initials, followed by a five
      digit number ranging from 10000 through 99999 and then the
      employee's gender (M or F). A (hyphen) - is acceptable
      for the middle initial. */
   fname    varchar(20)     NOT NULL,
   minit    char(1) NULL,
   lname    varchar(30)     NOT NULL,
   job_id   smallint        NOT NULL
      DEFAULT 1
      /* Entry job_id for new hires. */
      REFERENCES jobs(job_id),
   job_lvl tinyint
      DEFAULT 10,
      /* Entry job_lvl for new hires. */
   pub_id  char(4) NOT NULL
      DEFAULT ('9952')
```

(continued)

(continued)

```
        REFERENCES publishers(pub_id),
        /* By default, the Parent Company Publisher is the company
        to whom each employee reports. */
    hire_date          datetime          NOT NULL
        DEFAULT (getdate())
        /* By default, the current system date is entered. */
)

/* **************** publishers table ******************** */
CREATE TABLE publishers
(
    pub_id  char(4) NOT NULL
          CONSTRAINT UPKCL_pubind PRIMARY KEY CLUSTERED
          CHECK (pub_id IN ('1389', '0736', '0877', '1622', '1756')
             OR pub_id LIKE '99[0-9][0-9]'),
    pub_name      varchar(40)     NULL,
    city          varchar(20)     NULL,
    state     char(2) NULL,
    country       varchar(30)     NULL
              DEFAULT('USA')
)
```

G. Use the uniqueidentifier data type in a column

This example creates a table with a **uniqueidentifier** column. It uses a PRIMARY KEY
constraint to protect the table against users inserting duplicated values, and it uses the
NEWID() function in the DEFAULT constraint to provide values for new rows.

```
CREATE TABLE Globally_Unique_Data
(guid uniqueidentifier
   CONSTRAINT Guid_Default
   DEFAULT NEWID(),
Employee_Name varchar(60),
CONSTRAINT Guid_PK PRIMARY KEY (Guid)
)
```

H. Use an expression for a computed column

This example illustrates the use of an expression (**(low + high)/2**) for calculating the
myavg computed column.

```
CREATE TABLE mytable
   (
    low int,
    high int,
    myavg AS (low + high)/2
   )
```

I. Use the USER_NAME function for a computed column

This example uses the USER_NAME function in the **myuser_name** column.

```
CREATE TABLE mylogintable
   (
    date_in datetime,
    user_id int,
    myuser_name AS USER_NAME()
   )
```

J. Use NOT FOR REPLICATION

This example shows using the IDENTITY property on a table subscribed to a replication. The table includes a CHECK constraint to ensure that the **SaleID** values generated on this system do not grow into the range assigned to the replication Publisher.

```
CREATE TABLE Sales
   (SaleID INT IDENTITY(100000,1) NOT FOR REPLICATION,
            CHECK NOT FOR REPLICATION (SaleID <= 199999),
    SalesRegion CHAR(2),
    CONSTRAINT ID_PK PRIMARY KEY (SaleID)
   )
```

Related Topics

ALTER TABLE, COLUMNPROPERTY, CREATE INDEX, CREATE RULE, CREATE VIEW, Data Types, DROP INDEX, DROP RULE, DROP TABLE, sp_addtype, sp_depends, sp_help, sp_helpconstraint, sp_rename, sp_spaceused

CREATE TRIGGER

Creates a trigger, which is a special kind of stored procedure that executes automatically when a user attempts the specified data-modification statement on the specified table. Microsoft SQL Server allows the creation of multiple triggers for any given INSERT, UPDATE, or DELETE statement.

Syntax

```
CREATE TRIGGER trigger_name
ON { table | view }
[ WITH ENCRYPTION ]
{
   { { FOR | AFTER | INSTEAD OF } { [ INSERT ] [ , ] [ UPDATE ] }
      [ WITH APPEND ]
      [ NOT FOR REPLICATION ]
```

(continued)

(continued)

```
    AS
    [ { IF UPDATE ( column )
        [ { AND | OR } UPDATE ( column ) ]
            [ ...n ]
    | IF ( COLUMNS_UPDATED ( ) { bitwise_operator } updated_bitmask )
            { comparison_operator } column_bitmask [ ...n ]
    } ]
    sql_statement [ ...n ]
    }
}
```

Arguments

trigger_name

Is the name of the trigger. A trigger name must conform to the rules for identifiers and must be unique within the database. Specifying the trigger owner name is optional.

Table | view

Is the table or view on which the trigger is executed and is sometimes called the trigger table or trigger view. Specifying the owner name of the table or view is optional.

WITH ENCRYPTION

Encrypts the **syscomments** entries that contain the text of CREATE TRIGGER. Using WITH ENCRYPTION prevents the trigger from being published as part of SQL Server replication.

AFTER

Specifies that the trigger is fired only when all operations specified in the triggering SQL statement have executed successfully. All referential cascade actions and constraint checks also must succeed before this trigger executes.

AFTER is the default, if FOR is the only keyword specified.

AFTER triggers cannot be defined on views.

INSTEAD OF

Specifies that the trigger is executed *instead of* the triggering SQL statement, thus overriding the actions of the triggering statements.

At most, one INSTEAD OF trigger per INSERT, UPDATE, or DELETE statement can be defined on a table or view. However, it is possible to define views on views where each view has its own INSTEAD OF trigger.

INSTEAD OF triggers are not allowed on updateable views WITH CHECK OPTION. SQL Server will raise an error if an INSTEAD OF trigger is added to an updateable view WITH CHECK OPTION specified. The user must remove that option using ALTER VIEW before defining the INSTEAD OF trigger.

{ [DELETE] [,] [INSERT] [,] [UPDATE] }

Are keywords that specify which data modification statements, when attempted against this table or view, activate the trigger. At least one option must be specified. Any combination of these in any order is allowed in the trigger definition. If more than one option is specified, separate the options with commas.

For INSTEAD OF triggers, the DELETE option is not allowed on tables that have a referential relationship specifying a cascade action ON DELETE. Similarly, the UPDATE option is not allowed on tables that have a referential relationship specifying a cascade action ON UPDATE.

WITH APPEND

Specifies that an additional trigger of an existing type should be added. Use of this optional clause is needed only when the compatibility level is 65 or lower. If the compatibility level is 70 or higher, the WITH APPEND clause is not needed to add an additional trigger of an existing type (this is the default behavior of CREATE TRIGGER with the compatibility level setting of 70 or higher.) For more information, see **sp_dbcmptlevel**.

WITH APPEND cannot be used with INSTEAD OF triggers or if AFTER trigger is explicitly stated. WITH APPEND can be used only when FOR is specified (without INSTEAD OF or AFTER) for backward compatibility reasons. WITH APPEND and FOR (which is interpreted as AFTER) will not be supported in future releases.

NOT FOR REPLICATION

Indicates that the trigger should not be executed when a replication process modifies the table involved in the trigger.

AS

Are the actions the trigger is to perform.

sql_statement

Is the trigger condition(s) and action(s). Trigger conditions specify additional criteria that determine whether the attempted DELETE, INSERT, or UPDATE statements cause the trigger action(s) to be carried out.

The trigger actions specified in the Transact-SQL statements go into effect when the DELETE, INSERT, or UPDATE operation is attempted.

Triggers can include any number and kind of Transact-SQL statements. A trigger is designed to check or change data based on a data modification statement; it should not return data to the user. The Transact-SQL statements in a trigger often include control-of-flow language. A few special tables are used in CREATE TRIGGER statements:

- **deleted** and **inserted** are logical (conceptual) tables. They are structurally similar to the table on which the trigger is defined, that is, the table on which the user action is attempted, and hold the old values or new values of the rows that may be changed by the user action. For example, to retrieve all values in the **deleted** table, use:

```
SELECT *
FROM deleted
```

- In a DELETE, INSERT, or UPDATE trigger, SQL Server does not allow **text**, **ntext**, or **image** column references in the **inserted** and **deleted** tables if the compatibility level is equal to 70. The **text**, **ntext**, and **image** values in the **inserted** and **deleted** tables cannot be accessed. To retrieve the new value in either an INSERT or UPDATE trigger, join the **inserted** table with the original update table. When the compatibility level is 65 or lower, null values are returned for **inserted** or **deleted text**, **ntext**, or **image** columns that allow null values; zero-length strings are returned if the columns are not nullable.

  If the compatibility level is 80 or higher, SQL Server allows the update of **text**, **ntext**, or **image** columns through the INSTEAD OF trigger on tables or views.

n

Is a placeholder indicating that multiple Transact-SQL statements can be included in the trigger. For the IF UPDATE (*column*) statement, multiple columns can be included by repeating the UPDATE (*column*) clause.

IF UPDATE (*column*)

Tests for an INSERT or UPDATE action to a specified column and is not used with DELETE operations. More than one column can be specified. Because the table name is specified in the ON clause, do not include the table name before the column name in an IF UPDATE clause. To test for an INSERT or UPDATE action for more than one column, specify a separate UPDATE(*column*) clause following the first one. IF UPDATE will return the TRUE value in INSERT actions because the columns have either explicit values or implicit (NULL) values inserted.

> **Note**   The IF UPDATE (*column*) clause functions identically to an IF, IF...ELSE or WHILE statement and can use the BEGIN...END block. For more information, see Control-of-Flow Language.

UPDATE(*column*) can be used anywhere inside the body of the trigger.

column

Is the name of the column to test for either an INSERT or UPDATE action. This column can be of any data type supported by SQL Server. However, computed columns cannot be used in this context. For more information, see Data Types.

IF (COLUMNS_UPDATED())

Tests, in an INSERT or UPDATE trigger only, whether the mentioned column or columns were inserted or updated. COLUMNS_UPDATED returns a **varbinary** bit pattern that indicates which columns in the table were inserted or updated.

The COLUMNS_UPDATED function returns the bits in order from left to right, with the least significant bit being the leftmost. The leftmost bit represents the first column in the table; the next bit to the right represents the second column, and so on. COLUMNS_UPDATED returns multiple bytes if the table on which the trigger is created contains more than 8 columns, with the least significant byte being the leftmost. COLUMNS_UPDATED will return the TRUE value for all columns in INSERT actions because the columns have either explicit values or implicit (NULL) values inserted.

COLUMNS_UPDATED can be used anywhere inside the body of the trigger.

bitwise_operator

Is the bitwise operator to use in the comparison.

updated_bitmask

Is the integer bitmask of those columns actually updated or inserted. For example, table **t1** contains columns **C1**, **C2**, **C3**, **C4**, and **C5**. To check whether columns **C2**, **C3**, and **C4** are all updated (with table **t1** having an UPDATE trigger), specify a value of 14. To check whether only column **C2** is updated, specify a value of 2.

comparison_operator

Is the comparison operator. Use the equal sign (=) to check whether all columns specified in *updated_bitmask* are actually updated. Use the greater than symbol (>) to check whether any or some of the columns specified in *updated_bitmask* are updated.

column_bitmask

Is the integer bitmask of those columns to check whether they are updated or inserted.

Remarks

Triggers are often used for enforcing business rules and data integrity. SQL Server provides declarative referential integrity (DRI) through the table creation statements (ALTER TABLE and CREATE TABLE); however, DRI does not provide cross-database referential integrity. To enforce referential integrity (rules about the relationships between the primary and foreign keys of tables), use primary and foreign key constraints (the PRIMARY KEY and FOREIGN KEY keywords of ALTER TABLE and CREATE TABLE). If constraints exist on the trigger table, they are checked after the INSTEAD OF trigger execution and prior to the AFTER trigger execution. If the constraints are violated, the INSTEAD OF trigger actions are rolled back and the AFTER trigger is not executed (fired).

The first and last AFTER triggers to be executed on a table may be specified by using **sp_settriggerorder**. Only one first and one last AFTER trigger for each of the INSERT, UPDATE, and DELETE operations may be specified on a table; if there are other AFTER triggers on the same table, they are executed randomly.

If an ALTER TRIGGER statement changes a first or last trigger, the first or last attribute set on the modified trigger is dropped, and the order value must be reset with **sp_settriggerorder**.

An AFTER trigger is executed only after the triggering SQL statement, including all referential cascade actions and constraint checks associated with the object updated or deleted, has executed successfully. The AFTER trigger sees the effects of the triggering statement as well as all referential cascade UPDATE and DELETE actions caused by the triggering statement.

Trigger Limitations

CREATE TRIGGER must be the first statement in the batch and can apply to only one table.

A trigger is created only in the current database; however, a trigger can reference objects outside the current database.

If the trigger owner name is specified (to qualify the trigger), qualify the table name in the same way.

The same trigger action can be defined for more than one user action (for example, INSERT and UPDATE) in the same CREATE TRIGGER statement.

INSTEAD OF DELETE/UPDATE triggers cannot be defined on a table that has a foreign key with a cascade on DELETE/UPDATE action defined.

Any SET statement can be specified inside a trigger. The SET option chosen remains in effect during the execution of the trigger and then reverts to its former setting.

When a trigger fires, results are returned to the calling application, just as with stored procedures. To eliminate having results returned to an application due to a trigger firing, do not include either SELECT statements that return results, or statements that perform variable assignment in a trigger. A trigger that includes either SELECT statements that return results to the user or statements that perform variable assignment requires special handling; these returned results would have to be written into every application in which modifications to the trigger table are allowed.
If variable assignment must occur in a trigger, use a SET NOCOUNT statement at the beginning of the trigger to eliminate the return of any result sets.

A TRUNCATE TABLE statement is not caught by a DELETE trigger. Although a TRUNCATE TABLE statement is, in effect, a DELETE without a WHERE clause (it removes all rows), it is not logged and thus cannot execute a trigger. Because permission for the TRUNCATE TABLE statement defaults to the table owner and is not transferable, only the table owner should be concerned about inadvertently circumventing a DELETE trigger with a TRUNCATE TABLE statement.

The WRITETEXT statement, whether logged or unlogged, does not activate a trigger.

These Transact-SQL statements are not allowed in a trigger:

ALTER DATABASE	CREATE DATABASE	DISK INIT
DISK RESIZE	DROP DATABASE	LOAD DATABASE
LOAD LOG	RECONFIGURE	RESTORE DATABASE
RESTORE LOG		

Note Because SQL Server does not support user-defined triggers on system tables, it is recommended that no user-defined triggers be created on system tables.

Multiple Triggers

SQL Server allows multiple triggers to be created for each data modification event (DELETE, INSERT, or UPDATE). For example, if CREATE TRIGGER FOR UPDATE is executed for a table that already has an UPDATE trigger, then an additional update trigger is created. In earlier versions, only one trigger for each data modification event (INSERT, UPDATE, DELETE) was allowed for each table.

Note The default behavior for CREATE TRIGGER (with the compatibility level of 70) is to add additional triggers to existing triggers, if the trigger names differ. If trigger names are the same, SQL Server returns an error message. However, if the compatibility level is equal to or less than 65, any new triggers created with the CREATE TRIGGER statement replace any existing triggers of the same type, even if the trigger names are different. For more information, see sp_dbcmptlevel.

Recursive Triggers

SQL Server also allows recursive invocation of triggers when the **recursive triggers** setting is enabled in **sp_dboption**.

Recursive triggers allow two types of recursion to occur:

- Indirect recursion
- Direct recursion

With indirect recursion, an application updates table **T1**, which fires trigger **TR1**, updating table **T2**. In this scenario, trigger **T2** then fires and updates table **T1**.

With direct recursion, the application updates table **T1**, which fires trigger **TR1**, updating table **T1**. Because table **T1** was updated, trigger **TR1** fires again, and so on.

This example uses both indirect and direct trigger recursion. Assume that two update triggers, **TR1** and **TR2**, are defined on table **T1**. Trigger **TR1** updates table **T1** recursively. An UPDATE statement executes each **TR1** and **TR2** one time. In addition, the execution of **TR1** triggers the execution of **TR1** (recursively) and **TR2**. The **inserted** and **deleted** tables for a given trigger contain rows corresponding only to the UPDATE statement that invoked the trigger.

Note The above behavior occurs only if the **recursive triggers** setting of **sp_dboption** is enabled. There is no defined order in which multiple triggers defined for a given event are executed. Each trigger should be self-contained.

Disabling the **recursive triggers** setting only prevents direct recursions. To disable indirect recursion as well, set the **nested triggers** server option to 0 using **sp_configure**.

If any of the triggers do a ROLLBACK TRANSACTION, regardless of the nesting level, no further triggers are executed.

Nested Triggers

Triggers can be nested to a maximum of 32 levels. If a trigger changes a table on which there is another trigger, the second trigger is activated and can then call a third trigger, and so on. If any trigger in the chain sets off an infinite loop, the nesting level is exceeded and the trigger is canceled. To disable nested triggers, set the **nested triggers** option of **sp_configure** to 0 (off). The default configuration allows nested triggers. If nested triggers is off, recursive triggers is also disabled, regardless of the **recursive triggers** setting of **sp_dboption**.

Deferred Name Resolution

SQL Server allows Transact-SQL stored procedures, triggers, and batches to refer to tables that do not exist at compile time. This ability is called deferred name resolution. However, if the Transact-SQL stored procedure, trigger, or batch refers to a table defined in the stored procedure or trigger, a warning is issued at creation time only if the compatibility level setting (set by executing **sp_dbcmptlevel**) is equal to 65. A warning is issued at compile time if a batch is used. An error message is returned at run time if the table referenced does not exist. For more information, see Deferred Name Resolution and Compilation.

Permissions

CREATE TRIGGER permissions default to the table owner on which the trigger is defined, the **sysadmin** fixed server role, and members of the **db_owner** and **db_ddladmin** fixed database roles, and are not transferable.

To retrieve data from a table or view, a user must have SELECT statement permission on the table or view. To update the content of a table or view, a user must have INSERT, DELETE, and UPDATE statement permissions on the table or view.

If an INSTEAD OF trigger exists on a view, the user must have INSERT, DELETE, and UPDATE privileges on that view to issue INSERT, DELETE, and UPDATE statements against the view, regardless of whether the execution actually performs such an operation on the view.

Examples

A. Use a trigger with a reminder message

This example trigger prints a message to the client when anyone tries to add or change data in the **titles** table.

> **Note** Message 50009 is a user-defined message in **sysmessages**. For more information about creating user-defined messages, see sp_addmessage.

```
USE pubs
IF EXISTS (SELECT name FROM sysobjects
        WHERE name = 'reminder' AND type = 'TR')
    DROP TRIGGER reminder
GO
CREATE TRIGGER reminder
ON titles
FOR INSERT, UPDATE
AS RAISERROR (50009, 16, 10)
GO
```

B. Use a trigger with a reminder e-mail message

This example sends an e-mail message to a specified person (MaryM) when the **titles** table changes.

```
USE pubs
IF EXISTS (SELECT name FROM sysobjects
        WHERE name = 'reminder' AND type = 'TR')
    DROP TRIGGER reminder
GO
CREATE TRIGGER reminder
ON titles
FOR INSERT, UPDATE, DELETE
AS
    EXEC master..xp_sendmail 'MaryM',
        'Don''t forget to print a report for the distributors.'
GO
```

C. Use a trigger business rule between the employee and jobs tables

Because CHECK constraints can reference only the columns on which the column- or table-level constraint is defined, any cross-table constraints (in this case, business rules) must be defined as triggers.

This example creates a trigger that, when an employee job level is inserted or updated, checks that the specified employee job level (**job_lvls**), on which salaries are based, is within the range defined for the job. To get the appropriate range, the **jobs** table must be referenced.

```
USE pubs
IF EXISTS (SELECT name FROM sysobjects
        WHERE name = 'employee_insupd' AND type = 'TR')
    DROP TRIGGER employee_insupd
GO
CREATE TRIGGER employee_insupd
```

(continued)

(continued)

```
ON employee
FOR INSERT, UPDATE
AS
/* Get the range of level for this job type from the jobs table. */
DECLARE @min_lvl tinyint,
   @max_lvl tinyint,
   @emp_lvl tinyint,
   @job_id smallint
SELECT @min_lvl = min_lvl,
   @max_lvl = max_lvl,
   @emp_lvl = i.job_lvl,
   @job_id = i.job_id
FROM employee e INNER JOIN inserted i ON e.emp_id = i.emp_id
   JOIN jobs j ON j.job_id = i.job_id
IF (@job_id = 1) and (@emp_lvl <> 10)
BEGIN
   RAISERROR ('Job id 1 expects the default level of 10.', 16, 1)
   ROLLBACK TRANSACTION
END
ELSE
IF NOT (@emp_lvl BETWEEN @min_lvl AND @max_lvl)
BEGIN
   RAISERROR ('The level for job_id:%d should be between %d and %d.',
      16, 1, @job_id, @min_lvl, @max_lvl)
   ROLLBACK TRANSACTION
END
```

D. Use deferred name resolution

This example creates two triggers to illustrate deferred name resolution.

```
USE pubs
IF EXISTS (SELECT name FROM sysobjects
      WHERE name = 'trig1' AND type = 'TR')
   DROP TRIGGER trig1
GO
-- Creating a trigger on a nonexistent table.
CREATE TRIGGER trig1
on authors
FOR INSERT, UPDATE, DELETE
AS
   SELECT a.au_lname, a.au_fname, x.info
   FROM authors a INNER JOIN does_not_exist x
```

(continued)

(continued)

```
        ON a.au_id = x.au_id
GO
-- Here is the statement to actually see the text of the trigger.
SELECT o.id, c.text
FROM sysobjects o INNER JOIN syscomments c
    ON o.id = c.id
WHERE o.type = 'TR' and o.name = 'trig1'

-- Creating a trigger on an existing table, but with a nonexistent
-- column.
USE pubs
IF EXISTS (SELECT name FROM sysobjects
        WHERE name = 'trig2' AND type = 'TR')
    DROP TRIGGER trig2
GO
CREATE TRIGGER trig2
ON authors
FOR INSERT, UPDATE
AS
    DECLARE @fax varchar(12)
    SELECT @fax = phone
    FROM authors
GO
-- Here is the statement to actually see the text of the trigger.
SELECT o.id, c.text
FROM sysobjects o INNER JOIN syscomments c
    ON o.id = c.id
WHERE o.type = 'TR' and o.name = 'trig2'
```

E. Use COLUMNS_UPDATED

This example creates two tables: an **employeeData** table and an **auditEmployeeData** table. The **employeeData** table, which holds sensitive employee payroll information, can be modified by members of the human resources department. If the employee's social security number (SSN), yearly salary, or bank account number is changed, an audit record is generated and inserted into the **auditEmployeeData** audit table.

By using the COLUMNS_UPDATED() function, it is possible to test quickly for any changes to these columns that contain sensitive employee information. This use of COLUMNS_UPDATED() only works if you are trying to detect changes to the first 8 columns in the table.

```
USE pubs
IF EXISTS(SELECT TABLE_NAME FROM INFORMATION_SCHEMA.TABLES
   WHERE TABLE_NAME = 'employeeData')
   DROP TABLE employeeData
IF EXISTS(SELECT TABLE_NAME FROM INFORMATION_SCHEMA.TABLES
   WHERE TABLE_NAME = 'auditEmployeeData')
   DROP TABLE auditEmployeeData
GO
CREATE TABLE employeeData (
   emp_id int NOT NULL,
   emp_bankAccountNumber char (10) NOT NULL,
   emp_salary int NOT NULL,
   emp_SSN char (11) NOT NULL,
   emp_lname nchar (32) NOT NULL,
   emp_fname nchar (32) NOT NULL,
   emp_manager int NOT NULL
   )
GO
CREATE TABLE auditEmployeeData (
   audit_log_id uniqueidentifier DEFAULT NEWID(),
   audit_log_type char (3) NOT NULL,
   audit_emp_id int NOT NULL,
   audit_emp_bankAccountNumber char (10) NULL,
   audit_emp_salary int NULL,
   audit_emp_SSN char (11) NULL,
   audit_user sysname DEFAULT SUSER_SNAME(),
   audit_changed datetime DEFAULT GETDATE()
   )
GO
CREATE TRIGGER updEmployeeData
ON employeeData
FOR update AS
/*Check whether columns 2, 3 or 4 has been updated. If any or all of columns 2, 3 or 4
have been changed, create an audit record. The bitmask is: power(2,(2-1))+power(2,(3-
1))+power(2,(4-1)) = 14. To check if all columns 2, 3, and 4 are updated, use = 14 in
place of >0 (below).*/

   IF (COLUMNS_UPDATED() & 14) > 0
/*Use IF (COLUMNS_UPDATED() & 14) = 14 to see if all of columns 2, 3, and 4 are updated.*/
      BEGIN
-- Audit OLD record.
      INSERT INTO auditEmployeeData
         (audit_log_type,
         audit_emp_id,
```

(continued)

(continued)

```
            audit_emp_bankAccountNumber,
            audit_emp_salary,
            audit_emp_SSN)
            SELECT 'OLD',
                del.emp_id,
                del.emp_bankAccountNumber,
                del.emp_salary,
                del.emp_SSN
            FROM deleted del

-- Audit NEW record.
        INSERT INTO auditEmployeeData
            (audit_log_type,
            audit_emp_id,
            audit_emp_bankAccountNumber,
            audit_emp_salary,
            audit_emp_SSN)
            SELECT 'NEW',
                ins.emp_id,
                ins.emp_bankAccountNumber,
                ins.emp_salary,
                ins.emp_SSN
            FROM inserted ins
    END
GO

/*Inserting a new employee does not cause the UPDATE trigger to fire.*/
INSERT INTO employeeData
    VALUES ( 101, 'USA-987-01', 23000, 'R-M53550M', N'Mendel', N'Roland', 32)
GO

/*Updating the employee record for employee number 101 to change the salary to 51000
causes the UPDATE trigger to fire and an audit trail to be produced.*/

UPDATE employeeData
    SET emp_salary = 51000
    WHERE emp_id = 101
GO
```

(continued)

(continued)

```
SELECT * FROM auditEmployeeData
GO

/*Updating the employee record for employee number 101 to change both the bank account
number and social security number (SSN) causes the UPDATE trigger to fire and an audit
trail to be produced.*/

UPDATE employeeData
   SET emp_bankAccountNumber = '133146A0', emp_SSN = 'R-M53550M'
   WHERE emp_id = 101
GO
SELECT * FROM auditEmployeeData
GO
```

F. Use COLUMNS_UPDATED to test more than 8 columns

If you must test for updates that affect columns other than the first 8 columns in a
table, you must use the SUBSTRING function to test the proper bit returned by
COLUMNS_UPDATED. This example tests for updates that affect columns 3, 5, or 9
in the **Northwind.dbo.Customers** table.

```
USE Northwind
DROP TRIGGER  tr1
GO
CREATE TRIGGER tr1 ON Customers
FOR UPDATE AS
   IF ( (SUBSTRING(COLUMNS_UPDATED(),1,1)=power(2,(3-1))
      + power(2,(5-1)))
      AND (SUBSTRING(COLUMNS_UPDATED(),2,1)=power(2,(1-1)))
      )
   PRINT 'Columns 3, 5 and 9 updated'
GO

UPDATE Customers
   SET ContactName=ContactName,
      Address=Address,
      Country=Country
GO
```

Related Topics

ALTER TABLE, ALTER TRIGGER, CREATE TABLE, DROP TRIGGER,
Programming Stored Procedures, sp_depends, sp_help, sp_helptext, sp_rename,
sp_settriggerorder, sp_spaceused, Using Identifiers

CREATE VIEW

Creates a virtual table that represents the data in one or more tables in an alternative way. CREATE VIEW must be the first statement in a query batch.

Syntax

```
CREATE VIEW [ < database_name > . ] [ < owner > . ] view_name [ ( column [ ,...n ] ) ]
[ WITH < view_attribute > [ ,...n ] ]
AS
select_statement
[ WITH CHECK OPTION ]

< view_attribute > ::=
    { ENCRYPTION | SCHEMABINDING | VIEW_METADATA }
```

Arguments

view_name

Is the name of the view. View names must follow the rules for identifiers. Specifying the view owner name is optional.

column

Is the name to be used for a column in a view. Naming a column in CREATE VIEW is necessary only when a column is derived from an arithmetic expression, a function, or a constant, when two or more columns may otherwise have the same name (usually because of a join), or when a column in a view is given a name different from that of the column from which derived. Column names can also be assigned in the SELECT statement.

If *column* is not specified, the view columns acquire the same names as the columns in the SELECT statement.

> **Note** In the columns for the view, the permissions for a column name apply across a CREATE VIEW or ALTER VIEW statement, regardless of the source of the underlying data. For example, if permissions are granted on the **title_id** column in a CREATE VIEW statement, an ALTER VIEW statement can name the **title_id** column with a different column name, such as **qty**, and still have the permissions associated with the view using **title_id**.

n

Is a placeholder that indicates that multiple columns can be specified.

AS

Are the actions the view is to perform.

select_statement

Is the SELECT statement that defines the view. It can use more than one table and other views. To select from the objects referenced in the SELECT clause of a view created, it is necessary to have the appropriate permissions.

A view does not have to be a simple subset of the rows and columns of one particular table. A view can be created using more than one table or other views with a SELECT clause of any complexity.

In an indexed view definition, the SELECT statement must be a single table statement or a multitable JOIN with optional aggregation.

There are a few restrictions on the SELECT clauses in a view definition. A CREATE VIEW statement cannot:

- Include COMPUTE or COMPUTE BY clauses.
- Include ORDER BY clause, unless there is also a TOP clause in the select list of the SELECT statement.
- Include the INTO keyword.
- Reference a temporary table or a table variable.

Because *select_statement* uses the SELECT statement, it is valid to use <join_hint> and <table_hint> hints as specified in the FROM clause. For more information, see FROM and SELECT.

Functions can be used in the *select_statement*.

select_statement can use multiple SELECT statements separated by UNION or UNION ALL.

WITH CHECK OPTION

Forces all data modification statements executed against the view to adhere to the criteria set within *select_statement*. When a row is modified through a view, the WITH CHECK OPTION ensures the data remains visible through the view after the modification is committed.

WITH ENCRYPTION

Indicates that SQL Server encrypts the system table columns containing the text of the CREATE VIEW statement. Using WITH ENCRYPTION prevents the view from being published as part of SQL Server replication.

SCHEMABINDING

Binds the view to the schema. When SCHEMABINDING is specified, the *select_statement* must include the two-part names (owner.object) of tables, views, or user-defined functions referenced.

Views or tables participating in a view created with the schema binding clause cannot be dropped unless that view is dropped or changed so that it no longer has schema binding. Otherwise, SQL Server raises an error. In addition, ALTER TABLE statements on tables that participate in views having schema binding will fail if these statements affect the view definition.

VIEW_METADATA

Specifies that SQL Server will return to the DBLIB, ODBC, and OLE DB APIs the metadata information about the view, instead of the base table or tables, when browse-mode metadata is being requested for a query that references the view. Browse-mode metadata is additional metadata returned by SQL Server to the client-side DB-LIB, ODBC, and OLE DB APIs, which allow the client-side APIs to implement updateable client-side cursors. Browse-mode meta data includes information about the base table that the columns in the result set belong to.

For views created with VIEW_METADATA option, the browse-mode meta data returns the view name as opposed to the base table names when describing columns from the view in the result set.

When a view is created WITH VIEW_METADATA, all its columns (except for **timestamp**) are updateable if the view has INSERT or UPDATE INSTEAD OF triggers. See Updateable Views later in this topic.

Remarks

A view can be created only in the current database. A view can reference a maximum of 1,024 columns.

When querying through a view, Microsoft SQL Server checks to make sure that all the database objects referenced anywhere in the statement exist, that they are valid in the context of the statement, and that data modification statements do not violate any data integrity rules. A check that fails returns an error message. A successful check translates the action into an action against the underlying table(s).

If a view depends on a table (or view) that was dropped, SQL Server produces an error message if anyone tries to use the view. If a new table (or view) is created, and the table structure does not change from the previous base table, to replace the one dropped, the view again becomes usable. If the new table (or view) structure changes, then the view must be dropped and recreated.

When a view is created, the name of the view is stored in the **sysobjects** table. Information about the columns defined in a view is added to the **syscolumns** table, and information about the view dependencies is added to the **sysdepends** table. In addition, the text of the CREATE VIEW statement is added to the **syscomments** table. This is similar to a stored procedure; when a view is executed for the first time, only its query tree is stored in the procedure cache. Each time a view is accessed, its execution plan is recompiled.

The result of a query using an index on a view defined with **numeric** or **float** expressions may be different from a similar query that does not use the index on the view. This difference may be the result of rounding errors during INSERT, DELETE, or UPDATE actions on underlying tables.

SQL Server saves the settings of SET QUOTED_IDENTIFIER and SET ANSI_NULLS when a view is created. These original settings are restored when the view is used. Therefore, any client session settings for SET QUOTED_IDENTIFIER and SET ANSI_NULLS is ignored when accessing the view.

Note Whether SQL Server interprets an empty string as a single space or as a true empty string is controlled by the setting of **sp_dbcmptlevel**. If the compatibility level is less than or equal to 65, SQL Server interprets empty strings as single spaces. If the compatibility level is equal to or higher than 70, SQL Server interprets empty strings as empty strings. For more information, see sp_dbcmptlevel.

Updateable Views

Microsoft SQL Server 2000 enhances the class of updateable views in two ways:

- **INSTEAD OF Triggers:** INSTEAD OF triggers can be created on a view in order to make a view updateable. The INSTEAD OF trigger is executed instead of the data modification statement on which the trigger is defined. This trigger allows the user to specify the set of actions that need to take place in order to process the data modification statement. Thus, if an INSTEAD OF trigger exists for a view on a given data modification statement (INSERT, UPDATE, or DELETE), the corresponding view is updateable through that statement. For more information about INSTEAD OF triggers, see Designing INSTEAD OF triggers.

- **Partitioned Views:** If the view is of a specified form called 'partitioned view,' the view is updateable, subject to certain restrictions. Partitioned views and their updateability are discussed later in this topic.

  When needed, SQL Server will distinguish **Local Partitioned Views** as the views in which all participating tables and the view are on the same SQL Server, and **Distributed Partitioned Views** as the views in which at least one of the tables in the view resides on a different (remote) server.

If a view does not have INSTEAD OF triggers, or if it is not a partitioned view, then it is updateable only if the following conditions are satisfied:

- The *select_statement* has no aggregate functions in the select list and does not contain the TOP, GROUP BY, UNION (unless the view is a partitioned view as described later in this topic), or DISTINCT clauses. Aggregate functions can be used in a subquery in the FROM clause as long as the values returned by the functions are not modified. For more information, see Aggregate Functions.

- *select_statement* has no derived columns in the select list. Derived columns are result set columns formed by anything other than a simple column expression, such as using functions or addition or subtraction operators.

- The FROM clause in the *select_statement* references at least one table. *select_statement* must have more than non-tabular expressions, which are expressions not derived from a table. For example, this view is not updateable:

```
CREATE VIEW NoTable AS
SELECT GETDATE() AS CurrentDate,
       @@LANGUAGE AS CurrentLanguage,
       CURRENT_USER AS CurrentUser
```

INSERT, UPDATE, and DELETE statements also must meet certain qualifications before they can reference a view that is updateable, as specified in the conditions above. UPDATE and INSERT statements can reference a view only if the view is updateable and the UPDATE or INSERT statement is written so that it modifies data in only one of the base tables referenced in the FROM clause of the view. A DELETE statement can reference an updateable view only if the view references exactly one table in its FROM clause.

Partitioned Views

A partitioned view is a view defined by a UNION ALL of member tables structured in the same way, but stored separately as multiple tables in either the same SQL Server or in a group of autonomous SQL Server 2000 servers, called Federated SQL Server 2000 Servers.

For example, if you have **Customers** table data distributed in three member tables in three server locations (**Customers_33** on **Server1**, **Customers_66** on **Server2**, and **Customers_99** on **Server3**), a partitioned view on **Server1** would be defined this way:

```
--Partitioned view as defined on Server1
CREATE VIEW Customers
AS
--Select from local member table
SELECT *
FROM CompanyData.dbo.Customers_33
UNION ALL
--Select from member table on Server2
SELECT *
FROM Server2.CompanyData.dbo.Customers_66
UNION ALL
--Select from mmeber table on Server3
SELECT *
FROM Server3.CompanyData.dbo.Customers_99
```

In general, a view is said to be a partitioned view if it is of the following form:

```
SELECT <select_list1>
FROM T1
UNION ALL
SELECT <select_list2>
FROM T2
UNION ALL
...
SELECT <select_listn>
FROM Tn
```

Conditions for Creating Partitioned Views

1. SELECT list

   - All columns in the member tables should be selected in the column list of the view definition.

   - The columns in the same ordinal position of each select_list should be of the same type, including collations. It is not sufficient for the columns to be implicitly convertible types, as is generally the case for UNION.

     Also, *at least one* column (for example <col>) must appear in all the SELECT lists in the same ordinal position. This <col> should be defined such that the member tables T1, ..., Tn have CHECK constraints C1, ..., Cn defined on <col> respectively.

     Constraint C1 defined on table T1 must follow this form:

```
C1 ::= < simple_interval > [ OR < simple_interval > OR ...]
< simple_interval > :: =
   < col > { < | > | <= | >= | = }
   | < col > BETWEEN < value1 > AND < value2 >
   | < col > IN ( value_list )
   | < col > { > | >= } < value1 > AND
      < col > { < | <= } < value2 >
```

   - The constraints should be such that any given value of <col> can satisfy *at most one* of the constraints C1, ..., Cn so that the constraints should form a set of disjointed or non-overlapping intervals. The column <col> on which the disjointed constraints are defined is called the 'partitioning column.' Note that the partitioning column may have different names in the underlying tables. The constraints should be in an **enabled** state in order for them to meet the above conditions of the partitioning column. If the constraints are disabled, re-enable constraint checking with either the WITH CHECK option or the CHECK *constraint_name* options of ALTER TABLE.

Here are some examples of valid sets of constraints:

```
{ [col < 10], [col between 11 and 20] , [col > 20] }
{ [col between 11 and 20], [col between 21 and 30], [col between 31 and 100] }
```

- The same column cannot be used multiple times in the SELECT list.

2. Partitioning column

- The partitioning column is a part of the PRIMARY KEY of the table.

- It cannot be a computed column.

- If there is more than one constraint on the same column in a member table, SQL Server ignores all the constraints and will not consider them when determining whether or not the view is a partitioned view. To meet the conditions of the partitioned view, there should be only one partitioning constraint on the partitioning column.

3. Member tables (or underlying tables T1, ..., T*n*)

- The tables can be either local tables or tables from other SQL Servers referenced either through a four-part name or an OPENDATASOURCE- or OPENROWSET-based name. (The OPENDATASOURCE and OPENROWSET syntax can specify a table name, but not a pass-through query.) For more information, see OPENDATASOURCE and OPENROWSET.

  If one or more of the member tables are remote, the view is called *distributed partitioned view*, and additional conditions apply. They are discussed later in this section.

- The same table cannot appear twice in the set of tables that are being combined with the UNION ALL statement.

- The member tables cannot have indexes created on computed columns in the table.

- The member tables should have all PRIMARY KEY constraints on an identical number of columns.

- All member tables in the view should have the same ANSI padding setting (which is set using the **user options** option in **sp_configure** or the SET option).

Conditions for Modifying Partitioned Views

Only the Developer and Enterprise Editions of SQL Server 2000 allow INSERT, UPDATE, and DELETE operations on partitioned views. To modify partitioned views, the statements must meet these conditions:

- The INSERT statement must supply values for all the columns in the view, even if the underlying member tables have a DEFAULT constraint for those columns or if they allow NULLs. For those member table columns that have DEFAULT definitions, the statements cannot use the keyword DEFAULT explicitly.

- The value being inserted into the partitioning column should satisfy at least one of the underlying constraints; otherwise, the INSERT action will fail with a constraint violation.

- UPDATE statements cannot specify the DEFAULT keyword as a value in the SET clause even if the column has a DEFAULT value defined in the corresponding member table.

- PRIMARY KEY columns cannot be modified through an UPDATE statement if the member tables have **text**, **ntext**, or **image** columns.

- Columns in the view that are an IDENTITY column in one or more of the member tables cannot be modified through an INSERT or UPDATE statement.

- If one of the member tables contains a **timestamp** column, the view cannot be modified through an INSERT or UPDATE statement.

- INSERT, UPDATE, and DELETE actions against a partitioned view are not allowed if there is a self-join with the same view or with any of the member tables in the statement.

> **Note**   To update a partitioned view, the user must have INSERT, UPDATE, and DELETE permissions on the member tables.

Additional Conditions for Distributed Partitioned Views

For distributed partitioned views (when one or more member tables are remote), the following additional conditions apply:

- A distributed transaction will be started to ensure atomicity across all nodes affected by the update.

- The XACT_ABORT SET option should be set to ON for INSERT, UPDATE, or DELETE statements to work.

- Any **smallmoney** and **smalldatetime** columns in remote tables that are referenced in a partitioned view are mapped as **money** and **datetime** respectively. Consequently, the corresponding columns (in the same ordinal position in the select list) in the local tables should be **money** and **datetime**.

- Any linked server in the partitioned view cannot be a loopback linked server (a linked server that points to the same SQL Server).

The setting of the SET ROWCOUNT option is ignored for INSERT, UPDATE, and DELETE actions that involve updateable partitioned views and remote tables.

When the member tables and partitioned view definition are in place, Microsoft SQL Server 2000 builds intelligent plans that use queries efficiently to access data from member tables. With the CHECK constraint definitions, the query processor maps the distribution of key values across the member tables. When a user issues a query, the query processor compares the map to the values specified in the WHERE clause, and builds an execution plan with a minimal amount of data transfer between member servers. Thus, although some member tables may be located in remote servers, SQL Server 2000 will resolve distributed queries so that the amount of distributed data that has to be transferred is minimal. For more information about how SQL Server 2000 resolves queries on partitioned views, see Resolving Distributed Partitioned Views.

Considerations for Replication

In order to create partitioned views on member tables that are involved in replication, the following considerations apply:

- If the underlying tables are involved in merge replication or transactional replication with updating subscribers, the uniqueidentifier column should also be included in the SELECT list.
- Any INSERT actions into the partitioned view must provide a NEWID() value for the uniqueidentifier column. Any UPDATE actions against the uniqueidentifier column must supply NEWID() as the value since the DEFAULT keyword cannot be used.
- The replication of updates made using the view is exactly the same as when replicating tables in two different databases; that is, the tables are served by different replication agents and the order of the updates is not guaranteed.

Permissions

CREATE VIEW permission defaults to the members of the **db_owner** and **db_ddladmin** fixed database roles. Members of the **sysadmin** fixed server role and the **db_owner** fixed database role can transfer CREATE VIEW permission to other users.

To create a view, the user must have CREATE VIEW permission along with SELECT permission on the tables, views, and table-valued functions being referenced in the view, and EXECUTE permission on the scalar-valued functions being invoked in the view.

In addition, to create a view WITH SCHEMABINDING, the user must have REFERENCES permissions on each table, view, and user-defined function that is referenced.

Examples

A. Use a simple CREATE VIEW

This example creates a view with a simple SELECT statement. A simple view is helpful when a combination of columns is queried frequently.

```
USE pubs
IF EXISTS (SELECT TABLE_NAME FROM INFORMATION_SCHEMA.VIEWS
      WHERE TABLE_NAME = 'titles_view')
   DROP VIEW titles_view
GO
CREATE VIEW titles_view
AS
SELECT title, type, price, pubdate
FROM titles
GO
```

B. Use WITH ENCRYPTION

This example uses the WITH ENCRYPTION option and shows computed columns, renamed columns, and multiple columns.

```
USE pubs
IF EXISTS (SELECT TABLE_NAME FROM INFORMATION_SCHEMA.VIEWS
      WHERE TABLE_NAME = 'accounts')
   DROP VIEW accounts
GO
CREATE VIEW accounts (title, advance, amt_due)
WITH ENCRYPTION
AS
SELECT title, advance, price * royalty * ytd_sales
FROM titles
WHERE price > $5
GO
```

Here is the query to retrieve the identification number and text of the encrypted stored procedure:

```
USE pubs
GO
SELECT c.id, c.text
FROM syscomments c, sysobjects o
WHERE c.id = o.id and o.name = 'accounts'
GO
```

Here is the result set:

> **Note** The **text** column output is shown on a separate line. When the procedure is executed, this information appears on the same line as the **id** column information.

```
id             text
------------ -------------------------------------------------------------
661577395
?????????????????????????????????????????????????????????????????????????…


(1 row(s) affected)
```

C. Use WITH CHECK OPTION

This example shows a view named **CAonly** that allows data modifications to apply only to authors within the state of California.

```
USE pubs
IF EXISTS (SELECT TABLE_NAME FROM INFORMATION_SCHEMA.VIEWS
      WHERE TABLE_NAME = 'CAonly')
   DROP VIEW CAonly
GO
CREATE VIEW CAonly
AS
SELECT au_lname, au_fname, city, state
FROM authors
WHERE state = 'CA'
WITH CHECK OPTION
GO
```

D. Use built-in functions within a view

This example shows a view definition that includes a built-in function. When you use functions, the derived column must include a column name in the CREATE VIEW statement.

```
USE pubs
IF EXISTS (SELECT TABLE_NAME FROM INFORMATION_SCHEMA.VIEWS
      WHERE TABLE_NAME = 'categories')
   DROP VIEW categories
GO
CREATE VIEW categories (category, average_price)
AS
SELECT type, AVG(price)
FROM titles
GROUP BY type
GO
```

E. Use @@ROWCOUNT function in a view

This example uses the @@ROWCOUNT function as part of the view definition.

```
USE pubs
IF EXISTS (SELECT TABLE_NAME FROM INFORMATION_SCHEMA.VIEWS
      WHERE TABLE_NAME = 'myview')
   DROP VIEW myview
GO
CREATE VIEW myview
AS
   SELECT au_lname, au_fname, @@ROWCOUNT AS bar
   FROM authors
   WHERE state = 'UT'
GO
SELECT *
FROM myview
```

F. Use partitioned data

This example uses tables named **SUPPLY1**, **SUPPLY2**, **SUPPLY3**, and **SUPPLY4**, which correspond to the supplier tables from four offices, located in different countries.

```
--create the tables and insert the values
CREATE TABLE SUPPLY1 (
   supplyID INT PRIMARY KEY CHECK (supplyID BETWEEN 1 and 150),
   supplier CHAR(50)
   )
CREATE TABLE SUPPLY2 (
   supplyID INT PRIMARY KEY CHECK (supplyID BETWEEN 151 and 300),
   supplier CHAR(50)
   )
CREATE TABLE SUPPLY3 (
   supplyID INT PRIMARY KEY CHECK (supplyID BETWEEN 301 and 450),
   supplier CHAR(50)
   )
CREATE TABLE SUPPLY4 (
   supplyID INT PRIMARY KEY CHECK (supplyID BETWEEN 451 and 600),
   supplier CHAR(50)
   )
INSERT SUPPLY1 VALUES ('1', 'CaliforniaCorp')
INSERT SUPPLY1 VALUES ('5', 'BraziliaLtd')
INSERT SUPPLY2 VALUES ('231', 'FarEast')
INSERT SUPPLY2 VALUES ('280', 'NZ')
```

(continued)

(continued)

```
INSERT SUPPLY3 VALUES ('321', 'EuroGroup')
INSERT SUPPLY3 VALUES ('442', 'UKArchip')
INSERT SUPPLY4 VALUES ('475', 'India')
INSERT SUPPLY4 VALUES ('521', 'Afrique')

--create the view that combines all supplier tables
CREATE VIEW all_supplier_view
AS
SELECT *
FROM SUPPLY1
   UNION ALL
SELECT *
FROM SUPPLY2
   UNION ALL
SELECT *
FROM SUPPLY3
   UNION ALL
SELECT *
FROM SUPPLY4
```

Related Topics

ALTER TABLE, ALTER VIEW, DELETE, DROP VIEW, INSERT, Programming
Stored Procedures, sp_depends, sp_help, sp_helptext, sp_rename, System Tables,
UPDATE, Using Identifiers, Using Views with Partitioned Data

DATABASEPROPERTY

Returns the named database property value for the given database and property name.

Important Use the Microsoft SQL Server 2000 function
DATABASEPROPERTYEX to obtain information about the current setting of
database options or the properties of a specified database. The
DATABASEPROPERTY function is provided for backward compatibility.

Syntax

```
DATABASEPROPERTY( database , property )
```

Arguments

database

Is an expression containing the name of the database for which to return the named
property information. *database* is **nvarchar(128)**.

property

Is an expression containing the name of the database property to return. *property* is **varchar(128)**, and can be one of these values.

Value	Description	Value returned
IsAnsiNullDefault	Database follows SQL-92 rules for allowing null values.	1 = TRUE 0 = FALSE NULL = Invalid input
IsAnsiNullsEnabled	All comparisons to a null evaluate to unknown.	1 = TRUE 0 = FALSE NULL = Invalid input
IsAnsiWarningsEnabled	Error or warning messages are issued when standard error conditions occur.	1 = TRUE 0 = FALSE NULL = Invalid input
IsAutoClose	Database shuts down cleanly and frees resources after the last user exits.	1 = TRUE 0 = FALSE NULL = Invalid input
IsAutoCreateStatistics	Existing statistics are automatically updated when the statistics become out-of-date because the data in the tables has changed.	1 = TRUE 0 = FALSE NULL = Invalid input
IsAutoShrink	Database files are candidates for automatic periodic shrinking.	1 = TRUE 0 = FALSE NULL = Invalid input
IsAutoUpdateStatistics	Auto update statistics database option is enabled.	1 = TRUE 0 = FALSE NULL = Invalid input
IsBulkCopy	Database allows nonlogged operations.	1 = TRUE 0 = FALSE NULL = Invalid input
IsCloseCursorsOnCommit Enabled	Cursors that are open when a transaction is committed are closed.	1 = TRUE 0 = FALSE NULL = Invalid input
IsDboOnly	Database is in DBO-only access mode.	1 = TRUE 0 = FALSE NULL = Invalid input

(continued)

(continued)

Value	Description	Value returned
IsDetached	Database was detached by a detach operation.	1 = TRUE 0 = FALSE NULL = Invalid input
IsEmergencyMode	Emergency mode is enabled to allow suspect database to be usable.	1 = TRUE 0 = FALSE NULL = Invalid input
IsFulltextEnabled	Database is full-text enabled.	1 = TRUE 0 = FALSE NULL = Invalid input
IsInLoad	Database is loading.	1 = TRUE 0 = FALSE NULL = Invalid input
IsInRecovery	Database is recovering.	1 = TRUE 0 = FALSE NULL[1] = Invalid input
IsInStandBy	Database is online as read-only, with restore log allowed.	1 = TRUE 0 = FALSE NULL = Invalid input
IsLocalCursorsDefault	Cursor declarations default to LOCAL.	1 = TRUE 0 = FALSE NULL = Invalid input
IsNotRecovered	Database failed to recover.	1 = TRUE 0 = FALSE NULL = Invalid input
IsNullConcat	Null concatenation operand yields NULL.	1 = TRUE 0 = FALSE NULL = Invalid input
IsOffline	Database is offline.	1 = TRUE 0 = FALSE NULL = Invalid input

(continued)

(continued)

Value	Description	Value returned
IsQuotedIdentifiersEnabled	Double quotation marks can be used on identifiers.	1 = TRUE 0 = FALSE NULL = Invalid input
IsReadOnly	Database is in a read-only access mode.	1 = TRUE 0 = FALSE NULL = Invalid input
IsRecursiveTriggersEnabled	Recursive firing of triggers is enabled.	1 = TRUE 0 = FALSE NULL = Invalid input
IsShutDown	Database encountered a problem at startup.	1 = TRUE 0 = FALSE NULL[1] = Invalid input
IsSingleUser	Database is in single-user access mode.	1 = TRUE 0 = FALSE NULL = Invalid input
IsSuspect	Database is suspect.	1 = TRUE 0 = FALSE NULL = Invalid input
IsTruncLog	Database truncates its logon checkpoints.	1 = TRUE 0 = FALSE NULL = Invalid input
Version	Internal version number of the Microsoft SQL Server code with which the database was created. For internal use only by SQL Server tools and in upgrade processing.	Version number = Database is open NULL = Database is closed

1 Returned value is also NULL if the database has never been started, or has been autoclosed.

Return Types
integer

Examples

This example returns the setting for the **IsTruncLog** property for the **master** database.

```
USE master
SELECT DATABASEPROPERTY('master', 'IsTruncLog')
```

Here is the result set:

```
-------------------
1
```

Related Topics

Control-of-Flow Language, DATABASEPROPERTYEX, DELETE, INSERT, Metadata Functions, SELECT, sp_dboption, UPDATE, WHERE

DATABASEPROPERTYEX

Returns the current setting of the specified database option or property for the specified database.

Syntax

```
DATABASEPROPERTYEX( database , property )
```

Arguments

database

Is an expression that evaluates to the name of the database for which a property setting is to be returned. *database* is **nvarchar(128)**.

property

Is an expression that indicates the option or property setting to be returned. *property* is **nvarchar(128)**, and can be one of these values.

Value	Description	Value returned
Collation	Default collation name for the database.	Collation name
IsAnsiNullDefault	Database follows SQL-92 rules for allowing null values.	1 = TRUE 0 = FALSE NULL = Invalid input
IsAnsiNullsEnabled	All comparisons to a null evaluate to unknown.	1 = TRUE 0 = FALSE NULL = Invalid input

(continued)

(continued)

Value	Description	Value returned
IsAnsiPaddingEnabled	Strings are padded to the same length before comparison or insert.	1 = TRUE 0 = FALSE NULL = Invalid input
IsAnsiWarningsEnabled	Error or warning messages are issued when standard error conditions occur.	1 = TRUE 0 = FALSE NULL = Invalid input
IsArithmeticAbortEnabled	Queries are terminated when an overflow or divide-by-zero error occurs during query execution.	1 = TRUE 0 = FALSE NULL = Invalid input
IsAutoClose	Database shuts down cleanly and frees resources after the last user exits.	1 = TRUE 0 = FALSE NULL = Invalid input
IsAutoCreateStatistics	Existing statistics are automatically updated when the statistics become out-of-date because the data in the tables has changed.	1 = TRUE 0 = FALSE NULL = Invalid input
IsAutoShrink	Database files are candidates for automatic periodic shrinking.	1 = TRUE 0 = FALSE NULL = Invalid input
IsAutoUpdateStatistics	Auto update statistics database option is enabled.	1 = TRUE 0 = FALSE NULL = Invalid input
IsCloseCursorsOnCommit Enabled	Cursors that are open when a transaction is committed are closed.	1 = TRUE 0 = FALSE NULL = Invalid input
IsFulltextEnabled	Database is full-text enabled.	1 = TRUE 0 = FALSE NULL = Invalid input
IsInStandBy	Database is online as read-only, with restore log allowed.	1 = TRUE 0 = FALSE NULL = Invalid input

(continued)

(continued)

Value	Description	Value returned
IsLocalCursorsDefault	Cursor declarations default to LOCAL.	1 = TRUE 0 = FALSE NULL = Invalid input
IsMergePublished	The tables of a database can be published for replication, if replication is installed.	1 = TRUE 0 = FALSE NULL = Invalid input
IsNullConcat	Null concatenation operand yields NULL.	1 = TRUE 0 = FALSE NULL = Invalid input
IsNumericRoundAbort Enabled	Errors are generated when loss of precision occurs in expressions.	1 = TRUE 0 = FALSE NULL = Invalid input
IsQuotedIdentifiersEnabled	Double quotation marks can be used on identifiers.	1 = TRUE 0 = FALSE NULL = Invalid input
IsRecursiveTriggersEnabled	Recursive firing of triggers is enabled.	1 = TRUE 0 = FALSE NULL = Invalid input
IsSubscribed	Database can be subscribed for publication.	1 = TRUE 0 = FALSE NULL = Invalid input
IsTornPageDetectionEnabled	Microsoft SQL Server detects incomplete I/O operations caused by power failures or other system outages.	1 = TRUE 0 = FALSE NULL = Invalid input
Recovery	Recovery model for the database.	FULL = full recovery model BULK_LOGGED = bulk logged model SIMPLE = simple recovery model

(continued)

(continued)

Value	Description	Value returned
SQLSortOrder	SQL Server sort order ID supported in previous versions of SQL Server.	0 = Database is using Windows collation >0 = SQL Server sort order ID
Status	Database status.	ONLINE = database is available for query OFFLINE = database was explicitly taken offline RESTORING = database is being restored RECOVERING = database is recovering and not yet ready for queries SUSPECT = database cannot be recovered
Updateability	Indicates whether data can be modified.	READ_ONLY = data can be read but not modified READ_WRITE = data can be read and modified
UserAccess	Indicates which users can access the database.	SINGLE_USER = only one **db_owner**, **dbcreator**, or **sysadmin** user at a time RESTRICTED_USER = only members of **db_owner**, **dbcreator**, and **sysadmin** roles MULTI_USER = all users
Version	Internal version number of the Microsoft SQL Server code with which the database was created. For internal use only by SQL Server tools and in upgrade processing.	Version number = Database is open NULL = Database is closed

Return Types

sql_variant

Remarks

This function returns only one property setting at a time.

DATABASEPROPERTY is supported for backward compatibility but does not provide information about the properties added in this release. Also, many properties supported by DATABASEPROPERTY have been replaced by new properties in DATABASEPROPERTYEX.

Examples

A. Retrieving the status of the autoshrink database option

This example returns the status of the **autoshrink** database option for the **Northwind** database.

```
SELECT DATABASEPROPERTYEX('Northwind', 'IsAutoShrink')
```

Here is the result set (indicates that **autoshrink** is off):

```
-------------------
0
```

B. Retrieving the default collation for a database

This example returns the name of the default collation for the **Northwind** database.

```
SELECT DATABASEPROPERTYEX('Northwind', 'Collation')
```

Here is the result set:

```
------------------------------
SQL_Latin1_General_CP1_CS_AS
```

Related Topics

ALTER DATABASE, COLLATE

DATALENGTH

Returns the number of bytes used to represent any expression.

Syntax

```
DATALENGTH ( expression )
```

Arguments

expression
　　Is an expression of any type.

Return Types

int

Remarks

DATALENGTH is especially useful with **varchar**, **varbinary**, **text**, **image**, **nvarchar**, and **ntext** data types because these data types can store variable-length data.

The DATALENGTH of NULL is NULL.

Note　Compatibility levels can affect return values. For more information about compatibility levels, see sp_dbcmptlevel.

Examples

This example finds the length of the **pub_name** column in the **publishers** table.

```
USE pubs
GO
SELECT length = DATALENGTH(pub_name), pub_name
FROM publishers
ORDER BY pub_name
GO
```

Here is the result set:

```
length       pub_name
-----------  -----------------------------------------------
20           Algodata Infosystems
16           Binnet & Hardley
21           Five Lakes Publishing
5            GGG&G
18           Lucerne Publishing
14           New Moon Books
17           Ramona Publishers
14           Scootney Books

(8 row(s) affected)
```

Related Topics

CAST and CONVERT, Data Types, System Functions

DATEADD

Returns a new **datetime** value based on adding an interval to the specified date.

Syntax

```
DATEADD ( datepart , number, date )
```

Arguments

datepart

Is the parameter that specifies on which part of the date to return a new value. The table lists the dateparts and abbreviations recognized by Microsoft SQL Server.

Datepart	Abbreviations
Year	yy, yyyy
quarter	qq, q
Month	mm, m
dayofyear	dy, y
Day	dd, d
Week	wk, ww
Hour	hh
minute	mi, n
second	ss, s
millisecond	ms

number

Is the value used to increment *datepart*. If you specify a value that is not an integer, the fractional part of the value is discarded. For example, if you specify **day** for *datepart* and **1.75** for *number*, *date* is incremented by 1.

date

Is an expression that returns a **datetime** or **smalldatetime** value, or a character string in a date format. For more information about specifying dates, see datetime and smalldatetime.

If you specify only the last two digits of the year, values less than or equal to the last two digits of the value of the **two digit year cutoff** configuration option are in the same century as the cutoff year. Values greater than the last two digits of the value of this option are in the century that precedes the cutoff year. For example, if **two digit year cutoff** is 2049 (default), 49 is interpreted as 2049 and 2050 is interpreted as 1950. To avoid ambiguity, use four-digit years.

Return Types

Returns **datetime**, but **smalldatetime** if the *date* argument is **smalldatetime**.

Examples

This example prints a listing of a time frame for titles in the **pubs** database. This time frame represents the existing publication date plus 21 days.

```
USE pubs
GO
SELECT DATEADD(day, 21, pubdate) AS timeframe
FROM titles
GO
```

Here is the result set:

```
timeframe
---------------------------
Jul  3 1991 12:00AM
Jun 30 1991 12:00AM
Jul 21 1991 12:00AM
Jul 13 1991 12:00AM
Jun 30 1991 12:00AM
Jul  9 1991 12:00AM
Mar 14 1997  5:09PM
Jul 21 1991 12:00AM
Jul  3 1994 12:00AM
Mar 14 1997  5:09PM
Nov 11 1991 12:00AM
Jul  6 1991 12:00AM
Oct 26 1991 12:00AM
Jul  3 1991 12:00AM
Jul  3 1991 12:00AM
Nov 11 1991 12:00AM
Jul  3 1991 12:00AM
Jul  3 1991 12:00AM

(18 row(s) affected)
```

Related Topics

CAST and CONVERT, Data Types, Date and Time Functions, Time Formats

DATEDIFF

Returns the number of date and time boundaries crossed between two specified dates.

Syntax

```
DATEDIFF ( datepart , startdate , enddate )
```

Arguments

datepart

Is the parameter that specifies on which part of the date to calculate the difference. The table lists dateparts and abbreviations recognized by Microsoft SQL Server.

Datepart	Abbreviations
Year	yy, yyyy
quarter	qq, q
Month	mm, m
dayofyear	dy, y
Day	dd, d
Week	wk, ww
Hour	hh
minute	mi, n
second	ss, s
millisecond	ms

startdate

Is the beginning date for the calculation. *startdate* is an expression that returns a **datetime** or **smalldatetime** value, or a character string in a date format.

Because **smalldatetime** is accurate only to the minute, when a **smalldatetime** value is used, seconds and milliseconds are always 0.

If you specify only the last two digits of the year, values less than or equal to the last two digits of the value of the **two digit year cutoff** configuration option are in the same century as the cutoff year. Values greater than the last two digits of the value of this option are in the century that precedes the cutoff year. For example, if the **two digit year cutoff** is 2049 (default), 49 is interpreted as 2049 and 2050 is interpreted as 1950. To avoid ambiguity, use four-digit years.

For more information about specifying time values, see Time Formats. For more information about specifying dates, see datetime and smalldatetime.

enddate

> Is the ending date for the calculation. *enddate* is an expression that returns a **datetime** or **smalldatetime** value, or a character string in a date format.

Return Types

integer

Remarks

startdate is subtracted from *enddate*. If *startdate* is later than *enddate*, a negative value is returned.

DATEDIFF produces an error if the result is out of range for integer values. For milliseconds, the maximum number is 24 days, 20 hours, 31 minutes and 23.647 seconds. For seconds, the maximum number is 68 years.

The method of counting crossed boundaries such as minutes, seconds, and milliseconds makes the result given by DATEDIFF consistent across all data types. The result is a signed integer value equal to the number of *datepart* boundaries crossed between the first and second date. For example, the number of weeks between Sunday, January 4, and Sunday, January 11, is 1.

Examples

This example determines the difference in days between the current date and the publication date for titles in the **pubs** database.

```
USE pubs
GO
SELECT DATEDIFF(day, pubdate, getdate()) AS no_of_days
FROM titles
GO
```

Related Topics

CAST and CONVERT, Data Types, Date and Time Functions

DATENAME

Returns a character string representing the specified datepart of the specified date.

Syntax

```
DATENAME ( datepart , date )
```

Arguments

datepart

Is the parameter that specifies the part of the date to return. The table lists dateparts and abbreviations recognized by Microsoft SQL Server.

Datepart	Abbreviations
year	yy, yyyy
quarter	qq, q
month	mm, m
dayofyear	dy, y
day	dd, d
week	wk, ww
weekday	dw
hour	hh
minute	mi, n
second	ss, s
millisecond	ms

The **weekday** (**dw**) datepart returns the day of the week (Sunday, Monday, and so on).

Is an expression that returns a **datetime** or **smalldatetime** value, or a character string in a date format. Use the **datetime** data type for dates after January 1, 1753. Store as character data for earlier dates. When entering **datetime** values, always enclose them in quotation marks. Because **smalldatetime** is accurate only to the minute, when a **smalldatetime** value is used, seconds and milliseconds are always 0. For more information about specifying dates, see datetime and smalldatetime. For more information about specifying time values, see Time Formats.

If you specify only the last two digits of the year, values less than or equal to the last two digits of the value of the **two digit year cutoff** configuration option are in the same century as the cutoff year. Values greater than the last two digits of the value of this option are in the century that precedes the cutoff year. For example, if **two digit year cutoff** is 2049 (default), 49 is interpreted as 2049 and 2050 is interpreted as 1950. To avoid ambiguity, use four-digit years.

Return Types

nvarchar

Remarks

SQL Server automatically converts between character and **datetime** values as necessary, for example, when you compare a character value with a **datetime** value.

Examples

This example extracts the month name from the date returned by GETDATE.

```
SELECT DATENAME(month, getdate()) AS 'Month Name'
```

Here is the result set:

```
Month Name
-------------------------------
February
```

Related Topics

CAST and CONVERT, Data Types, Date and Time Functions

DATEPART

Returns an integer representing the specified datepart of the specified date.

Syntax

```
DATEPART ( datepart , date )
```

Arguments

datepart

Is the parameter that specifies the part of the date to return. The table lists dateparts and abbreviations recognized by Microsoft SQL Server.

Datepart	Abbreviations
year	**yy, yyyy**
quarter	**qq, q**
month	**mm, m**
dayofyear	**dy, y**
day	**dd, d**

(continued)

(continued)

Datepart	Abbreviations
week	wk, ww
weekday	dw
hour	hh
minute	mi, n
second	ss, s
millisecond	ms

The **week** (**wk, ww**) datepart reflects changes made to SET DATEFIRST. January 1 of any year defines the starting number for the **week** datepart, for example: DATEPART(**wk**, 'Jan 1, xxxx') = 1, where xxxx is any year.

The **weekday** (**dw**) datepart returns a number that corresponds to the day of the week, for example: Sunday = 1, Saturday = 7. The number produced by the **weekday** datepart depends on the value set by SET DATEFIRST, which sets the first day of the week.

date

Is an expression that returns a **datetime** or **smalldatetime** value, or a character string in a date format. Use the **datetime** data type only for dates after January 1, 1753. Store dates as character data for earlier dates. When entering **datetime** values, always enclose them in quotation marks. Because **smalldatetime** is accurate only to the minute, when a **smalldatetime** value is used, seconds and milliseconds are always 0.

If you specify only the last two digits of the year, values less than or equal to the last two digits of the value of the **two digit year cutoff** configuration option are in the same century as the cutoff year. Values greater than the last two digits of the value of this option are in the century that precedes the cutoff year. For example, if **two digit year cutoff** is 2049 (default), 49 is interpreted as 2049 and 2050 is interpreted as 1950. To avoid ambiguity, use four-digit years.

For more information about specifying time values, see Time Formats. For more information about specifying dates, see datetime and smalldatetime.

Return Types

int

Remarks

The DAY, MONTH, and YEAR functions are synonyms for DATEPART(**dd**, *date*),
DATEPART(**mm**, *date*), and DATEPART(**yy**, *date*), respectively.

Examples

The GETDATE function returns the current date; however, the complete date is not
always the information needed for comparison (often only a portion of the date is
compared). This example shows the output of GETDATE as well as DATEPART.

```
SELECT GETDATE() AS 'Current Date'
GO
```

Here is the result set:

```
Current Date
---------------------------
Feb 18 1998 11:46PM

SELECT DATEPART(month, GETDATE()) AS 'Month Number'
GO
```

Here is the result set:

```
Month Number
------------
2
```

This example assumes the date May 29.

```
SELECT DATEPART(month, GETDATE())
GO
```

Here is the result set:

```
-----------
5

(1 row(s) affected)
```

In this example, the date is specified as a number. Notice that SQL Server interprets 0
as January 1, 1900.

```
SELECT DATEPART(m, 0), DATEPART(d, 0), DATEPART(yy, 0)
```

Here is the result set:

```
----- ------ ------
1     1       1900
```

Related Topics
CAST and CONVERT, Data Types, Date and Time Functions

datetime and smalldatetime

Date and time data types for representing date and time of day.

datetime

Date and time data from January 1, 1753 through December 31, 9999, to an accuracy of one three-hundredth of a second (equivalent to 3.33 milliseconds or 0.00333 seconds). Values are rounded to increments of .000, .003, or .007 seconds, as shown in the table.

Example	Rounded example
01/01/98 23:59:59.999	1998-01-02 00:00:00.000
01/01/98 23:59:59.995, 01/01/98 23:59:59.996, 01/01/98 23:59:59.997, or 01/01/98 23:59:59.998	1998-01-01 23:59:59.997
01/01/98 23:59:59.992, 01/01/98 23:59:59.993, 01/01/98 23:59:59.994	1998-01-01 23:59:59.993
01/01/98 23:59:59.990 or 01/01/98 23:59:59.991	1998-01-01 23:59:59.990

Microsoft SQL Server rejects all values it cannot recognize as dates between 1753 and 9999.

smalldatetime

Date and time data from January 1, 1900, through June 6, 2079, with accuracy to the minute. **smalldatetime** values with 29.998 seconds or lower are rounded down to the nearest minute; values with 29.999 seconds or higher are rounded up to the nearest minute.

```
--returns time as 12:35
SELECT CAST('2000-05-08 12:35:29.998' AS smalldatetime)
GO
--returns time as 12:36
SELECT CAST('2000-05-08 12:35:29.999' AS smalldatetime)
GO
```

Remarks

Values with the **datetime** data type are stored internally by Microsoft SQL Server as two 4-byte integers. The first 4 bytes store the number of days before or after the *base date*, January 1, 1900. The base date is the system reference date. Values for **datetime** earlier than January 1, 1753, are not permitted. The other 4 bytes store the time of day represented as the number of milliseconds after midnight.

The **smalldatetime** data type stores dates and times of day with less precision than **datetime**. SQL Server stores **smalldatetime** values as two 2-byte integers. The first 2 bytes store the number of days after January 1, 1900. The other 2 bytes store the number of minutes since midnight. Dates range from January 1, 1900, through June 6, 2079, with accuracy to the minute.

Related Topics

ALTER TABLE, CAST and CONVERT, CREATE TABLE, Data Type Conversion, Data Types, DECLARE @local_variable, DELETE, INSERT, SET @local_variable, UPDATE

DAY

Returns an integer representing the day datepart of the specified date.

Syntax

```
DAY ( date )
```

Arguments

date

    Is an expression of type **datetime** or **smalldatetime**.

Return Type

int

Remarks

This function is equivalent to DATEPART(**dd**, *date*).

Examples

This example returns the number of the day from the date 03/12/1998.

```
SELECT DAY('03/12/1998') AS 'Day Number'
GO
```

Here is the result set:

```
Day Number
-----------
12
```

In this example, the date is specified as a number. Notice that Microsoft SQL Server interprets 0 as January 1, 1900.

```
SELECT MONTH(0), DAY(0), YEAR(0)
```

Here is the result set.

```
----- ------ ------
1      1      1900
```

Related Topics

Date and Time Functions, datetime and smalldatetime, Expressions

---

DB_ID

Returns the database identification (ID) number.

Syntax

```
DB_ID ( [ 'database_name' ] )
```

Arguments

'*database_name*'
  Is the database name used to return the corresponding database ID. *database_name* is **nvarchar**. If *database_name* is omitted, the current database ID is returned.

Return Types

smallint

Examples

This example examines each database in **sysdatabases** using the database name to determine the database ID.

```
USE master
SELECT name, DB_ID(name) AS DB_ID
FROM sysdatabases
ORDER BY dbid
```

Here is the result set:

```
name                             DB_ID
-------------------------------- ------
master                           1
tempdb                           2
model                            3
msdb                             4
pubs                             5

(5 row(s) affected)
```

Related Topics

Metadata Functions

DB_NAME

Returns the database name.

Syntax

```
DB_NAME ( database_id )
```

Arguments

database_id

Is the identification number (ID) of the database to be returned. *database_id* is **smallint**, with no default. If no ID is specified, the current database name is returned.

Return Types

nvarchar(128)

Examples

This example examines each database in **sysdatabases** using the database identification number to determine the database name.

```
USE master
SELECT dbid, DB_NAME(dbid) AS DB_NAME
FROM sysdatabases
ORDER BY dbid
GO
```

Here is the result set:

```
dbid    DB_NAME
------  ------------------------------
1       master
2       tempdb
3       model
4       msdb
5       pubs

(5 row(s) affected)
```

Related Topics

Metadata Functions

DEALLOCATE

Removes a cursor reference. When the last cursor reference is deallocated, the data structures comprising the cursor are released by Microsoft SQL Server.

Syntax

```
DEALLOCATE { { [ GLOBAL ] cursor_name } | @cursor_variable_name }
```

Arguments

cursor_name
> Is the name of an already declared cursor. If both a global and a local cursor exist with *cursor_name* as their name, *cursor_name* refers to the global cursor if GLOBAL is specified and to the local cursor if GLOBAL is not specified.

@cursor_variable_name
> Is the name of a **cursor** variable. *@cursor_variable_name* must be of type **cursor**.

Remarks

Statements that operate on cursors use either a cursor name or a cursor variable to refer to the cursor. DEALLOCATE removes the association between a cursor and the cursor name or cursor variable. If a name or variable is the last one referencing the cursor, the cursor is deallocated and any resources used by the cursor are freed. Scroll locks used to protect the isolation of fetches are freed at DEALLOCATE. Transaction locks used to protect updates, including positioned updates made through the cursor, are held until the end of the transaction.

The DECLARE CURSOR statement allocates and associates a cursor with a cursor name:

```
DECLARE abc SCROLL CURSOR FOR
SELECT * FROM authors
```

After a cursor name is associated with a cursor, the name cannot be used for another cursor of the same scope (GLOBAL or LOCAL) until this cursor has been deallocated.

A cursor variable is associated with a cursor using one of two methods:

- By name using a SET statement that sets a cursor to a cursor variable:

```
DECLARE @MyCrsrRef CURSOR
SET @MyCrsrRef = abc
```

- A cursor can also be created and associated with a variable without having a cursor name defined:

```
DECLARE @MyCursor CURSOR
SET @MyCursor = CURSOR LOCAL SCROLL FOR
SELECT * FROM titles
```

A DEALLOCATE *@cursor_variable_name* statement removes only the reference of the named variable to the cursor. The variable is not deallocated until it goes out of scope at the end of the batch, stored procedure, or trigger. After a DEALLOCATE *@cursor_variable_name* statement, the variable can be associated with another cursor using the SET statement.

```
USE pubs
GO
DECLARE @MyCursor CURSOR
SET @MyCursor = CURSOR LOCAL SCROLL FOR
SELECT * FROM titles

DEALLOCATE @MyCursor

SET @MyCursor = CURSOR LOCAL SCROLL FOR
SELECT * FROM sales
GO
```

A cursor variable does not have to be explicitly deallocated. The variable is implicitly deallocated when it goes out of scope.

Permissions

DEALLOCATE permissions default to any valid user.

Examples

This script shows how cursors persist until the last name or until the variable referencing them has been deallocated.

```
USE pubs
GO
-- Create and open a global named cursor that
-- is visible outside the batch.
DECLARE abc CURSOR GLOBAL SCROLL FOR
SELECT * FROM authors
OPEN abc
GO
-- Reference the named cursor with a cursor variable.
DECLARE @MyCrsrRef1 CURSOR
SET @MyCrsrRef1 = abc
-- Now deallocate the cursor reference.
DEALLOCATE @MyCrsrRef1
-- Cursor abc still exists.
FETCH NEXT FROM abc
GO
-- Reference the named cursor again.
DECLARE @MyCrsrRef2 CURSOR
SET @MyCrsrRef2 = abc
-- Now deallocate cursor name abc.
DEALLOCATE abc
-- Cursor still exists, referenced by @MyCrsrRef2.
FETCH NEXT FROM @MyCrsrRef2
-- Cursor finally is deallocated when last referencing
-- variable goes out of scope at the end of the batch.
GO
-- Create an unnamed cursor.
DECLARE @MyCursor CURSOR
SET @MyCursor = CURSOR LOCAL SCROLL FOR
SELECT * FROM titles
-- The following statement deallocates the cursor
-- because no other variables reference it.
DEALLOCATE @MyCursor
GO
```

Related Topics

CLOSE, Cursors, DECLARE @local_variable, FETCH, OPEN

decimal and numeric

Numeric data types with fixed precision and scale.

decimal[(p[, s])] and **numeric**[(p[, s])]

Fixed precision and scale numbers. When maximum precision is used, valid values are from - 10^{38} +1 through 10^{38} - 1. The SQL-92 synonyms for **decimal** are **dec** and **dec**(p, s).

p (precision)

Specifies the maximum total number of decimal digits that can be stored, both to the left and to the right of the decimal point. The precision must be a value from 1 through the maximum precision. The maximum precision is 38.

s (scale)

Specifies the maximum number of decimal digits that can be stored to the right of the decimal point. Scale must be a value from 0 through p. The default scale is 0; therefore, $0 <= s <= p$. Maximum storage sizes vary, based on the precision.

Precision	Storage bytes
1–9	5
10–19	9
20–28	13
29–38	17

Related Topics

ALTER TABLE, CAST and CONVERT, CREATE TABLE, Data Type Conversion, Data Types, DECLARE @local_variable, DELETE, INSERT, SET @local_variable, Using Startup Options, UPDATE

DECLARE @local_variable

Variables are declared in the body of a batch or procedure with the DECLARE statement and are assigned values with either a SET or SELECT statement. Cursor variables can be declared with this statement and used with other cursor-related statements. After declaration, all variables are initialized as NULL.

Syntax

```
DECLARE
    {{ @local_variable data_type }
        | { @cursor_variable_name CURSOR }
        | { table_type_definition }
    } [ ,…n]

< table_type_definition > ::=
    TABLE ( { < column_definition > | < table_constraint > } [ ,… ]
        )

< column_definition > ::=
    column_name scalar_data_type
    [ COLLATE collation_name ]
    [ [ DEFAULT constant_expression ] | IDENTITY [ ( seed, increment ) ] ]
    [ ROWGUIDCOL ]
    [ < column_constraint > ]

< column_constraint > ::=
    { [ NULL | NOT NULL ]
    | [ PRIMARY KEY | UNIQUE ]
    | CHECK ( logical_expression )
    }

< table_constraint > ::=
    { { PRIMARY KEY | UNIQUE } ( column_name [ ,… ] )
    | CHECK ( search_condition )
    }
```

Arguments

@local_variable

Is the name of a variable. Variable names must begin with an at sign (@). Local variable names must conform to the rules for identifiers. For more information, see Using Identifiers.

data_type

Is any system-supplied or user-defined data type. A variable cannot be of **text**, **ntext**, or **image** data type. For more information about system data types, see Data Types. For more information about user-defined data types, see sp_addtype.

@cursor_variable_name

Is the name of a cursor variable. Cursor variable names must begin with an at sign (@) and conform to the rules for identifiers.

CURSOR

Specifies that the variable is a local, cursor variable.

table_type_definition

Defines the table data type. The table declaration includes column definitions, names, data types, and constraints. The only constraint types allowed are PRIMARY KEY, UNIQUE KEY, NULL, and CHECK.

table_type_definition is a subset of information used to define a table in CREATE TABLE. Elements and essential definitions are included here; for more information, see CREATE TABLE.

n

Is a placeholder indicating that multiple variables can be specified and assigned values. When declaring table variables, the table variable must be the only variable being declared in the DECLARE statement.

column_name

Is the name of the column in the table.

scalar_data_type

Specifies that the column is a scalar data type.

[COLLATE *collation_name*]

Specifies the collation for the column. *collation_name* can be either a Windows collation name or an SQL collation name, and is applicable only for columns of the **char**, **varchar**, **text**, **nchar**, **nvarchar**, and **ntext** data types. If not specified, the column is assigned either the collation of the user-defined data type (if the column is of a user-defined data type), or the default collation of the database.

For more information about the Windows and SQL collation names, see COLLATE.

DEFAULT

Specifies the value provided for the column when a value is not explicitly supplied during an insert. DEFAULT definitions can be applied to any columns except those defined as **timestamp**, or those with the IDENTITY property. DEFAULT definitions are removed when the table is dropped. Only a constant value, such as a character string; a system function, such as a SYSTEM_USER(); or NULL can be used as a default. To maintain compatibility with earlier versions of SQL Server, a constraint name can be assigned to a DEFAULT.

constant_expression

Is a constant, NULL, or a system function used as the default value for the column.

IDENTITY

Indicates that the new column is an identity column. When a new row is added to the table, SQL Server provides a unique, incremental value for the column. Identity columns are commonly used in conjunction with PRIMARY KEY constraints to serve as the unique row identifier for the table. The IDENTITY property can be assigned to **tinyint**, **smallint**, **int**, **decimal(p,0)**, or **numeric(p,0)** columns. Only one identity column can be created per table. Bound defaults and DEFAULT constraints cannot be used with an identity column. You must specify both the seed and increment, or neither. If neither is specified, the default is (1,1).

seed

Is the value used for the very first row loaded into the table.

increment

Is the incremental value added to the identity value of the previous row that was loaded.

ROWGUIDCOL

Indicates that the new column is a row global unique identifier column. Only one **uniqueidentifier** column per table can be designated as the ROWGUIDCOL column. The ROWGUIDCOL property can be assigned only to a **uniqueidentifier** column.

NULL | NOT NULL

Are keywords that determine whether or not null values are allowed in the column.

PRIMARY KEY

Is a constraint that enforces entity integrity for a given column or columns through a unique index. Only one PRIMARY KEY constraint can be created per table.

UNIQUE

Is a constraint that provides entity integrity for a given column or columns through a unique index. A table can have multiple UNIQUE constraints.

CHECK

Is a constraint that enforces domain integrity by limiting the possible values that can be entered into a column or columns.

logical_expression

Is a logical expression that returns TRUE or FALSE.

Remarks

Variables are often used in a batch or procedure as counters for WHILE, LOOP, or for an IF...ELSE block.

Variables can be used only in expressions, not in place of object names or keywords. To construct dynamic SQL statements, use EXECUTE.

The scope of a local variable is the batch, stored procedure, or statement block in which it is declared. For more information about using local variables in statement blocks, see Using BEGIN...END.

A cursor variable that currently has a cursor assigned to it can be referenced as a source in a:

- CLOSE statement.
- DEALLOCATE statement.
- FETCH statement.

- OPEN statement.
- Positioned DELETE or UPDATE statement.
- SET CURSOR variable statement (on the right side).

In all these statements, Microsoft SQL Server raises an error if a referenced cursor variable exists but does not have a cursor currently allocated to it. If a referenced cursor variable does not exist, SQL Server raises the same error raised for an undeclared variable of another type.

A cursor variable:

- Can be the target of either a cursor type or another cursor variable. For more information, see SET @local_variable.
- Can be referenced as the target of an output cursor parameter in an EXECUTE statement if the cursor variable does not have a cursor currently assigned to it.
- Should be regarded as a pointer to the cursor. For more information about cursor variables, see Transact-SQL Cursors.

Examples

A. Use DECLARE

This example uses a local variable named **@find** to retrieve author information for all authors with last names beginning with Ring.

```
USE pubs
DECLARE @find varchar(30)
SET @find = 'Ring%'
SELECT au_lname, au_fname, phone
FROM authors
WHERE au_lname LIKE @find
```

Here is the result set:

```
au_lname                                au_fname              phone
------------------------------------    --------------------  ------------
Ringer                                  Anne                  801 826-0752
Ringer                                  Albert                801 826-0752

(2 row(s) affected)
```

B. Use DECLARE with two variables

This example retrieves employee names from employees of Binnet & Hardley (**pub_id** = 0877) who were hired on or after January 1, 1993.

```
USE pubs
SET NOCOUNT ON
GO
DECLARE @pub_id char(4), @hire_date datetime
SET @pub_id = '0877'
SET @hire_date = '1/01/93'
-- Here is the SELECT statement syntax to assign values to two local
-- variables.
-- SELECT @pub_id = '0877', @hire_date = '1/01/93'
SET NOCOUNT OFF
SELECT fname, lname
FROM employee
WHERE pub_id = @pub_id and hire_date >= @hire_date
```

Here is the result set:

```
fname                  lname
-------------------    -----------------------------
Anabela                Domingues
Paul                   Henriot

(2 row(s) affected)
```

Related Topics

EXECUTE, Functions, SELECT, table

DECLARE CURSOR

Defines the attributes of a Transact-SQL server cursor, such as its scrolling behavior and the query used to build the result set on which the cursor operates. DECLARE CURSOR accepts both a syntax based on the SQL-92 standard and a syntax using a set of Transact-SQL extensions.

SQL-92 Syntax

```
DECLARE cursor_name [ INSENSITIVE ] [ SCROLL ] CURSOR
FOR select_statement
[ FOR { READ ONLY | UPDATE [ OF column_name [ ,...n ] ] } ]
```

Transact-SQL Extended Syntax

```
DECLARE cursor_name CURSOR
[ LOCAL | GLOBAL ]
[ FORWARD_ONLY | SCROLL ]
[ STATIC | KEYSET | DYNAMIC | FAST_FORWARD ]
[ READ_ONLY | SCROLL_LOCKS | OPTIMISTIC ]
[ TYPE_WARNING ]
FOR select_statement
[ FOR UPDATE [ OF column_name [ ,...n ] ] ]
```

SQL-92 Arguments

cursor_name

Is the name of the Transact-SQL server cursor defined. *cursor_name* must conform to the rules for identifiers. For more information about rules for identifiers, see Using Identifiers.

INSENSITIVE

Defines a cursor that makes a temporary copy of the data to be used by the cursor. All requests to the cursor are answered from this temporary table in **tempdb**; therefore, modifications made to base tables are not reflected in the data returned by fetches made to this cursor, and this cursor does not allow modifications. When SQL-92 syntax is used, if INSENSITIVE is omitted, committed deletes and updates made to the underlying tables (by any user) are reflected in subsequent fetches.

SCROLL

Specifies that all fetch options (FIRST, LAST, PRIOR, NEXT, RELATIVE, ABSOLUTE) are available. If SCROLL is not specified in an SQL-92 DECLARE CURSOR, NEXT is the only fetch option supported. SCROLL cannot be specified if FAST_FORWARD is also specified.

select_statement

Is a standard SELECT statement that defines the result set of the cursor. The keywords COMPUTE, COMPUTE BY, FOR BROWSE, and INTO are not allowed within *select_statement* of a cursor declaration.

Microsoft SQL Server implicitly converts the cursor to another type if clauses in *select_statement* conflict with the functionality of the requested cursor type. For more information, see Implicit Cursor Conversions.

READ ONLY

    Prevents updates made through this cursor. The cursor cannot be referenced in a WHERE CURRENT OF clause in an UPDATE or DELETE statement. This option overrides the default capability of a cursor to be updated.

UPDATE [OF *column_name* [,...*n*]]

    Defines updateable columns within the cursor. If OF *column_name* [,...*n*] is specified, only the columns listed allow modifications. If UPDATE is specified without a column list, all columns can be updated.

Transact-SQL Extended Arguments

cursor_name

    Is the name of the Transact-SQL server cursor defined. *cursor_name* must conform to the rules for identifiers. For more information about rules for identifiers, see Using Identifiers.

LOCAL

    Specifies that the scope of the cursor is local to the batch, stored procedure, or trigger in which the cursor was created. The cursor name is only valid within this scope. The cursor can be referenced by local cursor variables in the batch, stored procedure, or trigger, or a stored procedure OUTPUT parameter. An OUTPUT parameter is used to pass the local cursor back to the calling batch, stored procedure, or trigger, which can assign the parameter to a cursor variable to reference the cursor after the stored procedure terminates. The cursor is implicitly deallocated when the batch, stored procedure, or trigger terminates, unless the cursor was passed back in an OUTPUT parameter. If it is passed back in an OUTPUT parameter, the cursor is deallocated when the last variable referencing it is deallocated or goes out of scope.

GLOBAL

    Specifies that the scope of the cursor is global to the connection. The cursor name can be referenced in any stored procedure or batch executed by the connection. The cursor is only implicitly deallocated at disconnect.

    Note   If neither GLOBAL or LOCAL is specified, the default is controlled by the setting of the **default to local cursor** database option. In SQL Server version 7.0, this option defaults to FALSE to match earlier versions of SQL Server, in which all cursors were global. The default of this option may change in future versions of SQL Server. For more information, see Setting Database Options.

FORWARD_ONLY

Specifies that the cursor can only be scrolled from the first to the last row. FETCH NEXT is the only supported fetch option. If FORWARD_ONLY is specified without the STATIC, KEYSET, or DYNAMIC keywords, the cursor operates as a DYNAMIC cursor. When neither FORWARD_ONLY nor SCROLL is specified, FORWARD_ONLY is the default, unless the keywords STATIC, KEYSET, or DYNAMIC are specified. STATIC, KEYSET, and DYNAMIC cursors default to SCROLL. Unlike database APIs such as ODBC and ADO, FORWARD_ONLY is supported with STATIC, KEYSET, and DYNAMIC Transact-SQL cursors. FAST_FORWARD and FORWARD_ONLY are mutually exclusive; if one is specified the other cannot be specified.

STATIC

Defines a cursor that makes a temporary copy of the data to be used by the cursor. All requests to the cursor are answered from this temporary table in **tempdb**; therefore, modifications made to base tables are not reflected in the data returned by fetches made to this cursor, and this cursor does not allow modifications.

KEYSET

Specifies that the membership and order of rows in the cursor are fixed when the cursor is opened. The set of keys that uniquely identify the rows is built into a table in **tempdb** known as the **keyset**. Changes to nonkey values in the base tables, either made by the cursor owner or committed by other users, are visible as the owner scrolls around the cursor. Inserts made by other users are not visible (inserts cannot be made through a Transact-SQL server cursor). If a row is deleted, an attempt to fetch the row returns an @@FETCH_STATUS of -2. Updates of key values from outside the cursor resemble a delete of the old row followed by an insert of the new row. The row with the new values is not visible, and attempts to fetch the row with the old values return an @@FETCH_STATUS of -2. The new values are visible if the update is done through the cursor by specifying the WHERE CURRENT OF clause.

DYNAMIC

Defines a cursor that reflects all data changes made to the rows in its result set as you scroll around the cursor. The data values, order, and membership of the rows can change on each fetch. The ABSOLUTE fetch option is not supported with dynamic cursors.

FAST_FORWARD

Specifies a FORWARD_ONLY, READ_ONLY cursor with performance optimizations enabled. FAST_FORWARD cannot be specified if SCROLL or FOR_UPDATE is also specified. FAST_FORWARD and FORWARD_ONLY are mutually exclusive; if one is specified the other cannot be specified.

READ_ONLY

Prevents updates made through this cursor. The cursor cannot be referenced in a WHERE CURRENT OF clause in an UPDATE or DELETE statement. This option overrides the default capability of a cursor to be updated.

SCROLL_LOCKS

Specifies that positioned updates or deletes made through the cursor are guaranteed to succeed. Microsoft SQL Server locks the rows as they are read into the cursor to ensure their availability for later modifications. SCROLL_LOCKS cannot be specified if FAST_FORWARD is also specified.

OPTIMISTIC

Specifies that positioned updates or deletes made through the cursor do not succeed if the row has been updated since it was read into the cursor. SQL Server does not lock rows as they are read into the cursor. It instead uses comparisons of **timestamp** column values, or a checksum value if the table has no **timestamp** column, to determine whether the row was modified after it was read into the cursor. If the row was modified, the attempted positioned update or delete fails. OPTIMISTIC cannot be specified if FAST_FORWARD is also specified.

TYPE_WARNING

Specifies that a warning message is sent to the client if the cursor is implicitly converted from the requested type to another.

select_statement

Is a standard SELECT statement that defines the result set of the cursor. The keywords COMPUTE, COMPUTE BY, FOR BROWSE, and INTO are not allowed within *select_statement* of a cursor declaration.

SQL Server implicitly converts the cursor to another type if clauses in *select_statement* conflict with the functionality of the requested cursor type. For more information, see Implicit Cursor Conversions.

UPDATE [OF *column_name* [,...*n*]]

Defines updateable columns within the cursor. If OF *column_name* [,...*n*] is supplied, only the columns listed allow modifications. If UPDATE is specified without a column list, all columns can be updated, unless the READ_ONLY concurrency option was specified.

Remarks

DECLARE CURSOR defines the attributes of a Transact-SQL server cursor, such as its scrolling behavior and the query used to build the result set on which the cursor operates. The OPEN statement populates the result set, and FETCH returns a row from the result set. The CLOSE statement releases the current result set associated with the cursor. The DEALLOCATE statement releases the resources used by the cursor.

The first form of the DECLARE CURSOR statement uses the SQL-92 syntax for declaring cursor behaviors. The second form of DECLARE CURSOR uses Transact-SQL extensions that allow you to define cursors using the same cursor types used in the database API cursor functions of ODBC, ADO, and DB-Library.

You cannot mix the two forms. If you specify the SCROLL or INSENSITIVE keywords before the CURSOR keyword, you cannot use any keywords between the CURSOR and FOR *select_statement* keywords. If you specify any keywords between the CURSOR and FOR *select_statement* keywords, you cannot specify SCROLL or INSENSITIVE before the CURSOR keyword.

If a DECLARE CURSOR using Transact-SQL syntax does not specify READ_ONLY, OPTIMISTIC, or SCROLL_LOCKS, the default is as follows:

- If the SELECT statement does not support updates (insufficient permissions, accessing remote tables that do not support updates, and so on), the cursor is READ_ONLY.
- STATIC and FAST_FORWARD cursors default to READ_ONLY.
- DYNAMIC and KEYSET cursors default to OPTIMISTIC.

Cursor names can be referenced only by other Transact-SQL statements. They cannot be referenced by database API functions. For example, after declaring a cursor, the cursor name cannot be referenced from OLE DB, ODBC, ADO, or DB-Library functions or methods. The cursor rows cannot be fetched using the fetch functions or methods of the APIs; the rows can be fetched only by Transact-SQL FETCH statements.

After a cursor has been declared, these system stored procedures can be used to determine the characteristics of the cursor.

System stored procedure	Description
sp_cursor_list	Returns a list of cursors currently visible on the connection and their attributes.
sp_describe_cursor	Describes the attributes of a cursor, such as whether it is a forward-only or scrolling cursor.
sp_describe_cursor_columns	Describes the attributes of the columns in the cursor result set.
sp_describe_cursor_tables	Describes the base tables accessed by the cursor.

Variables may be used as part of the *select_statement* that declares a cursor. However, changes to those variables after the cursor has been declared will have no affect on the cursor's operation.

Permissions
DECLARE CURSOR permissions default to any user that has SELECT permissions on the views, tables, and columns used in the cursor.

Examples

A. Use simple cursor and syntax

The result set generated at the opening of this cursor includes all rows and all columns in the **authors** table of the **pubs** database. This cursor can be updated, and all updates and deletes are represented in fetches made against this cursor. FETCH NEXT is the only fetch available because the SCROLL option has not been specified.

```
DECLARE authors_cursor CURSOR
   FOR SELECT * FROM authors
OPEN authors_cursor
FETCH NEXT FROM authors_cursor
```

B. Use nested cursors to produce report output

This example shows how cursors can be nested to produce complex reports. The inner cursor is declared for each author.

```
SET NOCOUNT ON

DECLARE @au_id varchar(11), @au_fname varchar(20), @au_lname varchar(40),
   @message varchar(80), @title varchar(80)

PRINT "-------- Utah Authors report --------"

DECLARE authors_cursor CURSOR FOR
SELECT au_id, au_fname, au_lname
FROM authors
WHERE state = "UT"
ORDER BY au_id

OPEN authors_cursor

FETCH NEXT FROM authors_cursor
INTO @au_id, @au_fname, @au_lname

WHILE @@FETCH_STATUS = 0
BEGIN
   PRINT " "
   SELECT @message = "----- Books by Author: " +
      @au_fname + " " + @au_lname

   PRINT @message
```

(continued)

(continued)

```
    -- Declare an inner cursor based
    -- on au_id from the outer cursor.

    DECLARE titles_cursor CURSOR FOR
    SELECT t.title
    FROM titleauthor ta, titles t
    WHERE ta.title_id = t.title_id AND
    ta.au_id = @au_id  -- Variable value from the outer cursor

    OPEN titles_cursor
    FETCH NEXT FROM titles_cursor INTO @title

    IF @@FETCH_STATUS <> 0
        PRINT "          <<No Books>>"

    WHILE @@FETCH_STATUS = 0
    BEGIN

        SELECT @message = "          " + @title
        PRINT @message
        FETCH NEXT FROM titles_cursor INTO @title

    END

    CLOSE titles_cursor
    DEALLOCATE titles_cursor

    -- Get the next author.
    FETCH NEXT FROM authors_cursor
    INTO @au_id, @au_fname, @au_lname
END

CLOSE authors_cursor
DEALLOCATE authors_cursor
GO

-------- Utah Authors report --------
```

(continued)

(continued)

```
----- Books by Author: Anne Ringer
        The Gourmet Microwave
        Is Anger the Enemy?

----- Books by Author: Albert Ringer
        Is Anger the Enemy?
        Life Without Fear
```

Related Topics

@@FETCH_STATUS, CLOSE, Cursors, DEALLOCATE, FETCH, OPEN, SELECT, sp_configure

DEGREES

Given an angle in radians, returns the corresponding angle in degrees.

Syntax

```
DEGREES ( numeric_expression )
```

Arguments

numeric_expression

Is an expression of the exact numeric or approximate numeric data type category, except for the **bit** data type.

Return Code Values

Returns the same type as *numeric_expression*.

Examples

This example returns the number of degrees in an angle of PI/2 radians.

```
SELECT 'The number of degrees in PI/2 radians is: ' +
CONVERT(varchar, DEGREES((PI()/2)))
GO
```

Here is the result set:

```
The number of degrees in PI/2 radians is 90

(1 row(s) affected)
```

Related Topics

Mathematical Functions

DELETE

Removes rows from a table.

Syntax

```
DELETE
    [ FROM ]
        { table_name WITH ( < table_hint_limited > [ ...n ] )
        | view_name
        | rowset_function_limited
        }

        [ FROM { < table_source > } [ ,...n ] ]
    [ WHERE
        { < search_condition >
        | { [ CURRENT OF
                { { [ GLOBAL ] cursor_name }
                    | cursor_variable_name
                }
            ] }
        }
    ]
    [ OPTION ( < query_hint > [ ,...n ] ) ]
< table_source > ::=
    table_name [ [ AS ] table_alias ] [ WITH ( < table_hint > [ ,...n ] ) ]
    | view_name [ [ AS ] table_alias ]
    | rowset_function [ [ AS ] table_alias ]
    | derived_table [ AS ] table_alias [ ( column_alias [ ,...n ] ) ]
    | < joined_table >
< joined_table > ::=
    < table_source > < join_type > < table_source > ON < search_condition >
    | < table_source > CROSS JOIN < table_source >
```

(continued)

(continued)

```
   | < joined_table >
< join_type > ::=
  [ INNER | { { LEFT | RIGHT | FULL } [OUTER] } ]
  [ < join_hint > ]
  JOIN
< table_hint_limited > ::=
  { FASTFIRSTROW
      | HOLDLOCK
      | PAGLOCK
      | READCOMMITTED
      | REPEATABLEREAD
      | ROWLOCK
      | SERIALIZABLE
      | TABLOCK
      | TABLOCKX
      | UPDLOCK
  }
< table_hint > ::=
  { INDEX ( index_val [ ,...n ] )
      | FASTFIRSTROW
      | HOLDLOCK
      | NOLOCK
      | PAGLOCK
      | READCOMMITTED
      | READPAST
      | READUNCOMMITTED
      | REPEATABLEREAD
      | ROWLOCK
      | SERIALIZABLE
      | TABLOCK
      | TABLOCKX
      | UPDLOCK
  }
< query_hint > ::=
  { { HASH | ORDER } GROUP
      | { CONCAT | HASH | MERGE } UNION
      | FAST number_rows
      | FORCE ORDER
      | MAXDOP
      | ROBUST PLAN
      | KEEP PLAN
  }
```

Arguments

FROM

> Is an optional keyword that can be used between the DELETE keyword and the target *table_name*, *view_name*, or *rowset_function_limited*.

table_name

> Is the name of the table from which the rows are to be removed.
>
> A **table** variable, within its scope, or a four-part table name (or view name) using the OPENDATASOURCE function as the server name also may be used as a table source in a DELETE statement.

WITH (<table_hint_limited> [...*n*])

> Specifies one or more table hints that are allowed for a target table. The WITH keyword and the parentheses are required. READPAST, NOLOCK, and READUNCOMMITTED are not allowed. For more information about table hints, see FROM.

view_name

> Is the name of a view. The view referenced by *view_name* must be updateable and reference exactly one base table in the FROM clause of the view. For more information about updateable views, see CREATE VIEW.
>
> > **Note**   If the table or view exists in another database or has an owner other than the current user, use a four-part qualified name in the format *server_name.database.[owner].object_name*. For more information, see Transact-SQL Syntax Conventions.

rowset_function_limited

> Is either the OPENQUERY or OPENROWSET function, subject to provider capabilities. For more information about capabilities needed by the provider, see UPDATE and DELETE Requirements for OLE DB Providers. For more information about the rowset functions, see OPENQUERY and OPENROWSET.

FROM <table_source>

> Specifies an additional FROM clause. This Transact-SQL extension to DELETE allows you to specify data from <table_sources> and delete corresponding rows from the table in the first FROM clause.
>
> This extension, specifying a join, can be used instead of a subquery in the WHERE clause to identify rows to be removed.

table_name [[AS] *table_alias*]

> Is the name of the table to provide criteria values for the delete operation.

view_name [[AS] *table_alias*]

> Is the name of the view to provide criteria values for the delete operation.
> A view with INSTEAD OF UPDATE trigger cannot be a target of an UPDATE with a FROM clause.

WITH (<table_hint>
>   Specifies one or more table hints. For more information about table hints, see
>   FROM.

rowset_function [[AS] *table_alias*]
>   Is the name of a rowset function and an optional alias. For more information
>   about a list of rowset functions, see Rowset Functions.

derived_table [AS] *table_alias*
>   Is a subquery that retrieves rows from the database. *derived_table* is used as
>   input to the outer query.

column_alias
>   Is an optional alias to replace a column name in the result set. Include one
>   column alias for each column in the select list, and enclose the entire list of
>   column aliases in parentheses.

<joined_table>
>   Is a result set that is the product of two or more tables, for example:

```
SELECT *
FROM tab1 LEFT OUTER JOIN tab2 ON tab1.c3 = tab2.c3
    RIGHT OUTER JOIN tab3 LEFT OUTER JOIN tab4
        ON tab3.c1 = tab4.c1
        ON tab2.c3 = tab4.c3
```

For multiple CROSS joins, use parentheses to change the natural order of the joins.

<join_type>
>   Specifies the type of join operation.

INNER
>   Specifies all matching pairs of rows are returned. Discards unmatched rows
>   from both tables. This is the default if no join type is specified.

LEFT [OUTER]
>   Specifies that all rows from the left table not meeting the specified condition
>   are included in the result set, and output columns from the right table are set to
>   NULL in addition to all rows returned by the inner join.

RIGHT [OUTER]
>   Specifies that all rows from the right table not meeting the specified condition
>   are included in the result set, and output columns from the left table are set to
>   NULL in addition to all rows returned by the inner join.

FULL [OUTER]
>   If a row from either the left or right table does not match the selection criteria,
>   specifies the row be included in the result set, and output columns that
>   correspond to the other table be set to NULL. This is in addition to all rows
>   usually returned by the inner join.

JOIN

> Is a keyword to indicate that an SQL-92 style join be used in the delete operation.

ON <search_condition>

> Specifies the condition on which the join is based. The condition can specify any predicate, although columns and comparison operators are often used, for example:

```
FROM Suppliers JOIN Products
   ON (Suppliers.SupplierID = Products.SupplierID)
```

> When the condition specifies columns, they need not have the same name or same data type; however, if the data types are not identical, they must be either compatible or types that Microsoft SQL Server can implicitly convert. If the data types cannot be implicitly converted, the condition must explicitly convert the data type using the CAST function.

> For more information about search conditions and predicates, see Search Condition.

CROSS JOIN

> Specifies the cross-product of two tables. Returns the same rows as if no WHERE clause was specified in an old-style, non-SQL-92-style join.

WHERE

> Specifies the conditions used to limit the number of rows that are deleted. If a WHERE clause is not supplied, DELETE removes all the rows from the table. There are two forms of delete operations based on what is specified in the WHERE clause:

- Searched deletes specify a search condition to qualify the rows to delete.

- Positioned deletes use the CURRENT OF clause to specify a cursor. The delete operation occurs at the current position of the cursor. This can be more accurate than a searched DELETE that uses a WHERE *search_condition* clause to qualify the rows to be deleted. A searched DELETE deletes multiple rows if the search condition does not uniquely identify a single row.

<search_condition>

> Specifies the restricting conditions for the rows to be deleted. There is no limit to the number of predicates that can be included in a search condition. For more information, see Search Condition.

CURRENT OF

> Specifies that the DELETE is done at the current position of the specified cursor.

GLOBAL

> Specifies that *cursor_name* refers to a global cursor.

cursor_name

Is the name of the open cursor from which the fetch is made. If both a global and a local cursor with the name *cursor_name* exist, this argument refers to the global cursor if GLOBAL is specified, and to the local cursor otherwise. The cursor must allow updates.

cursor_variable_name

Is the name of a cursor variable. The cursor variable must reference a cursor that allows updates.

OPTION (<query_hint> [,...*n*])

Are keywords indicating that optimizer hints are used to customize SQL Server's processing of the statement.

{HASH | ORDER} GROUP

Specifies that the aggregations specified in the GROUP BY or COMPUTE clause of the query should use hashing or ordering.

{MERGE | HASH | CONCAT} UNION

Specifies that all UNION operations should be performed by merging, hashing, or concatenating UNION sets. If more than one UNION hint is specified, the query optimizer selects the least expensive strategy from those hints specified.

Note   If a <joint_hint> is also specified for any particular pair of joined tables in the FROM clause, it takes precedence over any <join_hint> specified in the OPTION clause.

FAST *number_rows*

Specifies that the query is optimized for fast retrieval of the first *number_rows* (a nonnegative integer). After the first *number_rows* are returned, the query continues execution and produces its full result set.

FORCE ORDER

Specifies that the join order indicated by the query syntax is preserved during query optimization.

MAXDOP *number*

Overrides the **max degree of parallelism** configuration option (of **sp_configure**) only for the query specifying this option. All semantic rules used with **max degree of parallelism** configuration option are applicable when using the MAXDOP query hint. For more information, see max degree of parallelism Option.

ROBUST PLAN

Forces the query optimizer to attempt a plan that works for the maximum potential row size at the expense of performance. If such a plan is not possible, the query optimizer returns an error rather than deferring error detection to query execution. Rows may contain variable-length columns; SQL Server allows rows to be defined that have a maximum potential size beyond the ability of SQL Server to process them. Usually, despite the maximum potential size, an application stores rows that have actual sizes within the limits that SQL Server can process. If SQL Server encounters a row that is too long, an execution error is returned.

KEEP PLAN

Forces the query optimizer to relax the estimated recompile threshold for a query. The estimated recompile threshold is the point at which a query is automatically recompiled when the estimated number of indexed column changes (update, delete or insert) have been made to a table. Specifying KEEP PLAN ensures that a query will not be recompiled as frequently when there are multiple updates to a table.

Remarks

DELETE may be used in the body of a user-defined function if the object modified is a **table** variable.

A four-part table name (or view name) using the OPENDATASOURCE function as the server name may be used as a table source in all places a table name can appear.

The DELETE statement may fail if it violates a trigger or attempts to remove a row referenced by data in another table with a FOREIGN KEY constraint. If the DELETE removes multiple rows, and any one of the removed rows violates a trigger or constraint, the statement is canceled, an error is returned, and no rows are removed.

When an INSTEAD-OF trigger is defined on DELETE actions against a table or view, the trigger executes *instead of* the DELETE statement. Earlier versions of SQL Server only support AFTER triggers on DELETE and other data modification statements.

When a DELETE statement encounters an arithmetic error (overflow, divide by zero, or a domain error) occurring during expression evaluation, SQL Server handles these errors as if SET ARITHABORT is ON. The remainder of the batch is canceled, and an error message is returned.

The setting of the SET ROWCOUNT option is ignored for DELETE statements against remote tables and local and remote partitioned views.

If you want to delete all the rows in a table, TRUNCATE TABLE is faster than DELETE. DELETE physically removes rows one at a time and records each deleted row in the transaction log. TRUNCATE TABLE deallocates all pages associated with the table. For this reason, TRUNCATE TABLE is faster and requires less transaction log space than DELETE. TRUNCATE TABLE is functionally equivalent to DELETE with no WHERE clause, but TRUNCATE TABLE cannot be used with tables referenced by foreign keys. Both DELETE and TRUNCATE TABLE make the space occupied by the deleted rows available for the storage of new data.

Permissions

DELETE permissions default to members of the **sysadmin** fixed server role, the **db_owner** and **db_datawriter** fixed database roles, and the table owner. Members of the **sysadmin**, **db_owner**, and the **db_securityadmin** roles, and the table owner can transfer permissions to other users.

SELECT permissions are also required if the statement contains a WHERE clause.

Examples

A. Use DELETE with no parameters

This example deletes all rows from the **authors** table.

```
USE pubs
DELETE authors
```

B. Use DELETE on a set of rows

Because **au_lname** may not be unique, this example deletes all rows in which **au_lname** is McBadden.

```
USE pubs
DELETE FROM authors
WHERE au_lname = 'McBadden'
```

C. Use DELETE on the current row of a cursor

This example shows a delete made against a cursor named **complex_join_cursor**. It affects only the single row currently fetched from the cursor.

```
USE pubs
DELETE FROM authors
WHERE CURRENT OF complex_join_cursor
```

D. Use DELETE based on a subquery or use the Transact-SQL extension

This example shows the Transact-SQL extension used to delete records from a base table that is based on a join or correlated subquery. The first DELETE shows the SQL-92-compatible subquery solution, and the second DELETE shows the Transact-SQL extension. Both queries remove rows from the **titleauthors** table based on the titles stored in the **titles** table.

```
/* SQL-92-Standard subquery */
USE pubs
DELETE FROM titleauthor
WHERE title_id IN
    (SELECT title_id
    FROM titles
    WHERE title LIKE '%computers%')

/* Transact-SQL extension */
USE pubs
DELETE titleauthor
FROM titleauthor INNER JOIN titles
    ON titleauthor.title_id = titles.title_id
WHERE titles.title LIKE '%computers%'
```

E. Use DELETE and a SELECT with the TOP Clause

Because a SELECT statement can be specified in a DELETE statement, the TOP clause can also be used within the SELECT statement. For example, this example deletes the top 10 authors from the **authors** table.

```
DELETE authors
FROM (SELECT TOP 10 * FROM authors) AS t1
WHERE authors.au_id = t1.au_id
```

Related Topics

CREATE TABLE, CREATE TRIGGER, Cursors, DROP TABLE, INSERT, SELECT, TRUNCATE TABLE, UPDATE

DENY

Creates an entry in the security system that denies a permission from a security account in the current database and prevents the security account from inheriting the permission through its group or role memberships.

Syntax

Statement permissions:

```
DENY { ALL | statement [ ,...n ] }
TO security_account [ ,...n ]
```

Object permissions:

```
DENY
    { ALL [ PRIVILEGES ] | permission [ ,...n ] }
    {
        [ ( column [ ,...n ] ) ] ON { table | view }
        | ON { table | view } [ ( column [ ,...n ] ) ]
        | ON { stored_procedure | extended_procedure }
        | ON { user_defined_function }
    }
TO security_account [ ,...n ]
[ CASCADE ]
```

Arguments

ALL

Specifies that all applicable permissions are denied. For statement permissions, ALL can be used only by members of the **sysadmin** role. For object permissions, ALL can be used by members of the **sysadmin** and **db_owner** roles, and database object owners.

statement

Is the statement for which permission is denied. The statement list can include:

- CREATE DATABASE
- CREATE DEFAULT
- CREATE FUNCTION
- CREATE PROCEDURE
- CREATE RULE
- CREATE TABLE
- CREATE VIEW
- BACKUP DATABASE
- BACKUP LOG

n

Is a placeholder indicating that the item can be repeated in a comma-separated list.

TO

Specifies the security account list.

security_account

Is the name of the security account in the current database affected by the denied permission. The security account can be a:

- Microsoft SQL Server user.

- SQL Server role.

- Microsoft Windows NT user.

- Windows NT group.

When a permission is denied from a SQL Server user or Windows NT user account, the specified *security_account* is the only account affected by the permission. If a permission is denied from a SQL Server role or a Windows NT group, the permission affects all users in the current database who are members of the group or role, regardless of the permissions that have been granted to the members of the group or role. If there are permission conflicts between a group or role and its members, the most restrictive permission (DENY) takes precedence.

Two special security accounts can be used with DENY. Permissions denied from the **public** role are applied to all users in the database. Permissions denied from the **guest** user are used by all users who do not have a user account in the database.

When denying permissions to a Windows NT local or global group, specify the domain or computer name the group is defined on, followed by a backslash, then the group name. However, to deny permissions to a Windows NT built-in local group, specify BUILTIN instead of the domain or computer name.

PRIVILEGES

Is an optional keyword that can be included for SQL-92 compliance.

permission

Is a denied object permission. When permissions are denied on a table or a view, the permission list can include one or more of these statements: SELECT, INSERT, DELETE, or UPDATE.

Object permissions denied on a table can also include REFERENCES, and object permissions denied on a stored procedure or extended stored procedure can include EXECUTE. When permissions are denied on columns, the permissions list can include SELECT or UPDATE.

column

Is the name of the column in the current database for which permissions are denied.

table

Is the name of the table in the current database for which permissions are denied.

view

Is the name of the view in the current database for which permissions are denied.

stored_procedure

Is the name of the stored procedure in the current database for which permissions are denied.

extended_procedure

Is the name of an extended stored procedure for which permissions are denied.

user_defined_function

Is the name of the user-defined function for which permissions are being denied.

CASCADE

Specifies that permissions are denied from *security_account* as well as any other security accounts granted permissions by *security_account*. Use CASCADE when denying a grantable permission. If CASCADE is not specified and the specified user is granted WITH GRANT OPTION permission, an error is returned.

Remarks

If the DENY statement is used to prevent a user from gaining a permission and the user is later added to a group or role with the permission granted, the user does not gain access to the permission.

If a user activates an application role, the effect of DENY is null for any objects the user accesses using the application role. Although a user may be denied access to a specific object in the current database, if the application role has access to the object, the user also has access while the application role is activated.

Use the REVOKE statement to remove a denied permission from a user account. The security account does not gain access to the permission unless the permission has been granted to a group or role in which the user is a member. Use the GRANT statement to both remove a denied permission, and explicitly apply the permission to the security account.

Note   DENY is a new keyword in SQL Server version 6.*x* compatibility mode. DENY is needed to specifically deny a permission from a user account, because in SQL Server version 7.0 REVOKE removes only previously granted or denied permissions. Existing SQL Server 6.*x* scripts that use REVOKE may have to be changed to use DENY to maintain behavior.

Permissions

DENY permissions default to members of the **sysadmin**, **db_owner**, or **db_securityadmin** roles, and database object owners.

Examples

A. Deny statement permissions

This example denies multiple statement permissions to multiple users. Users cannot use the CREATE DATABASE or CREATE TABLE statements unless they are explicitly granted the permission.

```
DENY CREATE DATABASE, CREATE TABLE
TO Mary, John, [Corporate\BobJ]
```

B. Deny object permissions within the permission hierarchy

This example shows the preferred ordering of permissions. First, SELECT permissions are granted to the **public** role. After this, specific permissions are denied for users **Mary**, **John**, and **Tom**. These users then have no permissions to the **authors** table.

```
USE pubs
GO

GRANT SELECT
ON authors
TO public
GO

DENY SELECT, INSERT, UPDATE, DELETE
ON authors
TO Mary, John, Tom
```

C. Deny permissions to a SQL Server role

This example denies CREATE TABLE permissions to all members of the **Accounting** role. Even if existing users of **Accounting** have been explicitly granted CREATE TABLE permission, the DENY overrides that permission.

```
DENY CREATE TABLE TO Accounting
```

Related Topics

Backward Compatibility, GRANT, Denying Permissions, REVOKE, sp_helprotect

DIFFERENCE

Returns the difference between the SOUNDEX values of two character expressions as an integer.

Syntax

```
DIFFERENCE ( character_expression , character_expression )
```

Arguments

character_expression

Is an expression of type **char** or **varchar**.

Return Types

int

Remarks

The integer returned is the number of characters in the SOUNDEX values that are the same. The return value ranges from 0 through 4, with 4 indicating the SOUNDEX values are identical.

Examples

In the first part of this example, the SOUNDEX values of two very similar strings are compared, and DIFFERENCE returns a value of 4. In the second part of this example, the SOUNDEX values for two very different strings are compared, and DIFFERENCE returns a value of 0.

```
USE pubs
GO
-- Returns a DIFFERENCE value of 4, the least possible difference.
SELECT SOUNDEX('Green'),
  SOUNDEX('Greene'), DIFFERENCE('Green','Greene')
GO
-- Returns a DIFFERENCE value of 0, the highest possible difference.
SELECT SOUNDEX('Blotchet-Halls'),
  SOUNDEX('Greene'), DIFFERENCE('Blotchet-Halls', 'Greene')
GO
```

Here is the result set:

```
----- ----- -----------
G650  G650  4

(1 row(s) affected)


----- ----- -----------
B432  G650  0

(1 row(s) affected)
```

Related Topics

SOUNDEX, String Functions

DROP DATABASE

Removes one or more databases from Microsoft SQL Server. Removing a database deletes the database and the disk files used by the database.

Syntax

```
DROP DATABASE database_name [ ,...n ]
```

Arguments

database_name
> Specifies the name of the database to be removed. Execute **sp_helpdb** from the **master** database to see a list of databases.

Remarks

To use DROP DATABASE, the database context of the connection must be in the **master** database.

DROP DATABASE removes damaged databases marked as suspect and removes the specified database. Before dropping a database used in replication, first remove replication. Any database published for transactional replication, or published or subscribed to merge replication cannot be dropped. For more information, see Administering and Monitoring Replication. If a database is damaged and replication cannot first be removed, in most cases you still can drop the database by marking it as an offline database.

A dropped database can be re-created only by restoring a backup. You cannot drop a database currently in use (open for reading or writing by any user). When a database is dropped, the **master** database should be backed up.

System databases (**msdb**, **master**, **model**, **tempdb**) cannot be dropped.

Permissions

DROP DATABASE permissions default to the database owner, members of the **sysadmin** and **dbcreator** fixed server roles, and are not transferable.

Examples

A. Drop a single database

This example removes all references for the **publishing** database from the system tables.

```
DROP DATABASE publishing
```

B. Drop multiple databases

This example removes all references for each of the listed databases from the system tables.

```
DROP DATABASE pubs, newpubs
```

Related Topics

ALTER DATABASE, CREATE DATABASE, sp_dropdevice, sp_helpdb, sp_renamedb, USE

DROP DEFAULT

Removes one or more user-defined defaults from the current database.

The DROP DEFAULT statement does not apply to DEFAULT constraints. For more information about dropping DEFAULT constraints (created by using the DEFAULT option of either the CREATE TABLE or ALTER TABLE statements), see ALTER TABLE in this volume.

Syntax

```
DROP DEFAULT { default } [ ,...n ]
```

Arguments

default

Is the name of an existing default. To see a list of defaults that exist, execute **sp_help**. Defaults must conform to the rules for identifiers. For more information, see Using Identifiers. Specifying the default owner name is optional.

n

Is a placeholder indicating that multiple defaults can be specified.

Remarks

Before dropping a default, unbind the default by executing **sp_unbindefault** (if the default is currently bound to a column or a user-defined data type).

After a default is dropped from a column that allows null values, NULL is inserted in that position when rows are added and no value is explicitly supplied. After a default is dropped from a NOT NULL column, an error message is returned when rows are added and no value is explicitly supplied. These rows are added later as part of the normal INSERT statement behavior.

Permissions

DROP DEFAULT permissions default to the owner of the default, and are not transferable. However, members of the **db_owner** and **db_ddladmin** fixed database roles and the **sysadmin** fixed server role can drop any default object by specifying the owner in DROP DEFAULT.

Examples

A. Drop a default

If a default has not been bound to a column or to a user-defined data type, it can simply be dropped using DROP DEFAULT. This example removes the user-created default named **datedflt**.

```
USE pubs
IF EXISTS (SELECT name FROM sysobjects
        WHERE name = 'datedflt'
            AND type = 'D')
   DROP DEFAULT datedflt
GO
```

B. Drop a default that has been bound to a column

This example unbinds the default associated with the **phone** column of the **authors** table and then drops the default named **phonedflt**.

```
USE pubs
IF EXISTS (SELECT name FROM sysobjects
        WHERE name = 'phonedflt'
            AND type = 'D')
   BEGIN
      EXEC sp_unbindefault 'authors.phone'
      DROP DEFAULT phonedflt
   END
GO
```

Related Topics

CREATE DEFAULT, sp_helptext, sp_help, sp_unbindefault

DROP FUNCTION

Removes one or more user-defined functions from the current database. User-defined functions are created using CREATE FUNCTION and modified using ALTER FUNCTION.

Syntax

```
DROP FUNCTION { [ owner_name . ] function_name } [ ,...n ]
```

Arguments

function_name

Is the name of the user-defined function or functions to be removed. Specifying the owner name is optional; the server name and database name cannot be specified.

n

Is a placeholder indicating that multiple user-defined functions can be specified.

Permissions

DROP FUNCTION permissions default to the function owner, and are not transferable. However, members of the **sysadmin** fixed server role and the **db_owner** and **db_ddladmin** fixed database roles can drop any object by specifying the owner in DROP FUNCTION.

Related Topics

ALTER FUNCTION, CREATE FUNCTION, User-defined Functions

DROP INDEX

Removes one or more indexes from the current database.

The DROP INDEX statement does not apply to indexes created by defining PRIMARY KEY or UNIQUE constraints (created by using the PRIMARY KEY or UNIQUE options of either the CREATE TABLE or ALTER TABLE statements, respectively). For more information about PRIMARY or UNIQUE KEY constraints, see CREATE TABLE or ALTER TABLE in this volume.

Syntax

```
DROP INDEX 'table.index | view.index' [ ,...n ]
```

Arguments

table | view

Is the table or indexed view in which the indexed column is located. To see a list of indexes that exist on a table or view, use **sp_helpindex** and specify the table or view name. Table and view names must conform to the rules for identifiers. For more information, see Using Identifiers. Specifying the table or view owner name is optional.

index

Is the name of the index to be dropped. Index names must conform to the rules for identifiers.

n

Is a placeholder indicating that multiple indexes can be specified.

Remarks

After DROP INDEX is executed, all the space previously occupied by the index is regained. This space can then be used for any database object.

DROP INDEX cannot be specified on an index on a system table.

To drop the indexes created to implement PRIMARY KEY or UNIQUE constraints, the constraint must be dropped. For more information about dropping constraints, see ALTER TABLE in this volume.

Nonclustered indexes have different pointers to data rows depending on whether or not a clustered index is defined for the table. If there is a clustered index the leaf rows of the nonclustered indexes use the clustered index keys to point to the data rows. If the table is a heap, the leaf rows of nonclustered indexes use row pointers. If you drop a clustered index on a table with nonclustered indexes, all the nonclustered indexes are rebuilt to replace the clustered index keys with row pointers.

Similarly, when the clustered index of an indexed view is dropped, all nonclustered indexes on the same view are dropped automatically.

Sometimes indexes are dropped and re-created to reorganize the index, for example to apply a new fillfactor or to reorganize data after a bulk load. It is more efficient to use CREATE INDEX and the WITH DROP_EXISTING clause for this, especially for clustered indexes. Dropping a clustered index causes all the nonclustered indexes to be rebuilt. If the clustered index is then re-created, the nonclustered indexes are rebuilt once again to replace the row pointers with clustered index keys. The WITH DROP_EXISTING clause of CREATE INDEX has optimizations to prevent this overhead of rebuilding the nonclustered indexes twice. DBCC DBREINDEX can also be used and has the advantage that it does not require that the structure of the index be known.

Permissions

DROP INDEX permissions default to the table owner, and are not transferable. However, members of the **db_owner** and **db_ddladmin** fixed database role or **sysadmin** fixed server role can drop any object by specifying the owner in DROP INDEX.

Examples

This example removes the index named **au_id_ind** in the **authors** table.

```
USE pubs
IF EXISTS (SELECT name FROM sysindexes
        WHERE name = 'au_id_ind')
  DROP INDEX authors.au_id_ind
GO
```

Related Topics

CREATE INDEX, DBCC DBREINDEX, sp_helpindex, sp_spaceused

DROP PROCEDURE

Removes one or more stored procedures or procedure groups from the current database.

Syntax

```
DROP PROCEDURE { procedure } [ ,...n ]
```

Arguments

procedure

Is name of the stored procedure or stored procedure group to be removed. Procedure names must conform to the rules for identifiers. For more information, see Using Identifiers. Specifying the procedure owner name is optional, and a server name or database name cannot be specified.

n

Is a placeholder indicating that multiple procedures can be specified.

Remarks

To see a list of procedure names, use **sp_help**. To display the procedure definition (which is stored in the **syscomments** system table), use **sp_helptext**. When a stored procedure is dropped, information about the procedure is removed from the **sysobjects** and **syscomments** system tables.

Individual procedures in the group cannot be dropped; the entire procedure group is dropped.

User-defined system procedures (prefixed with **sp_**) are dropped from the **master** database whether or not it is the current database. If the system procedure is not found in the current database, Microsoft SQL Server tries to drop it from the **master** database.

Permissions

DROP PROCEDURE permissions default to the procedure owner and are not transferable. However, members of the **db_owner** and **db_ddladmin** fixed database roles and the **sysadmin** fixed server role can drop any object by specifying the owner in DROP PROCEDURE.

Examples

This example removes the **byroyalty** stored procedure (in the current database).

```
DROP PROCEDURE byroyalty
GO
```

Related Topics

ALTER PROCEDURE, CREATE PROCEDURE, sp_depends, sp_helptext, sp_rename, syscomments, sysobjects, USE

DROP RULE

Removes one or more user-defined rules from the current database.

Syntax

```
DROP RULE { rule } [ ,...n ]
```

Arguments

rule

Is the rule to be removed. Rule names must conform to the rules for identifiers. For more information about rules for identifiers, see Using Identifiers. Specifying the rule owner name is optional.

n

Is a placeholder indicating that multiple rules can be specified.

Remarks

To drop a rule, first unbind it if the rule is currently bound to a column or to a user-defined data type. Use **sp_unbindrule** to unbind the rule. If the rule is bound when attempting to drop it, an error message is displayed and the DROP RULE statement is canceled.

After a rule is dropped, new data entered into the columns previously governed by the rule is entered without the rule's constraints. Existing data is not affected in any way.

The DROP RULE statement does not apply to CHECK constraints. For more information about dropping CHECK constraints, see ALTER TABLE in this volume.

Permissions

DROP RULE permissions default to the rule owner and are not transferable. However, members of the **db_owner** and **db_ddladmin** fixed database roles and the **sysadmin** fixed server role can drop any object by specifying the owner in DROP RULE.

Examples

This example unbinds and then drops the rule named **pub_id_rule**.

```
USE pubs
IF EXISTS (SELECT name FROM sysobjects
        WHERE name = 'pub_id_rule'
            AND type = 'R')
   BEGIN
      EXEC sp_unbindrule 'publishers.pub_id'
      DROP RULE pub_id_rule
   END
GO
```

Related Topics

CREATE RULE, sp_bindrule, sp_help, sp_helptext, sp_unbindrule, USE

DROP STATISTICS

Drops statistics for multiple collections within the specified tables (in the current database).

Syntax

```
DROP STATISTICS table.statistics_name | view.statistics_name [ ,...n ]
```

Arguments

table | view

Is the name of the target table or indexed view for which statistics should be dropped. Table and view names must conform to the rules for identifiers. For more information, see Using Identifiers. Specifying the table or view owner name is optional.

statistics_name

Is the name of the statistics group to drop. Statistics names must conform to the rules for identifiers.

n

Is a placeholder indicating that more than one *statistics_name* group (collection) can be specified.

Remarks

Be careful when dropping statistics because dropping statistics may affect the plan chosen by the query optimizer.

For more information about displaying statistics, see DBCC SHOW_STATISTICS in this volume. For more information about updating statistics, see UPDATE STATISTICS and the **auto update statistics** option of **sp_dboption** in this volume. For more information about creating statistics, see CREATE STATISTICS, CREATE INDEX, and the **auto create statistics** option of **sp_dboption** in this volume.

Permissions

DROP STATISTICS permissions default to the table or view owner, and are not transferable. However, members of the **db_owner** and **db_ddladmin** fixed database roles and **sysadmin** fixed server role can drop any object by specifying the owner in DROP STATISTICS.

Examples

This example drops the **anames** statistics group (collection) of the **authors** table and the **tnames** statistics (collection) of the **titles** table.

```
-- Create the statistics groups.
CREATE STATISTICS anames
    ON authors (au_lname, au_fname)
    WITH SAMPLE 50 PERCENT
GO
CREATE STATISTICS tnames
    ON titles (title_id)
    WITH FULLSCAN
GO
DROP STATISTICS authors.anames, titles.tnames
GO
```

Related Topics

CREATE INDEX, CREATE STATISTICS, DBCC SHOW_STATISTICS,
sp_autostats, sp_createstats, sp_dboption, UPDATE STATISTICS, USE

DROP TABLE

Removes a table definition and all data, indexes, triggers, constraints, and permission
specifications for that table. Any view or stored procedure that references the dropped
table must be explicitly dropped by using the DROP VIEW or DROP PROCEDURE
statement.

Syntax

```
DROP TABLE table_name
```

Arguments

table_name
   Is the name of the table to be removed.

Remarks

DROP TABLE cannot be used to drop a table referenced by a FOREIGN KEY
constraint. The referencing FOREIGN KEY constraint or the referencing table must
first be dropped.

A table owner can drop a table in any database. When a table is dropped, rules or
defaults on it lose their binding, and any constraints or triggers associated with it are
automatically dropped. If you re-create a table, you must rebind the appropriate rules
and defaults, re-create any triggers, and add all necessary constraints.

You cannot use the DROP TABLE statement on system tables.

If you delete all rows in a table (DELETE *tablename*) or use the TRUNCATE TABLE
statement, the table exists until it is dropped.

Permissions

DROP TABLE permissions default to the table owner, and are not transferable.
However, members of the **sysadmin** fixed server role or the **db_owner** and
db_dlladmin fixed database roles can drop any object by specifying the owner in the
DROP TABLE statement.

Examples

A. Drop a table in the current database

This example removes the **titles1** table and its data and indexes from the current database.

```
DROP TABLE titles1
```

B. Drop a table in another database

This example drops the **authors2** table in the **pubs** database. It can be executed from any database.

```
DROP TABLE pubs.dbo.authors2
```

Related Topics

ALTER TABLE, CREATE TABLE, DELETE, sp_depends, sp_help, sp_spaceused, TRUNCATE TABLE

DROP TRIGGER

Removes one or more triggers from the current database.

Syntax

```
DROP TRIGGER { trigger } [ ,...n ]
```

Arguments

trigger

Is the name of the trigger(s) to remove. Trigger names must conform to the rules for identifiers. For more information about rules for identifiers, see Using Identifiers. Specifying the trigger owner name is optional. To see a list of currently created triggers, use sp_helptrigger.

n

Is a placeholder indicating that multiple triggers can be specified.

Remarks

You can remove a trigger by dropping it or by dropping the trigger table. When a table is dropped, all associated triggers are also dropped. When a trigger is dropped, information about the trigger is removed from the **sysobjects** and **syscomments** system tables.

Use DROP TRIGGER and CREATE TRIGGER to rename a trigger. Use ALTER TRIGGER to change the definition of a trigger.

For more information about determining dependencies for a specific trigger, see **sp_depends** in this volume.

For more information about viewing the text of the trigger, see **sp_helptext** in this volume.

For more information about viewing a list of existing triggers, see **sp_helptrigger** in this volume.

Permissions

DROP TRIGGER permissions default to the trigger table owner, and are not transferable. However, members of the **db_owner** and **db_dlladmin** fixed database role or **sysadmin** fixed server role can drop any object by explicitly specifying the owner in the DROP TRIGGER statement.

Examples

This example drops the **employee_insupd** trigger.

```
USE pubs
IF EXISTS (SELECT name FROM sysobjects
      WHERE name = 'employee_insupd' AND type = 'TR')
   DROP TRIGGER employee_insupd
GO
```

Related Topics

ALTER TRIGGER, CREATE TRIGGER, sp_help, syscomments, sysobjects

DROP VIEW

Removes one or more views from the current database. DROP VIEW can be executed against indexed views.

Syntax

```
DROP VIEW { view } [ ,...n ]
```

Arguments

view

Is the name of the view(s) to be removed. View names must conform to the rules for identifiers. For more information, see Using Identifiers. Specifying the view owner name is optional. To see a list of currently created views, use sp_help.

n

Is a placeholder indicating that multiple views can be specified.

Remarks

When you drop a view, the definition of the view and other information about the view is deleted from the **sysobjects**, **syscolumns**, **syscomments**, **sysdepends**, and **sysprotects** system tables. All permissions for the view are also deleted.

Any view on a dropped table (dropped by using the DROP TABLE statement) must be dropped explicitly by using DROP VIEW.

When executed against an indexed view, DROP VIEW automatically drops all indexes on a view. Use **sp_helpindex** to display all indexes on a view.

When querying through a view, Microsoft SQL Server checks to make sure that all the database objects referenced anywhere in the statement exist, that they are valid in the context of the statement, and that data modification statements do not violate any data integrity rules. A check that fails returns an error message. A successful check translates the action into an action against the underlying table(s).

If the underlying table(s) or view(s) have changed since the view was originally created, it may be useful to drop and re-create the view.

For more information about determining dependencies for a specific view, see sp_depends.

For more information about viewing the text of the view, see sp_helptext.

Permissions

DROP VIEW permissions default to the view owner, and are not transferable. However, members of the **db_owner** and **db_ddladmin** fixed database role and **sysadmin** fixed server role can drop any object by explicitly specifying the owner in DROP VIEW.

Examples

This example removes the view **titles_view**.

```
USE pubs
IF EXISTS (SELECT TABLE_NAME FROM INFORMATION_SCHEMA.VIEWS
        WHERE TABLE_NAME = 'titles_view')
   DROP VIEW titles_view
GO
```

Related Topics

ALTER VIEW, CREATE VIEW, syscolumns, syscomments, sysdepends, sysobjects, sysprotects, USE

DUMP

Makes a backup copy of a database (DUMP DATABASE) or makes a copy of the transaction log (DUMP TRANSACTION) in a form that can be read into Microsoft SQL Server using the BACKUP or LOAD statements.

Important The DUMP statement is included in SQL Server version 2000 for backward compatibility. It is recommended that the BACKUP statement be used instead of the DUMP statement. In a future version of SQL Server, DUMP will not be supported.

Related Topics

BACKUP, LOAD, sp_addumpdevice, sp_dropdevice, sp_helpdb, sp_helpdevice, sp_spaceused

---

ELSE (IF...ELSE)

Imposes conditions on the execution of a Transact-SQL statement. The Transact-SQL statement (*sql_statement*) following the *Boolean_expression* is executed if the *Boolean_expression* evaluates to TRUE. The optional ELSE keyword is an alternate Transact-SQL statement that is executed when *Boolean_expression* evaluates to FALSE or NULL.

Syntax

```
IF Boolean_expression { sql_statement | statement_block }
[
    ELSE
    { sql_statement | statement_block } ]
```

Arguments

Boolean_expression

Is an expression that returns TRUE or FALSE. If the Boolean expression contains a SELECT statement, the SELECT statement must be enclosed in parentheses.

{*sql_statement | statement_block*}

Is any valid Transact-SQL statement or statement grouping as defined with a statement block. To define a statement block (batch), use the control-of-flow language keywords BEGIN and END. Although all Transact-SQL statements are valid within a BEGIN...END block, certain Transact-SQL statements should not be grouped together within the same batch (statement block).

Result Types

Boolean

Examples

This example produces a list of traditional cookbooks priced between $10 and $20 when one or more books meet these conditions. Otherwise, SQL Server prints a message that no books meet the condition and a list of traditional cookbooks that costs less than $10 is produced.

```
USE pubs
GO
DECLARE @msg varchar(255)
IF (SELECT COUNT(price)
    FROM titles
    WHERE title_id LIKE 'TC%' AND price BETWEEN 10 AND 20) > 0

    BEGIN
      SET NOCOUNT ON
      SET @msg = 'There are several books that are a good value between $10 and $20. These
books are: '
          PRINT @msg
      SELECT title
      FROM titles
      WHERE title_id LIKE 'TC%' AND price BETWEEN 10 AND 20
    END
ELSE
    BEGIN
      SET NOCOUNT ON
      SET @msg = 'There are no books between $10 and $20. You might consider the following
books that are under $10.'
          PRINT @msg
      SELECT title
      FROM titles
      WHERE title_id LIKE 'TC%' AND price < 10
    END
```

Here is the result set:

```
There are several books that are a good value between $10 and $20. These books are:
title
----------------------------------------------------------------------------
Fifty Years in Buckingham Palace Kitchens
Sushi, Anyone?

(2 row(s) affected)
```

Related Topics
ALTER TRIGGER, Batches, Control-of-Flow Language, CREATE TRIGGER,
IF...ELSE

END (BEGIN...END)

Encloses a series of Transact-SQL statements that will execute as a group.
BEGIN...END blocks can be nested.

Syntax

```
BEGIN
    { sql_statement | statement_block }
END
```

Arguments

{*sql_statement* | *statement_block*}

Is any valid Transact-SQL statement or statement grouping as defined with a
statement block. To define a statement block (batch), use the control-of-flow
language keywords BEGIN and END. Although all Transact-SQL statements are
valid within a BEGIN...END block, certain Transact-SQL statements should not be
grouped together within the same batch (statement block).

Result Types

Boolean

Examples

This example produces a list of business books that are priced less than $20 when one
or more books meet these conditions. Otherwise, SQL Server prints a message that no
books meet the conditions and a list of all books that cost less than $20 is produced.

```
SET NOCOUNT OFF
GO
USE pubs
GO
SET NOCOUNT ON
GO
DECLARE @msg varchar(255)
IF (SELECT COUNT(price)
    FROM titles
    WHERE title_id LIKE 'BU%' AND price < 20) > 0
```

(continued)

(continued)

```
   BEGIN
     SET @msg = 'There are several books that are a good value at under $20. These books
are: '
        PRINT @msg
     SET NOCOUNT OFF
      SELECT title
      FROM titles
      WHERE price < 20
   END
ELSE
   BEGIN
     SET @msg = 'There are no books under $20. '
        PRINT @msg
     SELECT title
     FROM titles
     WHERE title_id
     LIKE 'BU%'
     AND
     PRICE <10
   END
```

Here is the result set:

```
There are several books that are a good value at under $20. These books are:
title
---------------------------------------------------------------------------
The Busy Executive's Database Guide
Cooking with Computers: Surreptitious Balance Sheets
You Can Combat Computer Stress!
Straight Talk About Computers
Silicon Valley Gastronomic Treats
The Gourmet Microwave
Is Anger the Enemy?
Life Without Fear
Prolonged Data Deprivation: Four Case Studies
Emotional Security: A New Algorithm
Fifty Years in Buckingham Palace Kitchens
Sushi, Anyone?

(12 row(s) affected)
```

Related Topics

ALTER TRIGGER, Batches, BEGIN...END, Control-of-Flow Language, CREATE
TRIGGER, ELSE (IF...ELSE), IF...ELSE, WHILE

EXECUTE

Executes a scalar-valued, user-defined function, a system procedure, a user-defined stored procedure, or an extended stored procedure. Also supports the execution of a character string within a Transact-SQL batch.

To invoke a function, use the syntax described for EXECUTE *stored_procedure*.

Syntax

Execute a stored procedure:

```
[ [ EXEC [ UTE ] ]
   {
     [ @return_status = ]
        { procedure_name [ ;number ] | @procedure_name_var
   }
   [ [ @parameter = ] { value | @variable [ OUTPUT ] | [ DEFAULT ] ]
     [ ,...n ]
[ WITH RECOMPILE ]
```

Execute a character string:

```
EXEC [ UTE ] ( { @string_variable | [ N ] 'tsql_string' } [ + ...n ] )
```

Arguments

@return_status

Is an optional integer variable that stores the return status of a stored procedure. This variable must be declared in the batch, stored procedure, or function before it is used in an EXECUTE statement.

When used to invoke a scalar-valued user-defined function, the *@return_status* variable can be of any scalar data type.

procedure_name

Is the fully qualified or nonfully qualified name of the stored procedure to call. Procedure names must conform to the rules for identifiers. For more information, see Using Identifiers. The names of extended stored procedures are always case-sensitive, regardless of the code page or sort order of the server.

A procedure that has been created in another database can be executed if the user executing the procedure owns the procedure or has the appropriate permission to execute it in that database. A procedure can be executed on another server running Microsoft SQL Server if the user executing the procedure has the appropriate permission to use that server (remote access) and to execute the procedure in that database. If a server name is specified but no database name is specified, SQL Server looks for the procedure in the user's default database.

;*number*

Is an optional integer used to group procedures of the same name so they can be dropped with a single DROP PROCEDURE statement. This parameter is not used for extended stored procedures.

Procedures used in the same application are often grouped this way. For example, the procedures used with the orders application may be named **orderproc**;1, **orderproc**;2, and so on. The statement DROP PROCEDURE **orderproc** drops the entire group. After the procedures have been grouped, individual procedures within the group cannot be dropped. For example, the statement DROP PROCEDURE **orderproc**;2 is not allowed. For more information about procedure groups, see CREATE PROCEDURE.

@*procedure_name_var*

Is the name of a locally defined variable that represents a stored procedure name.

@*parameter*

Is the parameter for a procedure, as defined in the CREATE PROCEDURE statement. Parameter names must be preceded by the at sign (@). When used with the @*parameter_name* = *value* form, parameter names and constants do not have to be supplied in the order in which they are defined in the CREATE PROCEDURE statement. However, if the @*parameter_name* = *value* form is used for any parameter, it must be used for all subsequent parameters.

Parameters are nullable by default. If a NULL parameter value is passed and that parameter is used in a CREATE or ALTER TABLE statement in which the column referenced does not allow NULLs (for example, inserting into a column that does not allow NULLs), SQL Server generates an error. To prevent passing a parameter value of NULL to a column that does not allow NULLs, either add programming logic to the procedure or use a default value (with the DEFAULT keyword of CREATE or ALTER TABLE) for the column.

value

Is the value of the parameter to the procedure. If parameter names are not specified, parameter values must be supplied in the order defined in the CREATE PROCEDURE statement.

If the value of a parameter is an object name, character string, or qualified by a database name or owner name, the entire name must be enclosed in single quotation marks. If the value of a parameter is a keyword, the keyword must be enclosed in double quotation marks.

If a default is defined in the CREATE PROCEDURE statement, a user can execute the procedure without specifying a parameter. The default must be a constant and can include the wildcard characters %, _, [ ], and [^] if the procedure uses the parameter name with the LIKE keyword.

The default can also be NULL. Usually, the procedure definition specifies the action that should be taken if a parameter value is NULL.

@variable
> Is the variable that stores a parameter or a return parameter.

OUTPUT
> Specifies that the stored procedure returns a parameter. The matching parameter in the stored procedure must also have been created with the keyword OUTPUT. Use this keyword when using cursor variables as parameters.
>
> If OUTPUT parameters are being used and the intent is to use the return values in other statements within the calling batch or procedure, the value of the parameter must be passed as a variable (that is, *@parameter* = *@variable*). You cannot execute a procedure specifying OUTPUT for a parameter that is not defined as an OUTPUT parameter in the CREATE PROCEDURE statement. Constants cannot be passed to stored procedures using OUTPUT; the return parameter requires a variable name. The variable's data type must be declared and a value assigned before executing the procedure. Return parameters can be of any data type except the **text** or **image** data types.

DEFAULT
> Supplies the default value of the parameter as defined in the procedure. When the procedure expects a value for a parameter that does not have a defined default and either a parameter is missing or the DEFAULT keyword is specified, an error occurs.

n
> Is a placeholder indicating that the preceding item(s) can be repeated multiple times. For example, EXECUTE can specify one or more *@parameter*, *value*, or *@variable* items.

WITH RECOMPILE
> Forces a new plan to be compiled. Use this option if the parameter you are supplying is atypical or if the data has significantly changed. The changed plan is used in subsequent executions. This option is not used for extended stored procedures. It is recommended that you use this option sparingly because it is expensive.

@string_variable
> Is the name of a local variable. *@string_variable* can be of **char**, **varchar**, **nchar**, or **nvarchar** data type with a maximum value of the server's available memory. If the string is greater than 4,000 characters, concatenate multiple local variables to use for the EXECUTE string. For more information about system-supplied SQL Server data types, see Data Types.

[N]'*tsql_string*'
> Is a constant string. *tsql_string* can be of **nvarchar** or **varchar** data type. If the N is included, the string is interpreted as **nvarchar** data type with a maximum value of the server's available memory. If the string is greater than 4,000 characters, concatenate multiple local variables to use for the EXECUTE string.

Remarks

If the first three characters of the procedure name are **sp_**, SQL Server searches the **master** database for the procedure. If no qualified procedure name is provided, SQL Server searches for the procedure as if the owner name is **dbo**. To resolve the stored procedure name as a user-defined stored procedure with the same name as a system stored procedure, provide the fully qualified procedure name.

Parameters can be supplied either by using *value* or by using *@parameter_name* = *value*. A parameter is not part of a transaction; therefore, if a parameter is changed in a transaction that is later rolled back, the parameter's value does not revert to its previous value. The value returned to the caller is always the value at the time the procedure returns.

Nesting occurs when one stored procedure calls another. The nesting level is incremented when the called procedure begins execution, and it is decremented when the called procedure has finished. Exceeding the maximum of 32 nesting levels causes the entire calling procedure chain to fail. The current nesting level is stored in the @@NESTLEVEL function.

SQL Server currently uses return values 0 through -14 to indicate the execution status of stored procedures. Values from -15 through -99 are reserved for future use. For more information about a list of reserved return status values, see RETURN.

Because remote stored procedures and extended stored procedures are not within the scope of a transaction (unless issued within a BEGIN DISTRIBUTED TRANSACTION statement or when used with various configuration options), commands executed through calls to them cannot be rolled back. For more information, see System Stored Procedures and BEGIN DISTRIBUTED TRANSACTION.

When using cursor variables, if you execute a procedure that passes in a cursor variable with a cursor allocated to it an error occurs.

You do not have to specify the EXECUTE keyword when executing stored procedures if the statement is the first one in a batch.

Using EXECUTE with a Character String

Use the string concatenation operator (+) to create large strings for dynamic execution. Each string expression can be a mixture of Unicode and non-Unicode data types.

Although each [N] *'tsql_string'* or *@string_variable* must be less than 8,000 bytes, the concatenation is performed logically in the SQL Server parser and never materializes in memory. For example, this statement never produces the expected 16,000 concatenated character string:

```
EXEC('name_of_8000_char_string' + 'another_name_of_8000_char_string')
```

Statement(s) inside the EXECUTE statement are not compiled until the EXECUTE statement is executed.

Changes in database context last only until the end of the EXECUTE statement. For example, after the EXEC in this example, the database context is **master**:

```
USE master EXEC ("USE pubs") SELECT * FROM authors
```

Permissions

EXECUTE permissions for a stored procedure default to the owner of the stored procedure, who can transfer them to other users. Permissions to use the statement(s) within the EXECUTE string are checked at the time EXECUTE is encountered, even if the EXECUTE statement is included within a stored procedure. When a stored procedure is run that executes a string, permissions are checked in the context of the user who executes the procedure, not in the context of the user who created the procedure. However, if a user owns two stored procedures in which the first procedure calls the second, then EXECUTE permission checking is not performed for the second stored procedure.

Examples

A. Use EXECUTE to pass a single parameter

The **showind** stored procedure expects one parameter (**@tabname**), a table name. The following examples execute the **showind** stored procedure with **titles** as its parameter value.

> **Note**   The **showind** stored procedure is shown for illustrative purposes only and does not exist in the **pubs** database.

```
EXEC showind titles
```

The variable can be explicitly named in the execution:

```
EXEC showind @tabname = titles
```

If this is the first statement in a batch or an **isql** script, EXEC is not required:

```
showind titles
```

-or-

```
showind @tabname = titles
```

B. Use multiple parameters and an output parameter

This example executes the **roy_check** stored procedure, which passes three parameters. The third parameter, **@pc**, is an OUTPUT parameter. After the procedure has been executed, the return value is available in the variable **@percent**.

Note The **roy_check** stored procedure is shown for illustrative purposes only and does not exist in the **pubs** database.

```
DECLARE @percent int
EXECUTE roy_check 'BU1032', 1050, @pc = @percent OUTPUT
SET Percent = @percent
```

C. Use EXECUTE '*tsql_string*' with a variable

This example shows how EXECUTE handles dynamically built strings containing variables. This example creates the **tables_cursor** cursor to hold a list of all user-defined tables (*type* = U).

Note This example is shown for illustrative purposes only.

```
DECLARE tables_cursor CURSOR
   FOR
   SELECT name FROM sysobjects WHERE type = 'U'
OPEN tables_cursor
DECLARE @tablename sysname
FETCH NEXT FROM tables_cursor INTO @tablename
WHILE (@@FETCH_STATUS <> -1)
BEGIN
   /* A @@FETCH_STATUS of -2 means that the row has been deleted.
   There is no need to test for this because this loop drops all
   user-defined tables. */.
   EXEC ('DROP TABLE ' + @tablename)
   FETCH NEXT FROM tables_cursor INTO @tablename
END
PRINT 'All user-defined tables have been dropped from the database.'
DEALLOCATE tables_cursor
```

D. Use EXECUTE with a remote stored procedure

This example executes the **checkcontract** stored procedure on the remote server **SQLSERVER1** and stores the return status indicating success or failure in **@retstat**.

```
DECLARE @retstat int
EXECUTE @retstat = SQLSERVER1.pubs.dbo.checkcontract '409-56-4008'
```

E. Use EXECUTE with an extended stored procedure

This example uses the **xp_cmdshell** extended stored procedure to list a directory of all files with an .exe file name extension.

```
USE master
EXECUTE xp_cmdshell 'dir *.exe'
```

F. Use EXECUTE with a stored procedure variable

This example creates a variable that represents a stored procedure name.

```
DECLARE @proc_name varchar(30)
SET @proc_name = 'sp_who'
EXEC @proc_name
```

G. Use EXECUTE with DEFAULT

This example creates a stored procedure with default values for the first and third parameters. When the procedure is run, these defaults are inserted for the first and third parameters if no value is passed in the call or if the default is specified. Note the various ways the DEFAULT keyword can be used.

```
USE pubs
IF EXISTS (SELECT name FROM sysobjects
      WHERE name = 'proc_calculate_taxes' AND type = 'P')
   DROP PROCEDURE proc_calculate_taxes
GO
-- Create the stored procedure.
CREATE PROCEDURE proc_calculate_taxes (@p1 smallint = 42, @p2 char(1),
      @p3 varchar(8) = 'CAR')
   AS
   SELECT *
   FROM mytable
```

The **proc_calculate_taxes** stored procedure can be executed in many combinations:

```
EXECUTE proc_calculate_taxes @p2 = 'A'
EXECUTE proc_calculate_taxes 69, 'B'
EXECUTE proc_calculate_taxes 69, 'C', 'House'
EXECUTE proc_calculate_taxes @p1 = DEFAULT, @p2 = 'D'
EXECUTE proc_calculate_taxes DEFAULT, @p3 = 'Local', @p2 = 'E'
EXECUTE proc_calculate_taxes 69, 'F', @p3 = DEFAULT
EXECUTE proc_calculate_taxes 95, 'G', DEFAULT
EXECUTE proc_calculate_taxes DEFAULT, 'H', DEFAULT
EXECUTE proc_calculate_taxes DEFAULT, 'I', @p3 = DEFAULT
```

Related Topics

+ (String Concatenation), [ ] (Wildcard - Character(s) to Match), @@NESTLEVEL,
ALTER PROCEDURE, DECLARE @local_variable, DROP PROCEDURE,
Functions, sp_depends, sp_helptext

EXISTS

Specifies a subquery to test for the existence of rows.

Syntax

```
EXISTS subquery
```

Arguments

subquery

Is a restricted SELECT statement (the COMPUTE clause, and the INTO keyword
are not allowed). For more information, see the discussion of subqueries in
SELECT.

Result Types

Boolean

Result Values

Returns TRUE if a subquery contains any rows.

Examples

A. Use NULL in subquery to still return a result set

This example returns a result set with NULL specified in the subquery and still
evaluates to TRUE by using EXISTS.

```
USE Northwind
GO
SELECT CategoryName
FROM Categories
WHERE EXISTS (SELECT NULL)
ORDER BY CategoryName ASC
GO
```

B. Compare queries using EXISTS and IN

This example compares two queries that are semantically equivalent. The first query
uses EXISTS and the second query uses IN. Note that both queries return the same
information.

```
USE pubs
GO
SELECT DISTINCT pub_name
FROM publishers
WHERE EXISTS
    (SELECT *
    FROM titles
    WHERE pub_id = publishers.pub_id
    AND type = 'business')
GO

-- Or, using the IN clause:

USE pubs
GO
SELECT distinct pub_name
FROM publishers
WHERE pub_id IN
    (SELECT pub_id
    FROM titles
    WHERE type = 'business')
GO
```

Here is the result set for either query:

```
pub_name
-----------------------------------------
Algodata Infosystems
New Moon Books

(2 row(s) affected)
```

C. Compare queries using EXISTS and = ANY

This example shows two queries to find authors who live in the same city as a publisher. The first query uses = ANY and the second uses EXISTS. Note that both queries return the same information.

```
USE pubs
GO
SELECT au_lname, au_fname
FROM authors
WHERE exists
    (SELECT *
    FROM publishers
```

(continued)

(continued)

```
    WHERE authors.city = publishers.city)
GO


-- Or, using = ANY

USE pubs
GO
SELECT au_lname, au_fname
FROM authors
WHERE city = ANY
   (SELECT city
   FROM publishers)
GO
```

Here is the result set for either query:

```
au_lname                                  au_fname
----------------------------------------- --------------------

Carson                                    Cheryl
Bennet                                    Abraham

(2 row(s) affected)
```

D. Compare queries using EXISTS and IN

This example shows queries to find titles of books published by any publisher located in a city that begins with the letter B.

```
USE pubs
GO
SELECT title
FROM titles
WHERE EXISTS
   (SELECT *
   FROM publishers
   WHERE pub_id = titles.pub_id
   AND city LIKE 'B%')
GO

-- Or, using IN:

USE pubs
GO
SELECT title
```

(continued)

(continued)

```
FROM titles
WHERE pub_id IN
    (SELECT pub_id
    FROM publishers
    WHERE city LIKE 'B%')
GO
```

Here is the result set for either query:

```
title
-----------------------------------------------------------------------
The Busy Executive's Database Guide
Cooking with Computers: Surreptitious Balance Sheets
You Can Combat Computer Stress!
Straight Talk About Computers
But Is It User Friendly?
Secrets of Silicon Valley
Net Etiquette
Is Anger the Enemy?
Life Without Fear
Prolonged Data Deprivation: Four Case Studies
Emotional Security: A New Algorithm

(11 row(s) affected)
```

E. Use NOT EXISTS

NOT EXISTS works the opposite as EXISTS. The WHERE clause in NOT EXISTS is satisfied if no rows are returned by the subquery. This example finds the names of publishers who do not publish business books.

```
USE pubs
GO
SELECT pub_name
FROM publishers
WHERE NOT EXISTS
    (SELECT *
    FROM titles
    WHERE pub_id = publishers.pub_id
    AND type = 'business')
ORDER BY pub_name
GO
```

Here is the result set:

```
pub_name
------------------------------------------
Binnet & Hardley
Five Lakes Publishing
GGG&G
Lucerne Publishing
Ramona Publishers
Scootney Books


(6 row(s) affected)
```

Related Topics

Expressions, Functions, WHERE

EXP

Returns the exponential value of the given **float** expression.

Syntax

```
EXP ( float_expression )
```

Arguments

float_expression
    Is an expression of type **float**.

Return Types

float

Examples

This example declares a variable and returns the exponential value of the given variable (378.615345498) with a text description.

```
DECLARE @var float
SET @var = 378.615345498
SELECT 'The EXP of the variable is: ' + CONVERT(varchar,EXP(@var))
GO
```

Here is the result set:

```
The EXP of the variable is: 2.69498e+164

(1 row(s) affected)
```

Related Topics

CAST and CONVERT, float and real, Mathematical Functions, money and smallmoney

---

Expressions

A combination of symbols and operators that Microsoft SQL Server evaluates to obtain a single data value. Simple expressions can be a single constant, variable, column, or scalar function. Operators can be used to join two or more simple expressions into a complex expression.

Syntax

```
{ constant
  | scalar_function
  | [ alias. ] column
  | local_variable
  | ( expression )
  | ( scalar_subquery )
  | { unary_operator } expression
  | expression { binary_operator } expression
}
```

Arguments

constant

Is a symbol that represents a single, specific data value. *constant* is one or more alphanumeric characters (letters a–z, A–Z, and numbers 0–9) or symbols (exclamation point (!), at sign (@), number sign (#), and so on). Character and datetime values are enclosed in quotation marks, while binary strings and numeric constants are not. For more information, see Constants.

scalar_function

Is a unit of Transact-SQL syntax that provides a specific service and returns a single value. *scalar_function* can be built-in scalar functions, such as the SUM, GETDATE, or CAST functions, or scalar user-defined functions.

[alias.]

Is the alias, or correlation name, assigned to a table by the AS keyword in the FROM clause.

column

Is the name of a column. Only the name of the column is allowed in an expression; a four-part name cannot be specified.

local_variable

Is the name of a user-defined variable. For more information, see DECLARE @local_variable.

(*expression*)

> Is any valid SQL Server expression as defined in this topic. The parentheses are grouping operators that ensure that all the operators in the expression within the parentheses are evaluated before the resulting expression is combined with another.

(*scalar_subquery*)

> Is a subquery that returns one value. For example:

```
SELECT MAX(UnitPrice)
FROM Products
```

{*unary_operator*}

> Is an operator that has only one numeric operand:

- + indicates a positive number.

- - indicates a negative number.

- ~ indicates the one's complement operator.

> Unary operators can be applied only to expressions that evaluate to any of the data types of the numeric data type category.

{*binary_operator*}

> Is an operator that defines the way two expressions are combined to yield a single result. *binary _operator* can be an arithmetic operator, the assignment operator (=), a bitwise operator, a comparison operator, a logical operator, the string concatenation operator (+), or a unary operator. For more information about operators, see Operators.

Expression Results

For a simple expression built of a single constant, variable, scalar function, or column name, the data type, collation, precision, scale, and value of the expression is the data type, collation, precision, scale, and value of the referenced element.

When two expressions are combined using comparison or logical operators, the resulting data type is Boolean and the value is one of three values: TRUE, FALSE, or UNKNOWN. For more information about Boolean data types, see Operators.

When two expressions are combined using arithmetic, bitwise, or string operators, the operator determines the resulting data type.

Complex expressions made up of many symbols and operators evaluate to a single-valued result. The data type, collation, precision, and value of the resulting expression is determined by combining the component expressions, two at a time, until a final result is reached. The sequence in which the expressions are combined is defined by the precedence of the operators in the expression.

Remarks

Two expressions can be combined by an operator if they both have data types supported by the operator and at least one of these conditions is TRUE:

- The expressions have the same data type.
- The data type with the lower precedence can be implicitly converted to the data type with the higher data type precedence.
- The CAST function can explicitly convert the data type with the lower precedence to either the data type with the higher precedence or to an intermediate data type that can be implicitly converted to the data type with the higher precedence.

If there is no supported implicit or explicit conversion, the two expressions cannot be combined.

The collation of any expression that evaluates to a character string is set following the rules of collation precedence. For more information, see Collation Precedence.

In a programming language such as C or Microsoft Visual Basic, an expression always evaluates to a single result. Expressions in a Transact-SQL select list have a variation on this rule: The expression is evaluated individually for each row in the result set. A single expression may have a different value in each row of the result set, but each row has only one value for the expression. For example, in this SELECT statement both the reference to ProductID and the term 1+2 in the select list are expressions:

```
SELECT ProductID, 1+2
FROM Northwind.dbo.Products
```

The expression 1+2 evaluates to 3 in each row in the result set. Although the expression ProductID generates a unique value in each result set row, each row only has one value for ProductID.

Related Topics

CASE, CAST and CONVERT, COALESCE, Data Type Conversion, Data Type Precedence, Data Types, Functions, LIKE, NULLIF, SELECT, WHERE

FETCH

Retrieves a specific row from a Transact-SQL server cursor.

Syntax

```
FETCH
      [ [ NEXT | PRIOR | FIRST | LAST
            | ABSOLUTE { n | @nvar }
            | RELATIVE { n | @nvar }
        ]
        FROM
      ]
{ { [ GLOBAL ] cursor_name } | @cursor_variable_name }
[ INTO @variable_name [ ,...n ] ]
```

Arguments

NEXT

Returns the result row immediately following the current row, and increments the current row to the row returned. If FETCH NEXT is the first fetch against a cursor, it returns the first row in the result set. NEXT is the default cursor fetch option.

PRIOR

Returns the result row immediately preceding the current row, and decrements the current row to the row returned. If FETCH PRIOR is the first fetch against a cursor, no row is returned and the cursor is left positioned before the first row.

FIRST

Returns the first row in the cursor and makes it the current row.

LAST

Returns the last row in the cursor and makes it the current row.

ABSOLUTE {n | @nvar}

If n or @nvar is positive, returns the row n rows from the front of the cursor and makes the returned row the new current row. If n or @nvar is negative, returns the row n rows before the end of the cursor and makes the returned row the new current row. If n or @nvar is 0, no rows are returned. n must be an integer constant and @nvar must be **smallint**, **tinyint**, or **int**.

RELATIVE {n | @nvar}

If n or @nvar is positive, returns the row n rows beyond the current row and makes the returned row the new current row. If n or @nvar is negative, returns the row n rows prior to the current row and makes the returned row the new current row. If n or @nvar is 0, returns the current row. If FETCH RELATIVE is specified with n or @nvar set to negative numbers or 0 on the first fetch done against a cursor, no rows are returned. n must be an integer constant and @nvar must be **smallint**, **tinyint**, or **int**.

GLOBAL
> Specifies that *cursor_name* refers to a global cursor.

cursor_name
> Is the name of the open cursor from which the fetch should be made. If both a global and a local cursor exist with *cursor_name* as their name, *cursor_name* to the global cursor if GLOBAL is specified and to the local cursor if GLOBAL is not specified.

@cursor_variable_name
> Is the name of a cursor variable referencing the open cursor from which the fetch should be made.

INTO *@variable_name*[*,...n*]
> Allows data from the columns of a fetch to be placed into local variables. Each variable in the list, from left to right, is associated with the corresponding column in the cursor result set. The data type of each variable must either match or be a supported implicit conversion of the data type of the corresponding result set column. The number of variables must match the number of columns in the cursor select list.

Remarks

If the SCROLL option is not specified in an SQL-92 style DECLARE CURSOR statement, NEXT is the only FETCH option supported. If SCROLL is specified in an SQL-92 style DECLARE CURSOR, all FETCH options are supported.

When the Transact_SQL DECLARE cursor extensions are used, these rules apply:

* If either FORWARD-ONLY or FAST_FORWARD is specified, NEXT is the only FETCH option supported.

* If DYNAMIC, FORWARD_ONLY or FAST_FORWARD are not specified, and one of KEYSET, STATIC, or SCROLL are specified, all FETCH options are supported.

* DYNAMIC SCROLL cursors support all the FETCH options except ABSOLUTE.

The @@FETCH_STATUS function reports the status of the last FETCH statement. The same information is recorded in the **fetch_status** column in the cursor returned by **sp_describe_cursor**. This status information should be used to determine the validity of the data returned by a FETCH statement prior to attempting any operation against that data. For more information, see @@FETCH_STATUS.

Permissions

FETCH permissions default to any valid user.

Examples

A. Use FETCH in a simple cursor

This example declares a simple cursor for the rows in the **authors** table with a last name beginning with B, and uses FETCH NEXT to step through the rows.
The FETCH statements return the value for the column specified in the DECLARE CURSOR as a single-row result set.

```
USE pubs
GO
DECLARE authors_cursor CURSOR FOR
SELECT au_lname FROM authors
WHERE au_lname LIKE "B%"
ORDER BY au_lname

OPEN authors_cursor

-- Perform the first fetch.
FETCH NEXT FROM authors_cursor

-- Check @@FETCH_STATUS to see if there are any more rows to fetch.
WHILE @@FETCH_STATUS = 0
BEGIN
   -- This is executed as long as the previous fetch succeeds.
   FETCH NEXT FROM authors_cursor
END

CLOSE authors_cursor
DEALLOCATE authors_cursor
GO

au_lname
----------------------------------------
Bennet
au_lname
----------------------------------------
Blotchet-Halls
au_lname
----------------------------------------
```

B. Use FETCH to store values in variables

This example is similar to the last example, except the output of the FETCH statements is stored in local variables rather than being returned directly to the client. The PRINT statement combines the variables into a single string and returns them to the client.

```
USE pubs
GO


-- Declare the variables to store the values returned by FETCH.
DECLARE @au_lname varchar(40), @au_fname varchar(20)



DECLARE authors_cursor CURSOR FOR
SELECT au_lname, au_fname FROM authors
WHERE au_lname LIKE "B%"
ORDER BY au_lname, au_fname

OPEN authors_cursor

-- Perform the first fetch and store the values in variables.
-- Note: The variables are in the same order as the columns
-- in the SELECT statement.

FETCH NEXT FROM authors_cursor
INTO @au_lname, @au_fname

-- Check @@FETCH_STATUS to see if there are any more rows to fetch.
WHILE @@FETCH_STATUS = 0
BEGIN

   -- Concatenate and display the current values in the variables.
   PRINT "Author: " + @au_fname + " " +  @au_lname

   -- This is executed as long as the previous fetch succeeds.
   FETCH NEXT FROM authors_cursor
   INTO @au_lname, @au_fname
END

CLOSE authors_cursor
DEALLOCATE authors_cursor
GO

Author: Abraham Bennet
Author: Reginald Blotchet-Halls
```

C. Declare a SCROLL cursor and use the other FETCH options

This example creates a SCROLL cursor to allow full scrolling capabilities through the LAST, PRIOR, RELATIVE, and ABSOLUTE options.

```
USE pubs
GO

-- Execute the SELECT statement alone to show the
-- full result set that is used by the cursor.
SELECT au_lname, au_fname FROM authors
ORDER BY au_lname, au_fname

-- Declare the cursor.
DECLARE authors_cursor SCROLL CURSOR FOR
SELECT au_lname, au_fname FROM authors
ORDER BY au_lname, au_fname

OPEN authors_cursor

-- Fetch the last row in the cursor.
FETCH LAST FROM authors_cursor

-- Fetch the row immediately prior to the current row in the cursor.
FETCH PRIOR FROM authors_cursor

-- Fetch the second row in the cursor.
FETCH ABSOLUTE 2 FROM authors_cursor

-- Fetch the row that is three rows after the current row.
FETCH RELATIVE 3 FROM authors_cursor

-- Fetch the row that is two rows prior to the current row.
FETCH RELATIVE -2 FROM authors_cursor

CLOSE authors_cursor
DEALLOCATE authors_cursor
GO

au_lname                                       au_fname
---------------------------------------------- --------------------
Bennet                                         Abraham
Blotchet-Halls                                 Reginald
Carson                                         Cheryl
DeFrance                                       Michel
```

(continued)

(continued)

```
del Castillo                              Innes
Dull                                      Ann
Green                                     Marjorie
Greene                                    Morningstar
Gringlesby                                Burt
Hunter                                    Sheryl
Karsen                                    Livia
Locksley                                  Charlene
MacFeather                                Stearns
McBadden                                  Heather
O'Leary                                   Michael
Panteley                                  Sylvia
Ringer                                    Albert
Ringer                                    Anne
Smith                                     Meander
Straight                                  Dean
Stringer                                  Dirk
White                                     Johnson
Yokomoto                                  Akiko


au_lname                                  au_fname
----------------------------------------  --------------------
Yokomoto                                  Akiko
au_lname                                  au_fname
----------------------------------------  --------------------
White                                     Johnson
au_lname                                  au_fname
----------------------------------------  --------------------
Blotchet-Halls                            Reginald
au_lname                                  au_fname
----------------------------------------  --------------------
del Castillo                              Innes
au_lname                                  au_fname
----------------------------------------  --------------------
Carson                                    Cheryl
```

Related Topics

CLOSE, Cursors, DEALLOCATE, DECLARE CURSOR, OPEN

FILE_ID

Returns the file identification (ID) number for the given logical file name in the current database.

Syntax

```
FILE_ID ( 'file_name' )
```

Arguments

'file_name'

Is the name of the file for which to return the file ID. *file_name* is **nchar(128)**.

Return Types

smallint

Remarks

file_name corresponds to the **name** column in **sysfiles**.

Examples

This example returns the file ID (1) for the **master** database.

```
USE master
SELECT FILE_ID('master')
```

Related Topics

Control-of-Flow Language, DELETE, INSERT, Metadata Functions, SELECT, UPDATE, WHERE

FILE_NAME

Returns the logical file name for the given file identification (ID) number.

Syntax

```
FILE_NAME ( file_id )
```

Arguments

file_id

Is the file identification number for which to return the file name. *file_id* is **smallint**.

Return Types

nvarchar(128)

Remarks

file_ID corresponds to the **fileid** column in **sysfiles**.

Examples

This example returns the file name for a *file_ID* of 1 (the **master** database file).

```
USE master
SELECT FILE_NAME(1)
```

Related Topics

Control-of-Flow Language, DELETE, INSERT, Metadata Functions, SELECT, UPDATE, WHERE

FILEGROUP_ID

Returns the filegroup identification (ID) number for the given filegroup name.

Syntax

```
FILEGROUP_ID ( 'filegroup_name' )
```

Arguments

'filegroup_name'
  Is the filegroup name for which to return the filegroup ID. *filegroup_name* is **nvarchar(128)**.

Return Types

smallint

Remarks

filegroup_name corresponds to the **groupname** column in **sysfilegroups**.

Examples

This example returns the filegroup ID for the filegroup named **default**.

```
USE master
SELECT FILEGROUP_ID('default')
```

Related Topics

Control-of-Flow Language, DELETE, INSERT, Metadata Functions, SELECT, UPDATE, WHERE

FILEGROUP_NAME

Returns the filegroup name for the given filegroup identification (ID) number.

Syntax

```
FILEGROUP_NAME ( filegroup_id )
```

Arguments

filegroup_id

Is the filegroup ID number for which to return the filegroup name. *filegroup_id* is **smallint**.

Return Types

nvarchar(128)

Remarks

filegroup_id corresponds to the **groupid** column in **sysfilegroups**.

Examples

This example returns the filegroup name for the filegroup ID 1 (the default).

```
USE master
SELECT FILEGROUP_NAME(1)
```

Related Topics

Control-of-Flow Language, DELETE, INSERT, Metadata Functions, SELECT, UPDATE, WHERE

FILEGROUPPROPERTY

Returns the specified filegroup property value when given a filegroup and property name.

Syntax

```
FILEGROUPPROPERTY ( filegroup_name , property )
```

Arguments

filegroup_name

Is an expression containing the name of the filegroup for which to return the named property information. *filegroup_name* is **nvarchar(128)**.

property

Is an expression containing the name of the filegroup property to return. *property* is **varchar**(128), and can be one of these values.

Value	Description	Value returned
IsReadOnly	Filegroup name is read-only.	1 = True 0 = False NULL = Invalid input
IsUserDefinedFG	Filegroup name is a user-defined filegroup.	1 = True 0 = False NULL = Invalid input
IsDefault	Filegroup name is the default filegroup.	1 = True 0 = False NULL = Invalid input

Return Types

int

Examples

This example returns the setting for the **IsUserDefinedFG** property for the primary filegroup.

```
USE master
SELECT FILEGROUPPROPERTY('primary', 'IsUserDefinedFG')
```

Related Topics

Control-of-Flow Language, DELETE, INSERT, Metadata Functions, SELECT, UPDATE, WHERE

FILEPROPERTY

Returns the specified file name property value when given a file name and property name.

Syntax

```
FILEPROPERTY ( file_name , property )
```

Arguments

file_name

Is an expression containing the name of the file associated with the current database for which to return property information. *file_name* is **nchar(128)**.

property

Is an expression containing the name of the file property to return. *property* is **varchar(128)**, and can be one of these values.

Value	Description	Value returned
IsReadOnly	File is read-only.	1 = True 0 = False NULL = Invalid input
IsPrimaryFile	File is the primary file.	1 = True 0 = False NULL = Invalid input
IsLogFile	File is a log file.	1 = True 0 = False NULL = Invalid input
SpaceUsed	Amount of space used by the specified file.	Number of pages allocated in the file

Return Types

int

Examples

This example returns the setting for the **IsPrimaryFile** property for the master file name in the **master** database.

```
USE master
SELECT FILEPROPERTY('master', 'IsPrimaryFile')
```

Related Topics

Control-of-Flow Language, DELETE, INSERT, Metadata Functions, SELECT, UPDATE, WHERE

float and real

Approximate number data types for use with floating point numeric data. Floating point data is approximate; not all values in the data type range can be precisely represented.

Syntax

```
float [ ( n ) ]
```

Is a floating point number data from - 1.79E + 308 through 1.79E + 308. n is the number of bits used to store the mantissa of the **float** number in scientific notation and thus dictates the precision and storage size. n must be a value from **1** through **53**.

n is	Precision	Storage size
1–24	7 digits	4 bytes
25–53	15 digits	8 bytes

The Microsoft SQL Server **float[(n)]** data type conforms to the SQL-92 standard for all values of n from **1** to **53**. The synonym for **double precision** is **float(53)**.

real

Floating point number data from −3.40E + 38 through 3.40E + 38. Storage size is 4 bytes. In SQL Server, the synonym for real is **float(24)**.

Related Topics

ALTER TABLE, CAST and CONVERT, CREATE TABLE, Data Type Conversion, Data Types, DECLARE @local_variable, DELETE, INSERT, SET @local_variable, UPDATE

FLOOR

Returns the largest integer less than or equal to the given numeric expression.

Syntax

```
FLOOR ( numeric_expression )
```

Arguments

numeric_expression

Is an expression of the exact numeric or approximate numeric data type category, except for the **bit** data type.

Return Types

Returns the same type as *numeric_expression*.

Examples

This example shows positive numeric, negative numeric, and currency values with the FLOOR function.

```
SELECT FLOOR(123.45), FLOOR(-123.45), FLOOR($123.45)
```

The result is the integer portion of the calculated value in the same data type as *numeric_expression*.

```
---------      ---------      -----------
123            -124           123.0000
```

Related Topics

Mathematical Functions

---

fn_helpcollations

Returns a list of all the collations supported by Microsoft SQL Server 2000.

Syntax

```
fn_helpcollations ()
```

Tables Returned

fn_helpcollations returns the following information.

Column name	Data type	Description
Name	sysname	Standard collation name
Description	nvarchar(1000)	Description of the collation

Related Topics

COLLATE, COLLATIONPROPERTY

fn_listextendedproperty

Returns extended property values of database objects.

Syntax

```
fn_listextendedproperty (
    { default | [ @name = ] 'property_name' | NULL }
    , { default | [ @level0type = ] 'level0_object_type' | NULL }
    , { default | [ @level0name = ] 'level0_object_name' | NULL }
    , { default | [ @level1type = ] 'level1_object_type' | NULL }
    , { default | [ @level1name = ] 'level1_object_name' | NULL }
    , { default | [ @level2type = ] 'level2_object_type' | NULL }
    , { default | [ @level2name = ] 'level2_object_name' | NULL }
    )
```

Arguments

{default|[@**name** =] 'property_name'|NULL}

Is the name of the property. *property_name* is **sysname**. Valid inputs are default, NULL, or a property name.

{default|[@**level0type** =] 'level0_object_type'|NULL}

Is the user or user-defined type. *level0_object_type* is **varchar(128)**, with a default of NULL. Valid inputs are USER, TYPE, default, and NULL.

{default|[@**level0name** =] 'level0_object_name'|NULL}

Is the name of the level 0 object type specified. *level0_object_name* is **sysname** with a default of NULL. Valid inputs are default, NULL, or an object name.

{default|[@**level1type** =] 'level1_object_type'|NULL}

Is the type of level 1 object. *level1_object_type* is **varchar(128)** with a default of NULL. Valid inputs are TABLE, VIEW, PROCEDURE, FUNCTION, DEFAULT, RULE, default, and NULL.

Note   Default maps to NULL and 'default' maps to the object type DEFAULT.

{default|[**@level1name** =] '*level1_object_name*'|NULL}
> Is the name of the level 1 object type specified. *level1_object_name* is **sysname** with a default of NULL. Valid inputs are default, NULL, or an object name.

{default|[**@level2type** =] '*level2_object_type*'|NULL}
> Is the type of level 2 object. *level2_object_type* is **varchar(128)** with a default of NULL. Valid inputs are COLUMN, PARAMETER, INDEX, CONSTRAINT, TRIGGER, DEFAULT, default (which maps to NULL), and NULL.

{default|[**@level2name** =] '*level2_object_name*'|NULL}
> Is the name of the level 2 object type specified. *level2_object_name* is **sysname** with a default of NULL. Valid inputs are default, NULL, or an object name.

Tables Returned

This is the format of the tables returned by fn_listextendedproperty.

Column name	Data type
objtype	**sysname**
objname	**sysname**
name	**sysname**
value	**sql_variant**

If the table returned is empty, either the object does not have extended properties or the user does not have permissions to list the extended properties on the object.

Remarks

Extended properties are not allowed on system objects.

If the value for *property_name* is NULL or default, fn_listextendedproperty returns all the properties for the object.

When the object type is specified and the value of the corresponding object name is NULL or default, fn_listextendedproperty returns all extended properties for all objects of the type specified.

The objects are distinguished according to levels, with level 0 as the highest and level 2 the lowest. If a lower level object (level 1 or 2) type and name are specified, the parent object type and name should be given values that are not NULL or default. Otherwise, the function will return an error.

Permissions to list extended properties of certain level object types vary.

- For level 0 objects, a user can list extended properties specifying the type "user" if that person is the user identified in the level 0 name, or if that user is a member of the **db_owner** and **db_ddladmin** fixed database role.

- All users can list extended properties using the level 0 object type "type."

- For level 1 objects, a user can list extended properties on any of the valid type values if the user is the object owner, or if the user has any permission on the object.

- For level 2 objects, a user can list extended properties on any of valid type values if the current user has any permission on the parent object (level 1 and 0).

Examples

This example lists all extended properties for the database.

```
SELECT *
FROM   ::fn_listextendedproperty(NULL, NULL, NULL, NULL, NULL, NULL, NULL)
```

-or-

```
SELECT *
FROM   ::fn_listextendedproperty(default, default, default, default, default, default, default)
```

This example lists all extended properties for all columns in table 'T1.'

```
CREATE table T1 (id int , name char (20))

EXEC  sp_addextendedproperty 'caption', 'Employee ID', 'user', dbo, 'table', 'T1',
'column', id

EXEC  sp_addextendedproperty 'caption', 'Employee Name', 'user', dbo, 'table', 'T1',
'column', name

SELECT *
FROM   ::fn_listextendedproperty (NULL, 'user', 'dbo', 'table', 'T1', 'column', default)
```

Here is the result set:

objtype	objname	name	value
COLUMN	id	caption	Employee ID
COLUMN	name	caption	Employee Name

Related Topics

Property Management, sp_addextendedproperty

fn_servershareddrives

Returns the names of shared drives used by the clustered server.

Syntax

```
fn_servershareddrives()
```

Tables Returned

If the current server instance is not a clustered server, fn_servershareddrives returns an empty rowset.

If the current server is a clustered server, fn_servershareddrives returns the following information:

Name	Data type	Description
DriveName	nchar(1)	Name of the shared drive

Remarks

fn_servershareddrives returns a list of shared drives used by this clustered server. These shared drives belong to the same cluster group as the SQL Server resource. Further, the SQL Server resource is dependent on these drives.

This function is helpful in identifying drives available to users.

Examples

Here is a query on a clustered server instance.

```
SELECT *
FROM ::fn_servershareddrives()
```

Here is the result set:

```
DriveName
--------
m
n
```

Related Topics

Failover Clustering, fn_virtualservernodes

fn_trace_geteventinfo

Returns information about the events traced.

Syntax

```
fn_trace_geteventinfo ( [ @traceid = ] trace_id )
```

Arguments

[**@traceid =**] *trace_id*

Is the ID of the trace. *trace_id* is **int**, with no default. The user employs this *trace_id* value to identify, modify, and control the trace.

Tables Returned

Column name	Data type	Description
EventID	**int**	ID of the traced event
ColumnID	**int**	ID numbers of all columns collected for each event

Remarks

fn_trace_geteventinfo is a Microsoft SQL Server 2000 built-in function that performs many of the actions previously executed by extended stored procedures available in earlier versions of SQL Server. Use fn_trace_geteventinfo instead of:

- **xp_trace_geteventclassrequired**
- **xp_trace_getqueuecreateinfo**
- **xp_trace_getqueueproperties**

To obtain information previously returned by the **xp_trace_geteventclassrequired**, for example, execute a query in the following form:

```
SELECT *
FROM ::fn_trace_geteventinfo(trace_id)
WHERE EventID= 'x'
```

Related Topics

sp_trace_generateevent, sp_trace_setevent, sp_trace_setfilter

fn_trace_getfilterinfo

Returns information about the filters applied to a specified trace.

Syntax

```
fn_trace_getfilterinfo( [ @traceid = ] trace_id )
```

Arguments

[@**traceid** =] *trace_id*

Is the ID of the trace. *trace_id* is **int**, with no default. The user employs this *trace_id* value to identify, modify, and control the trace.

Tables Returned

This function returns the following information. For more information about the columns, see sp_trace_setfilter.

Column name	Data type	Description
Column ID	**int**	The ID of the column on which the filter is applied.
Logical Operator	**int**	Specifies whether the AND or OR operator is applied.
Comparison Operator	**int**	Specifies the type of comparison made (=, <>, <, >, <=, >=, LIKE, or NOT LIKE).
Value	**sql_variant**	Specifies the value on which the filter is applied.

Remarks

fn_trace_getfilterinfo is a Microsoft SQL Server 2000 built-in function that performs many of the actions previously executed by extended stored procedures available in earlier versions of SQL Server. Use fn_trace_getfilterinfo instead of the **xp_trace_get*filter** extended stored procedures. For more information, see Creating and Managing Traces and Templates.

To use fn_trace_getfilterinfo to obtain information about the filters applied or available for certain traces, execute a query that follows this form:

```
SELECT *
FROM ::fn_trace_getfilterinfo(trace_id)
WHERE
```

Related Topics

sp_trace_setfilter

fn_trace_getinfo

Returns information about a specified trace or existing traces.

Syntax

```
fn_trace_getinfo( [ @traceid = ] trace_id )
```

Arguments

[@**traceid** =] *trace_id*

Is the ID of the trace, and is an integer. To return information on all traces, specify the default value for this parameter. The keyword 'default' must be used, as in

```
SELECT * FROM :: fn_trace_getinfo(default)
```

When the value of 0 is explicitly supplied, the function will return all traces as if the function was called with the 'default' keyword. The user employs this *trace_id* value to identify, modify, and control the trace.

Tables Returned

If a *trace_id* is specified, fn_trace_getinfo returns a table with information about the specified trace. If no *trace_id* is specified, this function returns information about all active traces.

Column name	Data type	Description
TraceId	**int**	The ID of the trace.
Property	**int**	The property of the trace as represented by the following integers: 1 - Trace Options (See @options in **sp_trace_create**) 2 - FileName 3 - MaxSize 4 - StopTime 5 - Current Trace status
Value	**sql_variant**	The information about the property of the trace specified.

Remarks

fn_trace_getinfo is a Microsoft SQL Server 2000 built-in function that performs many of the actions previously executed by extended stored procedures available in earlier versions of SQL Server. Use fn_trace_getinfo instead of:

- **xp_trace_getqueuecreateinfo**
- **xp_trace_getqueuedestination**
- **xp_trace_getqueueproperties**

To obtain information previously returned by the **xp_trace_getqueueproperties**, for example, execute a query in the following form:

```
SELECT *
FROM ::fn_trace_getinfo(trace_id)
WHERE Property=4
```

Related Topics

sp_trace_generateevent, sp_trace_setevent, sp_trace_setfilter, sp_trace_setstatus

---

fn_trace_gettable

Returns trace file information in a table format.

Syntax

```
fn_trace_gettable( [ @filename = ] filename , [ @numfiles = ] number_files )
```

Arguments

[**@filename =**] *filename*
Specifies the initial trace to be read. *filename* is **nvarchar(256)**, with no default.

[**@numfiles =**] *number_files*
Specifies the number of rollover files, including the initial file specified in *filename*, to be read. *number_files* is **int**. Users may specify the default value "default" to tell SQL Server to read all rollover files until the end of the trace.

```
SELECT * FROM ::fn_trace_gettable('c:\my_trace.trc', default)
GO
```

-or-

```
SELECT * FROM ::fn_trace_gettable(('c:\my_trace.trc', -1)
GO
```

Tables Returned

fn_trace_gettable returns a table with all the valid columns. For information, see sp_trace_setevent.

Examples

This example calls the function as part of a SELECT..INTO statement and returns a table that can be loaded into SQL Profiler.

```
USE pubs
SELECT * INTO temp_trc
FROM ::fn_trace_gettable(c:\my_trace.trc", default)
```

Related Topics

sp_trace_generateevent, sp_trace_setevent, sp_trace_setfilter, sp_trace_setstatus

---

fn_virtualfilestats

Returns I/O statistics for database files, including log files.

Syntax

```
fn_virtualfilestats ( [@DatabaseID=] database_id
    , [ @FileID = ] file_id )
```

Arguments

[@**DatabaseID**=] *database_id*
    Is the ID of the database. *database_id* is **int**, with no default.

[@**FileID** =] *file_id*
    Is the ID of the file. *file_id* is **int**, with no default.

Tables Returned

Column Name	Data type	Description
DbId	**smallint**	Database ID
FileId	**smallint**	File ID
TimeStamp	**int**	Time at which the data was taken
NumberReads	**bigint**	Number of reads issued on the file
NumberWrites	**bigint**	Number of writes made on the file
BytesRead	**bigint**	Number of bytes read issued on the file
BytesWritten	**bigint**	Number of bytes written made on the file
IoStallMS	**bigint**	Total amount of time, in milliseconds, that users waited for the I/Os to complete on the file

Remarks

fn_virtualfilestats is a system table-valued function that gives statistical information, such as the total number of I/Os performed on a file. The function helps keep track of the length of time users have to wait to read or write to a file. The function also helps identify the files that encounter large numbers of I/O activity.

Examples

```
SELECT *
FROM :: fn_virtualfilestats(1, 1)
```

fn_virtualservernodes

Returns the list of nodes on which the virtual server can run. Such information is useful in failover clustering environments.

Syntax

```
fn_virtualservernodes()
```

Tables Returned

If the current server instance is not a clustered server, fn_virtualservernodes returns an empty rowset.

If the current server is a clustered server, fn_virtualservernodes returns the list of nodes on which this virtual server has been defined.

Examples

Here is a query on a clustered server instance.

```
SELECT *
FROM ::fn_virtualservernodes()
```

Here is the result set:

```
NodeName
--------
ntmachine1
ntmachine2
```

Related Topics

Failover Clustering, fn_serversharedrives

FORMATMESSAGE

Constructs a message from an existing message in **sysmessages**. The functionality of
FORMATMESSAGE resembles that of the RAISERROR statement; however,
RAISERROR prints the message immediately, and FORMATMESSAGE returns the
edited message for further processing.

Syntax

```
FORMATMESSAGE ( msg_number , param_value [ ,...n ] )
```

Arguments

msg_number
> Is the ID of the message stored in **sysmessages**. If the message does not exist in
> **sysmessages**, NULL is returned.

param_value
> Is one or more parameter values for use in the message. The values must be
> specified in the order in which the placeholder variables appear in the message.
> The maximum number of values is 20.

Return Types

nvarchar

Remarks

Like the RAISERROR statement, FORMATMESSAGE edits the message by
substituting the supplied parameter values for placeholder variables in the message.
For more information about the placeholders allowed in error messages and the editing
process, see RAISERROR.

FORMATMESSAGE looks up the message in the current language of the user. If there
is no localized version of the message, the U.S. English version is used.

For localized messages, the supplied parameter values must correspond to the
parameter placeholders in the U.S. English version. That is, parameter 1 in the
localized version must correspond to parameter 1 in the U.S. English version,
parameter 2 must correspond to parameter 2, and so on.

Examples

This example uses a hypothetical message 50001, stored in **sysmessages** as "The number of rows in %s is %1d." FORMATMESSAGE substitutes the values Table1 and 5 for the parameter placeholders. The resulting string, "The number of rows in Table1 is 5." is stored in the local variable **@var1**.

```
DECLARE @var1 VARCHAR(100)
SELECT @var1 = FORMATMESSAGE(50001, 'Table1', 5)
```

Related Topics

sp_addmessage, System Functions

FREETEXT

Is a predicate used to search columns containing character-based data types for values that match the meaning and not the exact wording of the words in the search condition. When FREETEXT is used, the full-text query engine internally "word-breaks" the *freetext_string* into a number of search terms and assigns each term a weight and then finds the matches.

Syntax

```
FREETEXT ( { column | * } , 'freetext_string' )
```

Arguments

column

Is the name of a specific column that has been registered for full-text searching. Columns of the character string data types are valid columns for full-text searching.

*

Specifies that all columns that have been registered for full-text searching should be used to search for the given *freetext_string*.

freetext_string

Is text to search for in the specified *column*. Any text, including words, phrases or sentences, can be entered. There is no concern about syntax.

Remarks

Full-text queries using FREETEXT are less precise than those full-text queries using CONTAINS. The Microsoft SQL Server full-text search engine identifies important words and phrases. No special meaning is given to any of the reserved keywords or wildcard characters that typically have meaning when specified in the <contains_search_condition> parameter of the CONTAINS predicate.

FREETEXT is not recognized as a keyword if the compatibility level is less than 70. For more information, see sp_dbcmptlevel.

Examples

A. Use FREETEXT to search for words containing specified character values

This example searches for all product categories containing the words related to bread, candy, dry, and meat in the product description, such as breads, candies, dried, and meats.

```
USE Northwind
GO
SELECT CategoryName
FROM Categories
WHERE FREETEXT (Description, 'sweetest candy bread and dry meat' )
GO
```

B. Use variables in full-text search

This example uses a variable instead of a specific search term.

```
USE pubs
GO
DECLARE @SearchWord varchar(30)
SET @SearchWord ='Moon'
SELECT pr_info FROM pub_info WHERE FREETEXT(pr_info, @SearchWord)
```

Related Topics

CONTAINS, CONTAINSTABLE, Data Types, FREETEXTTABLE, WHERE

FREETEXTTABLE

Returns a table of zero, one, or more rows for those columns containing character-based data types for values that match the meaning, but not the exact wording, of the text in the specified *freetext_string*. FREETEXTTABLE can be referenced in the FROM clause of a SELECT statement like a regular table name.

Queries using FREETEXTTABLE specify freetext-type full-text queries that return a relevance ranking value (RANK) for each row.

Syntax

```
FREETEXTTABLE ( table , { column | * } , 'freetext_string' [ , top_n_by_rank ] )
```

Arguments

table

> Is the name of the table that has been marked for full-text querying. *table* can be a one-, two-, or three-part database object name. For more information, see Transact-SQL Syntax Conventions. *table* cannot specify a server name and cannot be used in queries against linked servers.

column

> Is the name of the column to search that resides within *table*. Columns of the character string data types are valid columns for full-text searching.

*

> Specifies that all columns that have been registered for full-text searching should be used to search for the given *freetext_string*.

freetext_string

> Is the text to search for in the specified *column*. Variables cannot be used.

top_n_by_rank

> When an integer value, *n*, is specified, FREETEXTTABLE returns only the top *n* matches, ordered by rank.

Remarks

FREETEXTTABLE uses the same search conditions as the FREETEXT predicate.

Like CONTAINSTABLE, the table returned has columns named **KEY** and **RANK**, which are referenced within the query to obtain the appropriate rows and use the row ranking values.

FREETEXTTABLE is not recognized as a keyword if the compatibility level is less than 70. For more information, see sp_dbcmptlevel.

Permissions

FREETEXTTABLE can be invoked only by users with appropriate SELECT privileges for the specified table or the referenced columns of the table.

Examples

This example returns the category name and description of all categories that relate to sweet, candy, bread, dry, and meat.

```
USE Northwind
SELECT FT_TBL.CategoryName,
   FT_TBL.Description,
   KEY_TBL.RANK
FROM Categories AS FT_TBL INNER JOIN
```

(continued)

(continued)

```
    FREETEXTTABLE(Categories, Description,
    'sweetest candy bread and dry meat') AS KEY_TBL
    ON FT_TBL.CategoryID = KEY_TBL.[KEY]
GO
```

Related Topics

CONTAINS, CONTAINSTABLE, FREETEXT, Full-text Querying SQL Server Data, Rowset Functions, SELECT, WHERE

FROM

Specifies the tables, views, derived tables, and joined tables used in DELETE, SELECT, and UPDATE statements.

Syntax

```
[ FROM { < table_source > } [ ,...n ] ]

< table_source > ::=
    table_name [ [ AS ] table_alias ] [ WITH ( < table_hint > [ ,...n ] ) ]
    | view_name [ [ AS ] table_alias ] [ WITH ( < view_hint > [ ,...n ] ) ]
    | rowset_function [ [ AS ] table_alias ]
    | user_defined_function [ [ AS ] table_alias ]
    | derived_table [ AS ] table_alias [ ( column_alias [ ,...n ] ) ]
    | < joined_table >
< joined_table > ::=
    < table_source > < join_type > < table_source > ON < search_condition >
    | < table_source > CROSS JOIN < table_source >
    | [ ( ] < joined_table > [ ) ] ]
< join_type > ::=
    [ INNER | { { LEFT | RIGHT | FULL } [ OUTER] } ]
    [ < join_hint > ]
    JOIN
```

Arguments

<table_source>

Specifies a table or view, both with or without an alias, to use in the Transact-SQL statement. A maximum of 256 tables can be used in the statement. A **table** variable may be specified as a table source.

If the table or view exists in another database on the same computer running Microsoft SQL Server, use a fully qualified name in the form *database.owner.object_name*. If the table or view exists outside the local server on a linked server, use a four-part name in the form *linked_server.catalog.schema.object*. A four-part table (or view) name constructed using the OPENDATASOURCE function as the server part of the name also may be used to specify the table source. For more information about the function, see OPENDATASOURCE.

table_name

Is the name of a table. The order of the tables and views after the FROM keyword does not affect the result set returned. Errors are reported when duplicate names appear in the FROM clause.

[AS] *table_alias*

Is an alias for *table_name*, *view_name*, or *rowset_function*, used either for convenience or to distinguish a table or view in a self-join or subquery. An alias is often a shortened table name used to refer to specific columns of the tables in a join. If the same column name exists in more than one table in the join, SQL Server requires that the column name must be qualified by a table name or alias. (The table name cannot be used if an alias is defined).

WITH (< table_hint >)

Specifies a table scan, one or more indexes to be used by the query optimizer, or a locking method to be used by the query optimizer with this table and for this statement. For more information, see Table Hints.

view_name

Is the name of a view. A view is a "virtual table", usually created as a subset of columns from one or more tables.

WITH (< view_hint >)

Specifies a scan of the indexed view. By default, the view is expanded before the query optimizer processes the query. View hints are allowed only in SELECT statements, and cannot be used in UPDATE, DELETE, and INSERT statements.

rowset_function

Specifies one of the rowset functions, which return an object that can be used in place of a table reference. For more information about a list of rowset functions, see Rowset Functions.

user_defined_function

Specifies a user-defined function that returns a table. If the user-defined function is a built-in user-defined function, it must be preceded by two colons, as in

```
FROM ::fn_listextendedproperty
```

derived_table

Is a subquery that retrieves rows from the database. *derived_table* is used as input to the outer query.

column_alias

Is an optional alias to replace a column name in the result set. Include one column alias for each column in the select list, and enclose the entire list of column aliases in parentheses.

< joined_table >

Is a result set that is the product of two or more tables, for example:

```
SELECT *
FROM tab1 LEFT OUTER JOIN tab2 ON tab1.c3 = tab2.c3
    RIGHT OUTER JOIN tab3 LEFT OUTER JOIN tab4
        ON tab3.c1 = tab4.c1
        ON tab2.c3 = tab4.c3
```

For multiple CROSS joins, use parentheses to change the natural order of the joins.

< *join*_type >

Specifies the type of join operation.

INNER

Specifies all matching pairs of rows are returned. Discards unmatched rows from both tables. This is the default if no join type is specified.

FULL [OUTER]

Specifies that a row from either the left or right table that does not meet the join condition is included in the result set, and output columns that correspond to the other table are set to NULL. This is in addition to all rows usually returned by the INNER JOIN.

> **Note** It is possible to specify outer joins as specified here or by using the old nonstandard *= and =* operators in the WHERE clause. The two methods cannot both be used in the same statement.

LEFT [OUTER]

Specifies that all rows from the left table not meeting the join condition are included in the result set, and output columns from the other table are set to NULL in addition to all rows returned by the inner join.

RIGHT [OUTER]

Specifies all rows from the right table not meeting the join condition are included in the result set, and output columns that correspond to the other table are set to NULL, in addition to all rows returned by the inner join.

<join_hint>

Specifies that the SQL Server query optimizer use one join hint, or execution algorithm, per join specified in the query FROM clause. For more information, see Join Hints later in this topic.

JOIN

Indicates that the specified join operation should take place between the given tables or views.

ON <search_condition>

> Specifies the condition on which the join is based. The condition can specify any predicate, although columns and comparison operators are often used, for example:

```
SELECT ProductID, Suppliers.SupplierID
  FROM Suppliers JOIN Products
  ON (Suppliers.SupplierID = Products.SupplierID)
```

> When the condition specifies columns, the columns do not have to have the same name or same data type; however, if the data types are not identical, they must be either compatible or types that Microsoft SQL Server can implicitly convert. If the data types cannot be implicitly converted, the condition must explicitly convert the data type using the CAST function.

> There may be predicates involving only one of the joined tables in the ON clause. Such predicates also may be in the WHERE clause in the query. Although the placement of such predicates does not make a difference in the case of INNER joins, they may cause a different result if OUTER joins are involved. This is because the predicates in the ON clause are applied to the table prior to the join, while the WHERE clause is semantically applied on the result of the join.

> For more information about search conditions and predicates, see Search Condition.

CROSS JOIN

> Specifies the cross-product of two tables. Returns the same rows as if no WHERE clause was specified in an old-style, non-SQL-92-style join.

Table Hints

A table hint specifies a table scan, one or more indexes to be used by the query optimizer, or a locking method to be used by the query optimizer with this table and for this SELECT. Although this is an option, the query optimizer can usually pick the best optimization method without hints being specified.

> **CAUTION**   Because the query optimizer of SQL Server usually selects the best execution plan for a query, it is recommended that <join_hint>, <query_hint>, <table_hint>, and <view_hint> only be used as a last resort by experienced developers and database administrators.

The table hints are ignored if the table is not accessed by the query plan. This may be a result of the optimizer's choice not to access the table at all, or because an indexed view is accessed instead. In the latter case, the use of an indexed view may be prevented by using the OPTION (EXPAND VIEWS) query hint.

The use of commas between table hints is optional but encouraged. Separation of hints by spaces rather than commas is supported for backward compatibility.

The use of the WITH keyword is encouraged, although it is not currently required. In future releases of SQL Server, WITH may be a required keyword.

In SQL Server 2000, all lock hints are propagated to all the base tables and views that are referenced in a view. In addition, SQL Server performs the corresponding lock consistency checks.

If a table (including system tables) contains computed columns and the computed columns are computed by expressions or functions accessing columns in other tables, the table hints are not used on those tables (the table hints are not propagated). For example, a NOLOCK table hint is specified on a table in the query. This table has computed columns that are computed by a combination of expressions and functions (accessing columns in another table). The tables referenced by the expressions and functions do not use the NOLOCK table hint when accessed.

SQL Server does not allow more than one table hint from each of the following groups for each table in the FROM clause:

- Granularity hints: PAGLOCK, NOLOCK, ROWLOCK, TABLOCK, or TABLOCKX.

- Isolation level hints: HOLDLOCK, NOLOCK, READCOMMITTED, REPEATABLEREAD, SERIALIZABLE.

The NOLOCK, READUNCOMMITTED, and READPAST table hints are not allowed for tables that are targets of delete, insert, or update operations.

Syntax

```
< table_hint > ::=
    { INDEX ( index_val [ ,...n ] )
        | FASTFIRSTROW
        | HOLDLOCK
        | NOLOCK
        | PAGLOCK
        | READCOMMITTED
        | READPAST
        | READUNCOMMITTED
        | REPEATABLEREAD
        | ROWLOCK
        | SERIALIZABLE
        | TABLOCK
        | TABLOCKX
        | UPDLOCK
        | XLOCK
    }
```

Arguments

INDEX (*index_val* [,...*n*])

Specifies the name or ID of the indexes to be used by SQL Server when processing the statement. Only one index hint per table can be specified.

If a clustered index exists, INDEX(0) forces a clustered index scan and INDEX(1) forces a clustered index scan or seek. If no clustered index exists, INDEX(0) forces a table scan and INDEX(1) is interpreted as an error.

The alternative INDEX = syntax (which specifies a single index hint) is supported only for backward compatibility.

If multiple indexes are used in the single hint list, the duplicates are ignored and the rest of the listed indexes are used to retrieve the rows of the table. The order of the indexes in the index hint is significant. A multiple index hint also enforces index ANDing and SQL Server applies as many conditions as possible on each index accessed. If the collection of hinted indexes is not covering, a fetch is performed after retrieving all the indexed columns.

Note   If an index hint referring to multiple indexes is used on the *fact table* in a *star join*, SQL Server ignores the index hint and returns a warning message. Also, *index ORing* is disallowed for a table with an index hint specified.

The maximum number of indexes in the table hint is 250 nonclustered indexes.

FASTFIRSTROW

Equivalent to OPTION (FAST 1). For more information, see FAST in the OPTION clause in SELECT.

HOLDLOCK

Equivalent to SERIALIZABLE. (For more information, see SERIALIZABLE later in this topic.) The HOLDLOCK option applies only to the table or view for which it is specified and only for the duration of the transaction defined by the statement in which it is used. HOLDLOCK cannot be used in a SELECT statement that includes the FOR BROWSE option.

NOLOCK

Equivalent to READUNCOMMITTED. For more information, see READUNCOMMITTED later in this topic.

PAGLOCK

Takes shared page locks where a single shared table lock is normally taken.

READCOMMITTED

Specifies that a scan is performed with the same locking semantics as a transaction running at READ COMMITTED isolation level. For more information about isolation levels, see SET TRANSACTION ISOLATION LEVEL.

READPAST

Specifies that locked rows are skipped (read past). For example, assume table **T1** contains a single integer column with the values of 1, 2, 3, 4, 5. If transaction A changes the value of 3 to 8 but has not yet committed, a SELECT * FROM T1 (READPAST) yields values 1, 2, 4, 5. READPAST applies only to transactions operating at READ COMMITTED isolation and reads past only row-level locks. This lock hint is used primarily to implement a work queue on a SQL Server table.

READUNCOMMITTED

Specifies that dirty reads are allowed. This means that no shared locks are issued and no exclusive locks are honored. Allowing dirty reads can result in higher concurrency, but at the cost of lower consistency. If READUNCOMMITTED is specified, it is possible to read an uncommitted transaction or to read a set of pages rolled back in the middle of the read; therefore, error messages may result. For more information about isolation levels, see SET TRANSACTION ISOLATION LEVEL.

> **Note** If you receive the error message 601 when READUNCOMMITTED is specified, resolve it as you would a deadlock error (1205), and retry your statement.

REPEATABLEREAD

Specifies that a scan is performed with the same locking semantics as a transaction running at REPEATABLE READ isolation level. For more information about isolation levels, see SET TRANSACTION ISOLATION LEVEL.

ROWLOCK

Specifies that a shared row lock is taken when a single shared page or table lock is normally taken.

SERIALIZABLE

Equivalent to HOLDLOCK. Makes shared locks more restrictive by holding them until the completion of a transaction (instead of releasing the shared lock as soon as the required table or data page is no longer needed, whether or not the transaction has been completed). The scan is performed with the same semantics as a transaction running at the SERIALIZABLE isolation level. For more information about isolation levels, see SET TRANSACTION ISOLATION LEVEL.

TABLOCK

Specifies that a shared lock is taken on the table held until the end-of-statement. If HOLDLOCK is also specified, the shared table lock is held until the end of the transaction.

TABLOCKX

Specifies that an exclusive lock is taken on the table held until the end-of-statement or end-of-transaction.

UPDLOCK

Specifies that update locks instead of shared locks are taken while reading the table, and that they are held until the end-of-statement or end-of-transaction.

XLOCK

Specifies that exclusive locks should be taken and held until the end of transaction on all data processed by the statement. If specified with PAGLOCK or TABLOCK, the exclusive locks apply to the appropriate level of granularity.

View Hints

View hints can be used only for indexed views. (An indexed view is a view with a unique clustered index created on it.) If a query contains references to columns that are present both in an indexed view and base tables, and Microsoft SQL Server query optimizer determines that using the indexed view provides the best method for executing the query, then the optimizer utilizes the index on the view. This function is supported only on the Enterprise and Developer Editions of the Microsoft SQL Server 2000.

However, in order for the optimizer to consider indexed views, the following SET options must be set to ON:

ANSI_NULLS	ARITHABORT
ANSI_PADDING	CONCAT_NULL_YIELDS_NULL
ANSI_WARNINGS	QUOTED_IDENTIFIERS

In addition, the NUMERIC_ROUNDABORT option must be set to OFF.

To force the optimizer to use an index for an indexed view, specify the NOEXPAND option. This hint may be used only if the view is also named in the query. SQL Server 2000 does not provide a hint to force a particular indexed view to be used in a query that does not name the view directly in the FROM clause; however, the query optimizer considers the use of indexed views even if they are not referenced directly in the query.

View hints are allowed only in SELECT statements; they cannot be used in views that are the table source in INSERT, UPDATE, and DELETE statements.

Syntax

```
< view_hint > ::=
{ NOEXPAND [ , INDEX ( index_val [ ,…n ] ) ] }
```

Arguments

NOEXPAND

Specifies that the indexed view is not expanded when the query optimizer processes the query. The query optimizer treats the view like a table with clustered index.

INDEX (*index_val* [,...*n*])

Specifies the name or ID of the indexes to be used by SQL Server when it processes the statement. Only one index hint per view can be specified.

INDEX(0) forces a clustered index scan and INDEX(1) forces a clustered index scan or seek.

If multiple indexes are used in the single hint list, the duplicates are ignored and the rest of the listed indexes are used to retrieve the rows of the indexed view. The ordering of the indexes in the index hint is significant. A multiple index hint also enforces index ANDing and SQL Server applies as many conditions as possible on each index accessed. If the collection of hinted indexes does not contain all columns referenced in the query, a fetch is performed after retrieving all the indexed columns.

Join Hints

Join hints, which are specified in a query's FROM clause, enforce a join strategy between two tables. If a join hint is specified for any two tables, the query optimizer automatically enforces the join order for all joined tables in the query, based on the position of the ON keywords. In the case of CROSS JOINS, when the ON clauses are not used, parentheses can be used to indicate the join order.

> **CAUTION** Because the SQL Server query optimizer usually selects the best execution plan for a query, it is recommended that <join_hint>, <query_hint>, and <table_hint> be used only as a last resort by experienced database administrators.

Syntax

```
< join_hint > ::=
    { LOOP | HASH | MERGE | REMOTE }
```

Arguments

LOOP | HASH | MERGE

Specifies that the join in the query should use looping, hashing, or merging. Using LOOP | HASH | MERGE JOIN enforces a particular join between two tables.

REMOTE

Specifies that the join operation is performed on the site of the right table. This is useful when the left table is a local table and the right table is a remote table. REMOTE should be used only when the left table has fewer rows than the right table.

If the right table is local, the join is performed locally. If both tables are remote but from different data sources, REMOTE causes the join to be performed on the right table's site. If both tables are remote tables from the same data source, REMOTE is not necessary.

REMOTE cannot be used when one of the values being compared in the join predicate is cast to a different collation using the COLLATE clause.

REMOTE can be used only for INNER JOIN operations.

Remarks

The FROM clause supports the SQL-92-SQL syntax for joined tables and derived tables. SQL-92 syntax provides the INNER, LEFT OUTER, RIGHT OUTER, FULL OUTER, and CROSS join operators.

Although the outer join operators from earlier versions of SQL Server are supported, you cannot use both outer join operators and SQL-92-style joined tables in the same FROM clause.

UNION and JOIN within a FROM clause are supported within views as well as in derived tables and subqueries.

A self-join is a table that joins upon itself. Inserts or updates that are based on a self-join follow the order in the FROM clause.

Since Microsoft SQL Server 2000 considers distribution and cardinality statistics from linked servers that provide column distribution statistics, the REMOTE join hint is not really necessary to force evaluating a join remotely. The SQL Server query processor considers remote statistics and determines if a remote-join strategy is appropriate. REMOTE join hint is useful for providers that do not provide column distribution statistics. For more information, see Distribution Statistics Requirements for OLE DB Providers.

Permissions

FROM permissions default to the permissions for the DELETE, SELECT, or UPDATE statement.

Examples

A. Use a simple FROM clause

This example retrieves the **pub_id** and **pub_name** columns from the **publishers** table.

```
USE pubs
SELECT pub_id, pub_name
FROM publishers
ORDER BY pub_id
```

Here is the result set:

```
pub_id pub_name
------ --------------------
0736   New Moon Books
0877   Binnet & Hardley
1389   Algodata Infosystems
1622   Five Lakes Publishing
1756   Ramona Publishers
9901   GGG&G
9952   Scootney Books
9999   Lucerne Publishing

(8 row(s) affected)
```

B. Use the TABLOCK and HOLDLOCK optimizer hints

The following partial transaction shows how to place an explicit shared table lock on **authors** and how to read the index. The lock is held throughout the entire transaction.

```
USE pubs
BEGIN TRAN
SELECT COUNT(*)
FROM authors WITH (TABLOCK, HOLDLOCK)
```

C. Use the SQL-92 CROSS JOIN syntax

This example returns the cross product of the two tables **authors** and **publishers**. A list of all possible combinations of **au_lname** rows and all **pub_name** rows are returned.

```
USE pubs
SELECT au_lname, pub_name
FROM authors CROSS JOIN publishers
ORDER BY au_lname ASC, pub_name ASC
```

Here is the result set:

```
au_lname                                    pub_name
------------------------------------------- --------------------------------
Bennet                                      Algodata Infosystems
Bennet                                      Binnet & Hardley
Bennet                                      Five Lakes Publishing
Bennet                                      GGG&G
Bennet                                      Lucerne Publishing
Bennet                                      New Moon Books
Bennet                                      Ramona Publishers
Bennet                                      Scootney Books
```

(continued)

(continued)

```
Blotchet-Halls                      Algodata Infosystems
Blotchet-Halls                      Binnet & Hardley
Blotchet-Halls                      Five Lakes Publishing
Blotchet-Halls                      GGG&G
Blotchet-Halls                      Lucerne Publishing
Blotchet-Halls                      New Moon Books
Blotchet-Halls                      Ramona Publishers
Blotchet-Halls                      Scootney Books
Carson                              Algodata Infosystems
Carson                              Binnet & Hardley
Carson                              Five Lakes Publishing
...
Stringer                            Scootney Books
White                               Algodata Infosystems
White                               Binnet & Hardley
White                               Five Lakes Publishing
White                               GGG&G
White                               Lucerne Publishing
White                               New Moon Books
White                               Ramona Publishers
White                               Scootney Books
Yokomoto                            Algodata Infosystems
Yokomoto                            Binnet & Hardley
Yokomoto                            Five Lakes Publishing
Yokomoto                            GGG&G
Yokomoto                            Lucerne Publishing
Yokomoto                            New Moon Books
Yokomoto                            Ramona Publishers
Yokomoto                            Scootney Books

(184 row(s) affected)
```

D. Use the SQL-92 FULL OUTER JOIN syntax

This example returns the book title and its corresponding publisher in the **titles** table. It also returns any publishers who have not published books listed in the **titles** table, and any book titles with a publisher other than the one listed in the **publishers** table.

```
USE pubs
-- The OUTER keyword following the FULL keyword is optional.
SELECT SUBSTRING(titles.title, 1, 10) AS Title,
    publishers.pub_name AS Publisher
FROM publishers FULL OUTER JOIN titles
```

(continued)

(continued)

```
   ON titles.pub_id = publishers.pub_id
WHERE titles.pub_id IS NULL
   OR publishers.pub_id IS NULL
ORDER BY publishers.pub_name
```

Here is the result set:

```
Title       Publisher
----------  ----------------------------------------
NULL        Five Lakes Publishing
NULL        GGG&G
NULL        Lucerne Publishing
NULL        Ramona Publishers
NULL        Scootney Books

(5 row(s) affected)
```

E. Use the SQL-92 LEFT OUTER JOIN syntax

This example joins two tables on **au_id** and preserves the unmatched rows from the left table. The **authors** table is matched with the **titleauthor** table on the **au_id** columns in each table. All authors, published and unpublished, appear in the result set.

```
USE pubs
-- The OUTER keyword following the LEFT keyword is optional.
SELECT SUBSTRING(authors.au_lname, 1, 10) AS Last,
    authors.au_fname AS First, titleauthor.title_id
FROM authors LEFT OUTER JOIN titleauthor
    ON authors.au_id = titleauthor.au_id
```

Here is the result set:

```
Last        First                 title_id
----------  --------------------  --------
White       Johnson               PS3333
Green       Marjorie              BU1032
Green       Marjorie              BU2075
Carson      Cheryl                PC1035
...                    ...
McBadden    Heather               NULL
Ringer      Anne                  PS2091
Ringer      Albert                PS2091
Ringer      Albert                PS2106

(29 row(s) affected)
```

F. Use the SQL-92 INNER JOIN syntax

This example returns all publisher names with the corresponding book titles each publisher has published.

```
USE pubs
-- By default, SQL Server performs an INNER JOIN if only the JOIN
-- keyword is specified.
SELECT SUBSTRING(titles.title, 1, 30) AS Title, publishers.pub_name
FROM publishers INNER JOIN titles
   ON titles.pub_id = publishers.pub_id
ORDER BY publishers.pub_name
```

Here is the result set:

```
Title                          pub_name
------------------------------ ----------------------------------------
The Busy Executive's Database  Algodata Infosystems
Cooking with Computers: Surrep Algodata Infosystems
Straight Talk About Computers  Algodata Infosystems
But Is It User Friendly?       Algodata Infosystems
Secrets of Silicon Valley      Algodata Infosystems
Net Etiquette                  Algodata Infosystems
Silicon Valley Gastronomic Tre Binnet & Hardley
The Gourmet Microwave          Binnet & Hardley
The Psychology of Computer Coo Binnet & Hardley
Computer Phobic AND Non-Phobic Binnet & Hardley
Onions, Leeks, and Garlic: Coo Binnet & Hardley
Fifty Years in Buckingham Pala Binnet & Hardley
Sushi, Anyone?                 Binnet & Hardley
You Can Combat Computer Stress New Moon Books
Is Anger the Enemy?            New Moon Books
Life Without Fear              New Moon Books
Prolonged Data Deprivation: Fo New Moon Books
Emotional Security: A New Algo  New Moon Books

(18 row(s) affected)
```

G. Use the SQL-92 RIGHT OUTER JOIN syntax

This example joins two tables on **pub_id** and preserves the unmatched rows from the right table. The **publishers** table is matched with the **titles** table on the **pub_id** column in each table. All publishers appear in the result set, whether or not they have published any books.

```
USE pubs
SELECT SUBSTRING(titles.title, 1, 30) AS 'Title', publishers.pub_name
FROM titles RIGHT OUTER JOIN publishers
   ON titles.pub_id = publishers.pub_id
ORDER BY publishers.pub_name
```

Here is the result set:

```
Title                           pub_name
------------------------------  ----------------------------------------
The Busy Executive's Database   Algodata Infosystems
Cooking with Computers: Surrep  Algodata Infosystems
Straight Talk About Computers   Algodata Infosystems
But Is It User Friendly?        Algodata Infosystems
Secrets of Silicon Valley       Algodata Infosystems
Net Etiquette                   Algodata Infosystems
Silicon Valley Gastronomic Tre  Binnet & Hardley
The Gourmet Microwave           Binnet & Hardley
The Psychology of Computer Coo  Binnet & Hardley
Computer Phobic AND Non-Phobic  Binnet & Hardley
Onions, Leeks, and Garlic: Coo  Binnet & Hardley
Fifty Years in Buckingham Pala  Binnet & Hardley
Sushi, Anyone?                  Binnet & Hardley
NULL                            Five Lakes Publishing
NULL                            GGG&G
NULL                            Lucerne Publishing
You Can Combat Computer Stress  New Moon Books
Is Anger the Enemy?             New Moon Books
Life Without Fear               New Moon Books
Prolonged Data Deprivation: Fo  New Moon Books
Emotional Security: A New Algo  New Moon Books
NULL                            Ramona Publishers
NULL                            Scootney Books

(23 row(s) affected)
```

H. Use HASH and MERGE join hints

This example performs a three-table join among the **authors**, **titleauthors**, and **titles** tables to produce a list of authors and the books they have written. The query optimizer joins **authors** and **titleauthors** (A x TA) using a MERGE join. Next, the results of the **authors** and **titleauthors** MERGE join (A x TA) are HASH joined with the **titles** table to produce (A x TA) x T.

> **Important**   After a join hint is specified, the INNER keyword is no longer optional and must be explicitly stated for an INNER JOIN to be performed.

```
USE pubs
SELECT SUBSTRING((RTRIM(a.au_fname) + ' ' + LTRIM(a.au_lname)), 1, 25)
   AS Name, SUBSTRING(t.title, 1, 20) AS Title
FROM authors a INNER MERGE JOIN titleauthor ta
   ON a.au_id = ta.au_id INNER HASH JOIN titles t
   ON t.title_id = ta.title_id
ORDER BY au_lname ASC, au_fname ASC
```

Here is the result set:

```
Warning: The join order has been enforced because a local join hint is used.
Name                         Title
---------------------------- --------------------

Abraham Bennet               The Busy Executive's
Reginald Blotchet-Halls      Fifty Years in Bucki
Cheryl Carson                But Is It User Frien
Michel DeFrance              The Gourmet Microwav
Innes del Castillo           Silicon Valley Gastr
...                   ...
Johnson White                Prolonged Data Depri
Akiko Yokomoto               Sushi, Anyone?


(25 row(s) affected)
```

I. Use a derived table

This example uses a derived table, a SELECT statement after the FROM clause, to return all authors' first and last names and the book numbers for each title the author has written.

```
USE pubs
SELECT RTRIM(a.au_fname) + ' ' + LTRIM(a.au_lname) AS Name, d1.title_id
FROM authors a, (SELECT title_id, au_id FROM titleauthor) AS d1
WHERE a.au_id = d1.au_id
ORDER BY a.au_lname, a.au_fname
```

Here is the result set:

```
Name                                                          title_id
------------------------------------------------------------- --------
Abraham Bennet                                                BU1032
Reginald Blotchet-Halls                                       TC4203
Cheryl Carson                                                 PC1035
Michel DeFrance                                               MC3021
Innes del Castillo                                            MC2222
Ann Dull                                                      PC8888
Marjorie Green                                                BU1032
```

(continued)

(continued)

Marjorie Green	BU2075
Burt Gringlesby	TC7777
Sheryl Hunter	PC8888
Livia Karsen	PS1372
Charlene Locksley	PC9999
Charlene Locksley	PS7777
Stearns MacFeather	BU1111
Stearns MacFeather	PS1372
Michael O'Leary	BU1111
Michael O'Leary	TC7777
Sylvia Panteley	TC3218
Albert Ringer	PS2091
Albert Ringer	PS2106
Anne Ringer	MC3021
Anne Ringer	PS2091
Dean Straight	BU7832
Johnson White	PS3333
Akiko Yokomoto	TC7777

(25 row(s) affected)

Related Topics

CONTAINSTABLE, DELETE, FREETEXTTABLE, INSERT, OPENQUERY, OPENROWSET, Operators, UPDATE, WHERE

FULLTEXTCATALOGPROPERTY

Returns information about full-text catalog properties.

Syntax

```
FULLTEXTCATALOGPROPERTY ( catalog_name , property )
```

Arguments

catalog_name

Is an expression containing the name of the full-text catalog.

property

Is an expression containing the name of the full-text catalog property. The table lists the properties and provides descriptions of the information returned.

Property	Description
PopulateStatus	0 = Idle 1 = Full population in progress 2 = Paused 3 = Throttled 4 = Recovering 5 = Shutdown 6 = Incremental population in progress 7 = Building index 8 = Disk is full. Paused. 9 = Change tracking
ItemCount	Number of full-text indexed items currently in the full-text catalog.
IndexSize	Size of the full-text index in megabytes.
UniqueKeyCount	Number of unique words (keys) that make up the full-text index in this catalog. This is an approximation of the number of nonnoise words stored in the full-text catalog.
LogSize	Size, in bytes, of the combined set of error logs associated with a Microsoft Search Service full-text catalog.
PopulateCompletionAge	The difference in seconds between the completion of the last full-text index population and 01/01/1990 00:00:00.

Return Types

int

Remarks

It is important that applications do not wait in a tight loop, checking for the **PopulateStatus** property to become idle (indicating that population has completed) because this takes CPU cycles away from the database and full-text search processes and causes time outs.

Examples

This example returns the number of full-text indexed items in the **Cat_Desc** full-text catalog.

```
USE Northwind
GO
SELECT fulltextcatalogproperty('Cat_Desc', 'ItemCount')
```

Here is the result set:

```
-----------
9
```

Related Topics

FULLTEXTSERVICEPROPERTY, Metadata Functions, sp_help_fulltext_catalogs

FULLTEXTSERVICEPROPERTY

Returns information about full-text service-level properties.

Syntax

```
FULLTEXTSERVICEPROPERTY ( property )
```

Arguments

property

Is an expression containing the name of the full-text service-level property. The table lists the properties and provides descriptions of the information returned.

Property	Value
ResourceUsage	A value from 1 (background) through 5 (dedicated).
ConnectTimeout	The number of seconds that Microsoft Search Service will wait for all connections to the Microsoft SQL Server database server for full-text index population before timing out.
IsFulltextInstalled	The full-text component is installed with the current instance of SQL Server.
	1 = Full-text is installed. 0 = Full-text is not installed. NULL = Invalid input, or error.
DataTimeout	The number of seconds that Microsoft Search Service will wait for data to be returned by Microsoft SQL Server database server for full-text index population before timing out.

Return Types

int

Examples

This example verifies that Microsoft Search Service is installed.

```
SELECT fulltextserviceproperty('IsFulltextInstalled')
```

Here is the result set:

```
-----------
1
```

Related Topics

FULLTEXTCATALOGPROPERTY, Metadata Functions, sp_fulltext_service

GETANSINULL

Returns the default nullability for the database for this session.

Syntax

```
GETANSINULL ( [ 'database' ] )
```

Arguments

'database'

Is the name of the database for which to return nullability information. *database* is either **char** or **nchar**. If **char**, *database* is implicitly converted to **nchar**.

Return Types

int

Remarks

When the nullability of the given database allows null values and the column or data type nullability is not explicitly defined, GETANSINULL returns 1. This is the ANSI NULL default.

To activate the ANSI NULL default behavior, one of these conditions must be set:

- **sp_dboption** *'database_name'*, **'ANSI null default'**, **true**
- SET ANSI_NULL_DFLT_ON ON
- SET ANSI_NULL_DFLT_OFF OFF

Examples

This example checks the default nullability for the **pubs** database.

```
USE pubs
GO
SELECT GETANSINULL('pubs')
GO
```

Here is the result set:

```
------
1

(1 row(s) affected)
```

Related Topics

System Functions

GETDATE

Returns the current system date and time in the Microsoft SQL Server standard internal format for **datetime** values.

Syntax

```
GETDATE ( )
```

Return Types

datetime

Remarks

Date functions can be used in the SELECT statement select list or in the WHERE clause of a query.

In designing a report, GETDATE can be used to print the current date and time every time the report is produced. GETDATE is also useful for tracking activity, such as logging the time a transaction occurred on an account.

Examples

A. Use GET DATE to return the current date and time

This example finds the current system date and time.

```
SELECT GETDATE()
GO
```

Here is the result set:

```
-------------------------
July 29 1998   2:50    PM

(1 row(s) affected)
```

B. Use GETDATE with CREATE TABLE

This example creates the **employees** table and uses GETDATE for a default value for the employee hire date.

```
USE pubs
GO
CREATE TABLE employees
(
 emp_id char(11) NOT NULL,
 emp_lname varchar(40) NOT NULL,
 emp_fname varchar(20) NOT NULL,
 emp_hire_date datetime DEFAULT GETDATE(),
 emp_mgr varchar(30)
)
GO
```

Related Topics

Date and Time Functions

GETUTCDATE

Returns the **datetime** value representing the current UTC time (Universal Time Coordinate or Greenwich Mean Time). The current UTC time is derived from the current local time and the time zone setting in the operating system of the computer on which SQL Server is running.

Syntax

```
GETUTCDATE()
```

Return Types

datetime

Remarks

GETUTCDATE is a nondeterministic function. Views and expressions that reference this column cannot be indexed.

GETUTCDATE cannot be called inside a user-defined function.

GO

Signals the end of a batch of Transact-SQL statements to the Microsoft SQL Server utilities.

Syntax

```
GO
```

Remarks

GO is not a Transact-SQL statement; it is a command recognized by the **osql** and **isql** utilities and SQL Query Analyzer.

SQL Server utilities interpret GO as a signal that they should send the current batch of Transact-SQL statements to SQL Server. The current batch of statements is composed of all statements entered since the last GO, or since the start of the ad hoc session or script if this is the first GO. SQL Query Analyzer and the **osql** and **isql** command prompt utilities implement GO differently. For more information, see osql Utility, iSQL Utility, and SQL Query Analyzer.

A Transact-SQL statement cannot occupy the same line as a GO command. However, the line can contain comments.

Users must follow the rules for batches. For example, any execution of a stored procedure after the first statement in a batch must include the EXECUTE keyword. The scope of local (user-defined) variables is limited to a batch, and cannot be referenced after a GO command.

```
USE pubs
GO
DECLARE @MyMsg VARCHAR(50)
SELECT @MyMsg = 'Hello, World.'
GO -- @MyMsg is not valid after this GO ends the batch.

-- Yields an error because @MyMsg not declared in this batch.
PRINT @MyMsg
GO

SELECT @@VERSION;
-- Yields an error: Must be EXEC sp_who if not first statement in
-- batch.
sp_who
GO
```

SQL Server applications can send multiple Transact-SQL statements to SQL Server for execution as a batch. The statements in the batch are then compiled into a single execution plan. Programmers executing ad hoc statements in the SQL Server utilities, or building scripts of Transact-SQL statements to run through the SQL Server utilities, use GO to signal the end of a batch.

Applications based on the DB-Library, ODBC, or OLE DB APIs receive a syntax error if they attempt to execute a GO command. The SQL Server utilities never send a GO command to the server.

Permissions

GO is a utility command that requires no permissions. It can be executed by any user.

Examples

This example creates two batches. The first batch contains only a USE **pubs** statement to set the database context. The remaining statements use a local variable, so all local variable declarations must be grouped in a single batch. This is done by not having a GO command until after the last statement that references the variable.

```
USE pubs
GO
DECLARE @NmbrAuthors int
SELECT @NmbrAuthors = COUNT(*)
FROM authors
PRINT 'The number of authors as of ' +
     CAST(GETDATE() AS char(20)) + ' is ' +
     CAST(@NmbrAuthors AS char (10))
GO
```

Related Topics

Batches, Batch Processing, Writing Readable Code

GOTO

Alters the flow of execution to a label. The Transact-SQL statement(s) following GOTO are skipped and processing continues at the label. GOTO statements and labels can be used anywhere within a procedure, batch, or statement block. GOTO statements can be nested.

Syntax
Define the label:

```
label :
```

Alter the execution:

```
GOTO label
```

Arguments

label

Is the point after which processing begins if a GOTO is targeted to that label. Labels must follow the rules for identifiers. A label can be used as a commenting method whether or not GOTO is used.

Remarks

GOTO can exist within conditional control-of-flow statements, statement blocks, or procedures, but it cannot go to a label outside of the batch. GOTO branching can go to a label defined before or after GOTO.

Permissions

GOTO permissions default to any valid user.

Examples

This example shows GOTO looping as an alternative to using WHILE.

> **Note**   The **tnames_cursor** cursor is not defined. This example is for illustration only.

```
USE pubs
GO
DECLARE @tablename sysname
SET @tablename = N'authors'
table_loop:
   IF (@@FETCH_STATUS <> -2)
   BEGIN
      SELECT @tablename = RTRIM(UPPER(@tablename))
      EXEC ("SELECT """ + @tablename + """ = COUNT(*) FROM "
            + @tablename )
      PRINT " "
   END
   FETCH NEXT FROM tnames_cursor INTO @tablename
IF (@@FETCH_STATUS <> -1) GOTO table_loop
GO
```

Related Topics

BEGIN...END, BREAK, CONTINUE, Control-of-Flow Language, IF...ELSE, WAITFOR, Using Identifiers, WHILE

GRANT

Creates an entry in the security system that allows a user in the current database to work with data in the current database or execute specific Transact-SQL statements.

Syntax

Statement permissions:

```
GRANT { ALL | statement [ ,...n ] }
TO security_account [ ,...n ]
```

Object permissions:

```
GRANT
    { ALL [ PRIVILEGES ] | permission [ ,...n ] }
    {
        [ ( column [ ,...n ] ) ] ON { table | view }
        | ON { table | view } [ ( column [ ,...n ] ) ]
        | ON { stored_procedure | extended_procedure }
        | ON { user_defined_function }
    }
TO security_account [ ,...n ]
[ WITH GRANT OPTION ]
[ AS { group | role } ]
```

Arguments

ALL

Specifies that all applicable permissions are being granted. For statement permissions, ALL can be used only by members of the **sysadmin** role. For object permissions, ALL can be used by members of the **sysadmin** and **db_owner** roles, and database object owners.

statement

Is the statement for which permission is being granted. The statement list can include:

- CREATE DATABASE
- CREATE DEFAULT
- CREATE FUNCTION
- CREATE PROCEDURE
- CREATE RULE
- CREATE TABLE
- CREATE VIEW
- BACKUP DATABASE
- BACKUP LOG

n

A placeholder indicating that the item can be repeated in a comma-separated list.

TO

Specifies the security account list.

security_account

Is the security account to which the permissions are applied. The security account can be a:

- Microsoft SQL Server user.
- SQL Server role.
- Microsoft Windows NT user.
- Windows NT group.

When a permission is granted to a SQL Server user or Windows NT user account, the specified *security_account* is the only account affected by the permission. If a permission is granted to a SQL Server role or a Windows NT group, the permission affects all users in the current database who are members of the group or role. If there are permission conflicts between a group or role and its members, the most restrictive permission (DENY) takes precedence. *security_account* must exist in the current database; permissions cannot be granted to a user, role, or group in another database, unless the user has already been created or given access to the current database.

Two special security accounts can be used with GRANT. Permissions granted to the **public** role are applied to all users in the database. Permissions granted to the **guest** user are used by all users who do not have a user account in the database.

When granting permissions to a Windows NT local or global group, specify the domain or computer name the group is defined on, followed by a backslash, then the group name. However, to grant permissions to a Windows NT built-in local group, specify BUILTIN instead of the domain or computer name.

PRIVILEGES

Is an optional keyword that can be included for SQL-92 compliance.

permission

Is an object permission that is being granted. When object permissions are granted on a table, table-valued function, or a view, the permission list can include one or more of these permissions: SELECT, INSERT, DELETE, REFERENCES, or UPDATE. A column-list can be supplied along with SELECT and UPDATE permissions. If a column-list is not supplied with SELECT and UPDATE permissions, then the permission applies to all the columns in the table, view, or table-valued function.

Object permissions granted on a stored procedure can include only EXECUTE. Object permissions granted on a scalar-valued function can include EXECUTE and REFERENCES.

SELECT permission is needed on a column in order to access that column in a SELECT statement. UPDATE permission is needed on a column in order to update that column using an UPDATE statement.

The REFERENCES permission on a table is needed in order to create a FOREIGN KEY constraint that references that table.

The REFERENCES permission is needed on an object in order to create a FUNCTION or VIEW with the WITH SCHEMABINDING clause that references that object.

column

Is the name of a column in the current database for which permissions are being granted.

table

Is the name of the table in the current database for which permissions are being granted.

view

Is the name of the view in the current database for which permissions are being granted.

stored_procedure

Is the name of the stored procedure in the current database for which permissions are being granted.

extended_procedure

Is the name of the extended stored procedure for which permissions are being granted.

user_defined_function

Is the name of the user-defined function for which permissions are being granted.

WITH GRANT OPTION

Specifies that the *security_account* is given the ability to grant the specified object permission to the other security accounts. The WITH GRANT OPTION clause is valid only with object permissions.

AS {*group* | *role*}

Specifies the optional name of the security account in the current database that has the authority to execute the GRANT statement. AS is used when permissions on an object are granted to a group or role, and the object permissions need to be further granted to users who are not members of the group or role. Because only a user, rather than a group or role, can execute a GRANT statement, a specific member of the group or role grants permissions on the object under the authority of the group or role.

Remarks

Cross-database permissions are not allowed; permissions can be granted only to users in the current database for objects and statements in the current database. If a user needs permissions to objects in another database, create the user account in the other database, or grant the user account access to the other database, as well as the current database.

> **Note** System stored procedures are the exception because EXECUTE permissions are already granted to the **public** role, allowing everyone to execute them. However, after a system stored procedure is executed, it checks the user's role membership. If the user is not a member of the appropriate fixed server or database role necessary to run the stored procedure, the stored procedure does not continue.

The REVOKE statement can be used to remove granted permissions, and the DENY statement can be used to prevent a user from gaining permissions through a GRANT to their user account.

A granted permission removes the denied or revoked permission at the level granted (user, group, or role). The same permission denied at another level such as group or role containing the user takes precedence. However, although the same permission revoked at another level still applies, it does not prevent the user from accessing the object.

If a user activates an application role, the effect of GRANT is null for any objects the user accesses using the application role. Therefore, although a user may be granted access to a specific object in the current database, if the user uses an application role that does not have access to the object, the user also does not have access while the application role is activated.

The **sp_helprotect** system stored procedure reports permissions on a database object or user.

Permissions

GRANT permissions depend on the statement permissions being granted and the object involved in the permissions. The members of the **sysadmin** role can grant any permissions in any database. Object owners can grant permissions for the objects they own. Members of the **db_owner** or **db_securityadmin** roles can grant any permissions on any statement or object in their database.

Statements that require permissions are those that add objects in the database or perform administrative activities with the database. Each statement that requires permissions has a certain set of roles that automatically have permissions to execute the statement. For example, the CREATE TABLE permission defaults to members of the **sysadmin** and **db_owner** and **db_ddladmin** roles. The permissions to execute the SELECT statement for a table default to the **sysadmin** and **db_owner** roles, and the owner of the object.

There are some Transact-SQL statements that cannot be granted as permissions; the ability to execute these statements requires membership in a fixed role that has implied permissions to execute special statements. For example, to execute the SHUTDOWN statement, the user must be added as member of the **serveradmin** role.

Members of the **dbcreator**, **processadmin**, **securityadmin**, and **serveradmin** fixed server roles have permissions to execute only these Transact-SQL statements.

Statement	dbcreator	processadmin	securityadmin	serveradmin	bulkadmin
ALTER DATABASE	X				
CREATE DATABASE	X				
BULK INSERT					X
DBCC				X (1)	
DENY			X (2)		
GRANT			X (2)		
KILL		X			
RECONFIGURE				X	
RESTORE	X				
REVOKE			X (2)		
SHUTDOWN				X	

1 For more information, see the DBCC statement.
2 Applies to the CREATE DATABASE statement only.

Note Members of the **diskadmin** and **setupadmin** fixed server roles do not have permissions to execute any Transact-SQL statements, only certain system stored procedures. Members of the **sysadmin** fixed server role, however, have permissions to execute all Transact-SQL statements.

Members of the following fixed database roles have permissions to execute the specified Transact-SQL statements.

Statement	db_owner	db_datareader	db_datawriter	db_ddladmin	db_backup operator	db_security admin
ALTER DATABASE	X			X		
ALTER FUNCTION	X			X		
ALTER PROCEDURE	X			X		
ALTER TABLE	X [1]			X		
ALTER TRIGGER	X			X		
ALTER VIEW	X [1]			X		
BACKUP	X				X	
CHECKPOINT	X				X	
CREATE DEFAULT	X			X		
CREATE FUNCTION	X			X		
CREATE INDEX	X [1]			X		
CREATE PROCEDURE	X			X		
CREATE RULE	X			X		
CREATE TABLE	X			X		
CREATE TRIGGER	X [1]			X		
CREATE VIEW	X			X		
DBCC	X				X [2]	

(continued)

(continued)

Statement	db_owner	db_datareader	db_datawriter	db_ddladmin	db_backup operator	db_security admin
DELETE	X (1)		X			
DENY	X					X
DENY on object	X					
DROP	X (1)			X		
EXECUTE	X (1)					
GRANT	X					X
GRANT on object	X (1)					
INSERT	X (1)		X			
READTEXT	X (1)	X				
REFERENCES	X (1)			X		
RESTORE	X					
REVOKE	X					X
REVOKE on object	X (1)					
SELECT	X (1)	X				
SETUSER	X					
TRUNCATE TABLE	X (1)			X		
UPDATE	X (1)		X			
UPDATE STATISTICS	X (1)					
UPDATETEXT	X (1)		X			
WRITETEXT	X (1)		X			

1 Permission applies to the object owner as well.
2 For more information, see the DBCC statement.

Note Members of the **db_accessadmin** fixed database role do not have permissions to execute any Transact-SQL statements, only certain system stored procedures.

The Transact-SQL statements that do not require permissions to be executed (automatically granted to **public**) are:

BEGIN TRANSACTION	COMMIT TRANSACTION
PRINT	RAISERROR
ROLLBACK TRANSACTION	SAVE TRANSACTION
SET	

For more information about the permissions required to execute the system stored procedures, see the appropriate system stored procedure.

Examples

A. Grant statement permissions

This example grants multiple statement permissions to the users **Mary** and **John**, and the **Corporate\BobJ** Windows NT group.

```
GRANT CREATE DATABASE, CREATE TABLE
TO Mary, John, [Corporate\BobJ]
```

B. Grant object permissions within the permission hierarchy

This example shows the preferred ordering of permissions. First, SELECT permissions are granted to the **public** role. Then, specific permissions are granted to users **Mary**, **John**, and **Tom**. These users then have all permissions to the **authors** table.

```
USE pubs
GO

GRANT SELECT
ON authors
TO public
GO

GRANT INSERT, UPDATE, DELETE
ON authors
TO Mary, John, Tom
GO
```

C. Grant permissions to a SQL Server role

This example grants CREATE TABLE permissions to all members of the **Accounting** role.

```
GRANT CREATE TABLE TO Accounting
```

D. Grant permissions using the AS option

The **Plan_Data** table is owned by the user **Jean**. **Jean** grants SELECT permissions, specifying the WITH GRANT OPTION clause, on **Plan_Data** to the **Accounting** role. The user **Jill**, who is member of **Accounting**, wants to grant SELECT permissions on the **Plan_Data** table to the user **Jack**, who is not a member of **Accounting**.

Because the permission to GRANT other users SELECT permissions to the **Plan_Data** table were granted to the **Accounting** role and not **Jill** explicitly, **Jill** cannot grant permissions for the table based on the permissions granted through being a member of the **Accounting** role. **Jill** must use the AS clause to assume the grant permissions of the **Accounting** role.

```
/* User Jean */
GRANT SELECT ON Plan_Data TO Accounting WITH GRANT OPTION

/* User Jill */
GRANT SELECT ON Plan_Data TO Jack AS Accounting
```

Related Topics

Granting Permissions, DENY, REVOKE, sp_addgroup, sp_addlogin, sp_adduser, sp_changegroup, sp_changedbowner, sp_dropgroup, sp_dropuser, sp_helpgroup, sp_helpprotect, sp_helpuser

GROUP BY

Divides a table into groups. Groups can consist of column names or results or computed columns. For more information, see SELECT.

GROUPING

Is an aggregate function that causes an additional column to be output with a value of 1 when the row is added by either the CUBE or ROLLUP operator, or 0 when the row is not the result of CUBE or ROLLUP.

Grouping is allowed only in the select list associated with a GROUP BY clause that contains either the CUBE or ROLLUP operator.

Syntax

```
GROUPING ( column_name )
```

Arguments

column_name

Is a column in a GROUP BY clause to check for CUBE or ROLLUP null values.

Return Types

int

Remarks

Grouping is used to distinguish the null values returned by CUBE and ROLLUP from standard null values. The NULL returned as the result of a CUBE or ROLLUP operation is a special use of NULL. It acts as a column placeholder in the result set and means "all."

Examples

This example groups **royalty** and aggregate **advance** amounts. The GROUPING function is applied to the **royalty** column.

```
USE pubs
SELECT royalty, SUM(advance) 'total advance',
   GROUPING(royalty) 'grp'
   FROM titles
   GROUP BY royalty WITH ROLLUP
```

The result set shows two null values under **royalty**. The first NULL represents the group of null values from this column in the table. The second NULL is in the summary row added by the ROLLUP operation. The summary row shows the total **advance** amounts for all **royalty** groups and is indicated by 1 in the **grp** column.

Here is the result set:

```
royalty      total advance        grp
---------    --------------------  ---
NULL         NULL                  0
10           57000.0000            0
12           2275.0000             0
14           4000.0000             0
16           7000.0000             0
24           25125.0000            0
NULL         95400.0000            1
```

Related Topics

Aggregate Functions, SELECT

HAS_DBACCESS

Returns information about whether the user has access to the specified database.

Syntax

```
HAS_DBACCESS ( 'database_name' )
```

Arguments

database_name
    Is the name of the database for which the user wants access information.
    database_name is **sysname**.

Return Types

int

Remarks

HAS_DBACCESS returns 1 if the user has access to the database, 0 if the user has no access to the database, and NULL if the database name is invalid.

HAVING

Specifies a search condition for a group or an aggregate. HAVING can be used only with the SELECT statement. It is usually used in a GROUP BY clause. When GROUP BY is not used, HAVING behaves like a WHERE clause. For more information, see SELECT.

HOST_ID

Returns the workstation identification number.

Syntax

```
HOST_ID ( )
```

Return Types

char(8)

Remarks

When the parameter to a system function is optional, the current database, host computer, server user, or database user is assumed. Built-in functions must always be followed by parentheses.

System functions can be used in the select list, in the WHERE clause, and anywhere an expression is allowed.

Examples

This example creates a table that uses HOST_ID() in a DEFAULT definition to record the terminal ID of computers that insert rows into a table recording orders.

```
CREATE TABLE Orders
    (OrderID     INT        PRIMARY KEY,
     CustomerID  NCHAR(5)   REFERENCES Customers(CustomerID),
     TerminalID  CHAR(8)    NOT NULL DEFAULT HOST_ID(),
     OrderDate   DATETIME   NOT NULL,
     ShipDate    DATETIME   NULL,
     ShipperID   INT        NULL REFERENCES Shippers(ShipperID))
GO
```

Related Topics

Expressions, System Functions

HOST_NAME

Returns the workstation name.

Syntax

```
HOST_NAME ( )
```

Return Types

nchar

Remarks

When the parameter to a system function is optional, the current database, host computer, server user, or database user is assumed. Built-in functions must always be followed by parentheses.

System functions can be used in the select list, in the WHERE clause, and anywhere an expression is allowed.

Examples

This example creates a table that uses HOST_NAME() in a DEFAULT definition to record the workstation name of computers that insert rows into a table recording orders.

```
CREATE TABLE Orders
    (OrderID      INT        PRIMARY KEY,
     CustomerID   NCHAR(5)   REFERENCES Customers(CustomerID),
     Workstation  NCHAR(30)  NOT NULL DEFAULT HOST_NAME(),
     OrderDate    DATETIME   NOT NULL,
     ShipDate     DATETIME   NULL,
     ShipperID    INT        NULL REFERENCES Shippers(ShipperID))
```

Related Topics

Expressions, System Functions

IDENT_CURRENT

Returns the last identity value generated for a specified table in any session and any scope.

Syntax

```
IDENT_CURRENT('table_name')
```

Arguments

table_name
> Is the name of the table whose identity value will be returned. *table_name* is **varchar**, with no default.

Return Types

sql_variant

Remarks

IDENT_CURRENT is similar to the Microsoft SQL Server 2000 identity functions SCOPE_IDENTITY and @@IDENTITY. All three functions return last-generated identity values. However, the scope and session on which 'last' is defined in each of these functions differ.

- IDENT_CURRENT returns the last identity value generated for a specific table in any session and any scope.

- @@IDENTITY returns the last identity value generated for any table in the current session, across all scopes.

- SCOPE_IDENTITY returns the last identity value generated for any table in the current session and the current scope.

Examples

This example illustrates the different identity values returned by IDENT_CURRENT, @@IDENTITY, and SCOPE_IDENTITY.

```
USE pubs
DROP TABLE t6
DROP TABLE t7
GO
CREATE TABLE t6(id int IDENTITY)
CREATE TABLE t7(id int IDENTITY(100,1))
GO
CREATE TRIGGER t6ins ON t6 FOR INSERT
AS
BEGIN
   INSERT t7 DEFAULT VALUES
END
GO
--end of trigger definition

SELECT* FROM t6
--id is empty.

SELECT* FROM t7
--id is empty.

--Do the following in Session 1
INSERT t6 DEFAULT VALUES
SELECT @@IDENTITY
/*Returns the value 100, which was inserted by the trigger.*/

SELECT SCOPE_IDENTITY()
/* Returns the value 1, which was inserted by the
INSERT stmt 2 statements before this query.*/

SELECT IDENT_CURRENT('t7')
/* Returns value inserted into t7, i.e. in the trigger.*/

SELECT IDENT_CURRENT('t6')
/* Returns value inserted into t6, which was the INSERT statement 4 stmts before this
query.*/
```

(continued)

(continued)

```
-- Do the following in Session 2
SELECT @@IDENTITY
/* Returns NULL since there has been no INSERT action
so far in this session.*/

SELECT SCOPE_IDENTITY()
/* Returns NULL since there has been no INSERT action
so far in this scope in this session.*/

SELECT IDENT_CURRENT('t7')
/* Returns the last value inserted into t7.*/
```

Related Topics

@@IDENTITY, SCOPE_IDENTITY

IDENT_INCR

Returns the increment value (returned as **numeric**(@@MAXPRECISION,0)) specified during the creation of an identity column in a table or view that has an identity column.

Syntax

```
IDENT_INCR ( 'table_or_view' )
```

Arguments

'*table_or_view*'

Is an expression specifying the table or view to check for a valid identity increment value. *table_or_view* can be a character string constant enclosed in quotation marks, a variable, a function, or a column name. *table_or_view* is **char**, **nchar**, **varchar**, or **nvarchar**.

Return Types

numeric

Examples

This example returns 1 for the **jobs** table in the **pubs** database because the **jobs** table includes an identity column with an increment value of 1.

```
USE pubs
SELECT TABLE_NAME, IDENT_INCR(TABLE_NAME) AS IDENT_INCR
FROM INFORMATION_SCHEMA.TABLES
WHERE IDENT_INCR(TABLE_NAME) IS NOT NULL
```

Here is the result set:

```
TABLE_NAME                                                       IDENT_INCR
- - - - - - - - - - - - - - - - - - - - - - - - - - - - - - - -  - - - - - - - - - - -
jobs                                                             1

(1 row(s) affected)
```

Related Topics

Expressions, System Functions

IDENT_SEED

Returns the seed value (returned as **numeric**(@@MAXPRECISION,0)) specified
during the creation of an identity column in a table or a view that has an identity
column.

Syntax

```
IDENT_SEED ( 'table_or_view' )
```

Arguments

'table_or_view'

Is an expression specifying the table or view to check for a valid identity seed
value. *table_or_view* can be a character string constant enclosed in quotation
marks, a variable, a function, or a column name. *table_or_view* is **char**, **nchar**,
varchar, or **nvarchar**.

Return Types

numeric

Examples

This example returns 1 for the **jobs** table in the **pubs** database because the **jobs** table
includes an identity column with a seed value of 1.

```
USE pubs
SELECT TABLE_NAME, IDENT_SEED(TABLE_NAME) AS IDENT_SEED
FROM INFORMATION_SCHEMA.TABLES
WHERE IDENT_SEED(TABLE_NAME) IS NOT NULL
```

Here is the result set:

```
TABLE_NAME                                                        IDENT_SEED
-------------------------------------------------------------     -----------
jobs                                                              1

(1 row(s) affected)
```

Related Topics

Expressions, System Functions

IDENTITY (Property)

Creates an identity column in a table. This property is used with the CREATE TABLE and ALTER TABLE Transact-SQL statements.

Note   The IDENTITY property is not the same as the SQL-DMO **Identity** property that exposes the row identity property of a column.

Syntax

```
IDENTITY [ ( seed , increment ) ]
```

Arguments

seed

Is the value that is used for the very first row loaded into the table.

increment

Is the incremental value that is added to the identity value of the previous row that was loaded.

You must specify both the seed and increment or neither. If neither is specified, the default is (1,1).

Remarks

If an identity column exists for a table with frequent deletions, gaps can occur between identity values. If this is a concern, do not use the IDENTITY property. However, to ensure that no gaps have been created or to fill an existing gap, evaluate the existing identity values before explicitly entering one with SET IDENTITY_INSERT ON.

If you are reusing a removed identity value, use the sample code in Example B to check for the next available identity value. Replace *tablename*, *column_type*, and *max*(*column_type*) - 1 with your table name, identity column data type, and numeric value of the maximum allowable value (for that data type) -1.

Use DBCC CHECKIDENT to check the current identity value and compare it with the maximum value in the identity column.

When the IDENTITY property is used with CREATE TABLE, Microsoft SQL Server uses the NOT FOR REPLICATION option of CREATE TABLE to override the automatic incrementing of an identity column. Usually, SQL Server assigns each new row inserted in a table a value that is some increment greater than the previous highest value. However, if the new rows are replicated from another data source, the identity values must remain exactly as they were at the data source.

Examples

A. Use the IDENTITY property with CREATE TABLE

This example creates a new table using the IDENTITY property for an automatically incrementing identification number.

```
USE pubs
IF EXISTS(SELECT TABLE_NAME FROM INFORMATION_SCHEMA.TABLES
      WHERE TABLE_NAME = 'new_employees')
   DROP TABLE new_employees
GO
CREATE TABLE new_employees
(
 id_num int IDENTITY(1,1),
 fname varchar (20),
 minit char(1),
 lname varchar(30)
)

INSERT new_employees
   (fname, minit, lname)
VALUES
   ('Karin', 'F', 'Josephs')

INSERT new_employees
   (fname, minit, lname)
VALUES
   ('Pirkko', 'O', 'Koskitalo')
```

B. Use generic syntax for finding gaps in identity values

This example shows generic syntax for finding gaps in identity values when data is removed.

   Note   The first part of the following Transact-SQL script is designed for illustration purposes only. You can run the Transact-SQL script that starts with the comment: - - Create the img table.

```
-- Here is the generic syntax for finding identity value gaps in data.
-- This is the beginning of the illustrative example.
SET IDENTITY_INSERT tablename ON

DECLARE @minidentval column_type
DECLARE @nextidentval column_type
SELECT @minidentval = MIN(IDENTITYCOL) FROM tablename
IF @minidentval = IDENT_SEED('tablename')
   SELECT @nextidentval = MIN(IDENTITYCOL) + IDENT_INCR('tablename')
   FROM tablename t1
   WHERE IDENTITYCOL BETWEEN IDENT_SEED('tablename') AND
      MAX(column_type) AND
      NOT EXISTS (SELECT * FROM tablename t2
         WHERE t2.IDENTITYCOL = t1.IDENTITYCOL +
            IDENT_INCR('tablename'))
ELSE
   SELECT @nextidentval = IDENT_SEED('tablename')
SET IDENTITY_INSERT tablename OFF
-- Here is an example to find gaps in the actual data.
-- The table is called img and has two columns: the first column
-- called id_num, which is an increasing identification number, and the
-- second column called company_name.
-- This is the end of the illustration example.

-- Create the img table.
-- If the img table already exists, drop it.
-- Create the img table.
IF EXISTS(SELECT TABLE_NAME FROM INFORMATION_SCHEMA.TABLES
      WHERE TABLE_NAME = 'img')
   DROP TABLE img
GO
CREATE TABLE img (id_num int IDENTITY(1,1), company_name sysname)
INSERT img(company_name) VALUES ('New Moon Books')
INSERT img(company_name) VALUES ('Lucerne Publishing')
-- SET IDENTITY_INSERT ON and use in img table.
SET IDENTITY_INSERT img ON

DECLARE @minidentval smallint
DECLARE @nextidentval smallint
SELECT @minidentval = MIN(IDENTITYCOL) FROM img
 IF @minidentval = IDENT_SEED('img')
   SELECT @nextidentval = MIN(IDENTITYCOL) + IDENT_INCR('img')
   FROM img t1
```

(continued)

(continued)

```
   WHERE IDENTITYCOL BETWEEN IDENT_SEED('img') AND 32766 AND
      NOT  EXISTS (SELECT * FROM img t2
         WHERE t2.IDENTITYCOL = t1.IDENTITYCOL + IDENT_INCR('img'))
ELSE
   SELECT @nextidentval = IDENT_SEED('img')
SET IDENTITY_INSERT img OFF
```

Related Topics

ALTER TABLE, CREATE TABLE, DBCC CHECKIDENT, IDENT_INCR,
@@IDENTITY, IDENTITY (Function), IDENT_SEED, SELECT,
SET IDENTITY_INSERT

IDENTITY (Function)

Is used only in a SELECT statement with an INTO *table* clause to insert an identity column into a new table.

Although similar, the IDENTITY function is not the IDENTITY property that is used with CREATE TABLE and ALTER TABLE.

Syntax

```
IDENTITY ( data_type [ , seed , increment ] ) AS column_name
```

Arguments

data_type
  Is the data type of the identity column. Valid data types for an identity column are any data types of the integer data type category (except for the **bit** data type), or **decimal** data type.

seed
  Is the value to be assigned to the first row in the table. Each subsequent row is assigned the next identity value, which is equal to the last IDENTITY value plus the *increment* value. If neither *seed* nor *increment* is specified, both default to 1.

increment
  Is the increment to add to the *seed* value for successive rows in the table.

column_name
  Is the name of the column that is to be inserted into the new table.

Return Types

Returns the same as *data_type*.

Remarks

Because this function creates a column in a table, a name for the column must be specified in the select list in one of these ways:

```
--(1)
SELECT IDENTITY(int, 1,1) AS ID_Num
INTO NewTable
FROM OldTable

--(2)
SELECT ID_Num = IDENTITY(int, 1, 1)
INTO NewTable
FROM OldTable
```

Examples

This example inserts all rows from the **employee** table from the **pubs** database into a new table called **employees**. The IDENTITY function is used to start identification numbers at 100 instead of 1 in the **employees** table.

```
USE pubs
IF EXISTS(SELECT TABLE_NAME FROM INFORMATION_SCHEMA.TABLES
      WHERE TABLE_NAME = 'employees')
   DROP TABLE employees
GO
EXEC sp_dboption 'pubs', 'select into/bulkcopy', 'true'

SELECT emp_id AS emp_num,
   fname AS first,
   minit AS middle,
   lname AS last,
   IDENTITY(smallint, 100, 1) AS job_num,
   job_lvl AS job_level,
   pub_id,
   hire_date
INTO employees
FROM employee
GO
USE pubs
EXEC sp_dboption 'pubs', 'select into/bulkcopy', 'false'
```

Related Topics

CREATE TABLE, @@IDENTITY, IDENTITY (Property), SELECT @local_variable, Using System Functions

IF...ELSE

Imposes conditions on the execution of a Transact-SQL statement. The Transact-SQL statement following an IF keyword and its condition is executed if the condition is satisfied (when the Boolean expression returns TRUE). The optional ELSE keyword introduces an alternate Transact-SQL statement that is executed when the IF condition is not satisfied (when the Boolean expression returns FALSE).

Syntax

```
IF Boolean_expression
    { sql_statement | statement_block }
[ ELSE
    { sql_statement | statement_block } ]
```

Arguments

Boolean_expression

Is an expression that returns TRUE or FALSE. If the Boolean expression contains a SELECT statement, the SELECT statement must be enclosed in parentheses.

{*sql_statement | statement_block*}

Is any Transact-SQL statement or statement grouping as defined with a statement block. Unless a statement block is used, the IF or ELSE condition can affect the performance of only one Transact-SQL statement. To define a statement block, use the control-of-flow keywords BEGIN and END. CREATE TABLE or SELECT INTO statements must refer to the same table name if the CREATE TABLE or SELECT INTO statements are used in both the IF and ELSE areas of the IF...ELSE block.

Remarks

IF...ELSE constructs can be used in batches, in stored procedures (in which these constructs are often used to test for the existence of some parameter), and in ad hoc queries.

IF tests can be nested after another IF or following an ELSE. There is no limit to the number of nested levels.

Examples

A. Use one IF...ELSE block

This example shows an IF condition with a statement block. If the average price of the title is not less than $15, it prints the text: Average title price is more than $15.

```
USE pubs

IF (SELECT AVG(price) FROM titles WHERE type = 'mod_cook') < $15
```

(continued)

(continued)

```
BEGIN
   PRINT 'The following titles are excellent mod_cook books:'
   PRINT ' '
   SELECT SUBSTRING(title, 1, 35) AS Title
   FROM titles
   WHERE type = 'mod_cook'
END
ELSE
   PRINT 'Average title price is more than $15.'
```

Here is the result set:

```
The following titles are excellent mod_cook books:

Title
------------------------------------
Silicon Valley Gastronomic Treats
The Gourmet Microwave

(2 row(s) affected)
```

B. Use more than one IF...ELSE block

This example uses two IF blocks. If the average price of the title is not less than $15, it prints the text: Average title price is more than $15. If the average price of modern cookbooks is more than $15, the statement that the modern cookbooks are expensive is printed.

```
USE pubs

IF (SELECT AVG(price) FROM titles WHERE type = 'mod_cook') < $15
BEGIN
   PRINT 'The following titles are excellent mod_cook books:'
   PRINT ' '
   SELECT SUBSTRING(title, 1, 35) AS Title
   FROM titles
   WHERE type = 'mod_cook'
END
ELSE
   IF (SELECT AVG(price) FROM titles WHERE type = 'mod_cook') > $15
BEGIN
   PRINT 'The following titles are expensive mod_cook books:'
   PRINT ' '
   SELECT SUBSTRING(title, 1, 35) AS Title
   FROM titles
   WHERE type = 'mod_cook'
END
```

Related Topics

ALTER TRIGGER, BEGIN...END, CREATE TABLE, CREATE TRIGGER, ELSE (IF...ELSE), END (BEGIN...END), SELECT, WHILE

image

For more information about the **image** data type, see ntext, text, and image.

Related Topics

Data Type Conversion, Data Types

IN

Determines if a given value matches any value in a subquery or a list.

Syntax

```
test_expression [ NOT ] IN
    (
        subquery
        | expression [ ,...n ]
    )
```

Arguments

test_expression
　　Is any valid Microsoft SQL Server expression.

subquery
　　Is a subquery that has a result set of one column. This column must have the same data type as *test_expression*.

expression [,...n]
　　Is a list of expressions to test for a match. All expressions must be of the same type as *test_expression*.

Result Types

Boolean

Result Value

If the value of *test_expression* is equal to any value returned by *subquery* or is equal to any *expression* from the comma-separated list, the result value is TRUE. Otherwise, the result value is FALSE.

Using NOT IN negates the returned value.

Examples

A. Compare OR and IN

This example selects a list of the names and states of all authors who live in California, Indiana, or Maryland.

```
USE pubs

SELECT au_lname, state
FROM authors
WHERE state = 'CA' OR state = 'IN' OR state = 'MD'
```

However, you get the same results using IN:

```
USE pubs

SELECT au_lname, state
FROM authors
WHERE state IN ('CA', 'IN', 'MD')
```

Here is the result set from either query:

```
au_lname  state
--------  -----
White     CA
Green     CA
Carson    CA
O'Leary      CA
Straight     CA
Bennet    CA
Dull      CA
Gringlesby   CA
Locksley     CA
Yokomoto     CA
DeFrance     IN
Stringer     CA
MacFeather   CA
Karsen    CA
Panteley        MD
Hunter       CA
McBadden        CA

(17 row(s) affected)
```

B. Use IN with a subquery

This example finds all **au_ids** in the **titleauthor** table for authors who make less than 50 percent of the royalty on any one book, and then selects from the **authors** table all author names with **au_ids** that match the results from the **titleauthor** query.

The results show that several authors fall into the less-than-50-percent category.

```
USE pubs
SELECT au_lname, au_fname
FROM authors
WHERE au_id IN
    (SELECT au_id
    FROM titleauthor
    WHERE royaltyper < 50)
```

Here is the result set:

```
au_lname                                        au_fname
--------------------------------------------- ---------------------
Green                                           Marjorie
O'Leary                                         Michael
Gringlesby                                      Burt
Yokomoto                                        Akiko
MacFeather                                      Stearns
Ringer                                          Anne

(6 row(s) affected)
```

C. Use NOT IN with a subquery

NOT IN finds the authors who do not match the items in the values list. This example finds the names of authors who do not make less than 50 percent of the royalties on at least one book.

```
USE pubs
SELECT au_lname, au_fname
FROM authors
WHERE au_id NOT IN
    (SELECT au_id
    FROM titleauthor
    WHERE royaltyper < 50)
```

Here is the result set:

```
au_lname                                        au_fname
--------------------------------------------- ---------------------
White                                           Johnson
Carson                                          Cheryl
```

(continued)

(continued)

```
Straight                          Dean
Smith                             Meander
Bennet                            Abraham
Dull                              Ann
Locksley                          Charlene
Greene                            Morningstar
Blotchet-Halls                    Reginald
del Castillo                      Innes
DeFrance                          Michel
Stringer                          Dirk
Karsen                            Livia
Panteley                          Sylvia
Hunter                            Sheryl
McBadden                          Heather
Ringer                            Albert

(17 row(s) affected)
```

Related Topics

CASE, Expressions, Functions, Operators, SELECT, WHERE

INDEXKEY_PROPERTY

Returns information about the index key.

Syntax

```
INDEXKEY_PROPERTY ( table_ID , index_ID , key_ID , property )
```

Arguments

table_ID
   Is the table identification number. *table_ID* is **int**.

index_ID
   Is the index identification number. *index_ID* is **int**.

key_ID
   Is the index column position. *key_ID* is **int**.

property
> Is the name of the property for which information will be returned. *property* is a character string and can be one of these values.

Value	Description
ColumnId	Column ID at the *key_ID* position of the index.
IsDescending	Order in which the index column is stored. 1 = Descending 0 = Ascending

Return Types
int

Examples

```
SELECT indexkey_property(OBJECT_ID('authors'),2,2,'ColumnId')

SELECT indexkey_property(OBJECT_ID('authors'),2,2,'IsDescending')
```

INDEXPROPERTY

Returns the named index property value given a table identification number, index name, and property name.

Syntax

```
INDEXPROPERTY ( table_ID , index , property )
```

Arguments

table_ID
> Is an expression containing the identification number of the table or indexed view for which to provide index property information. *table_ID* is **int**.

index
> Is an expression containing the name of the index for which to return property information. *index* is **nvarchar(128)**.

property

Is an expression containing the name of the database property to return. *property* is **varchar(128)**, and can be one of these values.

Property	Description
IndexDepth	Depth of the index.
	Returns the number of levels the index has.
IndexFillFactor	Index specifies its own fill factor.
	Returns the fill factor used when the index was created or last rebuilt.
IndexID	Index ID of the index on a specified table or indexed view.
IsAutoStatistics	Index was generated by the **auto create statistics** option of **sp_dboption**.
	1 = True 0 = False NULL = Invalid input
IsClustered	Index is clustered.
	1 = True 0 = False NULL = Invalid input
IsFulltextKey	Index is the full-text key for a table.
	1 = True 0 = False NULL = Invalid input
IsHypothetical	Index is hypothetical and cannot be used directly as a data access path. Hypothetical indexes hold column level statistics.
	1 = True 0 = False NULL = Invalid input

(continued)

(continued)

Property	Description
IsPadIndex	Index specifies space to leave open on each interior node. 1 = True 0 = False NULL = Invalid input
IsPageLockDisallowed	1 = Page locking is disallowed through **sp_indexoption**. 0 = Page locking is allowed. NULL = Invalid input
IsRowLockDisallowed	1 = Row locking is disallowed through **sp_indexoption**. 0 = Row locking is allowed. NULL = Invalid input.
IsStatistics	Index was created by the CREATE STATISTICS statement or by the **auto create statistics** option of **sp_dboption**. Statistics indexes are used as a placeholder for column-level statistics. 1 = True 0 = False NULL = Invalid input
IsUnique	Index is unique. 1 = True 0 = False NULL = Invalid input

Return Types

int

Examples

This example returns the setting for the **IsPadIndex** property for the **UPKCL_auidind** index of the **authors** table.

```
USE pubs
SELECT INDEXPROPERTY(OBJECT_ID('authors'), 'UPKCL_auidind',
  'IsPadIndex')
```

Related Topics

Control-of-Flow Language, CREATE INDEX, DELETE, INSERT, Meta data
Functions, Operators (Logical Operators), UPDATE, WHERE

INDEX_COL

Returns the indexed column name.

Syntax

```
INDEX_COL ( 'table' , index_id , key_id )
```

Arguments

'table'
  Is the name of the table.

index_id
  Is the ID of the index.

key_id
  Is the ID of the key.

Return Types

nvarchar (256)

Examples

This example produces a list of indexes in the **authors** table.

```
USE pubs

-- Declare variables to use in this example.
DECLARE @id int, @type char(2),@msg varchar(80),
    @indid smallint, @indname sysname, @status int,
    @indkey int, @name varchar(30)
-- Obtain the identification number for the authors table to look up
-- its indexes in the sysindexes table.
SET NOCOUNT ON
SELECT @id = id, @type = type
FROM sysobjects
WHERE name = 'authors' and type = 'U'

-- Start printing the output information.
print 'Index information for the authors table'
print '---------------------------------------'
```

(continued)

(continued)

```
-- Loop through all indexes in the authors table.
-- Declare a cursor.
DECLARE i cursor
FOR
SELECT indid, name, status
FROM sysindexes
WHERE id = @id

-- Open the cursor and fetch next set of index information.
OPEN i

FETCH NEXT FROM i INTO @indid, @indname, @status

  IF @@FETCH_STATUS = 0
  PRINT ' '

  -- While there are still rows to retrieve from the cursor,
  -- find out index information and print it.
  WHILE @@FETCH_STATUS = 0
    BEGIN

    SET @msg = NULL
    -- Print the index name and the index number.
        SET @msg = ' Index number '  + CONVERT(varchar, @indid)+
      ' is '+@indname

    SET @indkey = 1
    -- @indkey (equivalent to key_id in the syntax diagram of
    -- INDEX_COL) can be from 1 to 16.
      WHILE @indkey <= 16 and INDEX_COL(@name, @indid, @indkey)
      IS NOT NULL

      BEGIN
      -- Print different information if @indkey <> 1.
        IF @indkey = 1
          SET @msg = @msg + ' on '
             + index_col(@name, @indid, @indkey)
        ELSE
          SET @msg = @msg + ', '
             + index_col(@name, @indid, @indkey)
```

(continued)

(continued)

```
        SET @indkey = @indkey + 1
     END

     PRINT @msg
     SET @msg = NULL
     FETCH NEXT FROM i INTO @indid, @indname, @status

   END
   CLOSE i
   DEALLOCATE i

SET NOCOUNT OFF
```

Here is the result set:

```
Index information for the authors table
---------------------------------------

Index number 1 is UPKCL_auidind
Index number 2 is aunmind
```

Related Topics

Expressions, Metadata Functions, WHERE

INSERT

Adds a new row to a table or a view.

Syntax

```
INSERT [ INTO]
   { table_name WITH ( < table_hint_limited > [ ...n ] )
      | view_name
      | rowset_function_limited
   }

   { [ ( column_list ) ]
     { VALUES
         ( { DEFAULT | NULL | expression } [ ,...n] )
         | derived_table
         | execute_statement
     }
```

(continued)

(continued)

```
    }
    | DEFAULT VALUES
< table_hint_limited > ::=
    { FASTFIRSTROW
        | HOLDLOCK
        | PAGLOCK
        | READCOMMITTED
        | REPEATABLEREAD
        | ROWLOCK
        | SERIALIZABLE
        | TABLOCK
        | TABLOCKX
        | UPDLOCK
    }
```

Arguments

[INTO]
> Is an optional keyword that can be used between INSERT and the target table.

table_name
> Is the name of a table or **table** variable that is to receive the data.

WITH (<table_hint_limited> [...*n*])
> Specifies one or more table hints that are allowed for a target table. The WITH
> keyword and the parentheses are required. READPAST, NOLOCK, and
> READUNCOMMITTED are not allowed. For more information about table hints,
> see FROM.

view_name
> Is the name and optional alias of a view. The view referenced by *view_name* must
> be updateable. The modifications made by the INSERT statement cannot affect
> more than one of the base tables referenced in the FROM clause of the view.
> For example, an INSERT into a multitable view must use a *column_list* that
> references only columns from one base table. For more information about
> updateable views, see CREATE VIEW.

rowset_function_limited
> Is either the OPENQUERY or OPENROWSET function. For more information,
> see OPENQUERY and OPENROWSET.

(column_list)
> Is a list of one or more columns in which to insert data. *column_list* must be
> enclosed in parentheses and delimited by commas.

If a column is not in *column_list*, Microsoft SQL Server must be able to provide a value based on the definition of the column; otherwise, the row cannot be loaded. SQL Server automatically provides a value for the column if the column:

- Has an IDENTITY property. The next incremental identity value is used.

- Has a default. The default value for the column is used.

- Has a **timestamp** data type. The current timestamp value is used.

- Is nullable. A null value is used.

column_list and VALUES list must be used when inserting explicit values into an identity column, and the SET IDENTITY_INSERT option must be ON for the table.

VALUES

Introduces the list of data values to be inserted. There must be one data value for each column in *column_list* (if specified) or in the table. The values list must be enclosed in parentheses.

If the values in the VALUES list are not in the same order as the columns in the table or do not have a value for each column in the table, *column_list* must be used to explicitly specify the column that stores each incoming value.

DEFAULT

Forces SQL Server to load the default value defined for a column. If a default does not exist for the column and the column allows NULLs, NULL is inserted. For a column defined with the **timestamp** data type, the next timestamp value is inserted. DEFAULT is not valid for an identity column.

expression

Is a constant, a variable, or an expression. The expression cannot contain a SELECT or EXECUTE statement.

derived_table

Is any valid SELECT statement that returns rows of data to be loaded into the table.

execute_statement

Is any valid EXECUTE statement that returns data with SELECT or READTEXT statements.

If *execute_statement* is used with INSERT, each result set must be compatible with the columns in the table or in *column_list*. *execute_statement* can be used to execute stored procedures on the same server or a remote server. The procedure in the remote server is executed, and the result sets are returned to the local server and loaded into the table in the local server. If *execute_statement* returns data with the READTEXT statement, each individual READTEXT statement can return a maximum of 1 MB (1024 KB) of data. *execute_statement* can also be used with extended procedures, and inserts the data returned by the main thread of the extended procedure. Output from threads other than the main thread are not inserted.

Note   For SQL Server version 7.0, *execute_statement* cannot contain an extended stored procedure that returns **text** or **image** columns. This behavior is a change from earlier versions of SQL Server.

DEFAULT VALUES
Forces the new row to contain the default values defined for each column.

Remarks

INSERT appends new rows to a table. To replace data in a table, the DELETE or TRUNCATE TABLE statements must be used to clear existing data before loading new data with INSERT. To modify column values in existing rows, use UPDATE. To create a new table and load it with data in one step, use the INTO option of the SELECT statement.

A **table** variable, in its scope, may be accessed like a regular table. Thus, **table** variable may be used as the table to which rows are to be added in an INSERT statement. For more information, see table.

A four-part name constructed with the OPENDATASOURCE function as the server-name part may be used as a table source in all places a table name can appear in INSERT statements.

Columns created with the **uniqueidentifier** data type store specially formatted 16-byte binary values. Unlike with identity columns, SQL Server does not automatically generate values for columns with the **uniqueidentifier** data type. During an insert operation, variables with a data type of **uniqueidentifier** and string constants in the form xxxxxxxx-xxxx-xxxx-xxxx-xxxxxxxxxxxx (36 characters including hyphens, where x is a hexadecimal digit in the range 0-9 or a-f) can be used for **uniqueidentifier** columns. For example, 6F9619FF-8B86-D011-B42D-00C04FC964FF is a valid value for a **uniqueidentifier** variable or column. Use the NEWID() function to obtain a globally unique ID (GUID).

When you insert rows, these rules apply:

- If a value is being loaded into columns with a **char**, **varchar**, or **varbinary** data type, the padding or truncation of trailing blanks (spaces for **char** and **varchar**, zeros for **varbinary**) is determined by the SET ANSI_PADDING setting defined for the column when the table was created. For more information, see SET ANSI_PADDING.

This table shows the default operation when SET ANSI_PADDING is OFF.

Data type	Default operation
Char	Pad value with spaces to the defined width of column.
Varchar	Remove trailing spaces to the last nonspace character or to a single space character for strings consisting of only spaces.
Varbinary	Remove trailing zeros.

- If an empty string (' ') is loaded into a column with a **varchar** or **text** data type, the default operation is to load a zero-length string. If the compatibility level for the database is less than 70, the value is converted to a single space. For more information, see sp_dbcmptlevel.

- If an INSERT statement violates a constraint or rule, or if it has a value incompatible with the data type of the column, the statement fails and SQL Server displays an error message.

- Inserting a null value into a **text** or **image** column does not create a valid text pointer, nor does it preallocate an 8-KB text page. For more information about inserting **text** and **image** data, see Using text, ntext, and image Functions.

- If INSERT is loading multiple rows with SELECT or EXECUTE, any violation of a rule or constraint that occurs from the values being loaded causes the entire statement to be terminated, and no rows are loaded.

- When inserting values into remote SQL Server tables, and not all values for all columns are specified, the user must identify the columns to which the specified values are to be inserted.

The setting of the SET ROWCOUNT option is ignored for INSERT statements against local and remote partitioned views. Also, this option is not supported for INSERT statements against remote tables in SQL Server 2000 when the compatibility level is set to 80.

When an INSTEAD-OF trigger is defined on INSERT actions against a table or view, the trigger executes *instead of* the INSERT statement. Previous versions of SQL Server only support AFTER triggers defined on INSERT and other data modification statements.

When an INSERT statement encounters an arithmetic error (overflow, divide by zero, or a domain error) occurring during expression evaluation, SQL Server handles these errors as if SET ARITHABORT is ON. The remainder of the batch is halted, and an error message is returned.

Permissions

INSERT permissions default to members of the **sysadmin** fixed server role, the **db_owner** and **db_datawriter** fixed database roles, and the table owner. Members of the **sysadmin**, **db_owner**, and the **db_securityadmin** roles, and the table owner can transfer permissions to other users.

Examples

A. Use a simple INSERT

This example creates the table **T1** and inserts one row.

```
IF EXISTS(SELECT TABLE_NAME FROM INFORMATION_SCHEMA.TABLES
      WHERE TABLE_NAME = 'T1')
   DROP TABLE T1
GO
CREATE TABLE T1 ( column_1 int, column_2 varchar(30))
INSERT T1 VALUES (1, 'Row #1')
```

B. Insert data that is not in the same order as the columns

This example uses *column_list* and VALUES list to explicitly specify the values that are inserted into each column.

```
IF EXISTS(SELECT TABLE_NAME FROM INFORMATION_SCHEMA.TABLES
      WHERE TABLE_NAME = 'T1')
   DROP TABLE T1
GO
CREATE TABLE T1 ( column_1 int, column_2 varchar(30))
INSERT T1 (column_2, column_1) VALUES ('Row #1',1)
```

C. Insert data with fewer values than columns

This example creates a table that has four columns. The INSERT statements insert rows that contain values for some of the columns, but not all of them.

```
IF EXISTS(SELECT TABLE_NAME FROM INFORMATION_SCHEMA.TABLES
      WHERE TABLE_NAME = 'T1')
   DROP TABLE T1
GO
CREATE TABLE T1
( column_1 int identity,
  column_2 varchar(30)
    CONSTRAINT default_name DEFAULT ('column default'),
  column_3 int NULL,
  column_4 varchar(40)
)
```

(continued)

(continued)

```
INSERT INTO T1 (column_4)
   VALUES ('Explicit value')
INSERT INTO T1 (column_2,column_4)
   VALUES ('Explicit value', 'Explicit value')
INSERT INTO T1 (column_2,column_3,column_4)
   VALUES ('Explicit value',-44,'Explicit value')
SELECT *
FROM T1
```

D. Load data into a table with an identity column

The first two INSERT statements allow identity values to be generated for the new rows. The third INSERT statement overrides the IDENTITY property for the column with the SET IDENTITY_INSERT statement, and inserts an explicit value into the identity column.

```
IF EXISTS(SELECT TABLE_NAME FROM INFORMATION_SCHEMA.TABLES
      WHERE TABLE_NAME = 'T1')
   DROP TABLE T1
GO
CREATE TABLE T1 ( column_1 int IDENTITY, column_2 varchar(30))
INSERT T1 VALUES ('Row #1')
INSERT T1 (column_2) VALUES ('Row #2')
SET IDENTITY_INSERT T1 ON
INSERT INTO T1 (column_1,column_2)
   VALUES (-99,'Explicit identity value')
SELECT *
FROM T1
```

E. Load data into a table through a view

The INSERT statement in this example specifies a view name; however, the new row is inserted in the view's underlying table. The order of VALUES list in the INSERT statement must match the column order of the view.

```
IF EXISTS(SELECT TABLE_NAME FROM INFORMATION_SCHEMA.TABLES
      WHERE TABLE_NAME = 'T1')
   DROP TABLE T1
GO
IF EXISTS(SELECT TABLE_NAME FROM INFORMATION_SCHEMA.VIEWS
      WHERE TABLE_NAME = 'V1')
   DROP VIEW V1
GO
CREATE TABLE T1 ( column_1 int, column_2 varchar(30))
GO
```

(continued)

(continued)

```
CREATE VIEW V1 AS SELECT column_2, column_1
FROM T1
GO
INSERT INTO V1
    VALUES ('Row 1',1)
SELECT *
FROM T1
```

F. Load data using the DEFAULT VALUES option

The CREATE TABLE statement in this example defines each column with a value that can be used when no explicit value for the column is specified in the INSERT statement. The DEFAULT VALUES option of the INSERT statement is used to add rows without supplying explicit values.

```
IF EXISTS(SELECT TABLE_NAME FROM INFORMATION_SCHEMA.TABLES
      WHERE TABLE_NAME = 'T1')
   DROP TABLE T1
GO
CREATE DEFAULT bound_default AS 'Bound default value'
GO
CREATE TABLE T1
( column_1 int identity,
  column_2 varchar(30)
    CONSTRAINT default_name DEFAULT ('column default'),
  column_3 timestamp,
  column_4 varchar(30),
  column_5 int NULL)
GO
USE master
EXEC sp_bindefault 'bound_default','T1.column_4'
INSERT INTO T1 DEFAULT VALUES
SELECT *
FROM T1
```

G. Load data using the SELECT and EXECUTE options

This example demonstrates three different methods for getting data from one table and loading it into another. Each is based on a multitable SELECT statement that includes an expression and a literal value in the column list.

The first INSERT statement uses a SELECT statement directly to retrieve data from the source table, **authors**, and store the result set in the **author_sales** table. The second INSERT executes a procedure that contains the SELECT statement, and the third INSERT executes the SELECT statement as a literal string.

```
IF EXISTS(SELECT TABLE_NAME FROM INFORMATION_SCHEMA.TABLES
      WHERE TABLE_NAME = 'author_sales')
   DROP TABLE author_sales
GO
IF EXISTS(SELECT name FROM sysobjects
      WHERE name = 'get_author_sales' AND type = 'P')
   DROP PROCEDURE get_author_sales
GO
USE pubs
CREATE TABLE author_sales
( data_source   varchar(20),
  au_id         varchar(11),
  au_lname      varchar(40),
  sales_dollars smallmoney
)
GO
CREATE PROCEDURE get_author_sales
AS
   SELECT 'PROCEDURE', authors.au_id, authors.au_lname,
      SUM(titles.price * sales.qty)
   FROM authors INNER JOIN titleauthor
      ON authors.au_id = titleauthor.au_id INNER JOIN titles
      ON titleauthor.title_id = titles.title_id INNER JOIN sales
      ON titles.title_id = sales.title_id
   WHERE authors.au_id like '8%'
   GROUP BY authors.au_id, authors.au_lname
GO
--INSERT...SELECT example
USE pubs
INSERT author_sales
   SELECT 'SELECT', authors.au_id, authors.au_lname,
      SUM(titles.price * sales.qty)
   FROM authors INNER JOIN titleauthor
      ON authors.au_id = titleauthor.au_id INNER JOIN titles
      ON titleauthor.title_id = titles.title_id INNER JOIN sales
      ON titles.title_id = sales.title_id
   WHERE authors.au_id LIKE '8%'
   GROUP BY authors.au_id, authors.au_lname

--INSERT...EXECUTE procedure example
INSERT author_sales EXECUTE get_author_sales
```

(continued)

(continued)

```
--INSERT...EXECUTE('string') example
INSERT author_sales
EXECUTE
('
SELECT ''EXEC STRING'', authors.au_id, authors.au_lname,
   SUM(titles.price * sales.qty)
   FROM authors INNER JOIN titleauthor
      ON authors.au_id = titleauthor.au_id INNER JOIN titles
      ON titleauthor.title_id = titles.title_id INNER JOIN sales
      ON titles.title_id = sales.title_id
   WHERE authors.au_id like ''8%''
   GROUP BY authors.au_id, authors.au_lname
')

--Show results.
SELECT * FROM author_sales
```

H. Insert data using the TOP clause in a SELECT statement

Because a SELECT statement can be specified in an INSERT statement, the TOP clause can also be used within the SELECT statement. The example inserts the top 10 authors from the **authors** table into a new table called **new_authors**.

```
IF EXISTS(SELECT TABLE_NAME FROM INFORMATION_SCHEMA.TABLES
      WHERE TABLE_NAME = 'new_authors')
   DROP TABLE new_authors
GO
USE pubs
CREATE TABLE new_authors
(
 au_id     id,
 au_lname  varchar(40),
 au_fname  varchar(20),
 phone     char(12),
 address   varchar(40),
 city      varchar(20),
 state     char(2),
 zip       char(5),
 contract  bit
)
INSERT INTO new_authors
SELECT TOP 10 *
FROM authors
```

Related Topics

CREATE TABLE, EXECUTE, FROM, IDENTITY (Property), NEWID, SELECT, SET ROWCOUNT

int, bigint, smallint, and tinyint

Exact number data types that use integer data.

bigint

Integer (whole number) data from -2^63 (-9223372036854775808) through 2^63-1 (9223372036854775807). Storage size is 8 bytes.

int

Integer (whole number) data from -2^31 (-2,147,483,648) through 2^31 - 1 (2,147,483,647). Storage size is 4 bytes. The SQL-92 synonym for **int** is **integer**.

smallint

Integer data from -2^15 (-32,768) through 2^15 - 1 (32,767). Storage size is 2 bytes.

tinyint

Integer data from 0 through 255. Storage size is 1 byte.

Remarks

The **bigint** data type is supported where integer values are supported. However, **bigint** is intended for special cases where the integer values may exceed the range supported by the **int** data type. The **int** data type remains the primary integer data type in SQL Server.

bigint fits between **smallmoney** and **int** in the data type precedence chart.

Functions will return **bigint** only if the parameter expression is a **bigint** data type. SQL Server will not automatically promote other integer data types (**tinyint**, **smallint**, and **int**) to **bigint**.

Related Topics

ALTER TABLE, CAST and CONVERT, CREATE TABLE, Data Type Conversion, Data Types, DECLARE @local_variable, DELETE, INSERT, SET @local_variable, UPDATE

IS_MEMBER

Indicates whether the current user is a member of the specified Microsoft
Windows NT group or Microsoft SQL Server role.

Syntax

```
IS_MEMBER ( { 'group' | 'role' } )
```

Arguments

'group'

Is the name of the Windows NT group being checked; must be in the format
Domain\Group. *group* is **sysname**.

'role'

Is the name of the SQL Server role being checked. *role* is **sysname** and can include
the database fixed roles or user-defined roles but not server roles.

Return Types

int

Remarks

IS_MEMBER returns these values.

Return value	Description
0	Current user is not a member of *group* or *role*.
1	Current user is a member of *group* or *role*.
NULL	Either *group* or *role* is not valid.

This function can be useful to programmatically detect whether the current user can
perform an activity that depends on the permissions applied to a group or role.

Examples

This example indicates whether the current user is a member of the **db_owner** fixed
database role.

```
IF IS_MEMBER ('db_owner') = 1
   print 'Current user is a member of the db_owner role'
ELSE IF IS_MEMBER ('db_owner') = 0
   print 'Current user is NOT a member of the db_owner role'
ELSE IF IS_MEMBER ('db_owner') IS NULL
   print 'ERROR: Invalid group / role specified'
```

Related Topics

IS_SRVROLEMEMBER, Security Functions

IS_SRVROLEMEMBER

Indicates whether the current user login is a member of the specified server role.

Syntax

```
IS_SRVROLEMEMBER ( 'role' [ , 'login' ] )
```

Arguments

'*role*'

Is the name of the server role being checked. *role* is **sysname**.

Valid values for *role* are:

- **sysadmin**
- **dbcreator**
- **diskadmin**
- **processadmin**
- **serveradmin**
- **setupadmin**
- **securityadmin**

'*login*'

Is the optional name of the login to check. *login* is **sysname**, with a default of NULL. If not specified, the login account for the current user is used.

Return Types

int

Remarks

IS_SRVROLEMEMBER returns these values.

Return value	Description
0	*login* is not a member of *role*.
1	*login* is a member of *role*.
NULL	*role* or *login* is not valid.

This function can be useful to programmatically detect whether the current user can perform an activity requiring the server role's permissions.

If a Windows NT user, such as **London\JoeB**, is specified for *login*, IS_SRVROLEMEMBER returns NULL if the user has not previously been granted or denied direct access to Microsoft SQL Server using **sp_grantlogin** or **sp_denylogin**.

Examples

This example indicates whether the current user is a member of the **sysadmin** fixed server role.

```
IF IS_SRVROLEMEMBER ('sysadmin') = 1
   print 'Current user''s login is a member of the sysadmin role'
ELSE IF IS_SRVROLEMEMBER ('sysadmin') = 0
   print 'Current user''s login is NOT a member of the sysadmin role'
ELSE IF IS_SRVROLEMEMBER ('sysadmin') IS NULL
   print 'ERROR: Invalid server role specified'
```

Related Topics

IS_MEMBER, Security Functions

ISDATE

Determines whether an input expression is a valid date.

Syntax

```
ISDATE ( expression )
```

Arguments

expression

Is an expression to be validated as a date. *expression* is any expression that returns a **varchar** data type.

Return Types

int

Remarks

ISDATE returns 1 if the input expression is a valid date; otherwise, it returns 0. This table shows the return values for a selection of examples.

Column value (varchar)	ISDATE return value
NULL	0
Abc	0
100, -100, 100 a, or 100.00	0
.01	0
-100.1234e-123	0
.231e90	0
$100.12345, - $100.12345, or $-1000.123	0
as100 or 1a00	0
1995-10-1,1/20/95,1995-10-1 12:00pm, Feb 7 1995 11:00pm, or 1995-10-1, or 1/23/95	1
13/43/3425 or 1995-10-1a	0
$1000, $100, or $100 a	0

Examples

A. Use ISDATE to check a variable

This example checks the **@datestring** local variable for valid date data.

```
DECLARE @datestring varchar(8)
SET @datestring = '12/21/98'
SELECT ISDATE(@datestring)
```

Here is the result set:

```
-----------
1
```

B. Use ISDATE to check a column for dates

This example creates the **test_dates** table and inserts two values. ISDATE is used to determine whether the values in the columns are dates.

```
USE tempdb
CREATE TABLE test_dates (Col_1 varchar(15), Col_2 datetime)
GO
INSERT INTO test_dates VALUES ('abc', 'July 13, 1998')
GO
SELECT ISDATE(Col_1) AS Col_1, ISDATE(Col_2) AS Col_2
    FROM test_dates
```

Here is the result set:

```
Col_1                    Col_2
----------------         --------------------
0                        1
```

Related Topics

char and varchar, System Functions

IS [NOT] NULL

Determines whether or not a given expression is NULL.

Syntax

```
expression IS [ NOT ] NULL
```

Arguments

expression

Is any valid Microsoft SQL Server expression.

NOT

Specifies that the Boolean result be negated. The predicate reverses its return values, returning TRUE if the value is not NULL, and FALSE if the value is NULL.

Result Types

Boolean

Return Code Values

If the value of *expression* is NULL, IS NULL returns TRUE; otherwise, it returns FALSE.

If the value of *expression* is NULL, IS NOT NULL returns FALSE; otherwise, it returns TRUE.

Remarks

To determine if an expression is NULL, use IS NULL or IS NOT NULL rather than comparison operators (such as = or !=). Comparison operators return UNKNOWN if either or both arguments are NULL.

Examples

This example returns the title number and the advance amount for all books in which either the advance amount is less than $5,000 or the advance is unknown (or NULL). Note that the results shown are those returned after Example C has been executed.

```
USE pubs
SELECT title_id, advance
FROM titles
WHERE advance < $5000 OR advance IS NULL
ORDER BY title_id
```

Here is the result set:

```
title_id advance
-------- --------------------------
MC2222   0.0000
MC3026   NULL
PC9999   NULL
PS2091   2275.0000
PS3333   2000.0000
PS7777   4000.0000
TC4203   4000.0000

(7 row(s) affected)
```

Related Topics

CASE, CREATE PROCEDURE, CREATE TABLE, Data Types, Expressions, INSERT, LIKE, Null Values, Operators (Logical Operators), SELECT, sp_help, UPDATE, WHERE

ISNULL

Replaces NULL with the specified replacement value.

Syntax

```
ISNULL ( check_expression , replacement_value )
```

Arguments

check_expression

Is the expression to be checked for NULL. *check_expression* can be of any type.

replacement_value

Is the expression to be returned if *check_expression* is NULL. *replacement_value* must have the same type as *check_expresssion*.

Return Types

Returns the same type as *check_expression*.

Remarks

The value of *check_expression* is returned if it is not NULL; otherwise, *replacement_value* is returned.

Examples

A. Use ISNULL with AVG

This example finds the average of the prices of all titles, substituting the value $10.00 for all NULL entries in the **price** column of the **titles** table.

```
USE pubs
GO
SELECT AVG(ISNULL(price, $10.00))
FROM titles
GO
```

Here is the result set:

```
--------------------------
14.24

(1 row(s) affected)
```

B. Use ISNULL

This example selects the title, type, and price for all books in the **titles** table. If the price for a given title is NULL, the price shown in the result set is 0.00.

```
USE pubs
GO
SELECT SUBSTRING(title, 1, 15) AS Title, type AS Type,
    ISNULL(price, 0.00) AS Price
FROM titles
GO
```

Here is the result set:

```
Title             Type         Price
---------------   ------------  ---------------------------
The Busy Execut   business     19.99
Cooking with Co   business     11.95
You Can Combat    business     2.99
Straight Talk A   business     19.99
Silicon Valley    mod_cook     19.99
The Gourmet Mic   mod_cook     2.99
The Psychology    UNDECIDED    0.00
But Is It User    popular_comp 22.95
Secrets of Sili   popular_comp 20.00
Net Etiquette     popular_comp 0.00
Computer Phobic   psychology   21.59
Is Anger the En   psychology   10.95
Life Without Fe   psychology   7.00
Prolonged Data    psychology   19.99
Emotional Secur   psychology   7.99
Onions, Leeks,    trad_cook    20.95
Fifty Years in    trad_cook    11.95
Sushi, Anyone?    trad_cook    14.99

(18 row(s) affected)
```

Related Topics

Expressions, IS [NOT] NULL, System Functions, WHERE

ISNUMERIC

Determines whether an expression is a valid numeric type.

Syntax

```
ISNUMERIC ( expression )
```

Arguments

expression

Is an expression to be evaluated.

Return Types

int

Remarks

ISNUMERIC returns 1 when the input expression evaluates to a valid integer, floating point number, **money** or **decimal** type; otherwise it returns 0. A return value of 1 guarantees that *expression* can be converted to one of these numeric types.

Examples

A. Use ISNUMERIC

This example returns 1 because the **zip** column contains valid numeric values.

```
USE pubs
SELECT ISNUMERIC(zip)
FROM authors
GO
```

B. Use ISNUMERIC and SUBSTRING

This example returns 0 for all titles in the **titles** table because none of the titles are valid numeric values.

```
USE pubs
GO
-- Because the title column is all character data, expect a result of 0
-- for the ISNUMERIC function.
SELECT SUBSTRING(title, 1, 15) type, price, ISNUMERIC(title)
FROM titles
GO
```

Here is the result set:

```
type            price
--------------- --------------------------- -----------
The Busy Execut 19.99                       0
Cooking with Co 11.95                       0
You Can Combat  2.99                        0
Straight Talk A 19.99                       0
Silicon Valley  19.99                       0
The Gourmet Mic 2.99                        0
The Psychology  (null)                      0
But Is It User  22.95                       0
Secrets of Sili 20.00                       0
Net Etiquette   (null)                      0
Computer Phobic 21.59                       0
Is Anger the En 10.95                       0
Life Without Fe 7.00                        0
Prolonged Data  19.99                       0
```

(continued)

(continued)

```
Emotional Secur 7.99                          0
Onions, Leeks,  20.95                         0
Fifty Years in  11.95                         0
Sushi, Anyone?  14.99                         0

(18 row(s) affected)
```

Related Topics

Expressions, System Functions

KILL

Terminates a user process based on the system process ID (SPID) or unit of work (UOW). If the specified SPID or UOW has a lot of work to undo, the KILL command may take some time to complete, particularly when it involves rolling back a long transaction.

In Microsoft SQL Server 2000, KILL can be used to terminate a normal connection, which internally terminates the transactions associated with the given SPID. In addition, the command can also be used to terminate all orphaned distributed transactions when Microsoft Distributed Transaction Coordinator (MS DTC) is in use. A distributed transaction is orphaned when it is not associated with any current SPID.

Syntax

```
KILL {spid | UOW} [WITH STATUSONLY]
```

Arguments

spid

Is the system process ID (SPID) of the process to terminate. The SPID value is a unique integer (**smallint**) assigned to each user connection when the connection is made, but the assignment is not permanent.

Use KILL *spid* to terminate regular non-distributed and distributed transactions associated with a given SPID.

UOW

Identifies the Unit of Work ID (UOW) of the DTC transaction. *UOW* is a character string that may be obtained from the **syslockinfo** table, which gives the UOW for every lock held by a DTC transaction. *UOW* also may be obtained from the error log or through the DTC monitor. For more information on monitoring distributed transactions, see the MS DTC user manual.

Use KILL *UOW* to terminate orphaned DTC transactions, which are not associated with any real SPID and instead are associated artificially with SPID = '-2'. For more information on SPID = '-2', see the Remarks section later in this topic.

WITH STATUSONLY

Specifies that SQL Server generate a progress report on a given *spid* or *UOW* that is being rolled back. The KILL command with WITH STATUSONLY does not terminate or roll back the *spid* or *UOW*. It only displays the current progress report.

For the KILL command with WITH STATUSONLY option to generate a report successfully, the *spid* or *UOW* must be currently in the rollback status. The progress report states the amount of rollback completed (in percent) and the estimated length of time left (in seconds), in this form:

```
Spid|UOW <xxx>: Transaction rollback in progress. Estimated rollback completion: yy%
Estimated time left: zz seconds.
```

If the rollback of the *spid* or *UOW* has completed when the KILL command with the WITH STATUSONLY option is executed, or if no *spid* or *UOW* is being rolled back, the KILL with WITH STATUSONLY will return the following error:

```
Status report cannot be obtained. KILL/ROLLBACK operator for Process ID|UOW <xxx> is
not in progress.
```

The same status report can be obtained by executing twice the KILL *spid|UOW* command without the WITH STATUSONLY option; however, this is not recommended. The second execution of the command may terminate a new process that may have been assigned to the released SPID.

Remarks

KILL is commonly used to terminate a process that is blocking other important processes with locks, or to terminate a process that is executing a query that is using necessary system resources. System processes and processes running an extended stored procedure cannot be terminated.

Use KILL very carefully, especially when critical processes are running. You cannot kill your own process. Other processes not to kill are:

- AWAITING COMMAND
- CHECKPOINT SLEEP
- LAZY WRITER
- LOCK MONITOR
- SELECT
- SIGNAL HANDLER

Execute **sp_who** to get a report on valid SPID values. If a rollback is in progress for a specific SPID, the **cmd** column for the specific the SPID in the **sp_who** result set will indicate 'KILLED/ROLLBACK'.

Use @@SPID to display the SPID value for the current session.

In SQL Server 2000, the KILL command can be used to resolve SPIDs associated with non-distributed and distributed transactions. KILL also can be used to resolve orphaned or in-doubt distributed transactions. A distributed transaction is orphaned when it is not associated with any current SPID.

The SPID value of '-2' is set aside as an indicator of connectionless, or orphaned, transactions. SQL Server assigns this value to all orphaned distributed transactions, making it easier to identify such transactions in **sp_lock** (**spid** column), **sp_who** (**blk** column), **syslockinfo**, and **sysprocesses**. This feature is useful when a particular connection has a lock on the database resource and is blocking the progress of a transaction. The user would be able to identify the SPID that owns the lock, and end the connection.

The KILL command can be used to resolve in-doubt transactions, which are unresolved distributed transactions resulting from unplanned restarts of the database server or DTC coordinator. For more information on resolving in-doubt transactions, see Troubleshooting DTC Transactions.

Permissions

KILL permissions default to the members of the **sysadmin** and **processadmin** fixed database roles, and are not transferable.

Examples

A. Use KILL to terminate a SPID

This example shows how to terminate SPID 53.

```
KILL 53
```

B. Use KILL spid WITH STATUSONLY to obtain a progress report

This example generates a status of the rollback process for the specific spid.

```
KILL 54
KILL 54 WITH STATUSONLY

--This is the progress report.
spid 54: Transaction rollback in progress. Estimated rollback completion: 80% Estimated
time left: 10 seconds.
```

C. Use KILL to terminate an orphan distributed transaction

This example shows how to terminate an orphan (SPID = -2) transaction with UOW = D5499C66-E398-45CA-BF7E-DC9C194B48CF.

```
KILL 'D5499C66-E398-45CA-BF7E-DC9C194B48CF'
```

Related Topics

Functions, SHUTDOWN, @@SPID, sp_lock, sp_who, Troubleshooting DTC
Transactions

LEFT

Returns the part of a character string starting at a specified number of characters from
the left.

Syntax

```
LEFT ( character_expression , integer_expression )
```

Arguments

character_expression

Is an expression of character or binary data. *character_expression* can be a
constant, variable, or column. *character_expression* must be of a data type that can
be implicitly convertible to **varchar**. Otherwise, use the CAST function to
explicitly convert *character_expression*.

integer_expression

Is a positive whole number. If *integer_expression* is negative, a null string is
returned.

Return Types

varchar

Remarks

Compatibility levels can affect return values. For more information about
compatibility levels, see sp_dbcmptlevel.

Examples

A. Use LEFT with a column

This example returns the five leftmost characters of each book title.

```
USE pubs
GO
SELECT LEFT(title, 5)
FROM titles
ORDER BY title_id
GO
```

Here is the result set:

```
-----
The B
Cooki
You C
Strai
Silic
The G
The P
But I
Secre
Net E
Compu
Is An
Life
Prolo
Emoti
Onion
Fifty
Sushi

(18 row(s) affected)
```

B. Use LEFT with a character string

This example uses LEFT to return the two leftmost characters of the character string abcdefg.

```
SELECT LEFT('abcdefg',2)
GO
```

Here is the result set:

```
--
ab

(1 row(s) affected)
```

Related Topics

Data Types, String Functions

LEN

Returns the number of characters, rather than the number of bytes, of the given string expression, excluding trailing blanks.

Syntax

```
LEN ( string_expression )
```

Arguments

string_expression
  Is the string expression to be evaluated.

Return Types

int

Examples

This example selects the number of characters and the data in **CompanyName** for companies located in Finland.

```
USE Northwind
GO
SELECT LEN(CompanyName) AS 'Length', CompanyName
FROM Customers
WHERE Country = 'Finland'
```

Here is the result set:

```
Length      CompanyName
----------- ------------------------------

14          Wartian Herkku
11          Wilman Kala
```

Related Topics

Data Types, String Functions

LIKE

Determines whether or not a given character string matches a specified pattern. A pattern can include regular characters and wildcard characters. During pattern matching, regular characters must exactly match the characters specified in the character string. Wildcard characters, however, can be matched with arbitrary fragments of the character string. Using wildcard characters makes the LIKE operator more flexible than using the = and != string comparison operators. If any of the arguments are not of character string data type, Microsoft SQL Server converts them to character string data type, if possible.

Syntax

```
match_expression [ NOT ] LIKE pattern [ ESCAPE escape_character ]
```

Arguments

match_expression
Is any valid SQL Server expression of character string data type.

pattern
Is the pattern to search for in *match_expression*, and can include these valid
SQL Server wildcard characters.

Wildcard character	Description	Example
%	Any string of zero or more characters.	WHERE title LIKE '%computer%' finds all book titles with the word 'computer' anywhere in the book title.
_ (underscore)	Any single character.	WHERE au_fname LIKE '_ean' finds all four-letter first names that end with ean (Dean, Sean, and so on).
[ ]	Any single character within the specified range ([a–f]) or set ([abcdef]).	WHERE au_lname LIKE '[C-P]arsen' finds author last names ending with arsen and beginning with any single character between C and P, for example Carsen, Larsen, Karsen, and so on.
[^]	Any single character not within the specified range ([^a–f]) or set ([^abcdef]).	WHERE au_lname LIKE 'de[^l]%' all author last names beginning with de and where the following letter is not l.

escape_character
Is any valid SQL Server expression of any of the data types of the character string
data type category. *escape_character* has no default and must consist of only one
character.

Result Types

Boolean

Result Value

LIKE returns TRUE if the *match_expression* matches the specified *pattern*.

Remarks

When you perform string comparisons with LIKE, all characters in the pattern string are significant, including leading or trailing spaces. If a comparison in a query is to return all rows with a string LIKE 'abc ' (abc followed by a single space), a row in which the value of that column is abc (abc without a space) is not returned. However, trailing blanks, in the expression to which the pattern is matched, are ignored. If a comparison in a query is to return all rows with the string LIKE 'abc' (abc without a space), all rows that start with abc and have zero or more trailing blanks are returned.

A string comparison using a pattern containing **char** and **varchar** data may not pass a LIKE comparison because of how the data is stored. It is important to understand the storage for each data type and where a LIKE comparison may fail. The following example passes a local **char** variable to a stored procedure and then uses pattern matching to find all of the books by a certain author. In this procedure, the author's last name is passed as a variable.

```
CREATE PROCEDURE find_books @AU_LNAME char(20)
AS
SELECT @AU_LNAME = RTRIM(@AU_LNAME) + '%'
SELECT t.title_id, t.title
FROM authors a, titleauthor ta, titles t
WHERE a.au_id = ta.au_id AND ta.title_id = t.title_id
    AND a.au_lname LIKE @AU_LNAME
```

In the **find_books** procedure, no rows are returned because the **char** variable (@AU_LNAME) contains trailing blanks whenever the name contains fewer than 20 characters. Because the **au_lname** column is **varchar**, there are no trailing blanks. This procedure fails because the trailing blanks are significant.

However, this example succeeds because trailing blanks are not added to a **varchar** variable:

```
USE pubs
GO
CREATE PROCEDURE find_books2 @au_lname varchar(20)
AS
SELECT t.title_id, t.title
FROM authors a, titleauthor ta, titles t
WHERE a.au_id = ta.au_id AND ta.title_id = t.title_id
    AND a.au_lname LIKE @au_lname + '%'

EXEC find_books2 'ring'
```

Here is the result set:

```
title_id title
-------- -------------------------------------------------------------
MC3021   The Gourmet Microwave
PS2091   Is Anger the Enemy?
PS2091   Is Anger the Enemy?
PS2106   Life Without Fear

(4 row(s) affected)
```

Pattern Matching with LIKE

It is recommended that LIKE be used when you search for **datetime** values, because **datetime** entries can contain a variety of dateparts. For example, if you insert the value 19981231 9:20 into a column named **arrival_time**, the clause WHERE *arrival_time* = 9:20 cannot find an exact match for the 9:20 string because SQL Server converts it to Jan 1, 1900 9:20AM. A match is found, however, by the clause WHERE *arrival_time* LIKE '%9:20%'.

LIKE supports ASCII pattern matching and Unicode pattern matching. When all arguments (*match_expression*, *pattern*, and *escape_character*, if present) are ASCII character data types, ASCII pattern matching is performed. If any of the arguments are of Unicode data type, all arguments are converted to Unicode and Unicode pattern matching is performed. When you use Unicode data (**nchar** or **nvarchar** data types) with LIKE, trailing blanks are significant; however, for non-Unicode data, trailing blanks are not significant. Unicode LIKE is compatible with the SQL-92 standard. ASCII LIKE is compatible with earlier versions of SQL Server.

Here is a series of examples that show the differences in rows returned between ASCII and Unicode LIKE pattern matching:

```
-- ASCII pattern matching with char column
CREATE TABLE t (col1 char(30))
INSERT INTO t VALUES ('Robert King')
SELECT *
FROM t
WHERE col1 LIKE '% King' -- returns 1 row

-- Unicode pattern matching with nchar column
CREATE TABLE t (col1 nchar(30))
INSERT INTO t VALUES ('Robert King')
SELECT *
FROM t
WHERE col1 LIKE '% King' -- no rows returned
```

(continued)

(continued)

```
-- Unicode pattern matching with nchar column and RTRIM
CREATE TABLE t (col1 nchar (30))
INSERT INTO t VALUES ('Robert King')
SELECT *
FROM t
WHERE RTRIM(col1) LIKE '% King'-- returns 1 row
```

Note When you perform string comparisons with LIKE, all characters in the pattern string are significant, including every leading or trailing blank (space).

Using the % Wildcard Character

If the LIKE '5%' symbol is specified, SQL Server searches for the number 5 followed by any string of zero or more characters.

For example, this query shows all system tables in a database, because they all begin with the letters sys:

```
SELECT TABLE_NAME
FROM INFORMATION_SCHEMA.TABLES
WHERE TABLE_NAME LIKE 'sys%'
```

Note Be aware that system tables can change from version to version. It is recommended that you use the Information Schema Views or applicable stored procedures to work with SQL Server system tables.

To see all objects that are not system tables, use NOT LIKE 'sys%'. If you have a total of 32 objects and LIKE finds 13 names that match the pattern, NOT LIKE finds the 19 objects that do not match the LIKE pattern.

You may not always find the same names with a pattern such as LIKE '[^s][^y][^s]%'. Instead of 19 names, you may get only 14, with all the names that begin with s or have y as the second letter or have s as the third letter eliminated from the results, as well as the system table names. This is because match strings with negative wildcards are evaluated in steps, one wildcard at a time. If the match fails at any point in the evaluation, it is eliminated.

Using Wildcard Characters as Literals

You can use the wildcard pattern matching characters as literal characters. To use a wildcard character as a literal character, enclose the wildcard character in brackets. The table shows several examples of using the LIKE keyword and the [ ] wildcard characters.

Symbol	Meaning
LIKE '5[%]'	5%
LIKE '[_]n'	_n
LIKE '[a-cdf]'	a, b, c, d, or f
LIKE '[-acdf]'	-, a, c, d, or f
LIKE '[[ ]'	[
LIKE ']'	]
LIKE 'abc[_]d%'	abc_d and abc_de
LIKE 'abc[def]'	abcd, abce, and abcf

Pattern Matching with the ESCAPE Clause

You can search for character strings that include one or more of the special wildcard characters. For example, the **discounts** table in the **customers** database may store discount values that include a percent sign (%). To search for the percent sign as a character instead of as a wildcard character, the ESCAPE keyword and escape character must be provided. For example, a sample database contains a column named **comment** that contains the text 30%. To search for any rows containing the string 30% anywhere in the **comment** column, specify a WHERE clause of WHERE comment LIKE '%30!%%' ESCAPE '!'. Unless ESCAPE and the escape character are specified, SQL Server returns any rows with the string 30.

This example shows how to search for the string "50% off when 100 or more copies are purchased" in the **notes** column of the **titles** table in the **pubs** database:

```
USE pubs
GO
SELECT notes
FROM titles
WHERE notes LIKE '50%% off when 100 or more copies are purchased'
   ESCAPE '%'
GO
```

Examples

A. Use LIKE with the % wildcard character

This example finds all phone numbers that have area code 415 in the authors table.

```
USE pubs
GO
SELECT phone
FROM authors
WHERE phone LIKE '415%'
ORDER by au_lname
GO
```

Here is the result set:

```
phone
------------
415 658-9932
415 548-7723
415 836-7128
415 986-7020
415 836-7128
415 534-9219
415 585-4620
415 354-7128
415 834-2919
415 843-2991
415 935-4228

(11 row(s) affected)
```

B. Use NOT LIKE with the % wildcard character

This example finds all phone numbers in the **authors** table that have area codes other than 415.

```
USE pubs
GO
SELECT phone
FROM authors
WHERE phone NOT LIKE '415%'
ORDER BY au_lname
GO
```

Here is the result set:

```
phone
------------
503 745-6402
219 547-9982
615 996-8275
615 297-2723
707 938-6445
707 448-4982
408 286-2428
301 946-8853
801 826-0752
801 826-0752
913 843-0462
408 496-7223

(12 row(s) affected)
```

C. Use the ESCAPE clause

This example uses the ESCAPE clause and the escape character to find the exact character string 10–15% in column **c1** of the **mytbl2** table.

```
USE pubs
GO
IF EXISTS(SELECT TABLE_NAME FROM INFORMATION_SCHEMA.TABLES
     WHERE TABLE_NAME = 'mytbl2')
   DROP TABLE mytbl2
GO
USE pubs
GO
CREATE TABLE mytbl2
(
 c1 sysname
)
GO
INSERT mytbl2 VALUES ('Discount is 10-15% off')
INSERT mytbl2 VALUES ('Discount is .10-.15 off')
GO
SELECT c1
FROM mytbl2
WHERE c1 LIKE '%10-15!% off%' ESCAPE '!'
GO
```

D. Use the [ ] wildcard characters

This example finds authors with the first name of Cheryl or Sheryl.

```
USE pubs
GO
SELECT au_lname, au_fname, phone
FROM authors
WHERE au_fname LIKE '[CS]heryl'
ORDER BY au_lname ASC, au_fname ASC
GO
```

This example finds the rows for authors with last names of Carson, Carsen, Karson, or Karsen.

```
USE pubs
GO
SELECT au_lname, au_fname, phone
FROM authors
WHERE au_lname LIKE '[CK]ars[eo]n'
ORDER BY au_lname ASC, au_fname ASC
GO
```

Related Topics

Expressions, Functions, SELECT, WHERE

LOAD

Loads a backup copy of one of the following:

- User database (LOAD DATABASE)
- Transaction log (LOAD TRANSACTION)
- Header information about the dump (LOAD HEADERONLY)

   Important   The LOAD statement is included in Microsoft SQL Server 2000 for backward compatibility. The LOAD statement is identical to the RESTORE statement. It is recommended that the RESTORE statement be used instead of the LOAD statement. In a future version of SQL Server, LOAD will not be supported.

Related Topics

BACKUP, CREATE DATABASE, RESTORE, sp_helpdevice

LOG

Returns the natural logarithm of the given **float** expression.

Syntax

```
LOG ( float_expression )
```

Arguments

float_expression
   Is an expression of the **float** data type.

Return Types

float

Examples

This example calculates the LOG for the given **float** expression.

```
DECLARE @var float
SET @var = 5.175643
SELECT 'The LOG of the variable is: ' + CONVERT(varchar,LOG(@var))
GO
```

Here is the result set:

```
The LOG of the variable is: 1.64396

(1 row(s) affected)
```

Related Topics

Mathematical Functions

LOG10

Returns the base-10 logarithm of the given **float** expression.

Syntax

```
LOG10 ( float_expression )
```

Arguments

float_expression
   Is an expression of the **float** data type.

Return Types

float

Examples

This example calculates the LOG10 of the given variable.

```
DECLARE @var float
SET @var = 145.175643
SELECT 'The LOG10 of the variable is: ' + CONVERT(varchar,LOG10(@var))
GO
```

Here is the result set:

```
The LOG10 of the variable is: 2.16189

(1 row(s) affected)
```

Related Topics

Mathematical Functions

LOWER

Returns a character expression after converting uppercase character data to lowercase.

Syntax

```
LOWER ( character_expression )
```

Arguments

character_expression

Is an expression of character or binary data. *character_expression* can be a constant, variable, or column. *character_expression* must be of a data type that is implicitly convertible to **varchar**. Otherwise, use CAST to explicitly convert *character_expression*.

Return Types

varchar

Examples

This example uses the LOWER function, the UPPER function, and nests the UPPER function inside the LOWER function in selecting book titles that have prices between $11 and $20.

```
USE pubs
GO
SELECT LOWER(SUBSTRING(title, 1, 20)) AS Lower,
   UPPER(SUBSTRING(title, 1, 20)) AS Upper,
   LOWER(UPPER(SUBSTRING(title, 1, 20))) As LowerUpper
FROM titles
WHERE price between 11.00 and 20.00
GO
```

Here is the result set:

```
Lower                    Upper                    LowerUpper
--------------------     --------------------     --------------------
the busy executive's     THE BUSY EXECUTIVE'S     the busy executive's
cooking with compute     COOKING WITH COMPUTE     cooking with compute
straight talk about      STRAIGHT TALK ABOUT      straight talk about
silicon valley gastr     SILICON VALLEY GASTR     silicon valley gastr
secrets of silicon v     SECRETS OF SILICON V     secrets of silicon v
prolonged data depri     PROLONGED DATA DEPRI     prolonged data depri
fifty years in bucki     FIFTY YEARS IN BUCKI     fifty years in bucki
sushi, anyone?           SUSHI, ANYONE?           sushi, anyone?

(8 row(s) affected)
```

Related Topics

Data Types, String Functions

LTRIM

Returns a character expression after removing leading blanks.

Syntax

```
LTRIM ( character_expression )
```

Arguments

character_expression

Is an expression of character or binary data. *character_expression* can be a constant, variable, or column. *character_expression* must be of a data type that is implicitly convertible to **varchar**. Otherwise, use CAST to explicitly convert *character_expression*.

Return Type

varchar

Remarks

Compatibility levels can affect return values. For more information about compatibility levels, see sp_dbcmptlevel.

Examples

This example uses LTRIM to remove leading spaces from a character variable.

```
DECLARE @string_to_trim varchar(60)
SET @string_to_trim = '     Five spaces are at the beginning of this
    string.'
SELECT 'Here is the string without the leading spaces: ' +
    LTRIM(@string_to_trim)
GO
```

Here is the result set:

```
-----------------------------------------------------------------
Here is the string without the leading spaces: Five spaces are at the beginning of this
string.

(1 row(s) affected)
```

Related Topics

Data Types, String Functions

MAX

Returns the maximum value in the expression.

Syntax

```
MAX ( [ ALL | DISTINCT ] expression )
```

Arguments

ALL
    Applies the aggregate function to all values. ALL is the default.

DISTINCT
    Specifies that each unique value is considered. DISTINCT is not meaningful with
    MAX and is available for SQL-92 compatibility only.

expression

Is a constant, column name, or function, and any combination of arithmetic, bitwise, and string operators. MAX can be used with numeric, character, and **datetime** columns, but not with **bit** columns. Aggregate functions and subqueries are not permitted.

Return Types

Returns a value same as *expression*.

Important Distinct aggregates, for example AVG(DISTINCT *column_name*), COUNT(DISTINCT *column_name*), MAX(DISTINCT *column_name*), MIN(DISTINCT *column_name*), and SUM(DISTINCT *column_name*), are not supported when using CUBE or ROLLUP. If used, Microsoft SQL Server returns an error message and cancels the query.

Remarks

MAX ignores any null values.

For character columns, MAX finds the highest value in the collating sequence.

Examples

This example returns the book with the highest (maximum) year-to-date sales.

```
USE pubs
GO
SELECT MAX(ytd_sales)
FROM titles
GO
```

Here is the result set:

```
-----------
22246

(1 row(s) affected)

Warning, null value eliminated from aggregate.
```

Related Topics

Aggregate Functions

MIN

Returns the minimum value in the expression.

Syntax

```
MIN ( [ ALL | DISTINCT ] expression )
```

Arguments

ALL

Applies the aggregate function to all values. ALL is the default.

DISTINCT

Specifies that each unique value is considered. DISTINCT is not meaningful with MIN and is available for SQL-92 compatibility only.

expression

Is a constant, column name, or function, and any combination of arithmetic, bitwise, and string operators. MIN can be used with numeric, **char**, **varchar**, or **datetime** columns, but not with **bit** columns. Aggregate functions and subqueries are not permitted.

Return Types

Returns a value same as *expression*.

> **Important**   Distinct aggregates, for example AVG(DISTINCT *column_name*), COUNT(DISTINCT *column_name*), MAX(DISTINCT *column_name*), MIN(DISTINCT *column_name*), and SUM(DISTINCT *column_name*), are not supported when using CUBE or ROLLUP. If used, Microsoft SQL Server returns an error message and ends the query.

Remarks

MIN ignores any null values.

With character data columns, MIN finds the value that is lowest in the sort sequence.

Examples

This example returns the book with the lowest (minimum) year-to-date sales.

```
USE pubs
GO
SELECT min(ytd_sales)
FROM titles
GO
```

Here is the result set:

```
- - - - - - - - - - -
111

(1 row(s) affected)
```

Related Topics

Aggregate Functions

money and smallmoney

Monetary data types for representing monetary or currency values.

money

Monetary data values from -2^63 (-922,337,203,685,477.5808) through 2^63 - 1 (+922,337,203,685,477.5807), with accuracy to a ten-thousandth of a monetary unit. Storage size is 8 bytes.

smallmoney

Monetary data values from -214,748.3648 through +214,748.3647, with accuracy to a ten-thousandth of a monetary unit. Storage size is 4 bytes.

Related Topics

ALTER TABLE, CAST and CONVERT, CREATE TABLE, Data Type Conversion, Data Types, DECLARE @local_variable, DELETE, INSERT, Monetary Data, SET @local_variable, UPDATE, Using Monetary Data

MONTH

Returns an integer that represents the month part of a specified date.

Syntax

```
MONTH ( date )
```

Arguments

date

Is an expression returning a **datetime** or **smalldatetime** value, or a character string in a date format. Use the **datetime** data type only for dates after January 1, 1753.

Return Types

int

Remarks

MONTH is equivalent to DATEPART(mm, *date*).

Always enclose **datetime** values in quotation marks. For earlier dates, store dates as character data.

Microsoft SQL Server recognizes a variety of date styles. For more information about date and time data, see CAST and CONVERT.

Examples

This example returns the number of the month from the date 03/12/1998.

```
SELECT "Month Number" = MONTH('03/12/1998')
GO
```

Here is the result set:

```
Month Number
------------
3
```

This example specifies the date as a number. Notice that SQL Server interprets 0 as January 1, 1900.

```
SELECT MONTH(0), DAY(0), YEAR(0)
```

Here is the result set.

```
----- ------ ------
1     1      1900
```

Related Topics

Data Types, Date and Time Functions, datetime and smalldatetime

NCHAR

Returns the Unicode character with the given integer code, as defined by the Unicode standard.

Syntax

```
NCHAR ( integer_expression )
```

Arguments

integer_expression

Is a positive whole number from 0 through 65535. If a value outside this range is specified, NULL is returned.

Return Types

nchar(1)

Examples

A. Use NCHAR and UNICODE

This example uses the UNICODE and NCHAR functions to print the UNICODE value and the NCHAR (Unicode character) of the second character of the København character string, and to print the actual second character, ø.

```
DECLARE @nstring nchar(8)
SET @nstring = N'København'
SELECT UNICODE(SUBSTRING(@nstring, 2, 1)),
    NCHAR(UNICODE(SUBSTRING(@nstring, 2, 1)))
GO
```

Here is the result set:

```
----------- -
248         ø

(1 row(s) affected)
```

B. Use SUBSTRING, UNICODE, CONVERT, and NCHAR

This example uses the SUBSTRING, UNICODE, CONVERT, and NCHAR functions to print the character number, the Unicode character, and the UNICODE value of each of the characters in the string København.

```
-- The @position variable holds the position of the character currently
-- being processed. The @nstring variable is the Unicode character
-- string to process.
DECLARE @position int, @nstring nchar(9)
-- Initialize the current position variable to the first character in
-- the string.
SET @position = 1
-- Initialize the character string variable to the string to process.
-- Notice that there is an N before the start of the string, which
-- indicates that the data following the N is Unicode data.
SET @nstring = N'København'
```

(continued)

(continued)

```
-- Print the character number of the position of the string you're at,
-- the actual Unicode character you're processing, and the UNICODE value -- for this
particular character.
PRINT 'Character #' + ' ' + 'Unicode Character' + ' ' + 'UNICODE Value'
WHILE @position <= DATALENGTH(@nstring)
   BEGIN
   SELECT @position,
      NCHAR(UNICODE(SUBSTRING(@nstring, @position, 1))),
      CONVERT(NCHAR(17), SUBSTRING(@nstring, @position, 1)),
      UNICODE(SUBSTRING(@nstring, @position, 1))
   SELECT @position = @position + 1
   END
GO
```

Here is the result set:

```
Character # Unicode Character UNICODE Value

----------- ------------------ -----------
1           K                  75

----------- ------------------ -----------
2           ø                  248

----------- ------------------ -----------
3           b                  98

----------- ------------------ -----------
4           e                  101

----------- ------------------ -----------
5           n                  110

----------- ------------------ -----------
6           h                  104

----------- ------------------ -----------
7           a                  97

----------- ------------------ -----------
8           v                  118
```

(continued)

(continued)

9	n	110
10	(null)	(null)
11	(null)	(null)
12	(null)	(null)
13	(null)	(null)
14	(null)	(null)
15	(null)	(null)
16	(null)	(null)
17	(null)	(null)
18	(null)	(null)

Related Topics

Data Types, String Functions, UNICODE

nchar and nvarchar

Character data types that are either fixed-length (**nchar**) or variable-length (**nvarchar**) Unicode data and use the UNICODE UCS-2 character set.

nchar(*n*)

Fixed-length Unicode character data of *n* characters. *n* must be a value from 1 through 4,000. Storage size is two times *n* bytes. The SQL-92 synonyms for **nchar** are **national char** and **national character**.

nvarchar(*n*)

Variable-length Unicode character data of *n* characters. *n* must be a value from 1 through 4,000. Storage size, in bytes, is two times the number of characters entered. The data entered can be 0 characters in length. The SQL-92 synonyms for **nvarchar** are **national char varying** and **national character varying**.

Remarks

When *n* is not specified in a data definition or variable declaration statement, the default length is 1. When *n* is not specified with the CAST function, the default length is 30.

Use **nchar** when the data entries in a column are expected to be consistently close to the same size.

Use **nvarchar** when the data entries in a column are expected to vary considerably in size.

Objects using **nchar** or **nvarchar** are assigned the default collation of the database, unless a specific collation is assigned using the COLLATE clause.

SET ANSI_PADDING OFF does not apply to **nchar** or **nvarchar**.
SET ANSI_PADDING is always ON for **nchar** and **nvarchar**.

Related Topics

ALTER TABLE, CAST and CONVERT, COLLATE, CREATE TABLE, Data Type Conversion, Data Types, DECLARE @local_variable, DELETE, INSERT, LIKE, SET ANSI_PADDING, SET @local_variable, sp_dbcmptlevel, UPDATE, Using Unicode Data, WHERE

NEWID

Creates a unique value of type **uniqueidentifier**.

Syntax

```
NEWID ( )
```

Return Types
uniqueidentifier

Examples

A. Use the NEWID function with a variable

This example uses NEWID to assign a value to a variable declared as the **uniqueidentifier** data type. The value of the **uniqueidentifier** data type variable is printed before the value is tested.

```
-- Creating a local variable with DECLARE/SET syntax.
DECLARE @myid uniqueidentifier
SET @myid = NEWID()
PRINT 'Value of @myid is: '+ CONVERT(varchar(255), @myid)
```

Here is the result set:

```
Value of @myid is: 6F9619FF-8B86-D011-B42D-00C04FC964FF
```

Note The value returned by NEWID is different for each computer. This number is shown only for illustration.

B. Use NEWID in a CREATE TABLE statement

This example creates **cust** table with a **uniqueidentifier** data type, and uses NEWID to fill the table with a default value. In assigning the default value of NEWID(), each new and existing row has a unique value for the **cust_id** column.

```
-- Creating a table using NEWID for uniqueidentifier data type.
CREATE TABLE cust
(
 cust_id uniqueidentifier NOT NULL
   DEFAULT newid(),
 company varchar(30) NOT NULL,
 contact_name varchar(60) NOT NULL,
 address varchar(30) NOT NULL,
 city varchar(30) NOT NULL,
 state_province varchar(10) NULL,
 postal_code varchar(10) NOT NULL,
 country varchar(20) NOT NULL,
 telephone varchar(15) NOT NULL,
 fax varchar(15) NULL
)
GO
-- Inserting data into cust table.
INSERT cust
(cust_id, company, contact_name, address, city, state_province,
 postal_code, country, telephone, fax)
VALUES
```

(continued)

(continued)

```
(newid(), 'Wartian Herkku', 'Pirkko Koskitalo', 'Torikatu 38', 'Oulu', NULL,
 '90110', 'Finland', '981-443655', '981-443655')
INSERT cust
(cust_id, company, contact_name, address, city, state_province,
postal_code, country, telephone, fax)
VALUES
(newid(), 'Wellington Importadora', 'Paula Parente', 'Rua do Mercado, 12', 'Resende',
'SP',
 '08737-363', 'Brazil', '(14) 555-8122', '')
INSERT cust
(cust_id, company, contact_name, address, city, state_province,
 postal_code, country, telephone, fax)
VALUES
(newid(), 'Cactus Comidas para llevar', 'Patricio Simpson', 'Cerrito 333', 'Buenos Aires',
NULL,
 '1010', 'Argentina', '(1) 135-5555', '(1) 135-4892')
INSERT cust
(cust_id, company, contact_name, address, city, state_province,
 postal_code, country, telephone, fax)
VALUES
(newid(), 'Ernst Handel', 'Roland Mendel', 'Kirchgasse 6', 'Graz', NULL,
 '8010', 'Austria', '7675-3425', '7675-3426')
INSERT cust
(cust_id, company, contact_name, address, city, state_province,
 postal_code, country, telephone, fax)
VALUES
(newid(), 'Maison Dewey', 'Catherine Dewey', 'Rue Joseph-Bens 532', 'Bruxelles', NULL,
 'B-1180', 'Belgium', '(02) 201 24 67', '(02) 201 24 68')
GO
```

C. Use uniqueidentifier and variable assignment

This example declares a local variable called **@myid** as a variable of **uniqueidentifier** data type. Then, the variable is assigned a value using the SET statement.

```
DECLARE @myid uniqueidentifier
SET @myid = 'A972C577-DFB0-064E-1189-0154C99310DAAC12'
GO
```

Related Topics

ALTER TABLE, CAST and CONVERT, CREATE TABLE, Data Types, Replication Overview, System Functions, uniqueidentifier

NOT

Negates a Boolean input.

Syntax

```
[ NOT ] boolean_expression
```

Arguments

boolean_expression
    Is any valid Microsoft SQL Server Boolean expression.

Result Types

Boolean

Result Value

NOT reverses the value of any Boolean expression.

Remarks

The use of NOT negates an expression.

This table shows the results of comparing TRUE and FALSE values using the NOT operator.

	NOT
TRUE	FALSE
FALSE	TRUE
UNKNOWN	UNKNOWN

Examples

This example finds all business and psychology books that do not have an advance over $5,500.

```
USE pubs
GO
SELECT title_id, type, advance
FROM titles
WHERE (type = 'business' OR type = 'psychology')
   AND NOT advance > $5500
ORDER BY title_id ASC
GO
```

Here is the result set:

```
title_id type          advance
-------- ------------  --------------------
BU1032   business      5000.0000
BU1111   business      5000.0000
BU7832   business      5000.0000
PS2091   psychology    2275.0000
PS3333   psychology    2000.0000
PS7777   psychology    4000.0000

(6 row(s) affected)
```

Related Topics

Expressions, Functions, Operators (Logical Operators), SELECT, WHERE

ntext, text, and image

Fixed and variable-length data types for storing large non-Unicode and Unicode character and binary data. Unicode data uses the UNICODE UCS-2 character set.

ntext

Variable-length Unicode data with a maximum length of 2^{30} - 1 (1,073,741,823) characters. Storage size, in bytes, is two times the number of characters entered. The SQL-92 synonym for **ntext** is **national text**.

text

Variable-length non-Unicode data in the code page of the server and with a maximum length of 2^{31}-1 (2,147,483,647) characters. When the server code page uses double-byte characters, the storage is still 2,147,483,647 bytes. Depending on the character string, the storage size may be less than 2,147,483,647 bytes.

image

Variable-length binary data from 0 through 2^{31}-1 (2,147,483,647) bytes.

Remarks

These functions and statements can be used with **ntext**, **text**, or **image** data.

Functions	Statements
DATALENGTH	READTEXT
PATINDEX	SET TEXTSIZE

(continued)

(continued)

Functions	Statements
SUBSTRING	UPDATETEXT
TEXTPTR	WRITETEXT
TEXTVALID	

Related Topics

ALTER TABLE, CAST and CONVERT, CREATE TABLE, Data Type Conversion, Data Types, DECLARE @local_variable, DELETE, INSERT, LIKE, SET @local_variable, UPDATE, Using Unicode Data

NULLIF

Returns a null value if the two specified expressions are equivalent.

Syntax

```
NULLIF ( expression , expression )
```

Arguments

expression

Is a constant, column name, function, subquery, or any combination of arithmetic, bitwise, and string operators.

Return Types

Returns the same type as the first *expression*.

NULLIF returns the first *expression* if the two expressions are not equivalent. If the expressions are equivalent, NULLIF returns a null value of the type of the first *expression*.

Remarks

NULLIF is equivalent to a searched CASE function in which the two expressions are equal and the resulting expression is NULL.

Examples

This example creates a **budgets** table to show a department (**dept**) its current budget
(**current_year**) and its previous budget (**previous_year**). For the current year, NULL
is used for departments with budgets that have not changed from the previous year,
and 0 is used for budgets that have not yet been determined. To find out the average of
only those departments that receive a budget as well as to include the budget value
from the previous year (use the **previous_year** value, where the **current_year** is 0),
combine the NULLIF and COALESCE functions.

```
USE pubs
IF EXISTS (SELECT TABLE_NAME FROM INFORMATION_SCHEMA.TABLES
      WHERE TABLE_NAME = 'budgets')
   DROP TABLE budgets
GO
SET NOCOUNT ON
CREATE TABLE budgets
(
   dept            tinyint   IDENTITY,
   current_year    decimal   NULL,
   previous_year   decimal   NULL
)
INSERT budgets VALUES(100000, 150000)
INSERT budgets VALUES(NULL, 300000)
INSERT budgets VALUES(0, 100000)
INSERT budgets VALUES(NULL, 150000)
INSERT budgets VALUES(300000, 250000)
GO
SET NOCOUNT OFF
SELECT AVG(NULLIF(COALESCE(current_year,
   previous_year), 0.00)) AS 'Average Budget'
FROM budgets
GO
```

Here is the result set:

```
Average Budget
-----------------------------------------
212500.000000

(1 row(s) affected)
```

Related Topics

CASE, decimal and numeric, System Functions

numeric

For more information about the **numeric** data type, see decimal and numeric.

Related Topics

Data Type Conversion, Data Types

OBJECT_ID

Returns the database object identification number.

Syntax

```
OBJECT_ID ( 'object' )
```

Arguments

'*object*'

    Is the object to be used. *object* is either **char** or **nchar**. If *object* is **char**, it is
implicitly converted to **nchar**.

Return Types

int

Remarks

When the parameter to a system function is optional, the current database, host
computer, server user, or database user is assumed. Built-in functions must always be
followed by parentheses.

When specifying a temporary table name, the database name must precede the
temporary table name, for example:

```
SELECT OBJECT_ID('tempdb..#mytemptable')
```

System functions can be used in the select list, in the WHERE clause, and anywhere
an expression is allowed. For more information, see Expressions and WHERE.

Examples

This example returns the object ID for the **authors** table in the **pubs** database.

```
USE master
SELECT OBJECT_ID('pubs..authors')
```

Here is the result set:

```
-----------
1977058079

(1 row(s) affected)
```

Related Topics

Metadata Functions

OBJECT_NAME

Returns the database object name.

Syntax

```
OBJECT_NAME ( object_id )
```

Arguments

object_id
    Is the ID of the object to be used. *object_id* is **int**.

Return Types

nchar

Remarks

When the parameter of a system function is optional, the current database, host computer, server user, or database user is assumed. Built-in functions must always be followed by parentheses.

System functions can be used in the select list, in the WHERE clause, and anywhere an expression is allowed. For more information, see Expressions and WHERE.

Examples

This example returns the OBJECT_NAME for the **authors** table in the **pubs** database.

```
USE pubs
SELECT TABLE_CATALOG, TABLE_NAME
FROM INFORMATION_SCHEMA.TABLES
WHERE TABLE_NAME = OBJECT_NAME(1977058079)
```

Here is the result set:

```
TABLE_CATALOG                    TABLE_NAME
------------------------------   --------------
pubs                             authors

(1 row(s) affected)
```

Related Topics

Metadata Functions

OBJECTPROPERTY

Returns information about objects in the current database.

Syntax

```
OBJECTPROPERTY ( id , property )
```

Arguments

id

Is an expression containing the ID of the object in the current database. *id* is **int**.

property

Is an expression containing the information to be returned for the object specified by *id*. *property* can be one of these values.

Note   Unless noted otherwise, the value NULL is returned when *property* is not a valid property name.

Property name	Object type	Description and values returned
CnstIsClustKey	Constraint	A primary key with a clustered index. 1 = True 0 = False
CnstIsColumn	Constraint	COLUMN constraint. 1 = True 0 = False

(continued)

(continued)

Property name	Object type	Description and values returned
CnstIsDeleteCascade	Constraint	A foreign key constraint with the ON DELETE CASCADE option.
CnstIsDisabled	Constraint	Disabled constraint. 1 = True 0 = False
CnstIsNonclustKey	Constraint	A primary key with a nonclustered index. 1 = True 0 = False
CnstIsNotTrusted	Constraint	Constraint was enabled without checking existing rows, so constraint may not hold for all rows. 1 = True 0 = False
CnstIsNotRepl	Constraint	The constraint is defined with the NOT FOR REPLICATION keywords.
CnstIsUpdateCascade	Constraint	A foreign key constraint with the ON UPDATE CASCADE option.
ExecIsAfterTrigger	Trigger	AFTER trigger.
ExecIsAnsiNullsOn	Procedure, Trigger, View	The setting of ANSI_NULLS at creation time. 1 = True 0 = False
ExecIsDeleteTrigger	Trigger	DELETE trigger. 1 = True 0 = False
ExecIsFirstDeleteTrigger	Trigger	The first trigger fired when a DELETE is executed against the table.
ExecIsFirstInsertTrigger	Trigger	The first trigger fired when an INSERT is executed against the table.

(continued)

(continued)

Property name	Object type	Description and values returned
ExecIsFirstUpdateTrigger	Trigger	The first trigger fired when an UPDATE is executed against the table.
ExecIsInsertTrigger	Trigger	INSERT trigger. 1 = True 0 = False
ExecIsInsteadOfTrigger	Trigger	INSTEAD OF trigger.
ExecIsLastDeleteTrigger	Trigger	The last trigger fired when a DELETE is executed against the table.
ExecIsLastInsertTrigger	Trigger	The last trigger fired when an INSERT is executed against the table.
ExecIsLastUpdateTrigger	Trigger	The last trigger fired when an UPDATE is executed against the table.
ExecIsQuotedIdentOn	Procedure, Trigger, View	The setting of QUOTED_IDENTIFIER at creation time. 1 = True 0 = False
ExecIsStartup	Procedure	Startup procedure. 1 = True 0 = False
ExecIsTriggerDisabled	Trigger	Disabled trigger. 1 = True 0 = False
ExecIsUpdateTrigger	Trigger	UPDATE trigger. 1 = True 0 = False

(continued)

(continued)

Property name	Object type	Description and values returned
HasAfterTrigger	Table, View	Table or view has an AFTER trigger. 1 = True 0 = False
HasInsertTrigger	Table, View	Table or view has an INSERT trigger. 1 = True 0 = False
HasInsteadOfTrigger	Table, View	Table or view has an INSTEAD OF trigger. 1 = True 0 = False
HasUpdateTrigger	Table, View	Table or view has an UPDATE trigger. 1 = True 0 = False
IsAnsiNullsOn	Function, Procedure, Table, Trigger, View	Specifies that the ANSI NULLS option setting for the table is ON, meaning all comparisons against a null value evaluate to UNKNOWN. This setting applies to all expressions in the table definition, including computed columns and constraints, for as long as the table exists. 1 = ON 0 = OFF
IsCheckCnst	Any	CHECK constraint. 1 = True 0 = False
IsConstraint	Any	Constraint. 1 = True 0 = False

(continued)

(continued)

Property name	Object type	Description and values returned
IsDefault	Any	Bound default.
		1 = True 0 = False
IsDefaultCnst	Any	DEFAULT constraint.
		1 = True 0 = False
IsDeterministic	Function, View	The determinism property of the function. Applies only to scalar- and table-valued functions.
		1 = Deterministic 0 = Not Deterministic NULL = Not a scalar- or table-valued function, or invalid object ID.
IsExecuted	Any	Specifies how this object can be executed (view, procedure, or trigger).
		1 = True 0 = False
IsExtendedProc	Any	Extended procedure.
		1 = True 0 = False
IsForeignKey	Any	FOREIGN KEY constraint.
		1 = True 0 = False
IsIndexed	Table, View	A table or view with an index.
IsIndexable	Table, View	A table or view on which an index may be created.

(continued)

(continued)

Property name	Object type	Description and values returned
IsInlineFunction	Function	Inline function. 1 = Inline function 0 = Not inline function NULL = Not a function, or invalid object ID.
IsMSShipped	Any	An object created during installation of Microsoft SQL Server 2000. 1 = True 0 = False
IsPrimaryKey	Any	PRIMARY KEY constraint. 1 = True 0 = False
IsProcedure	Any	Procedure. 1 = True 0 = False
IsQuotedIdentOn	Function, Procedure, Table, Trigger, View	Specifies that the quoted identifier setting for the table is ON, meaning double quotation marks delimit identifiers in all expressions involved in the table definition. 1 = ON 0 = OFF
IsReplProc	Any	Replication procedure. 1 = True 0 = False
IsRule	Any	Bound rule. 1 = True 0 = False

(continued)

(continued)

Property name	Object type	Description and values returned
IsScalarFunction	Function	Scalar-valued function. 1 = Scalar-valued 0 = Table-valued NULL = Not a function, or invalid object ID.
IsSchemaBound	Function, View	A schema bound function or view created with SCHEMABINDING. 1 = Schema-bound 0 = Not schema-bound NULL = Not a function or a view, or invalid object ID.
IsSystemTable	Table	System table. 1 = True 0 = False
IsTable	Table	Table. 1 = True 0 = False
IsTableFunction	Function	Table-valued function. 1 = Table-valued 0 = Scalar-valued NULL = Not a function, or invalid object ID.
IsTrigger	Any	Trigger. 1 = True 0 = False
IsUniqueCnst	Any	UNIQUE constraint. 1 = True 0 = False

(continued)

(continued)

Property name	Object type	Description and values returned
IsUserTable	Table	User-defined table. 1 = True 0 = False
IsView	View	View. 1 = True 0 = False
OwnerId	Any	Owner of the object. Nonnull = The database user ID of the object owner. NULL = Invalid input.
TableDeleteTrigger	Table	Table has a DELETE trigger. >1 = ID of first trigger with given type.
TableDeleteTriggerCount	Table	The table has the specified number of DELETE triggers. >1 = ID of first trigger with given type. NULL = Invalid input.
TableFullTextBackground UpdateIndexOn	Table	The table has full-text background update index enabled. 1 = TRUE 0 = FALSE
TableFulltextCatalogId	Table	The ID of the full-text catalog in which the full-text index data for the table resides. Nonzero = Full-text catalog ID, associated with the unique index that identifies the rows in a full-text indexed table. 0 = Table is not full-text indexed.

(continued)

(continued)

Property name	Object type	Description and values returned
TableFullTextChange TrackingOn	Table	The table has full-text change-tracking enabled. 1 = TRUE 0 = FALSE
TableFulltextKeyColumn	Table	The ID of the column associated with the single-column unique index that is participating in the full-text index definition. 0 = Table is not full-text indexed.
TableFullTextPopulate Status	Table	0 = No population 1 = Full population 2 = Incremental population
TableHasActiveFulltext Index	Tables	The table has an active full-text index. 1 = True 0 = False
TableHasCheckCnst	Table	The table has a CHECK constraint. 1 = True 0 = False
TableHasClustIndex	Table	The table has a clustered index. 1 = True 0 = False
TableHasDefaultCnst	Table	The table has a DEFAULT constraint. 1 = True 0 = False
TableHasDeleteTrigger	Table	The table has a DELETE trigger. 1 = True 0 = False

(continued)

(continued)

Property name	Object type	Description and values returned
TableHasForeignKey	Table	The table has a FOREIGN KEY constraint. 1 = True 0 = False
TableHasForeignRef	Table	Table is referenced by a FOREIGN KEY constraint. 1 = True 0 = False
TableHasIdentity	Table	The table has an identity column. 1 = True 0 = False
TableHasIndex	Table	The table has an index of any type. 1 = True 0 = False
TableHasInsertTrigger	Table	The object has an Insert trigger. 1 = True 0 = False NULL = Invalid input.
TableHasNonclustIndex	Table	The table has a nonclustered index. 1 = True 0 = False
TableHasPrimaryKey	Table	The table has a primary key. 1 = True 0 = False

(continued)

(continued)

Property name	Object type	Description and values returned
TableHasRowGuidCol	Table	The table has a ROWGUIDCOL for a **uniqueidentifier** column. 1 = True 0 = False
TableHasTextImage	Table	The table has a **text** column. 1 = True 0 = False
TableHasTimestamp	Table	The table has a **timestamp** column. 1 = True 0 = False
TableHasUniqueCnst	Table	The table has a UNIQUE constraint. 1 = True 0 = False
TableHasUpdateTrigger	Table	The object has an Update trigger. 1 = True 0 = False
TableInsertTrigger	Table	The table has an INSERT trigger. >1 = ID of first trigger with given type.
TableInsertTriggerCount	Table	The table has the specified number of INSERT triggers. >1 = ID of first trigger with given type.
TableIsFake	Table	The table is not real. It is materialized internally on demand by SQL Server. 1 = True 0 = False

(continued)

(continued)

Property name	Object type	Description and values returned
TableIsPinned	Table	The table is pinned to be held in the data cache. 1 = True 0 = False
TableTextInRowLimit	Table	The maximum bytes allowed for **text in row**, or 0 if **text in row** option is not set.
TableUpdateTrigger	Table	The table has an UPDATE trigger. >1 = ID of first trigger with given type.
TableUpdateTriggerCount	Table	The table has the specified number of UPDATE triggers. >1 = ID of first trigger with given type.

Return Types
int

Remarks
OBJECTPROPERTY(*view_id*, 'IsIndexable') may consume significant computer resources because evaluation of **IsIndexable** property requires the parsing of view definition, normalization, and partial optimization.

OBJECTPROPERTY(*table_id*, 'TableHasActiveFulltextIndex') will return '1' (True) when at least one column of a table is added for indexing. Full-text indexing becomes active for population as soon as the first column is added for indexing.

When the last column in an index is dropped, the index becomes inactive.

The actual creation of index still might fail if certain index key requirements are not met. See CREATE INDEX for details.

Examples

A. To find out if authors is a table

This example tests whether **authors** is a table.

```
IF OBJECTPROPERTY ( object_id('authors'),'ISTABLE') = 1
   print 'Authors is a table'

ELSE IF OBJECTPROPERTY ( object_id('authors'),'ISTABLE') = 0
   print 'Authors is not a table'

ELSE IF OBJECTPROPERTY ( object_id('authors'),'ISTABLE') IS NULL
   print 'ERROR: Authors is not an object'
```

B. To determine if text in row is enabled on a table

This example tests whether the **text in row** option is enabled in the **authors** table so that **text**, **ntext**, or **image** data can be stored in its data row.

```
USE pubs
SELECT OBJECTPROPERTY(OBJECT_ID('authors'),'TableTextInRowLimit')
```

The result set shows that **text in row** is not enabled on the table.

```
-----
0
```

C. To determine if a scalar-valued user-defined function is deterministic

This example tests whether the user-defined scalar-valued function fn_CubicVolume, which returns a decimal, is deterministic.

```
CREATE FUNCTION fn_CubicVolume
-- Input dimensions in centimeters.
   (@CubeLength decimal(4,1), @CubeWidth decimal(4,1),
   @CubeHeight decimal(4,1) )
RETURNS decimal(12,3) -- Cubic Centimeters.
WITH SCHEMABINDING
AS
BEGIN
   RETURN ( @CubeLength * @CubeWidth * @CubeHeight )
END

--Is it a deterministic function?
SELECT OBJECTPROPERTY(OBJECT_ID('fn_CubicVolume'), 'IsDeterministic')
```

The result set shows that fn_CubicVolume is a deterministic function.

```
-----
1
```

Related Topics
COLUMNPROPERTY, CREATE INDEX, Metadata Functions, TYPEPROPERTY

OPEN

Opens a Transact-SQL server cursor and populates the cursor by executing the
Transact-SQL statement specified on the DECLARE CURSOR or SET
cursor_variable statement.

Syntax

```
OPEN { { [ GLOBAL ] cursor_name } | cursor_variable_name }
```

Arguments

GLOBAL
> Specifies that *cursor_name* refers to a global cursor.

cursor_name
> Is the name of a declared cursor. If both a global and a local cursor exist with
> *cursor_name* as their name, *cursor_name* refers to the global cursor if GLOBAL is
> specified; otherwise, *cursor_name* refers to the local cursor.

cursor_variable_name
> Is the name of a cursor variable that references a cursor.

Remarks

If the cursor is declared with the INSENSITIVE or STATIC option, OPEN creates a
temporary table to hold the result set. OPEN fails if the size of any row in the result set
exceeds the maximum row size for Microsoft SQL Server tables. If the cursor is
declared with the KEYSET option, OPEN creates a temporary table to hold the keyset.
The temporary tables are stored in **tempdb**.

After a cursor has been opened, use the @@CURSOR_ROWS function to receive the
number of qualifying rows in the last opened cursor. Depending on the number of rows
expected in the result set, SQL Server may choose to populate a keyset-driven cursor
asynchronously on a separate thread. This allows fetches to proceed immediately, even
if the keyset is not fully populated. For more information, see Asynchronous
Population.

To set the threshold at which SQL Server generates keysets asynchronously, set the
cursor threshold configuration option. For more information, see sp_configure.

Examples

This example opens a cursor and fetches all the rows.

```
DECLARE Employee_Cursor CURSOR FOR
SELECT LastName, FirstName
FROM Northwind.dbo.Employees
WHERE LastName like 'B%'

OPEN Employee_Cursor

FETCH NEXT FROM Employee_Cursor
WHILE @@FETCH_STATUS = 0
BEGIN
    FETCH NEXT FROM Employee_Cursor
END

CLOSE Employee_Cursor
DEALLOCATE Employee_Cursor
```

Related Topics

CLOSE, @@CURSOR_ROWS, DEALLOCATE, DECLARE CURSOR, FETCH

OPENDATASOURCE

Provides ad hoc connection information as part of a four-part object name without using a linked server name.

Syntax

```
OPENDATASOURCE ( provider_name, init_string )
```

Arguments

provider_name

Is the name registered as the PROGID of the OLE DB provider used to access the data source. *provider_name* is a **char** data type, with no default value.

init_string

Is the connection string passed to the **IDataInitialize** interface of the destination provider. The provider string syntax is based on keyword-value pairs separated by semicolons, that is, "keyword1=value; keyword2=value."

The basic syntax is defined in the Microsoft Data Access SDK. Refer to the documentation on the provider for specific keyword-value pairs supported. This table lists the most commonly used keywords in the *init_string* argument.

Keyword	OLE DB property	Valid values and Description
Data Source	DBPROP_INIT_DATASOURCE	Name of the data source to connect to. Different providers interpret this in different ways. For SQL Server OLE DB provider, this indicates the name of the server. For Jet OLE DB provider, this indicates the full path of the .mdb file or .xls file.
Location	DBPROP_INIT_LOCATION	Location of the database to connect to.
Extended Properties	DBPROP_INIT_PROVIDERSTRING	The provider-specific connect-string.
Connect timeout	DBPROP_INIT_TIMEOUT	Time-out value after which the connection attempt fails.
User ID	DBPROP_AUTH_USERID	User ID to be used for the connection.
Password	DBPROP_AUTH_PASSWORD	Password to be used for the connection.
Catalog	DBPROP_INIT_CATALOG	The name of the initial or default catalog when connecting to the data source.

Remarks

The OPENDATASOURCE function can be used in the same Transact-SQL syntax locations as a linked server name. Thus, OPENDATASOURCE can be used as the first part of a four-part name that refers to a table or view name in a SELECT, INSERT, UPDATE, or DELETE statement, or to a remote stored procedure in an EXECUTE statement. When executing remote stored procedures, OPENDATASOURCE should refer to another SQL Server. OPENDATASOURCE does not accept variables for its arguments.

Like the OPENROWSET function, OPENDATASOURCE should only reference OLE DB data sources accessed infrequently. Define a linked server for any data sources accessed more than a few times. Neither OPENDATASOURCE, nor OPENROWSET provide all the functionality of linked server definitions, such as security management and the ability to query catalog information. All connection information, including passwords, must be provided each time OPENDATASOURCE is called.

Examples

This example accesses data from a table on another instance of SQL Server.

```
SELECT *
FROM    OPENDATASOURCE(
        'SQLOLEDB',
        'Data Source=ServerName;User ID=MyUID;Password=MyPass'
        ).Northwind.dbo.Categories
```

This is an example of a query against an Excel spreadsheet through the OLE DB provider for Jet.

```
SELECT *
FROM OpenDataSource( 'Microsoft.Jet.OLEDB.4.0',
  'Data Source="c:\Finance\account.xls";User ID=Admin;Password=;Extended properties=Excel
5.0')...xactions
```

Related Topics

Distributed Queries, OPENROWSET, sp_addlinkedserver

OPENQUERY

Executes the specified pass-through query on the given linked server, which is an OLE DB data source. The OPENQUERY function can be referenced in the FROM clause of a query as though it is a table name. The OPENQUERY function can also be referenced as the target table of an INSERT, UPDATE, or DELETE statement, subject to the capabilities of the OLE DB provider. Although the query may return multiple result sets, OPENQUERY returns only the first one.

Syntax

```
OPENQUERY ( linked_server , 'query' )
```

Arguments

linked_server
    Is an identifier representing the name of the linked server.

'*query*'
    Is the query string executed in the linked server.

Remarks

OPENQUERY does not accept variables for its arguments.

Examples

This example creates a linked server named **OracleSvr** against an Oracle database using the Microsoft OLE DB Provider for Oracle. Then this example uses a pass-through query against this linked server.

Note This example assumes that an Oracle database alias called ORCLDB has been created.

```
EXEC sp_addlinkedserver 'OracleSvr',
   'Oracle 7.3',
   'MSDAORA',
   'ORCLDB'
GO
SELECT *
FROM OPENQUERY(OracleSvr, 'SELECT name, id FROM joe.titles')
GO
```

Related Topics

DELETE, Distributed Queries, FROM, INSERT, OPENDATASOURCE, OPENROWSET, Rowset Functions, SELECT, sp_addlinkedserver, sp_serveroption, UPDATE, WHERE

OPENROWSET

Includes all connection information necessary to access remote data from an OLE DB data source. This method is an alternative to accessing tables in a linked server and is a one-time, ad hoc method of connecting and accessing remote data using OLE DB. The OPENROWSET function can be referenced in the FROM clause of a query as though it is a table name. The OPENROWSET function can also be referenced as the target table of an INSERT, UPDATE, or DELETE statement, subject to the capabilities of the OLE DB provider. Although the query may return multiple result sets, OPENROWSET returns only the first one.

Syntax

```
OPENROWSET ( 'provider_name'
  , { 'datasource' ; 'user_id' ; 'password'
    | 'provider_string' }
  , { [ catalog. ] [ schema. ] object
    | 'query' }
  )
```

Arguments

'*provider_name*'

Is a character string that represents the friendly name of the OLE DB provider as specified in the registry. *provider_name* has no default value.

'*datasource*'

Is a string constant that corresponds to a particular OLE DB data source. *datasource* is the DBPROP_INIT_DATASOURCE property to be passed to the provider's **IDBProperties** interface to initialize the provider. Typically, this string includes the name of the database file, the name of a database server, or a name that the provider understands to locate the database(s).

'*user_id*'

Is a string constant that is the username that is passed to the specified OLE DB provider. *user_id* specifies the security context for the connection and is passed in as the DBPROP_AUTH_USERID property to initialize the provider.

'*password*'

Is a string constant that is the user password to be passed to the OLE DB provider. *password* is passed in as the DBPROP_AUTH_PASSWORD property when initializing the provider.

'*provider_string*'

Is a provider-specific connection string that is passed in as the DBPROP_INIT_PROVIDERSTRING property to initialize the OLE DB provider. *provider_string* typically encapsulates all the connection information needed to initialize the provider.

catalog

Is the name of the catalog or database in which the specified object resides.

schema

Is the name of the schema or object owner for the specified object.

object

Is the object name that uniquely identifies the object to manipulate.

'*query*'

Is a string constant sent to and executed by the provider. Microsoft SQL Server does not process this query, but processes query results returned by the provider (a pass-through query). Pass-through queries are useful when used on providers that do not expose their tabular data through table names, but only through a command language. Pass-through queries are supported on the remote server, as long as the query provider supports the OLE DB **Command** object and its mandatory interfaces. For more information, see *SQL Server OLE DB Programmer's Reference*.

Remarks

Catalog and schema names are required if the OLE DB provider supports multiple catalogs and schemas in the specified data source. Values for *catalog* and *schema* can be omitted if the OLE DB provider does not support them.

If the provider supports only schema names, a two-part name of the form *schema.object* must be specified. If the provider supports only catalog names, a three-part name of the form *catalog.schema.object* must be specified.

OPENROWSET does not accept variables for its arguments.

Permissions

OPENROWSET permissions are determined by the permissions of the username being passed to the OLE DB provider.

Examples

A. Use OPENROWSET with a SELECT and the Microsoft OLE DB Provider for SQL Server

This example uses the Microsoft OLE DB Provider for SQL Server to access the **authors** table in the **pubs** database on a remote server named **seattle1**. The provider is initialized from the *datasource*, *user_id*, and *password*, and a SELECT is used to define the row set returned.

```
USE pubs
GO
SELECT a.*
FROM OPENROWSET('SQLOLEDB','seattle1';'sa';'MyPass',
    'SELECT * FROM pubs.dbo.authors ORDER BY au_lname, au_fname') AS a
GO
```

B. Use OPENROWSET with an object and the OLE DB Provider for ODBC

This example uses the OLE DB Provider for ODBC and the SQL Server ODBC driver to access the **authors** table in the **pubs** database on a remote server named **seattle1**. The provider is initialized with a *provider_string* specified in the ODBC syntax used by the ODBC provider, and the *catalog.schema.object* syntax is used to define the row set returned.

```
USE pubs
GO
SELECT a.*
FROM OPENROWSET('MSDASQL',
    'DRIVER={SQL Server};SERVER=seattle1;UID=sa;PWD=MyPass',
    pubs.dbo.authors) AS a
ORDER BY a.au_lname, a.au_fname
GO
```

C. Use the Microsoft OLE DB Provider for Jet

This example accesses the **orders** table in the Microsoft Access **Northwind** database through the Microsoft OLE DB Provider for Jet.

Note This example assumes that Access is installed.

```
USE pubs
GO
SELECT a.*
FROM OPENROWSET('Microsoft.Jet.OLEDB.4.0',
   'c:\MSOffice\Access\Samples\northwind.mdb';'admin';'mypwd', Orders)
   AS a
GO
```

D. Use OPENROWSET and another table in an INNER JOIN

This example selects all data from the **customers** table from the local SQL Server **Northwind** database and from the **orders** table from the Access **Northwind** database stored on the same computer.

Note This example assumes that Access is installed.

```
USE pubs
GO
SELECT c.*, o.*
FROM Northwind.dbo.Customers AS c INNER JOIN
   OPENROWSET('Microsoft.Jet.OLEDB.4.0',
   'c:\MSOffice\Access\Samples\northwind.mdb';'admin';'mypwd', Orders)
   AS o
   ON c.CustomerID = o.CustomerID
GO
```

Related Topics

DELETE, Distributed Queries, FROM, INSERT, OPENDATASOURCE, OPENQUERY, Rowset Functions, SELECT, sp_addlinkedserver, sp_serveroption, UPDATE, WHERE

OPENXML

OPENXML provides a rowset view over an XML document. Because OPENXML is a rowset provider, OPENXML can be used in Transact-SQL statements in which rowset providers such as a table, view, or the OPENROWSET function can appear.

Syntax

```
OPENXML(idoc int [in],rowpattern nvarchar[in],[flags byte[in]])
[WITH (SchemaDeclaration | TableName)]
```

Arguments

idoc

    Is the document handle of the internal representation of an XML document. The internal representation of an XML document is created by calling **sp_xml_preparedocument**.

rowpattern

    Is the XPath pattern used to identify the nodes (in the XML document whose handle is passed in the *idoc* parameter) to be processed as rows.

flags

    Indicates the mapping that should be used between the XML data and the relational rowset, and how the spill-over column should be filled. *flags* is an optional input parameter, and can be one of these values.

Byte Value	Description
0	Defaults to attribute-centric mapping.
1	Use the attribute-centric mapping. Can be combined with XML_ELEMENTS; in which case, attribute-centric mapping is applied first, and then element-centric mapping is applied for all columns not yet dealt with.
2	Use the element-centric mapping. Can be combined with XML_ATTRIBUTES; in which case, attribute-centric mapping is applied first, and then element-centric mapping is applied for all columns not yet dealt with.
8	Can be combined (logical OR) with XML_ATTRIBUTES or XML_ELEMENTS. In context of retrieval, this flag indicates that the consumed data should not be copied to the overflow property **@mp:xmltext**.

SchemaDeclaration

    Is the schema definition of the form:

    ColName ColType [ColPattern | MetaProperty][, ColName ColType [ColPattern | MetaProperty]...]

ColName

    Is the column name in the rowset.

ColType

    Is the SQL data type of the column in the rowset. If the column types differ from the underlying XML data type of the attribute, type coercion occurs. If the column is of type **timestamp**, the present value in the XML document is disregarded when selecting from an OPENXML rowset, and the autofill values are returned.

ColPattern
> Is an optional, general XPath pattern that describes how the XML nodes should be mapped to the columns. If the *ColPattern* is not specified, the default mapping (attribute-centric or element-centric mapping as specified by *flags*) takes place.
>
> The XPath pattern specified as *ColPattern* is used to specify the special nature of the mapping (in case of attribute-centric and element-centric mapping) that overwrites or enhances the default mapping indicated by *flags*.
>
> The general XPath pattern specified as *ColPattern* also supports the metaproperties.

MetaProperty
> Is one of the metaproperties provided by OPENXML. If the metaproperty is specified, the column contains information provided by the metaproperty. The metaproperties allow you to extract information (such as relative position, namespace information) about XML nodes, which provides more information than is visible in the textual representation.

TableName
> Is the table name that can be given (instead of *SchemaDeclaration*) if a table with the desired schema already exists and no column patterns are required.

The WITH clause provides a rowset format (and additional mapping information as necessary) using either *SchemaDeclaration* or specifying an existing *TableName*. If the optional WITH clause is not specified, the results are returned in an **edge table** format. Edge tables represent the fine-grained XML document structure (e.g. element/attribute names, the document hierarchy, the namespaces, PIs etc.) in a single table.

This table describes the structure of the edge table.

Column name	Data type	Description
id	**bigint**	Is the unique ID of the document node.
		The root element has an ID value 0. The negative ID values are reserved.
parentid	**bigint**	Identifies the parent of the node. The parent identified by this ID is not necessarily the parent element, but it depends on the NodeType of the node whose parent is identified by this ID. For example, if the node is a text node, the parent of it may be an attribute node.
		If the node is at the top level in the XML document, its **ParentID** is NULL.

(continued)

(continued)

Column name	Data type	Description
nodetype	**int**	Identifies the node type. Is an integer that corresponds to the XML DOM node type numbering (see DOM for node information). The node types are: **1** = Element node **2** = Attribute node **3** = Text node
localname	**nvarchar**	Gives the local name of the element or attribute. Is NULL if the DOM object does not have a name.
prefix	**nvarchar**	Is the namespace prefix of the node name.
namespaceuri	**nvarchar**	Is the namespace URI of the node. If the value is NULL, no namespace is present.
datatype	**nvarchar**	Is the actual data type of the element or attribute row and is NULL otherwise. The data type is inferred from the inline DTD or from the inline schema.
prev	**bigint**	Is the XML ID of the previous sibling element. Is NULL if there is no direct previous sibling.
text	**ntext**	Contains the attribute value or the element content in text form (or is NULL if the edge table entry does not need a value).

Examples

A. Use a simple SELECT statement with OPENXML

This example creates an internal representation of the XML image using **sp_xml_preparedocument**. A SELECT statement using an OPENXML rowset provider is then executed against the internal representation of the XML document.

The *flag* value is set to **1** indicating attribute-centric mapping. Therefore, the XML attributes map to the columns in the rowset. The *rowpattern* specified as **/ROOT/Customers** identifies the <Customers> nodes to be processed.

The optional *ColPattern* (column pattern) is not specified because the column name matches the XML attribute names.

The OPENXML rowset provider creates a two-column rowset (**CustomerID** and **ContactName**) from which the SELECT statement retrieves the necessary columns (in this case, all the columns).

```
DECLARE @idoc int
DECLARE @doc varchar(1000)
SET @doc ='
<ROOT>
<Customer CustomerID="VINET" ContactName="Paul Henriot">
   <Order CustomerID="VINET" EmployeeID="5" OrderDate="1996-07-04T00:00:00">
      <OrderDetail OrderID="10248" ProductID="11" Quantity="12"/>
      <OrderDetail OrderID="10248" ProductID="42" Quantity="10"/>
   </Order>
</Customer>
<Customer CustomerID="LILAS" ContactName="Carlos Gonzlez">
   <Order CustomerID="LILAS" EmployeeID="3" OrderDate="1996-08-16T00:00:00">
      <OrderDetail OrderID="10283" ProductID="72" Quantity="3"/>
   </Order>
</Customer>
</ROOT>'
--Create an internal representation of the XML document.
EXEC sp_xml_preparedocument @idoc OUTPUT, @doc
-- Execute a SELECT statement that uses the OPENXML rowset provider.
SELECT   *
FROM     OPENXML (@idoc, '/ROOT/Customer',1)
             WITH (CustomerID  varchar(10),
                   ContactName varchar(20))
```

Here is the result set:

```
CustomerID ContactName
---------- --------------------
VINET      Paul Henriot
LILAS      Carlos Gonzlez
```

If the same SELECT statement is executed with *flags* set to **2**, indicating element-centric mapping, the values of **CustomerID** and **ContactName** for both of the customers in the XML document are returned as NULL, because the <Customers> elements do not have any subelements.

Here is the result set:

```
CustomerID ContactName
---------- -----------
NULL       NULL
NULL       NULL
```

B. Specify ColPattern for mapping between columns and the XML attributes

This query returns customer ID, order date, product ID and quantity attributes from the XML document. The *rowpattern* identifies the <OrderDetails> elements. **ProductID** and **Quantity** are the attributes of the <OrderDetails> element. However, the **OrderID**, **CustomerID** and **OrderDate** are the attributes of the parent element (<Orders>).

The optional *ColPattern* is specified, indicating that:

- The **OrderID**, **CustomerID** and **OrderDate** in the rowset map to the attributes of the parent of the nodes identified by *rowpattern* in the XML document.

- The **ProdID** column in the rowset maps to the **ProductID** attribute, and the **Qty** column in the rowset maps to the **Quantity** attribute of the nodes identified in *rowpattern*.

Although the element-centric mapping is specified by the *flags* parameter, the mapping specified in *ColPattern* overwrites this mapping.

```
declare @idoc int
declare @doc varchar(1000)
set @doc ='
<ROOT>
<Customer CustomerID="VINET" ContactName="Paul Henriot">
   <Order OrderID="10248" CustomerID="VINET" EmployeeID="5"
          OrderDate="1996-07-04T00:00:00">
      <OrderDetail ProductID="11" Quantity="12"/>
      <OrderDetail ProductID="42" Quantity="10"/>
   </Order>
</Customer>
<Customer CustomerID="LILAS" ContactName="Carlos Gonzlez">
   <Order OrderID="10283" CustomerID="LILAS" EmployeeID="3"
          OrderDate="1996-08-16T00:00:00">
      <OrderDetail ProductID="72" Quantity="3"/>
   </Order>
</Customer>
</ROOT>'
--Create an internal representation of the XML document.
exec sp_xml_preparedocument @idoc OUTPUT, @doc
-- SELECT stmt using OPENXML rowset provider
SELECT *
FROM   OPENXML (@idoc, '/ROOT/Customer/Order/OrderDetail',2)
         WITH (OrderID      int          '../@OrderID',
               CustomerID   varchar(10)  '../@CustomerID',
               OrderDate    datetime     '../@OrderDate',
               ProdID       int          '@ProductID',
               Qty          int          '@Quantity')
```

This is the result:

```
OrderID CustomerID            OrderDate             ProdID   Qty

-------------------------------------------------------------------
10248    VINET    1996-07-04 00:00:00.000            11       12
10248    VINET    1996-07-04 00:00:00.000            42       10
10283    LILAS    1996-08-16 00:00:00.000            72       3
```

C. Obtain result in an edge table format

In this example, the WITH clause is not specified in the OPENXML statement. As a result, the rowset generated by OPENXML has an edge table format. The SELECT statement returns all the columns in the edge table.

The sample XML document in the example consists of <Customers>, <Orders>, and <Order_0020_Details> elements.

First sp_xml_preparedocument is called to obtain a document handle. This document handle is passed to OPENXML.

In the OPENXML statement

- The *rowpattern* (/ROOT/Customers) identifies the <Customers> nodes to process.

- The WITH clause is not provided. Therefore OPENXML returns the rowset in an edge table format.

Finally the SELECT statement retrieves all the columns in the edge table.

```
declare @idoc int
declare @doc varchar(1000)
set @doc ='
<ROOT>
<Customers CustomerID="VINET" ContactName="Paul Henriot">
   <Orders CustomerID="VINET" EmployeeID="5" OrderDate=
           "1996-07-04T00:00:00">
      <Order_x0020_Details OrderID="10248" ProductID="11" Quantity="12"/>
      <Order_x0020_Details OrderID="10248" ProductID="42" Quantity="10"/>
   </Orders>
</Customers>
<Customers CustomerID="LILAS" ContactName="Carlos Gonzlez">
   <Orders CustomerID="LILAS" EmployeeID="3" OrderDate=
           "1996-08-16T00:00:00">
      <Order_x0020_Details OrderID="10283" ProductID="72" Quantity="3"/>
   </Orders>
</Customers>
</ROOT>'
```

(continued)

(continued)

```
--Create an internal representation of the XML document.
exec sp_xml_preparedocument @idoc OUTPUT, @doc
-- SELECT statement using OPENXML rowset provider
SELECT    *
FROM      OPENXML (@idoc, '/ROOT/Customers')
EXEC sp_xml_removedocument @idoc
```

The result is returned as an edge table.

Related Topics

Using OPENXML

OR

Combines two conditions. When more than one logical operator is used in a statement, OR operators are evaluated after AND operators. However, you can change the order of evaluation by using parentheses.

Syntax

```
boolean_expression OR boolean_expression
```

Arguments

boolean_expression
    Is any valid Microsoft SQL Server expression that returns TRUE, FALSE, or UNKNOWN.

Result Types

Boolean

Result Value

OR returns TRUE when either of the conditions is TRUE.

Remarks

This table shows the result of the OR operator.

	TRUE	FALSE	UNKNOWN
TRUE	TRUE	TRUE	TRUE
FALSE	TRUE	FALSE	UNKNOWN
UNKNOWN	TRUE	UNKNOWN	UNKNOWN

Examples

This example retrieves the book titles that carry an advance greater than $5,500 and are either business or psychology books. If the parentheses are not included, the WHERE clause retrieves all business books or psychology books that have an advance greater than $5,500.

```
USE pubs
GO
SELECT SUBSTRING(title, 1, 30) AS Title, type
FROM titles
WHERE (type = 'business' OR type = 'psychology') AND
    advance > $5500
ORDER BY title
GO
```

Here is the result set:

```
Title                           type
------------------------------- ------------
Computer Phobic AND Non-Phobic  psychology
Life Without Fear               psychology
You Can Combat Computer Stress  business

(3 row(s) affected)
```

Related Topics

Expressions, Functions, Operators (Logical Operators), SELECT, WHERE

ORDER BY

Specifies the sort order used on columns returned in a SELECT statement. For more information, see SELECT.

PARSENAME

Returns the specified part of an object name. Parts of an object that can be retrieved are the object name, owner name, database name, and server name.

> **Note** The PARSENAME function does not indicate whether or not an object by the specified name exists. It just returns the specified piece of the given object name.

Syntax

```
PARSENAME ( 'object_name' , object_piece )
```

Arguments

'object_name'

> Is the name of the object for which to retrieve the specified object part. *object_name* is **sysname**. This parameter is an optionally qualified object name. If all parts of the object name are qualified, this name can consist of four parts: the server name, the database name, the owner name, and the object name.

object_piece

> Is the object part to return. *object_piece* is **int**, and can have these values.

Value	Description
1	Object name
2	Owner name
3	Database name
4	Server name

Return Types

nchar

Remarks

PARSENAME returns NULL if any of the following conditions are met:

- Either *object_name* or *object_piece* is NULL.

- A syntax error occurs.

- The requested object part has a length of 0 and is an invalid Microsoft SQL Server identifier. A zero-length object name renders the entire qualified name invalid.

Examples

This example uses PARSENAME to return information about the **authors** table in the **pubs** database.

```
USE pubs
SELECT PARSENAME('pubs..authors', 1) AS 'Object Name'
SELECT PARSENAME('pubs..authors', 2) AS 'Owner Name'
SELECT PARSENAME('pubs..authors', 3) AS 'Database Name'
SELECT PARSENAME('pubs..authors', 4) AS 'Server Name'
```

Here is the result set:

```
Object Name
------------------------------
authors

(1 row(s) affected)

Owner Name
------------------------------
(null)

(1 row(s) affected)

Database Name
------------------------------
pubs

(1 row(s) affected)

Server Name
------------------------------
(null)

(1 row(s) affected)
```

Related Topics

ALTER TABLE, CREATE TABLE, System Functions

PATINDEX

Returns the starting position of the first occurrence of a pattern in a specified
expression, or zeros if the pattern is not found, on all valid text and character data types.

Syntax

```
PATINDEX ( '%pattern%' , expression )
```

Arguments

pattern

Is a literal string. Wildcard characters can be used; however, the % character must
precede and follow *pattern* (except when searching for first or last characters).
pattern is an expression of the short character data type category.

expression

Is an expression, usually a column that is searched for the specified pattern.
expression is of the character string data type category.

Return Types

int

Remarks

PATINDEX is useful with **text** data types; it can be used in a WHERE clause in addition to IS NULL, IS NOT NULL, and LIKE (the only other comparisons that are valid on **text** in a WHERE clause).

If either *pattern* or *expression* is NULL, PATINDEX returns NULL when the database compatibility level is 70. If the database compatibility level is 65 or earlier, PATINDEX returns NULL only when both *pattern* and *expression* are NULL.

Examples

A. Use a pattern with PATINDEX

This example finds the position at which the pattern "wonderful" begins in a specific row of the **notes** column in the **titles** table.

```
USE pubs
GO
SELECT PATINDEX('%wonderful%', notes)
FROM titles
WHERE title_id = 'TC3218'
GO
```

Here is the result set:

```
-----------
46

(1 row(s) affected)
```

If you do not restrict the rows to be searched by using a WHERE clause, the query returns all rows in the table and reports nonzero values for those rows in which the pattern was found and zero for all rows in which the pattern was not found.

B. Use wildcard characters with PATINDEX

This example uses wildcards to find the position at which the pattern "won_erful" begins in a specific row of the **notes** column in the **titles** table, where the underscore is a wildcard representing any character.

```
USE pubs
GO
SELECT PATINDEX('%won_erful%', notes)
FROM titles
WHERE title_id = 'TC3218'
GO
```

Here is the result set:

```
------------
46

(1 row(s) affected)
```

If you do not restrict the rows to be searched, the query returns all rows in the table and reports nonzero values for those rows in which the pattern was found.

Related Topics

Data Types, String Functions

PERMISSIONS

Returns a value containing a bitmap that indicates the statement, object, or column permissions for the current user.

Syntax

```
PERMISSIONS ( [ objectid [ , 'column' ] ] )
```

Arguments

objectid

Is the ID of an object. If *objectid* is not specified, the bitmap value contains statement permissions for the current user; otherwise, the bitmap contains object permissions on the object ID for the current user. The object specified must be in the current database. Use the OBJECT_ID function with an object name to determine the *objectid* value.

'column'

Is the optional name of a column for which permission information is being returned. The column must be a valid column name in the table specified by *objectid*.

Return Types

int

Remarks

PERMISSIONS can be used to determine whether the current user has the necessary permissions to execute a statement or to GRANT a permission on an object to another user.

The permissions information returned is a 32-bit bitmap.

The lower 16 bits reflect permissions granted to the security account for the current user, as well as permissions applied to Microsoft Windows NT groups or Microsoft SQL Server roles of which the current user is a member. For example, a returned value of 66 (hex value 0x42), when no *objectid* is specified, indicates the current user has permissions to execute the CREATE TABLE (decimal value 2) and BACKUP DATABASE (decimal value 64) statement permissions.

The upper 16 bits reflect the permissions that the current user can GRANT to other users. The upper 16 bits are interpreted exactly as those for the lower 16 bits described in the following tables, except they are shifted to the left by 16 bits (multiplied by 65536). For example, 0x8 (decimal value 8) is the bit indicating INSERT permissions when an *objectid* is specified. Whereas 0x80000 (decimal value 524288) indicates the ability to GRANT INSERT permissions because 524288 = 8 x 65536. Due to membership in roles, it is possible to not have a permission to execute a statement, but still be able to grant that permission to someone else.

The table shows the bits used for statement permissions (*objectid* is not specified).

Bit (dec)	Bit (hex)	Statement permission
1	0x1	CREATE DATABASE (**master** database only)
2	0x2	CREATE TABLE
4	0x4	CREATE PROCEDURE
8	0x8	CREATE VIEW
16	0x10	CREATE RULE
32	0x20	CREATE DEFAULT
64	0x40	BACKUP DATABASE
128	0x80	BACKUP LOG
256	0x100	Reserved

The table shows the bits used for object permissions that are returned when only *objectid* is specified.

Bit (dec)	Bit (hex)	Statement permission
1	0x1	SELECT ALL
2	0x2	UPDATE ALL
4	0x4	REFERENCES ALL
8	0x8	INSERT
16	0x10	DELETE
32	0x20	EXECUTE (procedures only)
4096	0x1000	SELECT ANY (at least one column)
8192	0x2000	UPDATE ANY
16384	0x4000	REFERENCES ANY

The table shows the bits used for column-level object permissions that are returned when both *objectid* and *column* are specified.

Bit (dec)	Bit (hex)	Statement permission
1	0x1	SELECT
2	0x2	UPDATE
4	0x4	REFERENCES

A NULL is returned if a specified parameter is NULL or invalid (for example, an *objectid* or *column* that does not exist). The bit values for permissions that do not apply (for example EXECUTE permissions, bit 0x20, for a table) are undefined.

Use the bitwise AND (&) operator to determine each bit set in the bitmap returned by the PERMISSIONS function.

The **sp_helprotect** system stored procedure can also be used to return a list of object permissions for a user in the current database.

Examples

A. Use PERMISSIONS function with statement permissions

This example determines whether the current user can execute the CREATE TABLE statement.

```
IF PERMISSIONS()&2=2
   CREATE TABLE test_table (col1 INT)
ELSE
   PRINT 'ERROR: The current user cannot create a table.'
```

B. Use PERMISSIONS function with object permissions

This example determines whether the current user can insert a row of data into the **authors** table.

```
IF PERMISSIONS(OBJECT_ID('authors'))&8=8
   PRINT 'The current user can insert data into authors.'
ELSE
   PRINT 'ERROR: The current user cannot insert data into authors.'
```

C. Use PERMISSIONS function with grantable permissions

This example determines whether the current user can grant the INSERT permission on the **authors** table to another user.

```
IF PERMISSIONS(OBJECT_ID('authors'))&0x80000=0x80000
   PRINT 'INSERT on authors is grantable.'
ELSE
   PRINT 'You may not GRANT INSERT permissions on authors.'
```

Related Topics

DENY, GRANT, OBJECT_ID, REVOKE, sp_helprotect, System Functions

---

PI

Returns the constant value of PI.

Syntax

```
PI ( )
```

Return Types

float

Examples

This example returns the value of PI.

```
SELECT PI()
GO
```

Here is the result set:

```
------------------------
3.14159265358979

(1 row(s) affected)
```

Related Topics

Mathematical Functions

POWER

Returns the value of the given expression to the specified power.

Syntax

```
POWER ( numeric_expression , y )
```

Arguments

numeric_expression

Is an expression of the exact numeric or approximate numeric data type category, except for the **bit** data type.

y

Is the power to which to raise *numeric_expression*. *y* can be an expression of the exact numeric or approximate numeric data type category, except for the **bit** data type.

Return Types

Same as *numeric_expression*.

Examples

A. Use POWER to show results of 0.0

This example shows a floating point underflow that returns a result of 0.0.

```
SELECT POWER(2.0, -100.0)
GO
```

Here is the result set:

```
--------------------------------------------
0.0

(1 row(s) affected)
```

B. Use POWER

This example returns POWER results for 2^1 to 2^4.

```
DECLARE @value int, @counter int
SET @value = 2
SET @counter = 1

WHILE @counter < 5
   BEGIN
      SELECT POWER(@value, @counter)
      SET NOCOUNT ON
      SET @counter = @counter + 1
      SET NOCOUNT OFF
   END
GO
```

Here is the result set:

```
-----------
2

(1 row(s) affected)


-----------
4

(1 row(s) affected)


-----------
8

(1 row(s) affected)


-----------
16

(1 row(s) affected)
```

Related Topics

decimal and numeric, float and real, "int, smallint, and tinyint," Mathematical Functions, money and smallmoney

Predicate

Is an expression that evaluates to TRUE, FALSE, or UNKNOWN. Predicates are used in the search condition of WHERE clauses and HAVING clauses, and the join conditions of FROM clauses.

Related Topics

BETWEEN, CONTAINS, EXISTS, FREETEXT, IN, IS [NOT] NULL, LIKE, Search Condition

PRINT

Returns a user-defined message to the client.

Syntax

```
PRINT 'any ASCII text' | @local_variable | @@FUNCTION | string_expr
```

Arguments

'*any ASCII text*'
    Is a string of text.

@local_variable
    Is a variable of any valid character data type. *@local_variable* must be **char** or **varchar**, or be able to be implicitly converted to those data types.

@@FUNCTION
    Is a function that returns string results. *@@FUNCTION* must be **char** or **varchar**, or be able to be implicitly converted to those data types.

string_expr
    Is an expression that returns a string. Can include concatenated literal values and variables. The message string can be up to 8,000 characters long; any characters after 8,000 are truncated.

Remarks

To print a user-defined error message having an error number that can be returned by @@ERROR, use RAISERROR instead of PRINT.

Examples

A. Conditionally executed print (IF EXISTS)

This example uses the PRINT statement to conditionally return a message.

```
IF EXISTS (SELECT zip FROM authors WHERE zip = '94705')
   PRINT 'Berkeley author'
```

B. Build and display a string

This example converts the results of the GETDATE function to a **varchar** data type and concatenates it with literal text to be returned by PRINT.

```
PRINT 'This message was printed on ' +
   RTRIM(CONVERT(varchar(30), GETDATE())) + '.'
```

Related Topics

Data Types, DECLARE @local_variable, Functions, RAISERROR

QUOTENAME

Returns a Unicode string with the delimiters added to make the input string a valid Microsoft SQL Server delimited identifier.

Syntax

```
QUOTENAME ( 'character_string' [ , 'quote_character' ] )
```

Arguments

'character_string'

Is a string of Unicode character data. *character_string* is **sysname**.

'quote_character'

Is a one-character string to use as the delimiter. Can be a single quotation mark ('), a left or right bracket ([]), or a double quotation mark ("). If *quote_character* is not specified, brackets are used.

Return Types

nvarchar(129)

Examples

This example takes the character string abc[]def and uses the [and] characters to create a valid SQL Server quoted (delimited) identifier.

```
SELECT QUOTENAME('abc[]def')
```

Here is the result set:

```
[abc[]]def]

(1 row(s) affected)
```

Notice that the right bracket in the string abc[]def is doubled to indicate an escape character.

Related Topics

String Functions

RADIANS

Returns radians when a numeric expression, in degrees, is entered.

Syntax

```
RADIANS ( numeric_expression )
```

Arguments

numeric_expression

Is an expression of the exact numeric or approximate numeric data type category, except for the **bit** data type.

Return Types

Returns the same type as *numeric_expression*.

Examples

A. Use RADIANS to show 0.0

This example returns a result of 0.0 because the numeric expression to convert to radians is too small for the RADIANS function.

```
SELECT RADIANS(1e-307)
GO
```

Here is the result set:

```
--------------------
0.0
(1 row(s) affected)
```

B. Use RADIANS

This example takes a **float** expression and returns the RADIANS of the given angle.

```
-- First value is -45.01.
DECLARE @angle float
SET @angle = -45.01
SELECT 'The RADIANS of the angle is: ' +
    CONVERT(varchar, RADIANS(@angle))
GO
-- Next value is -181.01.
DECLARE @angle float
SET @angle = -181.01
SELECT 'The RADIANS of the angle is: ' +
    CONVERT(varchar, RADIANS(@angle))
GO
-- Next value is 0.00.
DECLARE @angle float
SET @angle = 0.00
SELECT 'The RADIANS of the angle is: ' +
    CONVERT(varchar, RADIANS(@angle))
GO
-- Next value is 0.1472738.
DECLARE @angle float
SET @angle = 0.1472738
SELECT 'The RADIANS of the angle is: ' +
     CONVERT(varchar, RADIANS(@angle))
GO
-- Last value is 197.1099392.
DECLARE @angle float
SET @angle = 197.1099392
SELECT 'The RADIANS of the angle is: ' +
    CONVERT(varchar, RADIANS(@angle))
GO
```

Here is the result set:

```
-----------------------------------------
The RADIANS of the angle is: -0.785573
(1 row(s) affected)
-----------------------------------------
The RADIANS of the angle is: -3.15922
(1 row(s) affected)
-----------------------------------------
The RADIANS of the angle is: 0
(1 row(s) affected)
```

(continued)

(continued)

```
-----------------------------------------
The RADIANS of the angle is: 0.00257041
 (1 row(s) affected)
-----------------------------------------
The RADIANS of the angle is: 3.44022
 (1 row(s) affected)
```

Related Topics

CAST and CONVERT, decimal and numeric, float and real, "int, smallint, and tinyint," Mathematical Functions, money and smallmoney

RAISERROR

Returns a user-defined error message and sets a system flag to record that an error has occurred. Using RAISERROR, the client can either retrieve an entry from the **sysmessages** table or build a message dynamically with user-specified severity and state information. After the message is defined it is sent back to the client as a server error message.

Syntax

```
RAISERROR ( { msg_id | msg_str } { , severity , state }
   [ , argument [ ,...n ] ] )
   [ WITH option [ ,...n ] ]
```

Arguments

msg_id

Is a user-defined error message stored in the **sysmessages** table. Error numbers for user-defined error messages should be greater than 50,000. Ad hoc messages raise an error of 50,000.

msg_str

Is an ad hoc message with formatting similar to the PRINTF format style used in C. The error message can have up to 400 characters. If the message contains more than 400 characters, only the first 397 will be displayed and an ellipsis will be added to indicate that the message has been cut. All ad hoc messages have a standard message ID of 14,000.

This format is supported for *msg_str*:

% [[*flag*] [*width*] [*precision*] [{h I 1}]] *type*

The parameters that can be used in *msg_str* are:

flag

Is a code that determines the spacing and justification of the user-defined error message.

Code	Prefix or justification	Description
- (minus)	Left-justified	Left-justify the result within the given field width.
+ (plus)	+ (plus) or - (minus) prefix	Preface the output value with a plus (+) or minus (-) sign if the output value is of signed type.
0 (zero)	Zero padding	If width is prefaced with 0, zeros are added until the minimum width is reached. When 0 and - appear, 0 is ignored. When 0 is specified with an integer format (i, u, x, X, o, d), 0 is ignored.
# (number)	0x prefix for hexadecimal type of x or X	When used with the o, x, or X format, the # flag prefaces any nonzero value with 0, 0x, or 0X, respectively. When d, i, or u are prefaced by the # flag, the flag is ignored.
' ' (blank)	Space padding	Preface the output value with blank spaces if the value is signed and positive. This is ignored when included with the plus sign (+) flag.

width

Is an integer defining the minimum width. An asterisk (*) allows *precision* to determine the width.

precision

Is the maximum number of characters printed for the output field or the minimum number of digits printed for integer values. An asterisk (*) allows *argument* to determine the precision.

{h | l} type

Is used with character types d, i, o, x, X, or u, and creates **short int** (h) or **long int** (l) values.

Character type	Represents
d or I	Signed integer
o	Unsigned octal
p	Pointer
s	String
u	Unsigned integer
x or X	Unsigned hexadecimal

Note   The **float**, double-, and single character types are not supported.

severity

Is the user-defined severity level associated with this message. Severity levels from 0 through 18 can be used by any user. Severity levels from 19 through 25 are used only by members of the **sysadmin** fixed server role. For severity levels from 19 through 25, the WITH LOG option is required.

> **CAUTION**   Severity levels from 20 through 25 are considered fatal. If a fatal severity level is encountered, the client connection is terminated after receiving the message, and the error is logged in the error log and the application log.

state

Is an arbitrary integer from 1 through 127 that represents information about the invocation state of the error. A negative value for *state* defaults to 1.

argument

Is the parameters used in the substitution for variables defined in *msg_str* or the message corresponding to *msg_id*. There can be 0 or more substitution parameters; however, the total number of substitution parameters cannot exceed 20. Each substitution parameter can be a local variable or any of these data types: **int1**, **int2**, **int4**, **char**, **varchar**, **binary**, or **varbinary**. No other data types are supported.

option

Is a custom option for the error. *option* can be one of these values.

Value	Description
LOG	Logs the error in the server error log and the application log. Errors logged in the server error log are currently limited to a maximum of 440 bytes.
NOWAIT	Sends messages immediately to the client.
SETERROR	Sets @@ERROR value to *msg_id* or 50000, regardless of the severity level.

Remarks

If a **sysmessages** error is used and the message was created using the format shown for *msg_str*, the supplied arguments (*argument1*, *argument2*, and so on) are passed to the message of the supplied *msg_id*.

When you use RAISERROR to create and return user-defined error messages, use **sp_addmessage** to add user-defined error messages and **sp_dropmessage** to delete user-defined error messages.

When an error is raised, the error number is placed in the @@ERROR function, which stores the most recently generated error number. @@ERROR is set to 0 by default for messages with a severity from 1 through 10.

Examples

A. Create an ad hoc message

This example shows two errors that can be raised. The first is a simple error with a static message. The second error is dynamically built based on the attempted modification.

```
CREATE TRIGGER employee_insupd
ON employee
FOR INSERT, UPDATE
AS
/* Get the range of level for this job type from the jobs table. */
DECLARE @@MIN_LVL tinyint,
   @@MAX_LVL tinyint,
   @@EMP_LVL tinyint,
   @@JOB_ID smallint
SELECT @@MIN_LV1 = min_lvl,
   @@MAX_LV = max_lvl,
   @@ EMP_LVL = i.job_lvl,
   @@JOB_ID = i.job_id
FROM employee e, jobs j, inserted i
WHERE e.emp_id = i.emp_id AND i.job_id = j.job_id
IF (@@JOB_ID = 1) and (@@EMP_lV1 <> 10)
BEGIN
   RAISERROR ('Job id 1 expects the default level of 10.', 16, 1)
   ROLLBACK TRANSACTION
END
ELSE
IF NOT @@ EMP_LVL BETWEEN @@MIN_LVL AND @@MAX_LVL)
BEGIN
   RAISERROR ('The level for job_id:%d should be between %d and %d.',
      16, 1, @@JOB_ID, @@MIN_LVL, @@MAX_LVL)
   ROLLBACK TRANSACTION
END
```

B. Create an ad hoc message in sysmessages

This example shows how to achieve the same results with RAISERROR using parameters passed to a message stored in the **sysmessages** table by executing the **employee_insupd** trigger. The message was added to the **sysmessages** table with the **sp_addmessage** system stored procedure as message number 50005.

Note   This example is shown for illustration only.

```
RAISERROR (50005, 16, 1, @@JOB_ID, @@MIN_LVL, @@MAX_LVL)
```

Related Topics

DECLARE @local_variable, Functions, PRINT, sp_addmessage, sp_dropmessage, sysmessages, xp_logevent

---

RAND

Returns a random **float** value from 0 through 1.

Syntax

```
RAND ( [ seed ] )
```

Arguments

seed

Is an integer expression (**tinyint**, **smallint**, or **int**) that gives the seed or start value.

Return Types

float

Remarks

Repetitive invocations of RAND() in a single query will produce the same value.

Examples

This example produces four different random numbers generated with the RAND function.

```
DECLARE @counter smallint
SET @counter = 1
WHILE @counter < 5
   BEGIN
      SELECT RAND(@counter) Random_Number
      SET NOCOUNT ON
      SET @counter = @counter + 1
      SET NOCOUNT OFF
   END
GO
```

Here is the result set:

```
Random_Number
-------------------
0.71359199321292355
```

(continued)

(continued)

```
(1 row(s) affected)

Random_Number
------------------
0.7136106261841817

(1 row(s) affected)

Random_Number
------------------
0.71362925915543995

(1 row(s) affected)

Random_Number
------------------
0.7136478921266981
(1 row(s) affected)
```

Related Topics
Mathematical Functions

READTEXT

Reads **text**, **ntext**, or **image** values from a **text**, **ntext**, or **image** column, starting from a specified offset and reading the specified number of bytes.

Syntax
```
READTEXT { table.column text_ptr offset size } [ HOLDLOCK ]
```

Arguments
table.column
> Is the name of a table and column from which to read. Table and column names must conform to the rules for identifiers. Specifying the table and column names is required; however, specifying the database name and owner names is optional.

text_ptr
> Is a valid text pointer. *text_ptr* must be **binary(16)**.

offset

Is the number of bytes (when using the **text** or **image** data types) or characters (when using the **ntext** data type) to skip before starting to read the **text**, **image**, or **ntext** data. When using **ntext** data type, *offset* is the number of characters to skip before starting to read the data. When using **text** or **image** data types, *offset* is the number of bytes to skip before starting to read the data.

size

Is the number of bytes (when using the **text** or **image** data types) or characters (when using the **ntext** data type) of data to read. If *size* is 0, 4 KB bytes of data are read.

HOLDLOCK

Causes the text value to be locked for reads until the end of the transaction. Other users can read the value, but they cannot modify it.

Remarks

Use the TEXTPTR function to obtain a valid *text_ptr* value. TEXTPTR returns a pointer to the **text**, **ntext**, or **image** column in the specified row or to the **text**, **ntext**, or **image** column in the last row returned by the query if more than one row is returned. Because TEXTPTR returns a 16-byte binary string, it is best to declare a local variable to hold the text pointer and then use the variable with READTEXT. For more information about declaring a local variable, see DECLARE @local_variable.

In SQL Server 2000, in row text pointers may exist but be invalid. For more information about the **text in row** option, see sp_tableoption. For more information about invalidating text pointers, see sp_invalidate_textptr.

The value of the @@TEXTSIZE function supersedes the size specified for READTEXT if it is less than the specified size for READTEXT. The @@TEXTSIZE function is the limit on the number of bytes of data to be returned set by the SET TEXTSIZE statement. For more information about how to set the session setting for TEXTSIZE, see SET TEXTSIZE.

Permissions

READTEXT permissions default to users with SELECT permissions on the specified table. Permissions are transferable when SELECT permissions are transferred.

Examples

This example reads the second through twenty-sixth characters of the **pr_info** column in the **pub_info** table.

```
USE pubs
GO
DECLARE @ptrval varbinary(16)
SELECT @ptrval = TEXTPTR(pr_info)
    FROM pub_info pr INNER JOIN publishers p
        ON pr.pub_id = p.pub_id
        AND p.pub_name = 'New Moon Books'
READTEXT pub_info.pr_info @ptrval 1 25
GO
```

Related Topics

@@TEXTSIZE, UPDATETEXT, WRITETEXT

---

real

For more information about the **real** data type, see float and real.

Related Topics

Data Type Conversion, Data Types

RECONFIGURE

Updates the currently configured (the **config_value** column in the **sp_configure** result set) value of a configuration option changed with the **sp_configure** system stored procedure. Because some configuration options require a server stop and restart to update the currently running value, RECONFIGURE does not always update the currently running value (the **run_value** column in the **sp_configure** result set) for a changed configuration value.

Syntax

```
RECONFIGURE [ WITH OVERRIDE ]
```

Arguments

RECONFIGURE

Specifies that if the configuration setting does not require a server stop and restart, the currently running value should be updated. RECONFIGURE also checks the new configuration value for either invalid values (for example, a sort order value that does not exist in **syscharsets**) or nonrecommended values (for example, setting **allow updates** to 1). With those configuration options not requiring a server stop and restart, the currently running value and the currently configured values for the configuration option should be the same value after specifying RECONFIGURE.

WITH OVERRIDE

Disables the configuration value checking (for invalid values or for nonrecommended values) for the **allow updates**, **recovery interval**, or **time slice** advanced configuration options. In addition, RECONFIGURE WITH OVERRIDE forces the reconfiguration with the specified value. For example, the **min server memory** configuration option could be configured with a value greater than the value specified in the **max server memory** configuration option. However, this is considered a fatal error. Therefore, specifying RECONFIGURE WITH OVERRIDE would not disable configuration value checking. Any configuration option can be reconfigured using the WITH OVERRIDE option.

Remarks

sp_configure does not accept new configuration option values out of the documented valid ranges for each configuration option.

Permissions

RECONFIGURE permissions default to members of the **sysadmin** and **serveradmin** fixed server roles, and are not transferable.

Examples

This example sets the upper limit for the **network packet size** configuration option and uses RECONFIGURE WITH OVERRIDE to install it. Because the WITH OVERRIDE option is specified, Microsoft SQL Server does not check the value specified (8192) to see if it is a valid value for the **network packet size** configuration option.

```
EXEC sp_configure 'network packet size', 8192
RECONFIGURE WITH OVERRIDE
GO
```

Related Topics

Setting Configuration Options, sp_configure

REPLACE

Replaces all occurrences of the second given string expression in the first string expression with a third expression.

Syntax

```
REPLACE ( 'string_expression1' , 'string_expression2' , 'string_expression3' )
```

Arguments

'*string_expression1*'

Is the string expression to be searched. *string_expression1* can be of character or binary data.

'*string_expression2*'

Is the string expression to try to find. *string_expression2* can be of character or binary data.

'*string_expression3*'

Is the replacement string expression *string_expression3* can be of character or binary data.

Return Types

Returns character data if *string_expression* (1, 2, or 3) is one of the supported character data types. Returns binary data if *string_expression* (1, 2, or 3) is one of the supported **binary** data types.

Examples

This example replaces the string cde in abcdefghi with xxx.

```
SELECT REPLACE('abcdefghicde','cde','xxx')
GO
```

Here is the result set:

```
------------
abxxxfghixxx
(1 row(s) affected)
```

Related Topics

Data Types, String Functions

REPLICATE

Repeats a character expression for a specified number of times.

Syntax

```
REPLICATE ( character_expression , integer_expression )
```

Arguments

character_expression

Is an alphanumeric expression of character data. *character_expression* can be a constant, variable, or column of either character or binary data.

integer_expression

Is a positive whole number. If *integer_expression* is negative, a null string is returned.

Return Types

varchar

character_expression must be of a data type that is implicitly convertible to **varchar**. Otherwise, use the CAST function to convert explicitly *character_expression*.

Remarks

Compatibility levels can affect return values. For more information, see sp_dbcmptlevel.

Examples

A. Use REPLICATE

This example replicates each author's first name twice.

```
USE pubs
SELECT REPLICATE(au_fname, 2)
FROM authors
ORDER BY au_fname
```

Here is the result set:

```
--------------------
AbrahamAbraham
AkikoAkiko
AlbertAlbert
AnnAnn
AnneAnne
```

(continued)

(continued)

```
BurtBurt
CharleneCharlene
CherylCheryl
DeanDean
DirkDirk
HeatherHeather
InnesInnes
JohnsonJohnson
LiviaLivia
MarjorieMarjorie
MeanderMeander
MichaelMichael
MichelMichel
MorningstarMorningstar
ReginaldReginald
SherylSheryl
StearnsStearns
SylviaSylvia
(23 row(s) affected)
```

B. Use REPLICATE, SUBSTRING, and SPACE

This example uses REPLICATE, SUBSTRING, and SPACE to produce a telephone
and fax listing of all authors in the **authors** table.

```
-- Replicate phone number twice because the fax number is identical to
-- the author telephone number.
USE pubs
GO
SELECT SUBSTRING((UPPER(au_lname) + ',' + SPACE(1) + au_fname), 1, 35)
   AS Name, phone AS Phone, REPLICATE(phone,1) AS Fax
FROM authors
ORDER BY au_lname, au_fname
GO
```

Here is the result set:

```
Name                                Phone        Fax
-----------------------------       ------------ ------------------------
BENNET, Abraham                     415 658-9932 415 658-9932
BLOTCHET-HALLS, Reginald            503 745-6402 503 745-6402
CARSON, Cheryl                      415 548-7723 415 548-7723
DEFRANCE, Michel                    219 547-9982 219 547-9982
DEL CASTILLO, Innes                 615 996-8275 615 996-8275
DULL, Ann                           415 836-7128 415 836-7128
```

(continued)

(continued)

```
GREEN, Marjorie          415 986-7020 415 986-7020
GREENE, Morningstar      615 297-2723 615 297-2723
GRINGLESBY, Burt         707 938-6445 707 938-6445
HUNTER, Sheryl           415 836-7128 415 836-7128
KARSEN, Livia            415 534-9219 415 534-9219
LOCKSLEY, Charlene       415 585-4620 415 585-4620
MACFEATHER, Stearns      415 354-7128 415 354-7128
MCBADDEN, Heather        707 448-4982 707 448-4982
O'LEARY, Michael         408 286-2428 408 286-2428
PANTELEY, Sylvia         301 946-8853 301 946-8853
RINGER, Albert           801 826-0752 801 826-0752
RINGER, Anne             801 826-0752 801 826-0752
SMITH, Meander           913 843-0462 913 843-0462
STRAIGHT, Dean           415 834-2919 415 834-2919
STRINGER, Dirk           415 843-2991 415 843-2991
WHITE, Johnson           408 496-7223 408 496-7223
YOKOMOTO, Akiko          415 935-4228 415 935-4228
(23 row(s) affected)
```

C. Use REPLICATE and DATALENGTH

This example left pads numbers to a specified length as they are converted from a numeric data type to character or Unicode.

```
USE Northwind
GO
DROP TABLE t1
GO
CREATE TABLE t1
(
 c1 varchar(3),
 c2 char(3)
)
GO
INSERT INTO t1 VALUES ('2', '2')
INSERT INTO t1 VALUES ('37', '37')
INSERT INTO t1 VALUES ('597', '597')
GO
SELECT REPLICATE('0', 3 - DATALENGTH(c1)) + c1 AS [Varchar Column],
       REPLICATE('0', 3 - DATALENGTH(c2)) + c2 AS [Char Column]
FROM t1
GO
```

Related Topics

Data Types, String Functions

RESTORE

Restores backups taken using the BACKUP command. For more information about database back up and restore operations, see Backing Up and Restoring Databases.

Syntax

Restore an entire database:

```
RESTORE DATABASE { database_name | @database_name_var }
[ FROM < backup_device > [ ,...n ] ]
[ WITH
   [ RESTRICTED_USER ]
   [ [ , ] FILE = { file_number | @file_number } ]
   [ [ , ] PASSWORD = { password | @password_variable } ]
   [ [ , ] MEDIANAME = { media_name | @media_name_variable } ]
   [ [ , ] MEDIAPASSWORD = { mediapassword | @mediapassword_variable } ]
   [ [ , ] MOVE 'logical_file_name' TO 'operating_system_file_name' ]
        [ ,...n ]
   [ [ , ] KEEP_REPLICATION ]
   [ [ , ] { NORECOVERY | RECOVERY | STANDBY = undo_file_name } ]
   [ [ , ] { NOREWIND | REWIND } ]
   [ [ , ] { NOUNLOAD | UNLOAD } ]
   [ [ , ] REPLACE ]
   [ [ , ] RESTART ]
   [ [ , ] STATS [ = percentage ] ]
]
```

Restore part of a database:

```
RESTORE DATABASE { database_name | @database_name_var }
   < file_or_filegroup > [ ,...n ]
[ FROM < backup_device > [ ,...n ] ]
[ WITH
   { PARTIAL }
   [ [ , ] FILE = { file_number | @file_number } ]
   [ [ , ] PASSWORD = { password | @password_variable } ]
   [ [ , ] MEDIANAME = { media_name | @media_name_variable } ]
   [ [ , ] MEDIAPASSWORD = { mediapassword | @mediapassword_variable } ]
   [ [ , ] MOVE 'logical_file_name' TO 'operating_system_file_name' ]
        [ ,...n ]
```

(continued)

(continued)

```
  [ [ , ] NORECOVERY ]
  [ [ , ] { NOREWIND | REWIND } ]
  [ [ , ] { NOUNLOAD | UNLOAD } ]
  [ [ , ] REPLACE ]
  [ [ , ] RESTRICTED_USER ]
  [ [ , ] RESTART ]
  [ [ , ] STATS [= percentage ] ]
]
```

Restore specific files or filegroups:

```
RESTORE DATABASE { database_name | @database_name_var }
  < file_or_filegroup > [ ,...n ]
[ FROM < backup_device > [ ,...n ] ]
[ WITH
  [ RESTRICTED_USER ]
  [ [ , ] FILE = { file_number | @file_number } ]
  [ [ , ] PASSWORD = { password | @password_variable } ]
  [ [ , ] MEDIANAME = { media_name | @media_name_variable } ]
  [ [ , ] MEDIAPASSWORD = { mediapassword | @mediapassword_variable } ]
  [ [ , ] MOVE 'logical_file_name' TO 'operating_system_file_name' ]
       [ ,...n ]
  [ [ , ] NORECOVERY ]
  [ [ , ] { NOREWIND | REWIND } ]
  [ [ , ] { NOUNLOAD | UNLOAD } ]
  [ [ , ] REPLACE ]
  [ [ , ] RESTART ]
  [ [ , ] STATS [ = percentage ] ]
]
```

Restore a transaction log:

```
RESTORE LOG { database_name | @database_name_var }
[ FROM < backup_device > [ ,...n ] ]
[ WITH
  [ RESTRICTED_USER ]
  [ [ , ] FILE = { file_number | @file_number } ]
  [ [ , ] PASSWORD = { password | @password_variable } ]
  [ [ , ] MOVE 'logical_file_name' TO 'operating_system_file_name' ]
       [ ,...n ]
  [ [ , ] MEDIANAME = { media_name | @media_name_variable } ]
  [ [ , ] MEDIAPASSWORD = { mediapassword | @mediapassword_variable } ]
  [ [ , ] KEEP_REPLICATION ]
  [ [ , ] { NORECOVERY | RECOVERY | STANDBY = undo_file_name } ]
```

(continued)

(continued)

```
      [ [ , ] { NOREWIND | REWIND } ]
      [ [ , ] { NOUNLOAD | UNLOAD } ]
      [ [ , ] RESTART ]
      [ [ , ] STATS [= percentage ] ]
      [ [ , ] STOPAT = { date_time | @date_time_var }
          | [ , ] STOPATMARK = 'mark_name' [ AFTER datetime ]
          | [ , ] STOPBEFOREMARK = 'mark_name' [ AFTER datetime ]
      ]
]
< backup_device > ::=
    {
        { 'logical_backup_device_name' | @logical_backup_device_name_var }
        | { DISK | TAPE } =
            { 'physical_backup_device_name' | @physical_backup_device_name_var }
    }
< file_or_filegroup > ::=
    {
        FILE = { logical_file_name | @logical_file_name_var }
        |
        FILEGROUP = { logical_filegroup_name | @logical_filegroup_name_var }
    }
```

Arguments

DATABASE

Specifies the complete restore of the database from a backup. If a list of files and filegroups is specified, only those files and filegroups are restored.

{*database_name* | @*database_name_var*}

Is the database that the log or complete database is restored into. If supplied as a variable (@*database_name_var*), this name can be specified either as a string constant (@*database_name_var* = *database name*) or as a variable of character string data type, except for the **ntext** or **text** data types.

FROM

Specifies the backup devices from which to restore the backup. If the FROM clause is not specified, the restore of a backup does not take place. Instead, the database is recovered. Omitting the FROM clause can be used to attempt recovery of a database that has been restored with the NORECOVERY option, or to switch over to a standby server. If the FROM clause is omitted, NORECOVERY, RECOVERY, or STANDBY must be specified.

<backup_device>

Specifies the logical or physical backup devices to use for the restore operation. Can be one or more of the following:

{ '*logical_backup_device_name*' | @*logical_backup_device_name_var* }

Is the logical name, which must follow the rules for identifiers, of the backup device(s) created by **sp_addumpdevice** from which the database is restored. If supplied as a variable (@*logical_backup_device_name_var*), the backup device name can be specified either as a string constant (@*logical_backup_device_name_var* = *logical_backup_device_name*) or as a variable of character string data type, except for the **ntext** or **text** data types.

{DISK | TAPE } =

'*physical_backup_device_name*' | @*physical_backup_device_name_var*

Allows backups to be restored from the named disk or tape device. The device types of disk and tape should be specified with the actual name (for example, complete path and file name) of the device: DISK = 'C:\Program Files\ Microsoft SQL Server\MSSQL\BACKUP\Mybackup.dat' or TAPE = '\\.\TAPE0'. If specified as a variable (@*physical_backup_device_name_var*), the device name can be specified either as a string constant (@*physical_backup_device_name_var* = '*physcial_backup_device_name*') or as a variable of character string data type, except for the **ntext** or **text** data types.

If using either a network server with a UNC name or a redirected drive letter, specify a device type of disk. The account under which you are running SQL Server must have READ access to the remote computer or network server in order to perform a RESTORE operation.

n

Is a placeholder that indicates multiple backup devices and logical backup devices can be specified. The maximum number of backup devices or logical backup devices is 64.

RESTRICTED_USER

Restricts access for the newly restored database to members of the **db_owner**, **dbcreator**, or **sysadmin** roles. In SQL Server 2000, RESTRICTED_USER replaces the DBO_ONLY option. DBO_ONLY is available only for backward compatibility.

Use with the RECOVERY option.

For more information, see Setting Database Options.

FILE = { *file_number* | @*file_number* **}**

Identifies the backup set to be restored. For example, a *file_number* of 1 indicates the first backup set on the backup medium and a *file_number* of 2 indicates the second backup set.

PASSWORD = { *password* | *@password_variable* }

Provides the password for the backup set. PASSWORD is a character string. If a password was provided when the backup set was created, the password must be supplied to perform any restore operation from the backup set.

For more information about using passwords, see Permissions.

MEDIANAME = {*media_name* | *@media_name_variable*}

Specifies the name for the media. If provided, the media name must match the media name on the backup volume(s); otherwise, the restore operation terminates. If no media name is given in the RESTORE statement, the check for a matching media name on the backup volume(s) is not performed.

> **Important** Consistently using media names in backup and restore operations provides an extra safety check for the media selected for the restore operation.

MEDIAPASSWORD = { *mediapassword* | *@mediapassword_variable* }

Supplies the password for the media set. MEDIAPASSWORD is a character string.

If a password was provided when the media set was formatted, that password must be supplied to access any backup set on that media set.

MOVE '*logical_file_name*' TO '*operating_system_file_name*'

Specifies that the given *logical_file_name* should be moved to *operating_system_file_name*. By default, the *logical_file_name* is restored to its original location. If the RESTORE statement is used to copy a database to the same or different server, the MOVE option may be needed to relocate the database files and to avoid collisions with existing files. Each logical file in the database can be specified in different MOVE statements.

> **Note** Use RESTORE FILELISTONLY to obtain a list of the logical files from the backup set.

For more information, see Copying Databases.

n

Is a placeholder that indicates more than one logical file can be moved by specifying multiple MOVE statements.

NORECOVERY

Instructs the restore operation to not roll back any uncommitted transactions. Either the NORECOVERY or STANDBY option must be specified if another transaction log has to be applied. If neither NORECOVERY, RECOVERY, or STANDBY is specified, RECOVERY is the default.

SQL Server requires that the WITH NORECOVERY option be used on all but the final RESTORE statement when restoring a database backup and multiple transaction logs, or when multiple RESTORE statements are needed (for example, a full database backup followed by a differential database backup).

Note   When specifying the NORECOVERY option, the database is not usable in this intermediate, nonrecovered state.

When used with a file or filegroup restore operation, NORECOVERY forces the database to remain in the restoring state after the restore operation. This is useful in either of these situations:

- A restore script is being run and the log is always being applied.

- A sequence of file restores is used and the database is not intended to be usable between two of the restore operations.

RECOVERY

Instructs the restore operation to roll back any uncommitted transactions. After the recovery process, the database is ready for use.

If subsequent RESTORE operations (RESTORE LOG, or RESTORE DATABASE from differential) are planned, NORECOVERY or STANDBY should be specified instead.

If neither NORECOVERY, RECOVERY, or STANDBY is specified, RECOVERY is the default. When restoring backup sets from an earlier version of SQL Server, a database upgrade may be required. This upgrade is performed automatically when WITH RECOVERY is specified. For more information, see Transaction Log Backups.

STANDBY = *undo_file_name*

Specifies the undo file name so the recovery effects can be undone. The size required for the undo file depends on the volume of undo actions resulting from uncommitted transactions. If neither NORECOVERY, RECOVERY, or STANDBY is specified, RECOVERY is the default.

STANDBY allows a database to be brought up for read-only access between transaction log restores and can be used with either warm standby server situations or special recovery situations in which it is useful to inspect the database between log restores.

If the specified undo file name does not exist, SQL Server creates it. If the file does exist, SQL Server overwrites it.

The same undo file can be used for consecutive restores of the same database. For more information, see Using Standby Servers.

Important   If free disk space is exhausted on the drive containing the specified undo file name, the restore operation stops.

STANDBY is not allowed when a database upgrade is necessary.

KEEP_REPLICATION

Instructs the restore operation to preserve replication settings when restoring a published database to a server other than that on which it was created. KEEP_REPLICATION is to be used when setting up replication to work with log shipping. It prevents replication settings from being removed when a database or log backup is restored on a warm standby server and the database is recovered. Specifying this option when restoring a backup with the NORECOVERY option is not permitted.

NOUNLOAD

Specifies that the tape is not unloaded automatically from the tape drive after a RESTORE. NOUNLOAD remains set until UNLOAD is specified. This option is used only for tape devices. If a non-tape device is being used for RESTORE, this option is ignored.

NOREWIND

Specifies that SQL Server will keep the tape open after the backup operation. Keeping the tape open prevents other processes from accessing the tape. The tape will not be released until a REWIND or UNLOAD statement is issued, or the server is shut down. A list of currently open tapes can be found by querying the **sysopentapes** table in the **master** database.

NOREWIND implies NOUNLOAD. This option is used only for tape devices. If a non-tape device is being used for RESTORE, this option is ignored.

REWIND

Specifies that SQL Server will release and rewind the tape. If neither NOREWIND nor REWIND is specified, REWIND is the default. This option is used only for tape devices. If a non-tape device is being used for RESTORE, this option is ignored.

UNLOAD

Specifies that the tape is automatically rewound and unloaded when the RESTORE is finished. UNLOAD is set by default when a new user session is started. It remains set until NOUNLOAD is specified. This option is used only for tape devices. If a non-tape device is being used for RESTORE, this option is ignored.

REPLACE

Specifies that SQL Server should create the specified database and its related files even if another database already exists with the same name. In such a case, the existing database is deleted. When the REPLACE option is not specified, a safety check occurs (which prevents overwriting a different database by accident). The safety check ensures that the RESTORE DATABASE statement will not restore the database to the current server if:

1. The database named in the RESTORE statement already exists on the current server, and

2. The database name is different from the database name recorded in the backup set.

REPLACE also allows RESTORE to overwrite an existing file which cannot be verified as belonging to the database being restored. Normally, RESTORE will refuse to overwrite pre-existing files.

RESTART

Specifies that SQL Server should restart a restore operation that has been interrupted. RESTART restarts the restore operation at the point it was interrupted.

> **Important** This option can only be used for restores directed from tape media and for restores that span multiple tape volumes.

STATS [= *percentage*]

Displays a message each time another percentage completes and is used to gauge progress. If *percentage* is omitted, SQL Server displays a message after every 10 percent completed.

PARTIAL

Specifies a partial restore operation. Application or user errors often affect an isolated portion of the database, such as a table. Examples of this type of error include an invalid update or a table dropped by mistake. To support recovery from these events, SQL Server provides a mechanism to restore part of the database to another location so that the damaged or missing data can be copied back to the original database.

The granularity of the partial restore operation is the database filegroup. The primary file and filegroup are always restored, along with the files that you specify and their corresponding filegroups. The result is a subset of the database. Filegroups that are not restored are marked as offline and are not accessible.

For more information, see Partial Database Restore Operations.

<file_or_filegroup>

Specifies the names of the logical files or filegroups to include in the database restore. Multiple files or filegroups can be specified.

FILE = {*logical_file_name* | @*logical_file_name_var*}

Names one or more files to include in the database restore.

FILEGROUP = {*logical_filegroup_name* | @*logical_filegroup_name_var*}

Names one or more filegroups to include in the database restore.

When this option is used, the transaction log must be applied to the database files after the last file or filegroup restore operation to roll the files forward to be consistent with the rest of the database. If none of the files being restored have been modified since they were last backed up, a transaction log does not have to be applied. The RESTORE statement informs the user of this situation.

n

Is a placeholder indicating that multiple files and filegroups may be specified. There is no maximum number of files or filegroups.

LOG
>   Specifies that a transaction log backup is to be applied to this database. Transaction logs must be applied in sequential order. SQL Server checks the backed up transaction log to ensure that the transactions are being loaded into the correct database and in the correct sequence. To apply multiple transaction logs, use the NORECOVERY option on all restore operations except the last. For more information, see Transaction Log Backups.

STOPAT = *date_time* | *@date_time_var*
>   Specifies that the database be restored to the state it was in as of the specified date and time. If a variable is used for STOPAT, the variable must be **varchar**, **char**, **smalldatetime**, or **datetime** data type. Only transaction log records written before the specified date and time are applied to the database.
>
>   > **Note** If you specify a STOPAT time that is beyond the end of the RESTORE LOG operation, the database is left in an unrecovered state, just as if RESTORE LOG had been run with NORECOVERY.

STOPATMARK = '*mark_name*' [AFTER *datetime*]
>   Specifies recovery to the specified mark, including the transaction that contains the mark. If AFTER *datetime* is omitted, recovery stops at the first mark with the specified name. If AFTER *datetime* is specified, recovery stops at the first mark having the specified name exactly at or after *datetime*.

STOPBEFOREMARK = '*mark_name*' [AFTER *datetime*]
>   Specifies recovery to the specified mark but does not include the transaction that contains the mark. If AFTER *datetime* is omitted, recovery stops at the first mark with the specified name. If AFTER *datetime* is specified, recovery stops at the first mark having the specified name exactly at or after *datetime*.

Remarks

During the restore, the specified database must not be in use. Any data in the specified database is replaced by the restored data.

For more information about database recovery, see Backing Up and Restoring Databases.

Cross-platform restore operations, even between different processor types, can be performed as long as the collation of the database is supported by the operating system. For more information, see SQL Server Collation Fundamentals.

Restore Types

Here are the types of restores that SQL Server supports:

- Full database restore which restores the entire database.
- Full database restore and a differential database restore. Restore a differential backup by using the RESTORE DATABASE statement.

- Transaction log restore.

- Individual file and filegroup restores. Files and filegroups can be restored either from a file or filegroup backup operation, or from a full database backup operation. When restoring files or filegroups, you must apply a transaction log. In addition, file differential backups can be restored after a full file restore.

  For more information, see Transaction Log Backups.

- Create and maintain a warm standby server or standby server. For more information about standby servers, see Using Standby Servers.

To maintain backward compatibility, the following keywords can be used in the RESTORE statement syntax:

- LOAD keyword can be used in place of the RESTORE keyword.

- TRANSACTION keyword can be used in place of the LOG keyword.

- DBO_ONLY keyword can be used in place of the RESTRICTED_USER keyword.

Database Settings and Restoring

When using the RESTORE DATABASE statement, the restorable database options (which are all the settable options of ALTER DATABASE except **offline** and the **merge publish**, **published**, and **subscribed** replication options) are reset to the settings in force at the time the BACKUP operation ended.

Note This behavior differs from earlier versions of Microsoft SQL Server.

Using the WITH RESTRICTED_USER option, however, overrides this behavior for the user access option setting. This setting is always set following a RESTORE statement, which includes the WITH RESTRICTED_USER option.

For more information, see Backing Up and Restoring Replication Databases.

Restore History Tables

SQL Server includes the following restore history tables, which track the RESTORE activity for each computer system:

- restorefile
- restorefilegroup
- restorehistory

Note When a RESTORE is performed, the backup history tables are modified.

Restoring a damaged **master** database is performed using a special procedure. For more information, see Restoring the master Database.

Backups created with Microsoft SQL Server 2000 cannot be restored to an earlier version of SQL Server.

Permissions

If the database being restored does not exist, the user must have CREATE DATABASE permissions to be able to execute RESTORE. If the database exists, RESTORE permissions default to members of the **sysadmin** and **dbcreator** fixed server roles and the owner (dbo) of the database.

RESTORE permissions are given to roles in which membership information is always readily available to the server. Because fixed database role membership can be checked only when the database is accessible and undamaged, which is not always the case when RESTORE is executed, members of the **db_owner** fixed database role do not have RESTORE permissions.

In addition, the user may specify passwords for a media set, a backup set, or both. When a password is defined on a media set, it is not enough that a user is a member of appropriate fixed server and database roles to perform a backup. The user also must supply the media password to perform these operations. Similarly, RESTORE is not allowed unless the correct media password and backup set password are specified in the restore command.

Defining passwords for backup sets and media sets is an optional feature in the BACKUP statement. The passwords will prevent unauthorized restore operations and unauthorized appends of backup sets to media using SQL Server 2000 tools, but passwords do not prevent overwrite of media with the FORMAT option.

Thus, although the use of passwords can help protect the contents of media from unauthorized access using SQL Server tools, passwords do not protect contents from being destroyed. Passwords do not fully prevent unauthorized access to the contents of the media because the data in the backup sets is not encrypted and could theoretically be examined by programs specifically created for this purpose. For situations where security is crucial, it is important to prevent access to the media by unauthorized individuals.

It is an error to specify a password if none is defined.

Examples

Note   All examples assume that a full database backup has been performed.

A. Restore a full database

Note   The **MyNwind** database is shown for illustration.

This example restores a full database backup.

```
RESTORE DATABASE MyNwind
   FROM MyNwind_1
```

B. Restore a full database and a differential backup

This example restores a full database backup followed by a differential backup.
In addition, this example shows restoring the second backup set on the media.
The differential backup was appended to the backup device that contains the full
database backup.

```
RESTORE DATABASE MyNwind
    FROM MyNwind_1
    WITH NORECOVERY
RESTORE DATABASE MyNwind
    FROM MyNwind_1
    WITH FILE = 2
```

C. Restore a database using RESTART syntax

This example uses the RESTART option to restart a RESTORE operation interrupted
by a server power failure.

```
-- This database RESTORE halted prematurely due to power failure.
RESTORE DATABASE MyNwind
    FROM MyNwind_1
-- Here is the RESTORE RESTART operation.
RESTORE DATABASE MyNwind
    FROM MyNwind_1 WITH RESTART
```

D. Restore a database and move files

This example restores a full database and transaction log and moves the restored
database into the C:\Program Files\Microsoft SQL Server\MSSQL\Data directory.

```
RESTORE DATABASE MyNwind
    FROM MyNwind_1
    WITH NORECOVERY,
        MOVE 'MyNwind' TO 'c:\Program Files\Microsoft SQL Server\MSSQL\Data\NewNwind.mdf',
        MOVE 'MyNwindLog1' TO 'c:\Program Files\Microsoft
SQL Server\MSSQL\Data\NewNwind.ldf'
RESTORE LOG MyNwind
    FROM MyNwindLog1
    WITH RECOVERY
```

E. Make a copy of a database using BACKUP and RESTORE

This example uses both the BACKUP and RESTORE statements to make a copy of
the **Northwind** database. The MOVE statement causes the data and log file to be
restored to the specified locations. The RESTORE FILELISTONLY statement is used
to determine the number and names of the files in the database being restored.
The new copy of the database is named **TestDB**. For more information, see RESTORE
FILELISTONLY.

```
BACKUP DATABASE Northwind
   TO DISK = 'c:\Northwind.bak'
RESTORE FILELISTONLY
   FROM DISK = 'c:\Northwind.bak'
RESTORE DATABASE TestDB
   FROM DISK = 'c:\Northwind.bak'
   WITH MOVE 'Northwind' TO 'c:\test\testdb.mdf',
   MOVE 'Northwind_log' TO 'c:\test\testdb.ldf'
GO
```

F. Restore to a point-in-time using STOPAT syntax and restore with more than one device

This example restores a database to its state as of 12:00 A.M. on April 15, 1998, and shows a restore operation that involves multiple logs and multiple backup devices.

```
RESTORE DATABASE MyNwind
   FROM MyNwind_1, MyNwind_2
   WITH NORECOVERY
RESTORE LOG MyNwind
   FROM MyNwindLog1
   WITH NORECOVERY
RESTORE LOG MyNwind
   FROM MyNwindLog2
   WITH RECOVERY, STOPAT = 'Apr 15, 1998 12:00 AM'
```

G. Restore using TAPE syntax

This example restores a full database backup from a TAPE backup device.

```
RESTORE DATABASE MyNwind
   FROM TAPE = '\\.\tape0'
```

H. Restore using FILE and FILEGROUP syntax

This example restores a database with two files, one filegroup, and one transaction log.

```
RESTORE DATABASE MyNwind
   FILE = 'MyNwind_data_1',
   FILE = 'MyNwind_data_2',
   FILEGROUP = 'new_customers'
   FROM MyNwind_1
   WITH NORECOVERY
-- Restore the log backup.
RESTORE LOG MyNwind
   FROM MyNwindLog1
```

I. Restore the Transaction Log to the Mark

This example restores the transaction log to the mark named "RoyaltyUpdate."

```
BEGIN TRANSACTION RoyaltyUpdate
   WITH MARK 'Update royalty values'
GO
USE pubs
GO
UPDATE roysched
   SET royalty = royalty * 1.10
   WHERE title_id LIKE 'PC%'
GO
COMMIT TRANSACTION RoyaltyUpdate
GO
--Time passes. Regular database
--and log backups are taken.
--An error occurs.
USE master
GO

RESTORE DATABASE pubs
FROM Pubs1
WITH FILE = 3, NORECOVERY
GO
RESTORE LOG pubs
   FROM Pubs1
   WITH FILE = 4,
   STOPATMARK = 'RoyaltyUpdate'
```

Related Topics

BACKUP, bcp Utility, BEGIN TRANSACTION, Data Types, RESTORE
FILELISTONLY, RESTORE HEADERONLY, RESTORE LABELONLY, RESTORE
VERIFYONLY, sp_addumpdevice, Understanding Media Sets and Families, Using
Identifiers

RESTORE FILELISTONLY

Returns a result set with a list of the database and log files contained in the backup set.

Syntax

```
RESTORE FILELISTONLY
FROM < backup_device >
[ WITH
   [ FILE = file_number ]
   [ [ , ] PASSWORD = { password | @password_variable } ]
   [ [ , ] MEDIAPASSWORD = { mediapassword | @mediapassword_variable } ]
   [ [ , ] { NOUNLOAD | UNLOAD } ]
]
< backup_device > ::=
   {
       { 'logical_backup_device_name' | @logical_backup_device_name_var }
       | { DISK | TAPE } =
           { 'physical_backup_device_name' | @physical_backup_device_name_var }
   }
```

Arguments

<backup_device>
Specifies the logical or physical backup device(s) to use for the restore. Can be one or more of the following:

{ 'logical_backup_device_name' | @logical_backup_device_name_var}
Is the logical name, which must follow the rules for identifiers, of the backup device created by **sp_addumpdevice** from which the database is restored. If supplied as a variable (@logical_backup_device_name_var), the backup device name can be specified either as a string constant (@logical_backup_device_name_var = 'logical_backup_device_name') or as a variable of character string data type, except for the **ntext** or **text** data types.

{ DISK | TAPE } =
'physical_backup_device_name' | @physical_backup_device_name_var

Allows backups to be restored from the named disk or tape. The device types of disk and tape should be specified with the actual name (for example, complete path and file name) of the device: DISK = 'C:\Program Files\Microsoft SQL Server\MSSQL\BACKUP\Mybackup.dat' or TAPE = '\\.\TAPE0'. If specified as a variable (@physical_backup_device_name_var), the device name can be specified either as a string constant (@physical_backup_device_name_var = 'physical_backup_device_name') or as a variable of character string data type, except for the **ntext** or **text** data types.

743

If using either a network server with a UNC name or a redirected drive letter, specify a device type of disk.

FILE = *file_number*

Identifies the backup set to be processed. For example, a *file_number* of 1 indicates the first backup set and a *file_number* of 2 indicates the second backup set. If no *file_number* is supplied, the first backup set on the specified <backup_device> is assumed.

PASSWORD = { *password* | *@password_variable* }

Is the password for the backup set. PASSWORD is a character string. If a password was provided when the backup set was created, the password must be supplied to perform any restore operation from the backup set.

For more information about using passwords, see Permissions.

MEDIAPASSWORD = { *mediapassword* | *@mediapassword_variable* }

Is the password for the media set. MEDIAPASSWORD is a character string.

If a password was provided when the media set was formatted, that password must be supplied to create a backup set on that media set. In addition, that media password also must be supplied to perform any restore operation from the media set.

NOUNLOAD

Specifies that the tape is not unloaded automatically from the tape drive after a restore. NOUNLOAD remains set until UNLOAD is specified. This option is used only for tape devices.

UNLOAD

Specifies that the tape is automatically rewound and unloaded when the restore is finished. UNLOAD is set by default when a new user session is started. It remains set until NOUNLOAD is specified. This option is used only for tape devices.

Result Sets

A client can use RESTORE FILELISTONLY to obtain a list of the files contained in a backup set. This information is returned as a result set containing one row for each file.

Column name	Data type	Description
LogicalName	nvarchar(128)	Logical name of the file
PhysicalName	nvarchar(260)	Physical or operating-system name of the file
Type	char(1)	Data file (D) or a log file (L)
FileGroupName	nvarchar(128)	Name of the filegroup that contains the file
Size	numeric(20,0)	Current size in bytes
MaxSize	numeric(20,0)	Maximum allowed size in bytes

Permissions

Any user may use RESTORE FILELISTONLY.

In addition, the user may specify passwords for a media set, a backup set, or both. When a password is defined on a media set, it is not enough that a user is a member of appropriate fixed server and database roles to perform a backup. The user also must supply the media password to perform these operations. Similarly, restore is not allowed unless the correct media password and backup set password are specified in the restore command.

Defining passwords for backup sets and media sets is an optional feature in the BACKUP statement. The passwords will prevent unauthorized restore operations and unauthorized appends of backup sets to media using SQL Server 2000 tools, but passwords do not prevent overwrite of media with the FORMAT option.

Thus, although the use of passwords can help protect the contents of media from unauthorized access using SQL Server tools, passwords do not protect contents from being destroyed. Passwords do not fully prevent unauthorized access to the contents of the media because the data in the backup sets is not encrypted and could theoretically be examined by programs specifically created for this purpose. For situations where security is crucial, it is important to prevent access to the media by unauthorized individuals.

It is an error to specify a password if none is defined.

Related Topics

Backing Up and Restoring Databases, BACKUP, Data Types, RESTORE, RESTORE HEADERONLY, RESTORE LABELONLY, RESTORE VERIFYONLY, Understanding Media Sets and Families, Using Identifiers

RESTORE HEADERONLY

Retrieves all the backup header information for all backup sets on a particular backup device. The result from executing RESTORE HEADERONLY is a result set.

Syntax

```
RESTORE HEADERONLY
FROM < backup_device >
[ WITH { NOUNLOAD | UNLOAD }
    [ [ , ] FILE = file_number ]
    [ [ , ] PASSWORD = { password | @password_variable } ]
    [ [ , ] MEDIAPASSWORD = { mediapassword | @mediapassword_variable } ]
]
```

(continued)

(continued)

```
< backup_device > ::=
    {
        { 'logical_backup_device_name' | @logical_backup_device_name_var }
        | { DISK | TAPE } =
            { 'physical_backup_device_name' | @physical_backup_device_name_var }
    }
```

Arguments

<backup_device>

> Specifies the logical or physical backup device(s) to use for the restore. Can be one of the following:

> { *'logical_backup_device_name'* | *@logical_backup_device_name_var*}
>> Is the logical name, which must follow the rules for identifiers, of the backup device created by **sp_addumpdevice** from which the database is restored. If supplied as a variable (*@logical_backup_device_name_var*), the backup device name can be specified either as a string constant (*@logical_backup_device_name_var* = *'logical_backup_device_name'*) or as a variable of character string data type, except for the **ntext** or **text** data types.

> {DISK | TAPE } =
>> *'physical_backup_device_name'* | *@physical_backup_device_name_var*

>> Allows backups to be restored from the named disk or tape device. The device types of disk and tape should be specified with the actual name (for example, complete path and file name) of the device: DISK = 'C:\Program Files\ Microsoft SQL Server\MSSQL\BACKUP\Mybackup.dat' or TAPE = '\\.\TAPE0'. If specified as a variable (*@physical_backup_device_name_var*), the device name can be specified either as a string constant (*@physical_backup_device_name_var* = *'physical_backup_device_name'*) or as a variable of character string data type, except for the **ntext** or **text** data types.

>> If using either a network server with a UNC name or a redirected drive letter, specify a device type of disk.

NOUNLOAD

> Specifies that the tape is not unloaded automatically from the tape drive after a restore. NOUNLOAD remains set until UNLOAD is specified. This option is used only for tape devices.

UNLOAD

> Specifies that the tape is automatically rewound and unloaded when the restore is finished. UNLOAD is set by default when a new user session is started. It remains set until NOUNLOAD is specified. This option is used only for tape devices.

FILE = *file_number*
>   Identifies the backup set to be described. For example, a *file_number* of 1 indicates the first backup set and a *file_number* of 2 indicates the second backup set. If not specified, all sets on the device are described.

PASSWORD = { *password* | *@password_variable* }
>   Is the password for the backup set. PASSWORD is a character string. If a password was provided when the backup set was created, the password must be supplied to perform any restore operation from the backup set.
>
>   For more information about using passwords, see Permissions.

MEDIAPASSWORD = { *mediapassword* | *@mediapassword_variable* }
>   Is the password for the media set. MEDIAPASSWORD is a character string.
>
>   If a password was provided when the media set was formatted, that password must be supplied to create a backup set on that media set. In addition, that media password also must be supplied to perform any restore operation from the media set.

Result Sets

For each backup on a given device, the server sends a row of header information with the following columns:

> **Note** Because RESTORE HEADERONLY looks at all backup sets on the media, it can take some time to produce this result set when using high-capacity tape drives. To get a quick look at the media without getting information about every backup set, use RESTORE LABELONLY or specify the FILE = *file_number*.

Due to the nature of Microsoft Tape Format, it is possible for backup sets from other software programs to occupy space on the same media as Microsoft SQL Server 2000 backup sets. The result set returned by RESTORE HEADERONLY includes a row for each of these other backup sets.

Column name	Data type	Description for SQL Server backup sets	Description for other backup sets
BackupName	**nvarchar(128)**	Backup set name.	Data set name
BackupDescription	**nvarchar(255)**	Backup set description.	Data set description
BackupType	**smallint**	Backup type:	Backup type:
		1 = Database 2 = Transaction Log 4 = File 5 = Differential Database 6 = Differential File	1 = Normal 5 = Differential 16 = Incremental 17 = Daily
ExpirationDate	**datetime**	Expiration date for the backup set.	NULL
Compressed	**tinyint**	0 = No. SQL Server does not support software compression.	Whether the backup set is compressed using software-based compression: 1 = Yes 0 = No
Position	**smallint**	Position of the backup set in the volume (for use with the FILE = option).	Position of the backup set in the volume
DeviceType	**tinyint**	Number corresponding to the device used for the backup operation: Disk 2 = Logical 102 = Physical	NULL

(continued)

(continued)

Column name	Data type	Description for SQL Server backup sets	Description for other backup sets
		Tape 5 = Logical 105 = Physical	
		Pipe 6 = Logical 106 = Physical	
		Virtual Device 7 = Logical 107 = Physical	
		All physical device names and device numbers can be found in **sysdevices**.	
UserName	**nvarchar(128)**	Username that performed the backup operation.	Username that performed the backup operation
ServerName	**nvarchar(128)**	Name of the server that wrote the backup set.	NULL
DatabaseName	**nvarchar(128)**	Name of the database that was backed up.	NULL
DatabaseVersion	**int**	Version of the database from which the backup was created.	NULL
DatabaseCreationDate	**datetime**	Date and time the database was created.	NULL

(continued)

(continued)

Column name	Data type	Description for SQL Server backup sets	Description for other backup sets
BackupSize	**numeric(20,0)**	Size of the backup, in bytes.	NULL
FirstLSN	**numeric(25,0)**	Log sequence number of the first transaction in the backup set. NULL for file backups.	NULL
LastLSN	**numeric(25,0)**	Log sequence number of the last transaction in the backup set. NULL for file backups.	NULL
CheckpointLSN	**numeric(25,0)**	Log sequence number of the most recent checkpoint at the time the backup was created.	NULL
DatabaseBackupLSN	**numeric(25,0)**	Log sequence number of the most recent full database backup.	NULL
BackupStartDate	**datetime**	Date and time that the backup operation began.	Media Write Date
BackupFinishDate	**datetime**	Date and time that the backup operation finished.	Media Write Date
SortOrder	**smallint**	Server sort order. This column is valid for database backups only. Provided for backward compatibility.	NULL
CodePage	**smallint**	Server code page or character set used by the server.	NULL
UnicodeLocaleId	**int**	Server Unicode locale ID configuration option used for Unicode character data sorting. Provided for backward compatibility.	NULL

(continued)

(continued)

Column name	Data type	Description for SQL Server backup sets	Description for other backup sets
UnicodeComparisonStyle	int	Server Unicode comparison style configuration option, which provides additional control over the sorting of Unicode data. Provided for backward compatibility.	NULL
CompatibilityLevel	tinyint	Compatibility level setting of the database from which the backup was created.	NULL
SoftwareVendorId	int	Software vendor identification number. For SQL Server, this number is 4608 (or hexadecimal 0x1200).	Software vendor identification number
SoftwareVersionMajor	int	Major version number of the server that created the backup set.	Major version number of the software that created the backup set
SoftwareVersionMinor	int	Minor version number of the server that created the backup set.	Minor version number of the software that created the backup set
SoftwareVersionBuild	int	Build number of the server that created the backup set.	NULL
MachineName	nvarchar(128)	Name of the computer that performed the backup operation.	Type of the computer that performed the backup operation
Flags	int	Bit 0 (X1) indicates bulk-logged data is captured in this log backup.	NULL
BindingID	uniqueidentifier	Binding ID for the database.	NULL
RecoveryForkID	uniqueidentifier	ID for the current recovery fork for this backup.	NULL
Collation	nvarchar(128)	Collation used by the database.	NULL

Note If passwords are defined for the backup sets, RESTORE HEADERONLY will show complete information for only the backup set whose password matches the specified PASSWORD option of the command. RESTORE HEADERONLY also will show complete information for unprotected backup sets. The **BackupName** column for the other password-protected backup sets on the media will be set to '***Password Protected***', and all other columns will be NULL.

Permissions

Any user may use RESTORE HEADERONLY.

In addition, the user may specify passwords for a media set, a backup set, or both. When a password is defined on a media set, it is not enough that a user is a member of appropriate fixed server and database roles to perform a backup. The user also must supply the media password to perform these operations. Similarly, restore is not allowed unless the correct media password and backup set password are specified in the restore command.

Defining passwords for backup sets and media sets is an optional feature in the BACKUP statement. The passwords will prevent unauthorized restore operations and unauthorized appends of backup sets to media using SQL Server 2000 tools, but passwords do not prevent overwrite of media with the FORMAT option.

Thus, although the use of passwords can help protect the contents of media from unauthorized access using SQL Server tools, passwords do not protect contents from being destroyed. Passwords do not fully prevent unauthorized access to the contents of the media because the data in the backup sets is not encrypted and could theoretically be examined by programs specifically created for this purpose. For situations where security is crucial, it is important to prevent access to the media by unauthorized individuals.

It is an error to specify a password if none is defined.

Remarks

A client can use RESTORE HEADERONLY to retrieve all the backup header information for all backups on a particular backup device. The header information is sent as a row by the server for each backup on a given backup device in a table.

Important To maintain backward compatibility, the LOAD keyword can be used in place of the RESTORE keyword in the RESTORE statement syntax.

Related Topics

Backing Up and Restoring Databases, BACKUP, Data Types, RESTORE, RESTORE FILELISTONLY, RESTORE VERIFYONLY, RESTORE LABELONLY, Understanding Media Sets and Families, Using Identifiers

RESTORE LABELONLY

Returns a result set containing information about the backup media identified by the given backup device.

Syntax

```
RESTORE LABELONLY
FROM < backup_device >
[ WITH { NOUNLOAD | UNLOAD } ]
    [ [ , ] MEDIAPASSWORD = { mediapassword | @mediapassword_variable } ]
< backup_device > ::=
    {
        { 'logical_backup_device_name' | @logical_backup_device_name_var }
        | { DISK | TAPE } =
            { 'physical_backup_device_name' | @physical_backup_device_name_var }
    }
```

Arguments

\<backup_device>

Specifies the logical or physical backup device to use for the restore. Can be one of the following:

{ *'logical_backup_device__name'* | *@logical_backup_device_name_var*}

Is the logical name, which must follow the rules for identifiers, of the backup device created by **sp_addumpdevice** from which the database is restored. If supplied as a variable (*@logical_backup_device_name_var*), the backup device name can be specified either as a string constant (*@logical_backup_device_name_var* = *'logical_backup_device_name'*) or as a variable of character string data type, except for the **ntext** or **text** data types.

{DISK | TAPE } =
'physical_backup_device_name' | *@physical_backup_device_name_var*

Allows backups to be restored from the named disk or tape device. The device types of disk and tape should be specified with the actual name (for example, complete path and file name) of the device: DISK = 'C:\Program Files\ Microsoft SQL Server\MSSQL\BACKUP\Mybackup.dat' or TAPE = '\\.\TAPE0'. If specified as a variable (*@physical_backup_device_name_var*), the device name can be specified either as a string constant (*@physical_backup_device_name_var* = *'physical_backup_device_name_var'*) or as a variable of character string data type, except for the **ntext** or **text** data types.

If using either a network server with a UNC name or a redirected drive letter, specify a device type of disk.

NOUNLOAD

Specifies that the tape is not unloaded automatically from the tape drive after a restore. NOUNLOAD remains set until UNLOAD is specified. This option is used only for tape devices.

UNLOAD

Specifies that the tape is automatically rewound and unloaded when the restore is finished. UNLOAD is set by default when a new user session is started. It remains set until NOUNLOAD is specified. This option is used only for tape devices.

MEDIAPASSWORD = { *mediapassword* | @*mediapassword_variable* }

Is the password for the media set. MEDIAPASSWORD is a character string.

If a password was provided when the media set was formatted, that password must be supplied to create a backup set on that media set. In addition, that media password also must be supplied to perform any restore operation from the media set.

Result Sets

The result set from RESTORE LABELONLY consists of a single row with this information.

Column name	Data type	Description
MediaName	**nvarchar(128)**	Name of the media.
MediaSetId	**uniqueidentifier**	Unique identification number of the media set. This column is NULL if there is only one media family in the media set.
FamilyCount	**int**	Number of media families in the media set.
FamilySequenceNumber	**int**	Sequence number of this family.
MediaFamilyId	**uniqueidentifier**	Unique identification number for the media family.
MediaSequenceNumber	**int**	Sequence number of this media in the media family.
MediaLabelPresent	**tinyint**	Whether the media description contains: 1 = Microsoft Tape Format media label 0 = Media description
MediaDescription	**nvarchar(255)**	Media description, in free-form text, or the Microsoft Tape Format media label.
SoftwareName	**nvarchar(128)**	Name of the backup software that wrote the label.
SoftwareVendorId	**int**	Unique vendor identification number of the software vendor that wrote the backup.
MediaDate	**datetime**	Date and time the label was written.

Note If passwords are defined for the media set, RESTORE LABELONLY will return information only if the correct media password is specified in the MEDIAPASSWORD option of the command.

Permissions

Any user may use RESTORE LABELONLY.

In addition, the user may specify passwords for a media set, a backup set, or both. When a password is defined on a media set, it is not enough that a user is a member of appropriate fixed server and database roles to perform a backup. The user also must supply the media password to perform these operations. Similarly, restore is not allowed unless the correct media password and backup set password are specified in the restore command.

Defining passwords for backup sets and media sets is an optional feature in the BACKUP statement. The passwords will prevent unauthorized restore operations and unauthorized appends of backup sets to media using SQL Server 2000 tools, but passwords do not prevent overwrite of media with the FORMAT option.

Thus, although the use of passwords can help protect the contents of media from unauthorized access using SQL Server tools, passwords do not protect contents from being destroyed. Passwords do not fully prevent unauthorized access to the contents of the media because the data in the backup sets is not encrypted and could theoretically be examined by programs specifically created for this purpose. For situations where security is crucial, it is important to prevent access to the media by unauthorized individuals.

It is an error to specify a password if none is defined.

Remarks

Executing RESTORE LABELONLY is a quick way to find out what the backup media contains. Because RESTORE LABELONLY reads only the media header, this statement finishes quickly even when using high-capacity tape devices.

Related Topics

Backing Up and Restoring Databases, BACKUP, Data Types, RESTORE, RESTORE FILELISTONLY, RESTORE VERIFYONLY, Understanding Media Sets and Families, Using Identifiers

RESTORE VERIFYONLY

Verifies the backup but does not restore the backup. Checks to see that the backup set is complete and that all volumes are readable. However, RESTORE VERIFYONLY does not attempt to verify the structure of the data contained in the backup volumes. If the backup is valid, Microsoft SQL Server 2000 returns the message: "The backup set is valid."

Syntax

```
RESTORE VERIFYONLY
FROM < backup_device > [ ,...n ]
[ WITH
    [ FILE = file_number ]
    [ [ , ] { NOUNLOAD | UNLOAD } ]
    [ [ , ] LOADHISTORY ]
    [ [ , ] PASSWORD = { password | @password_variable } ]
    [ [ , ] MEDIAPASSWORD = { mediapassword | @mediapassword_variable } ]
    [ [ , ] { NOREWIND | REWIND } ]
]
< backup_device > ::=
    {
        { 'logical_backup_device_name' | @logical_backup_device_name_var }
        | { DISK | TAPE } =
            { 'physical_backup_device_name' | @physical_backup_device_name_var }
    }
```

Arguments

<backup_device>

Specifies the logical or physical backup device(s) to use for the restore. Can be one or more of the following:

{ *'logical_backup_device_name'* | *@logical_backup_device_name_var*}

Is the logical name, which must follow the rules for identifiers, of the backup device(s) created by **sp_addumpdevice** from which the database is restored. If supplied as a variable (*@logical_backup_device_name_var*), the backup device name can be specified either as a string constant (*@logical_backup_device_name_var* = '*logical_backup_device_name*') or as a variable of character string data type, except for the **ntext** or **text** data types.

{DISK | TAPE } =
: *'physical_backup_device_name'* | *@physical_backup_device_name_var*

Allows backups to be restored from the named disk or tape device. The device types of disk and tape should be specified with the actual name (for example, complete path and file name) of the device: DISK = 'C:\Program Files\ Microsoft SQL Server\MSSQL\BACKUP\Mybackup.dat' or TAPE = '\\.\TAPE0'. If specified as a variable (*@physical_backup_device_name_var*), the device name can be specified either as a string constant (*@physical_backup_device_name_var* = '*physical_backup_device_name*') or as a variable of character string data type, except for the **ntext** or **text** data types.

If using either a network server with a UNC name or a redirected drive letter, specify a device type of disk.

n
: Is a placeholder indicating that multiple backup devices and logical backup devices may be specified. The maximum number of backup devices or logical backup devices in a single RESTORE VERIFYONLY statement is 64.

  Note   In order to specify multiple backup devices for <backup_device>, all backup devices specified must be part of the same media set.

FILE = *file_number*
: Identifies the backup set to be restored or processed. For example, a *file_number* of 1 indicates the first backup set and a *file_number* of 2 indicates the second backup set. If no *file_number* is supplied, the first backup set on the specified <backup_device> is assumed.

NOUNLOAD
: Specifies that the tape is not unloaded automatically from the tape drive after a restore. NOUNLOAD remains set until UNLOAD is specified. This option is used only for tape devices. If a nontape device is being used for the restore, this option is ignored.

UNLOAD
: Specifies that the tape is automatically rewound and unloaded when the RESTORE is finished. UNLOAD is set by default when a new user session is started. It remains set until NOUNLOAD is specified. This option is used only for tape devices. If a nontape device is being used for the RESTORE, this option is ignored.

LOADHISTORY
: Specifies that the restore operation loads the information into the **msdb** history tables. The LOADHISTORY option loads information, for the single backup set being verified, about SQL Server backups stored on the media set to the backup and restore history tables in the **msdb** database. No information for non-SQL Server backups is loaded into these history tables. For more information about history tables, see System Tables.

PASSWORD = { *password* | *@password_variable* }

Is the password for the backup set. PASSWORD is a character string. If a password was provided when the backup set was created, the password must be supplied to perform any restore operation from the backup set.

For more information about using passwords, see Permissions.

MEDIAPASSWORD = { *mediapassword* | *@mediapassword_variable* }

Is the password for the media set. MEDIAPASSWORD is a character string data type, with a default of NULL.

If a password was provided when the media set was formatted, that password must be supplied to create a backup set on that media set. In addition, that media password also must be supplied to perform any restore operation from the media set.

NOREWIND

Specifies that SQL Server will keep the tape open after the backup operation. NOREWIND implies NOUNLOAD.

REWIND

Specifies that SQL Server will release and rewind the tape. If neither NOREWIND nor REWIND is specified, REWIND is the default.

Permissions

Any user may use RESTORE VERIFYONLY.

In addition, the user may specify passwords for a media set, a backup set, or both. When a password is defined on a media set, it is not enough that a user is a member of appropriate fixed server and database roles to perform a backup. The user also must supply the media password to perform these operations. Similarly, restore is not allowed unless the correct media password and backup set password are specified in the restore command.

Defining passwords for backup sets and media sets is an optional feature in the BACKUP statement. The passwords will prevent unauthorized restore operations and unauthorized appends of backup sets to media using SQL Server 2000 tools, but passwords do not prevent overwrite of media with the FORMAT option.

Thus, although the use of passwords can help protect the contents of media from unauthorized access using SQL Server tools, passwords do not protect contents from being destroyed. Passwords do not fully prevent unauthorized access to the contents of the media because the data in the backup sets is not encrypted and could theoretically be examined by programs specifically created for this purpose. For situations where security is crucial, it is important to prevent access to the media by unauthorized individuals.

It is an error to specify a password if none is defined.

Related Topics

Backing Up and Restoring Databases, BACKUP, Data Types, RESTORE, RESTORE FILELISTONLY, RESTORE HEADERONLY, RESTORE LABELONLY, System Tables, Understanding Media Sets and Families, Using Identifiers

RETURN

Exits unconditionally from a query or procedure. RETURN is immediate and complete and can be used at any point to exit from a procedure, batch, or statement block. Statements following RETURN are not executed.

Syntax

```
RETURN [ integer_expression ]
```

Arguments

integer_expression
Is the integer value returned. Stored procedures can return an integer value to a calling procedure or an application.

Return Types

Optionally returns **int**.

> **Note** Unless documented otherwise, all system stored procedures return a value of 0, which indicates success; a nonzero value indicates failure.

Remarks

When used with a stored procedure, RETURN cannot return a null value. If a procedure attempts to return a null value (for example, using RETURN **@status** and **@status** is NULL), a warning message is generated and a value of 0 is returned.

The return status value can be included in subsequent Transact-SQL statements in the batch or procedure that executed the current procedure, but it must be entered in the following form:

```
EXECUTE @return_status = procedure_name
```

> **Note** Whether Microsoft SQL Server 2000 interprets an empty string (NULL) as either a single space or as a true empty string is controlled by the compatibility level setting. If the compatibility level is less than or equal to 65, SQL Server interprets empty strings as single spaces. If the compatibility level is equal to 70, SQL Server interprets empty strings as empty strings. For more information, see sp_dbcmptlevel.

Examples

A. Return from a procedure

This example shows if no username is given as a parameter when **findjobs** is executed, RETURN causes the procedure to exit after a message has been sent to the user's screen. If a username is given, the names of all objects created by this user in the current database are retrieved from the appropriate system tables.

```
CREATE PROCEDURE findjobs @nm sysname = NULL
AS
IF @nm IS NULL
   BEGIN
      PRINT 'You must give a username'
      RETURN
   END
ELSE
   BEGIN
      SELECT o.name, o.id, o.uid
      FROM sysobjects o INNER JOIN master..syslogins l
         ON o.uid = l.sid
      WHERE l.name = @nm
   END
```

B. Return status codes

This example checks the state for the specified author's ID. If the state is California (CA), a status of 1 is returned. Otherwise, 2 is returned for any other condition (a value other than CA for **state** or an **au_id** that did not match a row).

```
CREATE PROCEDURE checkstate @param varchar(11)
AS
IF (SELECT state FROM authors WHERE au_id = @param) = 'CA'
   RETURN 1
ELSE
   RETURN 2
```

The following examples show the return status from the execution of **checkstate**. The first shows an author in California; the second, an author not in California; and the third, an invalid author. The **@return_status** local variable must be declared before it can be used.

```
DECLARE @return_status int
EXEC @return_status = checkstate '172-32-1176'
SELECT 'Return Status' = @return_status
GO
```

Here is the result set:

```
Return Status
-------------
1
```

Execute the query again, specifying a different author number.

```
DECLARE @return_status int
EXEC @return_status = checkstate '648-92-1872'
SELECT 'Return Status' = @return_status
GO
```

Here is the result set:

```
Return Status
-------------
2
```

Execute the query again, specifying another author number.

```
DECLARE @return_status int
EXEC @return_status = checkstate '12345678901'
SELECT 'Return Status' = @return_status
GO
```

Here is the result set:

```
Return Status
-------------
2
```

Related Topics

ALTER PROCEDURE, CREATE PROCEDURE, DECLARE @local_variable,
EXECUTE, SET @local_variable

REVERSE

Returns the reverse of a character expression.

Syntax

```
REVERSE ( character_expression )
```

Arguments

character_expression

Is an expression of character data. *character_expression* can be a constant,
variable, or column of either character or binary data.

Return Types
varchar

Remarks

character_expression must be of a data type that is implicitly convertible to **varchar**. Otherwise, use CAST to explicitly convert *character_expression*.

Examples

This example returns all author first names with the characters reversed.

```
USE pubs
GO
SELECT REVERSE(au_fname)
FROM authors
ORDER BY au_fname
GO
```

Here is the result set:

```
--------------------
maharbA
okikA
treblA
nnA
ennA
truB
enelrahC
lyrehC
naeD
kriD
rehtaeH
sennI
nosnhoJ
aiviL
eirojraM
rednaeM
leahciM
lehciM
ratsgninroM
dlanigeR
lyrehS
snraetS
aivlyS
(23 row(s) affected)
```

Related Topics

CAST and CONVERT, Data Types, String Functions

REVOKE

Removes a previously granted or denied permission from a user in the current database.

Syntax

Statement permissions:

```
REVOKE { ALL | statement [ ,...n ] }
FROM security_account [ ,...n ]
```

Object permissions:

```
REVOKE [ GRANT OPTION FOR ]
    { ALL [ PRIVILEGES ] | permission [ ,...n ] }
    {
        [ ( column [ ,...n ] ) ] ON { table | view }
        | ON { table | view } [ ( column [ ,...n ] ) ]
        | ON { stored_procedure | extended_procedure }
        | ON { user_defined_function }
    }
{ TO | FROM }
    security_account [ ,...n ]
[ CASCADE ]
[ AS { group | role } ]
```

Arguments

ALL

Specifies that all applicable permissions are being removed. For statement permissions, ALL can be used only by members of the **sysadmin** fixed server role. For object permissions, ALL can be used by members of the **sysadmin** fixed server and **db_owner** fixed database roles, and database object owners.

statement

Is a granted statement for which permission is being removed. The statement list can include:

- CREATE DATABASE
- CREATE DEFAULT
- CREATE FUNCTION
- CREATE PROCEDURE

- CREATE RULE
- CREATE TABLE
- CREATE VIEW
- BACKUP DATABASE
- BACKUP LOG

n

Is a placeholder indicating the item can be repeated in a comma-separated list.

FROM

Specifies the security account list.

security_account

Is the security account in the current database from which the permissions are being removed. The security account can be:

- Microsoft SQL Server user.
- SQL Server role.
- Microsoft Windows NT user.
- Windows NT group.

Permissions cannot be revoked from the system roles, such as **sysadmin**. When permissions are revoked from an SQL Server or Windows NT user account, the specified *security_account* is the only account affected by the permissions.

If permissions are revoked from an SQL Server role or a Windows NT group, the permissions affect all users in the current database who are members of the group or role, unless the user has already been explicitly granted or denied a permission.

There are two special security accounts that can be used with REVOKE. Permissions revoked from the **public** role are applied to all users in the database. Permissions revoked from the **guest** user are used by all users who do not have a user account in the database.

When revoking permissions to a Windows NT local or global group, specify the domain or computer name the group is defined on, followed by a backslash, then the group name, for example **London\JoeB**. However, to revoke permissions to a Windows NT built-in local group, specify BUILTIN instead of the domain or computer name, for example **BUILTIN\Users**.

GRANT OPTION FOR

Specifies that WITH GRANT OPTION permissions are being removed. Use the GRANT OPTION FOR keywords with REVOKE to remove the effects of the WITH GRANT OPTION setting specified in the GRANT statement. The user still has the permissions, but cannot grant the permissions to other users.

If the permissions being revoked were not originally granted using the WITH GRANT OPTION setting, GRANT OPTION FOR is ignored if specified, and permissions are revoked as usual.

If the permissions being revoked were originally granted using the WITH GRANT OPTION setting, specify both the CASCADE and GRANT OPTION FOR clauses; otherwise, an error is returned.

PRIVILEGES

Is an optional keyword that can be included for SQL-92 compliance.

permission

Is an object permission that is being revoked. When permissions are revoked on a table or a view, the permission list can include one or more of these statements: SELECT, INSERT, DELETE, or UPDATE.

Object permissions revoked on a table can also include REFERENCES, and object permissions revoked on a stored procedure or extended stored procedure can be EXECUTE. When permissions are revoked on columns, the permissions list can include SELECT or UPDATE.

column

Is the name of the column in the current database for which permissions are being removed.

table

Is the name of the table in the current database for which permissions are being removed.

view

Is the name of the view in the current database for which permissions are being removed.

stored_procedure

Is the name of the stored procedure in the current database for which permissions are being removed.

extended_procedure

Is the name of an extended stored procedure for which permissions are being removed.

user_defined_function

Is the name of the user-defined function for which permissions are being removed.

TO

Specifies the security account list.

CASCADE

Specifies that permissions are being removed from *security_account* as well as any other security accounts that were granted permissions by *security_account*. Use when revoking a grantable permission.

If the permissions being revoked were originally granted to *security_account* using the WITH GRANT OPTION setting, specify both the CASCADE and GRANT OPTION FOR clauses; otherwise, an error is returned. Specifying both the CASCADE and GRANT OPTION FOR clauses revokes only the permissions granted using the WITH GRANT OPTION setting from *security_account*, as well as any other security accounts that were granted permissions by *security_account.*

AS {*group* | *role*}

Specifies the optional name of the security account in the current database under whose authority the REVOKE statement will be executed. AS is used when permissions on an object are granted to a group or role, and the object permissions need to be revoked from other users. Because only a user, rather than a group or role, can execute a REVOKE statement, a specific member of the group or role revokes permissions from the object under the authority of the group or role.

Remarks

Only use REVOKE with permissions in the current database.

A revoked permission removes the granted or denied permission only at the level revoked (user, group, or role). For example, permission to view the **authors** table is explicitly granted to the **Andrew** user account, which is a member of the **employees** role only. If the **employees** role is revoked access to view the **authors** table, **Andrew** can still view the table because permission has been explicitly granted. **Andrew** is unable to view the **authors** table only if **Andrew** is revoked permission as well. If **Andrew** is never explicitly granted permissions to view **authors**, then revoking permission from the **employees** role prevents **Andrew** from viewing the table.

> **Note** REVOKE removes only previously granted or denied permissions. Scripts from Microsoft SQL Server 6.5 or earlier that use REVOKE may have to be changed to use DENY to maintain behavior.

If a user activates an application role, the effect of REVOKE is null for any objects the user accesses using the application role. Although a user may be revoked access to a specific object in the current database, if the application role has access to the object, the user also has access while the application role is activated.

Use **sp_helprotect** to report the permissions on a database object or user.

Permissions

REVOKE permissions default to members of the **sysadmin** fixed server role, **db_owner** and **db_securityadmin** fixed database roles, and database object owners.

Examples

A. Revoke statement permissions from a user account

This example revokes the CREATE TABLE permissions that have been granted to the users **Joe** and **Corporate\BobJ**. It removes the permissions that allow **Joe** and **Corporate\BobJ** to create a table. However, **Joe** and **Corporate\BobJ** can still create tables if CREATE TABLE permissions have been granted to any roles of which they are members.

```
REVOKE CREATE TABLE FROM Joe, [Corporate\BobJ]
```

B. Revoke multiple permissions from multiple user accounts

This example revokes multiple statement permissions from multiple users.

```
REVOKE CREATE TABLE, CREATE DEFAULT
FROM Mary, John
```

C. Revoke a denied permission

The user **Mary** is a member of the **Budget** role, which has been granted SELECT permissions on the **Budget_Data** table. The DENY statement has been used with **Mary** to prevent access to the **Budget_Data** table through the permissions granted to the **Budget** role.

This example removes the denied permission from **Mary** and, through the SELECT permissions applied to the **Budget** role, allows **Mary** to use the SELECT statement on the table.

```
REVOKE SELECT ON Budget_Data TO Mary
```

Related Topics

Backward Compatibility, Deactivating Established Access by Revoking Permissions, DENY, GRANT, sp_helprotect

RIGHT

Returns the part of a character string starting a specified number of *integer_expression* characters from the right.

Syntax

```
RIGHT ( character_expression , integer_expression )
```

Arguments

character_expression

Is an expression of character data. *character_expression* can be a constant, variable, or column of either character or binary data.

integer_expression

Is the starting position, expressed as a positive whole number. If *integer_expression* is negative, an error is returned.

Return Types

varchar

character_expression must be of a data type that is implicitly convertible to **varchar**. Otherwise, use CAST to explicitly convert *character_expression*.

Remarks

Compatibility levels can affect return values. For more information, see sp_dbcmptlevel.

Examples

This example returns the five rightmost characters of each author's first name.

```
USE pubs
GO
SELECT RIGHT(au_fname, 5)
FROM authors
ORDER BY au_fname
GO
```

Here is the result set:

```
------------------
raham
Akiko
lbert
Ann
Anne
Burt
rlene
heryl
Dean
Dirk
ather
Innes
```

(continued)

(continued)

```
hnson
Livia
jorie
ander
chael
ichel
gstar
inald
heryl
earns
ylvia
(23 row(s) affected)
```

Related Topics

CAST and CONVERT, Data Types, String Functions

ROLLBACK TRANSACTION

Rolls back an explicit or implicit transaction to the beginning of the transaction, or to a savepoint inside a transaction.

Syntax

```
ROLLBACK [ TRAN [ SACTION ]
    [ transaction_name | @tran_name_variable
    | savepoint_name | @savepoint_variable ] ]
```

Arguments

transaction_name
> Is the name assigned to the transaction on BEGIN TRANSACTION. *transaction_name* must conform to the rules for identifiers, but only the first 32 characters of the transaction name are used. When nesting transactions, *transaction_name* must be the name from the outermost BEGIN TRANSACTION statement.

@tran_name_variable
> Is the name of a user-defined variable containing a valid transaction name. The variable must be declared with a **char**, **varchar**, **nchar**, or **nvarchar** data type.

savepoint_name
> Is *savepoint_name* from a SAVE TRANSACTION statement. *savepoint_name* must conform to the rules for identifiers. Use *savepoint_name* when a conditional rollback should affect only part of the transaction.

@savepoint_variable
> Is name of a user-defined variable containing a valid savepoint name. The variable must be declared with a **char**, **varchar**, **nchar**, or **nvarchar** data type.

Remarks

ROLLBACK TRANSACTION erases all data modifications made since the start of the transaction or to a savepoint. It also frees resources held by the transaction.

ROLLBACK TRANSACTION without a *savepoint_name* or *transaction_name* rolls back to the beginning of the transaction. When nesting transactions, this same statement rolls back all inner transactions to the outermost BEGIN TRANSACTION statement. In both cases, ROLLBACK TRANSACTION decrements the @@TRANCOUNT system function to 0. ROLLBACK TRANSACTION *savepoint_name* does not decrement @@TRANCOUNT.

A ROLLBACK TRANSACTION statement specifying a *savepoint_name* does not free any locks.

ROLLBACK TRANSACTION cannot reference a *savepoint_name* in distributed transactions started either explicitly with BEGIN DISTRIBUTED TRANSACTION or escalated from a local transaction.

A transaction cannot be rolled back after a COMMIT TRANSACTION statement is executed.

Within a transaction, duplicate savepoint names are allowed, but a ROLLBACK TRANSACTION using the duplicate savepoint name rolls back only to the most recent SAVE TRANSACTION using that savepoint name.

In stored procedures, ROLLBACK TRANSACTION statements without a *savepoint_name* or *transaction_name* roll back all statements to the outermost BEGIN TRANSACTION. A ROLLBACK TRANSACTION statement in a stored procedure that causes @@TRANCOUNT to have a different value when the trigger completes than the @@TRANCOUNT value when the stored procedure was called produces an informational message. This message does not affect subsequent processing.

If a ROLLBACK TRANSACTION is issued in a trigger:

- All data modifications made to that point in the current transaction are rolled back, including any made by the trigger.

- The trigger continues executing any remaining statements after the ROLLBACK statement. If any of these statements modify data, the modifications are not rolled back. No nested triggers are fired by the execution of these remaining statements.

- The statements in the batch after the statement that fired the trigger are not executed.

@@TRANCOUNT is incremented by one when entering a trigger, even when in autocommit mode. (The system treats a trigger as an implied nested transaction.)

ROLLBACK TRANSACTION statements in stored procedures do not affect subsequent statements in the batch that called the procedure; subsequent statements in the batch are executed. ROLLBACK TRANSACTION statements in triggers terminate the batch containing the statement that fired the trigger; subsequent statements in the batch are not executed.

A ROLLBACK TRANSACTION statement does not produce any messages to the user. If warnings are needed in stored procedures or triggers, use the RAISERROR or PRINT statements. RAISERROR is the preferred statement for indicating errors.

The effect of a ROLLBACK on cursors is defined by these three rules:

1. With CURSOR_CLOSE_ON_COMMIT set ON, ROLLBACK closes but does not deallocate all open cursors.

2. With CURSOR_CLOSE_ON_COMMIT set OFF, ROLLBACK does not affect any open synchronous STATIC or INSENSITIVE cursors or asynchronous STATIC cursors that have been fully populated. Open cursors of any other type are closed but not deallocated.

3. An error that terminates a batch and generates an internal rollback deallocates all cursors that were declared in the batch containing the error statement. All cursors are deallocated regardless of their type or the setting of CURSOR_CLOSE_ON_COMMIT. This includes cursors declared in stored procedures called by the error batch. Cursors declared in a batch before the error batch are subject to rules 1 and 2. A deadlock error is an example of this type of error. A ROLLBACK statement issued in a trigger also automatically generates this type of error.

Permissions

ROLLBACK TRANSACTION permissions default to any valid user.

Related Topics

BEGIN DISTRIBUTED TRANSACTION, BEGIN TRANSACTION, COMMIT TRANSACTION, COMMIT WORK, Cursor Locking, ROLLBACK WORK, SAVE TRANSACTION, Transactions

ROLLBACK WORK

Rolls back a user-specified transaction to the beginning of a transaction.

Syntax

```
ROLLBACK [ WORK ]
```

Remarks

This statement functions identically to ROLLBACK TRANSACTION except that ROLLBACK TRANSACTION accepts a user-defined transaction name. With or without specifying the optional WORK keyword, this ROLLBACK syntax is SQL-92-compatible.

When nesting transactions, ROLLBACK WORK always rolls back to the outermost BEGIN TRANSACTION statement and decrements the @@TRANCOUNT system function to 0.

Permissions

ROLLBACK WORK permissions default to any valid user.

Related Topics

BEGIN DISTRIBUTED TRANSACTION, BEGIN TRANSACTION, COMMIT TRANSACTION, COMMIT WORK, ROLLBACK TRANSACTION, SAVE TRANSACTION, Transactions

ROUND

Returns a numeric expression, rounded to the specified length or precision.

Syntax

```
ROUND ( numeric_expression , length [ , function ] )
```

Arguments

numeric_expression

Is an expression of the exact numeric or approximate numeric data type category, except for the **bit** data type.

length

Is the precision to which *numeric_expression* is to be rounded. *length* must be **tinyint**, **smallint**, or **int**. When *length* is a positive number, *numeric_expression* is rounded to the number of decimal places specified by *length*. When *length* is a negative number, *numeric_expression* is rounded on the left side of the decimal point, as specified by *length*.

function

Is the type of operation to perform. *function* must be **tinyint**, **smallint**, or **int**. When *function* is omitted or has a value of 0 (default), *numeric_expression* is rounded. When a value other than 0 is specified, *numeric_expression* is truncated.

Return Types

Returns the same type as *numeric_expression*.

Remarks

ROUND always returns a value. If *length* is negative and larger than the number of digits before the decimal point, ROUND returns 0.

Example	Result
ROUND(748.58, -4)	0

ROUND returns a rounded *numeric_expression*, regardless of data type, when *length* is a negative number.

Examples	Result
ROUND(748.58, -1)	750.00
ROUND(748.58, -2)	700.00
ROUND(748.58, -3)	1000.00

Examples

A. Use ROUND and estimates

This example shows two expressions illustrating that with the ROUND function the last digit is always an estimate.

```
SELECT ROUND(123.9994, 3), ROUND(123.9995, 3)
GO
```

Here is the result set:

```
------------ -----------
123.9990    124.0000
```

B. Use ROUND and rounding approximations

This example shows rounding and approximations.

Statement	Result
SELECT ROUND(123.4545, 2)	123.4500
SELECT ROUND(123.45, -2)	100.00

C. Use ROUND to truncate

This example uses two SELECT statements to demonstrate the difference between rounding and truncation. The first statement rounds the result. The second statement truncates the result.

Statement	Result
SELECT ROUND(150.75, 0)	151.00
SELECT ROUND(150.75, 0, 1)	150.00

Related Topics

CEILING, Data Types, Expressions, FLOOR, Mathematical

Functions**ROWCOUNT_BIG**

Returns the number of rows affected by the last statement executed. This function operates like @@ROWCOUNT, except that the return type of ROWCOUNT_BIG is **bigint**.

Syntax

```
ROWCOUNT_BIG ( )
```

Return Types

bigint

Remarks

Following a SELECT statement, this function returns the number of rows returned by the SELECT statement.

Following INSERT, UPDATE, or DELETE statements, this function returns the number of rows affected by the data modification statement.

Following statements that do not return rows, such as an IF statement, this function returns zero (0).

Related Topics

COUNT_BIG, Data Types

RTRIM

Returns a character string after truncating all trailing blanks.

Syntax

```
RTRIM ( character_expression )
```

Arguments

character_expression
> Is an expression of character data. *character_expression* can be a constant, variable, or column of either character or binary data.

Return Types

varchar

Remarks

character_expression must be of a data type that is implicitly convertible to **varchar**. Otherwise, use the CAST function to explicitly convert *character_expression*.

> **Note** Compatibility levels can affect return values. For more information, see sp_dbcmptlevel.

Examples

This example demonstrates how to use RTRIM to remove trailing spaces from a character variable.

```
DECLARE @string_to_trim varchar(60)
SET @string_to_trim = 'Four spaces are after the period in this sentence.    '
SELECT 'Here is the string without the leading spaces: ' + CHAR(13) +
    RTRIM(@string_to_trim)
GO
```

Here is the result set:

```
(1 row(s) affected)
------------------------------------------------------------------------
Here is the string without the leading spaces: Four spaces are after the period in this
sentence.
(1 row(s) affected)
```

Related Topics

CAST and CONVERT, Data Types, String Functions

SAVE TRANSACTION

Sets a savepoint within a transaction.

Syntax

```
SAVE TRAN [ SACTION ] { savepoint_name | @savepoint_variable }
```

Arguments

savepoint_name

Is the name assigned to the savepoint. Savepoint names must conform to the rules for identifiers, but only the first 32 characters are used.

@savepoint_variable

Is the name of a user-defined variable containing a valid savepoint name. The variable must be declared with a **char**, **varchar**, **nchar**, **or nvarchar** data type.

Remarks

A user can set a savepoint, or marker, within a transaction. The savepoint defines a location to which a transaction can return if part of the transaction is conditionally canceled. If a transaction is rolled back to a savepoint, it must proceed to completion (with more Transact-SQL statements if needed and a COMMIT TRANSACTION statement), or it must be canceled altogether (by rolling the transaction back to its beginning). To cancel an entire transaction, use the form ROLLBACK TRANSACTION *transaction_name*. All the statements or procedures of the transaction are undone.

SAVE TRANSACTION is not supported in distributed transactions started either explicitly with BEGIN DISTRIBUTED TRANSACTION or escalated from a local transaction.

Important When a transaction begins, resources used during the transaction are held until the completion of the transaction (namely locks). When part of a transaction is rolled back to a savepoint, resources continue to be held until the completion of the transaction (or a rollback of the complete transaction).

Permissions

SAVE TRANSACTION permissions default to any valid user.

Examples

This example changes the royalty split for the two authors of *The Gourmet Microwave*. Because the database would be inconsistent between the two updates, they must be grouped into a user-defined transaction.

```
BEGIN TRANSACTION royaltychange
   UPDATE titleauthor
      SET royaltyper = 65
         FROM titleauthor, titles
            WHERE royaltyper = 75
               AND titleauthor.title_id = titles.title_id
               AND title = 'The Gourmet Microwave'
   UPDATE titleauthor
      SET royaltyper = 35
         FROM titleauthor, titles
            WHERE royaltyper = 25
               AND titleauthor.title_id = titles.title_id
               AND title = 'The Gourmet Microwave'
SAVE TRANSACTION percentchanged

/*
After having updated the royaltyper entries for the two authors, the
user inserts the savepoint percentchanged, and then determines how a
10-percent increase in the book's price would affect the authors' royalty earnings.
*/

UPDATE titles
   SET price = price * 1.1
      WHERE title = 'The Gourmet Microwave'
SELECT (price * royalty * ytd_sales) * royaltyper
   FROM titles, titleauthor
      WHERE title = 'The Gourmet Microwave'
         AND titles.title_id = titleauthor.title_id
/*
```

(continued)

(continued)

```
The transaction is rolled back to the savepoint
with the ROLLBACK TRANSACTION statement.
*/


ROLLBACK TRANSACTION percentchanged
COMMIT TRANSACTION


/* End of royaltychange. */
```

Related Topics

Batches, BEGIN TRANSACTION, COMMIT TRANSACTION, COMMIT WORK,
CREATE PROCEDURE, CREATE TRIGGER, DELETE, INSERT, ROLLBACK
TRANSACTION, ROLLBACK WORK, SELECT, Transaction Savepoints, UPDATE

SCOPE_IDENTITY

Returns the last IDENTITY value inserted into an IDENTITY column in the same
scope. A scope is a module—a stored procedure, trigger, function, or batch. Thus, two
statements are in the same scope if they are in the same stored procedure, function, or
batch.

Syntax

```
SCOPE_IDENTITY( )
```

Return Types

sql_variant

Remarks

SCOPE_IDENTITY, IDENT_CURRENT, and @@IDENTITY are similar functions
in that they return values inserted into IDENTITY columns.

IDENT_CURRENT is not limited by scope and session; it is limited to a specified
table. IDENT_CURRENT returns the value generated for a specific table in any
session and any scope. For more information, see IDENT_CURRENT.

SCOPE_IDENTITY and @@IDENTITY will return last identity values generated in
any table in the current session. However, SCOPE_IDENTITY returns values inserted
only within the current scope; @@IDENTITY is not limited to a specific scope.

For example, you have two tables, T1 and T2, and an INSERT trigger defined on T1.
When a row is inserted to T1, the trigger fires and inserts a row in T2. This scenario
illustrates two scopes: the insert on T1, and the insert on T2 as a result of the trigger.

Assuming that both T1 and T2 have IDENTITY columns, @@IDENTITY and SCOPE_IDENTITY will return different values at the end of an INSERT statement on T1.

@@IDENTITY will return the last IDENTITY column value inserted across any scope in the current session, which is the value inserted in T2.

SCOPE_IDENTITY() will return the IDENTITY value inserted in T1, which was the last INSERT that occurred in the same scope. The SCOPE_IDENTITY() function will return the NULL value if the function is invoked before any insert statements into an identity column occur in the scope.

See Examples for an illustration.

Examples

This example creates two tables, **TZ** and **TY**, and an INSERT trigger on **TZ**. When a row is inserted to table **TZ**, the trigger (**Ztrig**) fires and inserts a row in **TY**.

```
USE tempdb
GO
CREATE TABLE TZ (
   Z_id  int IDENTITY(1,1)PRIMARY KEY,
   Z_name varchar(20) NOT NULL)

INSERT TZ
   VALUES ('Lisa')
INSERT TZ
   VALUES ('Mike')
INSERT TZ
   VALUES ('Carla')

SELECT * FROM TZ

--Result set: This is how table TZ looks
Z_id   Z_name
-------------
1      Lisa
2      Mike
3      Carla

CREATE TABLE TY (
   Y_id  int IDENTITY(100,5)PRIMARY KEY,
   Y_name varchar(20) NULL)
```

(continued)

(continued)

```
INSERT TY (Y_name)
   VALUES ('boathouse')
INSERT TY (Y_name)
   VALUES ('rocks')
INSERT TY (Y_name)
   VALUES ('elevator')

SELECT * FROM TY
--Result set: This is how TY looks:
Y_id  Y_name
---------------
100   boathouse
105   rocks
110   elevator

/*Create the trigger that inserts a row in table TY
when a row is inserted in table TZ*/
CREATE TRIGGER Ztrig
ON TZ
FOR INSERT AS
   BEGIN
   INSERT TY VALUES ('')
   END

/*FIRE the trigger and find out what identity values you get
with the @@IDENTITY and SCOPE_IDENTITY functions*/
INSERT TZ VALUES ('Rosalie')

SELECT SCOPE_IDENTITY() AS [SCOPE_IDENTITY]
GO
SELECT@@IDENTITY AS [@@IDENTITY]
GO

--Here is the result set.
SCOPE_IDENTITY
4
/*SCOPE_IDENTITY returned the last identity value in the same scope, which was the insert
on table TZ*/

@@IDENTITY
115
/*@@IDENTITY returned the last identity value inserted to TY by the trigger, which fired
due to an earlier insert on TZ*/
```

Related Topics

@@IDENTITY

Search Condition

Is a combination of one or more predicates using the logical operators AND, OR, and NOT.

Syntax

```
< search_condition > ::=
    {  [ NOT ] < predicate > | ( < search_condition > ) }
       [ { AND | OR } [ NOT ] { < predicate > | ( < search_condition > ) } ]
    } [ ,...n ]
< predicate > ::=
    {  expression { = | < > | ! = | > | > = | ! > | < | < = | ! < } expression
     | string_expression [ NOT ] LIKE string_expression
        [ ESCAPE 'escape_character' ]
     | expression [ NOT ] BETWEEN expression AND expression
     | expression IS [ NOT ] NULL
     | CONTAINS
        ( { column | * } , '< contains_search_condition >' )
     | FREETEXT ( { column | * } , 'freetext_string' )
     | expression [ NOT ] IN ( subquery | expression [ ,...n ] )
     | expression { = | < > | ! = | > | > = | ! > | < | < = | ! < }
        { ALL | SOME | ANY} ( subquery )
     | EXISTS ( subquery )
    }
```

Arguments

< search_condition >

Specifies the conditions for the rows returned in the result set for a SELECT statement, query expression, or subquery. For an UPDATE statement, specifies the rows to be updated. For a DELETE statement, specifies the rows to be deleted. There is no limit to the number of predicates that can be included in a Transact-SQL statement search condition.

NOT

Negates the Boolean expression specified by the predicate. For more information, see NOT.

AND

Combines two conditions and evaluates to TRUE when both of the conditions are TRUE. For more information, see AND.

OR

> Combines two conditions and evaluates to TRUE when either condition is TRUE. For more information, see OR.

< predicate >

> Is an expression that returns TRUE, FALSE, or UNKNOWN.

expression

> Is a column name, a constant, a function, a variable, a scalar subquery, or any combination of column names, constants, and functions connected by an operator(s) or a subquery. The expression can also contain the CASE function.

=

> Is the operator used to test the equality between two expressions.

<>

> Is the operator used to test the condition of two expressions not being equal to each other.

!=

> Is the operator used to test the condition of two expressions not being equal to each other.

>

> Is the operator used to test the condition of one expression being greater than the other.

>=

> Is the operator used to test the condition of one expression being greater than or equal to the other expression.

!>

> Is the operator used to test the condition of one expression not being greater than the other expression.

<

> Is the operator used to test the condition of one expression being less than the other.

<=

> Is the operator used to test the condition of one expression being less than or equal to the other expression.

!<

> Is the operator used to test the condition of one expression not being less than the other expression.

string_expression

> Is a string of characters and wildcard characters.

[NOT] LIKE
Indicates that the subsequent character string is to be used with pattern matching. For more information, see LIKE.

ESCAPE *'escape_character'*
Allows a wildcard character to be searched for in a character string instead of functioning as a wildcard. *escape_character* is the character that is placed in front of the wildcard character to denote this special use.

[NOT] BETWEEN
Specifies an inclusive range of values. Use AND to separate the beginning and ending values. For more information, see BETWEEN.

IS [NOT] NULL
Specifies a search for null values, or for values that are not null, depending on the keywords used. An expression with a bitwise or arithmetic operator evaluates to NULL if any of the operands is NULL.

CONTAINS
Searches columns containing character-based data for precise or "fuzzy" (less precise) matches to single words and phrases, the proximity of words within a certain distance of one another, and weighted matches. Can only be used with SELECT statements. For more information, see CONTAINS.

FREETEXT
Provides a simple form of natural language query by searching columns containing character-based data for values that match the meaning rather than the exact words in the predicate. Can only be used with SELECT statements. For more information, see FREETEXT.

[NOT] IN
Specifies the search for an expression, based on the expression's inclusion in or exclusion from a list. The search expression can be a constant or a column name, and the list can be a set of constants or, more commonly, a subquery. Enclose the list of values in parentheses. For more information, see IN.

subquery
Can be considered a restricted SELECT statement and is similar to <query_expresssion> in the SELECT statement. The ORDER BY clause, the COMPUTE clause, and the INTO keyword are not allowed. For more information, see SELECT.

ALL
Used with a comparison operator and a subquery. Returns TRUE for <predicate> if all values retrieved for the subquery satisfy the comparison operation, or FALSE if not all values satisfy the comparison or if the subquery returns no rows to the outer statement. For more information, see ALL.

{ SOME | ANY }

Used with a comparison operator and a subquery. Returns TRUE for
<predicate> if any value retrieved for the subquery satisfies the comparison
operation, or FALSE if no values in the subquery satisfy the comparison or if
the subquery returns no rows to the outer statement. Otherwise, the expression
is unknown. For more information, see SOME | ANY.

EXISTS

Used with a subquery to test for the existence of rows returned by the subquery.
For more information, see EXISTS.

Remarks

The order of precedence for the logical operators is NOT (highest), followed by AND,
followed by OR. The order of evaluation at the same precedence level is from left to
right. Parentheses can be used to override this order in a search condition. For more
information about how the logical operators operate on truth values, see AND, OR,
and NOT.

Examples

A. Use WHERE with LIKE and ESCAPE syntax

This example assumes a **description** column exists in **finances** table. To search for the
rows in which the **description** column contains the exact characters g_, use the
ESCAPE option because _ is a wildcard character. Without specifying the ESCAPE
option, the query would search for any description values containing the letter g
followed by any single character other than the _ character.

```
SELECT *
FROM finances
WHERE description LIKE 'gs_' ESCAPE 'S'
GO
```

B. Use WHERE and LIKE syntax with Unicode data

This example uses the WHERE clause to retrieve the contact name, telephone, and
fax numbers for any companies containing the string snabbköp at the end of the
company name.

```
USE Northwind
SELECT CompanyName, ContactName, Phone, Fax
FROM Customers
WHERE CompanyName LIKE N'%snabbköp'
ORDER BY CompanyName ASC, ContactName ASC
```

Related Topics

Aggregate Functions, CASE, CONTAINSTABLE, Cursors, DELETE, Expressions, FREETEXTTABLE, FROM, Full-text Querying SQL Server Data, Operators (Logical), UPDATE

SELECT @local_variable

Specifies that the given local variable (created using DECLARE @*local_variable*) should be set to the specified expression.

It is recommended that SET @*local_variable* be used for variable assignment rather than SELECT @*local_variable*. For more information, see SET @local_variable.

Syntax

```
SELECT { @local_variable = expression } [ ,...n ]
```

Arguments

@*local_variable*
>   Is a declared variable for which a value is to be assigned.

expression
>   Is any valid Microsoft SQL Server expression, including a scalar subquery.

Remarks

SELECT @*local_variable* is usually used to return a single value into the variable. It can return multiple values if, for example, *expression* is the name of a column. If the SELECT statement returns more than one value, the variable is assigned the last value returned.

If the SELECT statement returns no rows, the variable retains its present value.
If *expression* is a scalar subquery that returns no value, the variable is set to NULL.

In the first example, a variable **@var1** is assigned Generic Name as its value.
The query against the **Customers** table returns no rows because the value specified for **CustomerID** does not exist in the table. The variable retains the Generic Name value.

```
USE Northwind
DECLARE @var1 nvarchar(30)
SELECT @var1 = 'Generic Name'

SELECT @var1 = CompanyName
FROM Customers
WHERE CustomerID = 'ALFKA'

SELECT @var1 AS 'Company Name'
```

This is the result:

```
Company Name
-------------------------------------------
Generic Name
```

In this example, a subquery is used to assign a value to **@var1**. Because the value requested for **CustomerID** does not exist, the subquery returns no value and the variable is set to NULL.

```
USE Northwind
DECLARE @var1 nvarchar(30)
SELECT @var1 = 'Generic Name'

SELECT @var1 =
   (SELECT CompanyName
   FROM Customers
   WHERE CustomerID = 'ALFKA')

SELECT @var1 AS 'Company Name'
```

This is the result:

```
Company Name
----------------------------
NULL
```

One SELECT statement can initialize multiple local variables.

Note A SELECT statement that contains a variable assignment cannot also be used to perform normal result set retrieval operations.

Related Topics

DECLARE @local_variable, Expressions, SELECT

SELECT

Retrieves rows from the database and allows the selection of one or many rows or columns from one or many tables. The full syntax of the SELECT statement is complex, but the main clauses can be summarized as:

```
SELECT select_list
[ INTO new_table ]
FROM table_source
[ WHERE search_condition ]
[ GROUP BY group_by_expression ]
[ HAVING search_condition ]
[ ORDER BY order_expression [ ASC | DESC ] ]
```

The UNION operator can be used between queries to combine their results into a single result set.

Syntax

```
SELECT statement ::=
   < query_expression >
   [ ORDER BY { order_by_expression | column_position [ ASC | DESC ] }
      [ ,...n ]]
   [ COMPUTE
      { { AVG | COUNT | MAX | MIN | SUM } ( expression ) } [ ,...n ]
      [ BY expression [ ,...n ] ]
   ]
   [ FOR { BROWSE | XML { RAW | AUTO | EXPLICIT }
         [ , XMLDATA ]
         [ , ELEMENTS ]
         [ , BINARY base64 ]
      }
]
   [ OPTION ( < query_hint > [ ,...n ]) ]
< query expression > ::=
   { < query specification > | ( < query expression > ) }
   [ UNION [ ALL ] < query specification | ( < query expression > ) [...n ] ]
< query specification > ::=
   SELECT [ ALL | DISTINCT ]
      [ { TOP integer | TOP integer PERCENT } [ WITH TIES ] ]
      < select_list >
   [ INTO new_table ]
   [ FROM { < table_source > } [ ,...n ] ]
   [ WHERE < search_condition > ]
   [ GROUP BY [ ALL ] group_by_expression [ ,...n ]
      [ WITH { CUBE | ROLLUP } ]
   ]
   [ HAVING < search_condition > ]
```

Because of the complexity of the SELECT statement, detailed syntax elements and arguments are shown by clause:

SELECT Clause
INTO Clause
FROM Clause
WHERE Clause
GROUP BY Clause
HAVING Clause

UNION Operator
ORDER BY Clause
COMPUTE Clause
FOR Clause
OPTION Clause

SELECT Clause

Specifies the columns to be returned by the query.

Syntax

```
SELECT [ ALL | DISTINCT ]
    [ TOP n [ PERCENT ] [ WITH TIES ] ]
    < select_list >
< select_list > ::=
    {  *
        | { table_name | view_name | table_alias }.*
        | { column_name | expression | IDENTITYCOL | ROWGUIDCOL }
            [ [ AS ] column_alias ]
        | column_alias = expression
    } [ ,...n ]
```

Arguments

ALL

Specifies that duplicate rows can appear in the result set. ALL is the default.

DISTINCT

Specifies that only unique rows can appear in the result set. Null values are considered equal for the purposes of the DISTINCT keyword.

TOP *n* [PERCENT]

Specifies that only the first n rows are to be output from the query result set. n is an integer between 0 and 4294967295. If PERCENT is also specified, only the first n percent of the rows are output from the result set. When specified with PERCENT, n must be an integer between 0 and 100.

If the query includes an ORDER BY clause, the first n rows (or n percent of rows) ordered by the ORDER BY clause are output. If the query has no ORDER BY clause, the order of the rows is arbitrary.

WITH TIES

Specifies that additional rows be returned from the base result set with the same value in the ORDER BY columns appearing as the last of the TOP n (PERCENT) rows. TOP ...WITH TIES can only be specified if an ORDER BY clause is specified.

< select_list >

The columns to be selected for the result set. The select list is a series of expressions separated by commas.

*

Specifies that all columns from all tables and views in the FROM clause should be returned. The columns are returned by table or view, as specified in the FROM clause, and in the order in which they exist in the table or view.

table_name | view_name | table_alias.*

Limits the scope of the * to the specified table or view.

column_name

Is the name of a column to return. Qualify *column_name* to prevent an ambiguous reference, such as occurs when two tables in the FROM clause have columns with duplicate names. For example, the **Customers** and **Orders** tables in the **Northwind** database both have a column named **ColumnID**. If the two tables are joined in a query, the customer ID can be specified in the select list as **Customers.CustomerID**.

expression

Is a column name, constant, function, any combination of column names, constants, and functions connected by an operator(s), or a subquery.

IDENTITYCOL

Returns the identity column. For more information, see IDENTITY (Property), ALTER TABLE, and CREATE TABLE.

If the more than one table in the FROM clause has a column with the IDENTITY property, IDENTITYCOL must be qualified with the specific table name, such as **T1.IDENTITYCOL**.

ROWGUIDCOL

Returns the row global unique identifier column.

If the more than one table in the FROM clause with the ROWGUIDCOL property, ROWGUIDCOL must be qualified with the specific table name, such as **T1.ROWGUIDCOL**.

column_alias

Is an alternative name to replace the column name in the query result set. For example, an alias such as "Quantity", or "Quantity to Date", or "Qty" can be specified for a column named **quantity**.

Aliases are used also to specify names for the results of expressions, for example:

```
USE Northwind
SELECT AVG(UnitPrice) AS 'Average Price'
FROM [Order Details]
```

column_alias can be used in an ORDER BY clause. However, it cannot be used in a WHERE, GROUP BY, or HAVING clause. If the query expression is part of a DECLARE CURSOR statement, *column_alias* cannot be used in the FOR UPDATE clause.

INTO Clause

Creates a new table and inserts the resulting rows from the query into it.

The user executing a SELECT statement with the INTO clause must have CREATE TABLE permission in the destination database. SELECT...INTO cannot be used with the COMPUTE. For more information, see Transactions and Explicit Transactions.

You can use SELECT...INTO to create an identical table definition (different table name) with no data by having a FALSE condition in the WHERE clause.

Syntax

```
[ INTO new_table ]
```

Arguments

new_table

Specifies the name of a new table to be created, based on the columns in the select list and the rows chosen by the WHERE clause. The format of *new_table* is determined by evaluating the expressions in the select list. The columns in *new_table* are created in the order specified by the select list. Each column in *new_table* has the same name, data type, and value as the corresponding expression in the select list.

When a computed column is included in the select list, the corresponding column in the new table is not a computed column. The values in the new column are the values that were computed at the time SELECT...INTO was executed.

In this release of SQL Server, the **select into/bulkcopy** database option has no effect on whether you can create a permanent table with SELECT INTO. The amount of logging for certain bulk operations, including SELECT INTO, depends on the recovery model in effect for the database. For more information, see Using Recovery Models.

In previous releases, creating a permanent table with SELECT INTO was allowed only if **select into/bulkcopy** was set.

select into/bulkcopy is available for backward compatibility purposes, but may not be supported in future releases. Refer to the Recovery Models and Backward Compatibility and ALTER DATABASE topics for more information.

FROM Clause

Specifies the table(s) from which to retrieve rows. The FROM clause is required except when the select list contains only constants, variables, and arithmetic expressions (no column names). For more information, see FROM.

Syntax

```
[ FROM { < table_source > } [ ,...n ] ]

< table_source > ::=
    table_name [ [ AS ] table_alias ] [ WITH ( < table_hint > [ ,...n ] ) ]
    | view_name [ [ AS ] table_alias ]
    | rowset_function [ [ AS ] table_alias ]
    | OPENXML
    | derived_table [ AS ] table_alias [ ( column_alias [ ,...n ] ) ]
    | < joined_table >
< joined_table > ::=
    < table_source > < join_type > < table_source > ON < search_condition >
    | < table_source > CROSS JOIN < table_source >
    | < joined_table >
< join_type > ::=
    [ INNER | { { LEFT | RIGHT | FULL } [ OUTER ] } ]
    [ < join_hint > ]
    JOIN
```

Arguments

< table_source >

Specifies tables, views, derived tables, and joined tables for the SELECT
statement.

table_name [[AS] *table_alias*]

Specifies the name of a table and an optional alias.

view_name [[AS] *table_alias*]

Specifies the name, a view, and an optional alias.

rowset_function [[AS] *table_alias*]

Is the name of a rowset function and an optional alias. For more information
about a list of rowset functions, see Rowset Functions.

OPENXML

Provides rowset view over an XML document. For more information see
OPENXML

WITH (< table_hint > [,...n])

Specifies one or more table hints. For more information about table hints,
see FROM.

derived_table [[AS] *table_alias*]

Is a nested SELECT statement, retrieving rows from the specified database and
table(s).

column_alias

Is an optional alias to replace a column name in the result set.

< joined_table >

Is a result set that is the product of two or more tables. For example:

```
SELECT *
FROM tab1 LEFT OUTER JOIN tab2 ON tab1.c3 = tab2.c3
    RIGHT OUTER JOIN tab3 LEFT OUTER JOIN tab4
        ON tab3.c1 = tab4.c1
        ON tab2.c3 = tab4.c3
```

For multiple CROSS joins, use parentheses to change the natural order of the joins.

< join_type >

Specifies the type of join operation.

INNER

Specifies that all matching pairs of rows are returned. Discards unmatched rows from both tables. This is the default if no join type is specified.

LEFT [OUTER]

Specifies that all rows from the left table not meeting the specified condition are included in the result set in addition to all rows returned by the inner join. Output columns from the left table are set to NULL.

RIGHT [OUTER]

Specifies that all rows from the right table not meeting the specified condition are included in the result set in addition to all rows returned by the inner join. Output columns from the right table are set to NULL.

FULL [OUTER]

If a row from either the left or right table does not match the selection criteria, specifies the row be included in the result set, and output columns that correspond to the other table be set to NULL. This is in addition to all rows usually returned by the inner join.

< join_hint >

Specifies a join hint or execution algorithm. If <join_hint> is specified, INNER, LEFT, RIGHT, or FULL must also be explicitly specified. For more information about join hints, see FROM.

JOIN

Indicates that the specified tables or views should be joined.

ON < search_condition >

Specifies the condition on which the join is based. The condition can specify any predicate, although columns and comparison operators are often used. For example:

```
SELECT ProductID, Suppliers.SupplierID
    FROM Suppliers JOIN Products
    ON (Suppliers.SupplierID = Products.SupplierID)
```

When the condition specifies columns, the columns do not have to have the same name or same data type. However, if the data types are not identical, they must be either compatible or types that Microsoft SQL Server can implicitly convert. If the data types cannot be implicitly converted, the condition must explicitly convert the data type using the CAST function.

For more information about search conditions and predicates, see Search Condition.

CROSS JOIN

Specifies the cross-product of two tables. Returns the same rows as if the tables to be joined were simply listed in the FROM clause and no WHERE clause was specified. For example, both of these queries return a result set that is a cross join of all the rows in **T1** and **T2**:

```
SELECT * FROM T1, T2
SELECT * FROM T1 CROSS JOIN T2
```

WHERE Clause

Specifies a search condition to restrict the rows returned.

Syntax

```
[ WHERE < search_condition > | < old_outer_join > ]
< old_outer_join > ::=
    column_name { * = | = * } column_name
```

Arguments

< search_condition >

Restricts the rows returned in the result set through the use of predicates. There is no limit to the number of predicates that can be included in a search condition. For more information about search conditions and predicates, see Search Condition.

< old_outer_join >

Specifies an outer join using the nonstandard product-specific syntax and the WHERE clause. The *= operator is used to specify a left outer join and the =* operator is used to specify a right outer join.

This example specifies a left outer join in which the rows from **Tab1,** that do not meet the specified condition, are included in the result set:

```
SELECT Tab1.name, Tab2.id
FROM Tab1, Tab2
WHERE Tab1.id *=Tab2.id
```

Note   Using this syntax for outer joins is discouraged because of the potential for ambiguous interpretation and because it is nonstandard. Instead, specify joins in the FROM clause.

It is possible to specify outer joins by using join operators in the FROM clause or by using the non-standard *= and =* operators in the WHERE clause. The two methods cannot both be used in the same statement.

GROUP BY Clause

Specifies the groups into which output rows are to be placed and, if aggregate functions are included in the SELECT clause <select list>, calculates a summary value for each group. When GROUP BY is specified, either each column in any non-aggregate expression in the select list should be included in the GROUP BY list, or the GROUP BY expression must match exactly the select list expression.

Note If the ORDER BY clause is not specified, groups returned using the GROUP BY clause are not in any particular order. It is recommended that you always use the ORDER BY clause to specify a particular ordering of the data.

Syntax

```
[ GROUP BY [ ALL ] group_by_expression [ ,...n ]
    [ WITH { CUBE | ROLLUP } ]
]
```

Arguments

ALL

Includes all groups and result sets, even those that do not have any rows that meet the search condition specified in the WHERE clause. When ALL is specified, null values are returned for the summary columns of groups that do not meet the search condition. You cannot specify ALL with the CUBE or ROLLUP operators.

GROUP BY ALL is not supported in queries that access remote tables if there is also a WHERE clause in the query.

group_by_expression

Is an expression on which grouping is performed. *group_by_expression* is also known as a grouping column. *group_by expression* can be a column or a nonaggregate expression that references a column. A column alias that is defined in the select list cannot be used to specify a grouping column.

Note Columns of type **text**, **ntext**, and **image** cannot be used in *group_by_expression*.

For GROUP BY clauses that do not contain CUBE or ROLLUP, the number of *group_by_expression* items is limited by the GROUP BY column sizes, the aggregated columns, and the aggregate values involved in the query. This limit originates from the limit of 8,060 bytes on the intermediate work table that is needed to hold intermediate query results. A maximum of 10 grouping expressions is permitted when CUBE or ROLLUP is specified.

CUBE

Specifies that in addition to the usual rows provided by GROUP BY, summary rows are introduced into the result set. A GROUP BY summary row is returned for every possible combination of group and subgroup in the result set. A GROUP BY summary row is displayed as NULL in the result, but is used to indicate all values. Use the GROUPING function to determine whether null values in the result set are GROUP BY summary values.

The number of summary rows in the result set is determined by the number of columns included in the GROUP BY clause. Each operand (column) in the GROUP BY clause is bound under the grouping NULL and grouping is applied to all other operands (columns). Because CUBE returns every possible combination of group and subgroup, the number of rows is the same, regardless of the order in which the grouping columns are specified.

ROLLUP

Specifies that in addition to the usual rows provided by GROUP BY, summary rows are introduced into the result set. Groups are summarized in a hierarchical order, from the lowest level in the group to the highest. The group hierarchy is determined by the order in which the grouping columns are specified. Changing the order of the grouping columns can affect the number of rows produced in the result set.

> **Important**   Distinct aggregates, for example, AVG(DISTINCT *column_name*), COUNT(DISTINCT *column_name*), and SUM(DISTINCT *column_name*), are not supported when using CUBE or ROLLUP. If used, SQL Server returns an error message and cancels the query.

HAVING Clause

Specifies a search condition for a group or an aggregate. HAVING is usually used with the GROUP BY clause. When GROUP BY is not used, HAVING behaves like a WHERE clause.

Syntax

```
[ HAVING < search_condition > ]
```

Arguments

< search_condition >

Specifies the search condition for the group or the aggregate to meet. When HAVING is used with GROUP BY ALL, the HAVING clause overrides ALL. For more information, see Search Condition.

The **text**, **image**, and **ntext** data types cannot be used in a HAVING clause.

> **Note**   Using the HAVING clause in the SELECT statement does not affect the way the CUBE operator groups the result set and returns summary aggregate rows.

UNION Operator

Combines the results of two or more queries into a single result set consisting of all the rows belonging to all queries in the union. This is different from using joins that combine columns from two tables.

Two basic rules for combining the result sets of two queries with UNION are:

- The number and the order of the columns must be identical in all queries.
- The data types must be compatible.

Syntax

```
{ < query specification > | ( < query expression > ) }
   UNION [ ALL ]
   < query specification | ( < query expression > )
     [ UNION [ ALL ] < query specification | ( < query expression > )
       [ ...n ] ]
```

Arguments

< query_specification > | (< query_expression >)

Is a query specification or query expression that returns data to be combined with the data from another query specification or query expression. The definitions of the columns that are part of a UNION operation do not have to be identical, but they must be compatible through implicit conversion.

The table shows the rules for comparing the data types and options of corresponding (*ith*) columns.

Data type of *ith* column	Data type of *ith* column of results table
Not data type-compatible (data conversion not handled implicitly by Microsoft SQL Server).	Error returned by SQL Server.
Both fixed-length **char** with lengths L1 and L2.	Fixed-length **char** with length equal to the greater of L1 and L2.
Both fixed-length **binary** with lengths L1 and L2.	Fixed-length **binary** with length equal to the greater of L1 and L2.
Either or both variable-length **char**.	Variable-length **char** with length equal to the maximum of the lengths specified for the *ith* columns.

(continued)

(continued)

Data type of *ith* column	Data type of *ith* column of results table
Either or both variable-length **binary**.	Variable-length **binary** with length equal to the maximum of the lengths specified for the *ith* columns.
Both numeric data types (for example, **smallint**, **int**, **float**, **money**).	Data type equal to the maximum precision of the two columns. For example, if the *ith* column of table A is of type **int** and the *ith* column of table B is of type **float**, then the data type of the *ith* column of the results table is **float** because **float** is more precise than **int**.
Both columns' descriptions specify NOT NULL.	Specifies NOT NULL.

UNION
> Specifies that multiple result sets are to be combined and returned as a single result set.

ALL
> Incorporates all rows into the results, including duplicates. If not specified, duplicate rows are removed.

ORDER BY Clause

Specifies the sort for the result set. The ORDER BY clause is invalid in views, inline functions, derived tables, and subqueries, unless TOP is also specified.

Syntax

```
[ ORDER BY { order_by_expression [ ASC | DESC ] }    [ ,...n] ]
```

Arguments

order_by_expression
> Specifies a column on which to sort. A sort column can be specified as a name or column alias (which can be qualified by the table or view name), an expression, or a nonnegative integer representing the position of the name, alias, or expression in select list.
>
> Multiple sort columns can be specified. The sequence of the sort columns in the ORDER BY clause defines the organization of the sorted result set.
>
> The ORDER BY clause can include items not appearing in the select list. However, if SELECT DISTINCT is specified, or if the SELECT statement contains a UNION operator, the sort columns must appear in the select list.
>
> Furthermore, when the SELECT statement includes a UNION operator, the column names or column aliases must be those specified in the first select list.
>
> **Note** **ntext**, **text**, or **image** columns cannot be used in an ORDER BY clause.

ASC
> Specifies that the values in the specified column should be sorted in ascending order, from lowest value to highest value.

DESC
> Specifies that the values in the specified column should be sorted in descending order, from highest value to lowest value.

Null values are treated as the lowest possible values.

There is no limit to the number of items in the ORDER BY clause. However, there is a limit of 8,060 bytes for the row size of intermediate worktables needed for sort operations. This limits the total size of columns specified in an ORDER BY clause.

COMPUTE Clause

Generates totals that appear as additional summary columns at the end of the result set. When used with BY, the COMPUTE clause generates control-breaks and subtotals in the result set. You can specify COMPUTE BY and COMPUTE in the same query.

Syntax

```
[ COMPUTE
    { { AVG | COUNT | MAX | MIN | STDEV | STDEVP
      | VAR | VARP | SUM }
        ( expression ) } [ ,...n ]
    [ BY expression [ ,...n ] ]
]
```

Arguments

AVG | COUNT | MAX | MIN | STDEV | STDEVP | VAR | VARP | SUM
> Specifies the aggregation to be performed. These row aggregate functions are used with the COMPUTE clause.

Row aggregate function	Result
AVG	Average of the values in the numeric expression
COUNT	Number of selected rows
MAX	Highest value in the expression
MIN	Lowest value in the expression
STDEV	Statistical standard deviation for all values in the expression

(continued)

(continued)

Row aggregate function	Result
STDEVP	Statistical standard deviation for the population for all values in the expression
SUM	Total of the values in the numeric expression
VAR	Statistical variance for all values in the expression
VARP	Statistical variance for the population for all values in the expression

There is no equivalent to COUNT(*). To find the summary information produced by GROUP BY and COUNT(*), use a COMPUTE clause without BY.

These functions ignore null values.

The DISTINCT keyword is not allowed with row aggregate functions when they are specified with the COMPUTE clause.

When you add or average integer data, SQL Server treats the result as an **int** value, even if the data type of the column is **smallint** or **tinyint**. For more information about the return types of added or average data, see SUM and AVG.

> **Note**   To reduce the possibility of overflow errors in ODBC and DB-Library programs, make all variable declarations for the results of averages or sums the data type **int**.

(*expression*)

An expression, such as the name of a column on which the calculation is performed. *expression* must appear in the select list and must be specified exactly the same as one of the expressions in the select list. A column alias specified in the select list cannot be used within *expression*.

> **Note**   **ntext**, **text**, or **image** data types cannot be specified in a COMPUTE or COMPUTE BY clause.

BY *expression*

Generates control-breaks and subtotals in the result set. *expression* is an exact copy of an *order_by_expression* in the associated ORDER BY clause. Typically, this is a column name or column alias. Multiple expressions can be specified. Listing multiple expressions after BY breaks a group into subgroups and applies the aggregate function at each level of grouping.

If you use COMPUTE BY, you must also use an ORDER BY clause. The expressions must be identical to or a subset of those listed after ORDER BY, and must be in the same sequence. For example, if the ORDER BY clause is:

```
ORDER BY a, b, c
```

The COMPUTE clause can be any (or all) of these:

```
COMPUTE BY a, b, c
COMPUTE BY a, b
COMPUTE BY a
```

Note In a SELECT statement with a COMPUTE clause, the order of columns in the select list overrides the order of the aggregate functions in the COMPUTE clause. ODBC and DB-Library programmers must be aware of this order requirement to put the aggregate function results in the correct place.

You cannot use COMPUTE in a SELECT INTO statement because statements including COMPUTE generate tables and their summary results are not stored in the database. Therefore, any calculations produced by COMPUTE do not appear in the new table created with the SELECT INTO statement.

You cannot use the COMPUTE clause when the SELECT statement is part of a DECLARE CURSOR statement.

FOR Clause

FOR clause is used to specify either the BROWSE or the XML option (BROWSE and XML are unrelated options).

Syntax

```
[ FOR { BROWSE | XML { RAW | AUTO | EXPLICIT }
        [ , XMLDATA ]
        [ , ELEMENTS ]
        [ , BINARY BASE64 ]
    }
]
```

Arguments

BROWSE

Specifies that updates be allowed while viewing the data in a DB-Library browse mode cursor. A table can be browsed in an application if the table includes a time-stamped column (defined with the **timestamp** data type), the table has a unique index, and the FOR BROWSE option is at the end of the SELECT statement(s) sent to SQL Server. For more information, see Browse Mode.

Note It is not possible to use the <lock_hint> HOLDLOCK in a SELECT statement that includes the FOR BROWSE option.

The FOR BROWSE option cannot appear in SELECT statements joined by the UNION operator.

XML

> Specifies that the results of a query are to be returned as an XML document. One of these XML modes must be specified: RAW, AUTO, EXPLICIT. For more information about XML data and SQL Server, see Retrieving XML Documents Using FOR XML.

RAW

> Takes the query result and transforms each row in the result set into an XML element with a generic identifier <row /> as the element tag. For more information, see Using RAW Mode.

AUTO

> Returns query results in a simple, nested XML tree. Each table in the FROM clause, for which at least one column is listed in the SELECT clause, is represented as an XML element. The columns listed in the SELECT clause are mapped to the appropriate element attributes. For more information, see Using AUTO Mode.

EXPLICIT

> Specifies that the shape of the resulting XML tree is defined explicitly. Using this mode, queries must be written in a particular way so that additional information about the desired nesting is specified explicitly. For more information, see Using EXPLICIT Mode.

XMLDATA

> Returns the schema, but does not add the root element to the result. If XMLDATA is specified, it is appended to the document.

ELEMENTS

> Specifies that the columns are returned as subelements. Otherwise, they are mapped to XML attributes.

BINARY BASE64

> Specifies that the query returns the binary data in binary base64-encoded format. In retrieving binary data using RAW and EXPLICIT mode, this option must be specified. This is the default in AUTO mode.

OPTION Clause

Specifies that the indicated query hint should be used throughout the entire query. Each query hint can be specified only once, although multiple query hints are permitted. Only one OPTION clause may be specified with the statement. The query hint affects all operators in the statement. If a UNION is involved in the main query, only the last query involving a UNION operator can have the OPTION clause. If one or more query hints causes the query optimizer to not generate a valid plan, error 8622 is produced.

> **CAUTION** Because the query optimizer usually selects the best execution plan for a query, it is recommended that <join_hint>, <query_hint>, and <table_hint> be used only as a last resort by experienced database administrators.

Syntax

```
[ OPTION ( < query_hint > [ ,...n ) ]
< query_hint > ::=
    {   { HASH | ORDER } GROUP
    | { CONCAT | HASH | MERGE } UNION
    | { LOOP | MERGE | HASH } JOIN
    | FAST number_rows
    | FORCE ORDER
    | MAXDOP number
    | ROBUST PLAN
    | KEEP PLAN
    | KEEPFIXED PLAN
    | EXPAND VIEWS
    }
```

Arguments

{ HASH | ORDER } GROUP

Specifies that aggregations described in the GROUP BY, DISTINCT, or COMPUTE clause of the query should use hashing or ordering.

{ MERGE | HASH | CONCAT } UNION

Specifies that all UNION operations are performed by merging, hashing, or concatenating UNION sets. If more than one UNION hint is specified, the query optimizer selects the least expensive strategy from those hints specified.

{ LOOP | MERGE | HASH } JOIN

Specifies that all join operations are performed by loop join, merge join, or hash join in the whole query. If more than one join hint is specified, the optimizer selects the least expensive join strategy from the allowed ones.

If, in the same query, a join hint is also specified for a specific pair of tables, this join hint takes precedence in the joining of the two tables although the query hints still must be honored. Thus, the join hint for the pair of tables may only restrict the selection of allowed join methods in the query hint. See Hints for details.

FAST number_rows

Specifies that the query is optimized for fast retrieval of the first number_rows (a nonnegative integer). After the first number_rows are returned, the query continues execution and produces its full result set.

FORCE ORDER

Specifies that the join order indicated by the query syntax is preserved during query optimization.

MAXDOP *number*

Overrides the **max degree of parallelism** configuration option (of **sp_configure**) only for the query specifying this option. All semantic rules used with **max degree of parallelism** configuration option are applicable when using the MAXDOP query hint. For more information, see max degree of parallelism Option.

ROBUST PLAN

Forces the query optimizer to attempt a plan that works for the maximum potential row size, possibly at the expense of performance. When the query is processed, intermediate tables and operators may need to store and process rows that are wider than any of the input rows. The rows may be so wide that, in some cases, the particular operator cannot process the row. If this happens, SQL Server produces an error during query execution. By using ROBUST PLAN, you instruct the query optimizer not to consider any query plans that may encounter this problem.

KEEP PLAN

Forces the query optimizer to relax the estimated recompile threshold for a query. The estimated recompile threshold is the point at which a query is automatically recompiled when the estimated number of indexed column changes (update, delete, or insert) have been made to a table. Specifying KEEP PLAN ensures that a query will not be recompiled as frequently when there are multiple updates to a table.

KEEPFIXED PLAN

Forces the query optimizer not to recompile a query due to changes in statistics or to the indexed column (update, delete, or insert). Specifying KEEPFIXED PLAN ensures that a query will be recompiled only if the schema of the underlying tables is changed or **sp_recompile** is executed against those tables.

EXPAND VIEWS

Specifies that the indexed views are expanded and the query optimizer will not consider any indexed view as a substitute for any part of the query. (A view is expanded when the view name is replaced by the view definition in the query text.) This query hint virtually disallows direct use of indexed views and indexes on indexed views in the query plan.

The indexed view is not expanded only if the view is directly referenced in the SELECT part of the query and WITH (NOEXPAND) or WITH (NOEXPAND, INDEX(index_val [,...*n*])) is specified. For more information about the query hint WITH (NOEXPAND), see FROM.

Only the views in the SELECT portion of statements, including those in INSERT, UPDATE, and DELETE statements are affected by the hint.

Remarks

The order of the clauses in the SELECT statement is significant. Any of the optional clauses can be omitted, but when used, they must appear in the appropriate order.

SELECT statements are allowed in user-defined functions only if the select lists of these statements contain expressions that assign values to variables that are local to the functions.

A **table** variable, in its scope, may be accessed like a regular table and thus may be used as a table source in a SELECT statement.

A four-part name constructed with the OPENDATASOURCE function as the server-name part may be used as a table source in all places a table name can appear in SELECT statements.

Some syntax restrictions apply to SELECT statements involving remote tables. For information, see External Data and Transact-SQL.

The length returned for **text** or **ntext** columns included in the select list defaults to the smallest of the actual size of the **text**, the default TEXTSIZE session setting, or the hard-coded application limit. To change the length of returned text for the session, use the SET statement. By default, the limit on the length of text data returned with a SELECT statement is 4,000 bytes.

SQL Server raises exception 511 and rolls back the current executing statement if either of these occur:

- The SELECT statement produces a result row or an intermediate work table row exceeding 8,060 bytes.
- The DELETE, INSERT, or UPDATE statement attempts action on a row exceeding 8,060 bytes.

In SQL Server, an error occurs if no column name is given to a column created by a SELECT INTO or CREATE VIEW statement.

Selecting Identity Columns

When selecting an existing identity column into a new table, the new column inherits the IDENTITY property, unless one of the following conditions is true:

- The SELECT statement contains a join, GROUP BY clause, or aggregate function.
- Multiple SELECT statements are joined with UNION.
- The identity column is listed more than once in the select list.
- The identity column is part of an expression.

If any of these conditions is true, the column is created NOT NULL instead of inheriting the IDENTITY property. All rules and restrictions for the identity columns apply to the new table.

Old-Style Outer Joins

Earlier versions of SQL Server supported the definition of outer joins that used the *= and =* operators in the WHERE clause. SQL Server version 7.0 supports the SQL-92 standard, which provides join operators in the FROM clause. It is recommended that queries be rewritten to use the SQL-92 syntax.

Processing Order of WHERE, GROUP BY, and HAVING Clauses

This list shows the processing order for a SELECT statement with a WHERE clause, a GROUP BY clause, and a HAVING clause:

1. The WHERE clause excludes rows not meeting its search condition.

2. The GROUP BY clause collects the selected rows into one group for each unique value in the GROUP BY clause.

3. Aggregate functions specified in the select list calculate summary values for each group.

4. The HAVING clause further excludes rows not meeting its search condition.

Permissions

SELECT permissions default to members of the **sysadmin** fixed server role, the **db_owner** and **db_datareader** fixed database roles, and the table owner. Members of the **sysadmin**, **db_owner**, and **db_securityadmin** roles, and the table owner can transfer permissions to other users.

If the INTO clause is used to create a permanent table, the user must have CREATE TABLE permission in the destination database.

Related Topics

CONTAINS, CONTAINSTABLE, CREATE TRIGGER, CREATE VIEW, DELETE, EXECUTE, Expressions, FREETEXT, FREETEXTTABLE, Full-text Querying SQL Server Data, INSERT, Join Fundamentals, SET TRANSACTION ISOLATION LEVEL, sp_dboption, Subquery Fundamentals, table, UNION, UPDATE, Using Variables and Parameters, WHERE

SELECT Examples

A. Use SELECT to retrieve rows and columns

This example shows three code examples. This first code example returns all rows (no WHERE clause is specified) and all columns (using the *) from the **authors** table in the **pubs** database.

```
USE pubs
SELECT *
FROM authors
ORDER BY au_lname ASC, au_fname ASC


-- Alternate way.
USE pubs
SELECT authors.*
FROM customers
ORDER BY au_lname ASC, au_fname ASC
```

This example returns all rows (no WHERE clause is specified), and only a subset of the columns (**au_lname**, **au_fname**, **phone**, **city**, **state**) from the **authors** table in the **pubs** database. In addition, column headings are added.

```
USE pubs
SELECT au_fname, au_lname, phone AS Telephone, city, state
FROM authors
ORDER BY au_lname ASC, au_fname ASC
```

This example returns only the rows for authors who live in California and do not have the last name McBadden.

```
USE pubs
SELECT au_fname, au_lname, phone AS Telephone
FROM authors
WHERE state = 'CA' and au_lname <> 'McBadden'
ORDER BY au_lname ASC, au_fname ASC
```

B. Use SELECT with column headings and calculations

These examples return all rows from **titles**. The first example returns total year-to-date sales and the amounts due to each author and publisher. In the second example, the total revenue is calculated for each book.

```
USE pubs
SELECT ytd_sales AS Sales,
    authors.au_fname + ' '+ authors.au_lname AS Author,
    ToAuthor = (ytd_sales * royalty) / 100,
    ToPublisher = ytd_sales - (ytd_sales * royalty) / 100
FROM titles INNER JOIN titleauthor
    ON titles.title_id = titleauthor.title_id INNER JOIN authors
    ON titleauthor.au_id = authors.au_id
ORDER BY Sales DESC, Author ASC
```

Here is the result set:

Sales	Author	ToAuthor	ToPublisher
22246	Anne Ringer	5339	16907
22246	Michel DeFrance	5339	16907
18722	Marjorie Green	4493	14229
15096	Reginald Blotchet-Halls	2113	12983
8780	Cheryl Carson	1404	7376
4095	Abraham Bennet	409	3686
4095	Akiko Yokomoto	409	3686
4095	Ann Dull	409	3686
4095	Burt Gringlesby	409	3686
4095	Dean Straight	409	3686
4095	Marjorie Green	409	3686
4095	Michael O'Leary	409	3686
4095	Sheryl Hunter	409	3686
4072	Johnson White	407	3665
3876	Michael O'Leary	387	3489
3876	Stearns MacFeather	387	3489
3336	Charlene Locksley	333	3003
2045	Albert Ringer	245	1800
2045	Anne Ringer	245	1800
2032	Innes del Castillo	243	1789
375	Livia Karsen	37	338
375	Stearns MacFeather	37	338
375	Sylvia Panteley	37	338
111	Albert Ringer	11	100
NULL	Charlene Locksley	NULL	NULL

```
(25 row(s) affected)
```

This is the query that calculates the revenue for each book:

```
USE pubs
SELECT 'Total income is', price * ytd_sales AS Revenue,
'for', title_id AS Book#
FROM titles
ORDER BY Book# ASC
```

Here is the result set:

```
Revenue                                Book#
---------------  --------------------  ----  ------
Total income is  81859.0500            for   BU1032
Total income is  46318.2000            for   BU1111
Total income is  55978.7800            for   BU2075
Total income is  81859.0500            for   BU7832
Total income is  40619.6800            for   MC2222
Total income is  66515.5400            for   MC3021
Total income is  NULL                  for   MC3026
Total income is  201501.0000           for   PC1035
Total income is  81900.0000            for   PC8888
Total income is  NULL                  for   PC9999
Total income is  8096.2500             for   PS1372
Total income is  22392.7500            for   PS2091
Total income is  777.0000              for   PS2106
Total income is  81399.2800            for   PS3333
Total income is  26654.6400            for   PS7777
Total income is  7856.2500             for   TC3218
Total income is  180397.2000           for   TC4203
Total income is  61384.0500            for   TC7777

(18 row(s) affected)
```

C. Use DISTINCT with SELECT

This example uses DISTINCT to prevent the retrieval of duplicate author ID numbers.

```
USE pubs
SELECT DISTINCT au_id
FROM authors
ORDER BY au_id
```

D. Create tables with SELECT INTO

This first example creates a temporary table named **#coffeetabletitles** in **tempdb**.
To use this table, always refer to it with the exact name shown, including the number sign (#).

```
USE pubs
DROP TABLE #coffeetabletitles
GO
SET NOCOUNT ON
SELECT * INTO #coffeetabletitles
FROM titles
WHERE price < $20
SET NOCOUNT OFF
SELECT name
FROM tempdb..sysobjects
WHERE name LIKE '#c%'
```

Here is the result set:

```
name
---------------------------------------------------------------------

#coffeetabletitles_____
_____000000000028

(1 row(s) affected)

CHECKPOINTing database that was changed.

(12 row(s) affected)

name
---------------------------------------------------------------------
newtitles

(1 row(s) affected)

CHECKPOINTing database that was changed.
```

This second example creates a permanent table named **newtitles**.

```
USE pubs
IF EXISTS (SELECT table_name FROM INFORMATION_SCHEMA.TABLES
      WHERE table_name = 'newtitles')
   DROP TABLE newtitles
GO
EXEC sp_dboption 'pubs', 'select into/bulkcopy', 'true'
USE pubs
SELECT * INTO newtitles
FROM titles
WHERE price > $25 OR price < $20
SELECT name FROM sysobjects WHERE name LIKE 'new%'
USE master
EXEC sp_dboption 'pubs', 'select into/bulkcopy', 'false'
```

Here is the result set:

```
name
------------------------------
newtitles

(1 row(s) affected)
```

E. Use correlated subqueries

This example shows queries that are semantically equivalent and illustrates the difference between using the EXISTS keyword and the IN keyword. Both are examples of a valid subquery retrieving one instance of each publisher name for which the book title is a business book, and the publisher ID numbers match between the **titles** and **publishers** tables.

```
USE pubs
SELECT DISTINCT pub_name
FROM publishers
WHERE EXISTS
   (SELECT *
   FROM titles
   WHERE pub_id = publishers.pub_id
   AND type = 'business')

-- Or
USE pubs
SELECT distinct pub_name
FROM publishers
WHERE pub_id IN
   (SELECT pub_id
   FROM titles
   WHERE type = 'business')
```

This example uses IN in a correlated (or repeating) subquery, which is a query that depends on the outer query for its values. It is executed repeatedly, once for each row that may be selected by the outer query. This query retrieves one instance of each author's first and last name for which the royalty percentage in the **titleauthor** table is 100 and for which the author identification numbers match in the **authors** and **titleauthor** tables.

```
USE pubs
SELECT DISTINCT au_lname, au_fname
FROM authors
WHERE 100 IN
   (SELECT royaltyper
   FROM titleauthor
   WHERE titleauthor.au_id = authors.au_id)
```

The above subquery in this statement cannot be evaluated independently of the outer query. It needs a value for **authors.au_id**, but this value changes as Microsoft SQL Server examines different rows in **authors**.

A correlated subquery can also be used in the HAVING clause of an outer query. This example finds the types of books for which the maximum advance is more than twice the average for the group.

```
USE pubs
SELECT t1.type
FROM titles t1
GROUP BY t1.type
HAVING MAX(t1.advance) >= ALL
   (SELECT 2 * AVG(t2.advance)
   FROM titles t2
   WHERE t1.type = t2.type)
```

This example uses two correlated subqueries to find the names of authors who have participated in writing at least one popular computing book.

```
USE pubs
SELECT au_lname, au_fname
FROM authors
WHERE au_id IN
   (SELECT au_id
   FROM titleauthor
   WHERE title_id IN
      (SELECT title_id
      FROM titles
      WHERE type = 'popular_comp'))
```

F. Use GROUP BY

This example finds the total year-to-date sales of each publisher in the database.

```
USE pubs
SELECT pub_id, SUM(ytd_sales) AS total
FROM titles
GROUP BY pub_id
ORDER BY pub_id
```

Here is the result set:

```
pub_id total
------ -----
0736   28286
0877   44219
1389   24941

(3 row(s) affected)
```

Because of the GROUP BY clause, only one row containing the sum of all sales is returned for each publisher.

G. Use GROUP BY with multiple groups

This example finds the average price and the sum of year-to-date sales, grouped by type and publisher ID.

```
USE pubs
SELECT type, pub_id, AVG(price) AS 'avg', sum(ytd_sales) AS 'sum'
FROM titles
GROUP BY type, pub_id
ORDER BY type, pub_id
```

Here is the result set:

```
type          pub_id  avg                    sum
------------  ------  ---------------------  -----------
business      0736    2.9900                 18722
business      1389    17.3100                12066
mod_cook      0877    11.4900                24278
popular_comp  1389    21.4750                12875
psychology    0736    11.4825                9564
psychology    0877    21.5900                375
trad_cook     0877    15.9633                19566
UNDECIDED     0877    NULL                   NULL


(8 row(s) affected)

Warning, null value eliminated from aggregate.
```

H. Use GROUP BY and WHERE

This example puts the results into groups after retrieving only the rows with advances greater than $5,000.

```
USE pubs
SELECT type, AVG(price)
FROM titles
WHERE advance > $5000
GROUP BY type
ORDER BY type
```

Here is the result set:

```
type
------------ --------------------------
business     2.99
mod_cook     2.99
popular_comp 21.48
psychology   14.30
trad_cook    17.97

(5 row(s) affected)
```

I. Use GROUP BY with an expression

This example groups by an expression. You can group by an expression if the expression does not include aggregate functions.

```
USE pubs
SELECT AVG(ytd_sales), ytd_sales * royalty
FROM titles
GROUP BY ytd_sales * royalty
ORDER BY ytd_sales * royalty
```

Here is the result set:

```
------------ -----------
NULL         NULL
111          1110
375          3750
2032         24384
2045         24540
3336         33360
3876         38760
4072         40720
4095         40950
8780         140480
15096        211344
18722        449328
22246        533904

(13 row(s) affected)
```

J. Compare GROUP BY and GROUP BY ALL

The first example produces groups only for those books that commanded royalties of 10 percent. Because no modern cookbooks have a royalty of 10 percent, there is no group in the results for the **mod_cook** type.

The second example produces groups for all types, including modern cookbooks and UNDECIDED, although the modern cookbook group does not include any rows that meet the qualification specified in the WHERE clause.

The column that holds the aggregate value (the average price) is NULL for groups that lack qualifying rows.

```
USE pubs
SELECT type, AVG(price)
FROM titles
WHERE royalty = 10
GROUP BY type
ORDER BY type
```

Here is the result set:

```
type
------------ ---------------------------
business     17.31
popular_comp 20.00
psychology   14.14
trad_cook    17.97

(4 row(s) affected)

-- Using GROUP BY ALL
USE pubs
SELECT type, AVG(price)
FROM titles
WHERE royalty = 10
GROUP BY all type
ORDER BY type
```

Here is the result set:

```
type
------------ ---------------------------
business     17.31
mod_cook     NULL
popular_comp 20.00
psychology   14.14
trad_cook    17.97
UNDECIDED    NULL

(6 row(s) affected)
```

K. Use GROUP BY with ORDER BY

This example finds the average price of each type of book and orders the results by average price.

```
USE pubs
SELECT type, AVG(price)
FROM titles
GROUP BY type
ORDER BY AVG(price)
```

Here is the result set:

```
type
------------ ---------------------------
UNDECIDED    NULL
mod_cook     11.49
psychology   13.50
business     13.73
trad_cook    15.96
popular_comp 21.48

(6 row(s) affected)
```

L. Use the HAVING clause

The first example shows a HAVING clause with an aggregate function. It groups the rows in the **titles** table by type and eliminates the groups that include only one book. The second example shows a HAVING clause without aggregate functions. It groups the rows in the **titles** table by type and eliminates those types that do not start with the letter p.

```
USE pubs
SELECT type
FROM titles
GROUP BY type
HAVING COUNT(*) > 1
ORDER BY type
```

Here is the result set:

```
type
------------
business
mod_cook
popular_comp
psychology
trad_cook

(5 row(s) affected)
```

This query uses the LIKE clause in the HAVING clause.

```
USE pubs
SELECT type
FROM titles
GROUP BY type
HAVING type LIKE 'p%'
ORDER BY type
```

Here is the result set:

```
type
------------
popular_comp
psychology

(2 row(s) affected)
```

M. Use HAVING and GROUP BY

This example shows using GROUP BY, HAVING, WHERE, and ORDER BY clauses in one SELECT statement. It produces groups and summary values but does so after eliminating the titles with prices under $5. It also organizes the results by **pub_id**.

```
USE pubs
SELECT pub_id, SUM(advance), AVG(price)
FROM titles
WHERE price >= $5
GROUP BY pub_id
HAVING SUM(advance) > $15000
   AND AVG(price) < $20
   AND pub_id > '0800'
ORDER BY pub_id
```

Here is the result set:

```
pub_id
------ -------------------------- ---------------------------
0877   26,000.00                  17.89
1389   30,000.00                  18.98

(2 row(s) affected)
```

N. Use HAVING with SUM and AVG

This example groups the **titles** table by publisher and includes only those groups of publishers who have paid more than $25,000 in total advances and whose books average more than $15 in price.

```
USE pubs
SELECT pub_id, SUM(advance), AVG(price)
FROM titles
GROUP BY pub_id
HAVING SUM(advance) > $25000
AND AVG(price) > $15
```

To see the publishers who have had year-to-date sales greater than $40,000, use this query:

```
USE pubs
SELECT pub_id, total = SUM(ytd_sales)
FROM titles
GROUP BY pub_id
HAVING SUM(ytd_sales) > 40000
```

If you want to make sure there are at least six books involved in the calculations for each publisher, use HAVING COUNT(*) > 5 to eliminate the publishers that return totals for fewer than six books. The query looks like this:

```
USE pubs
SELECT pub_id, SUM(ytd_sales) AS total
FROM titles
GROUP BY pub_id
HAVING COUNT(*) > 5
```

Here is the result set:

```
pub_idtotal
----- -----
0877     44219
1389     24941

(2 row(s) affected)
```

With this statement, two rows are returned. New Moon Books (0736) is eliminated.

O. Calculate group totals with **COMPUTE BY**

This example uses two code examples to show the use of COMPUTE BY. The first code example uses one COMPUTE BY with one aggregate function, and the second code example uses one COMPUTE BY item and two aggregate functions.

This example calculates the sum of the prices (for prices over $10) for each type of cookbook, in order first by type of book and then by price of book.

```
USE pubs
SELECT type, price
FROM titles
WHERE price > $10
    AND type LIKE '%cook'
ORDER BY type, price
COMPUTE SUM(price) BY type
```

Here is the result set:

```
type          price
------------  ----------------------
mod_cook      19.9900

(1 row(s) affected)


sum
----------------------
19.9900

(1 row(s) affected)

type          price
------------  ----------------------
trad_cook     11.9500
trad_cook     14.9900
trad_cook     20.9500

(3 row(s) affected)

sum
----------------------
47.8900

(1 row(s) affected)
```

This example retrieves the book type, publisher identification number, and price of all cookbooks. The COMPUTE BY clause uses two different aggregate functions.

```
USE pubs
SELECT type, pub_id, price
FROM titles
WHERE type LIKE '%cook'
ORDER BY type, pub_id
COMPUTE SUM(price), MAX(pub_id) BY type
```

Here is the result set:

```
type         pub_id price
------------ ------ ----------------------
mod_cook     0877   19.9900
mod_cook     0877   2.9900

(2 row(s) affected)


sum                  max
-------------------- ----
22.9800              0877

(1 row(s) affected)

type         pub_id price
------------ ------ ----------------------
trad_cook    0877   20.9500
trad_cook    0877   11.9500
trad_cook    0877   14.9900

(3 row(s) affected)


sum                  max
-------------------- ----
47.8900              0877

(1 row(s) affected)
```

P. Calculate grand values using COMPUTE without BY

The COMPUTE keyword can be used without BY to generate grand totals, grand counts, and so on.

This statement finds the grand total of the prices and advances for all types of books over $20.

```
USE pubs
SELECT type, price, advance
FROM titles
WHERE price > $20
COMPUTE SUM(price), SUM(advance)
```

You can use COMPUTE BY and COMPUTE without BY in the same query. This query finds the sum of prices and advances by type, and then computes the grand total of prices and advances for all types of books.

```
USE pubs
SELECT type, price, advance
FROM titles
WHERE type LIKE '%cook'
ORDER BY type, price
COMPUTE SUM(price), SUM(advance) BY type
COMPUTE SUM(price), SUM(advance)
```

Here is the result set:

```
type          price                 advance
-----------   -------------------   --------------------
mod_cook      2.9900                15000.0000
mod_cook      19.9900               .0000

(2 row(s) affected)

sum                   sum
-------------------   --------------------
22.9800               15000.0000

(1 row(s) affected)

type          price                 advance
-----------   -------------------   --------------------
trad_cook     11.9500               4000.0000
trad_cook     14.9900               8000.0000
trad_cook     20.9500               7000.0000
```

(continued)

```
(3 row(s) affected)

sum                     sum
-------------------- --------------------
47.8900                 19000.0000

(1 row(s) affected)

sum                     sum
-------------------- --------------------
70.8700                 34000.0000

(1 row(s) affected)
```

Q. Calculate computed sums on all rows

This example shows only three columns in the select list and gives totals based on all prices and all advances at the end of the results.

```
USE pubs
SELECT type, price, advance
FROM titles
COMPUTE SUM(price), SUM(advance)
```

Here is the result set:

```
type          price                 advance
------------- --------------------- --------------------
business      19.9900               5000.0000
business      11.9500               5000.0000
business      2.9900                10125.0000
business      19.9900               5000.0000
mod_cook      19.9900               .0000
mod_cook      2.9900                15000.0000
UNDECIDED     NULL                  NULL
popular_comp  22.9500               7000.0000
popular_comp  20.0000               8000.0000
popular_comp  NULL                  NULL
psychology    21.5900               7000.0000
psychology    10.9500               2275.0000
psychology    7.0000                6000.0000
psychology    19.9900               2000.0000
psychology    7.9900                4000.0000
trad_cook     20.9500               7000.0000
```

(continued)

(continued)

```
trad_cook    11.9500              4000.0000
trad_cook    14.9900              8000.0000

(18 row(s) affected)


sum                      sum
--------------------     ---------------------
236.2600                 95400.0000

(1 row(s) affected)

Warning, null value eliminated from aggregate.
```

R. Use more than one COMPUTE clause

This example finds the sum of the prices of all psychology books, as well as the sum of the prices of psychology books organized by publisher. You can use different aggregate functions in the same statement by including more than one COMPUTE BY clause.

```
USE pubs
SELECT type, pub_id, price
FROM titles
WHERE type = 'psychology'
ORDER BY type, pub_id, price
COMPUTE SUM(price) BY type, pub_id
COMPUTE SUM(price) BY type
```

Here is the result set:

```
type         pub_id price
-----------  ------ ---------------------
psychology   0736   7.0000
psychology   0736   7.9900
psychology   0736   10.9500
psychology   0736   19.9900

(4 row(s) affected)

sum
---------------------
45.9300

(1 row(s) affected)
```

(continued)

(continued)

```
type           pub_id price
------------   ------ ----------------------
psychology     0877   21.5900

(1 row(s) affected)

sum
---------------------
21.5900

(1 row(s) affected)

sum
---------------------
67.5200

(1 row(s) affected)
```

S. Compare GROUP BY with COMPUTE

The first example uses the COMPUTE clause to calculate the sum for the prices of the different types of cookbooks. The second example produces the same summary information using only GROUP BY.

```
USE pubs
-- Using COMPUTE
SELECT type, price
FROM titles
WHERE type like '%cook'
ORDER BY type, price
COMPUTE SUM(price) BY type
```

Here is the result set:

```
type           price
------------   ---------------------
mod_cook       2.9900
mod_cook       19.9900

(2 row(s) affected)
```

(continued)

(continued)

```
sum
---------------------
22.9800

(1 row(s) affected)

type         price
------------ ---------------------
trad_cook    11.9500
trad_cook    14.9900
trad_cook    20.9500

(3 row(s) affected)

sum
---------------------
47.8900

(1 row(s) affected)
```

This is the second query using GROUP BY:

```
USE pubs
-- Using GROUP BY
SELECT type, SUM(price)
FROM titles
WHERE type LIKE '%cook'
GROUP BY type
ORDER BY type
```

Here is the result set:

```
type
------------ ---------------------
mod_cook     22.9800
trad_cook    47.8900

(2 row(s) affected)
```

T. Use SELECT with GROUP BY, COMPUTE, and ORDER BY clauses

This example returns only those rows with current year-to-date sales, and then computes the average book cost and total advances in descending order by **type**. Four columns of data are returned, including a truncated title. All computed columns appear within the select list.

```
USE pubs
SELECT CAST(title AS char(20)) AS title, type, price, advance
FROM titles
WHERE ytd_sales IS NOT NULL
ORDER BY type DESC
COMPUTE AVG(price), SUM(advance) BY type
COMPUTE SUM(price), SUM(advance)
```

Here is the result set:

```
title                 type          price                  advance
--------------------  ------------  ---------------------  ----------------
Onions, Leeks, and G  trad_cook     20.9500                7000.0000
Fifty Years in Bucki  trad_cook     11.9500                4000.0000
Sushi, Anyone?        trad_cook     14.9900                8000.0000

(3 row(s) affected)

avg                   sum
--------------------  ---------------------
15.9633               19000.0000

(1 row(s) affected)

title                 type          price                  advance
--------------------  ------------  ---------------------  ----------------
Computer Phobic AND   psychology    21.5900                7000.0000
Is Anger the Enemy?   psychology    10.9500                2275.0000
Life Without Fear     psychology    7.0000                 6000.0000
Prolonged Data Depri  psychology    19.9900                2000.0000
Emotional Security:   psychology    7.9900                 4000.0000

(5 row(s) affected)

avg                   sum
--------------------  ---------------------
13.5040               21275.0000

(1 row(s) affected)
```

(continued)

(continued)

```
title                 type          price                 advance
--------------------  ------------  --------------------  ----------------
But Is It User Frien  popular_comp  22.9500               7000.0000
Secrets of Silicon V  popular_comp  20.0000               8000.0000

(2 row(s) affected)


avg                   sum
--------------------  --------------------
21.4750               15000.0000

(1 row(s) affected)


title                 type          price                 advance
--------------------  ------------  --------------------  ----------------
Silicon Valley Gastr  mod_cook      19.9900               .0000
The Gourmet Microwav  mod_cook      2.9900                15000.0000

(2 row(s) affected)


avg                   sum
--------------------  --------------------
11.4900               15000.0000

(1 row(s) affected)


title                 type          price                 advance
--------------------  ------------  --------------------  ----------------
The Busy Executive's  business      19.9900               5000.0000
Cooking with Compute  business      11.9500               5000.0000
You Can Combat Compu  business      2.9900                10125.0000
Straight Talk About   business      19.9900               5000.0000

(4 row(s) affected)


avg                   sum
--------------------  --------------------
13.7300               25125.0000

(1 row(s) affected)
```

(continued)

(continued)

```
sum                      sum
-------------------      --------------------
236.2600                 95400.0000

(1 row(s) affected)
```

U. Use SELECT statement with CUBE

This example shows two code examples. The first example returns a result set from a SELECT statement using the CUBE operator. The SELECT statement covers a one-to-many relationship between book titles and the quantity sold of each book. By using the CUBE operator, the statement returns an extra row.

```
USE pubs
SELECT SUBSTRING(title, 1, 65) AS title, SUM(qty) AS 'qty'
FROM sales INNER JOIN titles
    ON sales.title_id = titles.title_id
GROUP BY title
WITH CUBE
ORDER BY title
```

Here is the result set:

```
title                                                              qty
-----------------------------------------------------------------  ------
NULL                                                               493
But Is It User Friendly?                                          30
Computer Phobic AND Non-Phobic Individuals: Behavior Variations  20
Cooking with Computers: Surreptitious Balance Sheets             25
...
The Busy Executive's Database Guide                              15
The Gourmet Microwave                                            40
You Can Combat Computer Stress!                                  35

(17 row(s) affected)
```

NULL represents all values in the **title** column. The result set returns values for the quantity sold of each title and the total quantity sold of all titles. Applying the CUBE operator or ROLLUP operator returns the same result.

This example uses the **cube_examples** table to show how the CUBE operator affects the result set and uses an aggregate function (SUM). The **cube_examples** table contains a product name, a customer name, and the number of orders each customer has made for a particular product.

```
USE pubs
CREATE TABLE cube_examples
(product_name varchar(30)  NULL,
 customer_name varchar(30) NULL,
 number_of_orders int       NULL
)


INSERT cube_examples (product_name, customer_name, number_of_orders)
   VALUES ('Filo Mix', 'Romero y tomillo', 10)
INSERT cube_examples (product_name, customer_name, number_of_orders)
   VALUES ('Outback Lager', 'Wilman Kala', 10)
INSERT cube_examples (product_name, customer_name, number_of_orders)
   VALUES ('Filo Mix', 'Romero y tomillo', 20)
INSERT cube_examples (product_name, customer_name, number_of_orders)
   VALUES ('Ikura', 'Wilman Kala', 10)
INSERT cube_examples (product_name, customer_name, number_of_orders)
   VALUES ('Ikura', 'Romero y tomillo', 10)
INSERT cube_examples (product_name, customer_name, number_of_orders)
   VALUES ('Outback Lager', 'Wilman Kala', 20)
INSERT cube_examples (product_name, customer_name, number_of_orders)
   VALUES ('Filo Mix', 'Wilman Kala', 30)
INSERT cube_examples (product_name, customer_name, number_of_orders)
   VALUES ('Filo Mix', 'Eastern Connection', 40)
INSERT cube_examples (product_name, customer_name, number_of_orders)
   VALUES ('Outback Lager', 'Eastern Connection', 10)
INSERT cube_examples (product_name, customer_name, number_of_orders)
   VALUES ('Ikura', 'Wilman Kala', 40)
INSERT cube_examples (product_name, customer_name, number_of_orders)
   VALUES ('Ikura', 'Romero y tomillo', 10)
INSERT cube_examples (product_name, customer_name, number_of_orders)
   VALUES ('Filo Mix', 'Romero y tomillo', 50)
```

First, issue a typical query with a GROUP BY clause and the result set.

```
USE pubs
SELECT product_name, customer_name, SUM(number_of_orders)
FROM cube_examples
GROUP BY product_name, customer_name
ORDER BY product_name
```

The GROUP BY causes the result set to form groups within groups. Here is the result set:

product_name	customer_name	
Filo Mix	Eastern Connection	40
Filo Mix	Romero y tomillo	80
Filo Mix	Wilman Kala	30
Ikura	Romero y tomillo	20
Ikura	Wilman Kala	50
Outback Lager	Eastern Connection	10
Outback Lager	Wilman Kala	30

(7 row(s) affected)

Next, issue a query with a GROUP BY clause by using the CUBE operator. The result set should include the same information, and super-aggregate information for each of the GROUP BY columns.

```
USE pubs
SELECT product_name, customer_name, SUM(number_of_orders)
FROM cube_examples
GROUP BY product_name, customer_name
WITH CUBE
```

The result set for the CUBE operator holds the values from the simple GROUP BY result set above, and adds the super-aggregates for each column in the GROUP BY clause. NULL represents all values in the set from which the aggregate is computed. Here is the result set:

product_name	customer_name	
Filo Mix	Eastern Connection	40
Filo Mix	Romero y tomillo	80
Filo Mix	Wilman Kala	30
Filo Mix	NULL	150
Ikura	Romero y tomillo	20
Ikura	Wilman Kala	50
Ikura	NULL	70
Outback Lager	Eastern Connection	10
Outback Lager	Wilman Kala	30
Outback Lager	NULL	40
NULL	NULL	260
NULL	Eastern Connection	50
NULL	Romero y tomillo	100
NULL	Wilman Kala	110

(14 row(s) affected)

Line 4 of the result set indicates that a total of 150 orders for Filo Mix was placed for all customers.

Line 11 of the result set indicates that the total number of orders placed for all products by all customers is 260.

Lines 12–14 of the result set indicate that the total number of orders for each customer for all products are 100, 110, and 50, respectively.

V. Use CUBE on a result set with three columns

This example shows two code examples. The first code example produces a CUBE result set with three columns, and the second example produces a four-column CUBE result set.

The first SELECT statement returns the publication name, title, and quantity of books sold. The GROUP BY clause in this example includes two columns called **pub_name** and **title**. There are also two one-to-many relationships between **publishers** and **titles** and between **titles** and **sales**.

By using the CUBE operator, the result set contains more detailed information about the quantities of titles sold by publishers. NULL represents all values in the title column.

```
USE pubs
SELECT pub_name, title, SUM(qty) AS 'qty'
FROM sales INNER JOIN titles
   ON sales.title_id = titles.title_id INNER JOIN publishers
   ON publishers.pub_id = titles.pub_id
GROUP BY pub_name, title
WITH CUBE
```

Here is the result set:

```
pub_name              title                                        qty
-------------------   ------------------------------------------   ------
Algodata Infosystems  But Is It User Friendly?                       30
Algodata Infosystems  Cooking with Computers: Surreptitious Ba       25
Algodata Infosystems  Secrets of Silicon Valley                      50
Algodata Infosystems  Straight Talk About Computers                  15
Algodata Infosystems  The Busy Executive's Database Guide            15
Algodata Infosystems  NULL                                          135
Binnet & Hardley      Computer Phobic AND Non-Phobic Individu         20
Binnet & Hardley      Fifty Years in Buckingham Palace Kitche         20
...                                        ...
NULL                  Sushi, Anyone?                                 20
NULL                  The Busy Executive's Database Guide            15
NULL                  The Gourmet Microwave                          40
NULL                  You Can Combat Computer Stress!                35

(36 row(s) affected)
```

Increasing the number of columns in the GROUP BY clause shows why the CUBE operator is an *n*-dimensional operator. A GROUP BY clause with two columns returns three more kinds of groupings when the CUBE operator is used. The number of groupings can be more than three, depending on the distinct values in the columns.

The result set is grouped by the publisher name and then by the book title. The quantity of each title sold by each publisher is listed in the right-hand column.

NULL in the **title** column represents all titles. For more information about how to differentiate specific values and all values in the result set, see Example H. The CUBE operator returns these groups of information from one SELECT statement:

- Quantity of each title that each publisher has sold
- Quantity of each title sold
- Quantity of titles sold by each publisher
- Total number of titles sold by all publishers

Each column referenced in the GROUP BY clause has been cross-referenced with all other columns in the GROUP BY clause and the SUM aggregate has been reapplied, which produces additional rows in the result set. Information returned in the result set grows *n*-dimensionally along with the number of columns in the GROUP BY clause.

> **Note** Ensure that the columns following the GROUP BY clause have meaningful, real-life relationships with each other. For example, if you use **au_fname** and **au_lname**, the CUBE operator returns irrelevant information, such as the number of books sold by authors with the same first name. Using the CUBE operator on a real-life hierarchy, such as yearly sales and quarterly sales, produces meaningless rows in the result set. It is more efficient to use the ROLLUP operator.

In this second code example, the GROUP BY clause contains three columns cross-referenced by the CUBE operator. Three one-to-many relationships exist between **publishers** and **authors**, between **authors** and **titles**, and between **titles** and **sales**.

By using the CUBE operator, more detailed information is returned about the quantities of titles sold by publishers.

```
USE pubs
SELECT pub_name, au_lname, title, SUM(qty)
FROM authors INNER JOIN titleauthor
    ON authors.au_id = titleauthor.au_id INNER JOIN titles
    ON titles.title_id = titleauthor.title_id INNER JOIN publishers
    ON publishers.pub_id = titles.pub_id INNER JOIN sales
    ON sales.title_id = titles.title_id
GROUP BY pub_name, au_lname, title
WITH CUBE
```

The CUBE operator returns this information based on the cross-referenced groupings returned with the CUBE operator:

- Quantity of each title that each publisher has sold for each author
- Quantity of all titles each publisher has sold for each author
- Quantity of all titles each publisher has sold
- Total quantity of all titles sold by all publishers for all authors
- Quantity of each title sold by all publishers for each author
- Quantity of all titles sold by all publishers for each author
- Quantity of each title sold by each publisher for all authors
- Quantity of each title sold by all publishers for each author

Note The super-aggregate for all publishers, all titles, and all authors is greater than the total number of sales, because a number of books have more than one author.

A pattern emerges as the number of relationships grow. The pattern of values and NULL in the report shows which groups have been formed for a summary aggregate. Explicit information about the groups is provided by the GROUPING function.

W. Use the GROUPING function with CUBE

This example shows how the SELECT statement uses the SUM aggregate, the GROUP BY clause, and the CUBE operator. It also uses the GROUPING function on the two columns listed after the GROUP BY clause.

```
USE pubs
SELECT pub_name, GROUPING(pub_name),title, GROUPING(title),
   SUM(qty) AS 'qty'
FROM sales INNER JOIN titles
   ON sales.title_id = titles.title_id INNER JOIN publishers
   ON publishers.pub_id = titles.pub_id
GROUP BY pub_name, title
WITH CUBE
```

The result set has two columns containing 0 and 1 values, which are produced by the GROUPING(**pub_name**) and GROUPING(**title**) expressions.

Here is the result set:

```
pub_name                 title                      qty
------------------------  ---  ------------------------  ---  -----------
Algodata Infosystems      0    But Is It User Friendly?  0         30
Algodata Infosystems      0    Cooking with Computers: S 0         25
Algodata Infosystems      0    Secrets of Silicon Valley 0         50
```

(continued)

(continued)

```
Algodata Infosystems    0 Straight Talk About Compu    0        15
Algodata Infosystems    0 The Busy Executive's Data    0        15
Algodata Infosystems    0 NULL                         1       135
Binnet & Hardley        0 Computer Phobic AND Non-P    0        20
Binnet & Hardley        0 Fifty Years in Buckingham    0        20
...                                              ...
NULL                    1 The Busy Executive's Data    0        15
NULL                    1 The Gourmet Microwave        0        40
NULL                    1 You Can Combat Computer S    0        35

(36 row(s) affected)
```

X. Use the ROLLUP operator

This example shows two code examples. This first example retrieves the product name, customer name, and the sum of orders placed and uses the ROLLUP operator.

```
USE pubs
SELECT product_name, customer_name, SUM(number_of_orders)
   AS 'Sum orders'
FROM cube_examples
GROUP BY product_name, customer_name
WITH ROLLUP
```

Here is the result set:

```
product_name            customer_name                 Sum orders
--------------------    ----------------------------- ----------
Filo Mix                Eastern Connection            40
Filo Mix                Romero y tomillo              80
Filo Mix                Wilman Kala                   30
Filo Mix                NULL                          150
Ikura                   Romero y tomillo              20
Ikura                   Wilman Kala                   50
Ikura                   NULL                          70
Outback Lager           Eastern Connection            10
Outback Lager           Wilman Kala                   30
Outback Lager           NULL                          40
NULL                    NULL                          260

(11 row(s) affected)
```

This second example performs a ROLLUP operation on the company and department columns and totals the number of employees.

The ROLLUP operator produces a summary of aggregates. This is useful when summary information is needed but a full CUBE provides extraneous data or when you have sets within sets. For example, departments within a company are a set within a set.

```
USE pubs
CREATE TABLE personnel
(
 company_name varchar(20),
 department   varchar(15),
 num_employees int
)

INSERT personnel VALUES ('Du monde entier', 'Finance', 10)
INSERT personnel VALUES ('Du monde entier', 'Engineering', 40)
INSERT personnel VALUES ('Du monde entier', 'Marketing', 40)
INSERT personnel VALUES ('Piccolo und mehr', 'Accounting', 20)
INSERT personnel VALUES ('Piccolo und mehr', 'Personnel', 30)
INSERT personnel VALUES ('Piccolo und mehr', 'Payroll', 40)
```

In this query, the company name, department, and the sum of all employees for the company become part of the result set, in addition to the ROLLUP calculations.

```
SELECT company_name, department, SUM(num_employees)
FROM personnel
GROUP BY company_name, department WITH ROLLUP
```

Here is the result set:

```
company_name          department
--------------------  ----------------  -----------
Du monde entier       Engineering       40
Du monde entier       Finance           10
Du monde entier       Marketing         40
Du monde entier       NULL              90
Piccolo und mehr      Accounting        20
Piccolo und mehr      Payroll           40
Piccolo und mehr      Personnel         30
Piccolo und mehr      NULL              90
NULL                  NULL              180

(9 row(s) affected)
```

Y. Use the GROUPING function

This example adds three new rows to the **cube_examples** table. Each of the three records NULL in one or more columns to show only the ROLLUP function produces a value of 1 in the grouping column. In addition, this example modifies the SELECT statement that was used in the earlier example.

```
USE pubs
-- Add first row with a NULL customer name and 0 orders.
INSERT cube_examples (product_name, customer_name, number_of_orders)
   VALUES ('Ikura', NULL, 0)

-- Add second row with a NULL product and NULL customer with real value
-- for orders.
INSERT cube_examples (product_name, customer_name, number_of_orders)
   VALUES (NULL, NULL, 50)

-- Add third row with a NULL product, NULL order amount, but a real
-- customer name.
INSERT cube_examples (product_name, customer_name, number_of_orders)
VALUES (NULL, 'Wilman Kala', NULL)

SELECT product_name AS Prod, customer_name AS Cust,
   SUM(number_of_orders) AS 'Sum Orders',
   GROUPING(product_name) AS 'Grp prod_name',
   GROUPING(customer_name) AS 'Grp cust_name'
FROM cube_examples
GROUP BY product_name, customer_name
WITH ROLLUP
```

The GROUPING function can be used only with CUBE or ROLLUP. The GROUPING function returns 1 when an expression evaluates to NULL, because the column value is NULL and represents the set of all values. The GROUPING function returns 0 when the corresponding column (whether it is NULL or not) did not come from either the CUBE or ROLLUP options as a syntax value. The returned value has a **tinyint** data type.

Here is the result set:

Prod	Cust	Sum Orders	Grp prod_name	Grp cust_name
NULL	NULL	50	0	0
NULL	Wilman Kala	NULL	0	0
NULL	NULL	50	0	1
Filo Mix	Eastern Connection	40	0	0
Filo Mix	Romero y tomillo	80	0	0

(continued)

(continued)

```
Filo Mix        Wilman Kala        30        0        0
Filo Mix        NULL              150        0        1
Ikura           NULL                0        0        0
Ikura           Romero y tomillo   20        0        0
Ikura           Wilman Kala        50        0        0
Ikura           NULL               70        0        1
Outback Lager Eastern Connection  10        0        0
Outback Lager Wilman Kala          30        0        0
Outback Lager NULL                 40        0        1
NULL            NULL              310        1        1

(15 row(s) affected)
```

Z. Use SELECT with GROUP BY, an aggregate function, and ROLLUP

This example uses a SELECT query that contains an aggregate function and a
GROUP BY clause, which lists **pub_name**, **au_lname**, and **title**, in that order.

```
USE pubs
SELECT pub_name, au_lname, title, SUM(qty) AS 'SUM'
FROM authors INNER JOIN titleauthor
   ON authors.au_id = titleauthor.au_id INNER JOIN titles
   ON titles.title_id = titleauthor.title_id INNER JOIN publishers
   ON publishers.pub_id = titles.pub_id INNER JOIN sales
   ON sales.title_id = titles.title_id
GROUP BY pub_name, au_lname, title
WITH ROLLUP
```

By using the ROLLUP operator, these groupings are created by moving right to left
along the list of columns.

```
pub_name       au_lname       title SUM(qty)
pub_name       au_lname       NULL     SUM(qty)
pub_name       NULL           NULL     SUM(qty)
NULL           NULL           NULL     SUM(qty)
```

NULL represents all values for that column.

If you use the SELECT statement without the ROLLUP operator, the statement creates
a single grouping. The query returns a sum value for each unique combination of
pub_name, **au_lname**, and **title**.

```
pub_name       au_lname       title SUM(qty)
```

Compare these examples with the groupings created by using the CUBE operator on the same query.

pub_name	au_lname	title SUM(qty)
pub_name	au_lname	NULL SUM(qty)
pub_name	NULL	NULL SUM(qty)
NULL	NULL	NULL SUM(qty)
NULL	au_lname	title SUM(qty)
NULL	au_lname	NULL SUM(qty)
pub_name	NULL	title SUM(qty)
NULL	NULL	title SUM(qty)

The groupings correspond to the information returned in the result set. NULL in the result set represents all values in the column. The ROLLUP operator returns the following data when the columns (**pub_name**, **au_lname**, **title**) are in the order listed in the GROUP BY clause:

- Quantity of each title that each publisher has sold for each author
- Quantity of all titles each publisher has sold for each author
- Quantity of all titles each publisher has sold
- Total quantity of all titles sold by all publishers for all authors

Here is the result set:

pub_name	au_lname	title	SUM
Algodata Infosys	Bennet	The Busy Executive's Database Guide	15
Algodata Infosys	Bennet	NULL	15
Algodata Infosys	Carson	NULL	30
Algodata Infosys	Dull	Secrets of Silicon Valley	50
Algodata Infosys	Dull	NULL	50
...		...	
New Moon Books	White	Prolonged Data Deprivation: Four	15
New Moon Books	White	NULL	15
New Moon Books	NULL	NULL	316
NULL	NULL	NULL	791

```
(49 row(s) affected)
```

The GROUPING function can be used with the ROLLUP operator or with the CUBE operator. You can apply this function to one of the columns in the select list. The function returns either 1 or 0 depending upon whether the column is grouped by the ROLLUP operator.

a. Use the INDEX optimizer hint

This example shows two ways to use the INDEX optimizer hint. The first example shows how to force the optimizer to use a nonclustered index to retrieve rows from a table and the second example forces a table scan by using an index of 0.

```
-- Use the specifically named INDEX.
USE pubs
SELECT au_lname, au_fname, phone
FROM authors WITH (INDEX(aunmind))
WHERE au_lname = 'Smith'
```

Here is the result set:

```
au_lname                                au_fname              phone
------------------------------------    --------------------  ----------
Smith                                   Meander               913 843-0462

(1 row(s) affected)

-- Force a table scan by using INDEX = 0.
USE pubs
SELECT emp_id, fname, lname, hire_date
FROM employee (index = 0)
WHERE hire_date > '10/1/1994'
```

b. Use OPTION and the GROUP hints

This example shows how the OPTION (GROUP) clause is used with a GROUP BY clause.

```
USE pubs
SELECT a.au_fname, a.au_lname, SUBSTRING(t.title, 1, 15)
FROM authors a INNER JOIN titleauthor ta
   ON a.au_id = ta.au_id INNER JOIN titles t
   ON t.title_id = ta.title_id
GROUP BY a.au_lname, a.au_fname, t.title
ORDER BY au_lname ASC, au_fname ASC
OPTION (HASH GROUP, FAST 10)
```

c. Use the UNION query hint

This example uses the MERGE UNION query hint.

```
USE pubs
SELECT *
FROM authors a1
OPTION (MERGE UNION)
SELECT *
FROM authors a2
```

d. Use a simple UNION

The result set in this example includes the contents of the **ContactName**, **CompanyName**, **City**, and **Phone** columns of both the **Customers** and **SouthAmericanCustomers** tables.

```
USE Northwind
GO
IF EXISTS(SELECT TABLE_NAME FROM INFORMATION_SCHEMA.TABLES
      WHERE TABLE_NAME = 'SouthAmericanCustomers')
   DROP TABLE SouthAmericanCustomers
GO
-- Create SouthAmericanCustomers table.
SELECT ContactName, CompanyName, City, Phone
INTO SouthAmericanCustomers
FROM Customers
WHERE Country IN ('USA', 'Canada')
GO
-- Here is the simple union.
USE Northwind
SELECT ContactName, CompanyName, City, Phone
FROM Customers
WHERE Country IN ('USA', 'Canada')
UNION
SELECT ContactName, CompanyName, City, Phone
FROM SouthAmericanCustomers
ORDER BY CompanyName, ContactName ASC
GO
```

e. Use SELECT INTO with UNION

In this example, the INTO clause in the first SELECT statement specifies that the table named **CustomerResults** holds the final result set of the union of the designated columns of the **Customers** and **SouthAmericanCustomers** tables.

```
USE Northwind
IF EXISTS(SELECT TABLE_NAME FROM INFORMATION_SCHEMA.TABLES
      WHERE TABLE_NAME = 'CustomerResults')
   DROP TABLE CustomerResults
GO
USE Northwind
SELECT ContactName, CompanyName, City, Phone INTO CustomerResults
FROM Customers
WHERE Country IN ('USA', 'Canada')
UNION
SELECT ContactName, CompanyName, City, Phone
FROM SouthAmericanCustomers
ORDER BY CompanyName, ContactName ASC
GO
```

f. Use UNION of two SELECT statements with ORDER BY

The order of certain parameters used with the UNION clause is important. This example shows the incorrect and correct use of UNION in two SELECT statements in which a column is to be renamed in the output.

```
/* INCORRECT */
USE Northwind
GO
SELECT City
FROM Customers
ORDER BY Cities
UNION
SELECT Cities = City
FROM SouthAmericanCustomers
GO

/* CORRECT */
USE Northwind
GO
SELECT Cities = City
FROM Customers
    UNION
SELECT City
FROM SouthAmericanCustomers
ORDER BY Cities
GO
```

g. Use UNION of three SELECT statements showing the effects of ALL and parentheses

These examples use UNION to combine the results of three tables, in which all have the same 5 rows of data. The first example uses UNION ALL to show the duplicated records, and returns all 15 rows. The second example uses UNION without ALL to eliminate the duplicate rows from the combined results of the three SELECT statements, and returns 5 rows.

The final example uses ALL with the first UNION, and parentheses around the second UNION that is not using ALL. The second UNION is processed first because it is in parentheses, and returns 5 rows because the ALL option is not used and the duplicates are removed. These 5 rows are combined with the results of the first SELECT through the UNION ALL keywords, which does not remove the duplicates between the two sets of 5 rows. The final result has 10 rows.

```
USE Northwind
GO
IF EXISTS(SELECT TABLE_NAME FROM INFORMATION_SCHEMA.TABLES
     WHERE TABLE_NAME = 'CustomersOne')
  DROP TABLE CustomersOne
GO
IF EXISTS(SELECT TABLE_NAME FROM INFORMATION_SCHEMA.TABLES
     WHERE TABLE_NAME = 'CustomersTwo')
  DROP TABLE CustomersTwo
GO
IF EXISTS(SELECT TABLE_NAME FROM INFORMATION_SCHEMA.TABLES
     WHERE TABLE_NAME = 'CustomersThree')
  DROP TABLE CustomersThree
GO
USE Northwind
GO
SELECT ContactName, CompanyName, City, Phone INTO CustomersOne
FROM Customers
WHERE Country = 'Mexico'
GO
SELECT ContactName, CompanyName, City, Phone INTO CustomersTwo
FROM Customers
WHERE Country = 'Mexico'
GO
SELECT ContactName, CompanyName, City, Phone INTO CustomersThree
FROM Customers
WHERE Country = 'Mexico'
GO
-- Union ALL
SELECT ContactName
FROM CustomersOne
   UNION ALL
SELECT ContactName
FROM CustomersTwo
   UNION ALL
SELECT ContactName
FROM CustomersThree
GO

USE Northwind
GO
SELECT ContactName
FROM CustomersOne
   UNION
```

(continued)

(continued)

```
SELECT ContactName
FROM CustomersTwo
    UNION
SELECT ContactName
FROM CustomersThree
GO

USE Northwind
GO
SELECT ContactName
FROM CustomersOne
    UNION ALL
    (
        SELECT ContactName
        FROM CustomersTwo
            UNION
        SELECT ContactName
        FROM CustomersThree
    )
GO
```

Related Topics

CREATE TRIGGER, CREATE VIEW, DELETE, Distributed Queries, EXECUTE, Expressions, INSERT, LIKE, sp_dboption, Subquery Fundamentals, UNION, UPDATE, Using Variables and Parameters, WHERE

SERVERPROPERTY

Returns property information about the server instance.

Syntax

```
SERVERPROPERTY ( propertyname )
```

Arguments

propertyname

Is an expression containing the property information to be returned for the server. *propertyname* can be one of these values.

Property name	Values returned
Collation	The name of the default collation for the server.
	Returns NULL if invalid input or error.
	Base data type: **nvarchar**
Edition	The edition of the Microsoft SQL Server instance installed on the server.
	Returns:
	'Desktop Engine' 'Developer Edition' 'Enterprise Edition' 'Enterprise Evaluation Edition' 'Personal Edition' 'Standard Edition'
	Base data type: **nvarchar(128)**
Engine Edition	The engine edition of the SQL Server instance installed on the server.
	1 = Personal or Desktop Engine 2 = Standard 3 = Enterprise (returned for Enterprise, Enterprise Evaluation, and Developer)
	Base data type: **int**
InstanceName	The name of the instance to which the user is connected.
	Returns NULL if the instance name is the default instance, or invalid input or error.
	Base data type: **nvarchar**
IsClustered	The server instance is configured in a failover cluster.
	1 = Clustered. 0 = Not Clustered. NULL = Invalid input, or error.
	Base data type: **int**

(continued)

(continued)

Property name	Values returned
IsFullTextInstalled	The full-text component is installed with the current instance of SQL Server.
	1 = Full-text is installed. 0 = Full-text is not installed. NULL = Invalid input, or error.
	Base data type: **int**
IsIntegratedSecurityOnly	The server is in integrated security mode.
	1 = Integrated Security. 0 = Not Integrated Security. NULL = Invalid input, or error.
	Base data type: **int**
IsSingleUser	The server is in single user mode.
	1 = Single User. 0 = Not Single User NULL = Invalid input, or error.
	Base data type: **int**
IsSyncWithBackup	The database is either a published database or a distribution database, and can be restored without disrupting transactional replication.
	1 = True. 0 = False.
	Base data type: **int**

(continued)

(continued)

Property name	Values returned
LicenseType	Mode of this instance of SQL Server. PER_SEAT = Per-seat mode PER_PROCESSOR = Per-processor mode DISABLED = Licensing is disabled. Base data type: **nvarchar(128)**
MachineName	Windows NT computer name on which the server instance is running. For a clustered instance, an instance of SQL Server running on a virtual server on Microsoft Cluster Server, it returns the name of the virtual server. Returns NULL if invalid input or error. Base data type: **nvarchar**
NumLicenses	Number of client licenses registered for this instance of SQL Server, if in per-seat mode. Number of processors licensed for this instance of SQL Server, if in per-processor mode. Returns NULL if the server is none of the above. Base data type: **int**
ProcessID	Process ID of the SQL Server service. (**ProcessID** is useful in identifying which sqlservr.exe belongs to this instance.) Returns NULL if invalid input or error. Base data type: **int**
ProductVersion	The version of the instance of SQL Server, in the form of '*major.minor.build*'. Base data type: **varchar(128)**

(continued)

(continued)

Property name	Values returned
ProductLevel	The level of the version of the SQL Server instance.
	Returns: 'RTM' = shipping version. 'SP*n*' = service pack version 'B*n*', = beta version.
	Base data type: **nvarchar(128)**.
ServerName	Both the Windows NT server and instance information associated with a specified instance of SQL Server.
	Returns NULL if invalid input or error.
	Base data type: **nvarchar**

Return Types
sql_variant

Remarks

The **ServerName** property of the SERVERPROPERTY function and @@SERVERNAME return similar information. The **ServerName** property provides the Windows NT server and instance name that together make up the unique server instance. @@SERVERNAME provides the currently configured local server name.

ServerName property and @@SERVERNAME return the same information if the default server name at the time of installation has not been changed. The local server name can be configured by executing **sp_addserver** and **sp_dropserver**.

If the local server name has been changed from the default server name at install time, then @@SERVERNAME returns the new name.

Examples

This example used the SERVERPROPERTY function in a SELECT statement to return information about the current server. This scenario is useful when there are multiple instances of SQL Server installed on a Windows NT server, and the client needs to open another connection to the same instance used by the current connection.

```
SELECT CONVERT(char(20), SERVERPROPERTY('servername'))
```

Related Topics

@@SERVERNAME

SESSION_USER

Is a niladic function that allows a system-supplied value for the current session's username to be inserted into a table when no default value is specified. Also allows the username to be used in queries, error messages, and so on.

Syntax

```
SESSION_USER
```

Return Types

nchar

Remarks

Use SESSION_USER with DEFAULT constraints in either the CREATE TABLE or ALTER TABLE statements, or use as any standard function.

Examples

A. Use SESSION_USER to return the session's current username

This example declares a variable as **char**, assigns the current value of SESSION_USER, and then prints the variable with a text description.

```
DECLARE @session_usr char(30)
SET @session_usr = SESSION_USER
SELECT 'This session''s current user is: '+ @session_usr
GO
```

Here is the result set:

```
-----------------------------------------------------------------
This session's current user is: dbo


(1 row(s) affected)
```

B. Use SESSION_USER with DEFAULT constraints

This example creates a table using the SESSION_USER niladic function as a
DEFAULT constraint for the delivery person.

```
USE pubs
GO
CREATE TABLE deliveries2
(
 order_id int IDENTITY(5000, 1) NOT NULL,
 cust_id  int NOT NULL,
 order_date datetime NOT NULL DEFAULT GETDATE(),
 delivery_date datetime NOT NULL DEFAULT DATEADD(dd, 10, GETDATE()),
 delivery_person char(30) NOT NULL DEFAULT SESSION_USER
)
GO
INSERT deliveries2 (cust_id)
VALUES (7510)
INSERT deliveries2 (cust_id)
VALUES (7231)
INSERT deliveries2 (cust_id)
VALUES (7028)
INSERT deliveries2 (cust_id)
VALUES (7392)
INSERT deliveries2 (cust_id)
VALUES (7452)
GO
```

This query selects all information from the **deliveries2** table.

```
SELECT order_id AS 'Ord#', cust_id AS 'Cust#', order_date,
    delivery_date, delivery_person AS 'Delivery'
FROM deliveries2
ORDER BY order_id
GO
```

Here is the result set:

```
Ord#  Cust#  order_date          delivery_date         Delivery
----  ------ ------------------- --------------------- ----------------
5000  7510   Mar 4 1998 10:21AM  Mar 14 1998 10:21AM   dbo
5001  7231   Mar 4 1998 10:21AM  Mar 14 1998 10:21AM   dbo
5002  7028   Mar 4 1998 10:21AM  Mar 14 1998 10:21AM   dbo
5003  7392   Mar 4 1998 10:21AM  Mar 14 1998 10:21AM   dbo
5004  7452   Mar 4 1998 10:21AM  Mar 14 1998 10:21AM   dbo

(5 row(s) affected)
```

Related Topics

ALTER TABLE, CREATE TABLE, CURRENT_TIMESTAMP, CURRENT_USER, SYSTEM_USER, System Functions, USER, USER_NAME

SESSIONPROPERTY

Returns the SET options settings of a session.

Syntax

```
SESSIONPROPERTY ( option )
```

Arguments

option

Is the current option setting for this session. *option* may be any of the following values.

Option	Description
ANSI_NULLS	Specifies whether the SQL-92 compliant behavior of equals (=) and not equal to (<>) against null values is applied. 1 = ON 0 = OFF
ANSI_PADDING	Controls the way the column stores values shorter than the defined size of the column, and the way the column stores values that have trailing blanks in character and binary data. 1 = ON 0 = OFF
ANSI_WARNINGS	Specifies whether the SQL-92 standard behavior of raising error messages or warnings for certain conditions, including divide-by-zero and arithmetic overflow, is applied. 1 = ON 0 = OFF
ARITHABORT	Determines whether a query is terminated when an overflow or a divide-by-zero error occurs during query execution. 1 = ON 0 = OFF

(continued)

(continued)

Option	Description
CONCAT_NULL_YIELDS_NULL	Controls whether concatenation results are treated as null or empty string values. 1 = ON 0 = OFF
NUMERIC_ROUNDABORT	Specifies whether error messages and warnings are generated when rounding in an expression causes a loss of precision. 1 = ON 0 = OFF
QUOTED_IDENTIFIER	Specifies whether SQL-92 rules regarding the use of quotation marks to delimit identifiers and literal strings are to be followed. 1 = ON 0 = OFF
<Any other string>	NULL = Invalid input

Return Types

sql_variant

Remarks

SET options are figured by combining server-level, database-level, and user-specified options.

Examples

This example returns the setting for CONCAT_NULL_YIELDS_NULL option.

```
SELECT SESSIONPROPERTY ('CONCAT_NULL_YIELDS_NULL')
```

Related Topics

sql_variant

SET @local_variable

Sets the specified local variable, previously created with the DECLARE
@local_variable statement, to the given value.

Syntax

```
SET { { @local_variable = expression }
    | { @cursor_variable = { @cursor_variable | cursor_name
          | { CURSOR [ FORWARD_ONLY | SCROLL ]
                [ STATIC | KEYSET | DYNAMIC | FAST_FORWARD ]
                [ READ_ONLY | SCROLL_LOCKS | OPTIMISTIC ]
                [ TYPE_WARNING ]
            FOR select_statement
                [ FOR { READ ONLY | UPDATE [ OF column_name [ ,...n ] ] }
                ]
            }
        } }
    }
```

Arguments

@local_variable
> Is the name of a variable of any type except **cursor**, **text**, **ntext**, or **image**. Variable
> names must begin with one at sign (@). Variable names must conform to the rules
> for identifiers. For more information, see Using Identifiers.

expression
> Is any valid Microsoft SQL Server expression.

cursor_variable
> Is the name of a cursor variable. If the target cursor variable previously referenced
> a different cursor, that previous reference is removed.

cursor_name
> Is the name of a cursor declared using the DECLARE CURSOR statement.

CURSOR
> Specifies that the SET statement contains a declaration of a cursor.

SCROLL
> Specifies that the cursor supports all fetch options (FIRST, LAST, NEXT, PRIOR,
> RELATIVE, and ABSOLUTE). SCROLL cannot be specified if
> FAST_FORWARD is also specified.

FORWARD_ONLY

Specifies that the cursor supports only the FETCH NEXT option. The cursor can be retrieved only in one direction, from the first to the last row. If FORWARD_ONLY is specified without the STATIC, KEYSET, or DYNAMIC keywords, the cursor is implemented as DYNAMIC. When neither FORWARD_ONLY nor SCROLL is specified, FORWARD_ONLY is the default, unless the keywords STATIC, KEYSET, or DYNAMIC are specified. STATIC, KEYSET, and DYNAMIC cursors default to SCROLL. FAST_FORWARD and FORWARD_ONLY are mutually exclusive; if one is specified the other cannot be specified.

STATIC

Defines a cursor that makes a temporary copy of the data to be used by the cursor. All requests to the cursor are answered from this temporary table in **tempdb**; therefore, modifications made to base tables are not reflected in the data returned by fetches made to this cursor, and this cursor does not allow modifications.

KEYSET

Specifies that the membership and order of rows in the cursor are fixed when the cursor is opened. The set of keys that uniquely identify the rows is built into a table in **tempdb** known as the **keyset**. Changes to nonkey values in the base tables, either made by the cursor owner or committed by other users, are visible as the owner scrolls around the cursor. Inserts made by other users are not visible (inserts cannot be made through a Transact-SQL server cursor). If a row is deleted, an attempt to fetch the row returns an @@FETCH_STATUS of -2. Updates of key values from outside the cursor resemble a delete of the old row followed by an insert of the new row. The row with the new values is not visible, and attempts to fetch the row with the old values return an @@FETCH_STATUS of -2. The new values are visible if the update is done through the cursor by specifying the WHERE CURRENT OF clause.

DYNAMIC

Defines a cursor that reflects all data changes made to the rows in its result set as you scroll around the cursor. The data values, order, and membership of the rows can change on each fetch. The absolute and relative fetch options are not supported with dynamic cursors.

FAST_FORWARD

Specifies a FORWARD_ONLY, READ_ONLY cursor with optimizations enabled. FAST_FORWARD cannot be specified if SCROLL is also specified. FAST_FORWARD and FORWARD_ONLY are mutually exclusive, if one is specified the other cannot be specified.

READ_ONLY

Prevents updates from being made through this cursor. The cursor cannot be referenced in a WHERE CURRENT OF clause in an UPDATE or DELETE statement. This option overrides the default capability of a cursor to be updated.

SCROLL LOCKS

Specifies that positioned updates or deletes made through the cursor are guaranteed to succeed. SQL Server locks the rows as they are read into the cursor to ensure their availability for later modifications. SCROLL_LOCKS cannot be specified if FAST_FORWARD is also specified.

OPTIMISTIC

Specifies that positioned updates or deletes made through the cursor do not succeed if the row has been updated since it was read into the cursor. SQL Server does not lock rows as they are read into the cursor. It instead uses comparisons of **timestamp** column values, or a checksum value if the table has no **timestamp** column, to determine if the row was modified after it was read into the cursor. If the row was modified, the attempted positioned update or delete fails. OPTIMISTIC cannot be specified if FAST_FORWARD is also specified.

TYPE_WARNING

Specifies that a warning message is sent to the client if the cursor is implicitly converted from the requested type to another.

FOR *select_statement*

Is a standard SELECT statement that defines the result set of the cursor. The keywords COMPUTE, COMPUTE BY, FOR BROWSE, and INTO are not allowed within the *select_statement* of a cursor declaration.

If DISTINCT, UNION, GROUP BY, or HAVING are used, or an aggregate expression is included in the *select_list*, the cursor will be created as STATIC.

If each of the underlying tables does not have a unique index and an SQL-92 SCROLL cursor or a Transact-SQL KEYSET cursor is requested, it will automatically be a STATIC cursor.

If *select_statement* contains an ORDER BY in which the columns are not unique row identifiers, a DYNAMIC cursor is converted to a KEYSET cursor, or to a STATIC cursor if a KEYSET cursor cannot be opened. This also happens for a cursor defined using SQL-92 syntax but without the STATIC keyword.

READ ONLY

Prevents updates from being made through this cursor. The cursor cannot be referenced in a WHERE CURRENT OF clause in an UPDATE or DELETE statement. This option overrides the default capability of a cursor to be updated. This keyword varies from the earlier READ_ONLY by having a space instead of an underscore between READ and ONLY.

UPDATE [OF *column_name* [,...*n*]]

Defines updateable columns within the cursor. If OF *column_name* [,...*n*] is supplied, only the columns listed will allow modifications. If no list is supplied, all columns can be updated, unless the cursor has been defined as READ_ONLY.

Remarks

After declaration, all variables are initialized to NULL. Use the SET statement to assign a value that is not NULL to a declared variable. The SET statement that assigns a value to the variable returns a single value. When initializing multiple variables use a separate SET statement for each local variable.

Variables can be used only in expressions, not in place of object names or keywords. To construct dynamic SQL statements, use EXECUTE.

The syntax rules for SET @*cursor_variable* do not include the LOCAL and GLOBAL keywords. When the SET @*cursor_variable* = CURSOR... syntax is used, the cursor is created as GLOBAL or LOCAL, depending on the setting of the **default to local cursor** database option.

Cursor variables are always local, even if they reference a global cursor. When a cursor variable references a global cursor, the cursor has both a global and a local cursor reference. For more information, see Example C.

For more information, see DECLARE CURSOR.

Permissions

SET @*local_variable* permissions default to all users.

Examples

A. Print the value of a variable initialized with SET

This example creates the **@myvar** variable, places a string value into the variable, and prints the value of the **@myvar** variable.

```
DECLARE @myvar char(20)
SET @myvar = 'This is a test'
SELECT @myvar
GO
```

B. Use a local variable assigned a value with SET in a SELECT statement

This example creates a local variable named **@state** and uses this local variable in a SELECT statement to find all author first and last names where the author resides in the state of Utah.

```
USE pubs
GO
DECLARE @state char(2)
SET @state = 'UT'
SELECT RTRIM(au_fname) + ' ' + RTRIM(au_lname) AS Name, state
FROM authors
WHERE state = @state
GO
```

C. Use SET with a global cursor

This example creates a local variable and then sets the cursor variable to the global cursor name.

```
DECLARE my_cursor CURSOR GLOBAL FOR SELECT * FROM authors
   DECLARE @my_variable CURSOR
   SET @my_variable = my_cursor
                   /* There is a GLOBAL declared
                      reference (my_cursor) and a LOCAL variable
                      reference (@my_variable) to the my_cursor
                      cursor.                                    */
   DEALLOCATE my_cursor   /* There is now only a LOCAL variable
                      reference (@my_variable) to the my_cursor
                      cursor.                                    */
```

D. Define a cursor with SET

This example uses the SET statement to define a cursor.

```
DECLARE @CursorVar CURSOR

SET @CursorVar = CURSOR SCROLL DYNAMIC
FOR
SELECT LastName, FirstName
FROM Northwind.dbo.Employees
WHERE LastName like 'B%'

OPEN @CursorVar

FETCH NEXT FROM @CursorVar
WHILE @@FETCH_STATUS = 0
BEGIN
    FETCH NEXT FROM @CursorVar
END

CLOSE @CursorVar
DEALLOCATE @CursorVar
```

E. Assign a value from a query

This example uses a query to assign a value to a variable.

```
USE Northwind
GO
DECLARE @rows int
SET @rows = (SELECT COUNT(*) FROM Customers)
```

Related Topics
DECLARE @local_variable, EXECUTE, Expressions, SELECT, SET,
Using Variables and Parameters

SET

The Transact-SQL programming language provides several SET statements that alter
the current session handling of specific information.

The SET statements are grouped into these categories.

Category	Alters the current session settings for
Date and time	Handling date and time data.
Locking	Handling Microsoft SQL Server locking.
Miscellaneous	Miscellaneous SQL Server functionality.
Query execution	Query execution and processing.
SQL-92 settings	Using the SQL-92 default settings.
Statistics	Displaying statistics information.
Transactions	Handling SQL Server transactions.

Date and Time Statements
SET DATEFIRST
SET DATEFORMAT

Locking Statements
SET DEADLOCK_PRIORITY
SET LOCK_TIMEOUT

Miscellaneous Statements
SET CONCAT_NULL_YIELDS_NULL
SET CURSOR_CLOSE_ON_COMMIT
SET DISABLE_DEF_CNST_CHK
SET FIPS_FLAGGER
SET IDENTITY_INSERT
SET LANGUAGE
SET OFFSETS
SET QUOTED_IDENTIFIER

Query Execution Statements

SET ARITHABORT
SET ARITHIGNORE
SET FMTONLY
SET NOCOUNT
SET NOEXEC
SET NUMERIC_ROUNDABORT
SET PARSEONLY
SET QUERY_GOVERNOR_COST_LIMIT
SET ROWCOUNT
SET TEXTSIZE

SQL-92 Settings Statements

SET ANSI_DEFAULTS
SET ANSI_NULL_DFLT_OFF
SET ANSI_NULL_DFLT_ON
SET ANSI_NULLS
SET ANSI_PADDING
SET ANSI_WARNINGS

Statistics Statements

SET FORCEPLAN
SET SHOWPLAN_ALL
SET SHOWPLAN_TEXT
SET STATISTICS IO
SET STATISTICS PROFILE
SET STATISTICS TIME

Transactions Statements

SET IMPLICIT_TRANSACTIONS
SET REMOTE_PROC_TRANSACTIONS
SET TRANSACTION ISOLATION LEVEL
SET XACT_ABORT

Considerations When Using the SET Statements

- Except for SET FIPS_FLAGGER, SET OFFSETS, SET PARSEONLY, and SET QUOTED_IDENTIFIER, all other SET statements are set at execute or run time. SET FIPS_FLAGGER, SET OFFSETS, SET PARSEONLY, and SET QUOTED_IDENTIFIER are set at parse time.

- If a SET statement is set in a stored procedure, the value of the SET option is restored after control is returned from the stored procedure. Therefore, a SET statement specified in dynamic SQL does not affect the statements that follow the dynamic SQL statement.

- Stored procedures execute with the SET settings specified at execute time except for SET ANSI_NULLS and SET QUOTED_IDENTIFIER. Stored procedures specifying SET ANSI_NULLS or SET QUOTED_IDENTIFIER use the setting specified at stored procedure creation time. If used inside a stored procedure, any SET setting is ignored.

- The **user options** setting of **sp_configure** allows server-wide settings and works across multiple databases. This setting also behaves like an explicit SET statement, except that it occurs at login time.

- Database settings (set by using **sp_dboption**) are valid only at the database level and only take effect if explicitly set. Database settings override server option settings (set using **sp_configure**).

- With any of the SET statements with ON and OFF settings, it is possible to specify either an ON or OFF setting for multiple SET options. For example,

```
SET QUOTED_IDENTIFIER, ANSI_NULLS ON
```

sets both QUOTED_IDENTIFIER and ANSI_NULLS to ON.

- SET statement settings override database option settings (set by using **sp_dboption**). In addition, some connection settings are set ON automatically when a user connects to a database based on the values put into effect by the prior use of the **sp_configure user options** setting, or the values that apply to all ODBC and OLE/DB connections.

- When a global or shortcut SET statement (for example, SET ANSI_DEFAULTS) sets a number of settings, issuing the shortcut SET statement resets the prior settings for all those options affected by the shortcut SET statement. If an individual SET option (affected by a shortcut SET statement) is explicitly set after the shortcut SET statement is issued, the individual SET statement overrides the corresponding shortcut settings.

- When batches are used, the database context is determined by the batch established with the USE statement. Ad hoc queries and all other statements that are executed outside of the stored procedure and that are in batches inherit the option settings of the database and connection established with the USE statement.

- When a stored procedure is executed, either from a batch or from another stored procedure, it is executed under the option values that are currently set in the database that contains the stored procedure. For example, when stored procedure **db1.dbo.sp1** calls stored procedure **db2.dbo.sp2**, stored procedure **sp1** is executed under the current compatibility level setting of database **db1**, and stored procedure **sp2** is executed under the current compatibility level setting of database **db2**.

- When a Transact-SQL statement refers to objects that reside in multiple databases, the current database context and the current connection context (the database defined by the USE statement if it is in a batch, or the database that contains the stored procedure if it is in a stored procedure) applies to that statement.

- When creating and manipulating indexes on computed columns or indexed views, the SET options ARITHABORT, CONCAT_NULL_YIELDS_NULL, QUOTED_IDENTIFIER, ANSI_NULLS, ANSI_PADDING, and ANSI_WARNINGS must be set to ON. The option NUMERIC_ROUNDABORT must be set to OFF.

  If any of these options are not set to the required values, INSERT, UPDATE, and DELETE actions on indexed views or tables with indexes on computed columns will fail. SQL Server will raise an error listing all the options that are incorrectly set. Also, SQL Server will process SELECT statements on these tables or indexed views as though the indexes on computed columns or on the views do not exist.

SET ANSI_DEFAULTS

Controls a group of Microsoft SQL Server settings that collectively specify some SQL-92 standard behavior.

Syntax

```
SET ANSI_DEFAULTS { ON | OFF }
```

Remarks

When enabled (ON), this option enables the following SQL-92 settings:

SET ANSI_NULLS	SET CURSOR_CLOSE_ON_COMMIT
SET ANSI_NULL_DFLT_ON	SET IMPLICIT_TRANSACTIONS
SET ANSI_PADDING	SET QUOTED_IDENTIFIER
SET ANSI_WARNINGS	

Together, these SQL-92 standard SET options define the query processing environment for the duration of the user's work session, a running trigger, or a stored procedure. These SET options, however, do not include all of the options required to conform to the SQL-92 standard.

When dealing with indexes on computed columns and indexed views, four of these defaults (ANSI_NULLS, ANSI_PADDING, ANSI_WARNINGS, and QUOTED_IDENTIFIER) must be set to ON. These defaults are among seven SET options that must be assigned required values when creating and manipulating indexes on computed columns and indexed views. The other SET options are: ARITHABORT (ON), CONCAT_NULL_YIELDS_NULL (ON), and NUMERIC_ROUNDABORT (OFF). For more information about required SET option settings with indexed views and indexes on computed columns, see Considerations When Using SET Statements in SET.

The SQL Server ODBC driver and Microsoft OLE DB Provider for SQL Server automatically set ANSI_DEFAULTS to ON when connecting. The driver and Provider then set CURSOR_CLOSE_ON_COMMIT and IMPLICIT_TRANSACTIONS to OFF. The OFF settings for SET CURSOR_CLOSE_ON_COMMIT and SET IMPLICIT_TRANSACTIONS can be configured in ODBC data sources, in ODBC connection attributes, or in OLE DB connection properties that are set in the application before connecting to SQL Server. SET ANSI_DEFAULTS defaults to OFF for connections from DB-Library applications.

When SET ANSI_DEFAULTS is issued, SET QUOTED_IDENTIFIER is set at parse time, and these options are set at execute time:

SET ANSI_NULLS	SET ANSI_WARNINGS
SET ANSI_NULL_DFLT_ON	SET CURSOR_CLOSE_ON_COMMIT
SET ANSI_PADDING	SET IMPLICIT_TRANSACTIONS

Permissions

SET ANSI_DEFAULTS permissions default to all users.

Examples

This example sets SET ANSI_DEFAULTS ON and uses the DBCC USEROPTIONS statement to display the settings that are affected.

```
-- SET ANSI_DEFAULTS ON.
SET ANSI_DEFAULTS ON
GO
-- Display the current settings.
DBCC USEROPTIONS
GO
-- SET ANSI_DEFAULTS OFF.
SET ANSI_DEFAULTS OFF
GO
```

Related Topics

DBCC USEROPTIONS, SET, SET ANSI_NULL_DFLT_ON, SET ANSI_NULLS, SET ANSI_PADDING, SET ANSI_WARNINGS, SET CURSOR_CLOSE_ON_COMMIT, SET IMPLICIT_TRANSACTIONS, SET QUOTED_IDENTIFIER

SET ANSI_NULL_DFLT_OFF

Alters the session's behavior to override default nullability of new columns when the **ANSI null default** option for the database is **true**. For more information about setting the value for **ANSI null default**, see sp_dboption and Setting Database Options.

Syntax

```
SET ANSI_NULL_DFLT_OFF {ON | OFF}
```

Remarks

This setting only affects the nullability of new columns when the nullability of the column is not specified in the CREATE TABLE and ALTER TABLE statements. When SET ANSI_NULL_DFLT_OFF is ON, new columns created with the ALTER TABLE and CREATE TABLE statements are, by default, NOT NULL if the nullability status of the column is not explicitly specified. SET ANSI_NULL_DFLT_OFF has no effect on columns created with an explicit NULL or NOT NULL.

Both SET ANSI_NULL_DFLT_OFF and SET ANSI_NULL_DFLT_ON cannot be set ON simultaneously. If one option is set ON, the other option is set OFF. Therefore, either ANSI_NULL_DFLT_OFF or SET ANSI_NULL_DFLT_ON can be set ON, or both can be set OFF. If either option is ON, that setting (SET ANSI_NULL_DFLT_OFF or SET ANSI_NULL_DFLT_ON) takes effect. If both options are set OFF, Microsoft SQL Server uses the value of the **ANSI null default** option of **sp_dboption**.

For the most reliable operation of Transact-SQL scripts that may be used in databases with different nullability settings, it is best to always specify NULL or NOT NULL in CREATE TABLE and ALTER TABLE statements.

The setting of SET ANSI_NULL_DFLT_OFF is set at execute or run time and not at parse time.

Permissions

SET ANSI_NULL_DFLT_OFF permissions default to all users.

Examples

This example shows the effects of SET ANSI_NULL_DFLT_OFF with both settings for the **ANSI null default** database option.

```
USE pubs
GO
-- Set the 'ANSI null default' database option to true by executing
-- sp_dboption.
GO
EXEC sp_dboption 'pubs','ANSI null default','true'
GO
-- Create table t1.
CREATE TABLE t1 (a tinyint)
GO
-- NULL INSERT should succeed.
INSERT INTO t1 (a) VALUES (null)
GO
-- SET ANSI_NULL_DFLT_OFF to ON and create table t2.
SET ANSI_NULL_DFLT_OFF ON
GO
CREATE TABLE t2 (a tinyint)
GO
-- NULL INSERT should fail.
INSERT INTO t2 (a) VALUES (null)
GO
-- SET ANSI_NULL_DFLT_OFF to OFF and create table t3.
SET ANSI_NULL_DFLT_OFF off
GO
CREATE TABLE t3 (a tinyint)
GO
-- NULL INSERT should succeed.
INSERT INTO t3 (a) VALUES (null)
GO
-- This illustrates the effect of having both the sp_dboption and SET
-- option disabled.
-- Set the 'ANSI null default' database option to false.
EXEC sp_dboption 'pubs','ANSI null default','false'
GO
-- Create table t4.
CREATE TABLE t4 (a tinyint)
GO
-- NULL INSERT should fail.
INSERT INTO t4 (a) VALUES (null)
GO
```

(continued)

(continued)

```
-- SET ANSI_NULL_DFLT_OFF to ON and create table t5.
SET ANSI_NULL_DFLT_OFF ON
GO
CREATE TABLE t5 (a tinyint)
GO
-- NULL insert should fail.
INSERT INTO t5 (a) VALUES (null)
GO
-- SET ANSI_NULL_DFLT_OFF to OFF and create table t6.
SET ANSI_NULL_DFLT_OFF OFF
GO
CREATE TABLE t6 (a tinyint)
GO
-- NULL insert should fail.
INSERT INTO t6 (a) VALUES (null)
GO
-- Drop tables t1 through t6.
DROP TABLE t1
DROP TABLE t2
DROP TABLE t3
DROP TABLE t4
DROP TABLE t5
DROP TABLE t6
GO
```

Related Topics

ALTER TABLE, CREATE TABLE, SET, SET ANSI_NULL_DFLT_ON

SET ANSI_NULL_DFLT_ON

Alters the session's behavior to override default nullability of new columns when the **ANSI null default** option for the database is **false**. For more information about setting the value for **ANSI null default**, see sp_dboption and Setting Database Options.

Syntax

```
SET ANSI_NULL_DFLT_ON {ON | OFF}
```

Remarks

This setting only affects the nullability of new columns when the nullability of the column is not specified in the CREATE TABLE and ALTER TABLE statements. When SET ANSI_NULL_DFLT_ON is ON, new columns created with the ALTER TABLE and CREATE TABLE statements allow null values if the nullability status of the column is not explicitly specified. SET ANSI_NULL_DFLT_ON has no effect on columns created with an explicit NULL or NOT NULL.

Both SET ANSI_NULL_DFLT_OFF and SET ANSI_NULL_DFLT_ON cannot be set ON simultaneously. If one option is set ON, the other option is set OFF. Therefore, either ANSI_NULL_DFLT_OFF or ANSI_NULL_DFLT_ON can be set ON, or both can be set OFF. If either option is ON, that setting (SET ANSI_NULL_DFLT_OFF or SET ANSI_NULL_DFLT_ON) takes effect. If both options are set OFF, Microsoft SQL Server uses the value of the **ANSI null default** option of **sp_dboption**.

For the most reliable operation of Transact-SQL scripts used in databases with different nullability settings, it is best to specify NULL or NOT NULL in CREATE TABLE and ALTER TABLE statements.

The SQL Server ODBC driver and Microsoft OLE DB Provider for SQL Server automatically set ANSI_NULL_DFLT_ON to ON when connecting. SET ANSI_NULL_DFLT_ON defaults to OFF for connections from DB-Library applications.

When SET ANSI_DEFAULTS is ON, SET ANSI_NULL_DFLT_ON is enabled.

The setting of SET ANSI_NULL_DFLT_ON is set at execute or run time and not at parse time.

Permissions

SET ANSI_NULL_DFLT_ON permissions default to all users.

Examples

This example shows the effects of SET ANSI_NULL_DFLT_ON with both settings for the **ANSI null default** database option.

```
USE pubs
GO
-- The code from this point on demonstrates that SET ANSI_NULL_DFLT_ON
-- has an effect when the 'ANSI null default' for the database is false.
-- Set the 'ANSI null default' database option to false by executing
-- sp_dboption.
EXEC sp_dboption 'pubs','ANSI null default','false'
GO
```

(continued)

(continued)

```
-- Create table t1.
CREATE TABLE t1 (a tinyint)
GO
-- NULL INSERT should fail.
INSERT INTO t1 (a) VALUES (null)
GO
-- SET ANSI_NULL_DFLT_ON to ON and create table t2.
SET ANSI_NULL_DFLT_ON ON
GO
CREATE TABLE t2 (a tinyint)
GO
-- NULL insert should succeed.
INSERT INTO t2 (a) VALUES (null)
GO
-- SET ANSI_NULL_DFLT_ON to OFF and create table t3.
SET ANSI_NULL_DFLT_ON OFF
GO
CREATE TABLE t3 (a tinyint)
GO
-- NULL insert should fail.
INSERT INTO t3 (a) VALUES (null)
GO
-- The code from this point on demonstrates that SET ANSI_NULL_DFLT_ON
-- has no effect when the 'ANSI null default' for the database is true.
-- Set the 'ANSI null default' database option to true.
EXEC sp_dboption 'pubs','ANSI null default','true'
GO
-- Create table t4.
CREATE TABLE t4 (a tinyint)
GO
-- NULL INSERT should succeed.
INSERT INTO t4 (a) VALUES (null)
GO
-- SET ANSI_NULL_DFLT_ON to ON and create table t5.
SET ANSI_NULL_DFLT_ON ON
GO
CREATE TABLE t5 (a tinyint)
GO
-- NULL INSERT should succeed.
INSERT INTO t5 (a) VALUES (null)
GO
-- SET ANSI_NULL_DFLT_ON to OFF and create table t6.
```

(continued)

(continued)

```
SET ANSI_NULL_DFLT_ON OFF
GO
CREATE TABLE t6 (a tinyint)
GO
-- NULL INSERT should succeed.
INSERT INTO t6 (a) VALUES (null)
GO
-- Set the 'ANSI null default' database option to false.
EXEC sp_dboption 'pubs','ANSI null default','false'
GO
-- Drop tables t1 through t6.
DROP TABLE t1
DROP TABLE t2
DROP TABLE t3
DROP TABLE t4
DROP TABLE t5
DROP TABLE t6
GO
```

Related Topics

ALTER TABLE, CREATE TABLE, SET, SET ANSI_DEFAULTS, SET ANSI_NULL_DFLT_OFF

SET ANSI_NULLS

Specifies SQL-92 compliant behavior of the Equals (=) and Not Equal to (<>) comparison operators when used with null values.

Syntax

```
SET ANSI_NULLS {ON | OFF}
```

Remarks

The SQL-92 standard requires that an equals (=) or not equal to (<>) comparison against a null value evaluates to FALSE. When SET ANSI_NULLS is ON, a SELECT statement using WHERE *column_name* = NULL returns zero rows even if there are null values in *column_name*. A SELECT statement using WHERE *column_name* <> NULL returns zero rows even if there are nonnull values in *column_name*.

When SET ANSI_NULLS is OFF, the Equals (=) and Not Equal To (<>) comparison operators do not follow the SQL-92 standard. A SELECT statement using WHERE *column_name* = NULL returns the rows with null values in *column_name*. A SELECT statement using WHERE *column_name* <> NULL returns the rows with nonnull values in the column. In addition, a SELECT statement using WHERE column_name <> XYZ_value returns all rows that are not XYZ value and that are not NULL.

> **Note**   Whether Microsoft SQL Server interprets an empty string as either a single space or as a true empty string is controlled by the compatibility level setting of **sp_dbcmptlevel**. If the compatibility level is less than or equal to 65, SQL Server interprets empty strings as single spaces. If the compatibility level is equal to 70, SQL Server interprets empty strings as empty strings. For more information, see sp_dbcmptlevel.

When SET ANSI_NULLS is ON, all comparisons against a null value evaluate to UNKNOWN. When SET ANSI_NULLS is OFF, comparisons of all data against a null value evaluate to TRUE if the data value is NULL. If not specified, the setting of the **ANSI nulls** option of the current database applies. For more information about the **ANSI nulls** database option, see sp_dboption and Setting Database Options.

For a script to work as intended, regardless of the **ANSI nulls** database option or the setting of SET ANSI_NULLS, use IS NULL and IS NOT NULL in comparisons that may contain null values.

For stored procedures, SQL Server uses the SET ANSI_NULLS setting value from the initial creation time of the stored procedure. Whenever the stored procedure is subsequently executed, the setting of SET ANSI_NULLS is restored to its originally used value and takes effect. When invoked inside a stored procedure, the setting of SET ANSI_NULLS is not changed.

SET ANSI_NULLS should be set to ON for executing distributed queries.

SET ANSI_NULLS also must be ON when creating or manipulating indexes on computed columns or indexed views. If SET ANSI_NULLS is OFF, CREATE, UPDATE, INSERT, and DELETE statements on tables with indexes on computed columns or indexed views will fail. SQL Server will return an error listing all SET options violating the required values. In addition, when executing a SELECT statement, if SET ANSI_NULLS is OFF, SQL Server will ignore the index values on computed columns or views and resolve the select as though there were no such indexes on the tables or views.

> **Note**   ANSI_NULLS is one of seven SET options that must be set to required values when dealing with indexes on computed columns or indexed views. The options ANSI_PADDING, ANSI_WARNINGS, ARITHABORT, QUOTED_IDENTIFIER, and CONCAT_NULL_YIELDS_NULL also must be set to ON, while NUMERIC_ROUNDABORT must be set to OFF.

The SQL Server ODBC driver and Microsoft OLE DB Provider for SQL Server automatically set ANSI_NULLS to ON when connecting. This setting can be configured in ODBC data sources, in ODBC connection attributes, or in OLE DB connection properties that are set in the application before connecting to SQL Server. SET ANSI_NULLS defaults to OFF for connections from DB-Library applications.

When SET ANSI_DEFAULTS is ON, SET ANSI_NULLS is enabled.

The setting of SET ANSI_NULLS is set at execute or run time and not at parse time.

Permissions

SET ANSI_NULLS permissions default to all users.

Examples

This example uses the Equals (=) and Not Equal To (<>) comparison operators to make comparisons with NULL and nonnull values in a table. This example also demonstrates that IS NULL is not affected by the SET ANSI_NULLS setting.

```
-- Create table t1 and insert values.
CREATE TABLE t1 (a int null)
INSERT INTO t1 values (NULL)
INSERT INTO t1 values (0)
INSERT INTO t1 values (1)
GO
-- Print message and perform SELECT statements.
PRINT 'Testing default setting'
DECLARE @varname int
SELECT @varname = NULL
SELECT *
FROM t1
WHERE a = @varname
SELECT *
FROM t1
WHERE a <> @varname
SELECT *
FROM t1
WHERE a IS NULL
GO
-- SET ANSI_NULLS to ON and test.
```

(continued)

(continued)

```
PRINT 'Testing ANSI_NULLS ON'
SET ANSI_NULLS ON
GO
DECLARE @varname int
SELECT @varname = NULL
SELECT *
FROM t1
WHERE a = @varname
SELECT *
FROM t1
WHERE a <> @varname
SELECT *
FROM t1
WHERE a IS NULL
GO
-- SET ANSI_NULLS to OFF and test.
PRINT 'Testing SET ANSI_NULLS OFF'
SET ANSI_NULLS OFF
GO
DECLARE @varname int
SELECT @varname = NULL
SELECT *
FROM t1
WHERE a = @varname
SELECT *
FROM t1
WHERE a <> @varname
SELECT *
FROM t1
WHERE a IS NULL
GO
-- Drop table t1.
DROP TABLE t1
GO
```

Related Topics

= (Equals), IF...ELSE, <> (Not Equal To), SET, SET ANSI_DEFAULTS, WHERE,
WHILE

SET ANSI_PADDING

Controls the way the column stores values shorter than the defined size of the column, and the way the column stores values that have trailing blanks in **char**, **varchar**, **binary**, and **varbinary** data.

Syntax

```
SET ANSI_PADDING { ON | OFF }
```

Remarks

Columns defined with **char**, **varchar**, **binary**, and **varbinary** data types have a defined size.

This setting affects only the definition of new columns. After the column is created, Microsoft SQL Server stores the values based on the setting when the column was created. Existing columns are not affected by a later change to this setting.

> **! WARNING**   It is recommended that ANSI_PADDING always be set to ON.

This table shows the effects of the SET ANSI_PADDING setting when values are inserted into columns with **char**, **varchar**, **binary**, and **varbinary** data types.

Setting	char(*n*) NOT NULL or binary(*n*) NOT NULL	char(*n*) NULL or binary(*n*) NULL	varchar(*n*) or varbinary(*n*)
ON	Pad original value (with trailing blanks for **char** columns and with trailing zeros for **binary** columns) to the length of the column.	Follows same rules as for **char(*n*)** or **binary(*n*)** NOT NULL when SET ANSI_PADDING is ON.	Trailing blanks in character values inserted into **varchar** columns are not trimmed. Trailing zeros in binary values inserted into **varbinary** columns are not trimmed. Values are not padded to the length of the column.
OFF	Pad original value (with trailing blanks for **char** columns and with trailing zeros for **binary** columns) to the length of the column.	Follows same rules as for **varchar** or **varbinary** when SET ANSI_PADDING is OFF.	Trailing blanks in character values inserted into a **varchar** column are trimmed. Trailing zeros in binary values inserted into a **varbinary** column are trimmed.

> **Note**   When padded, **char** columns are padded with blanks, and **binary** columns are padded with zeros. When trimmed, **char** columns have the trailing blanks trimmed, and **binary** columns have the trailing zeros trimmed.

SET ANSI_PADDING must be ON when creating or manipulating indexes on computed columns or indexed views. For more information about required SET option settings with indexed views and indexes on computed columns, see Considerations When Using SET Statements in SET.

The SQL Server ODBC driver and Microsoft OLE DB Provider for SQL Server automatically set ANSI_PADDING to ON when connecting. This can be configured in ODBC data sources, in ODBC connection attributes, or OLE DB connection properties set in the application before connecting. SET ANSI_PADDING defaults to OFF for connections from DB-Library applications.

nchar, **nvarchar**, and **ntext** columns always display the SET ANSI_PADDING ON behavior, regardless of the current setting of SET ANSI_PADDING.

When SET ANSI_DEFAULTS is ON, SET ANSI_PADDING is enabled.

The setting of SET ANSI_PADDING is set at execute or run time and not at parse time.

Permissions

SET ANSI_PADDING permissions default to all users.

Examples

This example demonstrates how the setting affects each of these data types.

```
SET ANSI_PADDING ON
GO
PRINT 'Testing with ANSI_PADDING ON'
GO

CREATE TABLE t1
(charcol char(16) NULL,
varcharcol varchar(16) NULL,
varbinarycol varbinary(8))
GO
INSERT INTO t1 VALUES ('No blanks', 'No blanks', 0x00ee)
INSERT INTO t1 VALUES ('Trailing blank ', 'Trailing blank ', 0x00ee00)

SELECT 'CHAR'='>' + charcol + '<', 'VARCHAR'='>' + varcharcol + '<',
    varbinarycol
FROM t1
GO

SET ANSI_PADDING OFF
GO
```

(continued)

(continued)

```
PRINT 'Testing with ANSI_PADDING OFF'
GO

CREATE TABLE t2
(charcol char(16) NULL,
varcharcol varchar(16) NULL,
varbinarycol varbinary(8))
GO
INSERT INTO t2 VALUES ('No blanks', 'No blanks', 0x00ee)
INSERT INTO t2 VALUES ('Trailing blank ', 'Trailing blank ', 0x00ee00)

SELECT 'CHAR'='>' + charcol + '<', 'VARCHAR'='>' + varcharcol + '<',
    varbinarycol
FROM t2
GO

DROP TABLE t1
DROP TABLE t2
GO
```

Related Topics

CREATE TABLE, INSERT, SET, SET ANSI_DEFAULTS

SET ANSI_WARNINGS

Specifies SQL-92 standard behavior for several error conditions.

Syntax

```
SET ANSI_WARNINGS { ON | OFF }
```

Remarks

SET ANSI_WARNINGS affects these conditions:

- When ON, if null values appear in aggregate functions (such as SUM, AVG, MAX, MIN, STDEV, STDEVP, VAR, VARP, or COUNT) a warning message is generated. When OFF, no warning is issued.

- When ON, divide-by-zero and arithmetic overflow errors cause the statement to be rolled back and an error message is generated. When OFF, divide-by-zero and arithmetic overflow errors cause null values to be returned. The behavior in which a divide-by-zero or arithmetic overflow error causes null values to be returned occurs if an INSERT or UPDATE is attempted on a **character**, Unicode, or **binary** column in which the length of a new value exceeds the maximum size of the column. If SET ANSI_WARNINGS is ON, the INSERT or UPDATE is canceled as specified by the SQL-92 standard. Trailing blanks are ignored for character columns and trailing nulls are ignored for binary columns. When OFF, data is truncated to the size of the column and the statement succeeds.

  Note   When truncation happens in any conversion to or from **binary** or **varbinary** data, no warning or error is issued, regardless of SET options.

The **user options** option of **sp_configure** can be used to set the default setting for ANSI_WARNINGS for all connections to the server. For more information, see sp_configure or Setting Configuration Options.

SET ANSI_WARNINGS must be ON when creating or manipulating indexes on computed columns or indexed views. If SET ANSI_WARNINGS is OFF, CREATE, UPDATE, INSERT, and DELETE statements on tables with indexes on computed columns or indexed views will fail. For more information about required SET option settings with indexed views and indexes on computed columns, see Considerations When Using SET Statements in SET.

Microsoft SQL Server includes the **ANSI warnings** database option, which is equivalent to SET ANSI_WARNINGS. When SET ANSI_WARNINGS is ON, errors or warnings are raised in divide-by-zero, string too large for database column, and other similar errors. When SET ANSI_WARNINGS is OFF, these errors and warnings are not raised. The default value in the **model** database for SET ANSI_WARNINGS is OFF. If not specified, the setting of **ANSI warnings** applies. If SET ANSI_WARNINGS is OFF, SQL Server uses the **ANSI warnings** setting of **sp_dboption**. For more information, see sp_dboption or Setting Database Options.

ANSI_WARNINGS should be set to ON for executing distributed queries.

The SQL Server ODBC driver and Microsoft OLE DB Provider for SQL Server automatically set ANSI_WARNINGS to ON when connecting. This can be configured in ODBC data sources, in ODBC connection attributes, or OLE DB connection properties set in the application before connecting. SET ANSI_WARNINGS defaults to OFF for connections from DB-Library applications.

When SET ANSI_DEFAULTS is ON, SET ANSI_WARNINGS is enabled.

The setting of SET ANSI_WARNINGS is set at execute or run time and not at parse time.

If either SET ARITHABORT or SET ARITHIGNORE is OFF and SET ANSI_WARNINGS is ON, SQL Server still returns an error message when encountering divide-by-zero or overflow errors.

Permissions

SET ANSI_WARNINGS permissions default to all users.

Examples

This example demonstrates the three situations mentioned above with the SET ANSI_WARNINGS to ON and OFF.

```
USE pubs
GO
CREATE TABLE T1 ( a int, b int NULL, c varchar(20) )
GO
SET NOCOUNT ON
GO
INSERT INTO T1 VALUES (1, NULL, '')
INSERT INTO T1 VALUES (1, 0, '')
INSERT INTO T1 VALUES (2, 1, '')
INSERT INTO T1 VALUES (2, 2, '')
GO
SET NOCOUNT OFF
GO


PRINT '**** Setting ANSI_WARNINGS ON'
GO


SET ANSI_WARNINGS ON
GO


PRINT 'Testing NULL in aggregate'
GO
SELECT a, SUM(b) FROM T1 GROUP BY a
GO


PRINT 'Testing String Overflow in INSERT'
GO
INSERT INTO T1 VALUES (3, 3, 'Text string longer than 20 characters')
GO
```

(continued)

(continued)

```
PRINT 'Testing Divide by zero'
GO
SELECT a/b FROM T1
GO

PRINT '**** Setting ANSI_WARNINGS OFF'
GO
SET ANSI_WARNINGS OFF
GO

PRINT 'Testing NULL in aggregate'
GO
SELECT a, SUM(b) FROM T1 GROUP BY a
GO

PRINT 'Testing String Overflow in INSERT'
GO
INSERT INTO T1 VALUES (4, 4, 'Text string longer than 20 characters')
GO

PRINT 'Testing Divide by zero'
GO
SELECT a/b FROM T1
GO
DROP TABLE T1
GO
```

Related Topics

INSERT, SELECT, SET, SET ANSI_DEFAULTS

SET ARITHABORT

Terminates a query when an overflow or divide-by-zero error occurs during query execution.

Syntax

```
SET ARITHABORT { ON | OFF }
```

Remarks

If SET ARITHABORT is ON, these error conditions cause the query or batch to terminate. If the errors occur in a transaction, the transaction is rolled back. If SET ARITHABORT is OFF and one of these errors occurs, a warning message is displayed, and NULL is assigned to the result of the arithmetic operation.

> **Note** If neither SET ARITHABORT nor SET ARITHIGNORE is set, Microsoft SQL Server returns NULL and returns a warning message after the query is executed.

When an INSERT, DELETE or UPDATE statement encounters an arithmetic error (overflow, divide-by-zero, or a domain error) during expression evaluation when SET ARITHABORT is OFF, SQL Server inserts or updates a NULL value. If the target column is not nullable, the insert or update action fails and the user receives an error.

If either SET ARITHABORT or SET ARITHIGNORE is OFF and SET ANSI_WARNINGS is ON, SQL Server still returns an error message when encountering divide-by-zero or overflow errors.

The setting of SET ARITHABORT is set at execute or run time and not at parse time.

SET ARITHABORT must be ON when creating or manipulating indexes on computed columns or indexed views. If SET ARITHABORT is OFF, CREATE, UPDATE, INSERT, and DELETE statements on tables with indexes on computed columns or indexed views will fail. For more information about required SET option settings with indexed views and indexes on computed columns, see Considerations When Using SET Statements in SET.

Permissions

SET ARITHABORT permissions default to all users.

Example

This example demonstrates divide-by-zero and overflow errors with both SET ARITHABORT settings.

```
-- Create tables t1 and t2 and insert data values.
CREATE TABLE t1 (a tinyint, b tinyint)
CREATE TABLE t2 (a tinyint)
GO
INSERT INTO t1 VALUES (1, 0)
INSERT INTO t1 VALUES (255, 1)
GO
```

(continued)

(continued)

```
PRINT '*** SET ARITHABORT ON'
GO
-- SET ARITHABORT ON and testing.
SET ARITHABORT ON
GO

PRINT '*** Testing divide by zero during SELECT'
GO
SELECT a/b
FROM t1
GO
PRINT '*** Testing divide by zero during INSERT'
GO
INSERT INTO t2
SELECT a/b
FROM t1
GO

PRINT '*** Testing tinyint overflow'
GO
INSERT INTO t2
SELECT a+b
FROM t1
GO

PRINT '*** Resulting data - should be no data'
GO
SELECT *
FROM t2
GO

-- Truncate table t2.
TRUNCATE TABLE t2
GO

-- SET ARITHABORT OFF and testing.
PRINT '*** SET ARITHABORT OFF'
GO
SET ARITHABORT OFF
GO
-- This works properly.
PRINT '*** Testing divide by zero during SELECT'
```

(continued)

(continued)

```
GO
SELECT a/b
FROM t1
GO
-- This works as if SET ARITHABORT was ON.
PRINT '*** Testing divide by zero during INSERT'
GO
INSERT INTO t2
SELECT a/b
FROM t1
GO
PRINT '*** Testing tinyint overflow'
GO
INSERT INTO t2
SELECT a+b
FROM t1
GO

PRINT '*** Resulting data - should be 0 rows'
GO
SELECT *
FROM t2
GO
-- Drop tables t1 and t2.
DROP TABLE t1
DROP TABLE t2
GO
```

Related Topics

SET, SET ARITHIGNORE

SET ARITHIGNORE

Controls whether error messages are returned from overflow or divide-by-zero errors during a query.

Syntax

```
SET ARITHIGNORE { ON | OFF }
```

Remarks

The SET ARITHIGNORE setting only controls whether an error message is returned. Microsoft SQL Server returns a NULL in a calculation involving an overflow or divide-by-zero error, regardless of this setting. The SET ARITHABORT setting can be used to determine whether or not the query is terminated. This setting has no effect on errors occurring during INSERT, UPDATE, and DELETE statements.

If either SET ARITHABORT or SET ARITHIGNORE is OFF and SET ANSI_WARNINGS is ON, SQL Server still returns an error message when encountering divide-by-zero or overflow errors.

The setting of SET ARITHIGNORE is set at execute or run time and not at parse time.

Permissions

SET ARITHIGNORE permissions default to all users.

Examples

This example demonstrates both SET ARITHIGNORE settings with both types of query errors.

```
PRINT 'Setting ARITHIGNORE ON'
GO
-- SET ARITHIGNORE ON and testing.
SET ARITHIGNORE ON
GO
SELECT 1/0
GO
SELECT CAST(256 AS tinyint)
GO

PRINT 'Setting ARITHIGNORE OFF'
GO
-- SET ARITHIGNORE OFF and testing.
SET ARITHIGNORE OFF
GO
SELECT 1/0
GO
SELECT CAST(256 AS tinyint)
GO
```

Related Topics

SET, SET ARITHABORT

SET CONCAT_NULL_YIELDS_NULL

Controls whether or not concatenation results are treated as null or empty string values.

Syntax

```
SET CONCAT_NULL_YIELDS_NULL { ON | OFF }
```

Remarks

When SET CONCAT_NULL_YIELDS_NULL is ON, concatenating a null value with a string yields a NULL result. For example, SELECT 'abc' + NULL yields NULL. When SET CONCAT_NULL_YIELDS_NULL is OFF, concatenating a null value with a string yields the string itself (the null value is treated as an empty string). For example, SELECT 'abc' + NULL yields abc.

If not specified, the setting of the **concat null yields null** database option applies.

> **Note** SET CONCAT_NULL_YIELDS_NULL is the same setting as the **concat null yields null** setting of **sp_dboption**.

The setting of SET CONCAT_NULL_YIELDS_NULL is set at execute or run time and not at parse time.

SET CONCAT_NULL_YIELDS_NULL must be ON when creating or manipulating indexes on computed columns or indexed views. If SET CONCAT_NULL_YIELDS_NULL is OFF, CREATE, UPDATE, INSERT, and DELETE statements on tables with indexes on computed columns or indexed views will fail. For more information about required SET option settings with indexed views and indexes on computed columns, see Considerations When Using SET Statements in SET.

Related Topics

SET, Setting Database Options, sp_dboption

SET CONTEXT_INFO

Associates up to 128 bytes of binary information with the current session or connection.

Syntax

```
SET CONTEXT_INFO { binary | @binary_var }
```

Arguments

binary | *@binary_var*
> Specify a binary constant or **binary** or **varbinary** variable to associate with the current session or connection.

Remarks

Session context information is stored in the **context_info** column in the **master.dbo.sysprocesses** table. This is a **varbinary(128)** column.

SET CONTEXT_INFO cannot be specified in a user-defined function. You cannot supply a null value to SET CONTEXT_INFO because the **sysprocesses** table does not allow null values.

SET CONTEXT_INFO does not accept expressions other than constants or variable names. To set the context information to the result of a function call, you must first place the function call result in a **binary** or **varbinary** variable.

When you issue SET CONTEXT_INFO in a stored procedure or trigger, unlike in other SET statements, the new value set for the context information persists after the stored procedure or trigger completes.

SET CURSOR_CLOSE_ON_COMMIT

Controls whether or not a cursor is closed when a transaction is committed.

Syntax

```
SET CURSOR_CLOSE_ON_COMMIT { ON | OFF }
```

Remarks

When SET CURSOR_CLOSE_ON_COMMIT is ON, this setting closes any open cursors on commit or rollback in compliance with SQL-92. When SET CURSOR_CLOSE_ON_COMMIT is OFF, the cursor is not closed when a transaction is committed.

When SET CURSOR_CLOSE_ON_COMMIT is OFF, a ROLLBACK statement closes only open asynchronous cursors that are not fully populated.STATIC or INSENSITIVE cursors that were opened after modifications were made will no longer reflect the state of the data if the modifications are rolled back.

SET CURSOR_CLOSE_ON_COMMIT controls the same behavior as the **cursor close on commit** database option of **sp_dboption**. If CURSOR_CLOSE_ON_COMMIT is set to ON or OFF, that setting is used on the connection. If SET CURSOR_CLOSE_ON_COMMIT has not been specified, the **cursor close on commit** setting of **sp_dboption** applies.

The Microsoft OLE DB Provider for SQL Server and the SQL Server ODBC driver both set CURSOR_CLOSE_ON_COMMIT to OFF when they connect. DB-Library does not automatically set the CURSOR_CLOSE_ON_COMMIT value.

When SET ANSI_DEFAULTS is ON, SET CURSOR_CLOSE_ON_COMMIT is enabled.

The setting of SET CURSOR_CLOSE_ON_COMMIT is set at execute or run time and not at parse time.

Permissions

SET CURSOR_CLOSE_ON_COMMIT permissions default to all users.

Examples

This example defines a cursor in a transaction and attempts to use it after the transaction is committed.

```
SET NOCOUNT ON

CREATE TABLE t1 ( a int )
GO

INSERT INTO t1 values (1)
INSERT INTO t1 values (2)
GO

PRINT '-- SET CURSOR_CLOSE_ON_COMMIT ON'
GO
SET CURSOR_CLOSE_ON_COMMIT ON
GO

PRINT '-- BEGIN TRAN'
BEGIN TRAN

PRINT '-- Declare and open cursor'
DECLARE testcursor CURSOR FOR
SELECT a
FROM t1

OPEN testcursor

PRINT '-- Commit tran'
COMMIT TRAN
```

(continued)

(continued)

```
PRINT '-- Try to use cursor'

FETCH NEXT FROM testcursor

CLOSE testcursor
DEALLOCATE testcursor
GO

PRINT '-- SET CURSOR_CLOSE_ON_COMMIT OFF'
GO
SET CURSOR_CLOSE_ON_COMMIT OFF
GO

PRINT '-- BEGIN TRAN'
BEGIN TRAN

PRINT '-- Declare and open cursor'
DECLARE testcursor CURSOR FOR
SELECT a
FROM t1

OPEN testcursor

PRINT '-- Commit tran'
COMMIT TRAN

PRINT '-- Try to use cursor'

FETCH NEXT FROM testcursor

CLOSE testcursor
DEALLOCATE testcursor
GO

DROP TABLE t1
GO
```

Related Topics

BEGIN TRANSACTION, CLOSE, COMMIT TRANSACTION, ROLLBACK
TRANSACTION, SET, SET ANSI_DEFAULTS, Setting Database Options,
sp_dboption

SET DATEFIRST

Sets the first day of the week to a number from 1 through 7.

Syntax

```
SET DATEFIRST { number | @number_var }
```

Arguments

number | *@number_var*
Is an integer indicating the first day of the week, and can be one of these values.

Value	First day of the week is
1	Monday
2	Tuesday
3	Wednesday
4	Thursday
5	Friday
6	Saturday
7 (default, U.S. English)	Sunday

Remarks

Use the @@DATEFIRST function to check the current setting of SET DATEFIRST.

The setting of SET DATEFIRST is set at execute or run time and not at parse time.

Permissions

SET DATEFIRST permissions default to all users.

Examples

This example displays the day of the week for a date value and shows the effects of changing the DATEFIRST setting.

```
-- SET DATEFIRST to U.S. English default value of 7.
SET DATEFIRST 7
GO
SELECT CAST('1/1/99' AS datetime), DATEPART(dw, '1/1/99')
-- January 1, 1999 is a Friday. Because the U.S. English default
```

(continued)

(continued)

```
-- specifies Sunday as the first day of the week, DATEPART of 1/1/99
-- (Friday) yields a value of 6, because Friday is the sixth day of the
-- week when starting with Sunday as day 1.
SET DATEFIRST 3
-- Because Wednesday is now considered the first day of the week,
-- DATEPART should now show that 1/1/99 (a Friday) is the third day of the -- week. The
following DATEPART function should return a value of 3.
SELECT CAST('1/1/99' AS datetime), DATEPART(dw, '1/1/99')
GO
```

Related Topics

Data Types, @@DATEFIRST, datetime and smalldatetime, SET

SET DATEFORMAT

Sets the order of the dateparts (month/day/year) for entering **datetime** or **smalldatetime** data.

Syntax

```
SET DATEFORMAT { format | @format_var }
```

Arguments

format | @format_var

Is the order of the dateparts. Can be either Unicode or *DBCS* converted to Unicode. Valid parameters include mdy, dmy, ymd, ydm, myd, and dym. The U.S. English default is mdy.

Remarks

This setting is used only in the interpretation of character strings as they are converted to date values. It has no effect on the display of date values.

The setting of SET DATEFORMAT is set at execute or run time and not at parse time.

Permissions

SET DATEFORMAT permissions default to all users.

Examples

This example uses different date formats to handle date strings in different formats.

```
SET DATEFORMAT mdy
GO
DECLARE @datevar datetime
SET @datevar = '12/31/98'
SELECT @datevar
GO

SET DATEFORMAT ydm
GO
DECLARE @datevar datetime
SET @datevar = '98/31/12'
SELECT @datevar
GO

SET DATEFORMAT ymd
GO
DECLARE @datevar datetime
SET @datevar = '98/12/31'
SELECT @datevar
GO
```

Related Topics

Data Types, datetime and smalldatetime, SET

SET DEADLOCK_PRIORITY

Controls the way the session reacts when in a deadlock situation. Deadlock situations arise when two processes have data locked, and each process cannot release its lock until other processes have released theirs.

Syntax

```
SET DEADLOCK_PRIORITY { LOW | NORMAL | @deadlock_var }
```

Arguments

LOW

Specifies that the current session is the preferred deadlock victim. The deadlock victim's transaction is automatically rolled back by Microsoft SQL Server, and the deadlock error message 1205 is returned to the client application.

NORMAL

Specifies that the session return to the default deadlock-handling method.

@deadlock_var

Is a character variable specifying the deadlock-handling method. *@deadlock_var* is 3 if LOW is specified, and 6 if NORMAL is specified.

Remarks

The setting of SET DEADLOCK_PRIORITY is set at execute or run time and not at parse time.

Permissions

SET DEADLOCK_PRIORITY permissions default to all users.

Related Topics

@@LOCK_TIMEOUT, SET, SET LOCK_TIMEOUT

SET DISABLE_DEF_CNST_CHK

Specified interim deferred violation checking and was used for efficiency purposes in Microsoft SQL Server version 6.*x*.

Important   SET DISABLE_DEF_CNST_CHK is included for backward compatibility only. The functionality of this statement is now built into Microsoft SQL Server 2000. In a future version of SQL Server, SET DISABLE_DEF_CNST_CHK may not be supported.

Remarks

If the compatibility level is set to 60 or 65, executing this statement does nothing. However, if the compatibility level is set to 70, executing this statement does nothing, and SQL Server returns a warning message. For more information about setting compatibility levels, see sp_dbcmptlevel

Related Topics

CREATE TABLE, DELETE, INSERT, SET, UPDATE

SET FIPS_FLAGGER

Specifies checking for compliance with the *FIPS* 127-2 standard, which is based on the SQL-92 standard.

Syntax

```
SET FIPS_FLAGGER level
```

Arguments

level

Is the level of compliance against the FIPS 127-2 standard for which all database operations are checked. If a database operation conflicts with the level of SQL-92 standards chosen, Microsoft SQL Server generates a warning.

level must be one of these values.

Value	Description
ENTRY	Standards checking for SQL-92 entry-level compliance.
FULL	Standards checking for SQL-92 full compliance.
INTERMEDIATE	Standards checking for SQL-92 intermediate-level compliance.
OFF	No standards checking.

Remarks

The setting of SET FIPS_FLAGGER is set at parse time and not at execute or run time. Setting at parse time means that if the SET statement is present in the batch or stored procedure, it takes effect, regardless of whether code execution actually reaches that point; and the SET statement takes effect before any statements are executed. For example, even if the SET statement is in an IF...ELSE statement block that is never reached during execution, the SET statement still takes effect because the IF...ELSE statement block is parsed.

If SET FIPS_FLAGGER is set in a stored procedure, the value of SET FIPS_FLAGGER is restored after control is returned from the stored procedure. Therefore, a SET FIPS_FLAGGER statement specified in dynamic SQL does not have any effect on any statements following the dynamic SQL statement.

Permissions

SET FIPS_FLAGGER permissions default to all users.

Related Topics

SET

SET FMTONLY

Returns only meta data to the client.

Syntax

```
SET FMTONLY { ON | OFF }
```

Remarks

No rows are processed or sent to the client as a result of the request when SET FMTONLY is turned ON.

The setting of SET FMTONLY is set at execute or run time and not at parse time.

Permissions

SET FMTONLY permissions default to all users.

Examples

This example changes the SET FMTONLY setting to ON and executes a SELECT statement. The setting causes the statement to return the column information only; no rows of data are returned.

```
SET FMTONLY ON
GO
USE pubs
GO
SELECT *
FROM pubs.dbo.authors
GO
```

Related Topics

SET

SET FORCEPLAN

Makes the Microsoft SQL Server query optimizer process a join in the same order as tables appear in the FROM clause of a SELECT statement only.

Syntax

```
SET FORCEPLAN { ON | OFF }
```

Remarks

SET FORCEPLAN essentially overrides the logic used by the query optimizer to process a Transact-SQL SELECT statement. The data returned by the SELECT statement is the same regardless of this setting. The only difference is the way SQL Server processes the tables to satisfy the query.

Query optimizer hints can also be used in queries to affect how SQL Server processes the SELECT statement.

The setting of SET FORCEPLAN is set at execute or run time and not at parse time.

Permissions

SET FORCEPLAN permissions default to all users.

Examples

This example performs a join between three tables. The SHOWPLAN_TEXT setting is enabled so SQL Server returns information about how it is processing the query differently after the SET FORCE_PLAN setting is enabled.

```
-- SET SHOWPLAN_TEXT to ON.
SET SHOWPLAN_TEXT ON
GO
USE pubs
GO
-- Inner join.
SELECT a.au_lname, a.au_fname, t.title
FROM authors a INNER JOIN titleauthor ta
    ON a.au_id = ta.au_id INNER JOIN titles t
    ON ta.title_id = t.title_id
GO
-- SET FORCEPLAN to ON.
SET FORCEPLAN ON
GO
-- Reexecute inner join to see the effect of SET FORCEPLAN ON.
SELECT a.au_lname, a.au_fname, t.title
FROM authors a INNER JOIN titleauthor ta
    ON a.au_id = ta.au_id INNER JOIN titles t
    ON ta.title_id = t.title_id
GO
SET SHOWPLAN_TEXT OFF
GO
SET FORCEPLAN OFF
GO
```

SELECT, SET, SET SHOWPLAN_ALL, SET SHOWPLAN_TEXT

SET IDENTITY_INSERT

Allows explicit values to be inserted into the identity column of a table.

Syntax

```
SET IDENTITY_INSERT [ database. [ owner. ] ] { table } { ON | OFF }
```

Arguments

database
Is the name of the database in which the specified table resides.

owner
Is the name of the table owner.

table
Is the name of a table with an identity column.

Remarks

At any time, only one table in a session can have the IDENTITY_INSERT property set to ON. If a table already has this property set to ON, and a SET IDENTITY_INSERT ON statement is issued for another table, Microsoft SQL Server returns an error message that states SET IDENTITY_INSERT is already ON and reports the table it is set ON for.

If the value inserted is larger than the current identity value for the table, SQL Server automatically uses the new inserted value as the current identity value.

The setting of SET IDENTITY_INSERT is set at execute or run time and not at parse time.

Permissions

Execute permissions default to the **sysadmin** fixed server role, and the **db_owner** and **db_ddladmin** fixed database roles, and the object owner.

Examples

This example creates a table with an identity column and shows how the SET IDENTITY_INSERT setting can be used to fill a gap in the identity values caused by a DELETE statement.

```
-- Create products table.
CREATE TABLE products (id int IDENTITY PRIMARY KEY, product varchar(40))
GO
-- Inserting values into products table.
INSERT INTO products (product) VALUES ('screwdriver')
INSERT INTO products (product) VALUES ('hammer')
INSERT INTO products (product) VALUES ('saw')
INSERT INTO products (product) VALUES ('shovel')
GO

-- Create a gap in the identity values.
DELETE products
WHERE product = 'saw'
GO

SELECT *
FROM products
GO

-- Attempt to insert an explicit ID value of 3;
-- should return a warning.
INSERT INTO products (id, product) VALUES(3, 'garden shovel')
GO
-- SET IDENTITY_INSERT to ON.
SET IDENTITY_INSERT products ON
GO

-- Attempt to insert an explicit ID value of 3
INSERT INTO products (id, product) VALUES(3, 'garden shovel').
GO

SELECT *
FROM products
GO
-- Drop products table.
DROP TABLE products
GO
```

Related Topics

CREATE TABLE, IDENTITY (Property), INSERT, SET

SET IMPLICIT_TRANSACTIONS

Sets implicit transaction mode for the connection.

Syntax

```
SET IMPLICIT_TRANSACTIONS { ON | OFF }
```

Remarks

When ON, SET IMPLICIT_TRANSACTIONS sets the connection into implicit transaction mode. When OFF, it returns the connection to autocommit transaction mode.

When a connection is in implicit transaction mode and the connection is not currently in a transaction, executing any of the following statements starts a transaction:

ALTER TABLE	FETCH	REVOKE
CREATE	GRANT	SELECT
DELETE	INSERT	TRUNCATE TABLE
DROP	OPEN	UPDATE

If the connection is already in an open transaction, the statements do not start a new transaction.

Transactions that are automatically opened as the result of this setting being ON must be explicitly committed or rolled back by the user at the end of the transaction. Otherwise, the transaction and all the data changes it contains are rolled back when the user disconnects. After a transaction is committed, executing one of the statements above starts a new transaction.

Implicit transaction mode remains in effect until the connection executes a SET IMPLICIT_TRANSACTIONS OFF statement, which returns the connection to autocommit mode. In autocommit mode, all individual statements are committed if they complete successfully.

The Microsoft OLE DB Provider for SQL Server and the SQL Server ODBC driver automatically set IMPLICIT_TRANSACTIONS to OFF when connecting. SET IMPLICIT_TRANSACTIONS defaults to OFF for connections from DB-Library applications.

When SET ANSI_DEFAULTS is ON, SET IMPLICIT_TRANSACTIONS is enabled.

The setting of SET IMPLICIT_TRANSACTIONS is set at execute or run time and not at parse time.

Examples

This example demonstrates transactions that are started explicitly and implicitly with the IMPLICIT_TRANSACTIONS set ON. It uses the @@TRANCOUNT function to demonstrate open and closed transactions.

```
USE pubs
GO

CREATE table t1 (a int)
GO
INSERT INTO t1 VALUES (1)
GO

PRINT 'Use explicit transaction'
BEGIN TRAN
INSERT INTO t1 VALUES (2)
SELECT 'Tran count in transaction'= @@TRANCOUNT
COMMIT TRAN
SELECT 'Tran count outside transaction'= @@TRANCOUNT
GO

PRINT 'Setting IMPLICIT_TRANSACTIONS ON'
GO
SET IMPLICIT_TRANSACTIONS ON
GO

PRINT 'Use implicit transactions'
GO
-- No BEGIN TRAN needed here.
INSERT INTO t1 VALUES (4)
SELECT 'Tran count in transaction'= @@TRANCOUNT
COMMIT TRAN
SELECT 'Tran count outside transaction'= @@TRANCOUNT
GO

PRINT 'Use explicit transactions with IMPLICIT_TRANSACTIONS ON'
GO
BEGIN TRAN
INSERT INTO t1 VALUES (5)
SELECT 'Tran count in transaction'= @@TRANCOUNT
COMMIT TRAN
SELECT 'Tran count outside transaction'= @@TRANCOUNT
GO
```

(continued)

(continued)

```
SELECT * FROM t1
GO

-- Need to commit this tran too!
DROP TABLE t1
COMMIT TRAN
GO
```

Related Topics

ALTER TABLE, BEGIN TRANSACTION, CREATE TABLE, DELETE,
DROP TABLE, FETCH, GRANT, Implicit Transactions, INSERT, OPEN, REVOKE,
SELECT, SET, SET ANSI_DEFAULTS, @@TRANCOUNT, Transactions,
TRUNCATE TABLE, UPDATE

SET LANGUAGE

Specifies the language environment for the session. The session language determines
the **datetime** formats and system messages.

Syntax

```
SET LANGUAGE { [ N ] 'language' | @language_var }
```

Arguments

[N]*'language'* | @*language_var*
    Is the name of the language as stored in **syslanguages**. This argument can be either
    Unicode or DBCS converted to Unicode. To specify a language in Unicode, use
    N*'language'*. If specified as a variable, the variable must be **sysname**.

Remarks

The setting of SET LANGUAGE is set at execute or run time and not at parse time.

Permissions

SET LANGUAGE permissions default to all users.

Examples

This example sets the default language to **us_english**.

```
SET LANGUAGE us_english
GO
```

Related Topics

Data Types, sp_helplanguage, SET, SQL Server Language Support, syslanguages
(**master** database only)

SET LOCK_TIMEOUT

Specifies the number of milliseconds a statement waits for a lock to be released.

Syntax

```
SET LOCK_TIMEOUT timeout_period
```

Arguments

timeout_period
> Is the number of milliseconds that will pass before Microsoft SQL Server returns a
> locking error. A value of -1 (default) indicates no time-out period (that is, wait
> forever).
>
> When a wait for a lock exceeds the time-out value, an error is returned. A value
> of 0 means not to wait at all and return a message as soon as a lock is encountered.

Remarks

At the beginning of a connection, this setting has a value of -1. After it is changed, the
new setting stays in effect for the remainder of the connection.

The setting of SET LOCK_TIMEOUT is set at execute or run time and not at
parse time.

The READPAST locking hint provides an alternative to this SET option.

Permissions

SET LOCK_TIMEOUT permissions default to all users.

Examples

This example sets the lock time-out period to 1,800 milliseconds.

```
SET LOCK_TIMEOUT 1800
GO
```

Related Topics

Locking Hints, @@LOCK_TIMEOUT, SET

SET NOCOUNT

Stops the message indicating the number of rows affected by a Transact-SQL statement from being returned as part of the results.

Syntax

```
SET NOCOUNT { ON | OFF }
```

Remarks

When SET NOCOUNT is ON, the count (indicating the number of rows affected by a Transact-SQL statement) is not returned. When SET NOCOUNT is OFF, the count is returned.

The @@ROWCOUNT function is updated even when SET NOCOUNT is ON.

SET NOCOUNT ON eliminates the sending of DONE_IN_PROC messages to the client for each statement in a stored procedure. When using the utilities provided with Microsoft SQL Server to execute queries, the results prevent "nn rows affected" from being displayed at the end Transact-SQL statements such as SELECT, INSERT, UPDATE, and DELETE.

For stored procedures that contain several statements that do not return much actual data, this can provide a significant performance boost because network traffic is greatly reduced.

The setting of SET NOCOUNT is set at execute or run time and not at parse time.

Permissions

SET NOCOUNT permissions default to all users.

Examples

This example (when executed in the **osql** utility or SQL Query Analyzer) prevents the message (about the number of rows affected) from being displayed.

```
USE pubs
GO
-- Display the count message.
SELECT au_lname
FROM authors
GO
USE pubs
GO
-- SET NOCOUNT to ON and no longer display the count message.
SET NOCOUNT ON
```

(continued)

(continued)

```
GO
SELECT au_lname
FROM authors
GO
-- Reset SET NOCOUNT to OFF.
SET NOCOUNT OFF
GO
```

Related Topics

@@ROWCOUNT, SET

SET NOEXEC

Compiles each query but does not execute it.

Syntax

```
SET NOEXEC { ON | OFF }
```

Remarks

When SET NOEXEC is ON, Microsoft SQL Server compiles each batch of Transact-SQL statements but does not execute them. When SET NOEXEC is OFF, all batches are executed after compilation.

The execution of statements in SQL Server consists of two phases: compilation and execution. This setting is useful for having SQL Server validate the syntax and object names in Transact-SQL code when executing. It is also useful for debugging statements that would usually be part of a larger batch of statements.

The setting of SET NOEXEC is set at execute or run time and not at parse time.

Permissions

SET NOEXEC permissions default to all users.

Examples

This example uses NOEXEC with a valid query, a query with an invalid object name, and a query with incorrect syntax.

```
USE pubs
GO
PRINT 'Valid query'
GO
-- SET NOEXEC to ON.
SET NOEXEC ON
GO
-- Inner join.
SELECT a.au_lname, a.au_fname, t.title
FROM authors a INNER JOIN titleauthor ta
    ON a.au_id = ta.au_id INNER JOIN titles t
    ON ta.title_id = t.title_id
GO
-- SET NOEXEC to OFF.
SET NOEXEC OFF
GO
PRINT 'Invalid object name'
GO
-- SET NOEXEC to ON.
SET NOEXEC ON
GO
-- Function name used is a reserved keyword.

USE pubs
GO
CREATE FUNCTION values (@storeid varchar(30))
RETURNS TABLE
AS
RETURN (SELECT title, qty
    FROM sales s, titles t
    WHERE s.stor_id = @storeid and
    t.title_id = s.title_id)
-- SET NOEXEC to OFF.
SET NOEXEC OFF
GO
PRINT 'Invalid syntax'
GO
-- SET NOEXEC to ON.
SET NOEXEC ON
GO
-- Built-in function incorrectly invoked
SELECT *
```

(continued)

(continued)

```
FROM fn_helpcollations()
-- Reset SET NOEXEC to OFF.
SET NOEXEC OFF
GO
```

Related Topics

SET, SET SHOWPLAN_ALL, SET SHOWPLAN_TEXT

SET NUMERIC_ROUNDABORT

Specifies the level of error reporting generated when rounding in an expression causes a loss of precision.

Syntax

```
SET NUMERIC_ROUNDABORT { ON | OFF }
```

Remarks

When SET NUMERIC_ROUNDABORT is ON, an error is generated when a loss of precision occurs in an expression. When OFF, losses of precision do not generate error messages and the result is rounded to the precision of the column or variable storing the result.

Loss of precision occurs when attempting to store a value with a fixed precision in a column or variable with less precision.

If SET NUMERIC_ROUNDABORT is ON, SET ARITHABORT determines the severity of the generated error. This table shows the effects of these two settings when a loss of precision occurs.

Setting	SET NUMERIC_ROUNDABORT ON	SET NUMERIC_ROUNDABORT OFF
SET ARITHABORT ON	Error is generated; no result set returned.	No errors or warnings; result is rounded.
SET ARITHABORT OFF	Warning is returned; expression returns NULL.	No errors or warnings; result is rounded.

The setting of SET NUMERIC_ROUNDABORT is set at execute or run time and not at parse time.

SET NUMERIC_ROUNDABORT must be OFF when creating or manipulating indexes on computed columns or indexed views. If SET NUMERIC_ROUNDABORT is ON, CREATE, UPDATE, INSERT, and DELETE statements on tables with indexes on computed columns or indexed views will fail. For more information about required SET option settings with indexed views and indexes on computed columns, see Considerations When Using SET Statements in SET.

Permissions

SET NUMERIC_ROUNDABORT permissions default to all users.

Examples

This example shows two values with a precision of four decimal places that are added and stored in a variable with a precision of two decimal places. The expressions demonstrate the effects of the different SET NUMERIC_ROUNDABORT and SET ARITHABORT settings.

```
-- SET NOCOUNT to ON,
-- SET NUMERIC_ROUNDABORT to ON, and SET ARITHABORT to ON.
SET NOCOUNT ON
PRINT 'SET NUMERIC_ROUNDABORT ON'
PRINT 'SET ARITHABORT ON'
SET NUMERIC_ROUNDABORT ON
SET ARITHABORT ON
GO
DECLARE @result decimal(5,2),
@value_1 decimal(5,4), @value_2 decimal(5,4)
SET @value_1 = 1.1234
SET @value_2 = 1.1234
SELECT @result = @value_1 + @value_2
SELECT @result
GO
-- SET NUMERIC_ROUNDABORT to ON and SET ARITHABORT to OFF.
PRINT 'SET NUMERIC_ROUNDABORT ON'
PRINT 'SET ARITHABORT OFF'
SET NUMERIC_ROUNDABORT ON
SET ARITHABORT OFF
GO
DECLARE @result decimal(5,2),
@value_1 decimal(5,4), @value_2 decimal(5,4)
SET @value_1 = 1.1234
SET @value_2 = 1.1234
SELECT @result = @value_1 + @value_2
SELECT @result
```

(continued)

(continued)

```
GO
-- SET NUMERIC_ROUNDABORT to OFF and SET ARITHABORT to ON.
PRINT 'SET NUMERIC_ROUNDABORT OFF'
PRINT 'SET ARITHABORT ON'
SET NUMERIC_ROUNDABORT OFF
SET ARITHABORT ON
GO
DECLARE @result decimal(5,2),
@value_1 decimal(5,4), @value_2 decimal(5,4)
SET @value_1 = 1.1234
SET @value_2 = 1.1234
SELECT @result = @value_1 + @value_2
SELECT @result
GO
-- SET NUMERIC_ROUNDABORT to OFF and SET ARITHABORT to OFF.
PRINT 'SET NUMERIC_ROUNDABORT OFF'
PRINT 'SET ARITHABORT OFF'
SET NUMERIC_ROUNDABORT OFF
SET ARITHABORT OFF
GO
DECLARE @result decimal(5,2),
@value_1 decimal(5,4), @value_2 decimal(5,4)
SET @value_1 = 1.1234
SET @value_2 = 1.1234
SELECT @result = @value_1 + @value_2
SELECT @result
GO
```

Related Topics

Data Types, SET, SET ARITHABORT

SET OFFSETS

Returns the offset (position relative to the start of a statement) of specified keywords
in Transact-SQL statements to DB-Library applications.

Syntax

```
SET OFFSETS keyword_list
```

Arguments

keyword_list

Is a comma-separated list of Transact-SQL constructs including SELECT, FROM, ORDER, COMPUTE, TABLE, PROCEDURE, STATEMENT, PARAM, and EXECUTE.

Remarks

SET OFFSETS is used only in DB-Library applications.

The setting of SET OFFSETS is set at parse time and not at execute time or run time. Setting at parse time means that if the SET statement is present in the batch or stored procedure, it takes effect, regardless of whether code execution actually reaches that point; and the SET statement takes effect before any statements are executed. For example, even if the set statement is in an IF...ELSE statement block that is never reached during execution, the SET statement still takes effect because the IF...ELSE statement block is parsed.

If SET OFFSETS is set in a stored procedure, the value of SET OFFSETS is restored after control is returned from the stored procedure. Therefore, a SET OFFSETS statement specified in dynamic SQL does not have any effect on any statements following the dynamic SQL statement.

Permissions

SET OFFSETS permissions default to all users.

Related Topics

SET, SET PARSEONLY

SET PARSEONLY

Checks the syntax of each Transact-SQL statement and returns any error messages without compiling or executing the statement.

Syntax

```
SET PARSEONLY { ON | OFF }
```

Remarks

When SET PARSEONLY is ON, Microsoft SQL Server only parses the statement. When SET PARSEONLY is OFF, SQL Server compiles and executes the statement.

The setting of SET PARSEONLY is set at parse time and not at execute or run time.

Do not use PARSEONLY in a stored procedure or a trigger. SET PARSEONLY returns offsets if the OFFSETS option is ON and no errors occur.

Permissions

SET PARSEONLY permissions default to all users.

Related Topics

SET, SET OFFSETS

SET QUERY_GOVERNOR_COST_LIMIT

Overrides the currently configured value for the current connection.

Syntax

```
SET QUERY_GOVERNOR_COST_LIMIT value
```

Arguments

value

Is a numeric or integer value indicating if all queries are allowed to run (value of 0) or if no queries are allowed to run with an estimated cost greater than the specified nonzero value. If a numeric value is specified, Microsoft SQL Server truncates it to an integer.

Remarks

Using SET QUERY_GOVERNOR_COST_LIMIT applies to the current connection only and lasts the duration of the current connection. Use the **query governor cost limit** option of **sp_configure** to change the server-wide query governor cost limit value. For more information about configuring this option, see sp_configure and Setting Configuration Options.

The setting of SET QUERY_GOVERNOR_COST_LIMIT is set at execute or run time and not at parse time.

Permissions

SET QUERY_GOVERNOR_COST_LIMIT permissions default to members of the **sysadmin** fixed server role.

Related Topics

SET

SET QUOTED_IDENTIFIER

Causes Microsoft SQL Server to follow the SQL-92 rules regarding quotation mark delimiting identifiers and literal strings. Identifiers delimited by double quotation marks can be either Transact-SQL reserved keywords or can contain characters not usually allowed by the Transact-SQL syntax rules for identifiers.

Syntax

```
SET QUOTED_IDENTIFIER { ON | OFF }
```

Remarks

When SET QUOTED_IDENTIFIER is ON, identifiers can be delimited by double quotation marks, and literals must be delimited by single quotation marks. When SET QUOTED_IDENTIFIER is OFF, identifiers cannot be quoted and must follow all Transact-SQL rules for identifiers. For more information, see Using Identifiers. Literals can be delimited by either single or double quotation marks.

When SET QUOTED_IDENTIFIER is ON, all strings delimited by double quotation marks are interpreted as object identifiers. Therefore, quoted identifiers do not have to follow the Transact-SQL rules for identifiers. They can be reserved keywords and can include characters not usually allowed in Transact-SQL identifiers. Double quotation marks cannot be used to delimit literal string expressions; single quotation marks must be used to enclose literal strings. If a single quotation mark (') is part of the literal string, it can be represented by two single quotation marks ("). SET QUOTED_IDENTIFIER must be ON when reserved keywords are used for object names in the database.

When SET QUOTED_IDENTIFIER is OFF (default), literal strings in expressions can be delimited by single or double quotation marks. If a literal string is delimited by double quotation marks, the string can contain embedded single quotation marks, such as apostrophes.

SET QUOTED_IDENTIFIER must be ON when creating or manipulating indexes on computed columns or indexed views. If SET QUOTED_IDENTIFIER is OFF, CREATE, UPDATE, INSERT, and DELETE statements on tables with indexes on computed columns or indexed views will fail. For more information about required SET option settings with indexed views and indexes on computed columns, see Considerations When Using SET Statements in SET.

The SQL Server ODBC driver and Microsoft OLE DB Provider for SQL Server automatically set QUOTED_IDENTIFIER to ON when connecting. This can be configured in ODBC data sources, in ODBC connection attributes, or OLE DB connection properties. SET QUOTED_IDENTIFIER defaults to OFF for connections from DB-Library applications.

When a stored procedure is created, the SET QUOTED_IDENTIFIER and SET ANSI_NULLS settings are captured and used for subsequent invocations of that stored procedure.

When executed inside a stored procedure, the setting of SET QUOTED_IDENTIFIER is not changed.

When SET ANSI_DEFAULTS is ON, SET QUOTED_IDENTIFIER is enabled.

SET QUOTED_IDENTIFIER also corresponds to the **quoted identifier** setting of **sp_dboption**. If SET QUOTED_IDENTIFIER is OFF, SQL Server uses the **quoted identifier** setting of **sp_dboption**. For more information about database settings, see sp_dboption and Setting Database Options.

SET QUOTED_IDENTIFIER is set at parse time. Setting at parse time means that if the SET statement is present in the batch or stored procedure, it takes effect, regardless of whether code execution actually reaches that point; and the SET statement takes effect before any statements are executed.

Permissions

SET QUOTED_IDENTIFIER permissions default to all users.

Examples

A. Use the quoted identifier setting and reserved word object names

This example shows that the SET QUOTED_IDENTIFIER setting must be ON, and the keywords in table names must be in double quotation marks to create and use objects with reserved keyword names.

```
SET QUOTED_IDENTIFIER OFF
GO
-- Attempt to create a table with a reserved keyword as a name
-- should fail.
CREATE TABLE "select" ("identity" int IDENTITY, "order" int)
GO
SET QUOTED_IDENTIFIER ON
GO

-- Will succeed.
CREATE TABLE "select" ("identity" int IDENTITY, "order" int)
GO

SELECT "identity","order"
FROM "select"
ORDER BY "order"
```

(continued)

(continued)

```
GO

DROP TABLE "SELECT"
GO

SET QUOTED_IDENTIFIER OFF
GO
```

B. Use the quoted identifier setting with single and double quotes

This example shows the way single and double quotation marks are used in string expressions with SET QUOTED_IDENTIFIER set to ON and OFF.

```
SET QUOTED_IDENTIFIER OFF
GO
USE pubs
IF EXISTS(SELECT TABLE_NAME FROM INFORMATION_SCHEMA.VIEWS
      WHERE TABLE_NAME = 'Test')
   DROP TABLE Test
GO
USE pubs
CREATE TABLE Test ( Id int, String varchar (30) )
GO

-- Literal strings can be in single or double quotation marks.
INSERT INTO Test VALUES (1,"'Text in single quotes'")
INSERT INTO Test VALUES (2,'''Text in single quotes''')
INSERT INTO Test VALUES (3,'Text with 2 '''' single quotes')
INSERT INTO Test VALUES (4,'"Text in double quotes"')
INSERT INTO Test VALUES (5,"""Text in double quotes""")
INSERT INTO Test VALUES (6,"Text with 2 """" double quotes")
GO

SET QUOTED_IDENTIFIER ON
GO

-- Strings inside double quotation marks are now treated
-- as object names, so they cannot be used for literals.
INSERT INTO "Test" VALUES (7,'Text with a single '' quote')
GO

-- Object identifiers do not have to be in double quotation marks
-- if they are not reserved keywords.
SELECT *
```

(continued)

(continued)

```
FROM Test
GO


DROP TABLE Test
GO


SET QUOTED_IDENTIFIER OFF
GO
```

Here is the result set:

```
Id              String
-----------     -----------------------------
1               'Text in single quotes'
2               'Text in single quotes'
3               Text with 2 '' single quotes
4               "Text in double quotes"
5               "Text in double quotes"
6               Text with 2 "" double quotes
7               Text with a single ' quote
```

Related Topics

CREATE DATABASE, CREATE DEFAULT, CREATE PROCEDURE, CREATE
RULE, CREATE TABLE, CREATE TRIGGER, CREATE VIEW, Data Types,
EXECUTE, SELECT, SET, SET ANSI_DEFAULTS, sp_rename

SET REMOTE_PROC_TRANSACTIONS

Specifies that when a local transaction is active, executing a remote stored procedure
starts a Transact-SQL distributed transaction managed by the Microsoft Distributed
Transaction Manager (MS DTC).

Syntax

```
SET REMOTE_PROC_TRANSACTIONS { ON | OFF }
```

Arguments

ON | OFF

When ON, a Transact-SQL distributed transaction is started when a remote stored
procedure is executed from a local transaction. When OFF, calling a remote stored
procedures from a local transaction does not start a Transact-SQL distributed
transaction.

Remarks

When REMOTE_PROC_TRANSACTIONS is ON, calling a remote stored procedure starts a distributed transaction and enlists the transaction with MS DTC. The server making the remote stored procedure call is the transaction originator and controls the completion of the transaction. When a subsequent COMMIT TRANSACTION or ROLLBACK TRANSACTION statement is issued for the connection, the controlling server requests that MS DTC manage the completion of the distributed transaction across the servers involved.

After a Transact-SQL distributed transaction has been started, remote stored procedure calls can be made to other remote servers. The remote servers are all enlisted in the Transact-SQL distributed transaction and MS DTC ensures that the transaction is completed against each server.

REMOTE_PROC_TRANSACTIONS is a connection-level setting that can be used to override the server-level **sp_configure remote proc trans** option.

When REMOTE_PROC_TRANSACTIONS is set OFF, remote stored procedure calls are not made part of a local transaction. The modifications made by the remote stored procedure are committed or rolled back at the time the stored procedure completes. Subsequent COMMIT TRANSACTION or ROLLBACK TRANSACTION statements issued by the connection that called the remote stored procedure have no effect on the processing done by the procedure.

The REMOTE_PROC_TRANSACTIONS option is a compatibility option that affects only remote stored procedure calls made to remote servers defined using **sp_addserver**. For more information, see Remote Stored Procedure Architecture. The option does not apply to distributed queries that execute a stored procedure on a linked server defined using **sp_addlinkedserver**. For more information, see Distributed Query Architecture.

The setting of SET REMOTE_PROC_TRANSACTIONS is set at execute or run time and not at parse time.

Permissions

SET REMOTE_PROC_TRANSACTIONS permissions default to all users.

Related Topics

BEGIN DISTRIBUTED TRANSACTION, Distributed Transactions, SET, Transactions

SET ROWCOUNT

Causes Microsoft SQL Server to stop processing the query after the specified number of rows are returned.

Syntax

```
SET ROWCOUNT { number | @number_var }
```

Arguments

number | *@number_var*
Is the number (an integer) of rows to be processed before stopping the given query.

Remarks

It is recommended that DELETE, INSERT, and UPDATE statements currently using SET ROWCOUNT be rewritten to use the TOP syntax. For more information, see DELETE, INSERT, or UPDATE.

The setting of the SET ROWCOUNT option is ignored for INSERT, UPDATE, and DELETE statements against remote tables and local and remote partitioned views.

To turn this option off (so that all rows are returned), specify SET ROWCOUNT 0.

Note   Setting the SET ROWCOUNT option causes most Transact-SQL statements to stop processing when they have been affected by the specified number of rows. This includes triggers and data modification statements such as INSERT, UPDATE, and DELETE. The ROWCOUNT option has no effect on dynamic cursors, but it limits the rowset of keyset and insensitive cursors. This option should be used with caution and primarily with the SELECT statement.

SET ROWCOUNT overrides the SELECT statement TOP keyword if the rowcount is the smaller value.

The setting of SET ROWCOUNT is set at execute or run time and not at parse time.

Permissions

SET ROWCOUNT permissions default to all users.

Examples

SET ROWCOUNT stops processing after the specified number of rows. In this example, note that *x* rows meet the criteria of advances less than or equal to $5,000. However, from the number of rows returned by the update, you can see that not all rows were processed. ROWCOUNT affects all Transact-SQL statements.

```
USE pubs
GO
SELECT count(*) AS Cnt
FROM titles
WHERE advance >= 5000
GO
```

Here is the result set:

```
Cnt
-----------
11

(1 row(s) affected)
```

Now, set ROWCOUNT to 4 and update all rows with an advance of $5,000 or more.

```
-- SET ROWCOUNT to 4.
SET ROWCOUNT 4
GO
UPDATE titles
SET advance = 5000
WHERE advance >= 5000
GO
```

Related Topics

SET

SET SHOWPLAN_ALL

Causes Microsoft SQL Server not to execute Transact-SQL statements. Instead, SQL Server returns detailed information about how the statements are executed and provides estimates of the resource requirements for the statements.

Syntax

```
SET SHOWPLAN_ALL { ON | OFF }
```

Remarks

The setting of SET SHOWPLAN_ALL is set at execute or run time and not at parse time.

When SET SHOWPLAN_ALL is ON, SQL Server returns execution information for each statement without executing it, and Transact-SQL statements are not executed. After this option is set ON, information about all subsequent Transact-SQL statements are returned until the option is set OFF. For example, if a CREATE TABLE statement is executed while SET SHOWPLAN_ALL is ON, SQL Server returns an error message from a subsequent SELECT statement involving that same table; the specified table does not exist. Therefore, subsequent references to this table fail. When SET SHOWPLAN_ALL is OFF, SQL Server executes the statements without generating a report.

SET SHOWPLAN_ALL is intended to be used by applications written to handle its output. Use SET SHOWPLAN_TEXT to return readable output for Microsoft MS-DOS applications, such as the **osql** utility.

SET SHOWPLAN_TEXT and SET SHOWPLAN_ALL cannot be specified inside a stored procedure; they must be the only statements in a batch.

SET SHOWPLAN_ALL returns information as a set of rows that form a hierarchical tree representing the steps taken by the SQL Server query processor as it executes each statement. Each statement reflected in the output contains a single row with the text of the statement, followed by several rows with the details of the execution steps. The table shows the columns that the output contains.

Column name	Description
StmtText	For rows that are not of type PLAN_ROW, this column contains the text of the Transact-SQL statement. For rows of type PLAN_ROW, this column contains a description of the operation. This column contains the physical operator and may optionally also contain the logical operator. This column may also be followed by a description that is determined by the physical operator. For more information, see Logical and Physical Operators.
StmtId	Number of the statement in the current batch.
NodeId	ID of the node in the current query.
Parent	Node ID of the parent step.
PhysicalOp	Physical implementation algorithm for the node. For rows of type PLAN_ROWS only.
LogicalOp	Relational algebraic operator this node represents. For rows of type PLAN_ROWS only.
Argument	Provides supplemental information about the operation being performed. The contents of this column depend on the physical operator.

(continued)

(continued)

Column name	Description
DefinedValues	Contains a comma-separated list of values introduced by this operator. These values may be computed expressions which were present in the current query (for example, in the SELECT list or WHERE clause), or internal values introduced by the query processor in order to process this query. These defined values may then be referenced elsewhere within this query. For rows of type PLAN_ROWS only.
EstimateRows	Estimated number of rows output by this operator. For rows of type PLAN_ROWS only.
EstimateIO	Estimated I/O cost for this operator. For rows of type PLAN_ROWS only.
EstimateCPU	Estimated CPU cost for this operator. For rows of type PLAN_ROWS only.
AvgRowSize	Estimated average row size (in bytes) of the row being passed through this operator.
TotalSubtreeCost	Estimated (cumulative) cost of this operation and all child operations.
OutputList	Contains a comma-separated list of columns being projected by the current operation.
Warnings	Contains a comma-separated list of warning messages relating to the current operation. Warning messages may include the string "NO STATS:( )" with a list of columns. This warning message means that the query optimizer attempted to make a decision based on the statistics for this column, but none were available. Consequently, the query optimizer had to make a guess, which may have resulted in the selection of an inefficient query plan. For more information about creating or updating column statistics (which help the query optimizer choose a more efficient query plan), see UPDATE STATISTICS. This column may optionally include the string "MISSING JOIN PREDICATE", which means that a join (involving tables) is taking place without a join predicate. Accidentally dropping a join predicate may result in a query which takes much longer to run than expected, and returns a huge result set. If this warning is present, verify that the absence of a join predicate is intentional.
Type	Node type. For the parent node of each query, this is the Transact-SQL statement type (for example, SELECT, INSERT, EXECUTE, and so on). For subnodes representing execution plans, the type is PLAN_ROW.
Parallel	0 = Operator is not running in parallel. 1 = Operator is running in parallel.
EstimateExecutions	Estimated number of times this operator will be executed while running the current query.

Permissions

SET SHOWPLAN_ALL permissions default to all users.

Examples

The two statements that follow use the SET SHOWPLAN_ALL settings to show the way SQL Server analyzes and optimizes the use of indexes in queries.

The first query uses the Equals comparison operator (=) in the WHERE clause on an indexed column. This results in the Clustered Index Seek value in the **LogicalOp** column and the name of the index in the **Argument** column.

The second query uses the LIKE operator in the WHERE clause. This forces SQL Server to use a clustered index scan and find the data meeting the WHERE clause condition. This results in the Clustered Index Scan value in the **LogicalOp** column with the name of the index in the **Argument** column, and the Filter value in the **LogicalOp** column with the WHERE clause condition in the **Argument** column.

The values in the **EstimateRows** and the **TotalSubtreeCost** columns are smaller for the first indexed query, indicating that it is processed much faster and uses less resources than the nonindexed query.

```
USE pubs
GO
SET SHOWPLAN_ALL ON
GO
-- First query.
SELECT au_id
FROM authors
WHERE au_id = '409-56-7008'
GO
-- Second query.
SELECT city
FROM authors
WHERE city LIKE 'San%'
GO
SET SHOWPLAN_ALL OFF
GO
```

Related Topics

SET, SET SHOWPLAN_TEXT

SET SHOWPLAN_TEXT

Causes Microsoft SQL Server not to execute Transact-SQL statements. Instead,
SQL Server returns detailed information about how the statements are executed.

Syntax

```
SET SHOWPLAN_TEXT { ON | OFF }
```

Remarks

The setting of SET SHOWPLAN_TEXT is set at execute or run time and not at
parse time.

When SET SHOWPLAN_TEXT is ON, SQL Server returns execution information for
each Transact-SQL statement without executing it. After this option is set ON,
information about all subsequent Transact-SQL statements is returned until the option
is set OFF. For example, if a CREATE TABLE statement is executed while SET
SHOWPLAN_TEXT is ON, SQL Server returns an error message from a subsequent
SELECT statement involving that same table; the specified table does not exist.
Therefore, subsequent references to this table fail. When SET SHOWPLAN_TEXT is
OFF, SQL Server executes statements without generating a report.

SET SHOWPLAN_TEXT is intended to return readable output for Microsoft
MS-DOS applications such as the **osql** utility. SET SHOWPLAN_ALL returns more
detailed output intended to be used with programs designed to handle its output.

SET SHOWPLAN_TEXT and SET SHOWPLAN_ALL cannot be specified in a
stored procedure; they must be the only statements in a batch.

SET SHOWPLAN_TEXT returns information as a set of rows that form a hierarchical
tree representing the steps taken by the SQL Server query processor as it executes each
statement. Each statement reflected in the output contains a single row with the text of
the statement, followed by several rows with the details of the execution steps.
The table shows the column that the output contains.

Column name	Description
StmtText	For rows which are not of type PLAN_ROW, this column contains the text of the Transact-SQL statement. For rows of type PLAN_ROW, this column contains a description of the operation. This column contains the physical operator and may optionally also contain the logical operator. This column may also be followed by a description which is determined by the physical operator. For more information about physical operators, see the **Argument** column in SET SHOWPLAN_ALL.

For more information about the physical and logical operators that can be seen in
showplan output, see Logical and Physical Operators.

Permissions

SET SHOWPLAN_TEXT permissions default to all users.

Examples

This example shows how indexes are used by SQL Server as it processes the statements.

This is the query using an index:

```
SET SHOWPLAN_TEXT ON
GO
USE pubs
SELECT *
FROM roysched
WHERE title_id = 'PS1372'
GO
SET SHOWPLAN_TEXT OFF
GO
```

Here is the result set:

```
StmtText
-------------------------------------------------------
USE pubs

SELECT *
FROM roysched
WHERE title_id = 'PS1372'

(2 row(s) affected)

StmtText
----------------------------------------------------------------
  |--Bookmark Lookup(BOOKMARK:([Bmk1000]), OBJECT:([pubs].[dbo].[roysched]))
       |--Index Seek(OBJECT:([pubs].[dbo].[roysched].[titleidind]),
SEEK:([roysched].[title_id]='PS1372') ORDERED)

(2 row(s) affected)
```

Here is the query not using an index:

```
SET SHOWPLAN_TEXT ON
GO
USE pubs
SELECT *
FROM roysched
```

(continued)

(continued)

```
WHERE lorange < 5000
GO
SET SHOWPLAN_TEXT OFF
GO
```

Here is the result set:

```
StmtText
--------------------------------------------------
USE pubs

SELECT *
FROM roysched
WHERE lorange < 5000

(2 row(s) affected)

StmtText
-----------------------------------------------------------------------
  |--Table Scan(OBJECT:([pubs].[dbo].[roysched]), WHERE:([roysched].[lorange]<5000))

(1 row(s) affected)
```

Related Topics

Operators, SET, SET SHOWPLAN_ALL

SET STATISTICS IO

Causes Microsoft SQL Server to display information regarding the amount of disk activity generated by Transact-SQL statements.

Syntax

```
SET STATISTICS IO { ON | OFF }
```

Remarks

When STATISTICS IO is ON, statistical information is displayed. When OFF, the information is not displayed.

After this option is set ON, all subsequent Transact-SQL statements return the statistical information until the option is set to OFF.

There are five output items.

Output item	Meaning
Table	Name of the table.
scan count	Number of scans performed.
logical reads	Number of pages read from the data cache.
physical reads	Number of pages read from disk.
read-ahead reads	Number of pages placed into the cache for the query.

The setting of SET STATISTICS IO is set at execute or run time and not at parse time.

Permissions
SET STATISTICS IO permissions default to all users.

Related Topics
SET, SET SHOWPLAN_ALL, SET STATISTICS TIME

SET STATISTICS PROFILE

Displays the profile information for a statement. STATISTICS PROFILE works for ad hoc queries, views, triggers, and stored procedures.

Syntax
```
SET STATISTICS PROFILE { ON | OFF }
```

Remarks
When STATISTICS PROFILE is ON, each executed query returns its regular result set, followed by an additional result set that shows a profile of the query execution.

The additional result set contains the SHOWPLAN_ALL columns for the query and these additional columns.

Column name	Description
Rows	Actual number of rows produced by each operator
Executes	Number of times the operator has been executed

Permissions

SET STATISTICS PROFILE permissions default to all users.

Related Topics

SET, SET SHOWPLAN_ALL, SET STATISTICS TIME, SET STATISTICS IO

SET STATISTICS TIME

Displays the number of milliseconds required to parse, compile, and execute each statement.

Syntax

```
SET STATISTICS TIME { ON | OFF }
```

Remarks

When SET STATISTICS TIME is ON, the time statistics for a statement are displayed. When OFF, the time statistics are not displayed.

The setting of SET STATISTICS TIME is set at execute or run time and not at parse time.

Microsoft SQL Server is unable to provide accurate statistics in fiber mode, which is activated when you enable the **lightweight pooling** configuration option.

The **cpu** column in the **sysprocesses** table is only updated when a query executes with SET STATISTICS TIME ON. When SET STATISTICS TIME is OFF, a 0 is returned.

ON and OFF settings also affect the CPU column in the Process Info View for Current Activity in SQL Server Enterprise Manager.

Permissions

SET STATISTICS TIME permissions default to all users.

Related Topics

SET, SET STATISTICS IO

SET TEXTSIZE

Specifies the size of **text** and **ntext** data returned with a SELECT statement.

Syntax

```
SET TEXTSIZE { number }
```

Arguments

number

> Is the size (an integer) of **text** data, in bytes. The maximum setting for SET TEXTSIZE is 2 gigabytes (GB), specified in bytes. A setting of 0 resets the size to the default (4 KB).

Remarks

Setting SET TEXTSIZE affects the @@TEXTSIZE function.

The DB-Library variable DBTEXTLIMIT also limits the size of **text** data returned with a SELECT statement. If DBTEXTLIMIT is set to a smaller size than TEXTSIZE, only the amount specified by DBTEXTLIMIT is returned. For more information, see Programming DB-Library for C in *SQL Server Books Online*.

The SQL Server ODBC driver and Microsoft OLE DB Provider for SQL Server automatically set TEXTSIZE to 2147483647 when connecting.

The setting of set TEXTSIZE is set at execute or run time and not at parse time.

Permissions

SET TEXTSIZE permissions default to all users.

Related Topics

Data Types, SET, @@TEXTSIZE

SET TRANSACTION ISOLATION LEVEL

Controls the default transaction locking behavior for all Microsoft SQL Server SELECT statements issued by a connection.

Syntax

```
SET TRANSACTION ISOLATION LEVEL
    { READ COMMITTED
        | READ UNCOMMITTED
        | REPEATABLE READ
        | SERIALIZABLE
    }
```

Arguments

READ COMMITTED

Specifies that shared locks are held while the data is being read to avoid *dirty reads*, but the data can be changed before the end of the transaction, resulting in *nonrepeatable reads* or *phantom* data. This option is the SQL Server default.

READ UNCOMMITTED

Implements dirty read, or isolation level 0 locking, which means that no shared locks are issued and no exclusive locks are honored. When this option is set, it is possible to read uncommitted or dirty data; values in the data can be changed and rows can appear or disappear in the data set before the end of the transaction. This option has the same effect as setting NOLOCK on all tables in all SELECT statements in a transaction. This is the least restrictive of the four isolation levels.

REPEATABLE READ

Locks are placed on all data that is used in a query, preventing other users from updating the data, but new phantom rows can be inserted into the data set by another user and are included in later reads in the current transaction. Because concurrency is lower than the default isolation level, use this option only when necessary.

SERIALIZABLE

Places a range lock on the data set, preventing other users from updating or inserting rows into the data set until the transaction is complete. This is the most restrictive of the four isolation levels. Because concurrency is lower, use this option only when necessary. This option has the same effect as setting HOLDLOCK on all tables in all SELECT statements in a transaction.

Remarks

Only one of the options can be set at a time, and it remains set for that connection until it is explicitly changed. This becomes the default behavior unless an optimization option is specified at the table level in the FROM clause of the statement.

The setting of SET TRANSACTION ISOLATION LEVEL is set at execute or run time and not at parse time.

Examples

This example sets the TRANSACTION ISOLATION LEVEL for the session. For each Transact-SQL statement that follows, SQL Server holds all of the shared locks until the end of the transaction.

```
SET TRANSACTION ISOLATION LEVEL REPEATABLE READ
GO
BEGIN TRANSACTION
SELECT * FROM publishers
SELECT * FROM authors
...
COMMIT TRANSACTION
```

Related Topics

Adjusting Transaction Isolation Levels, DBCC USEROPTIONS, Isolation Levels, SELECT, SET

SET XACT_ABORT

Specifies whether Microsoft SQL Server automatically rolls back the current transaction if a Transact-SQL statement raises a run-time error.

Syntax

```
SET XACT_ABORT { ON | OFF }
```

Remarks

When SET XACT_ABORT is ON, if a Transact-SQL statement raises a run-time error, the entire transaction is terminated and rolled back. When OFF, only the Transact-SQL statement that raised the error is rolled back and the transaction continues processing. Compile errors, such as syntax errors, are not affected by SET XACT_ABORT.

It is required that XACT_ABORT be set ON for data modification statements in an implicit or explicit transaction against most OLE DB providers, including SQL Server. The only case where this option is not required is if the provider supports nested transactions. For more information, see Distributed Queries and Distributed Transactions.

The setting of SET XACT_ABORT is set at execute or run time and not at parse time.

Examples

This example causes a foreign key violation error in a transaction that has other Transact-SQL statements. In the first set of statements, the error is generated, but the other statements execute successfully and the transaction is successfully committed. In the second set of statements, the SET XACT_ABORT setting is turned ON. This causes the statement error to terminate the batch and the transaction is rolled back.

```
CREATE TABLE t1 (a int PRIMARY KEY)
CREATE TABLE t2 (a int REFERENCES t1(a))
GO
INSERT INTO t1 VALUES (1)
INSERT INTO t1 VALUES (3)
INSERT INTO t1 VALUES (4)
INSERT INTO t1 VALUES (6)
GO
```

(continued)

(continued)

```
SET XACT_ABORT OFF
GO
BEGIN TRAN
INSERT INTO t2 VALUES (1)
INSERT INTO t2 VALUES (2) /* Foreign key error */
INSERT INTO t2 VALUES (3)
COMMIT TRAN
GO

SET XACT_ABORT ON
GO

BEGIN TRAN
INSERT INTO t2 VALUES (4)
INSERT INTO t2 VALUES (5) /* Foreign key error */
INSERT INTO t2 VALUES (6)
COMMIT TRAN
GO

/* Select shows only keys 1 and 3 added.
   Key 2 insert failed and was rolled back, but
   XACT_ABORT was OFF and rest of transaction
   succeeded.
   Key 5 insert error with XACT_ABORT ON caused
   all of the second transaction to roll back. */

SELECT *
FROM t2
GO

DROP TABLE t2
DROP TABLE t1
GO
```

Related Topics

BEGIN TRANSACTION, COMMIT TRANSACTION, ROLLBACK TRANSACTION, SET, @@TRANCOUNT

SETUSER

Allows a member of the **sysadmin** fixed server role or **db_owner** fixed database role to impersonate another user.

> **Important**   SETUSER is included in Microsoft SQL Server 2000 only for backward compatibility, and its usage is not recommended. SETUSER may not be supported in a future release of SQL Server.

Syntax

```
SETUSER [ 'username' [ WITH NORESET ] ]
```

Arguments

'*username*'

Is the name of a SQL Server or Microsoft Windows NT user in the current database that is impersonated. When *username* is not specified, the original identity of the system administrator or database owner impersonating the user is reestablished.

WITH NORESET

Specifies that subsequent SETUSER statements (with no specified *username*) do not reset to the system administrator or database owner.

Remarks

SETUSER can be used by members of the **sysadmin** or **db_owner** roles to adopt the identity of another user in order to test the permissions of the other user.

Only use SETUSER with SQL Server users. It is not supported with Windows users. When SETUSER has been used to assume the identity of another user, any objects that are created are owned by the user being impersonated. For example, if the database owner assumes the identity of user **Margaret** and creates a table called **orders**, the **orders** table is owned by **Margaret** not the system administrator.

SETUSER is not required to create an object owned by another user, because the object can be created with a qualified name that specifies the other user as the owner of the new object. For example, if user **Andrew**, who is a member of the **db_owner** database role, creates a table **Margaret.customers**, user **Margaret** owns **customers** not user **Andrew**.

SETUSER remains in effect until another SETUSER statement is issued or until the current database is changed with the USE statement.

Permissions

SETUSER permissions default to members of the **sysadmin** fixed server role and are not transferable.

Examples

A. Use SETUSER

This example shows how the database owner can adopt the identity of another user. User **mary** has created a table called **computer_types**. Using SETUSER, the database owner impersonates **mary** to grant user **joe** access to the **computer_types** table.

```
SETUSER 'mary'
go
GRANT SELECT ON computer_types TO joe
go
SETUSER
```

B. Use the NORESET option

This example shows how a database owner must create some objects and then test their usability with minimal permissions. For simplicity, the database owner wants to maintain only the permission granted to **mary** for the entire session.

```
SETUSER 'mary' WITH NORESET
go
CREATE TABLE computer_types2
.
.
.
GRANT ...
go
SETUSER      /* This statement has no effect. */
```

> **Note** If SETUSER WITH NORESET is used, the database owner or system administrator must log off and then log on again to reestablish his or her own rights.

Related Topics

DENY, GRANT, REVOKE, USE

SHUTDOWN

Immediately stops Microsoft SQL Server.

Syntax

```
SHUTDOWN [ WITH NOWAIT ]
```

Arguments

WITH NOWAIT

> Shuts down SQL Server immediately, without performing checkpoints in every database. SQL Server exits after attempting to terminate all user processes, and a rollback operation occurs for each active transaction.

Remarks

Unless members of the **sysadmin** fixed server role specify the WITH NOWAIT option, SHUTDOWN tries to shut down SQL Server in an orderly fashion by:

1. Disabling logins (except for members of the **sysadmin** fixed server role). To see a listing of all current users, execute **sp_who**.
2. Waiting for currently executing Transact-SQL statements or stored procedures to finish. To see a listing of all active processes and locks, execute **sp_lock** and **sp_who**.
3. Performing a checkpoint in every database.

Using the SHUTDOWN statement minimizes the amount of automatic recovery work needed when members of the **sysadmin** fixed server role restart SQL Server.

These tools and methods can also be used to stop SQL Server. Each of these performs a checkpoint in all databases. All committed data from data cache is flushed, and then the server is stopped:

- By using SQL Server Enterprise Manager.
- By using **net stop mssqlserver** from a command prompt.
- By using Services in Control Panel.
- By using SQL Server Service Manager.

If **sqlservr.exe** was started from the command-prompt, pressing CTRL+C shuts down SQL Server. However, pressing CTRL+C does not perform a checkpoint.

> **Note**   The SQL Server Enterprise Manager, **net stop**, Control Panel, and SQL Server Service Manager methods of stopping SQL Server produce the identical service control message of SERVICE_CONTROL_STOP to SQL Server.

Permissions

SHUTDOWN permissions default to members of the **sysadmin** and **serveradmin** fixed server roles, and are not transferable.

Related Topics

CHECKPOINT, sp_lock, sp_who, sqlservr Application, Stopping SQL Server

SIGN

Returns the positive (+1), zero (0), or negative (–1) sign of the given expression.

Syntax

```
SIGN ( numeric_expression )
```

Arguments

numeric_expression
Is an expression of the exact numeric or approximate numeric data type category, except for the **bit** data type.

Return Types

float

Examples

This example returns the SIGN values of numbers from –1 to 1.

```
DECLARE @value real
SET @value = -1
WHILE @value < 2
    BEGIN
        SELECT SIGN(@value)
        SET NOCOUNT ON
        SELECT @value = @value + 1
        SET NOCOUNT OFF
    END
SET NOCOUNT OFF
GO
```

Here is the result set:

```
(1 row(s) affected)


------------------------
-1.0

(1 row(s) affected)


------------------------
0.0
```

(continued)

(continued)

```
(1 row(s) affected)


------------------------
1.0

(1 row(s) affected)
```

Related Topics

Mathematical Functions

SIN

Returns the trigonometric sine of the given angle (in radians) in an approximate numeric (**float**) expression.

Syntax

```
SIN ( float_expression )
```

Arguments

float_expression
   Is an expression of type **float**.

Return Types

float

Examples

This example calculates the SIN for a given angle.

```
DECLARE @angle float
SET @angle = 45.175643
SELECT 'The SIN of the angle is: ' + CONVERT(varchar,SIN(@angle))
GO
```

Here is the result set:

```
The SIN of the angle is: 0.929607

(1 row(s) affected)
```

Related Topics

Mathematical Functions

smalldatetime

For information about the **smalldatetime** data type, see datetime and smalldatetime.

Related Topics

Data Type Conversion, Data Types

smallint

For information about the **smallint** data type, see int, bigint, smallint, and tinyint.

Related Topics

Data Type Conversion, Data Types

smallmoney

For information about the **smallmoney** data type, see money and smallmoney.

Related Topics

Data Type Conversion, Data Types

SOME | ANY

Compares a scalar value with a single-column set of values.

Syntax

```
scalar_expression { = | < > | ! = | > | > = | ! > | < | < = | ! < }
    { SOME | ANY } ( subquery )
```

Arguments

scalar_expression
> Is any valid Microsoft SQL Server expression.

{ = | <> | != | > | >= | !> | < | <= | !< }
> Is any valid comparison operator.

SOME | ANY

Specifies that a comparison should be made.

subquery

Is a subquery that has a result set of one column. The data type of the column returned must be the same data type as *scalar_expression*.

Result Types

Boolean

Result Value

SOME or ANY returns TRUE when the comparison specified is TRUE for ANY pair (*scalar_expression*, *x*) where *x* is a value in the single-column set. Otherwise, returns FALSE.

Related Topics

CASE, Expressions, Functions, Operators (Logical Operators), SELECT, WHERE

SOUNDEX

Returns a four-character (SOUNDEX) code to evaluate the similarity of two strings.

Syntax

```
SOUNDEX ( CHARACTER_EXPRESSION )
```

Arguments

character_expression

Is an alphanumeric expression of character data. *character_expression* can be a constant, variable, or column.

Return Types

char

Remarks

SOUNDEX converts an alpha string to a four-character code to find similar-sounding words or names. The first character of the code is the first character of *character_expression* and the second through fourth characters of the code are numbers. Vowels in *character_expression* are ignored unless they are the first letter of the string. String functions can be nested.

Examples

This example shows the SOUNDEX function and the related DIFFERENCE function. In the first example, the standard SOUNDEX values are returned for all consonants. Returning the SOUNDEX for Smith and Smythe returns the same SOUNDEX result because all vowels, the letter y, doubled letters, and the letter h, are not included.

```
-- Using SOUNDEX
SELECT SOUNDEX ('Smith'), SOUNDEX ('Smythe')
```

Here is the result set:

```
----- -----
S530  S530

(1 row(s) affected)
```

The DIFFERENCE function compares the difference of the SOUNDEX pattern results. The first example shows two strings that differ only in vowels. The difference returned is 4 (lowest possible difference).

```
-- Using DIFFERENCE
SELECT DIFFERENCE('Smithers', 'Smythers')
GO
```

Here is the result set:

```
-----------
4

(1 row(s) affected)
```

In this example, the strings differ in consonants, so the difference returned is 2 (higher difference).

```
SELECT DIFFERENCE('Anothers', 'Brothers')
GO
```

Here is the result set:

```
-----------
2

(1 row(s) affected)
```

Related Topics

String Functions

SPACE

Returns a string of repeated spaces.

Syntax

```
SPACE ( integer_expression )
```

Arguments

integer_expression

Is a positive integer that indicates the number of spaces. If *integer_expression* is negative, a null string is returned.

Return Types

char

Remarks

To include spaces in Unicode data, use REPLICATE instead of SPACE.

Examples

This example trims the authors' last names and concatenates a comma, two spaces, and the authors' first names.

```
USE pubs
GO
SELECT RTRIM(au_lname) + ',' + SPACE(2) +  LTRIM(au_fname)
FROM authors
ORDER BY au_lname, au_fname
GO
```

Here is the result set:

```
Name
----------------------------------------------------------------

Bennet,  Abraham
Blotchet-Halls,  Reginald
Carson,  Cheryl
DeFrance,  Michel
del Castillo,  Innes
Dull,  Ann
Green,  Marjorie
Greene,  Morningstar
Gringlesby,  Burt
Hunter,  Sheryl
```

(continued)

(continued)

```
Karsen,  Livia
Locksley,  Charlene
MacFeather,  Stearns
McBadden,  Heather
O'Leary,  Michael
Panteley,  Sylvia
Ringer,  Albert
Ringer,  Anne
Smith,  Meander
Straight,  Dean
Stringer,  Dirk
White,  Olivier
Yokomoto,  Akiko

(23 row(s) affected)
```

Related Topics

String Functions

sql_variant

A data type that stores values of various SQL Server-supported data types, except **text**, **ntext**, **image**, **timestamp**, and **sql_variant**.

sql_variant may be used in columns, parameters, variables, and return values of user-defined functions. **sql_variant** allows these database objects to support values of other data types.

Syntax

```
sql_variant
```

Remarks

A column of type **sql_variant** may contain rows of different data types. For example, a column defined as **sql_variant** can store **int**, **binary**, and **char** values. The only types of values that cannot be stored using **sql_variant** are **text**, **ntext**, **image**, **timestamp**, and **sql_variant**.

sql_variant can have a maximum length of 8016 bytes.

An **sql_variant** data type must first be cast to its base data type value before participating in operations such as addition and subtraction.

sql_variant may be assigned a default value. This data type also may have NULL as its underlying value, but the NULL values will not have an associated base type. In addition, **sql_variant** may not have another **sql_variant** as its base type.

A UNIQUE, primary, or foreign key may include columns of type **sql_variant**, but the total length of the data values comprising the key of a given row should not be greater than the maximum length of an index (currently 900 bytes).

A table may have any number of **sql_variant** columns.

sql_variant cannot be used in CONTAINSTABLE and FREETEXTTABLE.

ODBC does not fully support sql_variant. Hence, queries of sql_variant columns are returned as binary data when using Microsoft OLE DB Provider for ODBC (MSDASQL). For example, an sql_variant column containing the character string data 'PS2091' is returned as 0x505332303931.

Comparing sql_variant values

The **sql_variant** data type belongs to the top of the data type hierarchy list for conversion. For **sql_variant** comparisons, the SQL Server data type hierarchy order is grouped into data type families.

Data Type Hierarchy	Data Type Family
sql_variant	sql_variant
datetime	datetime
smalldatetime	datetime
float	approximate number
real	approximate number
decimal	exact number
money	exact number
smallmoney	exact number
bigint	exact number
int	exact number
smallint	exact number
tinyint	exact number

(continued)

(continued)

Data Type Hierarchy	Data Type Family
bit	exact number
nvarchar	Unicode
nchar	Unicode
varchar	Unicode
char	Unicode
varbinary	binary
binary	binary
uniqueidentifier	uniqueidentifier

These rules apply to **sql_variant** comparisons:

- When **sql_variant** values of different base data types are compared, and the base data types are in different data type families, the value whose data type family is higher in the hierarchy chart is considered the higher of the two values.

- When **sql_variant** values of different base data types are compared, and the base data types are in the same data type family, the value whose base data type is lower in the hierarchy chart is implicitly converted to the other data type and the comparison is then made.

- When **sql_variant** values of the **char**, **varchar**, **nchar**, or **varchar** data types are compared, they are evaluated based on the following criteria: LCID, LCID version, comparison flags, and sort ID. Each of these criteria are compared as integer values, and in the order listed.

Related Topics

CAST and CONVERT, Using sql_variant_Data

SQL_VARIANT_PROPERTY

Returns the base data type and other information about a **sql_variant** value.

Syntax

```
SQL_VARIANT_PROPERTY ( expression, property )
```

Arguments

expression

Is an expression of type **sql_variant**.

property

Contains the name of the **sql_variant** property for which information is to be provided. *property* is **varchar(128)**, and can be any of the following values.

Value	Description	Base type of sql_variant returned
BaseType	The SQL Server data type, such as:	**sysname**
	char **int** **money** **nchar** **ntext** **numeric** **nvarchar** **real** **smalldatetime** **smallint** **smallmoney** **text** **timestamp** **tinyint** **uniqueidentifier** **varbinary** **varchar**	Invalid input = NULL
Precision	The number of digits of the numeric base data type:	**int**
	datetime = 23 **smalldatetime** = 16 **float** = 53 **real** = 24 **decimal** (p,s) and **numeric** (p,s) = p **money** = 19 **smallmoney** = 10 **int** = 10 **smallint** = 5 **tinyint** = 3 **bit** = 1 all other types = 0	Invalid input = NULL

(continued)

(continued)

Value	Description	Base type of sql_variant returned
Scale	The number of digits to the right of the decimal point of the numeric base data type: **decimal** (p,s) and **numeric** (p,s) = s **money** and **smallmoney** = 4 **datetime** = 3 all other types = 0	**int** Invalid input = NULL
TotalBytes	The number of bytes required to hold both the meta data and data of the value. This information would be useful in checking the maximum side of data in a **sql_variant** column. If the value is greater than 900, index creation will fail.	**int** Invalid input = NULL
Collation	Represents the collation of the particular **sql_variant** value.	**sysname** Invalid input = NULL
MaxLength	The maximum data type length, in bytes. For example, **MaxLength** of **nvarchar(50)** is 100, **MaxLength** of **int** is 4.	**int** Invalid input = NULL

Return Types

sql_variant

Examples

This example retrieves SQL_VARIANT_PROPERTY information on the colA value 46279.1 where colB =1689, given that tableA has colA that is of type **sql_variant** and colB.

```
CREATE TABLE tableA(colA sql_variant, colB int)
INSERT INTO tableA values ( cast (46279.1 as decimal(8,2)), 1689)
SELECT SQL_VARIANT_PROPERTY(colA,'BaseType'),
       SQL_VARIANT_PROPERTY(colA,'Precision'),
       SQL_VARIANT_PROPERTY(colA,'Scale')
FROM    tableA
WHERE   colB = 1689
```

Here is the result set. (Note that each of these three values is a **sql_variant**.)

```
decimal
8
2
```

Related Topics

sql_variant, Using sql_variant_Data

SQUARE

Returns the square of the given expression.

Syntax

```
SQUARE ( float_expression )
```

Arguments

float_expression
 Is an expression of type **float**.

Return Types

float

Examples

This example returns the volume of a cylinder having a radius of 1 inch and a height of 5 inches.

```
DECLARE @h float, @r float
SET @h = 5
SET @r = 1
SELECT PI()* SQUARE(@r)* @h AS 'Cyl Vol'
```

Here is the result:

```
Cyl Vol
--------------------------
15.707963267948966
```

Related Topics

Mathematical Functions

SQRT

Returns the square root of the given expression.

Syntax

```
SQRT ( float_expression )
```

Arguments

float_expression
    Is an expression of type **float**.

Return Types

float

Examples

This example returns the square root of numbers between 1.00 and 10.00.

```
DECLARE @myvalue float
SET @myvalue = 1.00
WHILE @myvalue < 10.00
   BEGIN
      SELECT SQRT(@myvalue)
      SELECT @myvalue = @myvalue + 1
   END
GO
```

Here is the result set:

```
-----------------------
1.0
-----------------------
1.4142135623731
-----------------------
1.73205080756888
-----------------------
2.0
-----------------------
2.23606797749979
-----------------------
2.44948974278318
-----------------------
2.64575131106459
-----------------------
2.82842712474619
-----------------------
3.0
```

Related Topics

Mathematical Functions

STATS_DATE

Returns the date that the statistics for the specified index were last updated.

Syntax

```
STATS_DATE ( table_id , index_id )
```

Arguments

table_id
>   Is the ID of the table used.

index_id
>   Is the ID of the index used.

Return Types

datetime

Remarks

System functions can be used in the select list, in the WHERE clause, and anywhere an expression is allowed.

Examples

This example returns the date of the last time that the statistics were updated for the specified object.

```
USE master
GO
SELECT 'Index Name' = i.name,
    'Statistics Date' = STATS_DATE(i.id, i.indid)
FROM sysobjects o, sysindexes i
WHERE o.name = 'employee' AND o.id = i.id
GO
```

Related Topics

System Functions, WHERE

STDEV

Returns the statistical standard deviation of all values in the given expression.

Syntax

```
STDEV ( expression )
```

Arguments

expression

> Is a numeric expression. Aggregate functions and subqueries are not permitted. *expression* is an expression of the exact numeric or approximate numeric data type category, except for the **bit** data type.

Return Types

float

Remarks

If STDEV is used on all items in a SELECT statement, each value in the result set is included in the calculation. STDEV can be used with numeric columns only. Null values are ignored.

Examples

This example returns the standard deviation for all royalty payments in the **titles** table.

```
USE pubs
SELECT STDEV(royalty)
FROM titles
```

Related Topics

Aggregate Functions

STDEVP

Returns the statistical standard deviation for the population for all values in the given expression.

Syntax

```
STDEVP ( expression )
```

Arguments

expression

> Is a numeric expression. Aggregate functions and subqueries are not permitted. *expression* is an expression of the exact numeric or approximate numeric data type category, except for the **bit** data type.

Return Types

float

Remarks

If STDEVP is used on all items in a SELECT statement, each value in the result set is included in the calculation. STDEVP can be used with numeric columns only. Null values are ignored.

Examples

This example returns the standard deviation for the population for all royalty values in the **titles** table.

```
USE pubs
SELECT STDEVP(royalty)
FROM titles
```

Related Topics

Aggregate Functions

STR

Returns character data converted from numeric data.

Syntax

```
STR ( float_expression [ , length [ , decimal ] ] )
```

Arguments

float_expression

Is an expression of approximate numeric (**float**) data type with a decimal point. Do not use a function or subquery as the *float_expression* in the STR function.

length

Is the total length, including decimal point, sign, digits, and spaces. The default is 10.

decimal

Is the number of places to the right of the decimal point.

Return Types

char

Remarks

If supplied, the values for *length* and *decimal* parameters to STR should be positive. The number is rounded to an integer by default or if the decimal parameter is 0. The specified length should be greater than or equal to the part of the number before the decimal point plus the number's sign (if any). A short *float_expression* is right-justified in the specified length, and a long *float_expression* is truncated to the specified number of decimal places. For example, STR(12,10) yields the result of 12, which is right-justified in the result set. However, STR(1223, 2) truncates the result set to **. String functions can be nested.

Note To convert to Unicode data, use STR inside a CONVERT or CAST conversion function.

Examples

A. Use STR

This example converts an expression consisting of five digits and a decimal point to a six-position character string. The fractional part of the number is rounded to one decimal place.

```
SELECT STR(123.45, 6, 1)
GO
```

Here is the result set:

```
------
 123.5

(1 row(s) affected)
```

When the expression exceeds the specified length, the string returns ** for the specified length.

```
SELECT STR(123.45, 2, 2)
GO
```

Here is the result set:

```
--
**

(1 row(s) affected)
```

Even when numeric data is nested within STR, the result is character data with the specified format.

```
SELECT STR (FLOOR (123.45), 8, 3)
GO
```

Here is the result set:

```
--------
 123.000

(1 row(s) affected)
```

B. Use the STR and CONVERT functions

This example compares the results of STR and CONVERT.

```
SELECT STR(3.147) AS 'STR',
       STR(3.147, 5, 2) AS '2 decimals',
       STR(3.147, 5, 3) AS '3 decimals'
GO
```

Here is the result set:

```
STR        2 decimals 3 decimals
---------- ---------- ----------
        3  3.15        3.147

(1 row(s) affected)

-- Use CONVERT.
SELECT CONVERT(char(1), 3.147) AS 'CHAR(1)',
       CONVERT(char(3), 3.147) AS 'CHAR(3)',
       CONVERT(char(5), 3.147) AS 'CHAR(5)'
GO
```

Here is the result set:

```
CHAR(1) CHAR(3) CHAR(5)
------- ------- -------
(null)  (null)  3.147

(1 row(s) affected)
```

Related Topics

String Functions

STUFF

Deletes a specified length of characters and inserts another set of characters at a specified starting point.

Syntax

```
STUFF ( character_expression , start , length , character_expression )
```

Arguments

character_expression

Is an expression of character data. *character_expression* can be a constant, variable, or column of either character or binary data.

start

Is an integer value that specifies the location to begin deletion and insertion. If *start* or *length* is negative, a null string is returned. If *start* is longer than the first *character_expression*, a null string is returned.

length

Is an integer that specifies the number of characters to delete. If *length* is longer than the first *character_expression*, deletion occurs up to the last character in the last *character_expression*.

Return Types

Returns character data if *character_expression* is one of the supported character data types. Returns binary data if *character_expression* is one of the supported binary data types.

Remarks

String functions can be nested.

Examples

This example returns a character string created by deleting three characters from the first string (abcdef) starting at position 2 (at b) and inserting the second string at the deletion point.

```
SELECT STUFF('abcdef', 2, 3, 'ijklmn')
GO
```

Here is the result set:

```
---------
aijklmnef

(1 row(s) affected)
```

Related Topics

Data Types, String Functions

SUBSTRING

Returns part of a character, binary, text, or image expression. For more information about the valid Microsoft SQL Server data types that can be used with this function, see Data Types.

Syntax

```
SUBSTRING ( expression , start , length )
```

Arguments

expression

Is a character string, binary string, text, image, a column, or an expression that includes a column. Do not use expressions that include aggregate functions.

start

Is an integer that specifies where the substring begins.

length

Is an integer that specifies the length of the substring (the number of characters or bytes to return).

> **Note** Because *start* and *length* specify the number of bytes when SUBSTRING is used on **text** data, DBCS data, such as Kanji, may result in split characters at the beginning or end of the result. This behavior is consistent with the way in which READTEXT handles DBCS. However, because of the occasional strange result, it is advisable to use **ntext** instead of **text** for DBCS characters.

Return Types

Returns character data if *expression* is one of the supported character data types. Returns binary data if *expression* is one of the supported **binary** data types.

The returned string is the same type as the given expression with the exceptions shown in the table.

Given expression	Return type
text	varchar
image	varbinary
ntext	nvarchar

Remarks

Offsets (*start* and *length*) using the **ntext**, **char**, or **varchar** data types must be specified in number of characters. Offsets using the **text**, **image**, **binary**, or **varbinary** data types must be specified in number of bytes.

Note Compatibility levels can affect return values. For more information about compatibility levels, see sp_dbcmptlevel.

Examples

A. Use SUBSTRING with a character string

This example shows how to return only a portion of a character string. From the **authors** table, this query returns the last name in one column with only the first initial in the second column.

```
USE pubs
SELECT au_lname, SUBSTRING(au_fname, 1, 1)
FROM authors
ORDER BY au_lname
```

Here is the result set:

```
au_lname
------------------------------------------------- -
Bennet                                            A
Blotchet-Halls                                    R
Carson                                            C
DeFrance                                          M
del Castillo                                      I
...
Yokomoto                                          A

(23 row(s) affected)
```

Here is how to display the second, third, and fourth characters of the string constant abcdef.

```
SELECT x = SUBSTRING('abcdef', 2, 3)
```

Here is the result set:

```
x
----------
bcd

(1 row(s) affected)
```

B. Use SUBSTRING with text, ntext, and image data

This example shows how to return the first 200 characters from each of a **text** and **image** data column in the **publishers** table of the **pubs** database. **text** data is returned as **varchar**, and **image** data is returned as **varbinary**.

```
USE pubs
SELECT pub_id, SUBSTRING(logo, 1, 10) AS logo,
    SUBSTRING(pr_info, 1, 10) AS pr_info
FROM pub_info
WHERE pub_id = '1756'
```

Here is the result set:

```
pub_id logo                   pr_info
------ ---------------------- ----------
1756   0x474946383961E3002500 This is sa

(1 row(s) affected)
```

This example shows the effect of SUBSTRING on both **text** and **ntext** data. First, this example creates a new table in the **pubs** database named **npr_info**. Second, the example creates the **pr_info** column in the **npr_info** table from the first 80 characters of the **pub_info.pr_info** column and adds an ü as the first character. Lastly, an INNER JOIN retrieves all publisher identification numbers and the SUBSTRING of both the **text** and **ntext** publisher information columns.

```
IF EXISTS (SELECT table_name FROM INFORMATION_SCHEMA.TABLES
      WHERE table_name = 'npub_info')
   DROP TABLE npub_info
GO
-- Create npub_info table in pubs database. Borrowed from instpubs.sql.
USE pubs
GO
CREATE TABLE npub_info
(
 pub_id          char(4)          NOT NULL
        REFERENCES publishers(pub_id)
        CONSTRAINT UPKCL_npubinfo PRIMARY KEY CLUSTERED,
 pr_info         ntext            NULL
)

GO

-- Fill the pr_info column in npub_info with international data.
RAISERROR('Now at the inserts to pub_info...',0,1)
```

(continued)

(continued)

```
GO

INSERT npub_info VALUES('0736', N'üThis is sample text data for New Moon Books, publisher
0736 in the pubs database')
INSERT npub_info values('0877', N'üThis is sample text data for Binnet & Hardley,
publisher 0877 in the pubs databa')
INSERT npub_info values('1389', N'üThis is sample text data for Algodata Infosystems,
publisher 1389 in the pubs da')
INSERT npub_info values('9952', N'üThis is sample text data for Scootney Books, publisher
9952 in the pubs database')
INSERT npub_info values('1622', N'üThis is sample text data for Five Lakes Publishing,
publisher 1622 in the pubs d')
INSERT npub_info values('1756', N'üThis is sample text data for Ramona Publishers,
publisher 1756 in the pubs datab')
INSERT npub_info values('9901', N'üThis is sample text data for GGG&G, publisher 9901 in
the pubs database. GGG&G i')
INSERT npub_info values('9999', N'üThis is sample text data for Lucerne Publishing,
publisher 9999 in the pubs data')
GO
-- Join between npub_info and pub_info on pub_id.
SELECT pr.pub_id, SUBSTRING(pr.pr_info, 1, 35) AS pr_info,
   SUBSTRING(npr.pr_info, 1, 35) AS npr_info
FROM pub_info pr INNER JOIN npub_info npr
   ON pr.pub_id = npr.pub_id
ORDER BY pr.pub_id ASC
```

Related Topics

String Functions

SUM

Returns the sum of all the values, or only the DISTINCT values, in the expression.
SUM can be used with numeric columns only. Null values are ignored.

Syntax

```
SUM ( [ ALL | DISTINCT ] expression )
```

Arguments

ALL

Applies the aggregate function to all values. ALL is the default.

DISTINCT

Specifies that SUM return the sum of unique values.

expression

Is a constant, column, or function, and any combination of arithmetic, bitwise, and string operators. *expression* is an expression of the exact numeric or approximate numeric data type category, except for the **bit** data type. Aggregate functions and subqueries are not permitted.

Return Types

Returns the summation of all *expression* values in the most precise *expression* data type.

Expression result	Return type
integer category	**int**
decimal category (p, s)	**decimal(38, s)**
money and **smallmoney** category	**money**
float and **real** category	**float**

Important Distinct aggregates, for example AVG(DISTINCT *column_name*), COUNT(DISTINCT *column_name*), MAX(DISTINCT *column_name*), MIN(DISTINCT *column_name*), and SUM(DISTINCT *column_name*), are not supported when using CUBE or ROLLUP. If used, Microsoft SQL Server returns an error message and cancels the query.

Examples

A. Use SUM for aggregates and row aggregates

These examples show the differences between aggregate functions and row aggregate functions. The first shows aggregate functions giving summary data only, and the second shows row aggregate functions giving detail and summary data.

```
USE pubs
GO
-- Aggregate functions
SELECT type, SUM(price), SUM(advance)
FROM titles
WHERE type LIKE '%cook'
GROUP BY type
ORDER BY type
GO
```

Here is the result set:

```
type
------------ -------------------------- --------------------------
mod_cook     22.98                      15,000.00
trad_cook    47.89                      19,000.00

(2 row(s) affected)

USE pubs
GO
-- Row aggregates
SELECT type, price, advance
FROM titles
WHERE type LIKE '%cook'
ORDER BY type
COMPUTE SUM(price), SUM(advance) BY type
```

Here is the result set:

```
type         price                      advance
------------ -------------------------- --------------------------
mod_cook     19.99                      0.00
mod_cook     2.99                       15,000.00

             sum
             ==========================
             22.98

                                        sum
                                        ==========================
                                        15,000.00

type         price                      advance
------------ -------------------------- --------------------------
trad_cook    20.95                      7,000.00
trad_cook    11.95                      4,000.00
trad_cook    14.99                      8,000.00

             sum
             ==========================
             47.89

                                        sum
                                        ==========================
                                        19,000.00

(7 row(s) affected)
```

B. Calculate group totals with more than one column

This example calculates the sum of the prices and advances for each type of book.

```
USE pubs
GO
SELECT type, SUM(price), SUM(advance)
FROM titles
GROUP BY type
ORDER BY type
GO
```

Here is the result set:

```
type
------------ --------------------------- ---------------------------
business     54.92                       25,125.00
mod_cook     22.98                       15,000.00
popular_comp 42.95                       15,000.00
psychology   67.52                       21,275.00
trad_cook    47.89                       19,000.00
UNDECIDED    (null)                      (null)

(6 row(s) affected)
```

Related Topics

Aggregate Functions

SUSER_ID

Returns the user's login identification number.

> **Important**   SUSER_ID always returns NULL when used in Microsoft
> SQL Server 2000. This system built-in function is included only for backward
> compatibility. Use SUSER_SID instead.

Syntax

```
SUSER_ID ( [ 'login' ] )
```

Arguments

'login'

Is the user's login identification name. *login*, which is optional, is **nchar**. If *login* is specified as **char**, it is implicitly converted to **nchar**. *login* can be any SQL Server login or Microsoft Windows NT user or group that has permission to connect to SQL Server. If *login* is not specified, the login identification number for the current user is returned.

Return Types

int

Remarks

In SQL Server 7.0, the security identification number (SID) replaces the server user identification number (SUID).

SUSER_SID returns a SUID only for a login that has an entry in the **syslogins** system table.

System functions can be used in the select list, in the WHERE clause, and anywhere an expression is allowed, and must always be followed by parentheses (even if no parameter is specified).

Examples

This example returns the login identification number for the **sa** login.

```
SELECT SUSER_ID('sa')
```

Related Topics

Managing Security, System Functions

SUSER_NAME

Returns the user's login identification name.

> **Important**   SUSER_NAME always returns NULL when used in Microsoft SQL Server 2000. This system built-in function is included only for backward compatibility. Use SUSER_SNAME instead.

Syntax

```
SUSER_NAME ( [ server_user_id ] )
```

Arguments

server_user_id
    Is the user's login identification number. *server_user_id*, which is optional, is **int**. *server_user_id* can be the login identification number of any SQL Server login or Microsoft Windows NT user or group that has permission to connect to SQL Server. If *server_user_id* is not specified, the login identification name for the current user is returned.

Return Types

nchar

Remarks

In SQL Server 7.0, the security identification number (SID) replaces the server user identification number (SUID).

SUSER_NAME returns a login name only for a login that has an entry in the **syslogins** system table.

System functions can be used in the select list, in the WHERE clause, and anywhere an expression is allowed, and must always be followed by parentheses (even if no parameter is specified).

Examples

This example returns the user's login identification name for a login identification number of 1.

```
SELECT SUSER_NAME(1)
```

Related Topics

Managing Security, System Functions

SUSER_SID

Returns the security identification number (SID) for the user's login name.

Syntax

```
SUSER_SID ( [ 'login' ] )
```

Arguments

'*login*'
    Is the user's login name. *login* is **sysname**. *login*, which is optional, can be a Microsoft SQL Server login or Microsoft Windows NT user or group. If *login* is not specified, information about the current user is returned.

Return Types

varbinary(85)

Remarks

When specifying a SQL Server login using SQL Server Authentication, the user must be granted permission to connect to SQL Server. Use **sp_addlogin** or SQL Server Enterprise Manager to grant this permission. However, when specifying a Windows NT user or group using Windows Authentication, this user or group does not have to be granted permission to connect to SQL Server.

SUSER_SID can be used as a DEFAULT constraint in either ALTER TABLE or CREATE TABLE.

System functions can be used in the select list, in the WHERE clause, and anywhere an expression is allowed, and must always be followed by parentheses (even if no parameter is specified).

Examples

A. Use SUSER_SID

This example returns the security identification number for the SQL Server **sa** login.

```
SELECT SUSER_SID('sa')
```

B. Use SUSER_SID with a Windows NT username

This example returns the security identification number for the Windows NT user **London\Workstation1**.

```
SELECT SUSER_SID('London\Workstation1')
```

C. Use SUSER_SID as a DEFAULT constraint

This example uses SUSER_SID as a DEFAULT constraint in a CREATE TABLE statement.

```
USE pubs
GO
CREATE TABLE sid_example
(
login_sid    varbinary(85) DEFAULT SUSER_SID(),
login_name   varchar(30) DEFAULT SYSTEM_USER,
login_dept   varchar(10) DEFAULT 'SALES',
login_date   datetime DEFAULT GETDATE()
)
GO
INSERT sid_example DEFAULT VALUES
GO
```

Related Topics

ALTER TABLE, binary and varbinary, CREATE TABLE, Managing Security, sp_addlogin, sp_grantlogin, System Functions

SUSER_SNAME

Returns the login identification name from a user's security identification number (SID).

Syntax

```
SUSER_SNAME ( [ server_user_sid ] )
```

Arguments

server_user_sid

Is the user security identification number. *server_user_sid*, which is optional, is **varbinary(85)**. *server_user_sid* can be the security identification number of any Microsoft SQL Server login or Microsoft Windows NT user or group. If *server_user_sid* is not specified, information about the current user is returned.

Return Types

nvarchar(256)

Remarks

When specifying a SQL Server login using SQL Server Authentication, the user must be granted permission to connect to SQL Server. Use **sp_addlogin** or SQL Server Enterprise Manager to grant this permission. However, when specifying a Windows NT user or group using Windows Authentication, this user or group does not have to be granted permission to connect to SQL Server.

SUSER_SNAME can be used as a DEFAULT constraint in either ALTER TABLE or CREATE TABLE.

System functions can be used in the select list, in the WHERE clause, and anywhere an expression is allowed, and must always be followed by parentheses (even if no parameter is specified).

Examples

A. Use SUSER_SNAME

This example returns the login name for the security identification number with a value of 0x01.

```
SELECT SUSER_SNAME(0x01)
```

B. Use SUSER_SNAME with a Windows NT user's security identification number

This example returns the login name for the Windows NT user's security identification number, obtained by using SUSER_SID.

```
SELECT SUSER_SNAME(0x010500000000000515000000a065cf7e784b9b5fe77c87705a2e0000)
```

C. Use SUSER_SNAME as a DEFAULT constraint

This example uses SUSER_SNAME as a DEFAULT constraint in a CREATE TABLE
statement.

```
USE pubs
GO
CREATE TABLE sname_example
(
login_sname sysname DEFAULT SUSER_SNAME(),
employee_id uniqueidentifier DEFAULT NEWID(),
login_date  datetime DEFAULT GETDATE()
)
GO
INSERT sname_example DEFAULT VALUES
GO
```

Related Topics

ALTER TABLE, binary and varbinary, CREATE TABLE, Managing Security,
sp_addlogin, sp_grantlogin, System Functions

SYSTEM_USER

Allows a system-supplied value for the current system username to be inserted into a
table when no default value is specified.

Syntax

```
SYSTEM_USER
```

Remarks

Use the SYSTEM_USER niladic function with DEFAULT constraints in either the
CREATE TABLE or ALTER TABLE statements, or use as any standard function.

If the current user is logged in to Microsoft SQL Server using Windows
Authentication, SYSTEM_USER returns the Windows 2000 or Windows NT 4.0 login
identification name, for example, DOMAIN\user_login_name. However, if the current
user is logged in to SQL Server using SQL Server Authentication, SYSTEM_USER
returns the SQL Server login identification name, for example, sa for a user logged
in as **sa**.

Examples

A. Use SYSTEM_USER to return the current system username

This example declares a **char** variable, puts the current value of SYSTEM_USER into the variable, and then prints the variable.

```
DECLARE @sys_usr char(30)
SET @sys_usr = SYSTEM_USER
SELECT 'The current system user is: '+ @sys_usr
GO
```

Here is the result set:

```
-----------------------------------------------------------
The current system user is: sa

(1 row(s) affected)
```

B. Use SYSTEM_USER with DEFAULT constraints

This example creates a table using SYSTEM_USER as a DEFAULT constraint for the receptionist for a patient row.

```
USE pubs
GO
CREATE TABLE appointments2
(
 patient_id int IDENTITY(2000, 1) NOT NULL,
 doctor_id  int NOT NULL,
 appt_date datetime NOT NULL DEFAULT GETDATE(),
 receptionist varchar(30) NOT NULL DEFAULT SYSTEM_USER
)
GO
INSERT appointments2 (doctor_id)
VALUES (151)
INSERT appointments2 (doctor_id, appt_date)
VALUES (293, '5/15/98')
INSERT appointments2 (doctor_id, appt_date)
VALUES (27882, '6/20/98')
INSERT appointments2 (doctor_id)
VALUES (21392)
INSERT appointments2 (doctor_id, appt_date)
VALUES (24283, '11/03/98')
GO
```

This is the query to select all the information from the **appointments2** table:

```
SELECT *
FROM appointments2
ORDER BY doctor_id
GO
```

Here is the result set:

```
patient_id  doctor_id   appt_date                 receptionist
----------  ----------  ------------------------  ----------------
2000        151         Mar  4 1998 10:36AM       sa
2001        293         May 15 1998 12:00AM       sa
2003        21392       Mar  4 1998 10:36AM       sa
2004        24283       Nov  3 1998 12:00AM       sa
2002        27882       Jun 20 1998 12:00AM       sa

(5 row(s) affected)
```

Related Topics

Allowing Null Values, ALTER TABLE, CREATE TABLE,
CURRENT_TIMESTAMP, CURRENT_USER, Managing Security,
SESSION_USER, System Functions, USER, Using Constraints, Defaults, and
Null Values

table

A special data type that can be used to store a result set for later processing. Its
primary use is for temporary storage of a set of rows, which are to be returned as the
result set of a table-valued function.

Syntax

Note Use DECLARE @*local_variable* to declare variables of type **table**.

```
table_type_definition ::=
    TABLE ( { column_definition | table_constraint } [ ,...n ] )

column_definition ::=
    column_name scalar_data_type
    [ COLLATE collation_definition ]
    [ [ DEFAULT constant_expression ] | IDENTITY [ ( seed , increment ) ] ]
    [ ROWGUIDCOL ]
    [ column_constraint ] [ ...n ]
```

(continued)

(continued)

```
column_constraint ::=
    { [ NULL | NOT NULL ]
    | [ PRIMARY KEY | UNIQUE ]
    | CHECK ( logical_expression )
    }

table_constraint ::=
    { { PRIMARY KEY | UNIQUE } ( column_name [ ,...n ] )
    | CHECK ( search_condition )
    }
```

Arguments

table_type_definition

Is the same subset of information used to define a table in CREATE TABLE. The table declaration includes column definitions, names, data types, and constraints. The only constraint types allowed are PRIMARY KEY, UNIQUE KEY, and NULL.

For more information about the syntax, see CREATE TABLE, CREATE FUNCTION, and DECLARE @*local_variable*.

collation_definition

Is the collation of the column consisting of a Microsoft Windows locale and a comparison style, a Windows locale and the binary notation, or a Microsoft SQL Server collation.

Remarks

Functions and variables can be declared to be of type **table**. **table** variables can be used in functions, stored procedures, and batches.

Use table variables instead of temporary tables, whenever possible. **table** variables provide the following benefits:

- A **table** variable behaves like a local variable. It has a well-defined scope, which is the function, stored procedure, or batch in which it is declared.

  Within its scope, a **table** variable may be used like a regular table. It may be applied anywhere a table or table expression is used in SELECT, INSERT, UPDATE, and DELETE statements. However, **table** may not be used in the following statements:

```
INSERT INTO table_variable EXEC stored_procedure
SELECT select_list INTO table_variable statements.
```

  table variables are cleaned up automatically at the end of the function, stored procedure, or batch in which they are defined.

- table variables used in stored procedures result in fewer recompilations of the stored procedures than when temporary tables are used.
- Transactions involving table variables last only for the duration of an update on the table variable. Thus, table variables require less locking and logging resources.

Assignment operation between table variables is not supported. In addition, because table variables have limited scope and are not part of the persistent database, they are not impacted by transaction rollbacks.

Related Topics

COLLATE, CREATE FUNCTION, CREATE TABLE, DECLARE @local_variable

TAN

Returns the tangent of the input expression.

Syntax

```
TAN ( float_expression )
```

Arguments

float_expression
  Is an expression of type **float** or **real**, interpreted as number of radians.

Return Types

float

Examples

This example returns the tangent of PI()/2.

```
SELECT TAN(PI()/2)
```

Here is the result set:

```
--------------------
1.6331778728383844E+16
```

Related Topics

Mathematical Functions

text

For information about the **text** data type, see ntext, text, and image.

Related Topics

Data Type Conversion, Data Types

TEXTPTR

Returns the text-pointer value that corresponds to a **text**, **ntext**, or **image** column in **varbinary** format. The retrieved text pointer value can be used in READTEXT, WRITETEXT, and UPDATETEXT statements.

Syntax

```
TEXTPTR ( column )
```

Arguments

column
> Is the **text**, **ntext**, or **image** column to be used.

Return Types

varbinary

Remarks

In Microsoft SQL Server 2000, for tables with in row text, TEXTPTR returns a handle for the text to be processed. You can obtain a valid text pointer even if the text value is null.

If the table does not have in row text, and if a **text**, **ntext**, or **image** column has not been initialized by an UPDATETEXT statement, TEXTPTR returns a null pointer.

Use TEXTVALID to check whether a text pointer exists. You cannot use UPDATETEXT, WRITETEXT, or READTEXT without a valid text pointer.

These functions and statements are also useful with **text**, **ntext**, and **image** data.

Function or statement	Description
PATINDEX(**'%**_pattern_**%'**, _expression_)	Returns the character position of a given character string in **text** or **ntext** columns.
DATALENGTH(_expression_)	Returns the length of data in **text**, **ntext**, and **image** columns.
SET TEXTSIZE	Returns the limit, in bytes, of the **text**, **ntext**, or **image** data to be returned with a SELECT statement.
SUBSTRING(_text_column_, _start_, _length_)	Returns a **varchar** string specified by the given _start_ offset and _length_. The length should be less than 8 KB.

Examples

A. Use TEXTPTR

This example uses the TEXTPTR function to locate the **image** column **logo** associated with New Moon Books in the **pub_info** table of the **pubs** database. The text pointer is put into a local variable **@ptrval**.

```
USE pubs
GO
DECLARE @ptrval varbinary(16)
SELECT @ptrval = TEXTPTR(logo)
FROM pub_info pr, publishers p
WHERE p.pub_id = pr.pub_id
    AND p.pub_name = 'New Moon Books'
GO
```

B. Use TEXTPTR with in row text

In SQL Server 2000, the in row text pointer must be used inside a transaction. Here is an example.

```
CREATE TABLE t1 (c1 int, c2 text)
EXEC sp_tableoption 't1', 'text in row', 'on'
INSERT t1 VALUES ('1', 'This is text.')
GO
BEGIN TRAN
    DECLARE @ptrval VARBINARY(16)
```

(continued)

(continued)

```
    SELECT @ptrval = TEXTPTR(c2)
    FROM t1
    WHERE c1 = 1
    READTEXT t1.c2 @ptrval 0 1
COMMIT
```

C. Return text data

This example selects the **pub_id** column and the 16-byte text pointer of the **pr_info** column from the **pub_info** table.

```
USE pubs
GO
SELECT pub_id, TEXTPTR(pr_info)
FROM pub_info
ORDER BY pub_id
GO
```

Here is the result set:

```
pub_id
------ ----------------------------------
0736   0x6c0000000000feffb801000001000100
0877   0x6d0000000000feffb801000001000300
1389   0x6e0000000000feffb801000001000500
1622   0x700000000000feffb801000001000900
1756   0x710000000000feffb801000001000b00
9901   0x720000000000feffb801000001000d00
9952   0x6f0000000000feffb801000001000700
9999   0x730000000000feffb801000001000f00

(8 row(s) affected)
```

This example shows how to return the first 8,000 bytes of text without using TEXTPTR.

```
USE pubs
GO
SET TEXTSIZE 8000
SELECT pub_id, pr_info
FROM pub_info
ORDER BY pub_id
GO
```

Here is the result set:

```
pub_id pr_info
------ ----------------------------------------------------------------------
0736   New Moon Books (NMB) has just released another top ten publication. With the latest
publication this makes NMB the hottest new publisher of the year!
0877   This is sample text data for Binnet & Hardley, publisher 0877 in the pubs database.
Binnet & Hardley is located in Washington, D.C.

This is sample text data for Binnet & Hardley, publisher 0877 in the pubs database. Binnet
& Hardley is located in Washi
1389   This is sample text data for Algodata Infosystems, publisher 1389 in the pubs
database. Algodata Infosystems is located in Berkeley, California.

9999   This is sample text data for Lucerne Publishing, publisher 9999 in the pubs
database. Lucerne publishing is located in Paris, France.

This is sample text data for Lucerne Publishing, publisher 9999 in the pubs database.
Lucerne publishing is located in

(8 row(s) affected)
```

D. Return specific text data

This example locates the **text** column (**pr_info**) associated with **pub_id** 0736 in the **pub_info** table of the **pubs** database. It first declares the local variable **@val**. The text pointer (a long binary string) is then put into **@val** and supplied as a parameter to the READTEXT statement, which returns 10 bytes starting at the fifth byte (offset of 4).

```
USE pubs
GO
DECLARE @val varbinary(16)
SELECT @val = TEXTPTR(pr_info)
FROM pub_info
WHERE pub_id = '0736'
READTEXT pub_info.pr_info @val 4 10
GO
```

Here is the result set:

```
(1 row(s) affected)

pr_info
--------------------------------------------------------------------
 is sample
```

Related Topics

DATALENGTH, PATINDEX, READTEXT, SET TEXTSIZE, Text and Image
Functions, UPDATETEXT, WRITETEXT

TEXTVALID

A **text**, **ntext**, or **image** function that checks whether a given text pointer is valid.

Syntax

```
TEXTVALID ( 'table.column' , text_ ptr )
```

Arguments

table
> Is the name of the table to be used.

column
> Is the name of the column to be used.

text_ptr
> Is the text pointer to be checked.

Return Types

int

Remarks

Returns 1 if the pointer is valid and 0 if the pointer is invalid. Note that the identifier
for the **text** column must include the table name. You cannot use UPDATETEXT,
WRITETEXT, or READTEXT without a valid text pointer.

These functions and statements are also useful with **text**, **ntext**, and **image** data.

Function or statement	Description
PATINDEX('*%pattern%*', *expression*)	Returns the character position of a given character string in **text** and **ntext** columns.
DATALENGTH(*expression*)	Returns the length of data in **text**, **ntext**, and **image** columns.
SET TEXTSIZE	Returns the limit, in bytes, of the **text**, **ntext**, or **image** data to be returned with a SELECT statement.

Examples

This example reports whether a valid text pointer exists for each value in the **logo** column of the **pub_info** table.

```
USE pubs
GO
SELECT pub_id, 'Valid (if 1) Text data'
   = TEXTVALID ('pub_info.logo', TEXTPTR(logo))
FROM pub_info
ORDER BY pub_id
GO
```

Here is the result set:

```
pub_id Valid (if 1) Text data
------ --------------------
0736   1
0877   1
1389   1
1622   1
1756   1
9901   1
9952   1
9999   1

(8 row(s) affected)
```

Related Topics

DATALENGTH, PATINDEX, SET TEXTSIZE, Text and Image Functions, TEXTPTR

---

timestamp

timestamp is a data type that exposes automatically generated binary numbers, which are guaranteed to be unique within a database. **timestamp** is used typically as a mechanism for version-stamping table rows. The storage size is 8 bytes.

Remarks

The Transact-SQL **timestamp** data type is not the same as the **timestamp** data type defined in the SQL-92 standard. The SQL-92 **timestamp** data type is equivalent to the Transact-SQL **datetime** data type.

A future release of Microsoft SQL Server may modify the behavior of the Transact-SQL **timestamp** data type to align it with the behavior defined in the standard. At that time, the current **timestamp** data type will be replaced with a **rowversion** data type.

Microsoft SQL Server 2000 introduces a **rowversion** synonym for the **timestamp** data type. Use **rowversion** instead of **timestamp** wherever possible in DDL statements. **rowversion** is subject to the behaviors of data type synonyms. For more information, see Data Type Synonyms.

In a CREATE TABLE or ALTER TABLE statement, you do not have to supply a column name for the **timestamp** data type:

```
CREATE TABLE ExampleTable (PriKey int PRIMARY KEY, timestamp)
```

If you do not supply a column name, SQL Server generates a column name of **timestamp**. The **rowversion** data type synonym does not follow this behavior. You must supply a column name when you specify **rowversion**.

A table can have only one **timestamp** column. The value in the **timestamp** column is updated every time a row containing a **timestamp** column is inserted or updated. This property makes a **timestamp** column a poor candidate for keys, especially primary keys. Any update made to the row changes the **timestamp** value, thereby changing the key value. If the column is in a primary key, the old key value is no longer valid, and foreign keys referencing the old value are no longer valid. If the table is referenced in a dynamic cursor, all updates change the position of the rows in the cursor. If the column is in an index key, all updates to the data row also generate updates of the index.

A nonnullable **timestamp** column is semantically equivalent to a **binary(8)** column. A nullable **timestamp** column is semantically equivalent to a **varbinary(8)** column.

Related Topics

ALTER TABLE, CAST and CONVERT, CREATE TABLE, Data Type Conversion, Data Types, DECLARE @local_variable, DELETE, INSERT, SET @local_variable, UPDATE

tinyint

For information about the **tinyint** data type, see int, bigint, smallint, and tinyint.

Related Topics

Data Type Conversion, Data Types

Trace Flags

Trace flags are used to temporarily set specific server characteristics or to switch off a particular behavior. For example, if trace flag 3205 is set when Microsoft SQL Server starts, hardware compression for tape drivers is disabled. Trace flags are often used to diagnose performance issues or to debug stored procedures or complex computer systems.

These trace flags are available in SQL Server.

Note   Trace flag behaviors may or may not be supported in future releases.

Trace flag	Description
260	Prints versioning information about extended stored procedure dynamic-link libraries (DLLs). For more information about **__GetXpVersion**(), see Creating Extended Stored Procedures.
1204	Returns the type of locks participating in the deadlock and the current command affected.
2528	Disables parallel checking of objects by DBCC CHECKDB, DBCC CHECKFILEGROUP, and DBCC CHECKTABLE. By default, the degree of parallelism is determined automatically by the query processor. The maximum degree of parallelism is configured in the same manner as that of parallel queries. For more information, see max degree of parallelism Option.
	Parallel DBCC should typically be left enabled. In the case of DBCC CHECKDB, the query processor re-evaluates and automatically adjusts parallelism with each table or batch of tables checked. In some cases, checking may commence while the server is virtually idle. An administrator who knows that the load will increase before checking is complete may want to manually decrease or disable parallelism.
	However, disabling parallel checking can cause a decrease in overall database performance. Decreasing the degree of parallelism increases the amount of transaction log that must be scanned. This in turn increases the demand for tempdb space and results in a non-linear increase in the time required for dbcc to complete its checks. If DBCC is run with the TABLOCK feature enabled and parallelism turned off, tables may be locked for longer periods of time.
3205	By default, if a tape drive supports hardware compression, either the DUMP or BACKUP statement uses it. With this trace flag, you can disable hardware compression for tape drivers. This is useful when you want to exchange tapes with other sites or tape drives that do not support compression.

Examples

A. Set trace flags using DBCC TRACEON

This example turns on trace flag 3205 by using DBCC TRACEON.

```
DBCC TRACEON (3205)
```

B. Set trace flags at the command prompt

This example turns on trace flag 3205 at the command prompt.

```
sqlservr -d"C:\Program Files\Microsoft SQL Server\MSSQL\Data\master.mdf" -T3205
```

Related Topics

Data Types, DBCC INPUTBUFFER, DBCC OUTPUTBUFFER, DBCC TRACEOFF, DBCC TRACEON, EXECUTE, SELECT, SET NOCOUNT, sp_dboption, SQL Server Backward Compatibility Details, sqlservr Application

---

Transactions

A transaction is a single unit of work. If a transaction is successful, all of the data modifications made during the transaction are committed and become a permanent part of the database. If a transaction encounters errors and must be canceled or rolled back, then all of the data modifications are erased.

Microsoft SQL Server operates in three transaction modes:

Autocommit transactions
    Each individual statement is a transaction.

Explicit transactions
    Each transaction is explicitly started with the BEGIN TRANSACTION statement and explicitly ended with a COMMIT or ROLLBACK statement.

Implicit transactions
    A new transaction is implicitly started when the prior transaction completes, but each transaction is explicitly completed with a COMMIT or ROLLBACK statement.

For more information, see Transactions.

Related Topics

BEGIN DISTRIBUTED TRANSACTION, BEGIN TRANSACTION, COMMIT TRANSACTION, COMMIT WORK, ROLLBACK TRANSACTION, ROLLBACK WORK, SAVE TRANSACTION, SET IMPLICIT_TRANSACTIONS, @@TRANCOUNT

TRIGGER_NESTLEVEL

Returns the number of triggers executed for the UPDATE, INSERT, or DELETE statement that fired the trigger. TRIGGER_NESTLEVEL is used in triggers to determine the current level of nesting.

Syntax

```
TRIGGER_NESTLEVEL ( [ object_id ] )
```

Arguments

object_id

Is the object ID of a trigger. If *object_id* is specified, the number of times the specified trigger has been executed for the statement is returned. If *object_id* is not specified, the number of times all triggers have been executed for the statement is returned.

When *object_id* is omitted (this is different from a null value), TRIGGER_NESTLEVEL returns the number of triggers on the call stack, including itself. Omission of *object_id* can occur when a trigger executes commands causing another trigger to be fired or creates a succession of firing triggers.

Remarks

TRIGGER_NESTLEVEL returns 0 if it is executed outside of a trigger and *object_id* is not NULL.

TRIGGER_NESTLEVEL optionally receives an object ID as its argument. When *object_id* is explicitly specified as NULL or an invalid object id is referenced, a value of NULL is returned regardless of whether TRIGGER_NESTLEVEL was used within or external to a trigger.

Examples

A. Test nesting level of a specific trigger

```
IF ( (SELECT trigger_nestlevel( object_ID('xyz') ) ) > 5 )
   RAISERROR('Trigger xyz nested more than 5 levels.',16,-1)
```

B. Test nesting level of all triggers executed

```
IF ( (SELECT trigger_nestlevel() ) > 5 )
   RAISERROR
      ('This statement nested over 5 levels of triggers.',16,-1)
```

Related Topics

CREATE TRIGGER

TRUNCATE TABLE

Removes all rows from a table without logging the individual row deletes.

Syntax

```
TRUNCATE TABLE name
```

Arguments

name

Is the name of the table to truncate or from which all rows are removed.

Remarks

TRUNCATE TABLE is functionally identical to DELETE statement with no WHERE clause: both remove all rows in the table. But TRUNCATE TABLE is faster and uses fewer system and transaction log resources than DELETE.

The DELETE statement removes rows one at a time and records an entry in the transaction log for each deleted row. TRUNCATE TABLE removes the data by deallocating the data pages used to store the table's data, and only the page deallocations are recorded in the transaction log.

TRUNCATE TABLE removes all rows from a table, but the table structure and its columns, constraints, indexes and so on remain. The counter used by an identity for new rows is reset to the seed for the column. If you want to retain the identity counter, use DELETE instead. If you want to remove table definition and its data, use the DROP TABLE statement.

You cannot use TRUNCATE TABLE on a table referenced by a FOREIGN KEY constraint; instead, use DELETE statement without a WHERE clause. Because TRUNCATE TABLE is not logged, it cannot activate a trigger.

TRUNCATE TABLE may not be used on tables participating in an indexed view.

Examples

This example removes all data from the **authors** table.

```
TRUNCATE TABLE authors
```

Permissions

TRUNCATE TABLE permissions default to the table owner, members of the **sysadmin** fixed server role, and the **db_owner** and **db_ddladmin** fixed database roles, and are not transferable.

Related Topics

DELETE, DROP TABLE

TYPEPROPERTY

Returns information about a data type.

Syntax

```
TYPEPROPERTY ( type , property )
```

Arguments

type

Is the name of the data type.

property

Is the type of information to be returned for the data type. *property* can be one of these values.

Property	Description	Value returned
Precision	Precision for the data type.	The number of digits or characters. NULL = Data type not found.
Scale	Scale for the data type.	The number of decimal places for the data type. NULL = Data type is not **numeric** or not found.
AllowsNull	Data type allows null values.	1 = True 0 = False NULL = Data type not found.
UsesAnsiTrim	ANSI padding setting was ON when the data type was created.	1 = True 0 = False NULL = Data type not found, or it is not a binary or string data type.

Return Types

int

Examples

This example returns the precision or number of digits for the **integer** data type.

```
SELECT TYPEPROPERTY( 'tinyint', 'PRECISION')
```

Related Topics

COLUMNPROPERTY, Metadata Functions, OBJECTPROPERTY

UNICODE

Returns the integer value, as defined by the Unicode standard, for the first character of the input expression.

Syntax

```
UNICODE ( 'ncharacter_expression' )
```

Arguments

'*ncharacter_expression*'
Is an **nchar** or **nvarchar** expression.

Return Types

int

Examples

A. Use UNICODE and NCHAR

This example uses the UNICODE and NCHAR functions to print the UNICODE value of the first character of the Åkergatan 24-character string, and to print the actual first character, Å.

```
DECLARE @nstring nchar(12)
SET @nstring = N'Åkergatan 24'
SELECT UNICODE(@nstring), NCHAR(UNICODE(@nstring))
```

Here is the result set:

```
----------- -
197          Å
```

B. Use SUBSTRING, UNICODE, and CONVERT

This example uses the SUBSTRING, UNICODE, and CONVERT functions to print the character number, the Unicode character, and the UNICODE value of each of the characters in the string Åkergatan 24.

```
-- The @position variable holds the position of the character currently
-- being processed. The @nstring variable is the Unicode character
-- string to process.
DECLARE @position int, @nstring nchar(12)
-- Initialize the current position variable to the first character in
-- the string.
SET @position = 1
-- Initialize the character string variable to the string to process.
-- Notice that there is an N before the start of the string, which
-- indicates that the data following the N is Unicode data.
SET @nstring = N'Åkergatan 24'
-- Print the character number of the position of the string you are at,
-- the actual Unicode character you are processing, and the UNICODE
-- value for this particular character.
PRINT 'Character #' + ' ' + 'Unicode Character' + ' ' + 'UNICODE Value'
WHILE @position <= DATALENGTH(@nstring)
-- While these are still characters in the character string,
   BEGIN
   SELECT @position,
       CONVERT(char(17), SUBSTRING(@nstring, @position, 1)),
       UNICODE(SUBSTRING(@nstring, @position, 1))
   SELECT @position = @position + 1
   END
```

Here is the result set:

```
Character # Unicode Character UNICODE Value

----------- ----------------- -----------
1           Å                 197

----------- ----------------- -----------
2           k                 107

----------- ----------------- -----------
3           e                 101

----------- ----------------- -----------
4           r                 114

----------- ----------------- -----------
5           g                 103

----------- ----------------- -----------
6           a                 97
```

(continued)

(continued)

7	t	116
8	a	97
9	n	110
10		32
11	2	50
12	4	52

Related Topics

Data Types, NCHAR, String Functions, Using Unicode Data

UNION

Combines the results of two or more queries into a single result set consisting of all the rows belonging to all queries in the union. For more information, see SELECT.

uniqueidentifier

A globally unique identifier (GUID).

Remarks

A column or local variable of **uniqueidentifier** data type can be initialized to a value in two ways:

- Using the NEWID function.
- Converting from a string constant in the following form (xxxxxxxx-xxxx-xxxx-xxxx-xxxxxxxxxxxx, in which each x is a hexadecimal digit in the range 0–9 or a–f). For example, 6F9619FF-8B86-D011-B42D-00C04FC964FF is a valid **uniqueidentifier** value.

Comparison operators can be used with **uniqueidentifier** values. However, ordering is not implemented by comparing the bit patterns of the two values. The only operations that are allowed against a **uniqueidentifier** value are comparisons (=, <>, <, >, <=, >=) and checking for NULL (IS NULL and IS NOT NULL). No other arithmetic operators are allowed. All column constraints and properties except IDENTITY are allowed on the **uniqueidentifier** data type.

Related Topics

ALTER TABLE, CAST and CONVERT, CREATE TABLE, Data Type Conversion, Data Types, DECLARE @local_variable, DELETE, INSERT, NEWID, Replication Overview, SET @local_variable, UPDATE

UPDATE

Changes existing data in a table.

Syntax

```
UPDATE
    {
     table_name WITH ( < table_hint_limited > [ ...n ] )
    | view_name
    | rowset_function_limited
    }
    SET
    { column_name = { expression | DEFAULT | NULL }
    | @variable = expression
    | @variable = column = expression } [ ,...n ]

  { { [ FROM { < table_source > } [ ,...n ] ]

    [ WHERE
        < search_condition > ] }
    |
    [ WHERE CURRENT OF
    { { [ GLOBAL ] cursor_name } | cursor_variable_name }
    ] }
      [ OPTION ( < query_hint > [ ,...n ] ) ]
< table_source > ::=
    table_name [ [ AS ] table_alias ] [ WITH ( < table_hint > [ ,...n ] ) ]
    | view_name [ [ AS ] table_alias ]
    | rowset_function [ [ AS ] table_alias ]
    | derived_table [ AS ] table_alias [ ( column_alias [ ,...n ] ) ]
```

(continued)

(continued)

```
    | < joined_table >
< joined_table > ::=
   < table_source > < join_type > < table_source > ON < search_condition >
   | < table_source > CROSS JOIN < table_source >
   | < joined_table >
< join_type > ::=
   [ INNER | { { LEFT | RIGHT | FULL } [ OUTER ] } ]
   [ < join_hint > ]
   JOIN
< table_hint_limited > ::=
   {   FASTFIRSTROW
      | HOLDLOCK
      | PAGLOCK
      | READCOMMITTED
      | REPEATABLEREAD
      | ROWLOCK
      | SERIALIZABLE
      | TABLOCK
      | TABLOCKX
      | UPDLOCK
   }
< table_hint > ::=
   {   INDEX ( index_val [ ,...n ] )
      | FASTFIRSTROW
      | HOLDLOCK
      | NOLOCK
      | PAGLOCK
      | READCOMMITTED
      | READPAST
      | READUNCOMMITTED
      | REPEATABLEREAD
      | ROWLOCK
      | SERIALIZABLE
      | TABLOCK
      | TABLOCKX
      | UPDLOCK
   }
< query_hint > ::=
   {   { HASH | ORDER } GROUP
      | { CONCAT | HASH | MERGE } UNION
      | {LOOP | MERGE | HASH } JOIN
      | FAST number_rows
```

(continued)

(continued)

```
    | FORCE ORDER
    | MAXDOP
    | ROBUST PLAN
    | KEEP PLAN
  }
```

Arguments

table_name

>   Is the name of the table to update. The name can be qualified with the linked
>   server, database, and owner name if the table is not in the current server or
>   database, or is not owned by the current user.

WITH (< table_hint_limited > [...*n*])

>   Specifies one or more table hints that are allowed for a target table. The WITH
>   keyword and the parentheses are required. READPAST, NOLOCK, and
>   READUNCOMMITTED are not allowed. For information about table hints,
>   see FROM.

view_name

>   Is the name of the view to update. The view referenced by *view_name* must be
>   updateable. The modifications made by the UPDATE statement cannot affect more
>   than one of the base tables referenced in the FROM clause of the view. For more
>   information on updateable views, see CREATE VIEW.

rowset_function_limited

>   Is either the OPENQUERY or OPENROWSET function, subject to provider
>   capabilities. For more information about capabilities needed by the provider, see
>   UPDATE and DELETE Requirements for OLE DB Providers. For more
>   information about the rowset functions, see OPENQUERY and OPENROWSET.

SET

>   Specifies the list of column or variable names to be updated.

column_name

>   Is a column that contains the data to be changed. *column_name* must reside in the
>   table or view specified in the UPDATE clause. Identity columns cannot be
>   updated.

>   If a qualified column name is specified, the qualifier must match the table or view
>   name in the UPDATE clause. For example, this is valid:

```
UPDATE authors
    SET authors.au_fname = 'Annie'
    WHERE au_fname = 'Anne'
```

A table alias specified in a FROM clause cannot be used as a qualifier in SET *column_name*. For example, this is not valid:

```
UPDATE titles
   SET t.ytd_sales = t.ytd_sales + s.qty
   FROM titles t, sales s
   WHERE t.title_id = s.title_id
   AND s.ord_date = (SELECT MAX(sales.ord_date) FROM sales)
```

To make the example work, remove the **t.** alias from the column name.

```
UPDATE titles
   SET ytd_sales = t.ytd_sales + s.qty
   FROM titles t, sales s
   WHERE t.title_id = s.title_id
   AND s.ord_date = (SELECT MAX(sales.ord_date) FROM sales)
```

expression

Is a variable, literal value, expression, or a parenthesized subSELECT statement that returns a single value. The value returned by *expression* replaces the existing value in *column_name* or @*variable*.

DEFAULT

Specifies that the default value defined for the column is to replace the existing value in the column. This can also be used to change the column to NULL if the column has no default and is defined to allow null values.

@*variable*

Is a declared variable that is set to the value returned by *expression*.

SET @*variable* = *column* = *expression* sets the variable to the same value as the column. This differs from SET @*variable* = *column*, *column* = *expression*, which sets the variable to the pre-update value of the column.

FROM < table_source >

Specifies that a table is used to provide the criteria for the update operation. For more information, see FROM.

table_name [[AS] *table_alias*]

Is the name of a table to provide criteria for the update operation.

If the table being updated is the same as the table in the FROM clause, and there is only one reference to the table in the FROM clause, *table_alias* may or may not be specified. If the table being updated appears more than one time in the FROM clause, one (and only one) reference to the table must not specify a table alias. All other references to the table in the FROM clause must include a table alias.

view_name [[AS] *table_alias*]

Is the name of a view to provide criteria for the update operation. A view with an INSTEAD OF UPDATE trigger cannot be a target of an UPDATE with a FROM clause.

WITH (< table_hint > [...*n*])

> Specifies one or more table hints for a source table. For information about table hints, see FROM in this volume.

rowset_function [[AS] *table_alias*]

> Is the name of any rowset function and an optional alias. For information about a list of rowset functions, see Rowset Functions.

derived_table

> Is a subquery that retrieves rows from the database. *derived_table* is used as input to the outer query.

column_alias

> Is an optional alias to replace a column name in the result set. Include one column alias for each column in the select list, and enclose the entire list of column aliases in parentheses.

< joined_table >

> Is a result set that is the product of two or more tables, for example:

```
SELECT *
FROM tab1 LEFT OUTER JOIN tab2 ON tab1.c3 = tab2.c3
    RIGHT OUTER JOIN tab3 LEFT OUTER JOIN tab4
        ON tab3.c1 = tab4.c1
        ON tab2.c3 = tab4.c3
```

For multiple CROSS joins, use parentheses to change the natural order of the joins.

< join_type >

> Specifies the type of join operation.

> INNER

>> Specifies that all matching pairs of rows are returned. Discards unmatched rows from both tables. This is the default if no join type is specified.

> LEFT [OUTER]

>> Specifies that all rows from the left table not meeting the specified condition are included in the result set in addition to all rows returned by the inner join. Output columns from the left table are set to NULL.

> RIGHT [OUTER]

>> Specifies that all rows from the right table not meeting the specified condition are included in the result set in addition to all rows returned by the inner join. Output columns from the right table are set to NULL.

> FULL [OUTER]

>> If a row from either the left or right table does not match the selection criteria, specifies the row be included in the result set, and output columns that correspond to the other table be set to NULL. This is in addition to all rows usually returned by the inner join.

< join_hint >

Specifies a join hint or execution algorithm. If <join_hint> is specified, INNER, LEFT, RIGHT, or FULL must also be explicitly specified. For more information about joint hints, see FROM.

JOIN

Indicates that the specified tables or views should be joined.

ON < search_condition >

Specifies the condition on which the join is based. The condition can specify any predicate, although columns and comparison operators are often used, for example:

```
FROM Suppliers JOIN Products
   ON (Suppliers.SupplierID = Products.SupplierID)
```

When the condition specifies columns, the columns do not have to have the same name or same data type; however, if the data types are not identical, they must be either compatible or types that Microsoft SQL Server can implicitly convert. If the data types cannot be implicitly converted, the condition must explicitly convert the data type using the CAST function.

For more information about search conditions and predicates, see Search Condition.

CROSS JOIN

Specifies the cross-product of two tables. Returns the same rows as if the tables to be joined were simply listed in the FROM clause and no WHERE clause was specified.

WHERE

Specifies the conditions that limit the rows that are updated. There are two forms of update based on which form of the WHERE clause is used:

- Searched updates specify a search condition to qualify the rows to delete.

- Positioned updates use the CURRENT OF clause to specify a cursor. The update operation occurs at the current position of the cursor.

< search_condition >

Specifies the condition to be met for the rows to be updated. The search condition can also be the condition upon which a join is based. There is no limit to the number of predicates that can be included in a search condition. For more information about predicates and search conditions, see Search Condition.

CURRENT OF

Specifies that the update is performed at the current position of the specified cursor.

GLOBAL

Specifies that *cursor_name* refers to a global cursor.

cursor_name

Is the name of the open cursor from which the fetch should be made. If both a global and a local cursor exist with *cursor_name* as their name, *cursor_name* refers to the global cursor if GLOBAL is specified. If GLOBAL is not specified, *cursor_name* refers to the local cursor. The cursor must allow updates.

cursor_variable_name

Is the name of a cursor variable. *cursor_variable_name* must reference a cursor that allows updates.

OPTION (< query_hint > [,...*n*])

Specifies that optimizer hints are used to customize SQL Server's processing of the statement.

{ HASH | ORDER } GROUP

Specifies that the aggregations specified in the GROUP BY or COMPUTE clause of the query should use hashing or ordering.

{ LOOP | MERGE | HASH |} JOIN

Specifies that all join operations are performed by loop join, merge join, or hash join in the whole query. If more than one join hint is specified, the query optimizer selects the least expensive join strategy for the allowed ones. If, in the same query, a join hint is also specified for a specific pair of tables, it takes precedence in the joining of the two tables.

{ MERGE | HASH | CONCAT } UNION

Specifies that all UNION operations should be performed by merging, hashing, or concatenating UNION sets. If more than one UNION hint is specified, the query optimizer selects the least expensive strategy from those hints specified.

Note If a join hint is also specified for any particular pair of joined tables in the FROM clause, it takes precedence over any join hint specified in the OPTION clause.

FAST number_rows

Specifies that the query is optimized for fast retrieval of the first *number_rows* (a nonnegative integer). After the first *number_rows* are returned, the query continues execution and produces its full result set.

FORCE ORDER

Specifies that the join order indicated by the query syntax should be preserved during query optimization.

MAXDOP *number*

Overrides the **max degree of parallelism** configuration option (of **sp_configure**) only for the query specifying this option. All semantic rules used with **max degree of parallelism** configuration option are applicable when using the MAXDOP query hint. For more information, see max degree of parallelism Option.

ROBUST PLAN

Forces the query optimizer to attempt a plan that works for the maximum potential row size at the expense of performance. If no such plan is possible, the query optimizer returns an error rather than deferring error detection to query execution. Rows may contain variable-length columns; SQL Server allows rows to be defined whose maximum potential size is beyond the ability of SQL Server to process. Usually, despite the maximum potential size, an application stores rows that have actual sizes within the limits that SQL Server can process. If SQL Server encounters a row that is too long, an execution error is returned.

KEEP PLAN

Forces the query optimizer to relax the estimated recompile threshold for a query. The estimated recompile threshold is the point at which a query is automatically recompiled when the estimated number of indexed column changes (update, delete or insert) have been made to a table. Specifying KEEP PLAN ensures that a query will be recompiled less frequently when there are multiple updates to a table.

Remarks

UPDATE statements are allowed in the body of user-defined functions only if the table being modified is a **table** variable.

A **table** variable, in its scope, may be accessed like a regular table. Thus, a **table** variable may be used as the table in which data is updated in an UPDATE statement.

A four-part name constructed with the OPENDATASOURCE function as the server-name part may be used as a table source in all places a table name can appear in UPDATE statements.

If an update to a row violates a constraint or rule, if it violates the NULL setting for the column, or if the new value is an incompatible data type, the statement is canceled, an error is returned, and no records are updated.

When an UPDATE statement encounters an arithmetic error (overflow, divide by zero, or a domain error) during expression evaluation, the update is not performed. The remainder of the batch is not executed, and an error message is returned.

If an update to a column or columns participating in a clustered index causes the size of the clustered index and the row to exceed 8,060 bytes, the update fails and an error message is returned.

When an INSTEAD-OF trigger is defined on UPDATE actions against a table, the trigger executes *instead of* the UPDATE statement. Previous versions of SQL Server only support AFTER triggers defined on UPDATE and other data modification statements.

If an update query could alter more than one row while updating both the clustering key and one or more **text**, **image**, or Unicode columns, the update operation fails and SQL Server returns an error message.

Modifying a **text**, **ntext**, or **image** column with UPDATE initializes the column, assigns a valid text pointer to it, and allocates at least one data page unless updating the column with NULL.

> **Note**   The UPDATE statement is logged. If you are replacing or modifying large blocks of **text**, **ntext**, or **image** data, use the WRITETEXT or UPDATETEXT statement instead of the UPDATE statement. The WRITETEXT and UPDATETEXT statements (by default) are not logged.

All **char** and **nchar** columns are right-padded to the defined length.

The setting of the SET ROWCOUNT option is ignored for UPDATE statements against remote tables and local and remote partitioned views.

If ANSI_PADDING is set OFF, all trailing spaces are removed from data inserted into **varchar** and **nvarchar** columns, except in strings containing only spaces. These strings are truncated to an empty string. If ANSI_PADDING is set ON, trailing spaces are inserted. The Microsoft SQL Server ODBC driver and OLE DB Provider for SQL Server automatically set ANSI_PADDING ON for each connection. This can be configured in ODBC data sources or by setting connection attributes or properties.

A positioned update using a WHERE CURRENT OF clause updates the single row at the current position of the cursor. This can be more accurate than a searched update that uses a WHERE <search_condition> clause to qualify the rows to be updated. A searched update modifies multiple rows when the search condition does not uniquely identify a single row.

The results of an UPDATE statement are undefined if the statement includes a FROM clause that is not specified in such a way that only one value is available for each column occurrence that is updated (in other words, if the UPDATE statement is not deterministic). For example, given the UPDATE statement in the following script, both rows in table **s** meet the qualifications of the FROM clause in the UPDATE statement, but it is undefined which row from **s** is used to update the row in table **t**.

```
CREATE TABLE s (ColA INT, ColB DECIMAL(10,3))
GO
CREATE TABLE t (ColA INT PRIMARY KEY, ColB DECIMAL(10,3))
GO
INSERT INTO s VALUES(1, 10.0)
INSERT INTO s VALUES(1, 20.0)
INSERT INTO t VALUES(1, 0.0)
GO
UPDATE t
SET t.ColB = t.ColB + s.ColB
FROM t INNER JOIN s ON (t.ColA = s.ColA)
GO
```

The same problem can occur when combining the FROM and WHERE CURRENT OF clauses. In this example, both rows in table **t2** meet the qualifications of the FROM clause in the UPDATE statement. It is undefined which row from **t2** is to be used to update the row in table **t1**.

```
CREATE TABLE t1(c1 INT PRIMARY KEY, c2 INT)
GO
CREATE TABLE t2(d1 INT PRIMARY KEY, d2 INT)
GO
INSERT INTO t1 VALUES (1, 10)
INSERT INTO t2 VALUES (1, 20)
INSERT INTO t2 VALUES (2, 30)
go

DECLARE abc CURSOR LOCAL FOR
SELECT * FROM t1

OPEN abc

FETCH abc

UPDATE t1 SET c2 = c2 + d2
FROM t2
WHERE CURRENT OF abc
GO
```

Setting Variables and Columns

Variable names can be used in UPDATE statements to show the old and new values affected. This should only be used when the UPDATE statement affects a single record; if the UPDATE statement affects multiple records, the variables only contain the values for one of the updated rows.

Permissions

UPDATE permissions default to members of the **sysadmin** fixed server role, the **db_owner** and **db_datawriter** fixed database roles, and the table owner. Members of the **sysadmin**, **db_owner**, and **db_securityadmin** roles, and the table owner can transfer permissions to other users.

SELECT permissions are also required for the table being updated if the UPDATE statement contains a WHERE clause, or if *expression* in the SET clause uses a column in the table.

Examples

A. Use a simple UPDATE

These examples show how all rows can be affected if a WHERE clause is eliminated from an UPDATE statement.

If all the publishing houses in the **publishers** table move their head offices to Atlanta, Georgia, this example shows how the **publishers** table can be updated.

```
UPDATE publishers
SET city = 'Atlanta', state = 'GA'
```

This example changes the names of all the publishers to NULL.

```
UPDATE publishers
SET pub_name = NULL
```

You can also use computed values in an update. This example doubles all prices in the **titles** table.

```
UPDATE titles
SET price = price * 2
```

B. Use the UPDATE statement with a WHERE clause

The WHERE clause specifies the rows to update. For example, consider the unlikely event that northern California is renamed Pacifica (abbreviated PC) and the people of Oakland vote to change the name of their city to Bay City. This example shows how to update the **authors** table for all former Oakland residents whose addresses are now out of date.

```
UPDATE authors
   SET state = 'PC', city = 'Bay City'
      WHERE state = 'CA' AND city = 'Oakland'
```

You must write another statement to change the name of the state for residents of other northern California cities.

C. Use the UPDATE statement using information from another table

This example modifies the **ytd_sales** column in the **titles** table to reflect the most recent sales recorded in the **sales** table.

```
UPDATE titles
   SET ytd_sales = titles.ytd_sales + sales.qty
      FROM titles, sales
         WHERE titles.title_id = sales.title_id
         AND sales.ord_date = (SELECT MAX(sales.ord_date) FROM sales)
```

This example assumes that only one set of sales is recorded for a given title on a given date and that updates are current. If this is not the case (if more than one sale for a given title can be recorded on the same day), the example shown here does not work correctly. It executes without error, but each title is updated with only one sale, regardless of how many sales actually occurred on that day. This is because a single UPDATE statement never updates the same row twice.

In the situation in which more than one sale for a given title can occur on the same day, all the sales for each title must be aggregated together within the UPDATE statement, as shown in this example:

```
UPDATE titles
   SET ytd_sales =
      (SELECT SUM(qty)
         FROM sales
            WHERE sales.title_id = titles.title_id
            AND sales.ord_date IN (SELECT MAX(ord_date) FROM sales))
   FROM titles, sales
```

D. Use UPDATE with the TOP clause in a SELECT statement

This example updates the **state** column for the first 10 authors from the **authors** table.

```
UPDATE authors
SET state = 'ZZ'
FROM (SELECT TOP 10 * FROM authors ORDER BY au_lname) AS t1
WHERE authors.au_id = t1.au_id
```

Related Topics

CREATE INDEX, CREATE TABLE, CREATE TRIGGER, Cursors, DELETE, INSERT, SET ROWCOUNT, Text and Image Functions

UPDATE STATISTICS

Updates information about the distribution of key values for one or more statistics groups (collections) in the specified table or indexed view. To create statistics on columns, see CREATE STATISTICS.

Syntax

```
UPDATE STATISTICS table | view
   [
      index
      | ( statistics_name [ ,...n ] )
   ]
   [  WITH
```

(continued)

(continued)

```
[
    [ FULLSCAN ]
    | SAMPLE number { PERCENT | ROWS } ]
    | RESAMPLE
]
[ [ , ] [ ALL | COLUMNS | INDEX ]
[ [ , ] NORECOMPUTE ]
]
```

Arguments

table | view

Is the name of the table or indexed view for which to update statistics. Table or view names must conform to the rules for identifiers. For more information, see Using Identifiers. Because index names are not unique within each database, *table* or *view* must be specified. Specifying the database, table, or view owner is optional. Indexed views are supported only on Microsoft SQL Server 2000, Enterprise Edition.

index

Is the index for which statistics are being updated. Index names must conform to the rules for identifiers. If *index* is not specified, the distribution statistics for all indexes in the specified table or indexed view are updated. To see a list of index names and descriptions, execute **sp_helpindex** with the table or view name.

statistics_name

Is the name of the statistics group (collection) to update. Statistics names must conform to the rules for identifiers. For more information about creating statistics groups, see CREATE STATISTICS.

n

Is a placeholder indicating that multiple *statistics_name* groups can be specified.

FULLSCAN

Specifies that all rows in *table* or *view* should be read to gather the statistics. FULLSCAN provides the same behavior as SAMPLE 100 PERCENT. FULLSCAN cannot be used with the SAMPLE option.

SAMPLE *number* { PERCENT | ROWS }

Specifies the percentage of the table or indexed view, or the number of rows to sample when collecting statistics for larger tables or views. Only integers are allowed for *number* whether it is PERCENT or ROWS. To use the default sampling behavior for larger tables or views, use SAMPLE *number* with PERCENT or ROWS. Microsoft SQL Server ensures a minimum number of values are sampled to ensure useful statistics. If the PERCENT, ROWS, or *number* option results in too few rows being sampled, SQL Server automatically corrects the sampling based on the number of existing rows in the table or view.

Note   The default behavior is to perform a sample scan on the target table or indexed view. SQL Server automatically computes the required sample size.

RESAMPLE

Specifies that statistics will be gathered using an inherited sampling ratio for all existing statistics including indexes. If the sampling ratio results in too few rows being sampled, SQL Server automatically corrects the sampling based on the number of existing rows in the table or view.

ALL | COLUMNS | INDEX

Specifies whether the UPDATE STATISTICS statement affects column statistics, index statistics, or all existing statistics. If no option is specified, the UPDATE STATISTICS statement affects all statistics. Only one type (ALL, COLUMNS, or INDEX) can be specified per UPDATE STATISTICS statement.

NORECOMPUTE

Specifies that statistics that become out of date are not automatically recomputed. Statistics become out of date depending on the number of INSERT, UPDATE, and DELETE operations performed on indexed columns. When specified, this option causes SQL Server to disable automatic statistics rebuilding. To restore automatic statistics recomputation, reissue UPDATE STATISTICS without the NORECOMPUTE option or execute **sp_autostats**.

Important   Disabling automatic statistics recomputation can cause the SQL Server query optimizer to choose a less optimal strategy for queries that involve the specified table.

Remarks

SQL Server keeps statistics about the distribution of the key values in each index and uses these statistics to determine which index(es) to use in query processing. Users can create statistics on nonindexed columns by using the CREATE STATISTICS statement. Query optimization depends on the accuracy of the distribution steps:

- If there is significant change in the key values in the index, rerun UPDATE STATISTICS on that index.
- If a large amount of data in an indexed column has been added, changed, or removed (that is, if the distribution of key values has changed), or the table has been truncated using the TRUNCATE TABLE statement and then repopulated, use UPDATE STATISTICS.

To see when the statistics were last updated, use the STATS_DATE function.

Statistics can be created or updated on tables with computed columns only if the conditions are such that an index can be created on these columns. For more information about the requirements and restrictions on creating indexes on computed columns, see CREATE INDEX.

Permissions

UPDATE STATISTICS permissions default to the table or view owner, and are not transferable.

Examples

A. Update all statistics for a single table

This example updates the distribution statistics for all indexes on the **authors** table.

```
UPDATE STATISTICS authors
```

B. Update only the statistics for a single index

This example updates only the distribution information for the **au_id_ind** index of the **authors** table.

```
UPDATE STATISTICS authors au_id_ind
```

C. Update statistics for specific statistics groups (collections) using 50 percent sampling

This example creates and then updates the statistics group for the **au_lname** and **au_fname** columns in the **authors** table.

```
CREATE STATISTICS anames
    ON authors (au_lname, au_fname)
    WITH SAMPLE 50 PERCENT
GO
-- Time passes. The UPDATE STATISTICS statement is then executed.
UPDATE STATISTICS authors(anames)
    WITH SAMPLE 50 PERCENT
GO
```

D. Update statistics for a specific statistics groups (collections) using FULLSCAN and NORECOMPUTE

This example updates the **anames** statistics group (collection) in the **authors** table, forces a full scan of all rows in the **authors** table, and turns off automatic statistics updating for the statistics group (collection).

```
UPDATE STATISTICS authors(anames)
    WITH FULLSCAN, NORECOMPUTE
GO
```

Related Topics

CREATE INDEX, CREATE STATISTICS, Cursors, DBCC SHOW_STATISTICS, DROP STATISTICS, EXECUTE, Functions, sp_autostats, sp_createstats, sp_dboption, sp_helpindex, sp_updatestats, STATS_DATE

UPDATETEXT

Updates an existing **text**, **ntext**, or **image** field. Use UPDATETEXT to change only a portion of a **text**, **ntext**, or **image** column in place. Use WRITETEXT to update and replace an entire **text**, **ntext**, or **image** field.

Syntax

```
UPDATETEXT { table_name.dest_column_name dest_text_ptr }
   { NULL | insert_offset }
   { NULL | delete_length }
   [ WITH LOG ]
   [ inserted_data
       | { table_name.src_column_name src_text_ptr } ]
```

Arguments

table_name.dest_column_name

Is the name of the table and **text**, **ntext**, or **image** column to be updated. Table names and column names must conform to the rules for identifiers. For more information, see Using Identifiers. Specifying the database name and owner names is optional.

dest_text_ptr

Is a text pointer value (returned by the TEXTPTR function) that points to the **text**, **ntext**, or **image** data to be updated. *dest_text_ptr* must be **binary(16)**.

insert_offset

Is the zero-based starting position for the update. For **text** or **image** columns, *insert_offset* is the number of bytes to skip from the start of the existing column before inserting new data. For **ntext** columns, *insert_offset* is the number of characters (each **ntext** character uses 2 bytes). The existing **text**, **ntext**, or **image** data beginning at this zero-based starting position is shifted to the right to make room for the new data. A value of 0 inserts the new data at the beginning of the existing data. A value of NULL appends the new data to the existing data value.

delete_length

Is the length of data to delete from the existing **text**, **ntext**, or **image** column, starting at the *insert_offset* position. The *delete_length* value is specified in bytes for **text** and **image** columns and in characters for **ntext** columns. Each **ntext** character uses 2 bytes. A value of 0 deletes no data. A value of NULL deletes all data from the *insert_offset* position to the end of the existing **text** or **image** column.

WITH LOG

Ignored in Microsoft SQL Server 2000. In this release, logging is determined by the recovery model in effect for the database.

inserted_data
>   Is the data to be inserted into the existing **text**, **ntext**, or **image** column at the *insert_offset* location. This is a single **char**, **nchar**, **varchar**, **nvarchar**, **binary**, **varbinary**, **text**, **ntext**, or **image** value. *inserted_data* can be a literal or a variable.

table_name.src_column_name
>   Is the name of the table and **text**, **ntext**, or **image** column used as the source of the inserted data. Table names and column names must conform to the rules for identifiers.

src_text_ptr
>   Is a text pointer value (returned by the TEXTPTR function) that points to a **text**, **ntext**, or **image** column used as the source of the inserted data.

Remarks

Newly inserted data can be a single *inserted_data* constant, table name, column name, or text pointer.

Update action	UPDATETEXT parameters
To replace existing data	Specify a nonnull *insert_offset* value, a nonzero *delete_length* value, and the new data to be inserted.
To delete existing data	Specify a nonnull *insert_offset* value and a nonzero *delete_length*. Do not specify new data to be inserted.
To insert new data	Specify the *insert_offset* value, a *delete_length* of 0, and the new data to be inserted.

In SQL Server 2000, in row text pointers to **text**, **ntext**, or **image** data may exist but be invalid. For information about the **text in row** option, see sp_tableoption. For information about invalidating text pointers, see sp_invalidate_textptr.

To initialize **text** columns to NULL, use UPDATETEXT when the compatibility level is equal to 65. If the compatibility level is equal to 70, use WRITETEXT to initialize text columns to NULL; otherwise, UPDATETEXT initializes **text** columns to an empty string. For information about setting the compatibility level, see sp_dbcmptlevel.

Permissions

UPDATETEXT permissions default to those users with SELECT permissions on the specified table. Permissions are transferable when SELECT permissions are transferred.

Examples

This example puts the text pointer into the local variable **@ptrval**, and then uses UPDATETEXT to update a spelling error.

```
USE pubs
GO
EXEC sp_dboption 'pubs', 'select into/bulkcopy', 'true'
GO
DECLARE @ptrval binary(16)
SELECT @ptrval = TEXTPTR(pr_info)
   FROM pub_info pr, publishers p
      WHERE p.pub_id = pr.pub_id
      AND p.pub_name = 'New Moon Books'
UPDATETEXT pub_info.pr_info @ptrval 88 1 'b'
GO
EXEC sp_dboption 'pubs', 'select into/bulkcopy', 'false'
GO
```

Related Topics

READTEXT, TEXTPTR, WRITETEXT

UPPER

Returns a character expression with lowercase character data converted to uppercase.

Syntax

```
UPPER ( character_expression )
```

Arguments

character_expression

    Is an expression of character data. *character_expression* can be a constant, variable, or column of either character or binary data.

Return Types

varchar

Remarks

character_expression must be of a data type that is implicitly convertible to **varchar**. Otherwise, use the CAST function to explicitly convert *character_expression*.

Examples

This example uses the UPPER and RTRIM functions to return the trimmed, uppercase author's last name concatenated with the author's first name.

```
USE pubs
GO
SELECT UPPER(RTRIM(au_lname)) + ', ' + au_fname AS Name
FROM authors
ORDER BY au_lname
GO
```

Here is the result set:

```
Name
------------------------------------------------------------
BENNET, Abraham
BLOTCHET-HALLS, Reginald
CARSON, Cheryl
DEFRANCE, Michel
DEL CASTILLO, Innes
DULL, Ann
GREEN, Marjorie
GREENE, Morningstar
GRINGLESBY, Burt
HUNTER, Sheryl
KARSEN, Livia
LOCKSLEY, Charlene
MACFEATHER, Stearns
MCBADDEN, Heather
O'LEARY, Michael
PANTELEY, Sylvia
RINGER, Albert
RINGER, Anne
SMITH, Meander
STRAIGHT, Dean
STRINGER, Dirk
WHITE, Johnson
YOKOMOTO, Akiko

(23 row(s) affected)
```

Related Topics

Data Types, String Functions

USE

Changes the database context to the specified database.

Syntax

```
USE { database }
```

Arguments

database

Is the name of the database to which the user context is switched. Database names must conform to the rules for identifiers.

Remarks

USE executes at both compile and execution time and takes effect immediately. Therefore, statements that appear in a batch after the USE statement are executed in the specified database.

When logging in to Microsoft SQL Server, users are usually connected to the **master** database automatically. Unless a default database has been set up for each user's login ID, each user must execute the USE statement to change from **master** to another database.

To change context to a different database, a user must have a security account for that database. The database owner provides the security accounts for the database.

Permissions

USE permissions default to those users who are assigned permissions by the **dbo** and **sysadmin** fixed server roles executing **sp_adduser**, or by the **sysadmin** fixed server role and the **db_accessadmin** and **db_owner** fixed database roles executing **sp_grantdbaccess**. Users without a security account in the destination database can still be allowed access if a guest user exists in that database.

Related Topics

CREATE DATABASE, DROP DATABASE, EXECUTE, sp_addalias, sp_adduser, sp_defaultdb, Using Identifiers

USER

Allows a system-supplied value for the current user's database username to be inserted into a table when no default value is specified.

Syntax

```
USER
```

Return Types

char

Remarks

USER provides the same functionality as the USER_NAME system function.

Use USER with DEFAULT constraints in either the CREATE TABLE or ALTER TABLE statements, or use as any standard function.

Examples

A. Use USER to return the current user's database username

This example declares a variable as **char**, assigns the current value of USER to it, and then prints the variable with a text description.

```
DECLARE @usr char(30)
SET @usr = user
SELECT 'The current user's database username is: '+ @usr
GO
```

Here is the result set:

```
---------------------------------------------------------------------
The current user's database username is: dbo

(1 row(s) affected)
```

B. Use USER with DEFAULT constraints

This example creates a table using USER as a DEFAULT constraint for the salesperson of a sales row.

```
USE pubs
GO
CREATE TABLE inventory2
(
 part_id int IDENTITY(100, 1) NOT NULL,
```

(continued)

(continued)

```
 description varchar(30) NOT NULL,
 entry_person varchar(30) NOT NULL DEFAULT USER
)
GO
INSERT inventory2 (description)
VALUES ('Red pencil')
INSERT inventory2 (description)
VALUES ('Blue pencil')
INSERT inventory2 (description)
VALUES ('Green pencil')
INSERT inventory2 (description)
VALUES ('Black pencil')
INSERT inventory2 (description)
VALUES ('Yellow pencil')
GO
```

This is the query to select all information from the **inventory2** table:

```
SELECT *
FROM inventory2
ORDER BY part_id
GO
```

Here is the result set (note the **entry-person** value):

```
part_id      description                    entry_person
----------   ----------------------------   ----------------------------
100          Red pencil                     dbo
101          Blue pencil                    dbo
102          Green pencil                   dbo
103          Black pencil                   dbo
104          Yellow pencil                  dbo

(5 row(s) affected)
```

Related Topics

ALTER TABLE, CREATE TABLE, Creating and Modifying PRIMARY KEY
Constraints, CURRENT_TIMESTAMP, CURRENT_USER, Modifying Column
Properties, Security Functions, SESSION_USER, SYSTEM_USER, USER_NAME

USER_ID

Returns a user's database identification number.

Syntax

```
USER_ID ( [ 'user' ] )
```

Arguments

'user'

Is the username to be used. *user* is **nchar**. If a **char** value is specified, it is implicitly converted to **nchar**.

Return Types

smallint

Remarks

When *user* is omitted, the current user is assumed. Parentheses are required.

USER_ID can be used in the select list, in the WHERE clause, and anywhere an expression is allowed. For more information, see Expressions.

Examples

This example returns the identification number for user **Harold**.

```
SELECT USER_ID('Harold')
```

Related Topics

Security Functions

USER_NAME

Returns a user database username from a given identification number.

Syntax

```
USER_NAME ( [ id ] )
```

Arguments

id

Is the identification number used to return a user's name. *id* is **int**.

Return Types

nvarchar(256)

Remarks

When *id* is omitted, the current user is assumed. Parentheses are required.

Examples

A. Use USER_NAME

This example returns the username for user number 13.

```
SELECT USER_NAME(13)
GO
```

B. Use USER_NAME without an ID

This example finds the name of the current user without specifying an ID.

```
SELECT user_name()
GO
```

Here is the result set (for a user who is a member of the **sysadmin** fixed server role):

```
--------------------------------
dbo

(1 row(s) affected)
```

C. Use USER_NAME in the WHERE clause

This example finds the row in **sysusers** in which the name is equal to the result of applying the system function USER_NAME to user identification number 1.

```
SELECT name
FROM sysusers
WHERE name = USER_NAME(1)
GO
```

Here is the result set:

```
name
-------------------------------
dbo

(1 row(s) affected)
```

Related Topics

ALTER TABLE, CREATE TABLE, CURRENT_TIMESTAMP, CURRENT_USER, Modifying Column Properties, SESSION_USER, System Functions, SYSTEM_USER

VAR

Returns the statistical variance of all values in the given expression.

Syntax

```
VAR ( expression )
```

Arguments

expression

Is an expression of the exact numeric or approximate numeric data type category, except for the **bit** data type. Aggregate functions and subqueries are not permitted.

Return Types

float

Remarks

If VAR is used on all items in a SELECT statement, each value in the result set is included in the calculation. VAR can be used with numeric columns only. Null values are ignored.

Examples

This example returns the variance for all royalty values in the **titles** table.

```
USE pubs
SELECT VAR(royalty)
FROM titles
```

Related Topics

Aggregate Functions

varbinary

For information about the **varbinary** data type, see binary and varbinary.

Related Topics

Data Type Conversion, Data Types

varchar

For information about the **varchar** data type, see char and varchar.

Related Topics

Data Type Conversion, Data Types

VARP

Returns the statistical variance for the population for all values in the given expression.

Syntax

```
VARP ( expression )
```

Arguments

expression

Is an expression of the exact numeric or approximate numeric data type category, except for the **bit** data type. Aggregate functions and subqueries are not permitted.

Return Types

float

Remarks

If VARP is used on all items in a SELECT statement, each value in the result set is included in the calculation. VARP can be used with numeric columns only. Null values are ignored.

Examples

This example returns the variance for the population for all royalty values in the **titles** table.

```
USE pubs
SELECT VARP(royalty)
FROM titles
```

Related Topics

Aggregate Functions

WAITFOR

Specifies a time, time interval, or event that triggers the execution of a statement block, stored procedure, or transaction.

Syntax

```
WAITFOR { DELAY 'time' | TIME 'time' }
```

Arguments

DELAY

Instructs Microsoft SQL Server to wait until the specified amount of time has passed, up to a maximum of 24 hours.

'*time*'

Is the amount of time to wait. *time* can be specified in one of the acceptable formats for **datetime** data, or it can be specified as a local variable. Dates cannot be specified; therefore, the date portion of the **datetime** value is not allowed.

TIME

Instructs SQL Server to wait until the specified time.

Remarks

After executing the WAITFOR statement, you cannot use your connection to SQL Server until the time or event that you specified occurs.

To see the active and waiting processes, use **sp_who**.

Examples

A. Use WAITFOR TIME

This example executes the stored procedure **update_all_stats** at 10:20 P.M.

```
BEGIN
    WAITFOR TIME '22:20'
    EXECUTE update_all_stats
END
```

For more information about using this procedure to update all statistics for a database, see the examples in UPDATE STATISTICS.

B. Use WAITFOR DELAY

This example shows how a local variable can be used with the WAITFOR DELAY option. A stored procedure is created to wait for a variable amount of time and then returns information to the user as to the number of hours, minutes, and seconds that have elapsed.

```
CREATE PROCEDURE time_delay @@DELAYLENGTH char(9)
AS
DECLARE @@RETURNINFO varchar(255)
BEGIN
    WAITFOR DELAY @@DELAYLENGTH
    SELECT @@RETURNINFO = 'A total time of ' +
                SUBSTRING(@@DELAYLENGTH, 1, 3) +
                ' hours, ' +
                SUBSTRING(@@DELAYLENGTH, 5, 2) +
                ' minutes, and ' +
                SUBSTRING(@@DELAYLENGTH, 8, 2) +
                ' seconds, ' +
                'has elapsed! Your time is up.'
    PRINT @@RETURNINFO
END
GO
-- This next statement executes the time_delay procedure.
EXEC time_delay '000:00:10'
GO
```

Here is the result set:

```
A total time of 000 hours, 00 minutes, and 10 seconds, has elapsed! Your time is up.
```

Related Topics

Control-of-Flow Language, datetime and smalldatetime, sp_who

WHERE

Specifies the condition for the rows returned by a query.

Syntax

```
WHERE < search_condition >
```

Arguments

<search_condition>

Defines the condition to be met for the rows to be returned. There is no limit to the number of predicates in <search_condition>.

Related Topics
DELETE, Predicate, Search Condition, SELECT, UPDATE

WHILE

Sets a condition for the repeated execution of an SQL statement or statement block.
The statements are executed repeatedly as long as the specified condition is true.
The execution of statements in the WHILE loop can be controlled from inside the loop
with the BREAK and CONTINUE keywords.

Syntax

```
WHILE Boolean_expression
    { sql_statement | statement_block }
    [ BREAK ]
    { sql_statement | statement_block }
    [ CONTINUE ]
```

Arguments

Boolean_expression
> Is an expression that returns TRUE or FALSE. If the Boolean expression contains a
> SELECT statement, the SELECT statement must be enclosed in parentheses.

{sql_statement | statement_block}
> Is any Transact-SQL statement or statement grouping as defined with a statement
> block. To define a statement block, use the control-of-flow keywords BEGIN
> and END.

BREAK
> Causes an exit from the innermost WHILE loop. Any statements appearing after
> the END keyword, marking the end of the loop, are executed.

CONTINUE
> Causes the WHILE loop to restart, ignoring any statements after the CONTINUE
> keyword.

Remarks

If two or more WHILE loops are nested, the inner BREAK exits to the next outermost
loop. First, all the statements after the end of the inner loop run, and then the next
outermost loop restarts.

Examples

A. Use BREAK and CONTINUE with nested IF...ELSE and WHILE

In this example, if the average price is less than $30, the WHILE loop doubles the prices and then selects the maximum price. If the maximum price is less than or equal to $50, the WHILE loop restarts and doubles the prices again. This loop continues doubling the prices until the maximum price is greater than $50, and then exits the WHILE loop and prints a message.

```
USE pubs
GO
WHILE (SELECT AVG(price) FROM titles) < $30
BEGIN
   UPDATE titles
      SET price = price * 2
   SELECT MAX(price) FROM titles
   IF (SELECT MAX(price) FROM titles) > $50
      BREAK
   ELSE
      CONTINUE
END
PRINT 'Too much for the market to bear'
```

B. Using WHILE within a procedure with cursors

The following WHILE construct is a section of a procedure named **count_all_rows**. For this example, this WHILE construct tests the return value of @@FETCH_STATUS, a function used with cursors. Because @@FETCH_STATUS may return -2, -1, or 0, all three cases must be tested. If a row is deleted from the cursor results since the time this stored procedure was executed, that row is skipped. A successful fetch (0) causes the SELECT within the BEGIN...END loop to execute.

```
USE pubs
DECLARE tnames_cursor CURSOR
FOR
   SELECT TABLE_NAME
   FROM INFORMATION_SCHEMA.TABLES
OPEN tnames_cursor
DECLARE @tablename sysname
--SET @tablename = 'authors'
FETCH NEXT FROM tnames_cursor INTO @tablename
WHILE (@@FETCH_STATUS <> -1)
BEGIN
   IF (@@FETCH_STATUS <> -2)
   BEGIN
      SELECT @tablename = RTRIM(@tablename)
```

(continued)

(continued)

```
      EXEC ('SELECT ''' + @tablename + ''' = count(*) FROM '
            + @tablename )
      PRINT ' '
  END
  FETCH NEXT FROM tnames_cursor INTO @tablename
END
CLOSE tnames_cursor
DEALLOCATE tnames_cursor
```

Related Topics

ALTER TRIGGER, Control-of-Flow Language, CREATE TRIGGER, Cursors,
SELECT

WRITETEXT

Permits nonlogged, interactive updating of an existing **text**, **ntext**, or **image** column.
This statement completely overwrites any existing data in the column it affects.
WRITETEXT cannot be used on **text**, **ntext**, and **image** columns in views.

Syntax

```
WRITETEXT { table.column text_ptr }
  [ WITH LOG ] { data }
```

Arguments

table.column
> Is the name of the table and **text**, **ntext**, or **image** column to update. Table and
> column names must conform to the rules for identifiers. For more information, see
> Using Identifiers. Specifying the database name and owner names is optional.

text_ptr
> Is a value that stores the pointer to the **text**, **ntext** or **image** data. *text_ptr* must be
> **binary(16)**. To create a text pointer, execute an INSERT or UPDATE statement
> with data that is not NULL for the **text**, **ntext**, or **image** column. For more
> information about creating a text pointer, see either INSERT or UPDATE.

WITH LOG
> Ignored in Microsoft SQL Server 2000. Logging is determined by the recovery
> model in effect for the database.

data
> Is the actual **text**, **ntext** or **image** data to store. *data* can be a literal or a variable.
> The maximum length of text that can be inserted interactively with WRITETEXT
> is approximately 120 KB for **text**, **ntext**, and **image** data.

Remarks

Use WRITETEXT to replace **text**, **ntext**, and **image** data and UPDATETEXT to modify **text**, **ntext**, and **image** data. UPDATETEXT is more flexible because it changes only a portion of a **text**, **ntext**, or **image** column rather than the entire column.

If the database recovery model is simple or bulk-logged, WRITETEXT is a nonlogged operation. This means **text**, **ntext**, or **image** data is not logged when it is written to the database; therefore, the transaction log does not fill up with the large amounts of data that often make up these data types.

For WRITETEXT to work properly, the column must already contain a valid text pointer.

If the table does not have in row text, SQL Server saves space by not initializing **text** columns when explicit or implicit null values are placed in **text** columns with INSERT, and no text pointer can be obtained for such nulls. To initialize **text** columns to NULL, use the UPDATE statement. If the table has in row text, there is no need to initialize the text column for nulls and you can always get a text pointer.

The DB-Library **dbwritetext** and **dbmoretext** functions and the ODBC **SQLPutData** function are faster and use less dynamic memory than WRITETEXT. These functions can insert up to 2 gigabytes of **text**, **ntext**, or **image** data.

In SQL Server 2000, in row text pointers to **text**, **ntext**, or **image** data may exist but be invalid. For information about the **text in row** option, see sp_tableoption. For information about invalidating text pointers, see sp_invalidate_textptr.

Permissions

WRITETEXT permissions default to those users with SELECT permissions on the specified table. Permissions are transferable when SELECT permissions are transferred.

Examples

This example puts the text pointer into the local variable **@ptrval**, and then WRITETEXT places the new text string into the row pointed to by **@ptrval**.

```
USE pubs
GO
EXEC sp_dboption 'pubs', 'select into/bulkcopy', 'true'
GO
DECLARE @ptrval binary(16)
SELECT @ptrval = TEXTPTR(pr_info)
```

(continued)

(continued)

```
FROM pub_info pr, publishers p
WHERE p.pub_id = pr.pub_id
   AND p.pub_name = 'New Moon Books'
WRITETEXT pub_info.pr_info @ptrval 'New Moon Books (NMB) has just released another top ten
publication. With the latest publication this makes NMB the hottest new publisher of the
year!'
GO
EXEC sp_dboption 'pubs', 'select into/bulkcopy', 'false'
GO
```

Related Topics

Data Types, DECLARE @local_variable, DELETE, SELECT, SET, UPDATETEXT

YEAR

Returns an integer that represents the year part of a specified date.

Syntax

```
YEAR ( date )
```

Arguments

date

An expression of type **datetime** or **smalldatetime**.

Return Types

int

Remarks

This function is equivalent to DATEPART(**yy**, *date*).

Examples

This example returns the number of the year from the date 03/12/1998.

```
SELECT "Year Number" = YEAR('03/12/1998')
GO
```

Here is the result set:

```
Year Number
------------
1998
```

This example specifies the date as a number. Notice that Microsoft SQL Server database interprets 0 as January 1, 1900.

```
SELECT MONTH(0), DAY(0), YEAR(0)
```

Here is the result set:

```
----- ------ ------
1     1       1900
```

Related Topics

Date and Time Functions

Northwind Sample Database

The **Northwind Traders** sample database contains the sales data for a fictitious company called Northwind Traders, which imports and exports specialty foods from around the world.

If you have made changes to the **Northwind** database, you can reinstall it by running a script from the Install directory of your Microsoft SQL Server 2000 installation:

1. At the command prompt, change to the Mssql\Install directory.

2. Use the **osql** utility to run the Instnwnd.sql script:

```
osql/Usa /Psapassword /Sservername /iinstnwnd.sql /oinstnwnd.rpt
```

3. Check Instnwnd.rpt for reported errors.

The database is created in the Data directory of your SQL Server installation.

Instnwnd.sql is a large file. If you want to view Instnwnd.sql using Notepad, first turn off the Notepad Word Wrap option. If Word Wrap is on, opening the file and each scrolling operation will take a long time. Even turning Word Wrap off after the file has been opened takes a long time.

Categories

Column_name	Data type	Nullable	Default	Check	Key/index
CategoryID	int	no	IDENTITY(1,1)		PK clust.
CategoryName	nvarchar(15)	no			Nonclust.
Description	ntext	yes			
Picture	image	yes			

Customers

Column_name	Data type	Nullable	Default	Check	Key/index
CustomerID	nchar(5)	no			PK clust.
CompanyName	nvarchar(40)	no			Nonclust.
ContactName	nvarchar(30)	yes			
ContactTitle	nvarchar(30)	yes			
Address	nvarchar(60)	yes			
City	nvarchar(15)	yes			Nonclust.
Region	nvarchar(15)	yes			Nonclust.
PostalCode	nvarchar(10)	yes			Nonclust.
Country	nvarchar(15)	yes			
Phone	nvarchar(24)	yes			
Fax	nvarchar(24)	yes			

CustomerCustomerDemo

Column_name	Data type	Nullable	Default	Check	Key/index
CustomerID	nchar(5)	no			Composite PK nonclust[1], FK **Customers(CustomerID)**
CustomerTypeID	nchar(10)	no			Composite PK nonclust[1], FK **CustomerDemographics (CustomerTypeID)**

1 The composite primary key is defined on **CustomerID**, **CustomerTypeID**.

CustomerDemographics

Column_name	Data type	Nullable	Default	Check	Key/index
CustomerTypeID	nchar(10)	no			PK nonclust.
CustomerDesc	ntext	yes			

Employees

Column_name	Data type	Nullable	Default	Check	Key/index
EmployeeID	**int**	no	IDENTITY (1,1)		PK clust.
LastName	**nvarchar(20)**	no			Nonclust.
FirstName	**nvarchar(10)**	no			
Title	**nvarchar(30)**	yes			
TitleOfCourtesy	**nvarchar(25)**	yes			
BirthDate	**datetime**	yes		yes[1]	
HireDate	**datetime**	yes			
Address	**nvarchar(60)**	yes			
City	**nvarchar(15)**	yes			
Region	**nvarchar(15)**	yes			
PostalCode	**nvarchar(10)**	yes			Nonclust.
Country	**nvarchar(15)**	yes			
HomePhone	**nvarchar(24)**	yes			
Extension	**nvarchar(4)**	yes			
Photo	**image**	yes			
Notes	**ntext**	yes			
ReportsTo	**int**	yes			FK **Employees(EmployeeID)**
Photopath	**nvarchar(255)**	yes			

1 The **BirthDate** CHECK constraint is defined as (**BirthDate** < GETDATE()).

Note Some entries in the **Address** column of the **Employees** table contain newline characters that may affect the format of the result set columns.

EmployeeTerritories

Column_name	Data type	Nullable	Default	Check	Key/index
EmployeeID	**int**	no			Composite PK nonclust.
TerritoryID	**nvarchar(20)**	no			Composite PK nonclust.

Order Details

Column_name	Data type	Nullable	Default	Check	Key/index
OrderID	**int**	no			Composite PK, clust[1], FK **Orders(OrderID)**[2]
ProductID	**int**	no			Composite PK, clust[1], FK **Products(ProductID)**[3]
UnitPrice	**money**	no	0	yes[4]	
Quantity	**smallint**	no	1	yes[5]	
Discount	**real**	no	0		

1 The composite, primary key, clustered index is defined on **OrderID** and **ProductID**.
2 There are also two nonclustered indexes on **OrderID**.
3 There are also two nonclustered indexes on **ProductID**.
4 The **UnitPrice** CHECK constraint is defined as (**UnitPrice** >= 0).
5 The **Quantity** CHECK constraint is defined as (**Quantity** > 0).
The table-level CHECK constraint is defined as (**Discount** >= 0 and **Discount** < = 1).

Orders

Column_name	Data type	Nullable	Default	Check	Key/index
OrderID	**int**	no	IDENTITY (1,1)		PK, clust.
CustomerID	**nchar(5)**	yes			FK **Customers(CustomerID)**[1]
EmployeeID	**int**	yes			FK **Employees(EmployeeID)**[2]
OrderDate	**datetime**	yes	GETDATE ()		Nonclust.
RequiredDate	**datetime**	yes			
ShippedDate	**datetime**	yes			Nonclust.
ShipVia	**int**	yes			FK **Shippers(ShipperID)**[3]
Freight	**money**	yes	0		
ShipName	**nvarchar(40)**	yes			
ShipAddress	**nvarchar(60)**	yes			

(continued)

(continued)

Column_name	Data type	Nullable	Default	Check	Key/index
ShipCity	**nvarchar(15)**	yes			
ShipRegion	**nvarchar(15)**	yes			
ShipPostalCode	**nvarchar(10)**	yes			Nonclust.
ShipCountry	**nvarchar(15)**	yes			

1 There are also two nonclustered indexes on **CustomerID**.
2 There are also two nonclustered indexes on **EmployeeID**.
3 There is also a nonclustered index on **ShipVia**.

Products

Column_name	Data type	Nullable	Default	Check	Key/index
ProductID	**int**	no	IDENTITY (1,1)		PK, clust.
ProductName	**nvarchar(40)**	no			Nonclust.
SupplierID	**int**	yes			FK **Suppliers(SupplierID)**, nonclust.[1]
CategoryID	**int**	yes			FK **Categories(CategoryID)**, nonclust.[2]
QuantityPerUnit	**nvarchar(20)**	yes			
UnitPrice	**money**	yes	0	yes[3]	
UnitsInStock	**smallint**	yes	0	yes[4]	
UnitsOnOrder	**smallint**	yes	0	yes[5]	
ReorderLevel	**smallint**	yes	0	yes[6]	
Discontinued	**bit**	no	0		

1 There are two nonclustered indexes on **SupplierID**.
2 There are two nonclustered indexes on **CategoryID**.
3 The **UnitPrice** CHECK constraint is defined as (**UnitPrice** >=).
4 The **UnitsInStock** CHECK constraint is defined as (**UnitsInStock** >=).
5 The **UnitsOnOrder** CHECK constraint is defined as (**UnitsOnOrder** >=).
6 The **ReorderLevel** CHECK constraint is defined as (**ReorderLevel** >=).

Region

Column_name	Data type	Nullable	Default	Check	Key/index
RegionID	**int**	no			PK nonclust.
RegionDescription	**nchar(50)**	no			

Shippers

Column_name	Data type	Nullable	Default	Check	Key/index
ShipperID	**int**	no	IDENTITY (1,1)		PK clust.
CompanyName	**nvarchar(40)**	no			
Phone	**nvarchar(24)**	yes			

Suppliers

Column_name	Data type	Nullable	Default	Check	Key/index
SupplierID	**int**	no	IDENTITY (1,1)		PK clust.
CompanyName	**nvarchar(40)**	no			Nonclust.
ContactName	**nvarchar(30)**	yes			
ContactTitle	**nvarchar(30)**	yes			
Address	**nvarchar(60)**	yes			
City	**nvarchar(15)**	yes			
Region	**nvarchar(15)**	yes			
PostalCode	**nvarchar(10)**	yes			Nonclust.
Country	**nvarchar(15)**	yes			
Phone	**nvarchar(24)**	yes			
Fax	**nvarchar(24)**	yes			
HomePage	**ntext**	yes			

Territories

Column_name	Data type	Nullable	Default	Check	Key/index
TerritoryID	nvarchar(20)	no			PK nonclust.
TerritoryDescription	nchar(50)	no			
RegionID	int	no			FK **Region (RegionID)**

Pubs Sample Database

The **pubs** sample database is modeled after a book publishing company and is used to demonstrate many of the options available for a Microsoft SQL Server database. The database and its tables are commonly used in the examples presented in the documentation content.

If you have made changes to the **pubs** database, you can reinstall it using files located in the Install directory of your SQL Server installation. The installation process requires two steps:

1. From the command prompt, use the **osql** utility to run the Instpubs.sql script. This drops the existing **pubs** database, creates a new one, and defines all the objects in the database.

2. From the command prompt, run Pubimage.bat. This inserts image values into the **pub_info** table.

authors

Column_name	Data type	Nullable	Default	Check	Key/index
au_id	**id**	no		yes [1]	PK, clust.
au_lname	**varchar(40)**	no			Composite, nonclust. [3]
au_fname	**varchar(20)**	no			Composite, nonclust. [3]
phone	**char(12)**	no	'UNKNOWN'		
address	**varchar(40)**	yes			
city	**varchar(20)**	yes			
state	**char(2)**	yes			
zip	**char(5)**	yes		yes [2]	
contract	**bit**	no			

1 The **au_id** CHECK constraint is defined as (**au_id** LIKE '[0-9][0-9][0-9]-[0-9][0-9]-[0-9][0-9][0-9][0-9]').
2 The **zip** CHECK constraint is defined as (**zip** LIKE '[0-9][0-9][0-9][0-9][0-9]').
3 The composite, nonclustered index is defined on **au_lname** and **au_fname**.

These tables show the contents of the **authors** table. The first column (**au_id**) is repeated in the second table, along with columns 5 through 9.

au_id (1)	au_lname (2)	au_fname (3)	phone (4)
172-32-1176	White	Johnson	408 496-7223
213-46-8915	Green	Marjorie	415 986-7020
238-95-7766	Carson	Cheryl	415 548-7723
267-41-2394	O'Leary	Michael	408 286-2428
274-80-9391	Straight	Dean	415 834-2919
341-22-1782	Smith	Meander	913 843-0462
409-56-7008	Bennet	Abraham	415 658-9932
427-17-2319	Dull	Ann	415 836-7128
472-27-2349	Gringlesby	Burt	707 938-6445
486-29-1786	Locksley	Charlene	415 585-4620
527-72-3246	Greene	Morningstar	615 297-2723
648-92-1872	Blotchet-Halls	Reginald	503 745-6402
672-71-3249	Yokomoto	Akiko	415 935-4228
712-45-1867	del Castillo	Innes	615 996-8275
722-51-5454	DeFrance	Michel	219 547-9982
724-08-9931	Stringer	Dirk	415 843-2991
724-80-9391	MacFeather	Stearns	415 354-7128
756-30-7391	Karsen	Livia	415 534-9219
807-91-6654	Panteley	Sylvia	301 946-8853
846-92-7186	Hunter	Sheryl	415 836-7128
893-72-1158	McBadden	Heather	707 448-4982
899-46-2035	Ringer	Anne	801 826-0752
998-72-3567	Ringer	Albert	801 826-0752

au_id (1)	address (5)	city (6)	state (7)	zip (8)	contract (9)
172-32-1176	10932 Bigge Rd.	Menlo Park	CA	94025	1
213-46-8915	309 63rd St. #411	Oakland	CA	94618	1
238-95-7766	589 Darwin Ln.	Berkeley	CA	94705	1
267-41-2394	22 Cleveland Av. #14	San Jose	CA	95128	1
274-80-9391	5420 College Av.	Oakland	CA	94609	1
341-22-1782	10 Mississippi Dr.	Lawrence	KS	66044	0
409-56-7008	6223 Bateman St.	Berkeley	CA	94705	1
427-17-2319	3410 Blonde St.	Palo Alto	CA	94301	1
472-27-2349	PO Box 792	Covelo	CA	95428	1
486-29-1786	18 Broadway Av.	San Francisco	CA	94130	1
527-72-3246	22 Graybar House Rd.	Nashville	TN	37215	0
648-92-1872	55 Hillsdale Bl.	Corvallis	OR	97330	1
672-71-3249	3 Silver Ct.	Walnut Creek	CA	94595	1
712-45-1867	2286 Cram Pl. #86	Ann Arbor	MI	48105	1
722-51-5454	3 Balding Pl.	Gary	IN	46403	1
724-08-9931	5420 Telegraph Av.	Oakland	CA	94609	0
724-80-9391	44 Upland Hts.	Oakland	CA	94612	1
756-30-7391	5720 McAuley St.	Oakland	CA	94609	1
807-91-6654	1956 Arlington Pl.	Rockville	MD	20853	1
846-92-7186	3410 Blonde St.	Palo Alto	CA	94301	1
893-72-1158	301 Putnam	Vacaville	CA	95688	0
899-46-2035	67 Seventh Av.	Salt Lake City	UT	84152	1
998-72-3567	67 Seventh Av.	Salt Lake City	UT	84152	1

discounts

Column_name	Data type	Nullable	Default	Check	Key/index
discounttype	varchar(40)	no			
stor_id	char(4)	yes			FK stores(stor_id)
lowqty	smallint	yes			
highqty	smallint	yes			
discount	float	no			

discounttype	stor_id	lowqty	highqty	discount
Initial Customer	NULL	NULL	NULL	10.5
Volume Discount	NULL	100	1000	6.7
Customer Discount	8042	NULL	NULL	5.0

employee

Column_name	Data type	Nullable	Default	Check	Key/index
emp_id	empid	no		yes [1]	PK, nonclust.
fname	varchar(20)	no			Composite, clust. [2]
minit	char(1)	yes			Composite, clust. [2]
lname	varchar(30)	no			Composite, clust. [2]
job_id	smallint	no	1		FK jobs(job_id)
job_lvl	tinyint	no	10		
pub_id	char(4)	no	'9952'		FK publishers(pub_id)
hire_date	datetime	no	GETDATE( )		

1 The CHECK constraint is defined as (emp_id LIKE '[A-Z][A-Z][A-Z][1-9][0-9][0-9][0-9][FM]') OR
(emp_id LIKE '[A-Z]-[A-Z][1-9][0-9][0-9][0-9][FM]').
2 The composite, clustered index is defined on lname, fname, and minit.

These tables show the contents of the **employee** table. The first column (**emp_id**) is repeated in the second table, along with columns 6 through 8.

emp_id (1)	fname (2)	minit (3)	lname (4)	job_id (5)
PMA42628M	Paolo	M	Accorti	13
PSA89086M	Pedro	S	Alfonso	14
VPA30890F	Victoria	P	Ashworth	6
H-B39728F	Helen	NULL	Bennett	12
L-B31947F	Lesley	NULL	Brown	7
F-C16315M	Francisco	NULL	Chang	4
PTC11962M	Philip	T	Cramer	2
A-C71970F	Aria	NULL	Cruz	10
AMD15433F	Ann	M	Devon	3
ARD36773F	Anabela	R	Domingues	8
PHF38899M	Peter	H	Franken	10
PXH22250M	Paul	X	Henriot	5
CFH28514M	Carlos	F	Hernández	5
PDI47470M	Palle	D	Ibsen	7
KJJ92907F	Karla	J	Jablonski	9
KFJ64308F	Karin	F	Josephs	14
MGK44605M	Matti	G	Karttunen	6
POK93028M	Pirkko	O	Koskitalo	10
JYL26161F	Janine	Y	Labrune	5
M-L67958F	Maria	NULL	Larsson	7
Y-L77953M	Yoshi	NULL	Latimer	12
LAL21447M	Laurence	A	Lebihan	5
ENL44273F	Elizabeth	N	Lincoln	14

(continued)

(continued)

emp_id (1)	fname (2)	minit (3)	lname (4)	job_id (5)
PCM98509F	Patricia	C	McKenna	11
R-M53550M	Roland	NULL	Mendel	11
RBM23061F	Rita	B	Müller	5
HAN90777M	Helvetius	A	Nagy	7
TPO55093M	Timothy	P	O'Rourke	13
SKO22412M	Sven	K	Ottlieb	5
MAP77183M	Miguel	A	Paolino	11
PSP68661F	Paula	S	Parente	8
M-P91209M	Manuel	NULL	Pereira	8
MJP25939M	Maria	J	Pontes	5
M-R38834F	Martine	NULL	Rancé	9
DWR65030M	Diego	W	Roel	6
A-R89858F	Annette	NULL	Roulet	6
MMS49649F	Mary	M	Saveley	8
CGS88322F	Carine	G	Schmitt	13
MAS70474F	Margaret	A	Smith	9
HAS54740M	Howard	A	Snyder	12
MFS52347M	Martín	F	Sommer	10
GHT50241M	Gary	H	Thomas	9
DBT39435M	Daniel	B	Tonini	11

emp_id (1)	job_lvl (6)	pub_id (7)	hire_date (8)
PMA42628M	35	0877	Aug 27 1992 12:00AM
PSA89086M	89	1389	Dec 24 1990 12:00AM
VPA30890F	140	0877	Sep 13 1990 12:00AM
H-B39728F	35	0877	Sep 21 1989 12:00AM
L-B31947F	120	0877	Feb 13 1991 12:00AM
F-C16315M	227	9952	Nov 3 1990 12:00AM
PTC11962M	215	9952	Nov 11 1989 12:00AM
A-C71970F	87	1389	Oct 26 1991 12:00AM
AMD15433F	200	9952	Jul 16 1991 12:00AM
ARD36773F	100	0877	Jan 27 1993 12:00AM
PHF38899M	75	0877	May 17 1992 12:00AM
PXH22250M	159	0877	Aug 19 1993 12:00AM
CFH28514M	211	9999	Apr 21 1989 12:00AM
PDI47470M	195	0736	May 9 1993 12:00AM
KJJ92907F	170	9999	Mar 11 1994 12:00AM
KFJ64308F	100	0736	Oct 17 1992 12:00AM
MGK44605M	220	0736	May 1 1994 12:00AM
POK93028M	80	9999	Nov 29 1993 12:00AM
JYL26161F	172	9901	May 26 1991 12:00AM
M-L67958F	135	1389	Mar 27 1992 12:00AM
Y-L77953M	32	1389	Jun 11 1989 12:00AM

(continued)

(continued)

emp_id (1)	job_lvl (6)	pub_id (7)	hire_date (8)
LAL21447M	175	0736	Jun 3 1990 12:00AM
ENL44273F	35	0877	Jul 24 1990 12:00AM
PCM98509F	150	9999	Aug 1 1989 12:00AM
R-M53550M	150	0736	Sep 5 1991 12:00AM
RBM23061F	198	1622	Oct 9 1993 12:00AM
HAN90777M	120	9999	Mar 19 1993 12:00AM
TPO55093M	100	0736	Jun 19 1988 12:00AM
SKO22412M	150	1389	Apr 5 1991 12:00AM
MAP77183M	112	1389	Dec 7 1992 12:00AM
PSP68661F	125	1389	Jan 19 1994 12:00AM
M-P91209M	101	9999	Jan 9 1989 12:00AM
MJP25939M	246	1756	Mar 1 1989 12:00AM
M-R38834F	75	0877	Feb 5 1992 12:00AM
DWR65030M	192	1389	Dec 16 1991 12:00AM
A-R89858F	152	9999	Feb 21 1990 12:00AM
MMS49649F	175	0736	Jun 29 1993 12:00AM
CGS88322F	64	1389	Jul 7 1992 12:00AM
MAS70474F	78	1389	Sep 29 1988 12:00AM
HAS54740M	100	0736	Nov 19 1988 12:00AM
MFS52347M	165	0736	Apr 13 1990 12:00AM
GHT50241M	170	0736	Aug 9 1988 12:00AM
DBT39435M	75	0877	Jan 1 1990 12:00AM

jobs

Column_name	Data type	Nullable	Default	Check	Key/index
job_id	smallint	no	IDENTITY(1,1)		PK, clust
stor_id	char(4)	no	yes [1]		
min_lvl	tinyint	no		yes [2]	
max_lvl	tinyint	no		yes [3]	

1 The DEFAULT constraint is defined as ("New Position - title not formalized yet").
2 The **min_lvl** CHECK constraint is defined as (**min_lvl** >= 10).
3 The **max_lvl** CHECK constraint is defined as (**max_lvl** <= 250).

This table shows the contents of the **jobs** table.

job_id	job_desc	min_lvl	max_lvl
1	New Hire - Job not specified	10	10
2	Chief Executive Officer	200	250
3	Business Operations Manager	175	225
4	Chief Financial Officer	175	250
5	Publisher	150	250
6	Managing Editor	140	225
7	Marketing Manager	120	200
8	Public Relations Manager	100	175
9	Acquisitions Manager	75	175
10	Productions Manager	75	165
11	Operations Manager	75	150
12	Editor	25	100
13	Sales Representative	25	100
14	Designer	25	100

pub_info

Column_name	Data type	Nullable	Default	Check	Key/index
pub_id	**char(4)**	no			PK, clust., FK **publishers(pub_id)**
logo	**image**	yes			
pr_info	**text**	yes			

This table shows the contents of the **pub_info** table.

pub_id	logo [1]	pr_info [2]
0736	Newmoon.bmp	This is sample text data for New Moon Books, publisher 0736 in the **pubs** database. New Moon Books is located in Boston, Massachusetts.
0877	Binnet.bmp	This is sample text data for Binnet & Hardley, publisher 0877 in the **pubs** database. Binnet & Hardley is located in Washington, D.C.
1389	Algodata.bmp	This is sample text data for Algodata Infosystems, publisher 1389 in the **pubs** database. Algodata Infosystems is located in Berkeley, California.
1622	5lakes.bmp	This is sample text data for Five Lakes Publishing, publisher 1622 in the **pubs** database. Five Lakes Publishing is located in Chicago, Illinois.
1756	Ramona.bmp	This is sample text data for Ramona Publishers, publisher 1756 in the **pubs** database. Ramona Publishers is located in Dallas, Texas.
9901	Gggg.bmp	This is sample text data for GGG&G, publisher 9901 in the **pubs** database. GGG&G is located in München, Germany.
9952	Scootney.bmp	This is sample text data for Scootney Books, publisher 9952 in the **pubs** database. Scootney Books is located in New York City, New York.
9999	Lucerne.bmp	This is sample text data for Lucerne Publishing, publisher 9999 in the **pubs** database. Lucerne Publishing is located in Paris, France.

1 The information shown here is not the actual data. It is the file name from which the bitmap (image data) was loaded.
2 The text shown here is incomplete. When displaying **text** data, the display is limited to a finite number of characters. This table shows the first 120 characters of the **text** column.

publishers

Column_name	Data type	Nullable	Default	Check	Key/index
pub_id	char(4)	no		yes [1]	PK, clust.
pub_name	varchar(40)	yes			
city	varchar(20)	yes			
state	char(2)	yes			
country	varchar(30)	yes	'USA'		

1 The **pub_id** CHECK constraint is defined as (**pub_id** = '1756' OR (**pub_id** = '1622' OR (**pub_id** = '0877' OR (**pub_id** = '0736' OR (**pub_id** = '1389')))) OR (**pub_id** LIKE '99[0-9][0-0]').

This table shows the contents of the **publishers** table.

pub_id	pub_name	city	state	country
0736	New Moon Books	Boston	MA	USA
0877	Binnet & Hardley	Washington	DC	USA
1389	Algodata Infosystems	Berkeley	CA	USA
1622	Five Lakes Publishing	Chicago	IL	USA
1756	Ramona Publishers	Dallas	TX	USA
9901	GGG&G	München	NULL	Germany
9952	Scootney Books	New York	NY	USA
9999	Lucerne Publishing	Paris	NULL	France

roysched

Column_name	Data type	Nullable	Default	Check	Key/index
title_id	tid	no			FK titles(**title_id**)
lorange	int	yes			
hirange	int	yes			
royalty	int	yes			

This table shows the contents of the **roysched** table.

title_id	lorange	hirange	royalty
BU1032	0	5000	10
BU1032	5001	50000	12
PC1035	0	2000	10
PC1035	2001	3000	12
PC1035	3001	4000	14
PC1035	4001	10000	16
PC1035	10001	50000	18
BU2075	0	1000	10
BU2075	1001	3000	12
BU2075	3001	5000	14
BU2075	5001	7000	16
BU2075	7001	10000	18
BU2075	10001	12000	20
BU2075	12001	14000	22
BU2075	14001	50000	24
PS2091	0	1000	10
PS2091	1001	5000	12
PS2091	5001	10000	14
PS2091	10001	50000	16
PS2106	0	2000	10
PS2106	2001	5000	12
PS2106	5001	10000	14
PS2106	10001	50000	16

(continued)

(continued)

title_id	lorange	hirange	royalty
MC3021	0	1000	10
MC3021	1001	2000	12
MC3021	2001	4000	14
MC3021	4001	6000	16
MC3021	6001	8000	18
MC3021	8001	10000	20
MC3021	10001	12000	22
MC3021	12001	50000	24
TC3218	0	2000	10
TC3218	2001	4000	12
TC3218	4001	6000	14
TC3218	6001	8000	16
TC3218	8001	10000	18
TC3218	10001	12000	20
TC3218	12001	14000	22
TC3218	14001	50000	24
PC8888	0	5000	10
PC8888	5001	10000	12
PC8888	10001	15000	14
PC8888	15001	50000	16
PS7777	0	5000	10
PS7777	5001	50000	12
PS3333	0	5000	10

(continued)

(continued)

title_id	lorange	hirange	royalty
PS3333	5001	10000	12
PS3333	10001	15000	14
PS3333	15001	50000	16
BU1111	0	4000	10
BU1111	4001	8000	12
BU1111	8001	10000	14
BU1111	12001	16000	16
BU1111	16001	20000	18
BU1111	20001	24000	20
BU1111	24001	28000	22
BU1111	28001	50000	24
MC2222	0	2000	10
MC2222	2001	4000	12
MC2222	4001	8000	14
MC2222	8001	12000	16
MC2222	12001	20000	18
MC2222	20001	50000	20
TC7777	0	5000	10
TC7777	5001	15000	12
TC7777	15001	50000	14
TC4203	0	2000	10
TC4203	2001	8000	12
TC4203	8001	16000	14

(continued)

(continued)

title_id	lorange	hirange	royalty
TC4203	16001	24000	16
TC4203	24001	32000	18
TC4203	32001	40000	20
TC4203	40001	50000	22
BU7832	0	5000	10
BU7832	5001	10000	12
BU7832	10001	15000	14
BU7832	15001	20000	16
BU7832	20001	25000	18
BU7832	25001	30000	20
BU7832	30001	35000	22
BU7832	35001	50000	24
PS1372	0	10000	10
PS1372	10001	20000	12
PS1372	20001	30000	14
PS1372	30001	40000	16
PS1372	40001	50000	18

sales

Column_name	Data type	Nullable	Key/index
stor_id	**char(4)**	no	Composite PK, clust. [1], FK **stores(stor_id)**
ord_num	**varchar(20)**	no	Composite PK, clust. [1]
ord_date	**datetime**	no	
qty	**smallint**	no	
payterms	**varchar(12)**	no	
title_id	**tid**	no	Composite PK, clust. [1], FK **titles(title_id)**

[1] The composite, primary key, clustered index is defined on **stor_id**, **ord_num**, and **title_id**.

This table shows the contents of the **sales** table.

stor_id	ord_num	ord_date	qty	payterms	title_id
6380	6871	Sep 14 1994 12:00AM	5	Net 60	BU1032
6380	722a	Sep 13 1994 12:00AM	3	Net 60	PS2091
7066	A2976	May 24 1993 12:00AM	50	Net 30	PC8888
7066	QA7442.3	Sep 13 1994 12:00AM	75	ON invoice	PS2091
7067	D4482	Sep 14 1994 12:00AM	10	Net 60	PS2091
7067	P2121	Jun 15 1992 12:00AM	40	Net 30	TC3218
7067	P2121	Jun 15 1992 12:00AM	20	Net 30	TC4203
7067	P2121	Jun 15 1992 12:00AM	20	Net 30	TC7777
7131	N914008	Sep 14 1994 12:00AM	20	Net 30	PS2091
7131	N914014	Sep 14 1994 12:00AM	25	Net 30	MC3021
7131	P3087a	May 29 1993 12:00AM	20	Net 60	PS1372
7131	P3087a	May 29 1993 12:00AM	25	Net 60	PS2106
7131	P3087a	May 29 1993 12:00AM	15	Net 60	PS3333
7131	P3087a	May 29 1993 12:00AM	25	Net 60	PS7777
7896	QQ2299	Oct 28 1993 12:00AM	15	Net 60	BU7832
7896	TQ456	Dec 12 1993 12:00AM	10	Net 60	MC2222
7896	X999	Feb 21 1993 12:00AM	35	ON invoice	BU2075
8042	423LL922	Sep 14 1994 12:00AM	15	ON invoice	MC3021
8042	423LL930	Sep 14 1994 12:00AM	10	ON invoice	BU1032
8042	P723	Mar 11 1993 12:00AM	25	Net 30	BU1111
8042	QA879.1	May 22 1993 12:00AM	30	Net 30	PC1035

stores

Column_name	Data type	Nullable	Default	Check	Key/index
stor_id	char(4)	no			PK, clust.
stor_name	varchar(40)	yes			
stor_address	varchar(40)	yes			
city	varchar(20)	yes			
state	char(2)	yes			
zip	char(5)	yes			

This table shows the contents of the **stores** table.

stor_id	stor_name	stor_address	city	state	zip
6380	Eric the Read Books	788 Catamaugus Ave.	Seattle	WA	98056
7066	Barnum's	567 Pasadena Ave.	Tustin	CA	92789
7067	News & Brews	577 First St.	Los Gatos	CA	96745
7131	Doc-U-Mat: Quality Laundry and Books	24-A Avrogado Way	Remulade	WA	98014
7896	Fricative Bookshop	89 Madison St.	Fremont	CA	90019
8042	Bookbeat	679 Carson St.	Portland	OR	89076

titleauthor

Column_name	Data type	Nullable	Default	Check	Key/index
au_id	id	no			Composite PK, clust. [1], FK **authors(au_id)** [2]
title_id	tid	no			Composite PK, clust. [1], FK **titles(title_id)** [3]
au_ord	tinyint	yes			
royaltyper	int	yes			

1 The composite, primary key, clustered index is defined on **au_id** and **title_id**.
2 This foreign key also has a nonclustered index on **au_id**.
3 This foreign key also has a nonclustered index on **title_id**.

This table shows the contents of the **titleauthor** table.

au_id	title_id	au_ord	royaltyper
172-32-1176	PS3333	1	100
213-46-8915	BU1032	2	40
213-46-8915	BU2075	1	100
238-95-7766	PC1035	1	100
267-41-2394	BU1111	2	40
267-41-2394	TC7777	2	30
274-80-9391	BU7832	1	100
409-56-7008	BU1032	1	60
427-17-2319	PC8888	1	50
472-27-2349	TC7777	3	30
486-29-1786	PC9999	1	100
486-29-1786	PS7777	1	100
648-92-1872	TC4203	1	100
672-71-3249	TC7777	1	40
712-45-1867	MC2222	1	100
722-51-5454	MC3021	1	75
724-80-9391	BU1111	1	60
724-80-9391	PS1372	2	25
756-30-7391	PS1372	1	75
807-91-6654	TC3218	1	100
846-92-7186	PC8888	2	50
899-46-2035	MC3021	2	25
899-46-2035	PS2091	2	50
998-72-3567	PS2091	1	50
998-72-3567	PS2106	1	100

titles

Column_name	Data type	Nullable	Default	Check	Key/index
title_id	tid	no			PK, clust.
title	varchar(80)	no			Nonclust.
type	char(12)	no	'UNDECIDED'		
pub_id	char(4)	yes			FK **publishers** (**pub_id**)
price	money	yes			
advance	money	yes			
royalty	int	yes			
ytd_sales	int	yes			
notes	varchar(200)	yes			
pubdate	datetime	no	GETDATE( )		

These tables show the contents of the **titles** table. The first column (**title_id**) is repeated in the tables that follow, along with columns 6 through 8, and 9 through 10.

title_id (1)	title (2)	type (3)	pub_id (4)	price (5)
BU1032	The Busy Executive's Database Guide	business	1389	19.99
BU1111	Cooking with Computers: Surreptitious Balance Sheets	business	1389	11.95
BU2075	You Can Combat Computer Stress!	business	0736	2.99
BU7832	Straight Talk About Computers	business	1389	19.99
MC2222	Silicon Valley Gastronomic Treats	mod_cook	0877	19.99
MC3021	The Gourmet Microwave	mod_cook	0877	2.99

(continued)

(continued)

title_id (1)	title (2)	type (3)	pub_id (4)	price (5)
MC3026	The Psychology of Computer Cooking	UNDECIDED	0877	NULL
PC1035	But Is It User Friendly?	popular_comp	1389	22.95
PC8888	Secrets of Silicon Valley	popular_comp	1389	20.00
PC9999	Net Etiquette	popular_comp	1389	NULL
PS1372	Computer Phobic and Non-Phobic Individuals: Behavior Variations	psychology	0877	21.59
PS2091	Is Anger the Enemy?	psychology	0736	10.95
PS2106	Life Without Fear	psychology	0736	7.00
PS3333	Prolonged Data Deprivation: Four Case Studies	psychology	0736	19.99
PS7777	Emotional Security: A New Algorithm	psychology	0736	7.99
TC3218	Onions, Leeks, and Garlic: Cooking Secrets of the Mediterranean	trad_cook	0877	20.95
TC4203	Fifty Years in Buckingham Palace Kitchens	trad_cook	0877	11.95
TC7777	Sushi, Anyone?	trad_cook	0877	14.99

title_id (1)	advance (6)	royalty (7)	ytd_sales (8)
BU1032	5,000.00	10	4095
BU1111	5,000.00	10	3876
BU2075	10,125.00	24	18722
BU7832	5,000.00	10	4095
MC2222	0.00	12	2032

(continued)

(continued)

title_id (1)	advance (6)	royalty (7)	ytd_sales (8)
MC3021	15,000.00	24	22246
MC3026	NULL	NULL	NULL
PC1035	7,000.00	16	8780
PC8888	8,000.00	10	4095
PC9999	NULL	NULL	NULL
PS1372	7,000.00	10	375
PS2091	2,275.00	12	2045
PS2106	6,000.00	10	111
PS3333	2,000.00	10	4072
PS7777	4,000.00	10	3336
TC3218	7,000.00	10	375
TC4203	4,000.00	14	15096
TC7777	8,000.00	10	4095

title_id (1)	notes (9)	pubdate (10)
BU1032	An overview of available database systems with emphasis on common business applications. Illustrated.	Jun 12 1991 12:00AM
BU1111	Helpful hints on how to use your electronic resources to the best advantage.	Jun 9 1991 12:00AM
BU2075	The latest medical and psychological techniques for living with the electronic office. Easy-to-understand explanations.	Jun 30 1991 12:00AM
BU7832	Annotated analysis of what computers can do for you: a no-hype guide for the critical user.	Jun 22 1991 12:00AM
MC2222	Favorite recipes for quick, easy, and elegant meals.	Jun 9 1991 12:00AM
MC3021	Traditional French gourmet recipes adapted for modern microwave cooking.	Jun 18 1991 12:00AM

(continued)

(continued)

title_id (1)	notes (9)	pubdate (10)
MC3026	NULL	Apr 28 1995 10:36AM
PC1035	A survey of software for the naive user, focusing on the "friendliness" of each.	Jun 30 1991 12:00AM
PC8888	Muckraking reporting on the world's largest computer hardware and software manufacturers.	Jun 12 1994 12:00AM
PC9999	A must-read for computer conferencing.	Apr 28 1995 10:36AM
PS1372	A must for the specialist, examining the difference between those who hate and fear computers and those who don't.	Oct 21 1991 12:00AM
PS2091	Carefully researched study of the effects of strong emotions on the body. Metabolic charts included.	Jun 15 1991 12:00AM
PS2106	New exercise, meditation, and nutritional techniques that can reduce the shock of daily interactions. Popular audience. Sample menus included, exercise video available separately.	Oct 5 1991 12:00AM
PS3333	What happens when the data runs dry? Searching evaluations of information-shortage effects.	Jun 12 1991 12:00AM
PS7777	Protecting yourself and your loved ones from undue emotional stress in the modern world. Use of computer and nutritional aids emphasized.	Jun 12 1991 12:00AM
TC3218	Profusely illustrated in color, this makes a wonderful gift book for a cuisine-oriented friend.	Oct 21 1991 12:00AM
TC4203	More anecdotes from the Queen's favorite cook describing life among English royalty. Recipes, techniques, tender vignettes.	Jun 12 1991 12:00AM
TC7777	Detailed instructions on how to make authentic Japanese sushi in your spare time.	Jun 12 1991 12:00AM

Index of T-SQL Programming Elements in Volume 5

Build
powerfully *robust*
services *faster!*

Writing code is an art form. Writing code for *services* requires total mastery of the art form. And with the expert guidance of Jeffrey Richter, author of *Programming Applications for Microsoft Windows*, and Jason Clark, a Windows 2000 security programming specialist for Microsoft, you'll master the intricacies of developing ultrascalable server software for Windows 2000. Each chapter teaches by example, skillfully demonstrating how to exploit the scalability, security, and administration features in the Windows 2000 operating system. Study the authors' sample code and custom C++ classes—and use them in your own development—to deliver powerfully robust services faster!

**Programming Server-Side Applications
for Microsoft® Windows® 2000**

U.S.A.	$ 49.99
U.K.	£32.99 (V.A.T. included)
Canada	$76.99
ISBN	0-7356-0753-2

Microsoft Press® products are available worldwide wherever quality computer books are sold. For more information, contact your book or computer retailer, software reseller, or local Microsoft Sales Office, or visit our Web site at mspress.microsoft.com. To locate your nearest source for Microsoft Press products, or to order directly, call 1-800-MSPRESS in the U.S. (in Canada, call 1-800-268-2222).

Prices and availability dates are subject to change.

Microsoft®

mspress.microsoft.com

Enable
seamless
business-to-business
data exchange
with XML, BizTalk™, and SOAP.

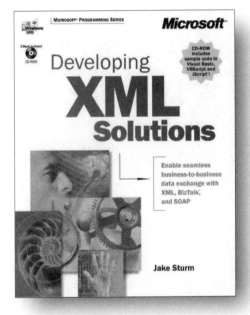

U.S.A. **$49.99**
U.K. £32.99 [V.A.T. included]
Canada $72.99
ISBN: 0-7356-0796-6

Extensible Markup Language (XML) has emerged as the most important format for moving data over the Web with the greatest variety of tools and platforms. DEVELOPING XML SOLUTIONS provides expert insights and practical guidance on how to use XML to access, manipulate, and exchange data among enterprise systems. This comprehensive developer's guidebook examines the newest XML-related technologies for data exchange, and it shows how XML fits into the Microsoft® DNA architecture for distributed computing. It also explores real-world technical examples in the Microsoft Visual Basic® programming language, Microsoft Visual Basic Scripting Edition (VBScript), and Microsoft JScript® to show how to create specific XML-enabled solutions for client/server and n-tier systems, and other scenarios.

Microsoft Press® products are available worldwide wherever quality computer books are sold. For more information, contact your book or computer retailer, software reseller, or local Microsoft Sales Office, or visit our Web site at mspress.microsoft.com. To locate your nearest source for Microsoft Press products, or to order directly, call 1-800-MSPRESS in the U.S. (in Canada, call 1-800-268-2222).

Prices and availability dates are subject to change.

Microsoft®

mspress.microsoft.com